Microsoft® Office 365™ EXCEL® 2016

INTRODUCTORY

Microsoft® Office 365™
EXCEL® 2016

INTRODUCTORY

Steven M. Freund

SHELLY CASHMAN SERIES®

Australia • Brazil • Japan • Korea • Mexico • Singapore • Spain • United Kingdom • United States

Microsoft® Excel® 2016: Introductory
Steven M. Freund

SVP, GM Skills & Global Product Management: Dawn Gerrain

Product Director: Kathleen McMahon

Senior Product Team Manager: Lauren Murphy

Associate Product Manager: William Guiliani

Senior Director, Development: Marah Bellegarde

Product Development Manager: Leigh Hefferon

Managing Content Developer: Emma F. Newsom

Developmental Editor: Karen Stevens

Product Assistant: Erica Chapman

Manuscript Quality Assurance: Jeffrey Schwartz, John Freitas, Serge Palladino, Susan Pedicini, Danielle Shaw, Susan Whalen

Senior Production Director: Wendy Troeger

Production Director: Patty Stephan

Senior Content Project Manager: Matthew Hutchinson

Manufacturing Planner: Julio Esperas

Designer: Diana Graham

Vice President, Marketing: Brian Joyner

Marketing Director: Michele McTighe

Marketing Manager: Stephanie Albracht

Cover image(s): Piotr Zajc/Shutterstock.com; Mrs. Opossum/Shutterstock.com

Compositor: Lumina Datamatics, Inc.

Mac users: If you're working through this book using a Mac, some of the steps may vary. Additional information for Mac users is included with the data files for this book.

For product information and technology assistance, contact us at
Cengage Learning Customer & Sales Support, 1-800-354-9706

For permission to use material from this text or product,
submit all requests online at **www.cengage.com/permissions.**
Further permissions questions can be e-mailed to
permissionrequest@cengage.com

Library of Congress Control Number: 2015955176

ISBN: 978-1-3058-7070-3

Cengage Learning
20 Channel Center Street
Boston, MA 02210
USA

Cengage Learning is a leading provider of customized learning solutions with employees residing in nearly 40 different countries and sales in more than 125 countries around the world. Find your local representative at **www.cengage.com.**

Cengage Learning products are represented in Canada by Nelson Education, Ltd.

To learn more about Cengage Learning, visit **www.cengage.com**

Purchase any of our products at your local college store or at our preferred online store **www.cengagebrain.com**

Printed in the United States of America
Print Number: 04 Print Year: 2017

Microsoft® Office 365™ EXCEL® 2016

INTRODUCTORY

Contents

Microsoft Excel 2016

MODULE ONE
Creating a Worksheet and a Chart

MODULE TWO
Formulas, Functions, and Formatting

MODULE THREE

Working with Large Worksheets, Charting, and What-If Analysis

Productivity Apps for School and Work

OneNote
Sway
Office Mix
Edge

Corinne Hoisington

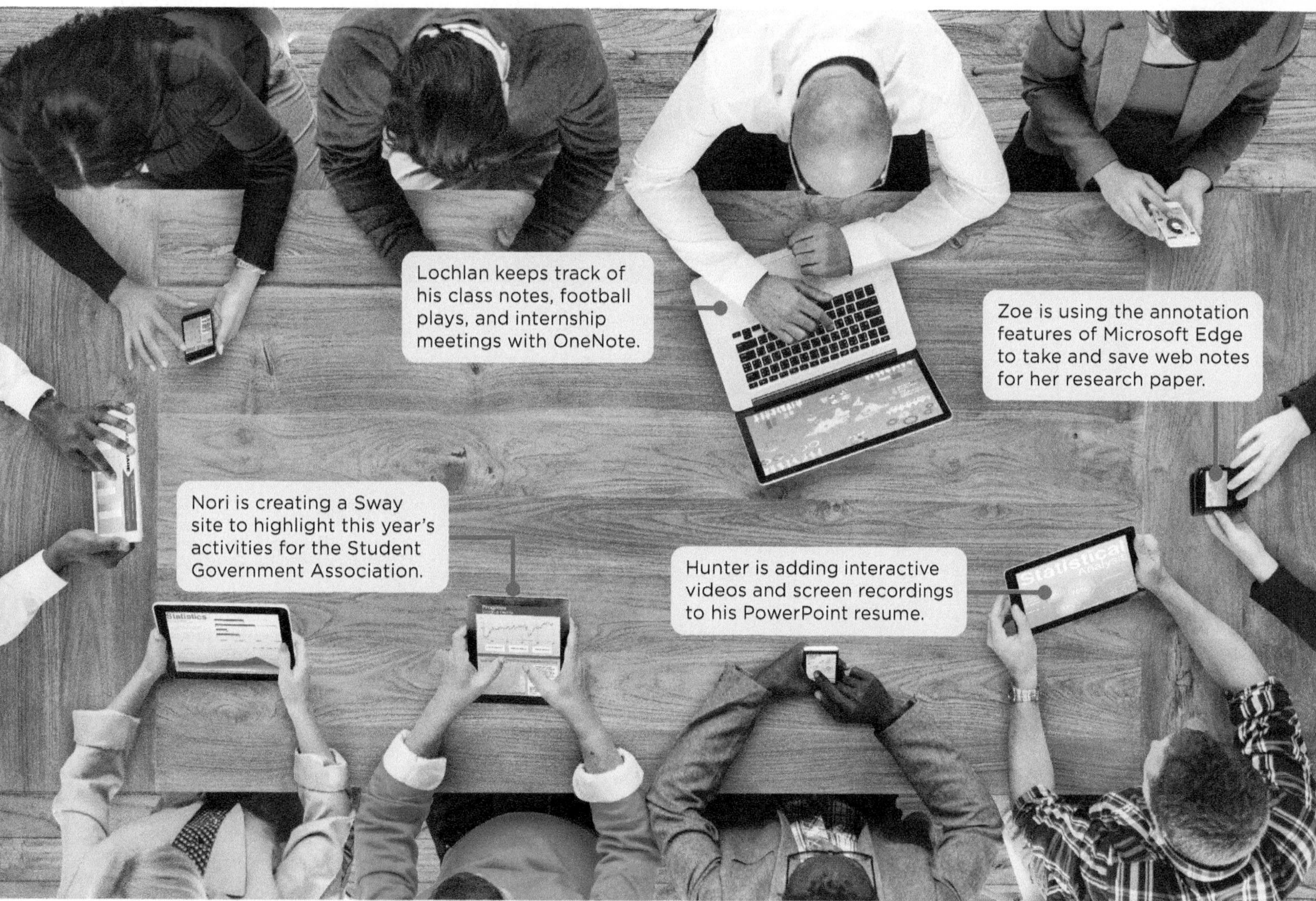

Being computer literate no longer means mastery of only Word, Excel, PowerPoint, Outlook, and Access. To become technology power users, Hunter, Nori, Zoe, and Lochlan are exploring Microsoft OneNote, Sway, Mix, and Edge in Office 2016 and Windows 10.

In this Module

Learn to use productivity apps!
Links to companion **Sways**, featuring **videos** with hands-on instructions, are located on www.cengagebrain.com.

Introduction to OneNote 2016

notebook | section tab | To Do tag | screen clipping | note | template | Microsoft OneNote Mobile app | sync | drawing canvas | inked handwriting | Ink to Text

Bottom Line

- OneNote is a note-taking app for your academic and professional life.
- Use OneNote to get organized by gathering your ideas, sketches, webpages, photos, videos, and notes in one place.

As you glance around any classroom, you invariably see paper notebooks and notepads on each desk. Because deciphering and sharing handwritten notes can be a challenge, Microsoft OneNote 2016 replaces physical notebooks, binders, and paper notes with a searchable, digital notebook. OneNote captures your ideas and schoolwork on any device so you can stay organized, share notes, and work with others on projects. Whether you are a student taking class notes as shown in **Figure 1** or an employee taking notes in company meetings, OneNote is the one place to keep notes for all of your projects.

Figure 1: OneNote 2016 notebook

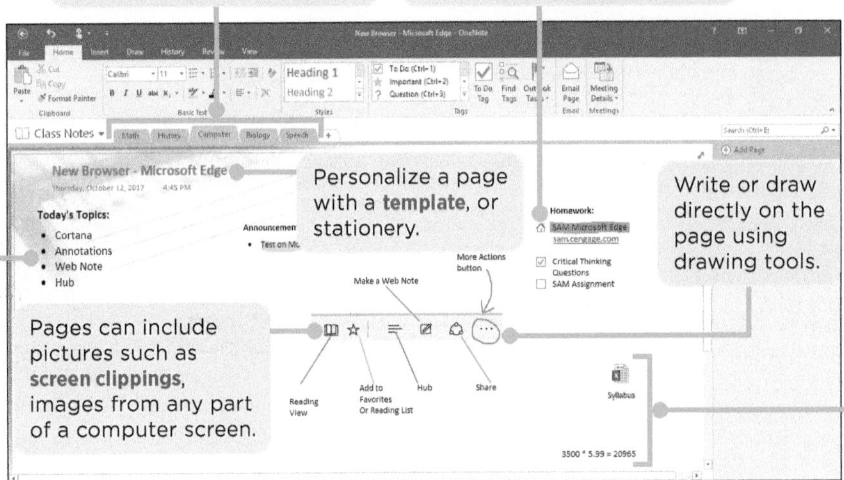

Creating a OneNote Notebook

OneNote is divided into sections similar to those in a spiral-bound notebook. Each OneNote notebook contains sections, pages, and other notebooks. You can use OneNote for school, business, and personal projects. Store information for each type of project in different notebooks to keep your tasks separate, or use any other organization that suits you. OneNote is flexible enough to adapt to the way you want to work.

When you create a notebook, it contains a blank page with a plain white background by default, though you can use templates, or stationery, to apply designs in categories such as Academic, Business, Decorative, and Planners. Start typing or use the buttons on the Insert tab to insert notes, which are small resizable windows that can contain text, equations, tables, on-screen writing, images, audio and video recordings, to-do lists, file attachments, and file printouts. Add as many notes as you need to each page.

Learn to use OneNote!
Links to companion **Sways**, featuring **videos** with hands-on instructions, are located on www.cengagebrain.com.

Syncing a Notebook to the Cloud

OneNote saves your notes every time you make a change in a notebook. To make sure you can access your notebooks with a laptop, tablet, or smartphone wherever you are, OneNote uses cloud-based storage, such as OneDrive or SharePoint. **Microsoft OneNote Mobile app**, a lightweight version of OneNote 2016 shown in **Figure 2**, is available for free in the Windows Store, Google Play for Android devices, and the AppStore for iOS devices.

If you have a Microsoft account, OneNote saves your notes on OneDrive automatically for all your mobile devices and computers, which is called **syncing**. For example, you can use OneNote to take notes on your laptop during class, and then open OneNote on your phone to study later. To use a notebook stored on your computer with your OneNote Mobile app, move the notebook to OneDrive. You can quickly share notebook content with other people using OneDrive.

Figure 2: Microsoft OneNote Mobile app

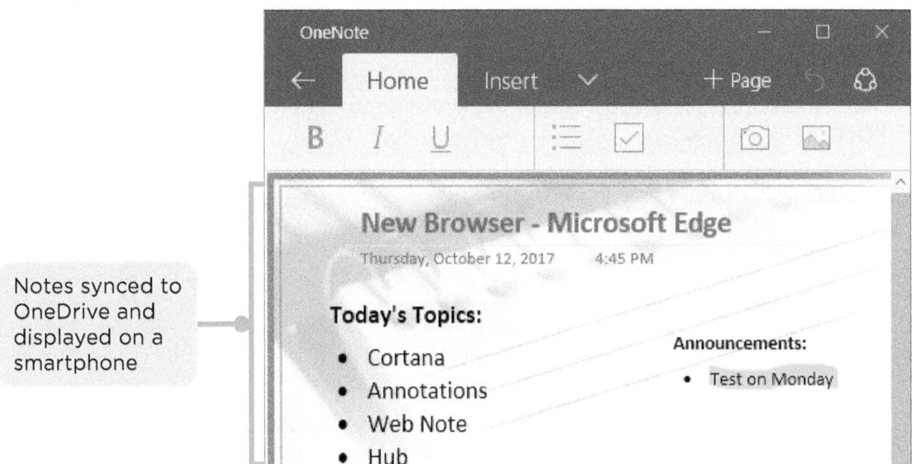

Taking Notes

Use OneNote pages to organize your notes by class and topic or lecture. Beyond simple typed notes, OneNote stores drawings, converts handwriting to searchable text and mathematical sketches to equations, and records audio and video.

OneNote includes drawing tools that let you sketch freehand drawings such as biological cell diagrams and financial supply-and-demand charts. As shown in Figure 3, the Draw tab on the ribbon provides these drawing tools along with shapes so you can insert diagrams and other illustrations to represent your ideas. When you draw on a page, OneNote creates a **drawing canvas**, which is a container for shapes and lines.

OneNote is ideal for taking notes during meetings, whether you are recording minutes, documenting a discussion, sketching product diagrams, or listing follow-up items. Use a meeting template to add pages with content appropriate for meetings.

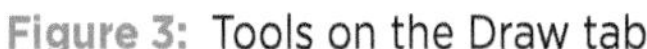

Figure 3: Tools on the Draw tab

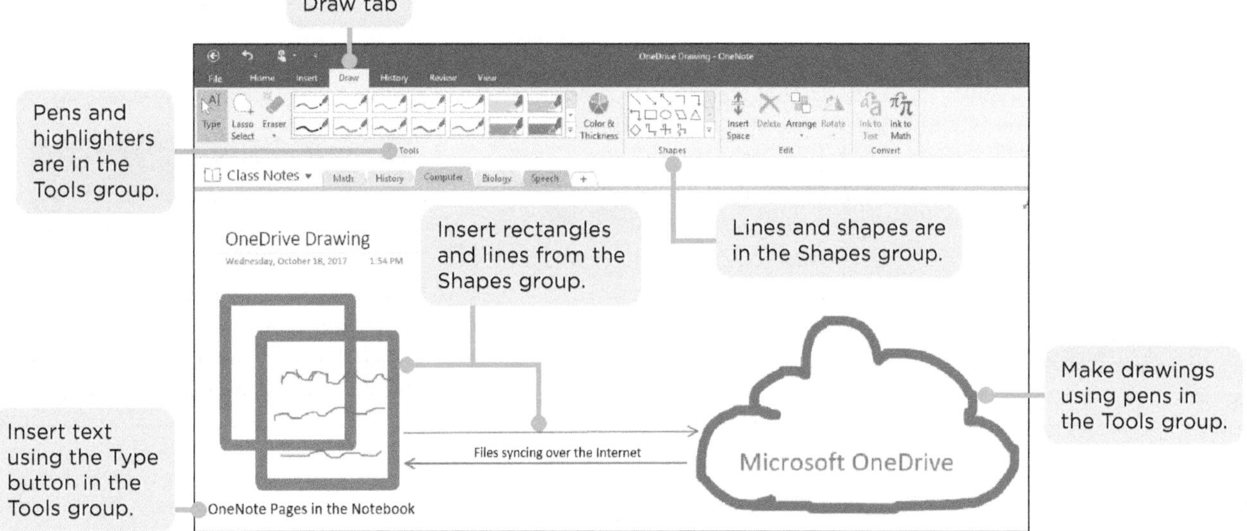

Converting Handwriting to Text

When you use a pen tool to write on a notebook page, the text you enter is called **inked handwriting**. OneNote can convert inked handwriting to typed text when you use the **Ink to Text** button in the Convert group on the Draw tab, as shown in Figure 4. After OneNote converts the handwriting to text, you can use the Search box to find terms in the converted text or any other note in your notebooks.

Figure 4: Converting handwriting to text

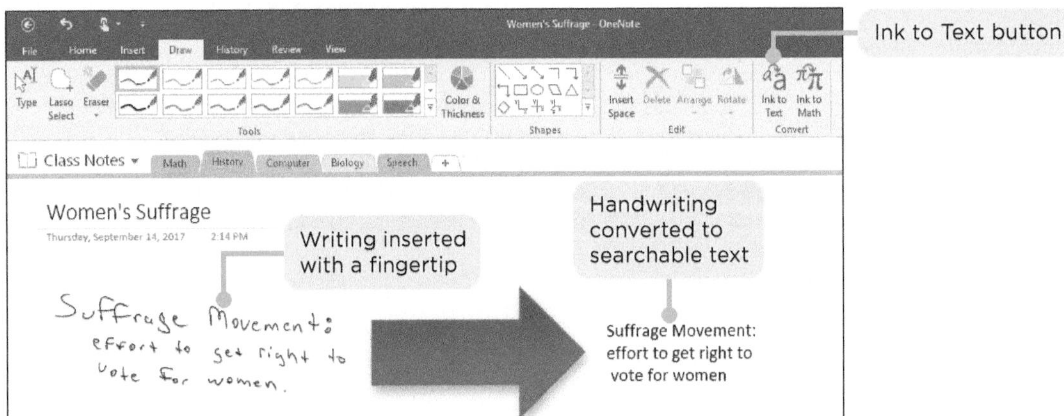

On the Job Now

Use OneNote as a place to brainstorm ongoing work projects. If a notebook contains sensitive material, you can password-protect some or all of the notebook so that only certain people can open it.

Recording a Lecture

If your computer or mobile device has a microphone or camera, OneNote can record the audio or video from a lecture or business meeting as shown in Figure 5. When you record a lecture (with your instructor's permission), you can follow along, take regular notes at your own pace, and review the video recording later. You can control the start, pause, and stop motions of the recording when you play back the recording of your notes.

Figure 5: Video inserted in a notebook

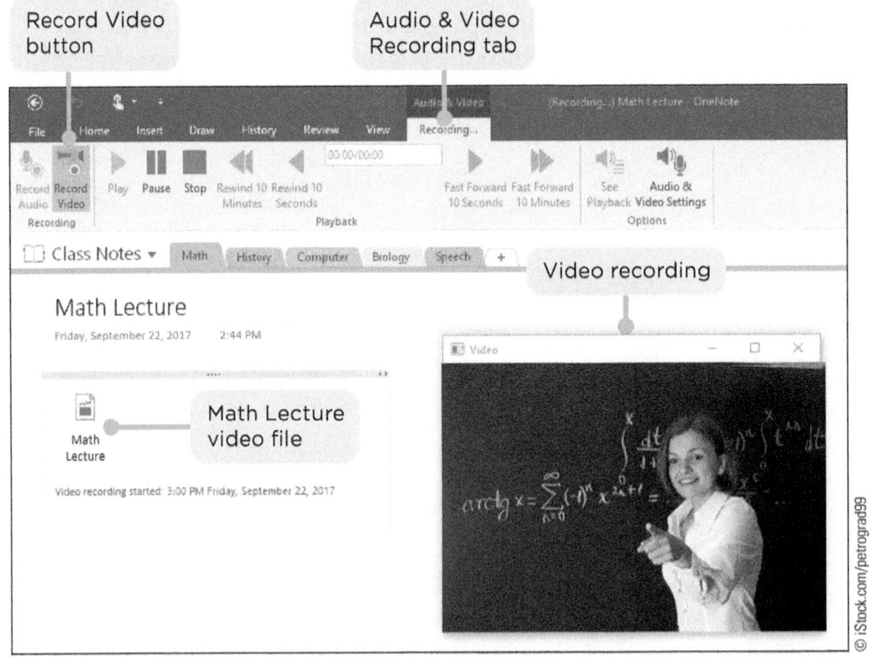

Try This Now

> **Learn to use OneNote!**
> Links to companion **Sways**, featuring **videos** with hands-on instructions, are located on www.cengagebrain.com.

1: Taking Notes for a Week

As a student, you can get organized by using OneNote to take detailed notes in your classes. Perform the following tasks:

a. Create a new OneNote notebook on your Microsoft OneDrive account (the default location for new notebooks). Name the notebook with your first name followed by "Notes," as in **Caleb Notes**.
b. Create four section tabs, each with a different class name.
c. Take detailed notes in those classes for one week. Be sure to include notes, drawings, and other types of content.
d. Sync your notes with your OneDrive. Submit your assignment in the format specified by your instructor.

2: Using OneNote to Organize a Research Paper

You have a research paper due on the topic of three habits of successful students. Use OneNote to organize your research. Perform the following tasks:

a. Create a new OneNote notebook on your Microsoft OneDrive account. Name the notebook **Success Research**.
b. Create three section tabs with the following names:
   - **Take Detailed Notes**
   - **Be Respectful in Class**
   - **Come to Class Prepared**
c. On the web, research the topics and find three sources for each section. Copy a sentence from each source and paste the sentence into the appropriate section. When you paste the sentence, OneNote inserts it in a note with a link to the source.
d. Sync your notes with your OneDrive. Submit your assignment in the format specified by your instructor.

3: Planning Your Career

Note: This activity requires a webcam or built-in video camera on any type of device.

Consider an occupation that interests you. Using OneNote, examine the responsibilities, education requirements, potential salary, and employment outlook of a specific career. Perform the following tasks:

a. Create a new OneNote notebook on your Microsoft OneDrive account. Name the notebook with your first name followed by a career title, such as **Kara - App Developer**.
b. Create four section tabs with the names **Responsibilities, Education Requirements, Median Salary**, and **Employment Outlook**.
c. Research the responsibilities of your career path. Using OneNote, record a short video (approximately 30 seconds) of yourself explaining the responsibilities of your career path. Place the video in the Responsibilities section.
d. On the web, research the educational requirements for your career path and find two appropriate sources. Copy a paragraph from each source and paste them into the appropriate section. When you paste a paragraph, OneNote inserts it in a note with a link to the source.
e. Research the median salary for a single year for this career. Create a mathematical equation in the Median Salary section that multiplies the amount of the median salary times 20 years to calculate how much you will possibly earn.
f. For the Employment Outlook section, research the outlook for your career path. Take at least four notes about what you find when researching the topic.
g. Sync your notes with your OneDrive. Submit your assignment in the format specified by your instructor.

Introduction to Sway

Sway site | responsive design | Storyline | card | Creative Commons license | animation emphasis effects | Docs.com

Bottom Line

- Drag photos, videos, and files from your computer and content from Facebook and Twitter directly to your Sway presentation.
- Run Sway in a web browser or as an app on your smartphone, and save presentations as webpages.

Expressing your ideas in a presentation typically means creating PowerPoint slides or a Word document. Microsoft Sway gives you another way to engage an audience. Sway is a free Microsoft tool available at Sway.com or as an app in Office 365. Using Sway, you can combine text, images, videos, and social media in a website called a **Sway site** that you can share and display on any device. To get started, you create a digital story on a web-based canvas without borders, slides, cells, or page breaks. A Sway site organizes the text, images, and video into a **responsive design**, which means your content adapts perfectly to any screen size as shown in Figure 6. You store a Sway site in the cloud on OneDrive using a free Microsoft account.

Figure 6: Sway site with responsive design

Learn to use Sway!
Links to companion **Sways**, featuring **videos** with hands-on instructions, are located on www.cengagebrain.com.

Creating a Sway Presentation

You can use Sway to build a digital flyer, a club newsletter, a vacation blog, an informational site, a digital art portfolio, or a new product rollout. After you select your topic and sign into Sway with your Microsoft account, a **Storyline** opens, providing tools and a work area for composing your digital story. See Figure 7. Each story can include text, images, and videos. You create a Sway by adding text and media content into a Storyline section, or **card**. To add pictures, videos, or documents, select a card in the left pane and then select the Insert Content button. The first card in a Sway presentation contains a title and background image.

Figure 7: Creating a Sway site

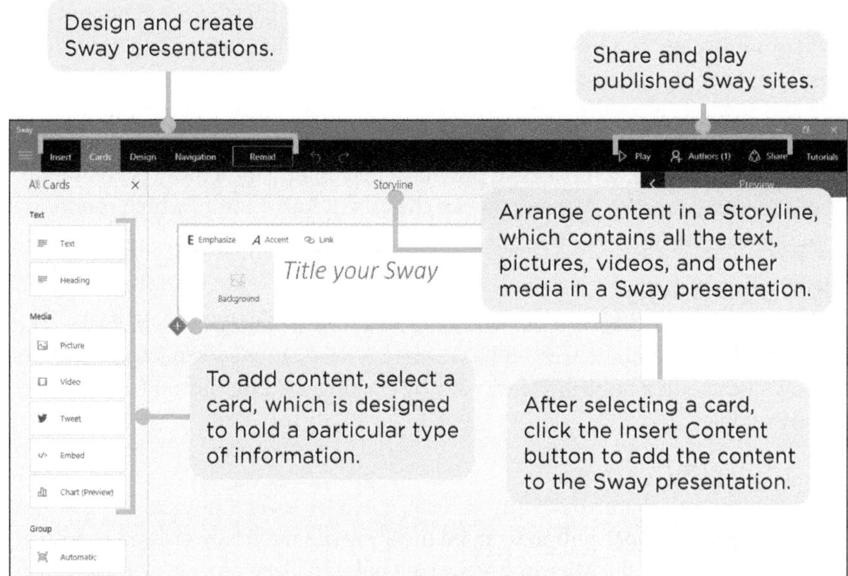

Adding Content to Build a Story

As you work, Sway searches the Internet to help you find relevant images, videos, tweets, and other content from online sources such as Bing, YouTube, Twitter, and Facebook. You can drag content from the search results right into the Storyline. In addition, you can upload your own images and videos directly in the presentation. For example, if you are creating a Sway presentation about the market for commercial drones, Sway suggests content to incorporate into the presentation by displaying it in the left pane as search results. The search results include drone images tagged with a **Creative Commons license** at online sources as shown in Figure 8. A Creative Commons license is a public copyright license that allows the free distribution of an otherwise copyrighted work. In addition, you can specify the source of the media. For example, you can add your own Facebook or OneNote pictures and videos in Sway without leaving the app.

On the Job Now

If you have a Microsoft Word document containing an outline of your business content, drag the outline into Sway to create a card for each topic.

Figure 8: Images in Sway search results

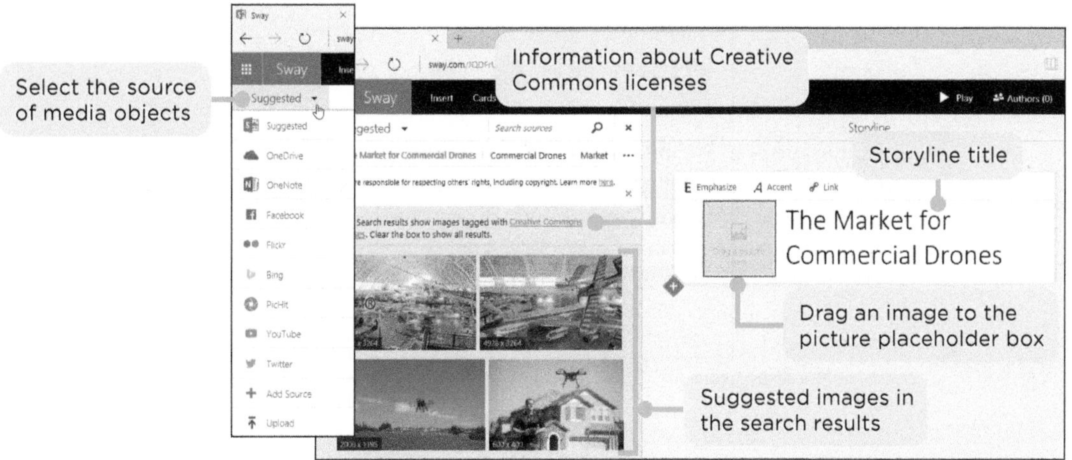

If your project team wants to collaborate on a Sway presentation, click the Authors button on the navigation bar to invite others to edit the presentation.

Designing a Sway

Sway professionally designs your Storyline content by resizing background images and fonts to fit your display, and by floating text, animating media, embedding video, and removing images as a page scrolls out of view. Sway also evaluates the images in your Storyline and suggests a color palette based on colors that appear in your photos. Use the Design button to display tools including color palettes, font choices, **animation emphasis effects**, and style templates to provide a personality for a Sway presentation. Instead of creating your own design, you can click the Remix button, which randomly selects unique designs for your Sway site.

Publishing a Sway

Use the Play button to display your finished Sway presentation as a website. The Address bar includes a unique web address where others can view your Sway site. As the author, you can edit a published Sway site by clicking the Edit button (pencil icon) on the Sway toolbar.

Sharing a Sway

When you are ready to share your Sway website, you have several options as shown in Figure 9. Use the Share slider button to share the Sway site publically or keep it private. If you add the Sway site to the Microsoft **Docs.com** public gallery, anyone worldwide can use Bing, Google, or other search engines to find, view, and share your Sway site. You can also share your Sway site using Facebook, Twitter, Google+, Yammer, and other social media sites. Link your presentation to any webpage or email the link to your audience. Sway can also generate a code for embedding the link within another webpage.

Figure 9: Sharing a Sway site

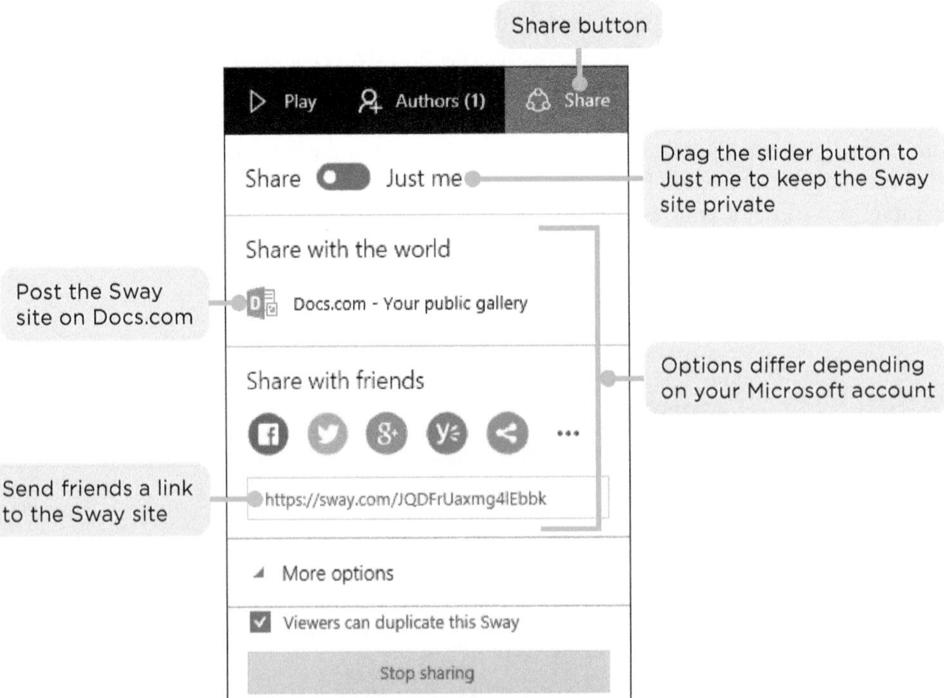

Try This Now

> **Learn to use Sway!**
> Links to companion **Sways**, featuring **videos** with hands-on instructions, are located on www.cengagebrain.com.

1: Creating a Sway Resume

Sway is a digital storytelling app. Create a Sway resume to share the skills, job experiences, and achievements you have that match the requirements of a future job interest. Perform the following tasks:

a. Create a new presentation in Sway to use as a digital resume. Title the Sway Storyline with your full name and then select a background image.
b. Create three separate sections titled **Academic Background, Work Experience**, and **Skills**, and insert text, a picture, and a paragraph or bulleted points in each section. Be sure to include your own picture.
c. Add a fourth section that includes a video about your school that you find online.
d. Customize the design of your presentation.
e. Submit your assignment link in the format specified by your instructor.

2: Creating an Online Sway Newsletter

Newsletters are designed to capture the attention of their target audience. Using Sway, create a newsletter for a club, organization, or your favorite music group. Perform the following tasks:

a. Create a new presentation in Sway to use as a digital newsletter for a club, organization, or your favorite music group. Provide a title for the Sway Storyline and select an appropriate background image.
b. Select three separate sections with appropriate titles, such as Upcoming Events. In each section, insert text, a picture, and a paragraph or bulleted points.
c. Add a fourth section that includes a video about your selected topic.
d. Customize the design of your presentation.
e. Submit your assignment link in the format specified by your instructor.

3: Creating and Sharing a Technology Presentation

To place a Sway presentation in the hands of your entire audience, you can share a link to the Sway presentation. Create a Sway presentation on a new technology and share it with your class. Perform the following tasks:

a. Create a new presentation in Sway about a cutting-edge technology topic. Provide a title for the Sway Storyline and select a background image.
b. Create four separate sections about your topic, and include text, a picture, and a paragraph in each section.
c. Add a fifth section that includes a video about your topic.
d. Customize the design of your presentation.
e. Share the link to your Sway with your classmates and submit your assignment link in the format specified by your instructor.

Introduction to Office Mix

Bottom Line
- Office Mix is a free PowerPoint add-in from Microsoft that adds features to PowerPoint.
- The Mix tab on the PowerPoint ribbon provides tools for creating screen recordings, videos, interactive quizzes, and live webpages.

add-in | clip | slide recording | Slide Notes | screen recording | free-response quiz

To enliven business meetings and lectures, Microsoft adds a new dimension to presentations with a powerful toolset called Office Mix, a free add-in for PowerPoint. (An **add-in** is software that works with an installed app to extend its features.) Using Office Mix, you can record yourself on video, capture still and moving images on your desktop, and insert interactive elements such as quizzes and live webpages directly into PowerPoint slides. When you post the finished presentation to OneDrive, Office Mix provides a link you can share with friends and colleagues. Anyone with an Internet connection and a web browser can watch a published Office Mix presentation, such as the one in Figure 10, on a computer or mobile device.

Figure 10: Office Mix presentation

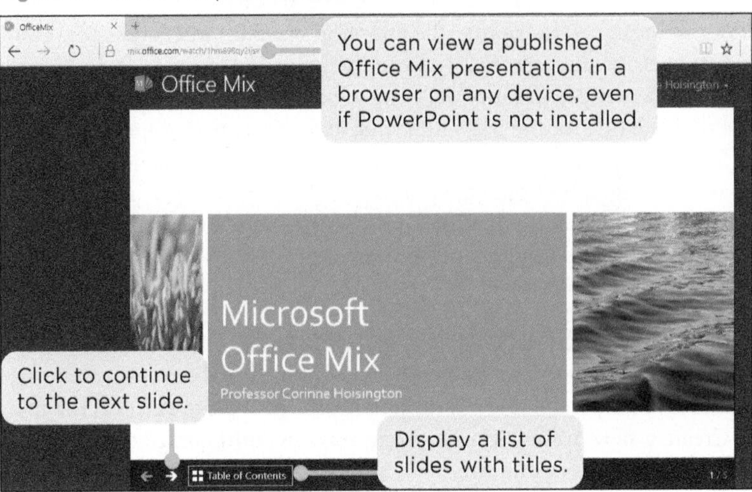

Learn to use Office Mix!
Links to companion **Sways**, featuring **videos** with hands-on instructions, are located on www.cengagebrain.com.

Adding Office Mix to PowerPoint

To get started, you create an Office Mix account at the website mix.office.com using an email address or a Facebook or Google account. Next, you download and install the Office Mix add-in (see Figure 11). Office Mix appears as a new tab named Mix on the PowerPoint ribbon in versions of Office 2013 and Office 2016 running on personal computers (PCs).

Figure 11: Getting started with Office Mix

Capturing Video Clips

A **clip** is a short segment of audio, such as music, or video. After finishing the content on a PowerPoint slide, you can use Office Mix to add a video clip to animate or illustrate the content. Office Mix creates video clips in two ways: by recording live action on a webcam and by capturing screen images and movements. If your computer has a webcam, you can record yourself and annotate the slide to create a **slide recording** as shown in **Figure 12**.

Companies are using Office Mix to train employees about new products, to explain benefit packages to new workers, and to educate interns about office procedures.

Figure 12: Making a slide recording

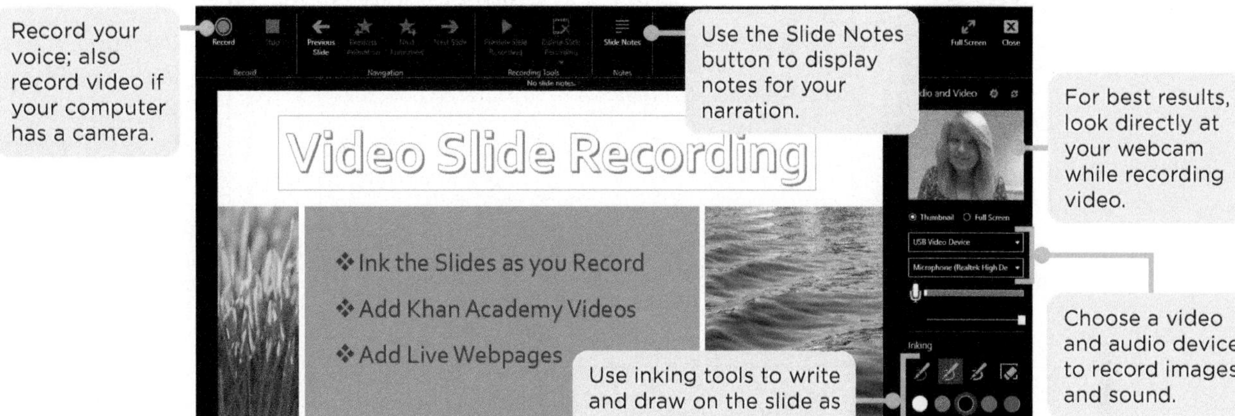

When you are making a slide recording, you can record your spoken narration at the same time. The **Slide Notes** feature works like a teleprompter to help you focus on your presentation content instead of memorizing your narration. Use the Inking tools to make annotations or add highlighting using different pen types and colors. After finishing a recording, edit the video in PowerPoint to trim the length or set playback options.

The second way to create a video is to capture on-screen images and actions with or without a voiceover. This method is ideal if you want to show how to use your favorite website or demonstrate an app such as OneNote. To share your screen with an audience, select the part of the screen you want to show in the video. Office Mix captures everything that happens in that area to create a **screen recording**, as shown in **Figure 13**. Office Mix inserts the screen recording as a video in the slide.

To make your video recordings accessible to people with hearing impairments, use the Office Mix closed-captioning tools. You can also use closed captions to supplement audio that is difficult to understand and to provide an aid for those learning to read.

Figure 13: Making a screen recording

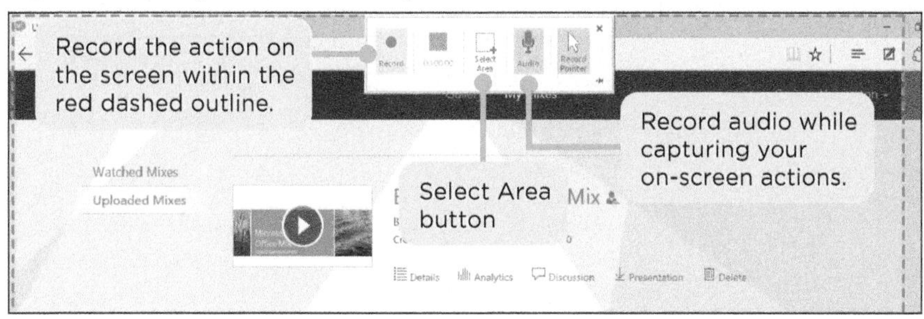

Inserting Quizzes, Live Webpages, and Apps

To enhance and assess audience understanding, make your slides interactive by adding quizzes, live webpages, and apps. Quizzes give immediate feedback to the user as shown in **Figure 14**. Office Mix supports several quiz formats, including a **free-response quiz** similar to a short answer quiz, and true/false, multiple-choice, and multiple-response formats.

Figure 14: Creating an interactive quiz

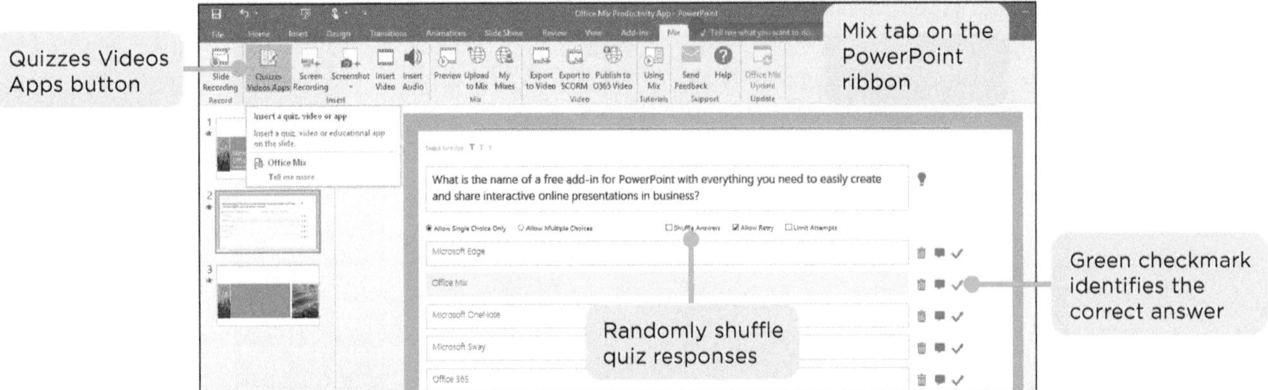

Sharing an Office Mix Presentation

When you complete your work with Office Mix, upload the presentation to your personal Office Mix dashboard as shown in **Figure 15**. Users of PCs, Macs, iOS devices, and Android devices can access and play Office Mix presentations. The Office Mix dashboard displays built-in analytics that include the quiz results and how much time viewers spent on each slide. You can play completed Office Mix presentations online or download them as movies.

Figure 15: Sharing an Office Mix presentation

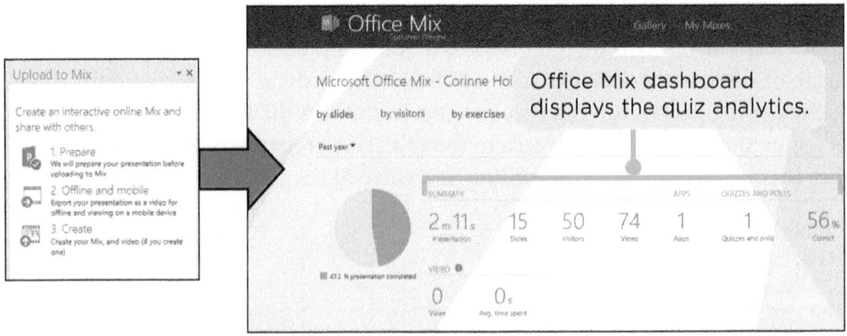

Try This Now

> **Learn to use Office Mix!**
> Links to companion **Sways**, featuring **videos** with hands-on instructions, are located on www.cengagebrain.com.

1: Creating an Office Mix Tutorial for OneNote

Note: This activity requires a microphone on your computer.

Office Mix makes it easy to record screens and their contents. Create PowerPoint slides with an Office Mix screen recording to show OneNote 2016 features. Perform the following tasks:

a. Create a PowerPoint presentation with the Ion Boardroom template. Create an opening slide with the title **My Favorite OneNote Features** and enter your name in the subtitle.
b. Create three additional slides, each titled with a new feature of OneNote. Open OneNote and use the Mix tab in PowerPoint to capture three separate screen recordings that teach your favorite features.
c. Add a fifth slide that quizzes the user with a multiple-choice question about OneNote and includes four responses. Be sure to insert a checkmark indicating the correct response.
d. Upload the completed presentation to your Office Mix dashboard and share the link with your instructor.
e. Submit your assignment link in the format specified by your instructor.

2: Teaching Augmented Reality with Office Mix

Note: This activity requires a webcam or built-in video camera on your computer.

A local elementary school has asked you to teach augmented reality to its students using Office Mix. Perform the following tasks:

a. Research augmented reality using your favorite online search tools.
b. Create a PowerPoint presentation with the Frame template. Create an opening slide with the title **Augmented Reality** and enter your name in the subtitle.
c. Create a slide with four bullets summarizing your research of augmented reality. Create a 20-second slide recording of yourself providing a quick overview of augmented reality.
d. Create another slide with a 30-second screen recording of a video about augmented reality from a site such as YouTube or another video-sharing site.
e. Add a final slide that quizzes the user with a true/false question about augmented reality. Be sure to insert a checkmark indicating the correct response.
f. Upload the completed presentation to your Office Mix dashboard and share the link with your instructor.
g. Submit your assignment link in the format specified by your instructor.

3: Marketing a Travel Destination with Office Mix

Note: This activity requires a webcam or built-in video camera on your computer.

To convince your audience to travel to a particular city, create a slide presentation marketing any city in the world using a slide recording, screen recording, and a quiz. Perform the following tasks:

a. Create a PowerPoint presentation with any template. Create an opening slide with the title of the city you are marketing as a travel destination and your name in the subtitle.
b. Create a slide with four bullets about the featured city. Create a 30-second slide recording of yourself explaining why this city is the perfect vacation destination.
c. Create another slide with a 20-second screen recording of a travel video about the city from a site such as YouTube or another video-sharing site.
d. Add a final slide that quizzes the user with a multiple-choice question about the featured city with five responses. Be sure to include a checkmark indicating the correct response.
e. Upload the completed presentation to your Office Mix dashboard and share your link with your instructor.
f. Submit your assignment link in the format specified by your instructor.

Introduction to Microsoft Edge

Reading view | Hub | Cortana | Web Note | Inking | sandbox

Bottom Line

- Microsoft Edge is the name of the new web browser built into Windows 10.
- Microsoft Edge allows you to search the web faster, take web notes, read webpages without distractions, and get instant assistance from Cortana.

Microsoft Edge is the default web browser developed for the Windows 10 operating system as a replacement for Internet Explorer. Unlike its predecessor, Edge lets you write on webpages, read webpages without advertisements and other distractions, and search for information using a virtual personal assistant. The Edge interface is clean and basic, as shown in **Figure 16**, meaning you can pay more attention to the webpage content.

Figure 16: Microsoft Edge tools

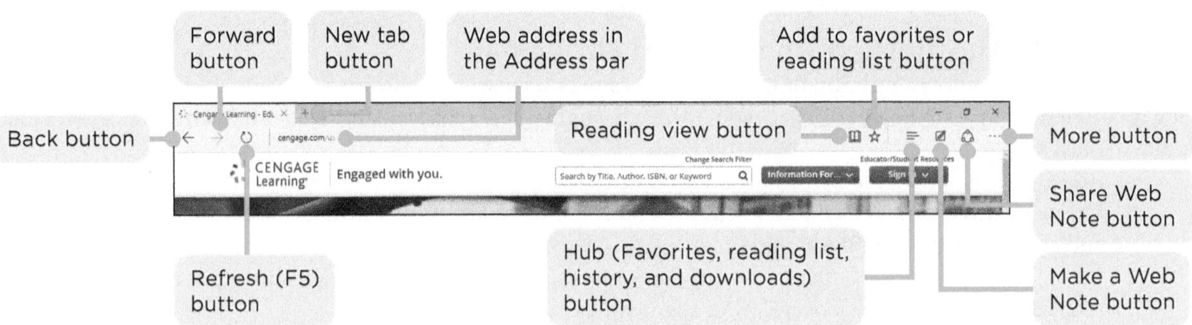

Learn to use Edge!
Links to companion **Sways**, featuring **videos** with hands-on instructions, are located on www.cengagebrain.com.

Browsing the Web with Microsoft Edge

One of the fastest browsers available, Edge allows you to type search text directly in the Address bar. As you view the resulting webpage, you can switch to **Reading view**, which is available for most news and research sites, to eliminate distracting advertisements. For example, if you are catching up on technology news online, the webpage might be difficult to read due to a busy layout cluttered with ads. Switch to Reading view to refresh the page and remove the original page formatting, ads, and menu sidebars to read the article distraction-free.

Consider the **Hub** in Microsoft Edge as providing one-stop access to all the things you collect on the web, such as your favorite websites, reading list, surfing history, and downloaded files.

On the Job Now

Businesses started adopting Internet Explorer more than 20 years ago simply to view webpages. Today, Microsoft Edge has a different purpose: to promote interaction with the web and share its contents with colleagues.

Locating Information with Cortana

Cortana, the Windows 10 virtual assistant, plays an important role in Microsoft Edge. After you turn on Cortana, it appears as an animated circle in the Address bar when you might need assistance, as shown in the restaurant website in **Figure 17**. When you click the Cortana icon, a pane slides in from the right of the browser window to display detailed information about the restaurant, including maps and reviews. Cortana can also assist you in defining words, finding the weather, suggesting coupons for shopping, updating stock market information, and calculating math.

Figure 17: Cortana providing restaurant information

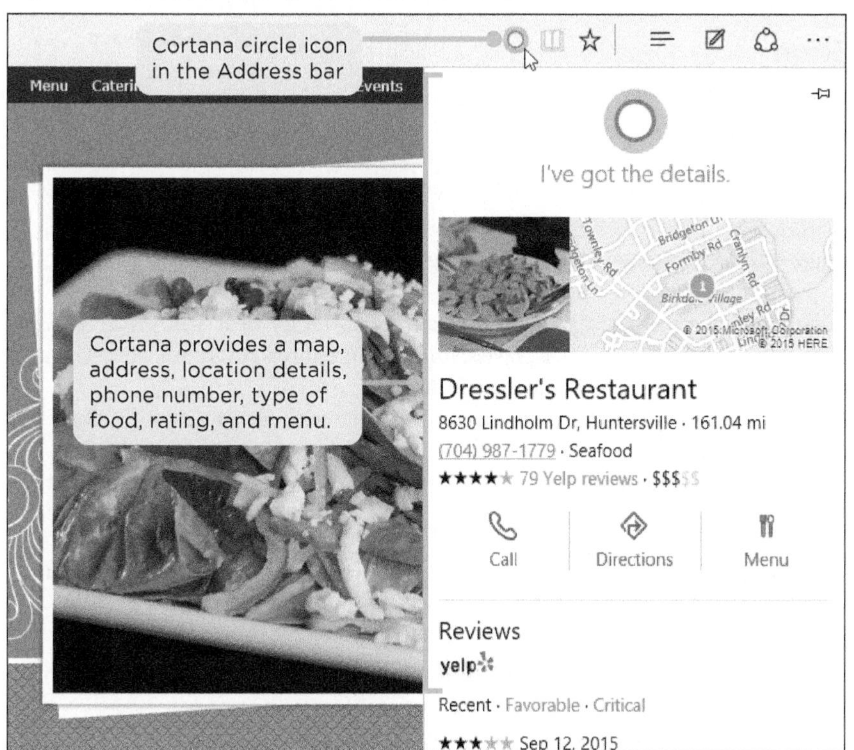

Annotating Webpages

One of the most impressive Microsoft Edge features are the **Web Note** tools, which you use to write on a webpage or to highlight text. When you click the Make a Web Note button, an **Inking** toolbar appears, as shown in Figure 18, that provides writing and drawing tools. These tools include an eraser, a pen, and a highlighter with different colors. You can also insert a typed note and copy a screen image (called a screen clipping). You can draw with a pointing device, fingertip, or stylus using different pen colors. Whether you add notes to a recipe, annotate sources for a research paper, or select a product while shopping online, the Web Note tools can enhance your productivity. After you complete your notes, click the Save button to save the annotations to OneNote, your Favorites list, or your Reading list. You can share the inked page with others using the Share Web Note button.

To enhance security, Microsoft Edge runs in a partial sandbox, an arrangement that prevents attackers from gaining control of your computer. Browsing within the **sandbox** protects computer resources and information from hackers.

Figure 18: Web Note tools in Microsoft Edge

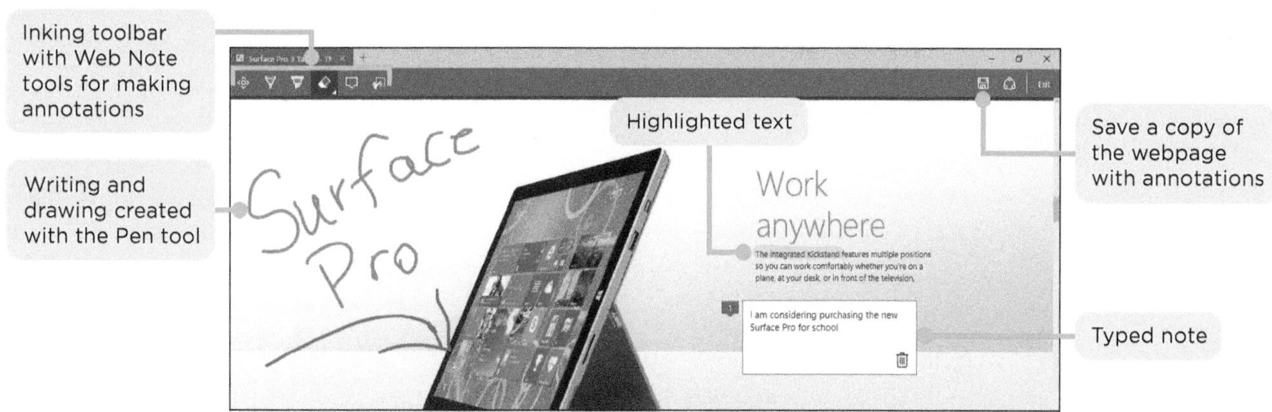

Try This Now

> **Learn to use Edge!**
> Links to companion **Sways**, featuring **videos** with hands-on instructions, are located on www.cengagebrain.com.

1: Using Cortana in Microsoft Edge

Note: This activity requires using Microsoft Edge on a Windows 10 computer.

Cortana can assist you in finding information on a webpage in Microsoft Edge. Perform the following tasks:

a. Create a Word document using the Word Screen Clipping tool to capture the following screenshots.
   - Screenshot A—Using Microsoft Edge, open a webpage with a technology news article. Right-click a term in the article and ask Cortana to define it.
   - Screenshot B—Using Microsoft Edge, open the website of a fancy restaurant in a city near you. Make sure the Cortana circle icon is displayed in the Address bar. (If it's not displayed, find a different restaurant website.) Click the Cortana circle icon to display a pane with information about the restaurant.
   - Screenshot C—Using Microsoft Edge, type **10 USD to Euros** in the Address bar without pressing the Enter key. Cortana converts the U.S. dollars to Euros.
   - Screenshot D—Using Microsoft Edge, type **Apple stock** in the Address bar without pressing the Enter key. Cortana displays the current stock quote.

b. Submit your assignment in the format specified by your instructor.

2: Viewing Online News with Reading View

Note: This activity requires using Microsoft Edge on a Windows 10 computer.

Reading view in Microsoft Edge can make a webpage less cluttered with ads and other distractions. Perform the following tasks:

a. Create a Word document using the Word Screen Clipping tool to capture the following screenshots.
   - Screenshot A—Using Microsoft Edge, open the website **mashable.com**. Open a technology article. Click the Reading view button to display an ad-free page that uses only basic text formatting.
   - Screenshot B—Using Microsoft Edge, open the website **bbc.com**. Open any news article. Click the Reading view button to display an ad-free page that uses only basic text formatting.
   - Screenshot C—Make three types of annotations (Pen, Highlighter, and Add a typed note) on the BBC article page displayed in Reading view.

b. Submit your assignment in the format specified by your instructor.

3: Inking with Microsoft Edge

Note: This activity requires using Microsoft Edge on a Windows 10 computer.

Microsoft Edge provides many annotation options to record your ideas. Perform the following tasks:

a. Open the website **wolframalpha.com** in the Microsoft Edge browser. Wolfram Alpha is a well-respected academic search engine. Type **US$100 1965 dollars in 2015** in the Wolfram Alpha search text box and press the Enter key.

b. Click the Make a Web Note button to display the Web Note tools. Using the Pen tool, draw a circle around the result on the webpage. Save the page to OneNote.

c. In the Wolfram Alpha search text box, type the name of the city closest to where you live and press the Enter key. Using the Highlighter tool, highlight at least three interesting results. Add a note and then type a sentence about what you learned about this city. Save the page to OneNote. Share your OneNote notebook with your instructor.

d. Submit your assignment link in the format specified by your instructor.

Office 2016 and Windows 10: Essential Concepts and Skills

Objectives

You will have mastered the material in this module when you can:

- Use a touch screen
- Perform basic mouse operations
- Start Windows and sign in to an account
- Identify the objects on the Windows 10 desktop
- Identify the apps in and versions of Microsoft Office 2016
- Run an app
- Identify the components of the Microsoft Office ribbon
- Create folders
- Save files
- Change screen resolution
- Perform basic tasks in Microsoft Office apps
- Manage files
- Use Microsoft Office Help and Windows Help

This introductory module uses Excel 2016 to cover features and functions common to Office 2016 apps, as well as the basics of Windows 10.

Roadmap

In this module, you will learn how to perform basic tasks in Windows and Excel. The following roadmap identifies general activities you will perform as you progress through this module:

1. SIGN IN to an account
2. USE WINDOWS
3. USE Features in Excel that are Common across Office APPS
4. FILE and Folder MANAGEMENT
5. SWITCH between APPS
6. SAVE and Manage FILES

7. CHANGE SCREEN RESOLUTION
8. EXIT APPS
9. USE ADDITIONAL Office APP FEATURES
10. USE Office and Windows HELP

At the beginning of the step instructions throughout each module, you will see an abbreviated form of this roadmap. The abbreviated roadmap uses colors to indicate module progress: gray means the module is beyond that activity, blue means the task being shown is covered in that activity, and black means that activity is yet to be covered. For example, the following abbreviated roadmap indicates the module would be showing a task in the USE APPS activity.

1 SIGN IN | 2 USE WINDOWS | 3 USE APPS | 4 FILE MANAGEMENT | 5 SWITCH APPS | 6 SAVE FILES
7 CHANGE SCREEN RESOLUTION | 8 EXIT APPS | 9 USE ADDITIONAL APP FEATURES | 10 USE HELP

Use the abbreviated roadmap as a progress guide while you read or step through the instructions in this module.

Introduction to the Windows 10 Operating System

Windows 10 is the newest version of Microsoft Windows, which is a popular and widely used operating system (Figure 1). An **operating system (OS)** is a set of programs that coordinate all the activities among computer or mobile device hardware.

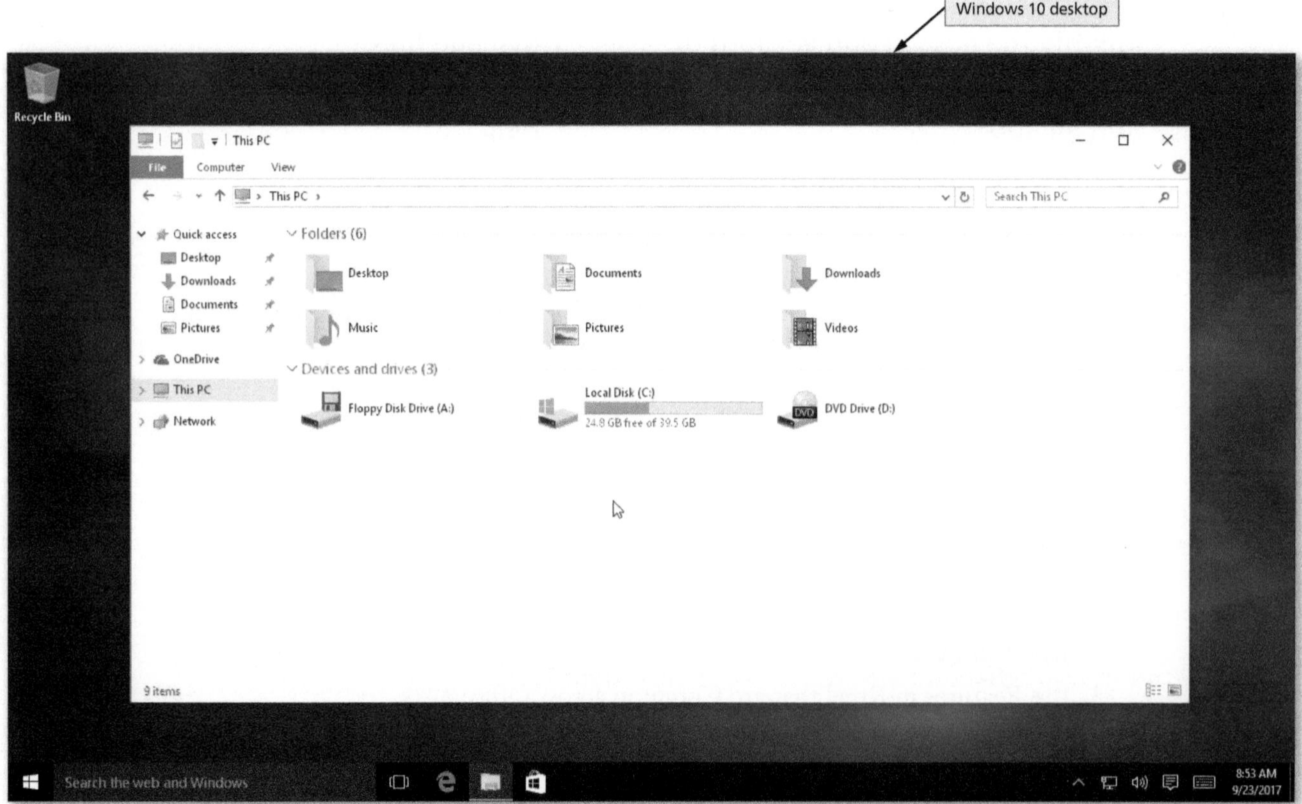

Figure 1

The Windows operating system simplifies the process of working with documents and apps by organizing the manner in which you interact with the computer. Windows is used to run apps. An application, or **app**, consists of programs designed to make users more productive and/or assist them with personal tasks, such as using spreadsheets or browsing the web.

If you are using your finger on a touch screen and are having difficulty completing the steps in this module, consider using a stylus. Many people find it easier to be precise with a stylus than with a finger. In addition, with a stylus you see the pointer. If you still are having trouble completing the steps with a stylus, try using a mouse.

Using a Touch Screen and a Mouse

Windows users who have computers or devices with touch screen capability can interact with the screen using gestures. A **gesture** is a motion you make on a touch screen with the tip of one or more fingers or your hand. Touch screens are convenient because they do not require a separate device for input. Table 1 presents common ways to interact with a touch screen.

Table 1 Touch Screen Gestures

Motion	Description	Common Uses	Equivalent Mouse Operation
Tap	Quickly touch and release one finger one time.	Activate a link (built-in connection). Press a button. Run a program or an app.	Click
Double-tap	Quickly touch and release one finger two times.	Run a program or an app. Zoom in (show a smaller area on the screen, so that contents appear larger) at the location of the double-tap.	Double-click
Press and hold	Press and hold one finger to cause an action to occur, or until an action occurs.	Display a shortcut menu (immediate access to allowable actions). Activate a mode enabling you to move an item with one finger to a new location.	Right-click
Drag, or slide	Press and hold one finger on an object and then move the finger to the new location.	Move an item around the screen. Scroll.	Drag
Swipe	Press and hold one finger and then move the finger horizontally or vertically on the screen.	Select an object. Swipe from edge to display a bar such as the Action Center, Apps bar, and Navigation bar (all discussed later).	Drag
Stretch	Move two fingers apart.	Zoom in (show a smaller area on the screen, so that contents appear larger).	None
Pinch	Move two fingers together.	Zoom out (show a larger area on the screen, so that contents appear smaller).	None

CONSIDER THIS

Will your screen look different if you are using a touch screen?

The Windows and Microsoft Office interface varies slightly if you are using a touch screen. For this reason, you might notice that your Windows or Excel screens looks slightly different from the screens in this book.

BTW
Pointer
If you are using a touch screen, the pointer may not appear on the screen as you perform touch gestures. The pointer will reappear when you begin using the mouse.

Windows users who do not have touch screen capabilities typically work with a mouse that has at least two buttons. For a right-handed user, the left button usually is the primary mouse button, and the right mouse button is the secondary mouse button. Left-handed people, however, can reverse the function of these buttons.

Table 2 explains how to perform a variety of mouse operations. Some apps also use keys in combination with the mouse to perform certain actions. For example, when you hold down the CTRL key while rolling the mouse wheel, text on the screen may become larger or smaller based on the direction you roll the wheel. The function of the mouse buttons and the wheel varies depending on the app.

Table 2 Mouse Operations

Operation	Mouse Action	Example*	Equivalent Touch Gesture
Point	Move the mouse until the pointer on the desktop is positioned on the item of choice.	Position the pointer on the screen.	None
Click	Press and release the primary mouse button, which usually is the left mouse button.	Select or deselect items on the screen or run an app or app feature.	Tap
Right-click	Press and release the secondary mouse button, which usually is the right mouse button.	Display a shortcut menu.	Press and hold
Double-click	Quickly press and release the primary mouse button twice without moving the mouse.	Run an app or app feature.	Double-tap
Triple-click	Quickly press and release the primary mouse button three times without moving the mouse.	Select a paragraph.	Triple-tap
Drag	Point to an item, hold down the primary mouse button, move the item to the desired location on the screen, and then release the mouse button.	Move an object from one location to another or draw pictures.	Drag or slide
Right-drag	Point to an item, hold down the secondary mouse button, move the item to the desired location on the screen, and then release the mouse button.	Display a shortcut menu after moving an object from one location to another.	Press and hold, then drag
Rotate wheel	Roll the wheel forward or backward.	Scroll vertically (up and down).	Swipe
Free-spin wheel	Whirl the wheel forward or backward so that it spins freely on its own.	Scroll through many pages in seconds.	Swipe
Press wheel	Press the wheel button while moving the mouse.	Scroll continuously.	None
Tilt wheel	Press the wheel toward the right or left.	Scroll horizontally (left and right).	None
Press thumb button	Press the button on the side of the mouse with your thumb.	Move forward or backward through webpages and/or control media, games, etc.	None

*Note: The examples presented in this column are discussed as they are demonstrated in this module.

Scrolling

A **scroll bar** is a horizontal or vertical bar that appears when the contents of an area may not be visible completely on the screen (Figure 2). A scroll bar contains **scroll arrows** and a **scroll box** that enable you to view areas that currently cannot be seen on the screen. Clicking the up and down scroll arrows moves the screen content up or down one line. You also can click above or below the scroll box to move up or down a section, or drag the scroll box up or down to move to a specific location.

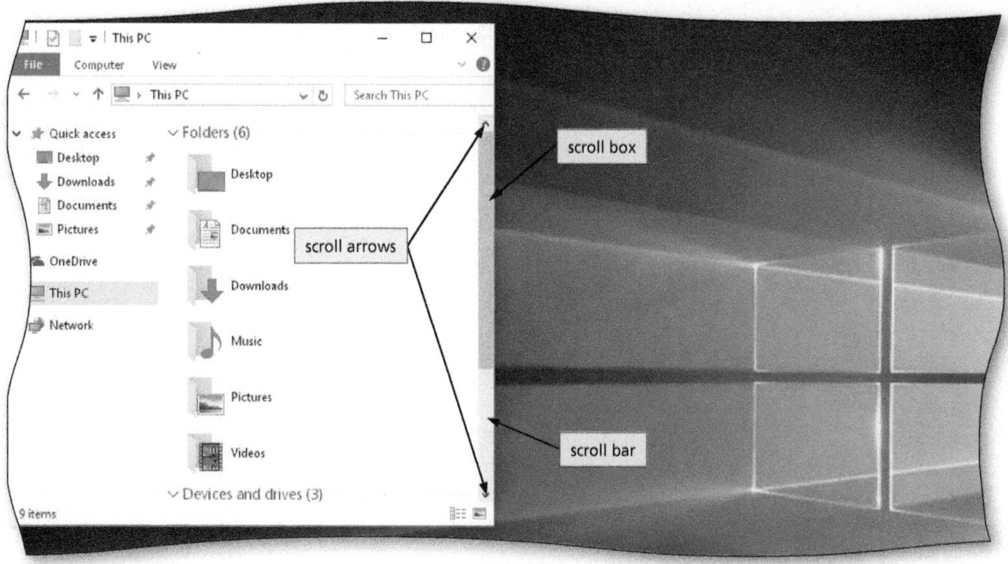

Figure 2

Keyboard Shortcuts

In many cases, you can use the keyboard instead of the mouse to accomplish a task. To perform tasks using the keyboard, you press one or more keyboard keys, sometimes identified as a **keyboard shortcut**. Some keyboard shortcuts consist of a single key, such as the F1 key. For example, to obtain help in many apps, you can press the F1 key. Other keyboard shortcuts consist of multiple keys, in which case a plus sign separates the key names, such as CTRL+ESC. This notation means to press and hold down the first key listed, press one or more additional keys, and then release all keys. For example, to display the Start menu, press CTRL+ESC, that is, hold down the CTRL key, press the ESC key, and then release both keys.

BTW

Minimize Wrist Injury

Computer users frequently switch between the keyboard and the mouse during a spreadsheet session; such switching strains the wrist. To help prevent wrist injury, minimize switching. For instance, if your fingers already are on the keyboard, use keyboard keys to scroll. If your hand already is on the mouse, use the mouse to scroll. If your hand is on the touch screen, use touch gestures to scroll.

Starting Windows

It is not unusual for multiple people to use the same computer in a work, educational, recreational, or home setting. Windows enables each user to establish a **user account**, which identifies to Windows the resources, such as apps and storage locations, a user can access when working with the computer.

Each user account has a user name and may have a password and an icon, as well. A **user name** is a unique combination of letters or numbers that identifies a specific user to Windows. A **password** is a private combination of letters, numbers, and special characters associated with the user name that allows access to a user's account resources. An icon is a small image that represents an object; thus, a **user icon** is a picture associated with a user name.

When you turn on a computer, Windows starts and displays a **lock screen** consisting of the time and date (Figure 3). To unlock the screen, click the lock screen. Depending on your computer's settings, Windows may or may not display a sign-in screen that shows the user names and user icons for users who have accounts on the computer. This **sign-in screen** enables you to sign in to your user account and makes the computer available for use. Clicking the user icon begins the process of signing in, also called logging on, to your user account.

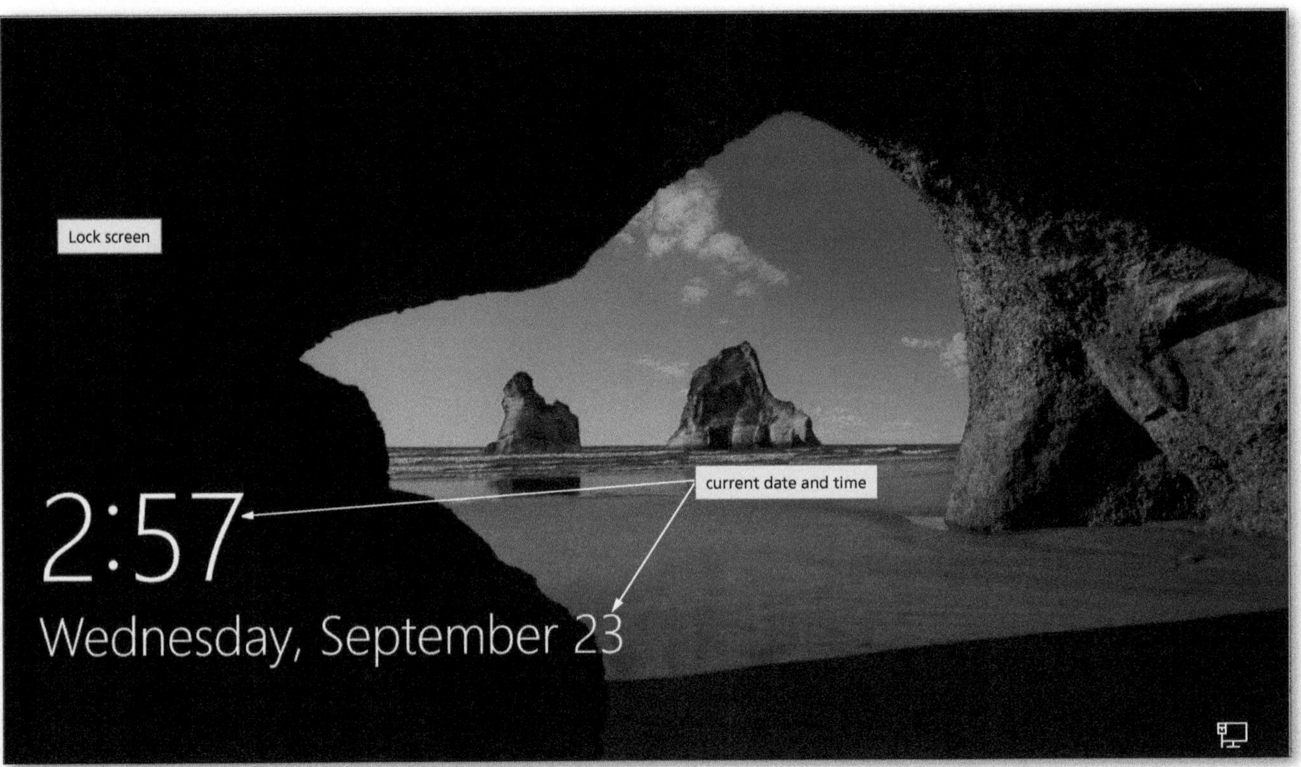

Figure 3

At the bottom of the sign-in screen is the 'Connect to Internet' button, 'Ease of access' button, and a Shut down button. Clicking the 'Connect to Internet' button displays a list of each network connection and its status. You also can connect to or disconnect from a network. Clicking the 'Ease of access' button displays the Ease of access menu, which provides tools to optimize a computer to accommodate the needs of the mobility, hearing, and vision impaired users. Clicking the Shut down button displays a menu containing commands related to putting the computer or mobile device in a low-power state, shutting it down, and restarting the computer or mobile device. The commands available on your computer or mobile device may differ.

- The Sleep command saves your work, turns off the computer fans and hard drive, and places the computer in a lower-power state. To wake the computer from sleep mode, press the power button or lift a laptop's cover, and sign in to your account.
- The Shut down command exits running apps, shuts down Windows, and then turns off the computer.
- The Restart command exits running apps, shuts down Windows, and then restarts Windows.

To Sign In to an Account

1 SIGN IN | 2 USE WINDOWS | 3 USE APPS | 4 FILE MANAGEMENT | 5 SWITCH APPS | 6 SAVE FILES
7 CHANGE SCREEN RESOLUTION | 8 EXIT APPS | 9 USE ADDITIONAL APP FEATURES | 10 USE HELP

The following steps, which use SCSeries as the user name, sign in to an account based on a typical Windows installation. ***Why?*** *After starting Windows, you might be required to sign in to an account to access the computer or mobile device's resources.* You may need to ask your instructor how to sign in to your account.

- Click the lock screen (shown in Figure 3) to display a sign-in screen.
- Click the user icon (for SCSeries, in this case) on the sign-in screen, which depending on settings, either will display a second sign-in screen that contains a Password text box (Figure 4) or will display the Windows desktop (Figure 5).

Q&A

Why do I not see a user icon?
Your computer may require you to type a user name instead of clicking an icon.

What is a text box?
A text box is a rectangular box in which you type text.

Why does my screen not show a Password text box?
Your account does not require a password.

- If Windows displays a sign-in screen with a Password text box, type your password in the text box.

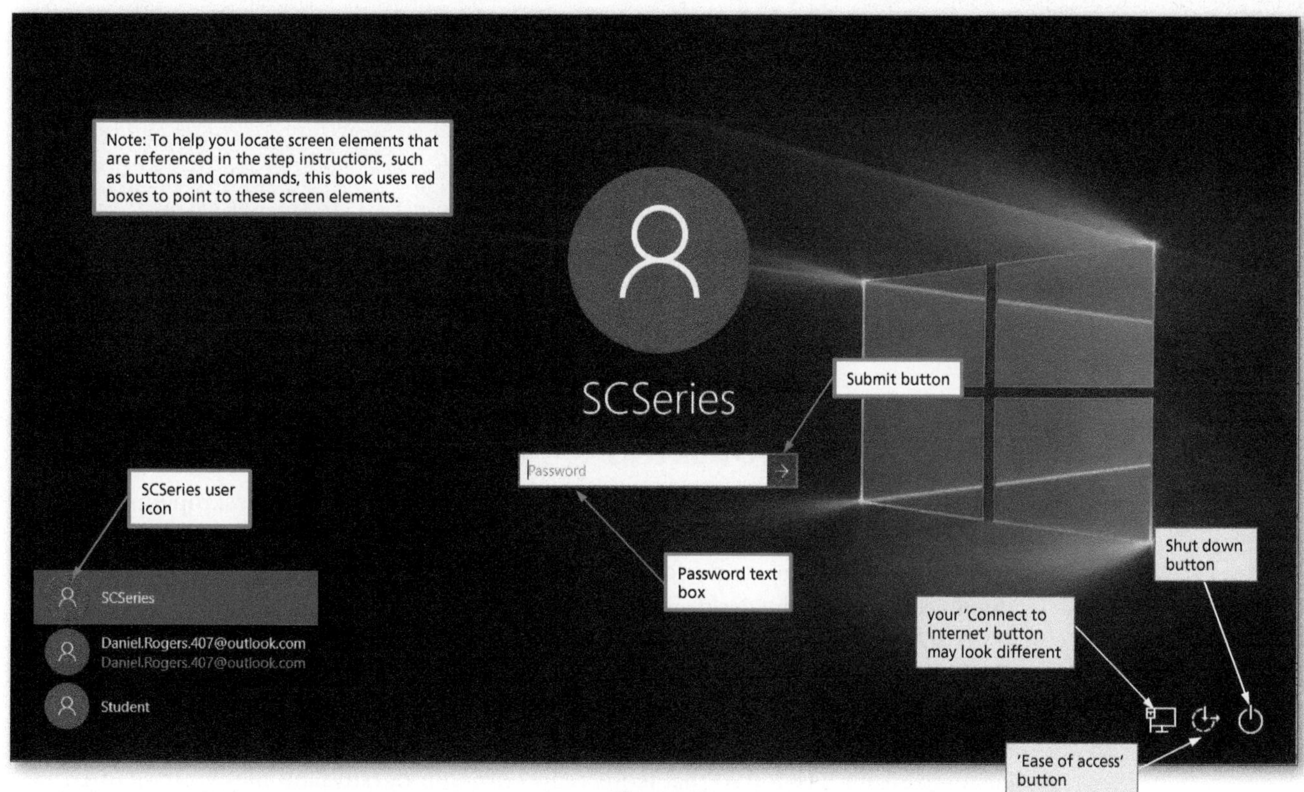

Figure 4

- Click the Submit button (shown in Figure 4) to sign in to your account and display the Windows desktop (Figure 5).

Q&A

Why does my desktop look different from the one in Figure 5?
The Windows desktop is customizable, and your school or employer may have modified the desktop to meet its needs. Also, your screen resolution, which affects the size of the elements on the screen, may differ from the screen resolution used in this book. Later in this module, you learn how to change screen resolution.

How do I type if my tablet has no keyboard?
You can use your fingers to press keys on a keyboard that appears on the screen, called an on-screen keyboard, or you can purchase a separate physical keyboard that attaches to or wirelessly communicates with the tablet.

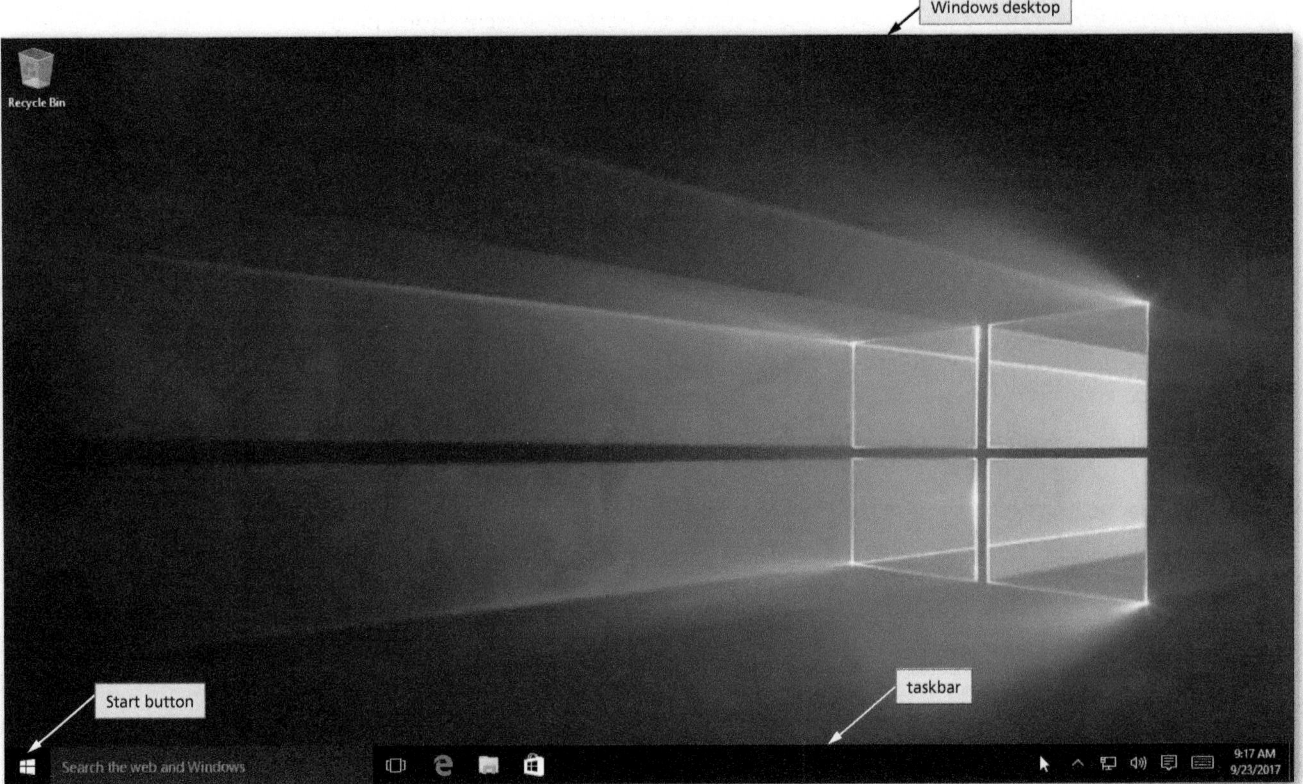

Figure 5

The Windows Desktop

The Windows 10 desktop (Figure 5) and the objects on the desktop emulate a work area in an office. Think of the Windows desktop as an electronic version of the top of your desk. You can perform tasks such as placing objects on the desktop, moving the objects around the desktop, and removing items from the desktop.

When you run an app in Windows 10, it appears on the desktop. Some icons also may be displayed on the desktop. For instance, the icon for the **Recycle Bin**, the location of files that have been deleted, appears on the desktop by default. A **file** is a named unit of storage. Files can contain text, images, audio, and video. You can customize your desktop so that icons representing programs and files you use often appear on your desktop.

Introduction to Microsoft Office 2016

Microsoft Office 2016 is the newest version of Microsoft Office, offering features that provide users with better functionality and easier ways to work with the various files they create. This version of Office also is designed to work more optimally on mobile devices and online.

Microsoft Office 2016 Apps

Microsoft Office 2016 includes a wide variety of apps, such as Word, PowerPoint, Excel, Access, Outlook, Publisher, and OneNote:

- **Microsoft Word 2016**, or Word, is a full-featured word processing app that allows you to create professional-looking documents and revise them easily.

- **Microsoft PowerPoint 2016**, or PowerPoint, is a complete presentation app that enables you to produce professional-looking presentations and then deliver them to an audience.
- **Microsoft Excel 2016**, or Excel, is a powerful spreadsheet app that allows you to organize data, complete calculations, make decisions, graph data, develop professional-looking reports, publish organized data to the web, and access real-time data from websites.
- **Microsoft Access 2016**, or Access, is a database management system that enables you to create a database; add, change, and delete data in the database; ask questions concerning the data in the database; and create forms and reports using the data in the database.
- **Microsoft Outlook 2016**, or Outlook, is a communications and scheduling app that allows you to manage email accounts, calendars, contacts, and access to other Internet content.
- **Microsoft Publisher 2016**, or Publisher, is a desktop publishing app that helps you create professional-quality publications and marketing materials that can be shared easily.
- **Microsoft OneNote 2016**, or OneNote, is a note taking app that allows you to store and share information in notebooks with other people.

Microsoft Office 2016 Suites

A **suite** is a collection of individual apps available together as a unit. Microsoft offers a variety of Office suites, including a stand-alone desktop app, Microsoft Office 365, and Microsoft Office Online. **Microsoft Office 365**, or Office 365, provides plans that allow organizations to use Office in a mobile setting while also being able to communicate and share files, depending upon the type of plan selected by the organization. **Microsoft Office Online** includes apps that allow you to edit and share files on the web using the familiar Office interface.

During the Office 365 installation, you select a plan, and depending on your plan, you receive different apps and services. Office Online apps do not require a local installation and can be accessed through OneDrive and your browser. **OneDrive** is a cloud storage service that provides storage and other services, such as Office Online, to computer and mobile device users.

CONSIDER THIS

How do you sign up for a OneDrive account?

- Use your browser to navigate to onedrive.live.com.
- Create a Microsoft account by clicking the Sign up button and then entering your information to create the account.
- Sign in to OneDrive using your new account or use it in Excel to save your files on OneDrive.

Apps in a suite, such as Microsoft Office, typically use a similar interface and share features. Once you are comfortable working with the elements and the interface and performing tasks in one app, the similarity can help you apply the knowledge and skills you have learned to another app(s) in the suite. For example, the process for saving a file in Excel is the same in Word, PowerPoint, and some of the other Office apps. While briefly showing how to use Excel, this module illustrates some of the common functions across the Office apps and identifies the characteristics unique to Excel.

Running and Using an App

To use an app, you must instruct the operating system to run the app. Windows provides many different ways to run an app, one of which is presented in this section (other ways to run an app are presented throughout this module). After an app is running, you can use it to perform a variety of tasks. The following pages use Excel to discuss some elements of the Office interface and to perform tasks that are common to other Office apps.

Excel

Excel is a powerful spreadsheet app that allows users to organize data, complete calculations, make decisions, graph data, develop professional-looking reports, publish organized data to the web, and access real-time data from websites (Figure 6). The four major parts of Excel are:

- **Workbooks and Worksheets:** A workbook is like a notebook. Inside the workbook are sheets, each of which is called a worksheet. Thus, a workbook is a collection of worksheets. Worksheets allow users to enter, calculate, manipulate, and analyze data, such as numbers and text. The terms worksheet and spreadsheet are interchangeable.
- **Charts:** Excel can draw a variety of charts, such as column charts and pie charts.
- **Tables:** Tables organize and store data within worksheets. For example, once a user enters data into a worksheet, an Excel table can sort the data, search for specific data, and select data that satisfies defined criteria.
- **Web Support:** Web support allows users to save Excel worksheets or parts of a worksheet in a format that a user can view in a browser, so that a user can view and manipulate the worksheet using a browser. Excel web support also provides access to real-time data, such as stock quotes, using web queries.

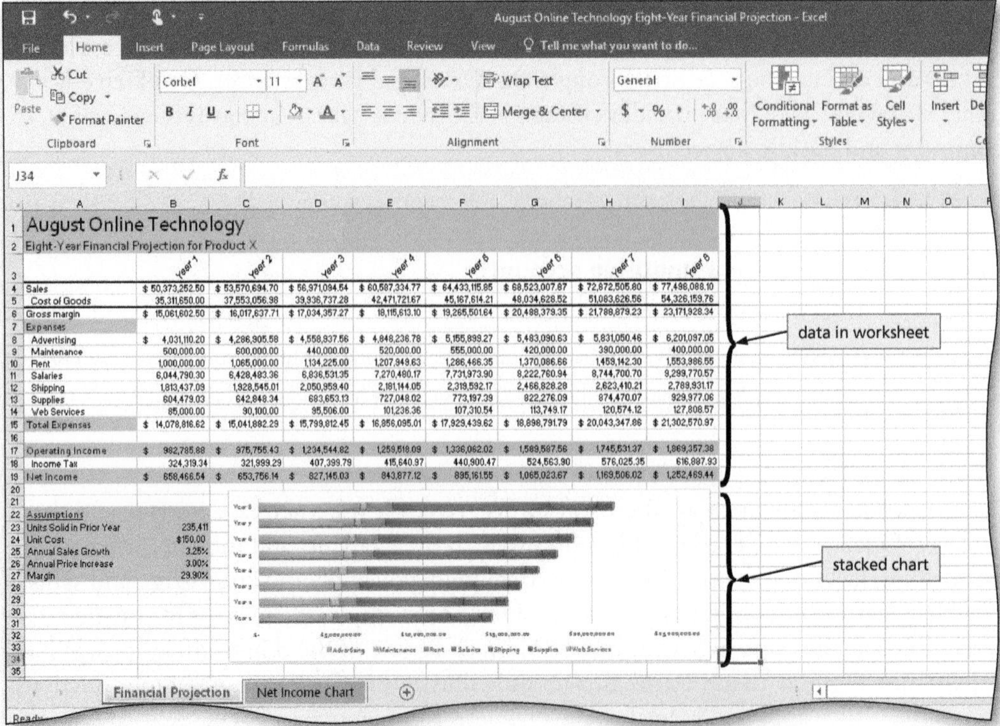

Figure 6

To Run an App Using the Start Menu and Create a Blank Document

Across the bottom of the Windows 10 desktop is the taskbar. The taskbar contains the **Start button**, which you use to access apps, files, folders, and settings. A **folder** is a named location on a storage medium that usually contains related documents.

Clicking the Start button displays the Start menu. The **Start menu** allows you to access programs, folders, and files on the computer or mobile device and contains commands that allow you to start programs, store and search for documents, customize the computer or mobile device, and sign out of a user account or shut down the computer or mobile device. A **menu** is a list of related items, including folders, programs, and commands. Each **command** on a menu performs a specific action, such as saving a file or obtaining help. ***Why?*** *When you install an app, for example, the app's name will be added to the All apps list on the Start menu.*

The following steps, which assume Windows is running, use the Start menu to run Excel and create a blank workbook based on a typical installation. You may need to ask your instructor how to run Excel on your computer. Although the steps illustrate running the Excel app, the steps to run any Office app are similar.

- Click the Start button on the Windows 10 taskbar to display the Start menu (Figure 7).

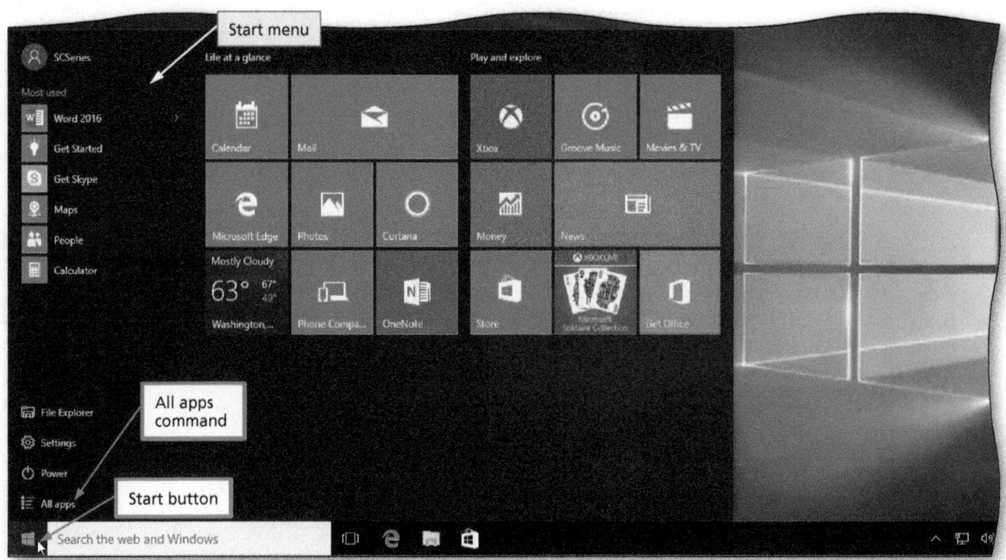

Figure 7

2

- Click All apps at the bottom of the left pane of the Start menu to display a list of apps installed on the computer or mobile device. If necessary, scroll to display the app you wish to run, Excel 2016, in this case (Figure 8).

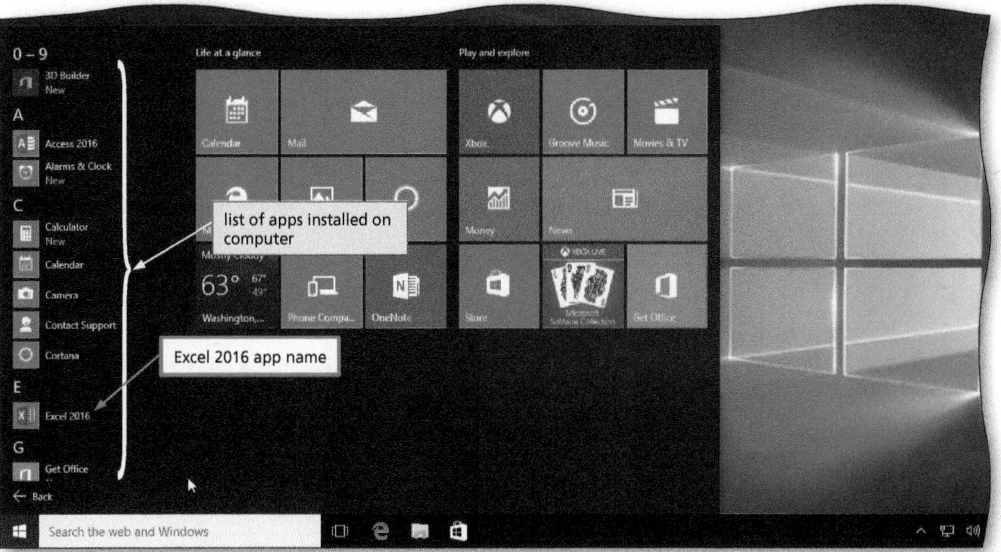

Figure 8

- If the app you wish to run is located in a folder, click or scroll to and then click the folder in the All apps list to display a list of the folder's contents.
- Click, or scroll to and then click, the app name (Excel 2016, in this case) in the list to run the selected app (Figure 9).

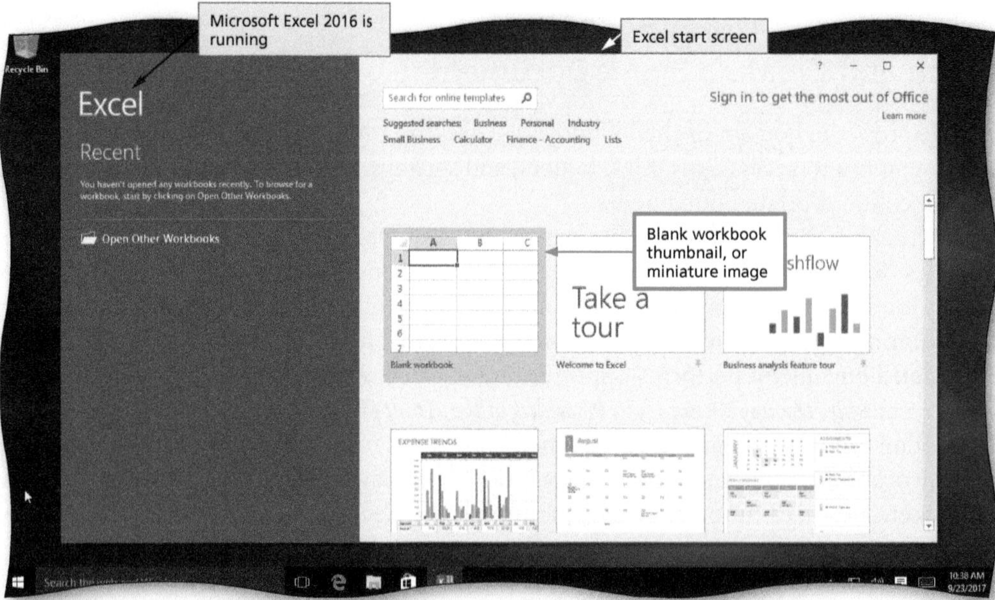

Figure 9

- Click the Blank workbook thumbnail on the Excel start screen to create a blank Excel workbook in the Excel window (Figure 10).

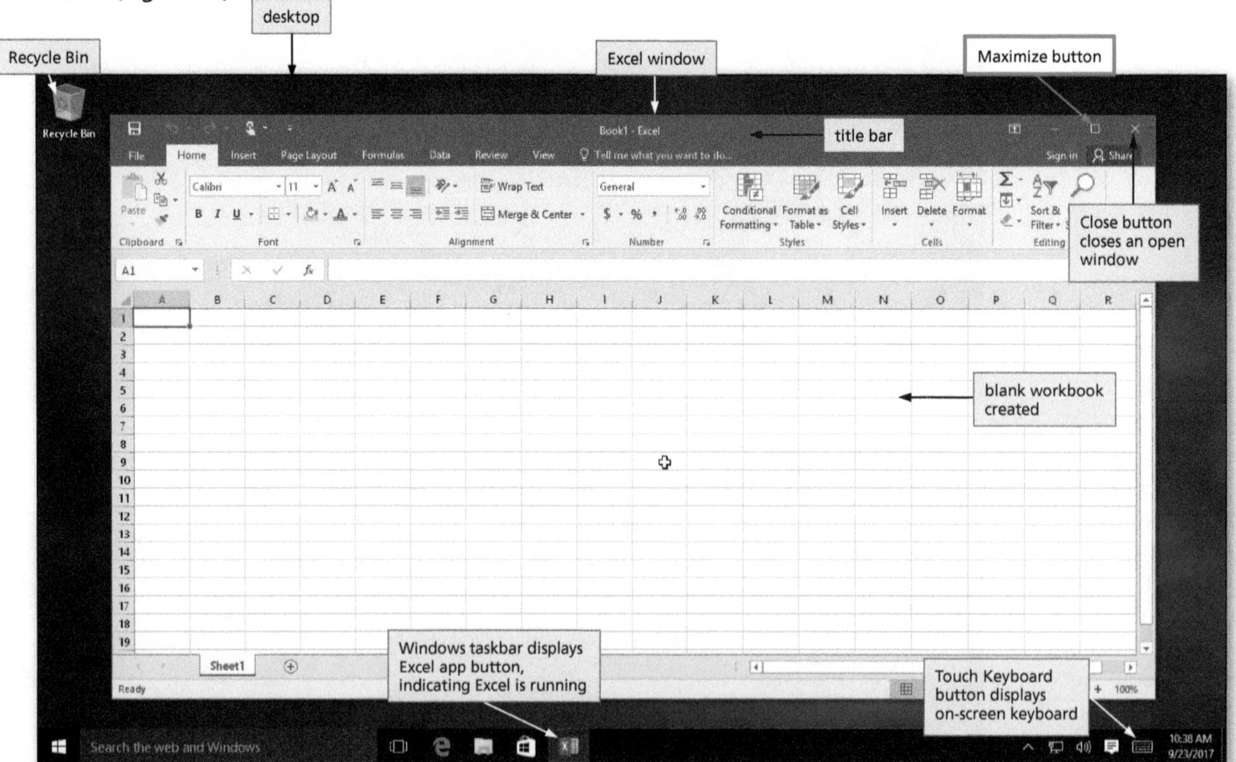

Figure 10

Q&A

What happens when you run an app?

Some apps provide a means for you to create a blank document, as shown in Figure 9; others immediately display a blank document in an app window, such as the Excel window shown in Figure 10. A **window** is a rectangular area that displays data and information. The top of a window has a **title bar**, which is a horizontal space that contains the window's name.

Other Ways

1. Type app name in search box, click app name in results list
2. Double-click file created in app you want to run

To Maximize a Window

Sometimes content is not visible completely in a window. One method of displaying the entire contents of a window is to **maximize** it, or enlarge the window so that it fills the entire screen. The following step maximizes the Excel window; however, any Office app's window can be maximized using this step. ***Why?*** *A maximized window provides the most space available for using the app.*

- If the Excel window is not maximized already, click the Maximize button (shown in Figure 10) next to the Close button on the Excel window's title bar to maximize the window (Figure 11).

Q&A What happened to the Maximize button?
It changed to a Restore Down button, which you can use to return a window to its size and location before you maximized it.

How do I know whether a window is maximized?
A window is maximized if it fills the entire display area and the Restore Down button is displayed on the title bar.

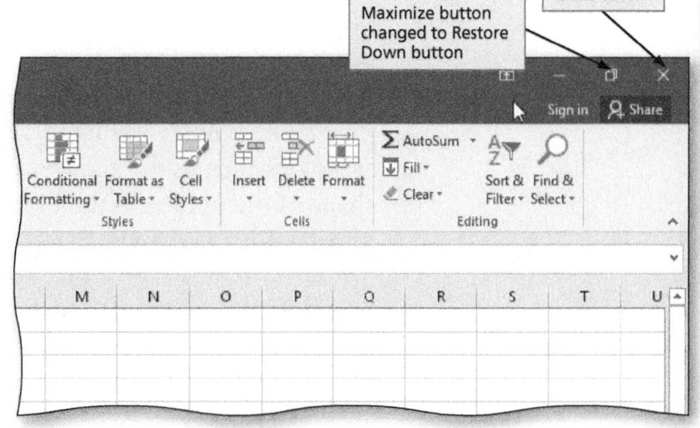

Figure 11

Other Ways

1. Double-click title bar
2. Drag title bar to top of screen

Excel Workbook Window, Ribbon, and Elements Common to Office Apps

The Excel window consists of a variety of components to make your work more efficient and worksheets more professional. These include the worksheet window, ribbon, Tell Me box, mini toolbar and shortcut menus, Quick Access Toolbar, and Microsoft Account area. Some of these components are common to other Office apps; others are unique to Excel.

Excel opens a new workbook with one worksheet. If necessary, you can add additional worksheets. Each worksheet has a sheet name that appears on a **sheet tab** at the bottom of the workbook. For example, Sheet1 is the name of the active worksheet displayed in the blank workbook shown in Figure 12. You can add more sheets to the workbook by clicking the New sheet button.

Worksheet The worksheet is organized into a rectangular grid containing vertical columns and horizontal rows. A column letter above the grid, called the **column heading**, identifies each column. A row number on the left side of the grid, called the **row heading**, identifies each row.

The intersection of each column and row is a cell. A **cell** is the basic unit of a worksheet into which you enter data. Each worksheet in a workbook has 16,384 columns and 1,048,576 rows for a total of 17,179,869,184 cells. Only a small fraction of the active worksheet appears on the screen at one time.

A cell is referred to by its unique address, or **cell reference**, which is the coordinates of the intersection of a column and a row. To identify a cell, specify the

BTW
Touch Keyboard
To display the on-screen touch keyboard, click the Touch Keyboard button on the Windows taskbar. When finished using the touch keyboard, click the X button on the touch keyboard to close the keyboard.

BTW
The Worksheet Size and Window
The 16,384 columns and 1,048,576 rows in Excel make for a huge worksheet that — if you could imagine — takes up the entire side of a building to display in its entirety. Your computer screen, by comparison, is a small window that allows you to view only a minute area of the worksheet at one time. While you cannot see the entire worksheet, you can move the window over the worksheet to view any part of it.

column letter first, followed by the row number. For example, cell reference C6 refers to the cell located at the intersection of column C and row 6 (Figure 12).

One cell on the worksheet, designated the **active cell**, is the one into which you can enter data. The active cell in Figure 12 is A1. The active cell is identified in three ways. First, a heavy border surrounds the cell; second, the active cell reference shows immediately above column A in the Name box; and third, the column heading A and row heading 1 are highlighted so that it is easy to see which cell is active (Figure 12).

The horizontal and vertical lines on the worksheet itself are called **gridlines**. Gridlines make it easier to see and identify each cell in the worksheet. If desired, you can turn the gridlines off so that they do not show on the worksheet. While learning Excel, gridlines help you to understand the structure of the worksheet.

The pointer in Figure 12 has the shape of a block plus sign. The pointer appears as a block plus sign whenever it is located in a cell on the worksheet. Another common shape of the pointer is the block arrow. The pointer turns into the block arrow when you move it outside the worksheet or when you drag cell contents between rows or columns.

Scroll Bars You use a scroll bar to display different portions of a document in the document window. At the right edge of the document window is a vertical scroll bar. If a document is too wide to fit in the document window, a horizontal scroll bar also appears at the bottom of the document window. On a scroll bar, the position of the scroll box reflects the location of the portion of the document that is displayed in the document window.

Status Bar The **status bar**, located at the bottom of the document window above the Windows taskbar, presents information about the document, the progress of current tasks, and the status of certain commands and keys; it also provides controls for viewing the document. As you type text or perform certain tasks, various indicators and buttons may appear on the status bar. The right side of the status bar includes buttons and controls you can use to change the view of a document and adjust the size of the displayed document.

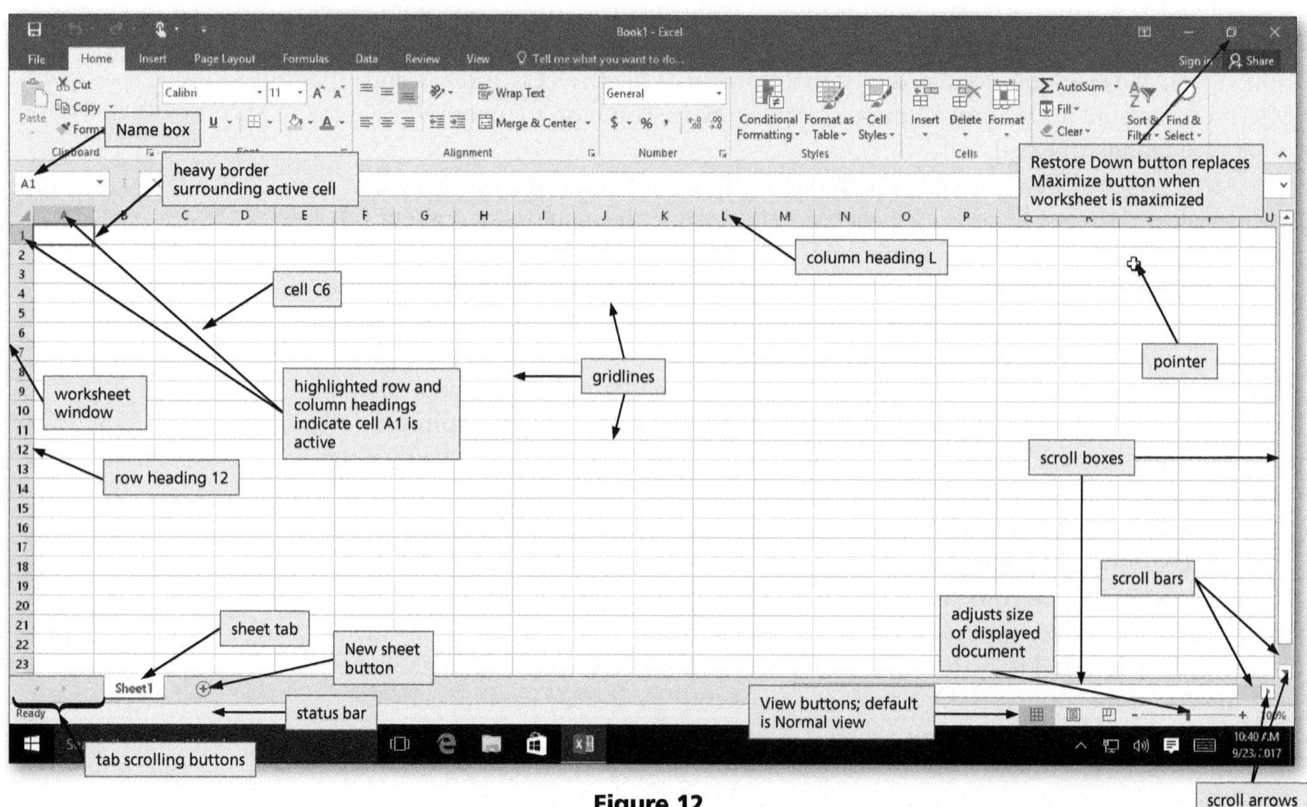

Figure 12

Ribbon The ribbon, located near the top of the window below the title bar, is the control center in Excel and other Office apps (Figure 13). The ribbon provides easy, central access to the tasks you perform while creating a document. The ribbon consists of tabs, groups, and commands. Each **tab** contains a collection of groups, and each **group** contains related commands. When you run an Office app, such as Excel, it initially displays several main tabs, also called default or top-level tabs. All Office apps have a Home tab, which contains the more frequently used commands. When you run Excel, the ribbon displays eight main tabs: File, Home, Insert, Page Layout, Formulas, Data, Review, and View. The Formulas and Data tabs are specific to Excel. The Formulas tab allows you to work with Excel formulas, and the Data tab allows you to work with data processing features such as importing and sorting data.

> BTW
> **Customizing the Ribbon**
> In addition to customizing the Quick Access Toolbar, you can add items to and remove items from the ribbon. To customize the ribbon, click File on the ribbon to open the Backstage view, click the Options tab in the Backstage view, and then click Customize Ribbon in the left pane of the Options dialog box. More information about customizing the ribbon is presented in a later module.

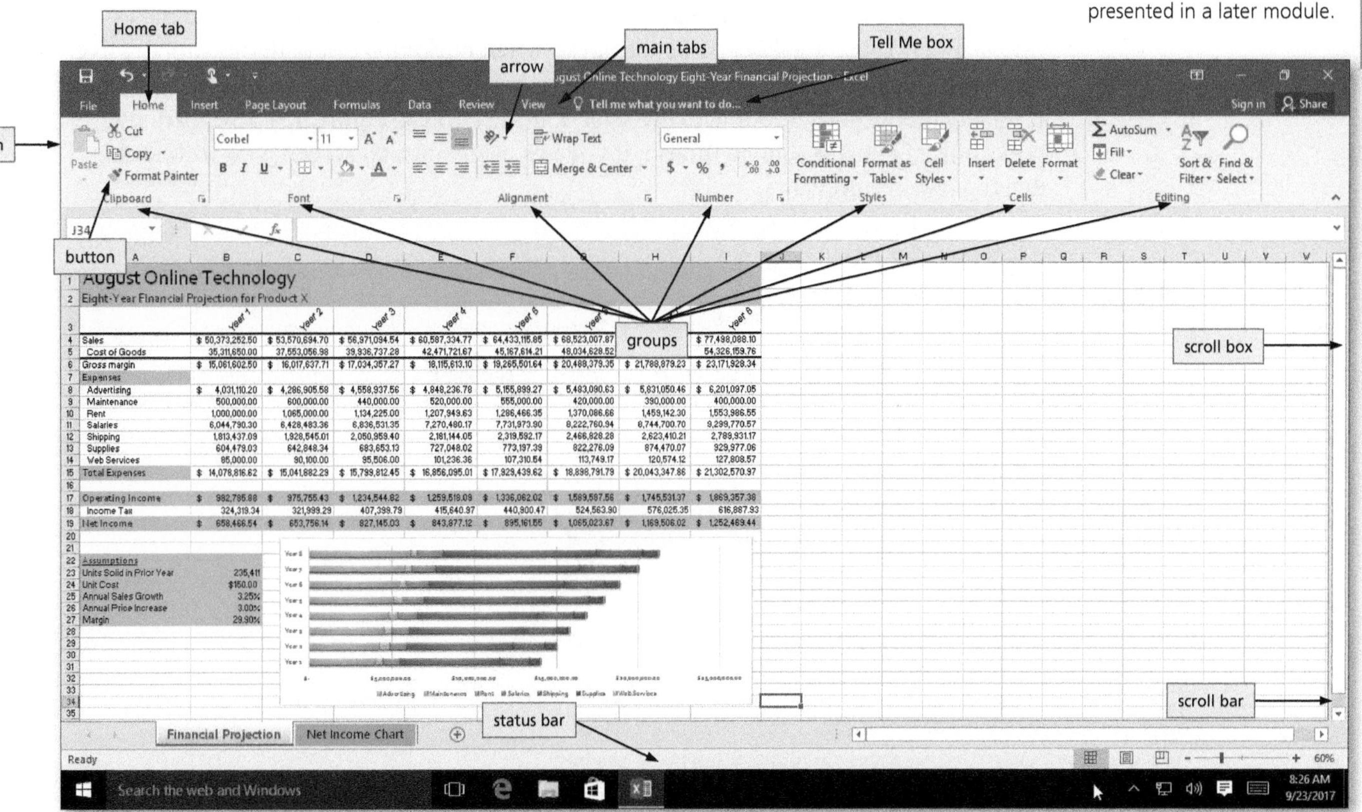

Figure 13

In addition to the main tabs, the Office apps display **tool tabs**, also called contextual tabs (Figure 14), when you perform certain tasks or work with objects such as pictures or tables. If you insert a chart in an Excel workbook, for example, the Chart Tools tab and its related subordinate Design and Format tabs appear, collectively referred to as the Chart Tools Design tab or Chart Tools Format tab. When you are finished working with the chart, the Chart Tools tab disappears from the ribbon. Excel and other Office apps determine when tool tabs should appear and disappear based on tasks you perform.

Items on the ribbon include buttons, boxes, and galleries (shown in Figures 13 and 14). A **gallery** is a set of choices, often graphical, arranged in a grid or in a list. You can scroll through choices in an in-ribbon gallery by clicking the gallery's scroll arrows. Or, you can click a gallery's More button to view more gallery options on the screen at a time.

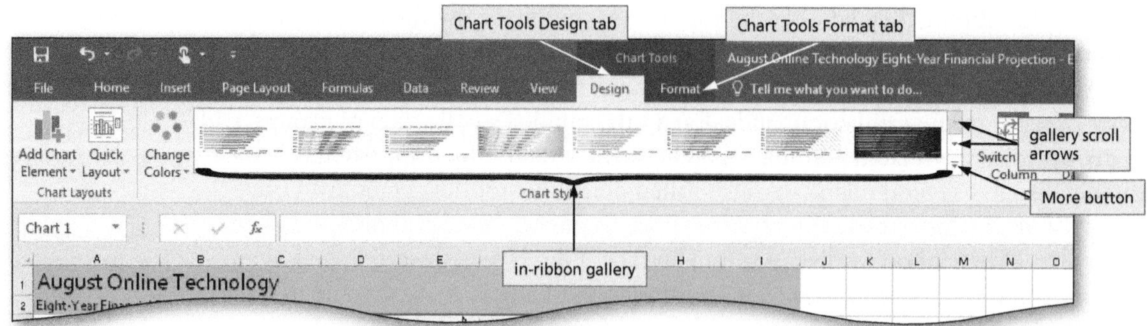

Figure 14

Some buttons and boxes have arrows that, when clicked, also display a gallery; others always cause a gallery to be displayed when clicked. Most galleries support **live preview**, which is a feature that allows you to point to a gallery choice and see its effect in the document — without actually selecting the choice (Figure 15). Live preview works only if you are using a mouse; if you are using a touch screen, you will not be able to view live previews.

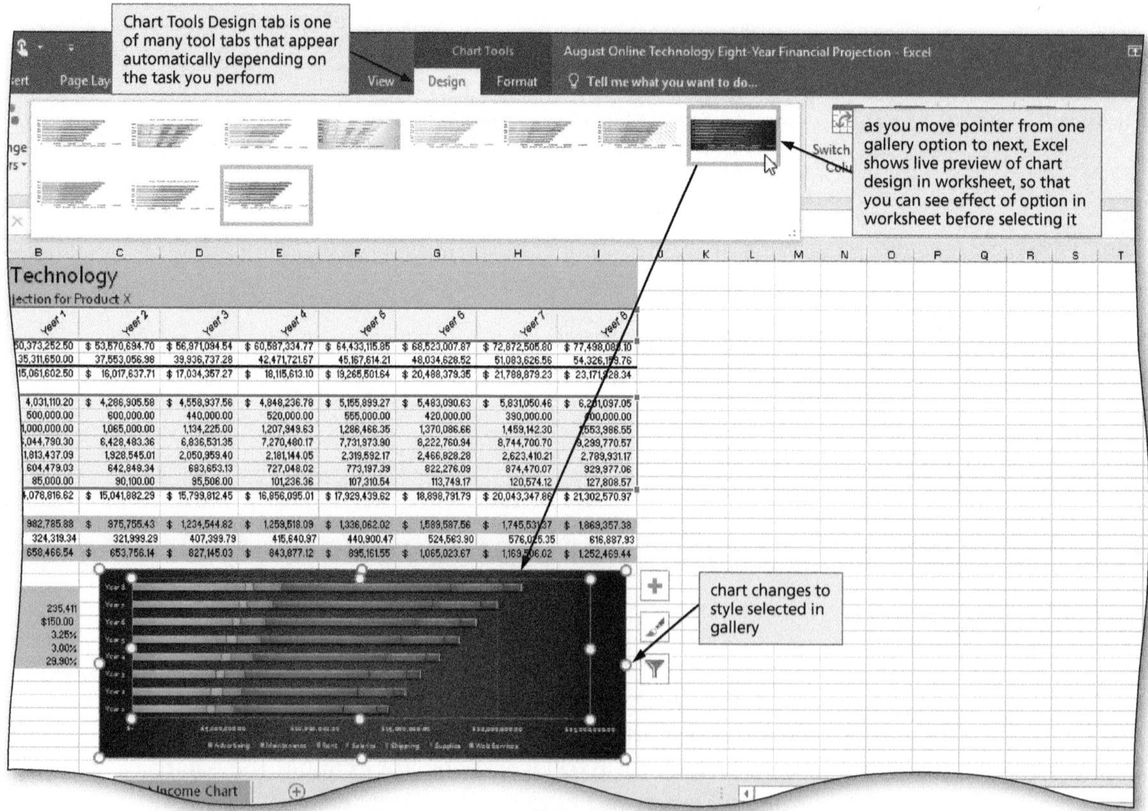

Figure 15

Some commands on the ribbon display an image to help you remember their function. When you point to a command on the ribbon, all or part of the command glows in a darker shade of gray, and a ScreenTip appears on the screen. A **ScreenTip** is an on-screen note that provides the name of the command, available keyboard shortcut(s), a description of the command, and sometimes instructions for how to obtain help about the command (Figure 16).

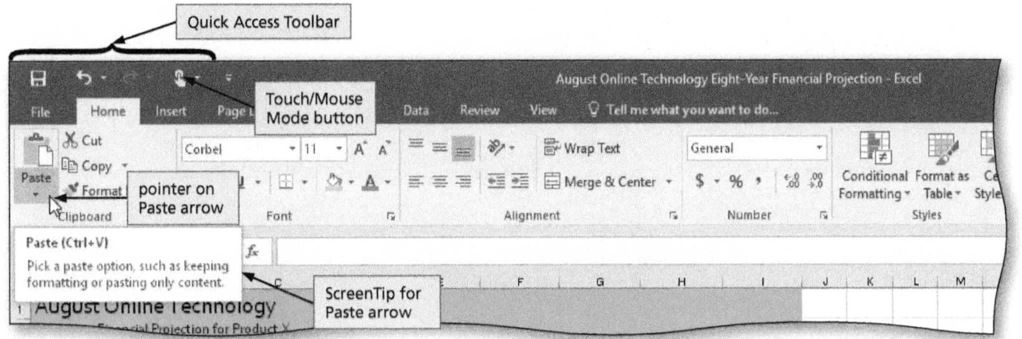

Figure 16

Some groups on the ribbon have a small arrow in the lower-right corner, called a **Dialog Box Launcher**, that when clicked, displays a dialog box or a task pane with additional options for the group (Figure 17). When presented with a dialog box, you make selections and must close the dialog box before returning to the document. A **task pane**, in contrast to a dialog box, is a window that can remain open and visible while you work in the document.

BTW

Touch Mode

The Office and Windows interfaces may vary if you are using touch mode. For this reason, you might notice that the function or appearance of your touch screen differs slightly from this module's presentation.

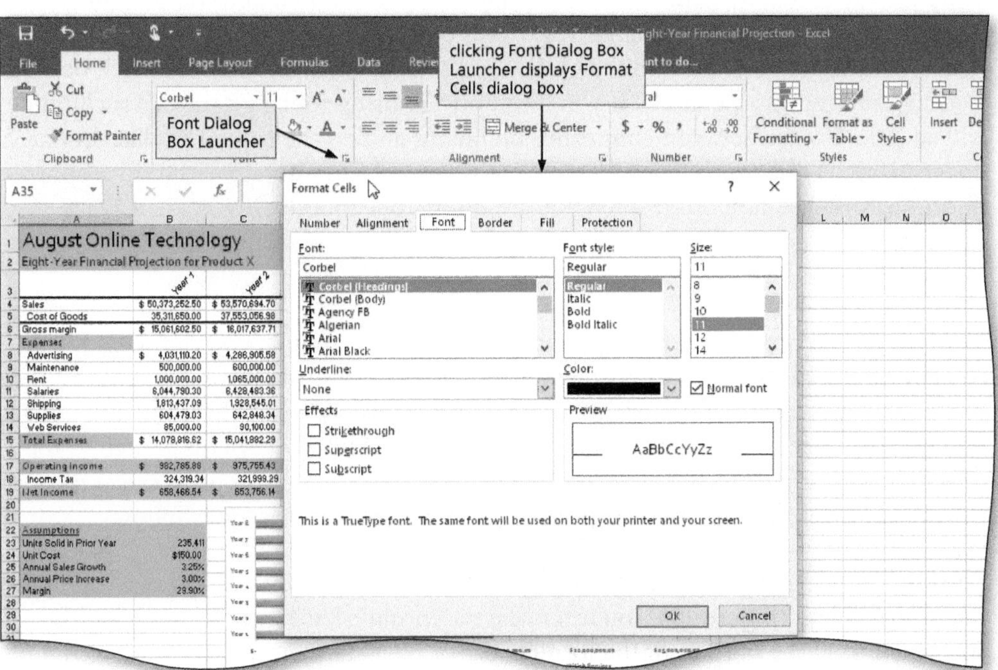

Figure 17

Mini Toolbar The **mini toolbar**, which appears automatically based on tasks you perform, contains commands related to changing the appearance of text in a document (Figure 18). If you do not use the mini toolbar, it disappears from the screen. The buttons, arrows, and boxes on the mini toolbar vary, depending on whether you are using Touch mode versus Mouse mode. If you right-click an item in the document window, Excel displays both the mini toolbar and a shortcut menu, which is discussed in a later section in this module.

BTW
Turning Off the Mini Toolbar
If you do not want the mini toolbar to appear, click File on the ribbon to open the Backstage view, click the Options tab in the Backstage view, if necessary, click General (Options dialog box), remove the check mark from the 'Show Mini Toolbar on selection' check box, and then click the OK button.

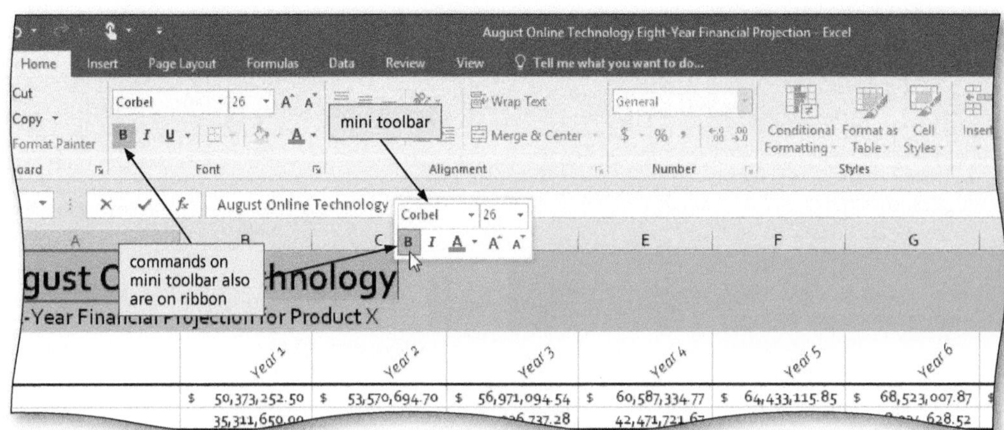

Figure 18

All commands on the mini toolbar also exist on the ribbon. The purpose of the mini toolbar is to minimize hand or mouse movement.

Quick Access Toolbar The **Quick Access Toolbar**, located initially (by default) above the ribbon at the left edge of the title bar, provides convenient, one-click access to frequently used commands (shown in Figure 16). The commands on the Quick Access Toolbar always are available, regardless of the task you are performing. The Touch/Mouse Mode button on the Quick Access Toolbar allows you to switch between Touch mode and Mouse mode. If you primarily are using touch gestures, Touch mode will add more space between commands on menus and on the ribbon so that they are easier to tap. While touch gestures are convenient ways to interact with Office apps, not all features are supported when you are using Touch mode. If you are using a mouse, Mouse mode will not add the extra space between buttons and commands. The Quick Access Toolbar is discussed in more depth later in the module.

KeyTips If you prefer using the keyboard instead of the mouse, you can press the ALT key on the keyboard to display **KeyTips**, or keyboard code icons, for certain commands (Figure 19). To select a command using the keyboard, press the letter or number displayed in the KeyTip, which may cause additional KeyTips related to the selected command to appear. To remove KeyTips from the screen, press the ALT key or the ESC key until all KeyTips disappear, or click anywhere in the app window.

Formula Bar As you type, Excel displays the entry in the **formula bar**, which appears below the ribbon (Figure 19). You can make the formula bar larger by dragging the sizing handle at the bottom of the formula bar or clicking the expand button to the right of the formula bar. Excel also displays the active cell reference in the **Name box** on the left side of the formula bar.

Tell Me Box The **Tell Me box**, which appears to the right of the tabs on the ribbon, is a type of search box that helps you to perform specific tasks in an Office app (Figure 19). As you type in the Tell Me box, the word-wheeling feature displays search results that are refined as you type. For example, if you want to center text in a document, you can type "center" in the Tell Me box and then select the appropriate command. The Tell Me box also lists the last five commands accessed from the box.

Microsoft Account Area In this area, you can use the Sign in link to sign in to your Microsoft account (Figure 19). Once signed in, you will see your account information, as well as a picture if you have included one in your Microsoft account.

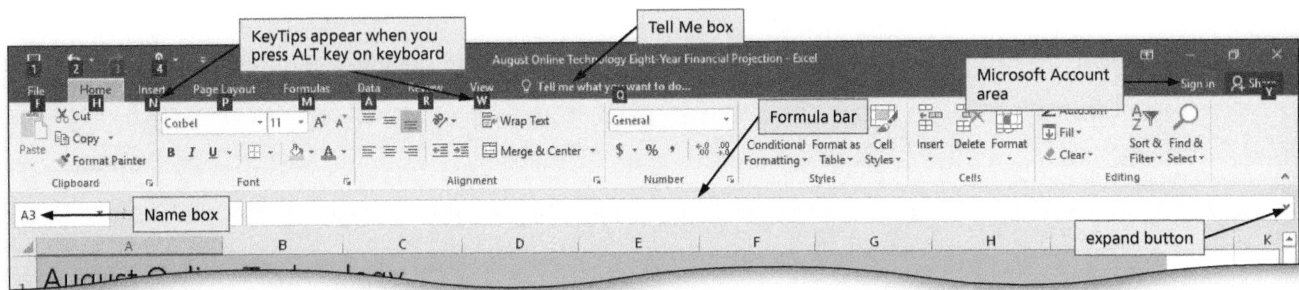

Figure 19

To Display a Different Tab on the Ribbon

1 SIGN IN | 2 USE WINDOWS | 3 USE APPS | 4 FILE MANAGEMENT | 5 SWITCH APPS | 6 SAVE FILES
7 CHANGE SCREEN RESOLUTION | 8 EXIT APPS | 9 USE ADDITIONAL APP FEATURES | 10 USE HELP

The tab currently displayed is called the **active tab.** The following step displays the Insert tab, that is, makes it the active tab. ***Why?*** *When working with an Office app, you may need to switch tabs to access other options for working with a document.*

- Click Insert on the ribbon to display the Insert tab (Figure 20).

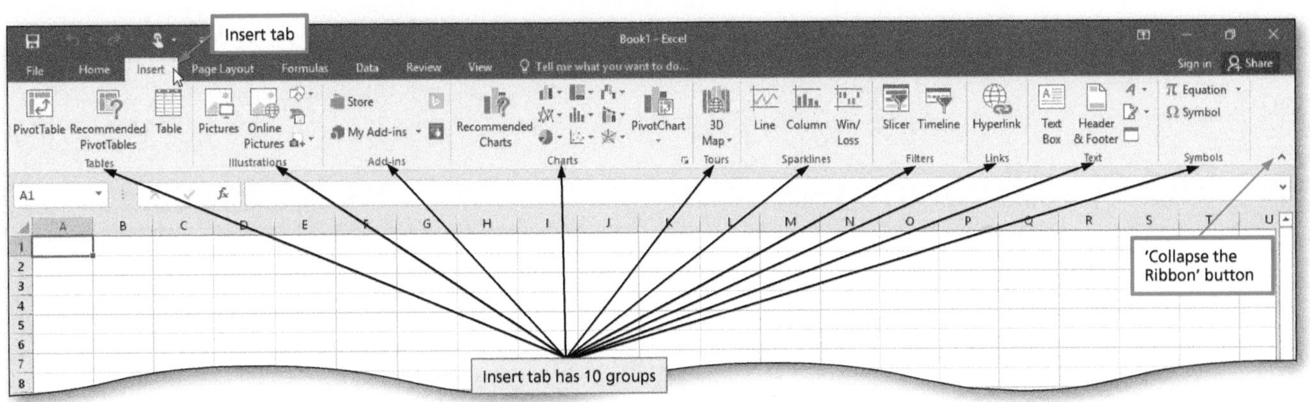

Figure 20

Experiment

- Click the other tabs on the ribbon to view their contents. When you are finished, click Insert on the ribbon to redisplay the Insert tab.

Other Ways

1. Press ALT, press letter corresponding to tab to display

To Collapse and Expand the Ribbon and Use Full Screen Mode

1 SIGN IN | 2 USE WINDOWS | 3 USE APPS | 4 FILE MANAGEMENT | 5 SWITCH APPS | 6 SAVE FILES
7 CHANGE SCREEN RESOLUTION | 8 EXIT APPS | 9 USE ADDITIONAL APP FEATURES | 10 USE HELP

To display more of a document or other item in the window of an Office app, some users prefer to collapse the ribbon, which hides the groups on the ribbon and displays only the main tabs, or to use **Full Screen mode**, which hides all the commands and just displays the document. Each time you run an Office app, such as Excel, the ribbon appears the same way it did the last time you used that Office app. The modules in this book, however, begin with the ribbon appearing as it did at the initial installation of Office or Excel.

The following steps collapse, expand, and restore the ribbon in Excel and then switch to Full Screen mode. ***Why?*** *If you need more space on the screen to work with your document, you may consider collapsing the ribbon or switching to Full Screen mode to gain additional workspace.*

- Click the 'Collapse the Ribbon' button on the ribbon (shown in Figure 20) to collapse the ribbon (Figure 21).

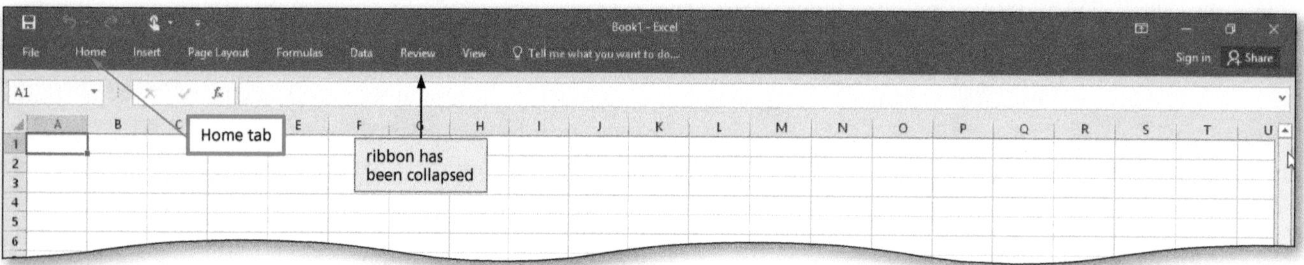

Figure 21

Q&A What happened to the 'Collapse the Ribbon' button?
The 'Pin the ribbon' button replaces the 'Collapse the Ribbon' button when the ribbon is collapsed. You will see the 'Pin the ribbon' button only when you expand a ribbon by clicking a tab.

- Click Home on the ribbon to expand the Home tab (Figure 22).

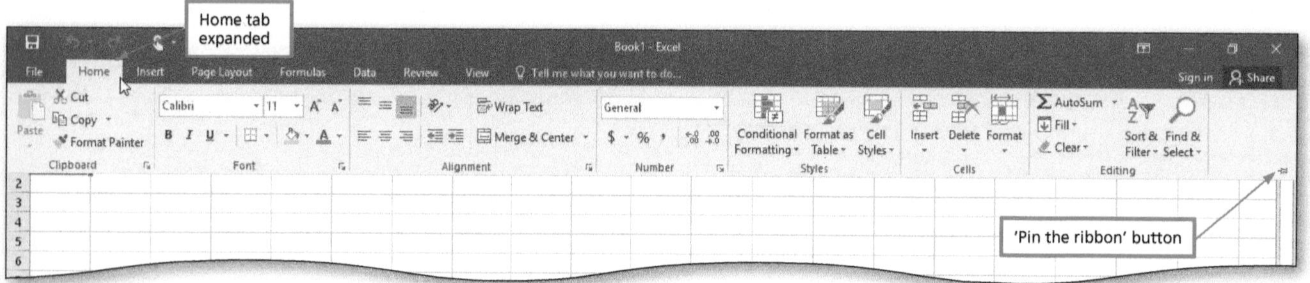

Figure 22

Q&A Why would I click the Home tab?
If you want to use a command on a collapsed ribbon, click the main tab to display the groups for that tab. After you select a command on the ribbon and resume working in the document, the groups will be collapsed once again. If you decide not to use a command on the ribbon, you can collapse the groups by clicking the same main tab or clicking in the app window.

Experiment

- Click Home on the ribbon to collapse the groups again. Click Home on the ribbon to expand the Home tab.

- Click the 'Pin the ribbon' button on the expanded Home tab to restore the ribbon.
- Click the 'Ribbon Display Options' button to display the Ribbon Display Options menu (Figure 23).

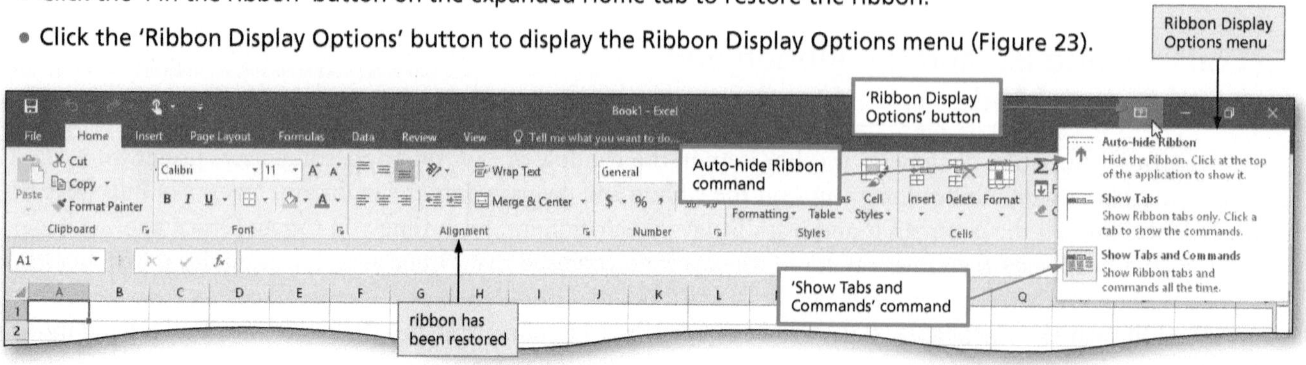

Figure 23

4

- Click Auto-hide Ribbon to use Full Screen mode, which hides all the commands from the screen (Figure 24).
- Click the ellipsis to display the ribbon temporarily.
- Click the 'Ribbon Display Options' button to display the Ribbon Display Options menu (shown in Figure 23).
- Click 'Show Tabs and Commands' on the Ribbon Display Options menu to exit Full Screen mode.

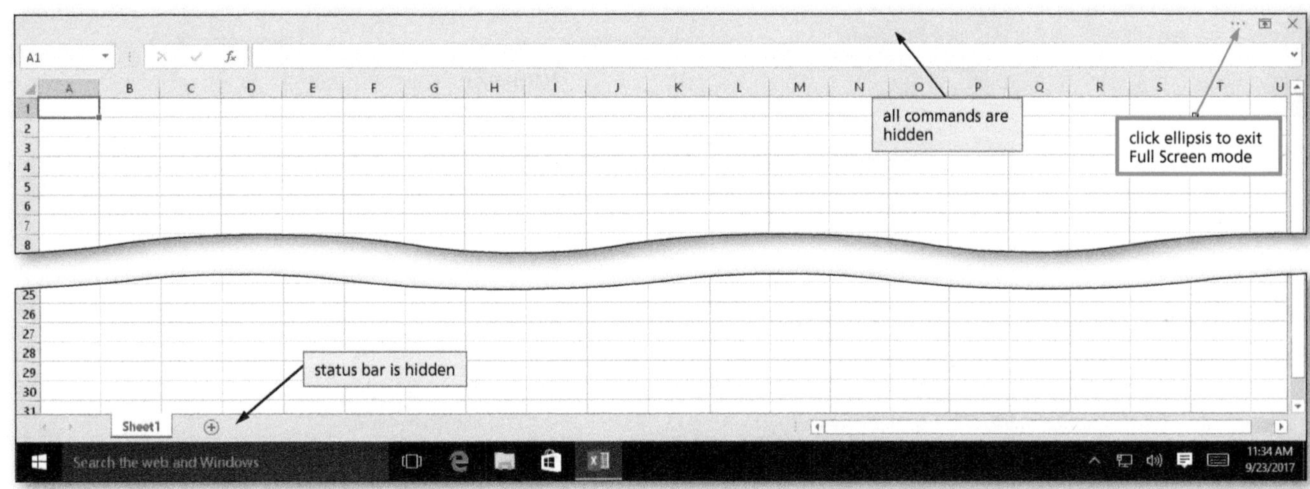

Figure 24

Other Ways

1. Double-click tab on ribbon

To Use a Shortcut Menu to Relocate the Quick Access Toolbar

1 SIGN IN | 2 USE WINDOWS | 3 USE APPS | 4 FILE MANAGEMENT | 5 SWITCH APPS | 6 SAVE FILES
7 CHANGE SCREEN RESOLUTION | 8 EXIT APPS | 9 USE ADDITIONAL APP FEATURES | 10 USE HELP

When you right-click certain areas of the Excel and other Office app windows, a shortcut menu will appear. A **shortcut menu** is a list of frequently used commands that relate to an object. ***Why?*** *You can use shortcut menus to access common commands quickly.* When you right-click the status bar, for example, a shortcut menu appears with commands related to the status bar. When you right-click the Quick Access Toolbar, a shortcut menu appears with commands related to the Quick Access Toolbar. The following steps use a shortcut menu to move the Quick Access Toolbar, which by default is located on the title bar.

- Right-click the Quick Access Toolbar to display a shortcut menu that presents a list of commands related to the Quick Access Toolbar (Figure 25).

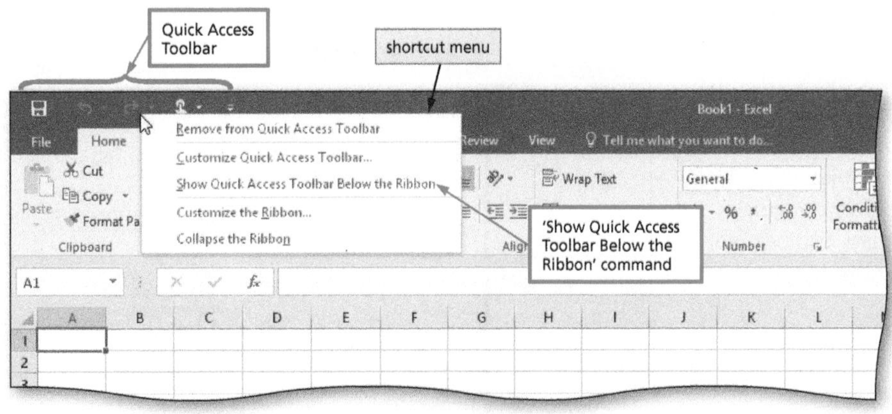

Figure 25

- Click 'Show Quick Access Toolbar Below the Ribbon' on the shortcut menu to display the Quick Access Toolbar below the ribbon (Figure 26).

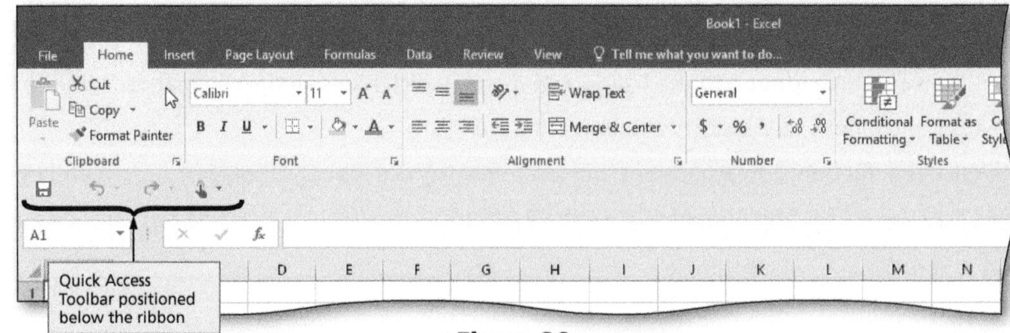

Figure 26

- Right-click the Quick Access Toolbar to display a shortcut menu (Figure 27).

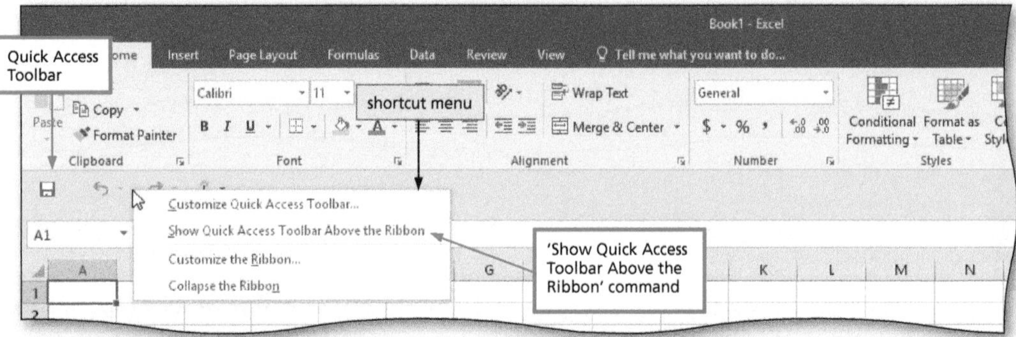

Figure 27

4

- Click 'Show Quick Access Toolbar Above the Ribbon' on the shortcut menu to return the Quick Access Toolbar to its original position (shown in Figure 25).

Other Ways

1. Click 'Customize Quick Access Toolbar' button on Quick Access Toolbar, click 'Show Below the Ribbon' or 'Show Above the Ribbon'

To Customize the Quick Access Toolbar

1 SIGN IN | 2 USE WINDOWS | 3 USE APPS | 4 FILE MANAGEMENT | 5 SWITCH APPS | 6 SAVE FILES
7 CHANGE SCREEN RESOLUTION | 8 EXIT APPS | 9 USE ADDITIONAL APP FEATURES | 10 USE HELP

The Quick Access Toolbar provides easy access to some of the more frequently used commands in the Office apps. By default, the Quick Access Toolbar contains buttons for the Save, Undo, and Redo commands. If your computer or mobile device has a touch screen, the Quick Access Toolbar also might display the Touch/Mouse Mode button. You can customize the Quick Access Toolbar by changing its location in the window, as shown in the previous steps, and by adding more buttons to reflect commands you would like to access easily. The following steps add the Quick Print button to the Quick Access Toolbar in the Excel window. ***Why?*** *Adding the Quick Print button to the Quick Access Toolbar speeds up the process of printing.*

- Click the 'Customize Quick Access Toolbar' button to display the Customize Quick Access Toolbar menu (Figure 28).

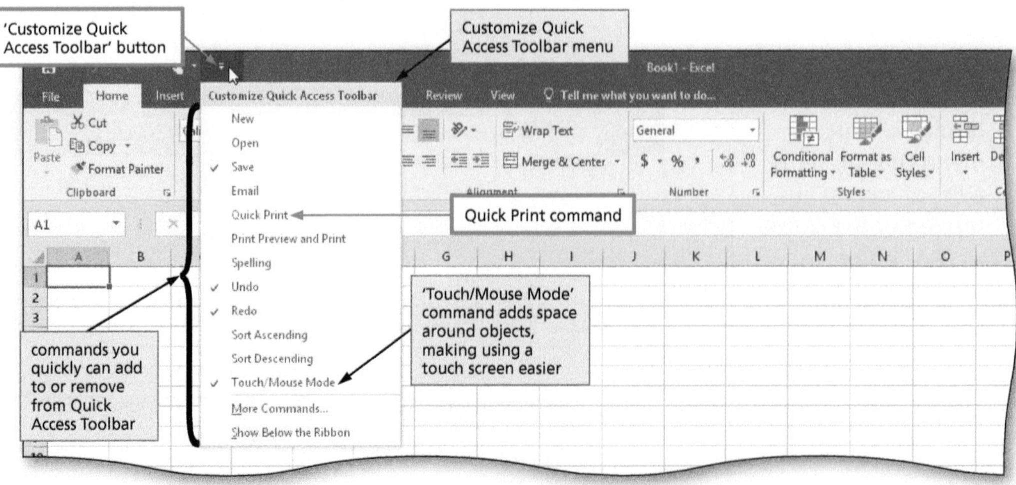

Figure 28

- Click Quick Print on the Customize Quick Access Toolbar menu to add the Quick Print button to the Quick Access Toolbar (Figure 29).

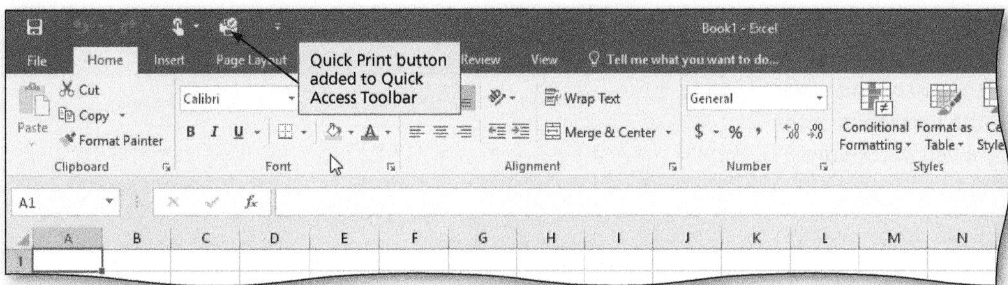

Figure 29

Q&A How would I remove a button from the Quick Access Toolbar?
You would right-click the button you wish to remove and then click 'Remove from Quick Access Toolbar' on the shortcut menu or click the 'Customize Quick Access Toolbar' button on the Quick Access Toolbar and then click the button name in the Customize Quick Access Toolbar menu to remove the check mark.

To Enter a Worksheet Title

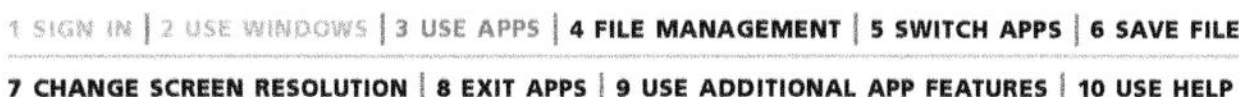

To enter data into a cell, you first must select it. The easiest way to select a cell (make it active) is to use the mouse to move the block plus sign pointer to the cell and then click. An alternative method is to use the arrow keys that are located just to the right of the typewriter keys on the keyboard. An arrow key selects the cell adjacent to the active cell in the direction of the arrow on the key.

In Excel, any set of characters containing a letter, hyphen (as in a telephone number), or space is considered text. **Text** is used to place titles, such as worksheet titles, column titles, and row titles, on the worksheet. The following steps enter the worksheet title in cell A1. ***Why?*** *A title informs others as to the contents of the worksheet.*

- If it is not already the active cell, click cell A1 to make it the active cell.
- Type **Silver Sky Hardware** in cell A1 (Figure 30).

Q&A What is the blinking vertical bar to the right of the text?
The blinking bar is the insertion point, which indicates where text will be inserted in the worksheet.

What if I make an error while typing?
You can press the BACKSPACE key until you have deleted the text in error and then retype the text correctly.

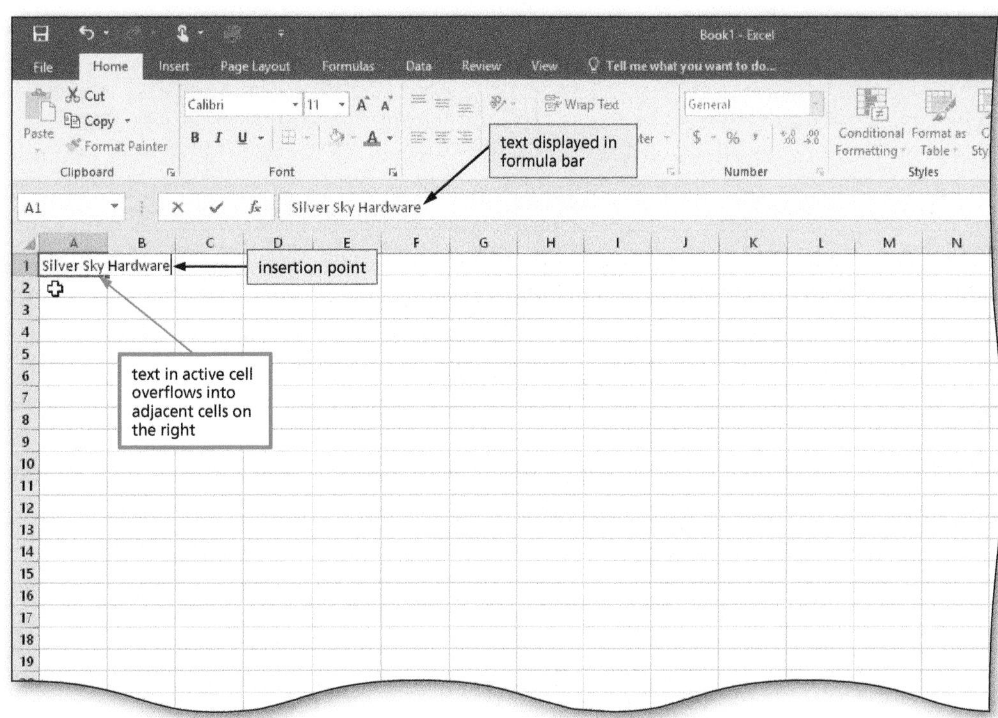

Figure 30

2

- Click the Enter button to complete the entry and enter the worksheet title in cell A1 (Figure 31).

Q&A Why do some commands on the ribbon appear dimmed?
Excel dims the commands that cannot be used at the current time.

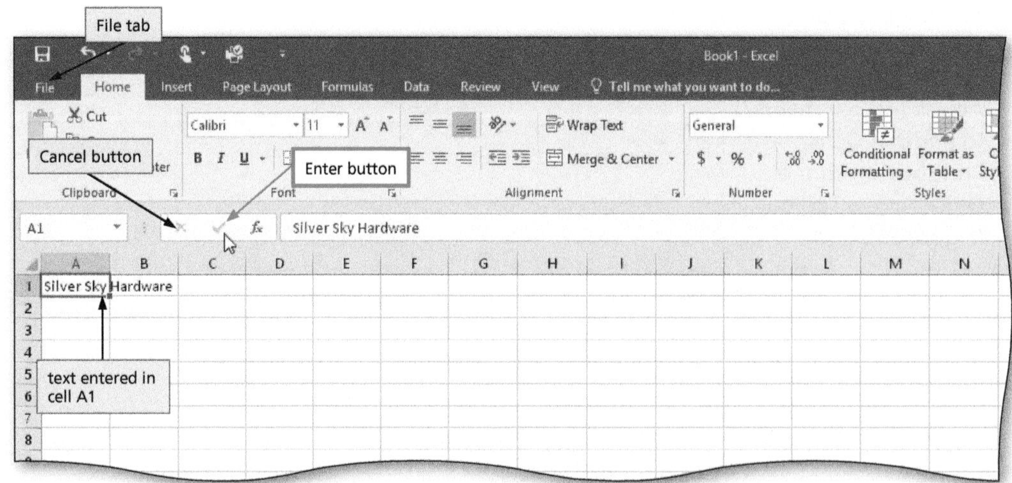

Figure 31

Document Properties

You can organize and identify your files by using **document properties**, which are the details about a file, such as the project author, title, and subject. For example, a class name or workbook topic can describe the file's purpose or content.

CONSIDER THIS

Why would you want to assign document properties to a document?
Document properties are valuable for a variety of reasons:

- Users can save time locating a particular file because they can view a file's document properties without opening the file.
- By creating consistent properties for files having similar content, users can better organize their files.
- Some organizations require users to add document properties so that other employees can view details about these files.

To Change Document Properties

1 SIGN IN | 2 USE WINDOWS | 3 USE APPS | 4 FILE MANAGEMENT | 5 SWITCH APPS | 6 SAVE FILES
7 CHANGE SCREEN RESOLUTION | 8 EXIT APPS | 9 USE ADDITIONAL APP FEATURES | 10 USE HELP

You can change the document properties while working with the file in an Office app. When you save the file, the Office app (Excel, in this case) will save the document properties with the file. The following steps change document properties. ***Why?*** *Adding document properties will help you identify characteristics of the file without opening it.*

- Click File on the ribbon (shown in Figure 31) to open the Backstage view and then, if necessary, click the Info tab in the Backstage view to display the Info gallery.

Q&A What is the purpose of the File tab on the ribbon and what is the Backstage view?
The File tab opens the Backstage view for each Office app, including Excel. The **Backstage view** contains a set of commands that enable you to manage documents (opening, saving, sharing, and printing) and provides data about the documents.

What is the purpose of the Info gallery in the Backstage view?
The Info tab, which is selected by default when you click File on the ribbon, displays the Info gallery, where you can protect a document, inspect a document, and manage versions of a document as well as view all the file properties, such as when the file was created.

- Click to the right of the Title property in the Properties list and then type `CIS 101 Assignment` in the text box (Figure 32).

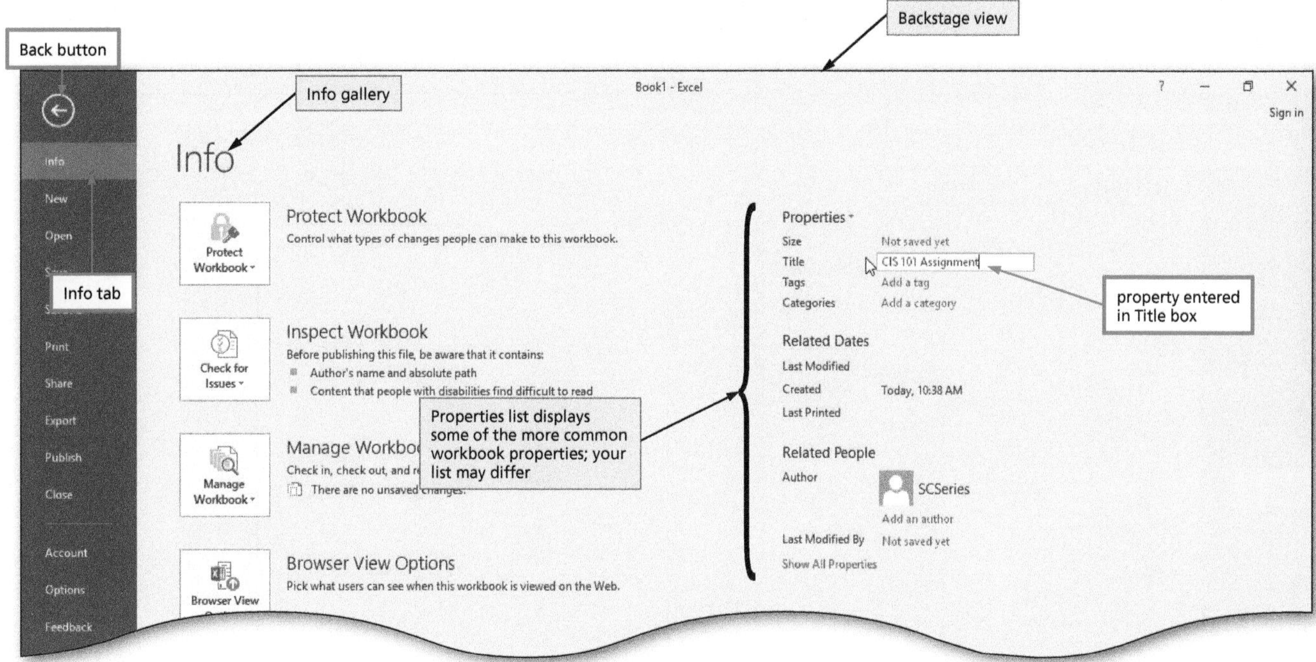

Figure 32

- Click the Back button in the upper-left corner of the Backstage view to return to the document window.

Printing, Saving, and Organizing Files

While you are creating a document, the computer or mobile device stores it in memory. When you save a document, the computer or mobile device places it on a storage medium, such as a hard disk, solid state drive (SSD), USB flash drive, or optical disc. The storage medium can be permanent in your computer, may be portable where you remove it from your computer, or may be on a web server you access through a network or the Internet.

A saved document is referred to as a file. A **file name** is the name assigned to a file when it is saved. When saving files, you should organize them so that you easily can find them later. Windows provides tools to help you organize files.

BTW
File Type
Depending on your Windows settings, the file type .xlsx may be displayed immediately to the right of the file name after you save the file. The file type .xlsx identifies an Excel 2016 workbook.

Printing a Document

After creating a document, you may want to print it. Printing a document enables you to distribute it to others in a form that can be read or viewed but typically not edited.

To Print a Document

1 SIGN IN | 2 USE WINDOWS | 3 USE APPS | 4 FILE MANAGEMENT | 5 SWITCH APPS | 6 SAVE FILES
7 CHANGE SCREEN RESOLUTION | 8 EXIT APPS | 9 USE ADDITIONAL APP FEATURES | 10 USE HELP

With the document opened, you may want to print it. ***Why?*** *Because you want to see how the text will appear on paper, you want to print a hard copy on a printer.* The following steps print a hard copy of the contents of the document.

- Click File on the ribbon to open the Backstage view.
- Click the Print tab in the Backstage view to display the Print gallery (Figure 33).

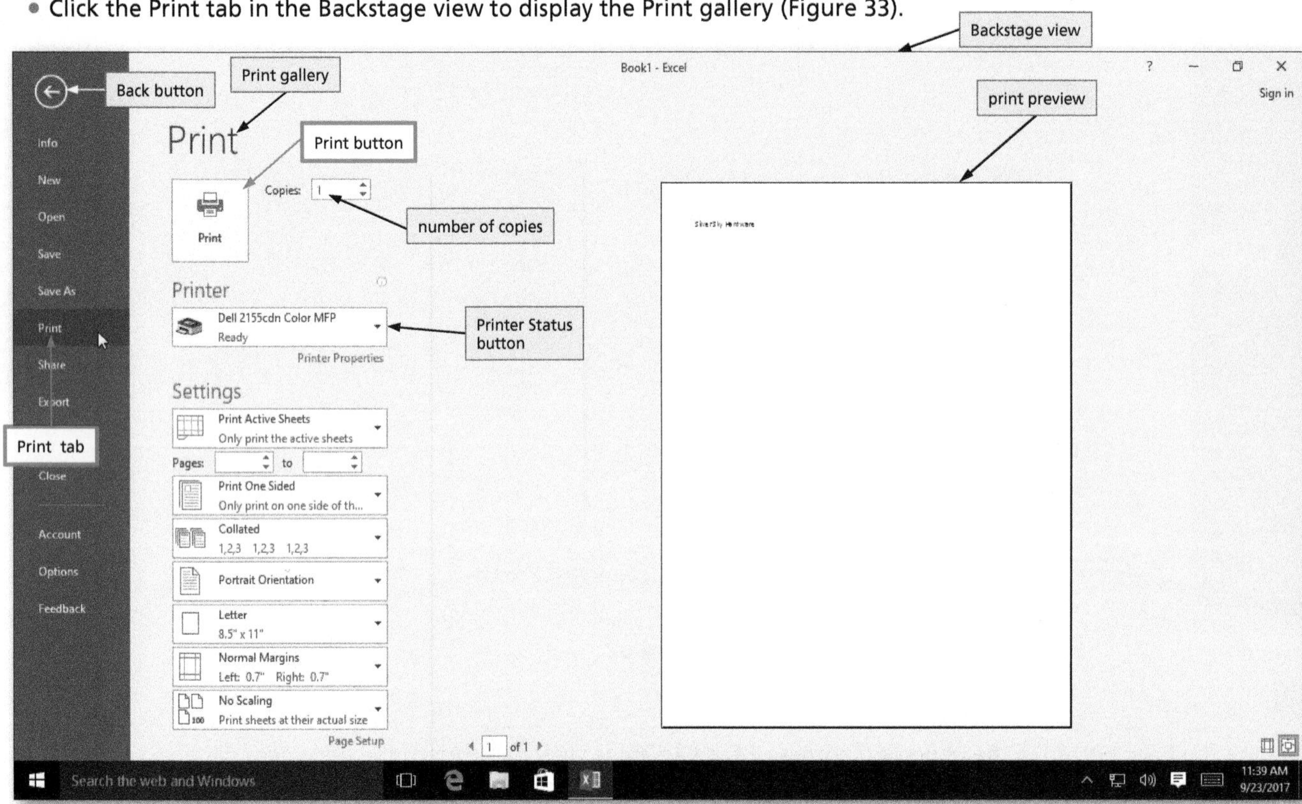

Figure 33

Q&A How can I print multiple copies of my document?
Increase the number in the Copies box in the Print gallery.

What if I decide not to print the document at this time?
Click the Back button in the upper-left corner of the Backstage view to return to the document window.

- Verify that the selected printer will print a hard copy of the document. If necessary, click the Printer Status button to display a list of available printer options and then click the desired printer to change the currently selected printer.

- Click the Print button in the Print gallery to print the document on the currently selected printer.
- When the printer stops, retrieve the hard copy (Figure 34).

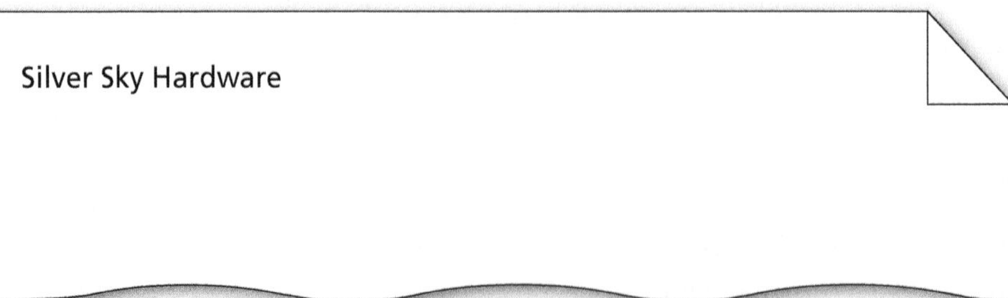

Figure 34

Q&A What if I want to print an electronic image of a document instead of a hard copy?
You would click the Printer Status button in the Print gallery and then select the desired electronic image option, such as Microsoft Print to PDF, which would create a PDF file.

Other Ways

1. Press CTRL+P

Organizing Files and Folders

A file contains data. This data can range from an inventory list to an accounting spreadsheet to an electronic math quiz. You should organize and store files in folders to avoid misplacing a file and to help you find a file quickly.

If you are taking an introductory computer class (CIS 101, for example), you may want to design a series of folders for the different subjects covered in the class. To accomplish this, you can arrange the folders in a hierarchy for the class, as shown in Figure 35. The hierarchy contains three levels. The first level contains the storage medium, such as a hard drive. The second level contains the class folder (CIS 101, in this case), and the third level contains seven folders, one each for a different Office app (Word, PowerPoint, Excel, Access, Outlook, Publisher, and OneNote).

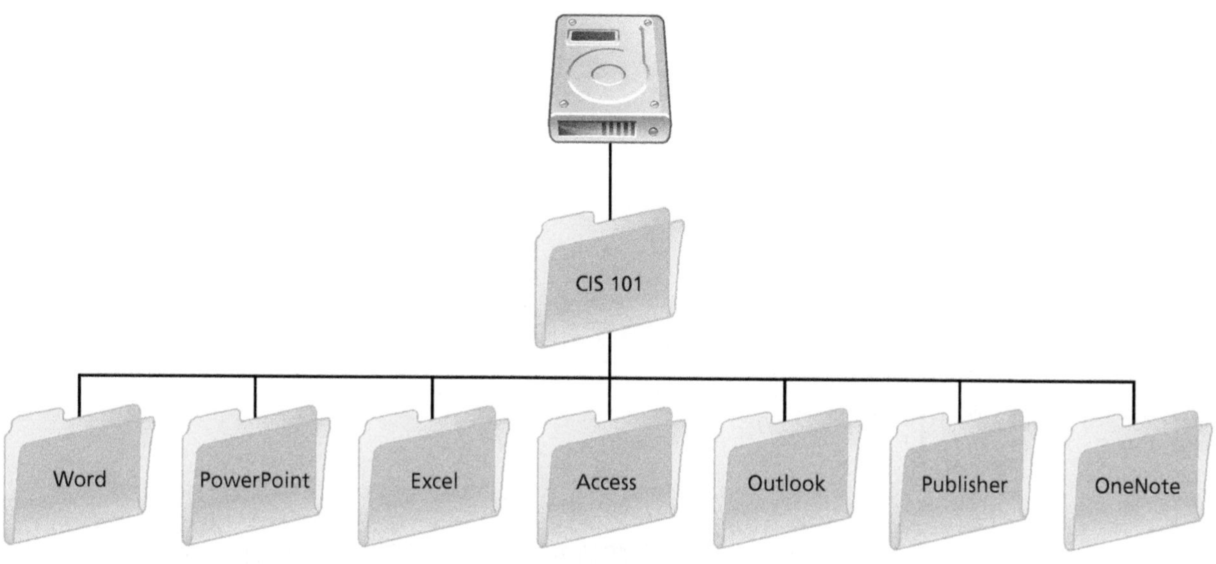

Figure 35

When the hierarchy in Figure 35 is created, the storage medium is said to contain the CIS 101 folder, and the CIS 101 folder is said to contain the separate Office folders (i.e., Word, PowerPoint, Excel, etc.). In addition, this hierarchy easily can be expanded to include folders from other classes taken during additional semesters.

The vertical and horizontal lines in Figure 35 form a pathway that allows you to navigate to a drive or folder on a computer or network. A **path** consists of a drive letter (preceded by a drive name when necessary) and colon, to identify the storage device, and one or more folder names. A hard drive typically has a drive letter of C. Each drive or folder in the hierarchy has a corresponding path.

By default, Windows saves documents in the Documents folder, music in the Music folder, photos in the Pictures folder, videos in the Videos folder, and downloads in the Downloads folder.

The following pages illustrate the steps to organize the folders for this class and save a file in a folder:

1. Create the folder identifying your class.
2. Create the Excel folder in the folder identifying your class.
3. Save a file in the Excel folder.
4. Verify the location of the saved file.

To Create a Folder

When you create a folder, such as the CIS 101 folder shown in Figure 35, you must name the folder. A folder name should describe the folder and its contents. A folder name can contain spaces and any uppercase or lowercase characters, except a backslash (\), slash (/), colon (:), asterisk (*), question mark (?), quotation marks ("), less than symbol (<), greater than symbol (>), or vertical bar (|). Folder names cannot be CON, AUX, COM1, COM2, COM3, COM4, LPT1, LPT2, LPT3, PRN, or NUL. The same rules for naming folders also apply to naming files.

The following steps create a class folder (CIS 101, in this case) in the Documents folder. ***Why?*** *When storing files, you should organize the files so that it will be easier to find them later.*

1

- Click the File Explorer button on the taskbar to run File Explorer.
- If necessary, double-click This PC in the navigation pane to expand the contents of your computer.
- Click the Documents folder in the navigation pane to display the contents of the Documents folder in the file list (Figure 36).

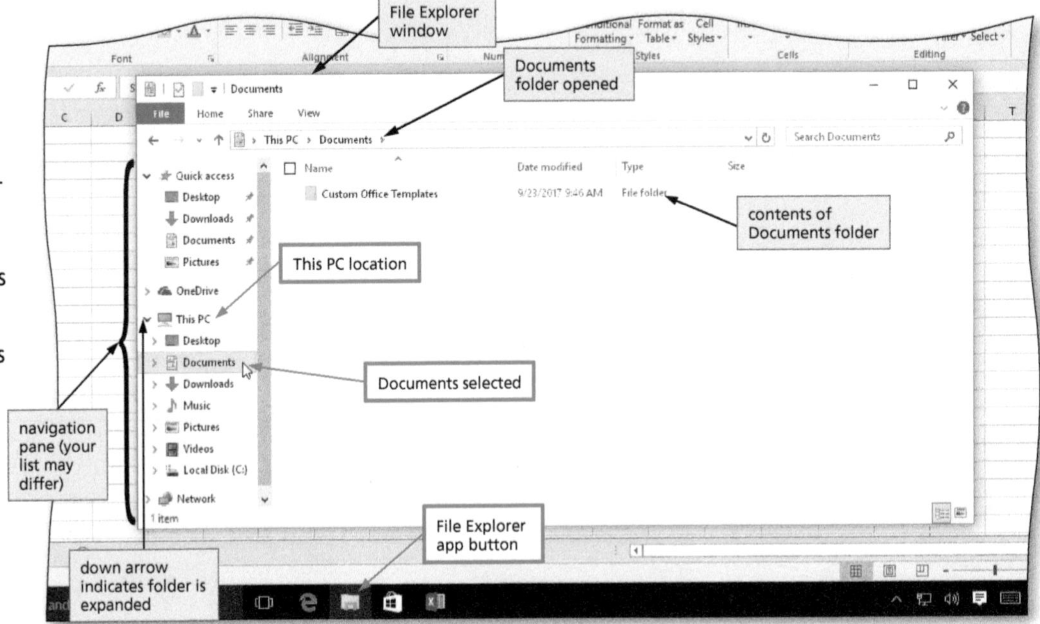

Figure 36

2

- Click the New folder button on the Quick Access Toolbar to create a new folder with the name, New folder, selected in a text box (Figure 37).

Q&A Why is the folder icon displayed differently on my computer or mobile device?
Windows might be configured to display contents differently on your computer or mobile device.

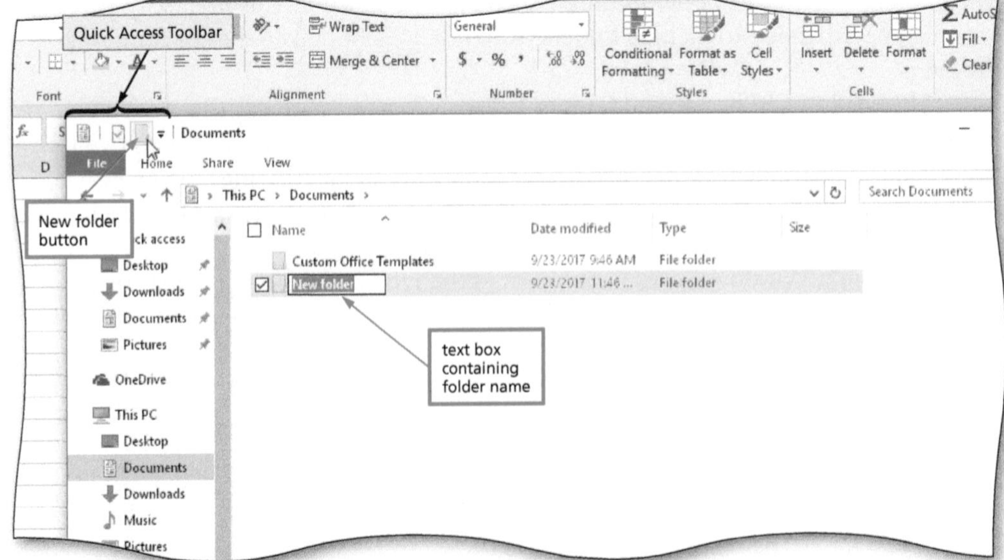

Figure 37

3

- Type **CIS 101** (or your class code) in the text box as the new folder name.

  If requested by your instructor, add your last name to the end of the folder name.

- Press the ENTER key to change the folder name from New folder to a folder name identifying your class (Figure 38).

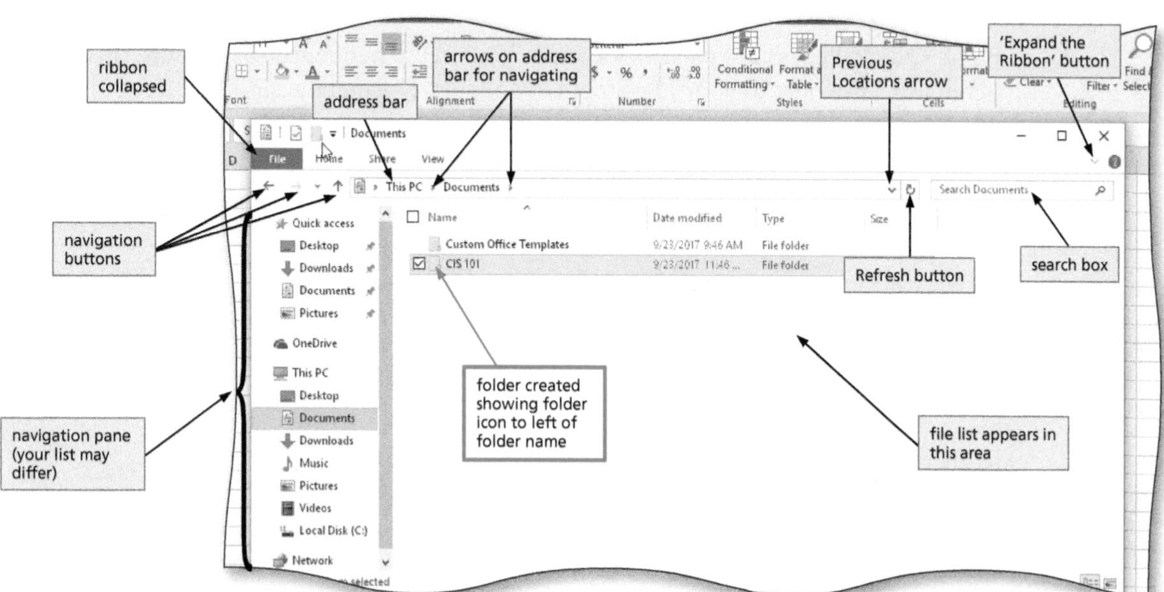

Figure 38

Q&A What happens when I press the ENTER key?

The class folder (CIS 101, in this case) is displayed in the file list, which contains the folder name, date modified, type, and size.

Other Ways

1. Press CTRL+SHIFT+N
2. Click New folder button (Home tab | New group)

Folder Windows

The File Explorer window (shown in Figure 38) is called a folder window. Recall that a folder is a specific named location on a storage medium that contains related files. Most users rely on **folder windows** for finding, viewing, and managing information on their computers. Folder windows have common design elements, including the following (shown in Figure 38):

- The **address bar** provides quick navigation options. The arrows on the address bar allow you to visit different locations on the computer or mobile device.
- The buttons to the left of the address bar allow you to navigate the contents of the navigation pane and view recent pages.
- The **Previous Locations arrow** displays the locations you have visited.
- The **Refresh button** on the right side of the address bar refreshes the contents of the folder list.

- The **Search box** contains the dimmed words, Search Documents. You can type a term in the search box for a list of files, folders, shortcuts, and elements containing that term within the location you are searching.
- The **ribbon** contains four tabs used to accomplish various tasks on the computer or mobile device related to organizing and managing the contents of the open window. This ribbon works similarly to the ribbon in the Office apps.
- The **navigation pane** on the left contains the Quick access area, the OneDrive area, the This PC area, and the Network area.
- The **Quick Access area** shows locations you access frequently. By default, this list contains links only to your Desktop, Downloads, Documents, and Pictures.

To Create a Folder within a Folder

1 SIGN IN | 2 USE WINDOWS | 3 USE APPS | 4 FILE MANAGEMENT | 5 SWITCH APPS | 6 SAVE FILES
7 CHANGE SCREEN RESOLUTION | 8 EXIT APPS | 9 USE ADDITIONAL APP FEATURES | 10 USE HELP

With the class folder created, you can create folders that will store the files you create using Excel. The following step creates an Excel folder in the CIS 101 folder (or the folder identifying your class). ***Why?*** *To be able to organize your files, you should create a folder structure.*

- Double-click the icon or folder name for the CIS 101 folder (or the folder identifying your class) in the file list to open the folder.
- Click the New folder button on the Quick Access Toolbar to create a new folder with the name, New folder, selected in a text box folder.
- Type **`Excel`** in the text box as the new folder name.
- Press the ENTER key to rename the folder (Figure 39).

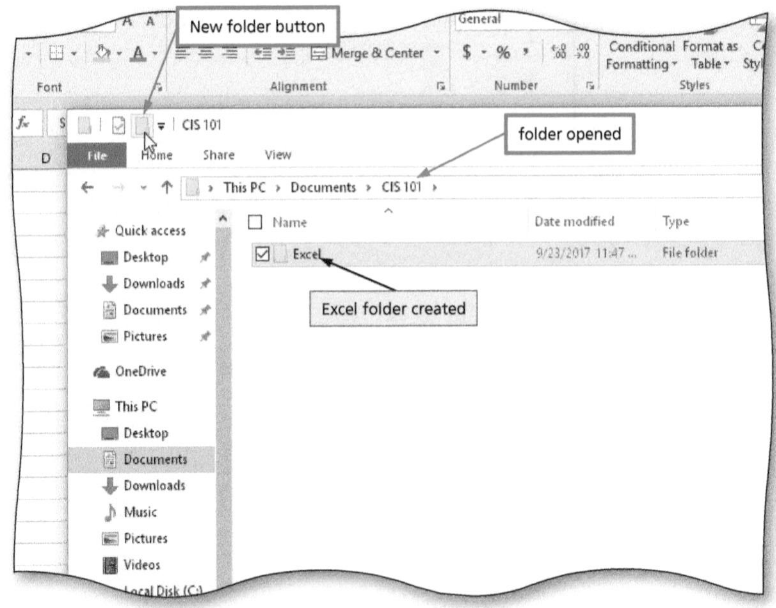

Figure 39

Other Ways

1. Press CTRL+SHIFT+N
2. Click New folder button (Home tab | New group)

To Expand a Folder, Scroll through Folder Contents, and Collapse a Folder

1 SIGN IN | 2 USE WINDOWS | 3 USE APPS | 4 FILE MANAGEMENT | 5 SWITCH APPS | 6 SAVE FILES
7 CHANGE SCREEN RESOLUTION | 8 EXIT APPS | 9 USE ADDITIONAL APP FEATURES | 10 USE HELP

Folder windows display the hierarchy of items and the contents of drives and folders in the file list. You might want to expand a folder in the navigation pane to view its contents, scroll through its contents, and collapse it when you are finished viewing its contents. ***Why?*** *When a folder is expanded, you can see all the folders it contains. By contrast, a collapsed folder hides the folders it contains.* The following steps expand, scroll through, and then collapse the folder identifying your class (CIS 101, in this case).

1

- Double-click the Documents folder in the This PC area of the navigation pane, which expands the folder to display its contents, indicated by a down arrow to the left of the Documents folder icon (Figure 40).

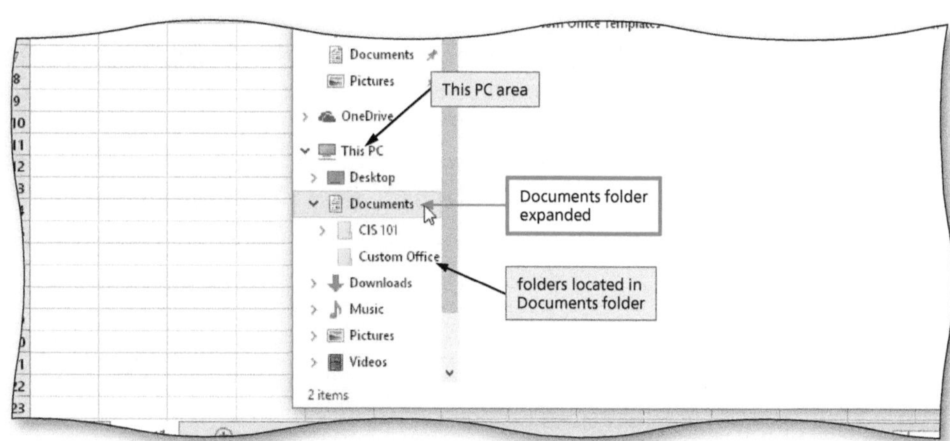

Figure 40

2

- Double-click the CIS 101 folder, which expands the folder to display its contents, indicated by a down arrow to the left of the folder icon (Figure 41).

Experiment

- Drag the scroll box down or click the down scroll arrow on the vertical scroll bar to display additional folders at the bottom of the navigation pane. Drag the scroll box up or click the scroll bar above the scroll box to move the scroll box to the top of the navigation pane. Drag the scroll box down the scroll bar until the scroll box is halfway down the scroll bar.

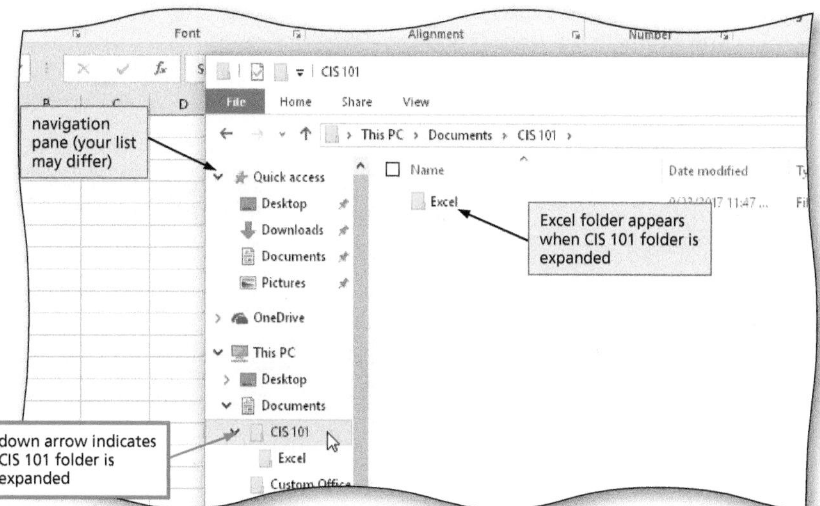

Figure 41

3

- Double-click the folder identifying your class (CIS 101, in this case) in the navigation pane to collapse the folder (Figure 42).

Q&A Why are some folders indented below others?

A folder contains the indented folders below it.

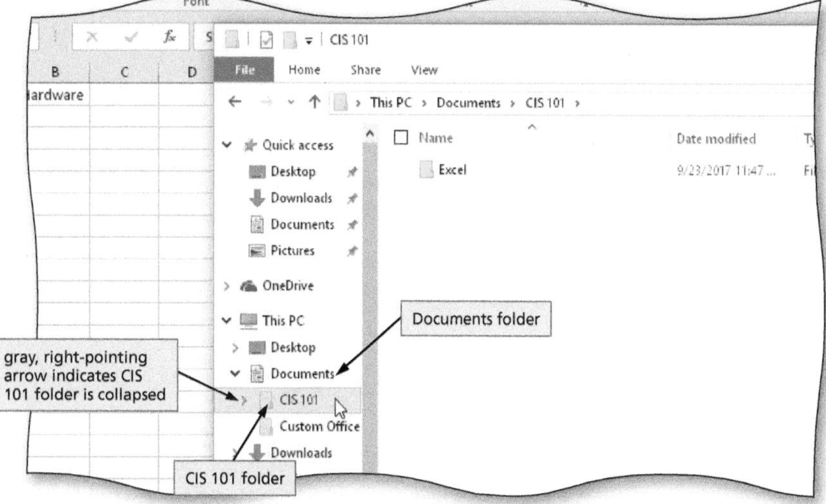

Figure 42

Other Ways

1. Point to display arrows in navigation pane, click arrow to expand or collapse
2. Select folder to expand or collapse using arrow keys, press RIGHT ARROW to expand; press LEFT ARROW to collapse

To Switch from One App to Another

The next step is to save the Excel file containing the title you typed earlier. However, Excel is not the active window. You can use the button on the taskbar and live preview to switch to Excel and then save the document in the Excel workbook window.

Why? *By clicking the appropriate app button on the taskbar, you can switch to the open app you want to use.* The steps below switch to the Excel window; however, the steps are the same for any active Office app currently displayed as a button on the taskbar.

1

- Point to the Excel app button on the taskbar to see a live preview of the open workbook(s) or the window title(s) of the open workbook(s), depending on your computer's configuration (Figure 43).

Q&A What if I am using a touch screen?
Live preview will not work if you are using a touch screen. If you are using a touch screen and do not have a mouse, proceed to Step 2.

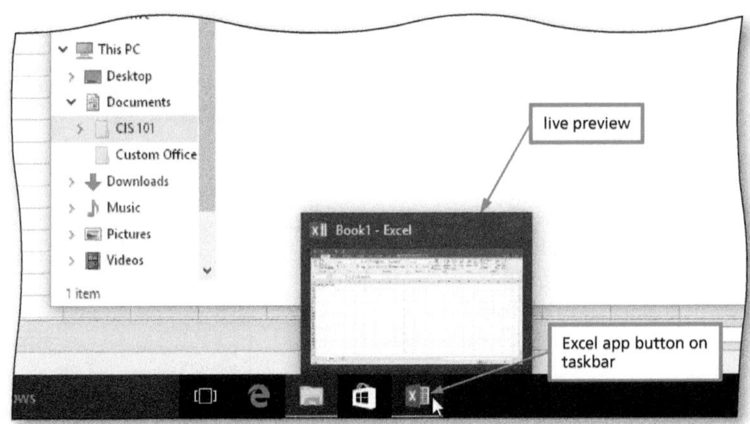

Figure 43

2

- Click the Excel app button or the live preview to make the app associated with the app button the active window (Figure 44).

Q&A What if multiple documents are open in an app?
Click the desired live preview to switch to the window you want to use.

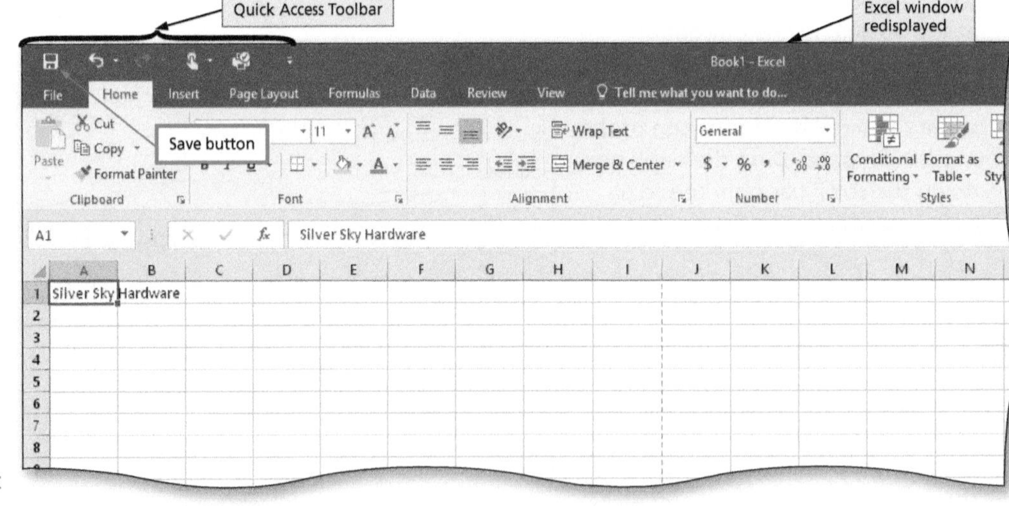

Figure 44

Other Ways

1. Press ALT+TAB until app you wish to display is selected

To Save a File in a Folder

With the Excel folder created, you can save the Excel workbooks shown in the Excel window in the Excel folder. ***Why?*** *Without saving a file, you may lose all the work you have completed and will be unable to reuse or share it with others later.* The following steps save a file in the Excel folder contained in your class folder (CIS 101, in this case) using the file name, Silver Sky Hardware.

- Click the Save button (shown in Figure 44) on the Quick Access Toolbar, which depending on settings, will display either the Save As gallery in the Backstage view (Figure 45) or the Save As dialog box (Figure 46).

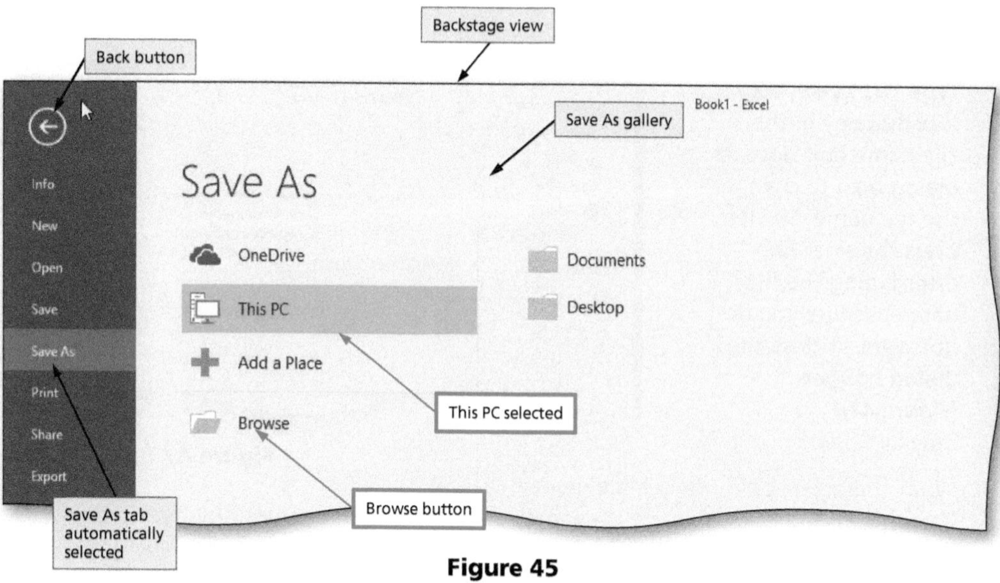

Figure 45

Q&A

What if the Save As gallery is not displayed in the Backstage view?
Click the Save As tab to display the Save As gallery.

How do I close the Backstage view?
Click the Back button in the upper-left corner of the Backstage view to return to the Excel window.

2

- If your screen displays the Backstage view, click the Browse button in the left pane to display the Save As dialog box (Figure 46). If your screen already displays the Save As dialog box, proceed to Step 3.

Q&A

What if I wanted to save on OneDrive instead?
You would click OneDrive. Saving on OneDrive is discussed in a later section in this module.

Why does a file name already appear in the File name box?
Excel automatically suggests a file name. Because the suggested file name is selected, you do not need to delete it; as soon as you begin typing, the new file name replaces the selected text.

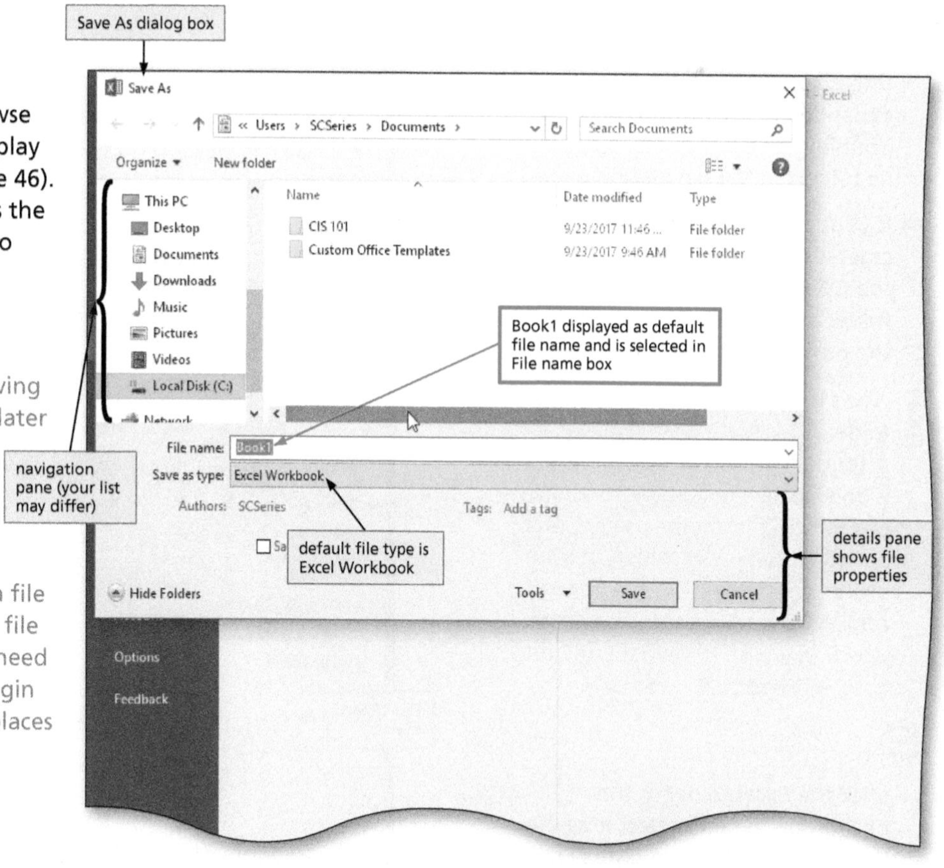

Save As dialog box

navigation pane (your list may differ)

Book1 displayed as default file name and is selected in File name box

default file type is Excel Workbook

details pane shows file properties

Figure 46

- Type **Silver Sky Hardware** in the File name box (Save As dialog box) to change the file name. Do not press the ENTER key after typing the file name because you do not want to close the dialog box yet (Figure 47).

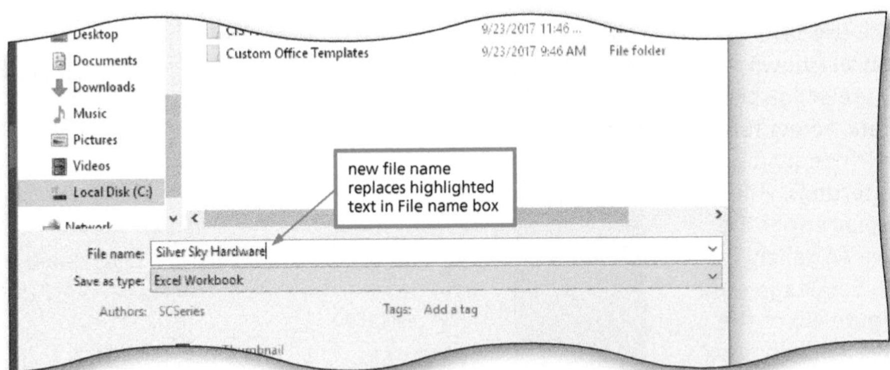

Figure 47

Q&A What characters can I use in a file name?
The only invalid characters are the same as those for folder names: the backslash (\), slash (/), colon (:), asterisk (*), question mark (?), quotation mark ("), less than symbol (<), greater than symbol (>), and vertical bar (|).

- Navigate to the desired save location (in this case, the Excel folder in the CIS 101 folder [or your class folder] in the Documents folder) by performing the tasks in Steps 4a and 4b.

- If the Documents folder is not displayed in the navigation pane, drag the scroll bar in the navigation pane until Documents appears.
- If the Documents folder is not expanded in the navigation pane, double-click Documents to display its folders in the navigation pane.
- If your class folder (CIS 101, in this case) is not expanded, double-click the CIS 101 folder to select the folder and display its contents in the navigation pane (Figure 48).

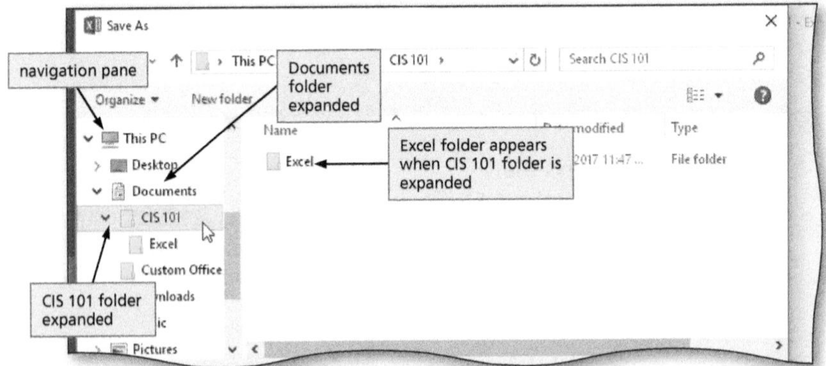

Figure 48

Q&A What if I do not want to save in a folder?
Although storing files in folders is an effective technique for organizing files, some users prefer not to store files in folders. If you prefer not to save this file in a folder, select the storage device on which you wish to save the file and then proceed to Step 5.

- Click the Excel folder in the navigation pane to select it as the new save location and display its contents in the file list (Figure 49).

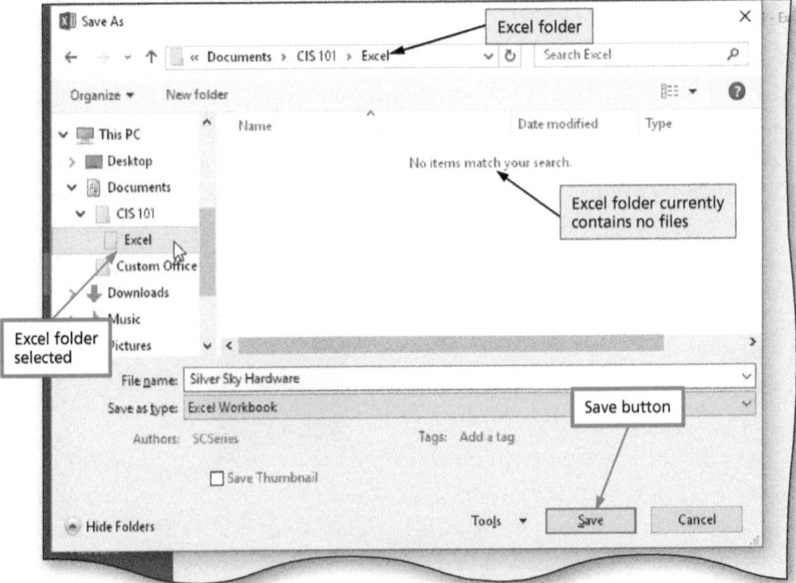

Figure 49

5

- Click the Save button (Save As dialog box) to save the document in the selected folder in the selected location with the entered file name (Figure 50).

Q&A How do I know that the file is saved?
While an Office app such as Excel is saving a file, it briefly displays a message on the status bar indicating the amount of the file saved. In addition, the file name appears on the title bar.

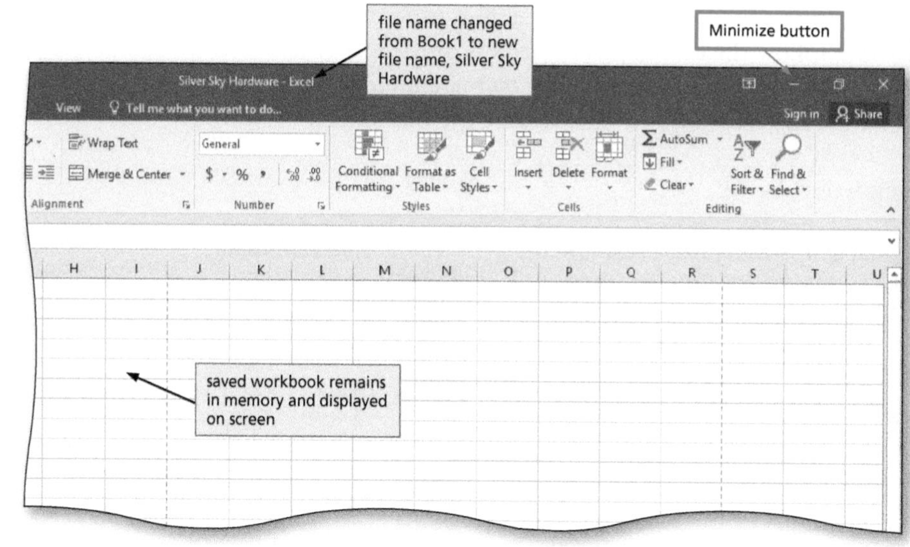

Figure 50

Other Ways

1. Click File on ribbon, click Save As in Backstage view, click Browse button, type file name (Save As dialog box), navigate to desired save location, click Save button
2. Press F12, type file name (Save As dialog box), navigate to desired save location, click Save button

CONSIDER THIS:

How often should you save a document?
It is important to save a document frequently for the following reasons:

- The document in memory might be lost if the computer is turned off or you lose electrical power while an app is running.
- If you run out of time before completing a project, you may finish it at a future time without starting over.

Navigating in Dialog Boxes

Navigating is the process of finding a location on a storage device. While saving the Silver Sky Hardware file, for example, Steps 4a and 4b navigated to the Excel folder located in the CIS 101 folder in the Documents folder. When performing certain functions in Windows apps, such as saving a file, opening a file, or inserting a picture in an existing workbook, you most likely will have to navigate to the location where you want to save the file or to the folder containing the file you want to open or insert. Most dialog boxes in Windows apps requiring navigation follow a similar procedure; that is, the way you navigate to a folder in one dialog box, such as the Save As dialog box, is similar to how you might navigate in another dialog box, such as the Open dialog box. If you chose to navigate to a specific location in a dialog box, you would follow the instructions in Steps 4a and 4b.

To Minimize and Restore a Window

1 SIGN IN | 2 USE WINDOWS | 3 USE APPS | 4 FILE MANAGEMENT | 5 SWITCH APPS | 6 SAVE FILES
7 CHANGE SCREEN RESOLUTION | 8 EXIT APPS | 9 USE ADDITIONAL APP FEATURES | 10 USE HELP

Before continuing, you can verify that the Excel file was saved properly. To do this, you will minimize the Excel window and then open the CIS 101 window so that you can verify the file is stored in the CIS 101 folder on the hard drive. A **minimized window** is an open window that is hidden from view but can be displayed quickly by clicking the window's button on the taskbar.

In the following example, Excel is used to illustrate minimizing and restoring windows; however, you would follow the same steps regardless of the Office app you are using. ***Why?*** *Before closing an app, you should make sure your file saved correctly so that you can find it later.* The following steps minimize the Excel window, verify that the file is saved, and then restore the minimized window.

1

- Click the Minimize button on the Excel window title bar (shown in Figure 50) to minimize the window (Figure 51).

Q&A Is the minimized window still available?
The minimized window, Excel in this case, remains available but no longer is the active window. It is minimized as a button on the taskbar.

- If the File Explorer window is not open on the screen, click the File Explorer button on the taskbar to make the File Explorer window the active window.

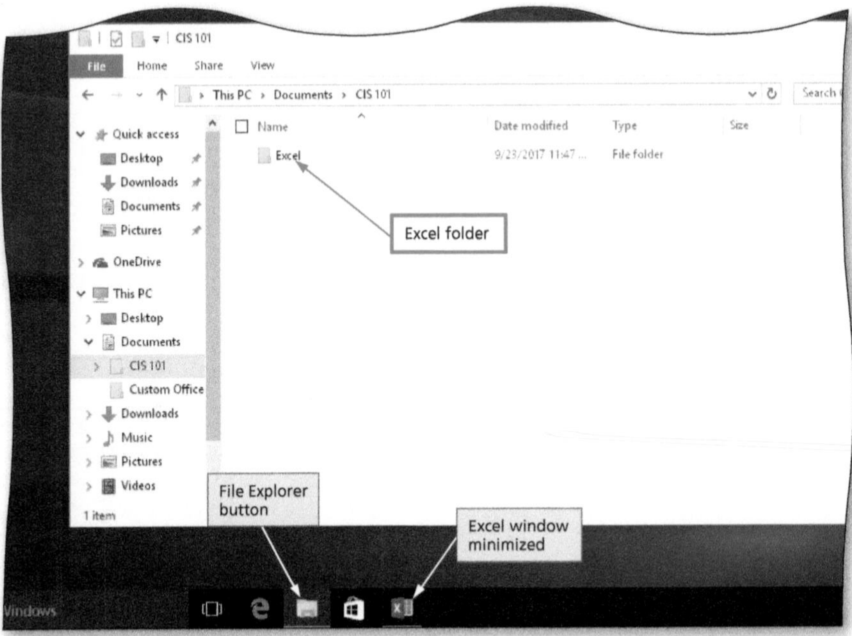

Figure 51

2

- Double-click the Excel folder in the file list to select the folder and display its contents (Figure 52).

Q&A Why does the File Explorer button on the taskbar change?
A selected app button indicates that the app is active on the screen. When the button is not selected, the app is running but not active.

3

- After viewing the contents of the selected folder, click the Excel button on the taskbar to restore the minimized window (as shown in Figure 50).

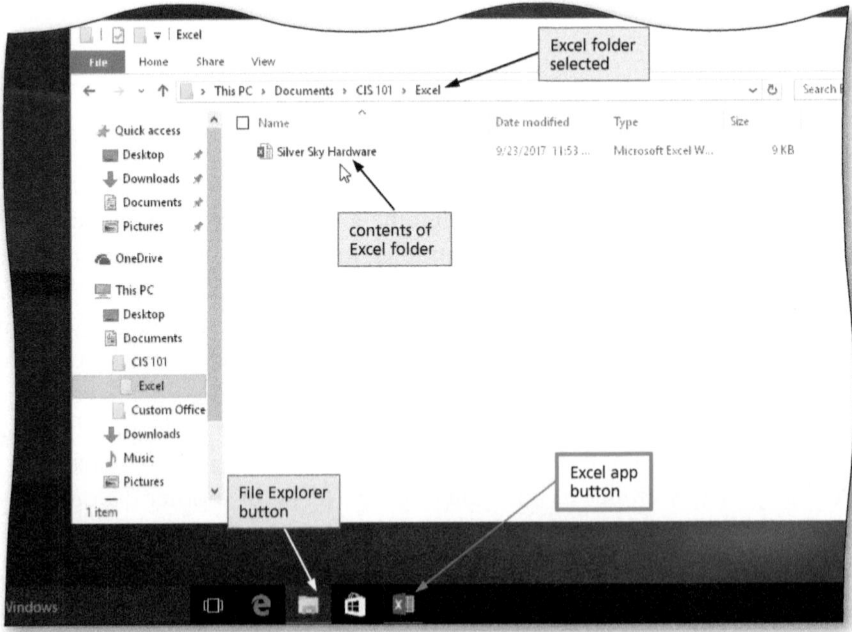

Figure 52

Other Ways

1. Right-click title bar, click Minimize on shortcut menu, click taskbar button in taskbar button area
2. Press WINDOWS+M, press WINDOWS+SHIFT+M
3. Click Excel app button on taskbar to minimize window. Click Excel app button again to restore window.

To Save a File on OneDrive

One of the features of Office is the capability to save files on OneDrive so that you can use the files on multiple computers or mobile devices without having to use an external storage device, such as a USB flash drive. Storing files on OneDrive also enables you to share files more efficiently with others, such as when using Office Online and Office 365.

In the following example, Excel is used to save a file on OneDrive. ***Why?*** *Storing files on OneDrive provides more portability options than are available from storing files in the Documents folder.*

You can save files directly on OneDrive from within an Office app. The following steps save the current Excel file on OneDrive. These steps require you have a Microsoft account and an Internet connection.

1

- Click File on the ribbon to open the Backstage view.
- Click the Save As tab in the Backstage view to display the Save As gallery.
- Click OneDrive in the left pane to display OneDrive saving options or a Sign In button, if you are not signed in already to your Microsoft account (Figure 53).

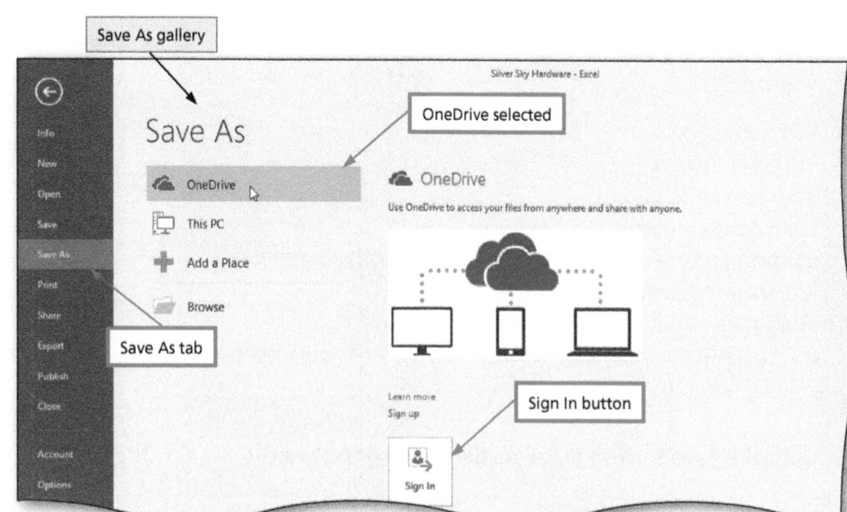

Figure 53

2

- If your screen displays a Sign In button (shown in Figure 53), click it to display the Sign in dialog box (Figure 54).

Q&A What if the Sign In button does not appear?
If you already are signed into your Microsoft account, the Sign In button will not be displayed. In this case, proceed to Step 3.

- Follow the instructions on the screen to sign in to your Microsoft account.

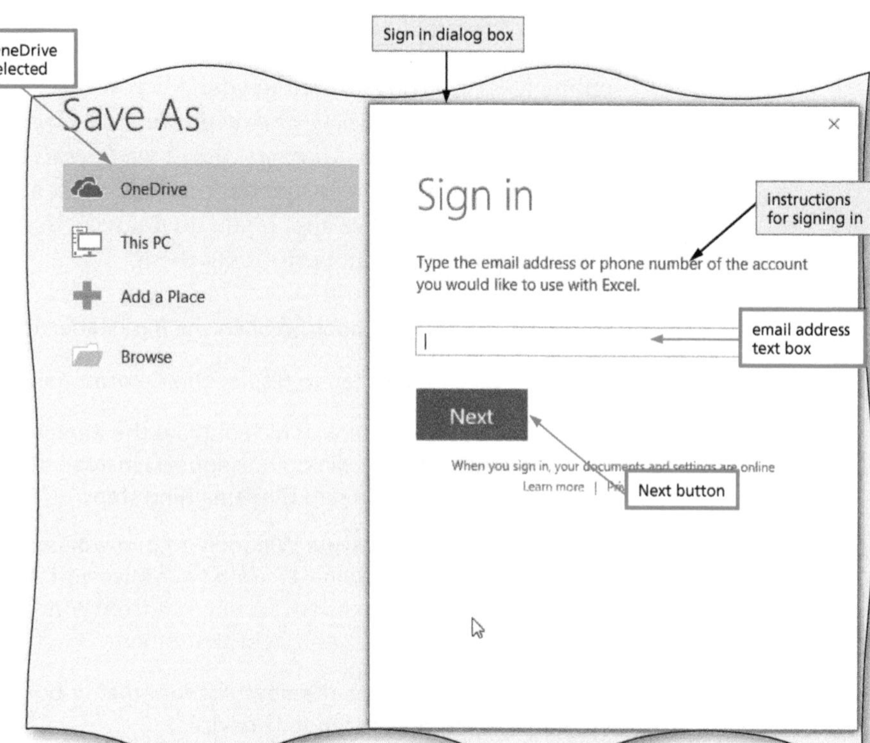

Figure 54

- If necessary, in the Backstage view, click OneDrive in the left pane in the Save As gallery to select OneDrive as the save location.
- Click the Documents folder in the right pane to display the Save As dialog box (Figure 55).

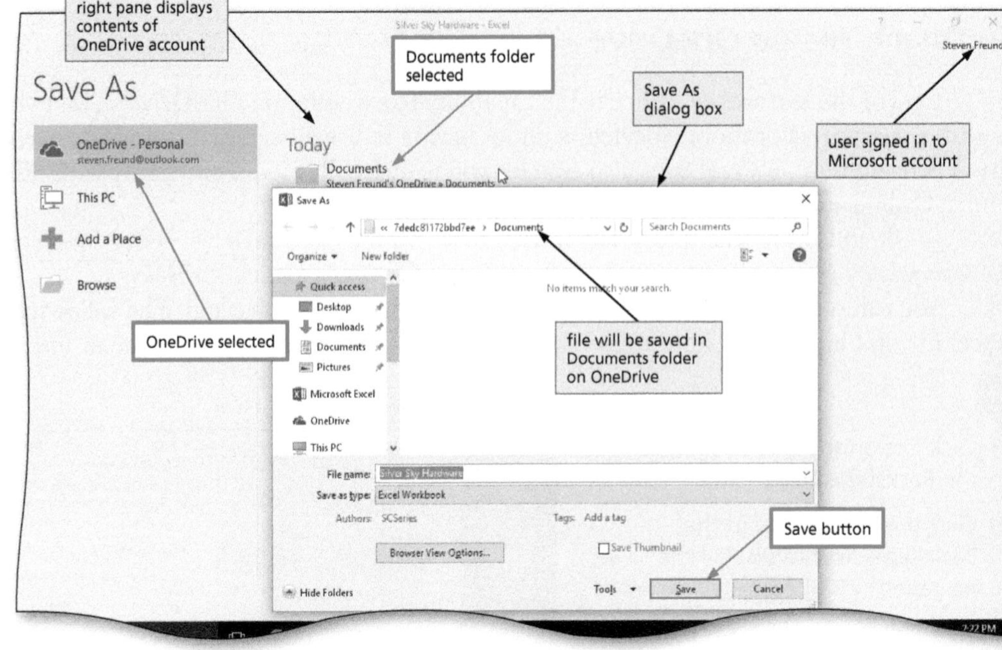

Figure 55

Q&A Why does the path in the OneDrive address bar in the Save As dialog box contain various letters and numbers?
The letters and numbers in the address bar uniquely identify the location of your OneDrive files and folders.

- Click the Save button (Save As dialog box) to save the file on OneDrive.

To Sign Out of a Microsoft Account

If you are using a public computer or otherwise wish to sign out of your Microsoft account, you should sign out of the account from the Accounts gallery in the Backstage view. Signing out of the account is the safest way to make sure that nobody else can access online files or settings stored in your Microsoft account. ***Why?*** *For security reasons, you should sign out of your Microsoft account when you are finished using a public or shared computer. Staying signed in to your Microsoft account might enable others to access your files.*

The following steps sign out of a Microsoft account from Excel. You would use the same steps in any Office app. If you do not wish to sign out of your Microsoft account, read these steps without performing them.

1. Click File on the ribbon to open the Backstage view.
2. Click the Account tab to display the Account gallery (Figure 56).
3. Click the Sign out link, which displays the Remove Account dialog box. If a Can't remove Windows accounts dialog box appears instead of the Remove Account dialog box, click the OK button and skip the remaining steps.

Q&A Why does a Can't remove Windows accounts dialog box appear?
If you signed in to Windows using your Microsoft account, then you also must sign out from Windows, rather than signing out from within Excel. When you are finished using Windows, be sure to sign out at that time.

4. Click the Yes button (Remove Account dialog box) to sign out of your Microsoft account on this computer or mobile device.

Q&A Should I sign out of Windows after removing my Microsoft account?
When you are finished using the computer, you should sign out of Windows for maximum security.

5 Click the Back button in the upper-left corner of the Backstage view to return to the document.

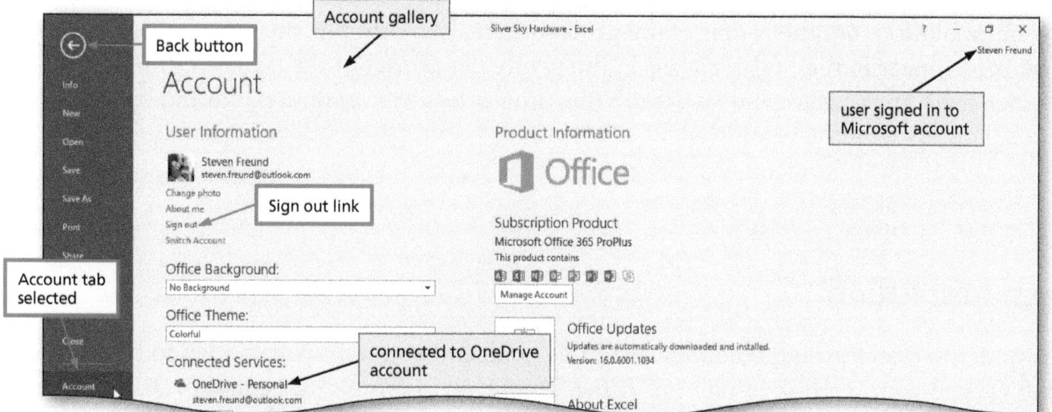

Figure 56

Screen Resolution

Screen resolution indicates the number of pixels (dots) that the computer uses to display the letters, numbers, graphics, and background you see on the screen. When you increase the screen resolution, Windows displays more information on the screen, but the information decreases in size. The reverse also is true: as you decrease the screen resolution, Windows displays less information on the screen, but the information increases in size.

Screen resolution usually is stated as the product of two numbers, such as 1366 × 768 (pronounced "thirteen sixty-six by seven sixty-eight"). A 1366 × 768 screen resolution results in a display of 1366 distinct pixels on each of 768 lines, or about 1,049,088 pixels. Changing the screen resolution affects how the ribbon appears in Office apps and some Windows dialog boxes. Figure 57, for example, shows the Excel ribbon at screen resolutions of 1366 × 768 and 1024 × 768. All of the same commands are available regardless of screen resolution. The app (Excel, in this case), however, makes changes to the groups and the buttons within the groups to accommodate the various screen resolutions. The result is that certain commands may need to be accessed differently depending on the resolution chosen. A command that is visible on the ribbon and available by clicking a button at one resolution may not be visible and may need to be accessed using its Dialog Box Launcher at a different resolution.

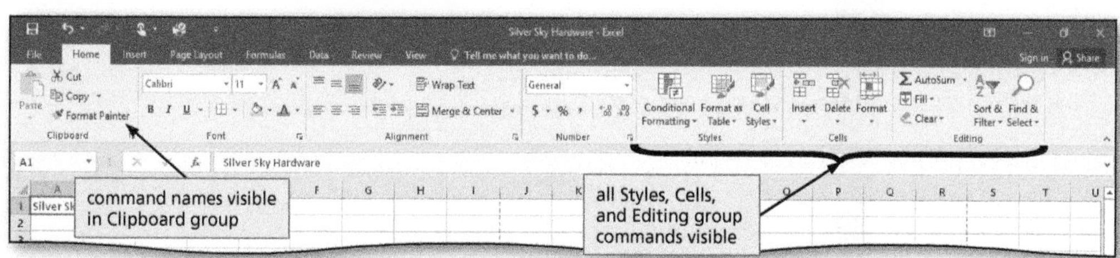

Figure 57(a) Ribbon at 1366 × 768 Resolution

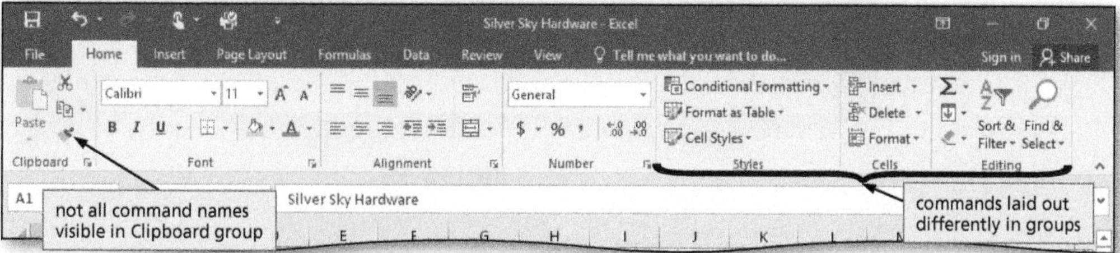

Figure 57(b) Ribbon at 1024 × 768 Resolution

Comparing the two ribbons in Figure 57, notice the changes in content and layout of the groups and galleries. In some cases, the content of a group is the same in each resolution, but the layout of the group differs. For example, the same gallery and buttons appear in the Styles groups in the two resolutions, but the layouts differ. In other cases, the content and layout are the same across the resolution, but the level of detail differs with the resolution.

To Change the Screen Resolution

1 SIGN IN | 2 USE WINDOWS | 3 USE APPS | 4 FILE MANAGEMENT | 5 SWITCH APPS | 6 SAVE FILES
7 CHANGE SCREEN RESOLUTION | 8 EXIT APPS | 9 USE ADDITIONAL APP FEATURES | 10 USE HELP

If you are using a computer to step through the modules in this book and you want your screen to match the figures, you may need to change your screen's resolution. ***Why?*** *The figures in this book use a screen resolution of 1366 × 768.* The following steps change the screen resolution to 1366 × 768. Your computer already may be set to 1366 × 768. Keep in mind that many computer labs prevent users from changing the screen resolution; in that case, read the following steps for illustration purposes.

- Click the Show desktop button, which is located at the far-right edge of the taskbar, to display the Windows desktop.
- Right-click an empty area on the Windows desktop to display a shortcut menu that contains a list of commands related to the desktop (Figure 58).

Q&A Why does my shortcut menu display different commands?
Depending on your computer's hardware and configuration, different commands might appear on the shortcut menu.

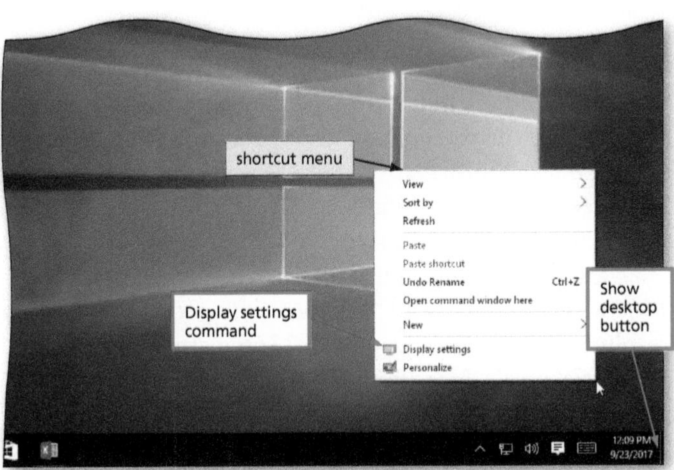

Figure 58

- Click Display settings on the shortcut menu to open the Settings app window. If necessary, scroll in the right pane to display the 'Advanced display settings' link (Figure 59).

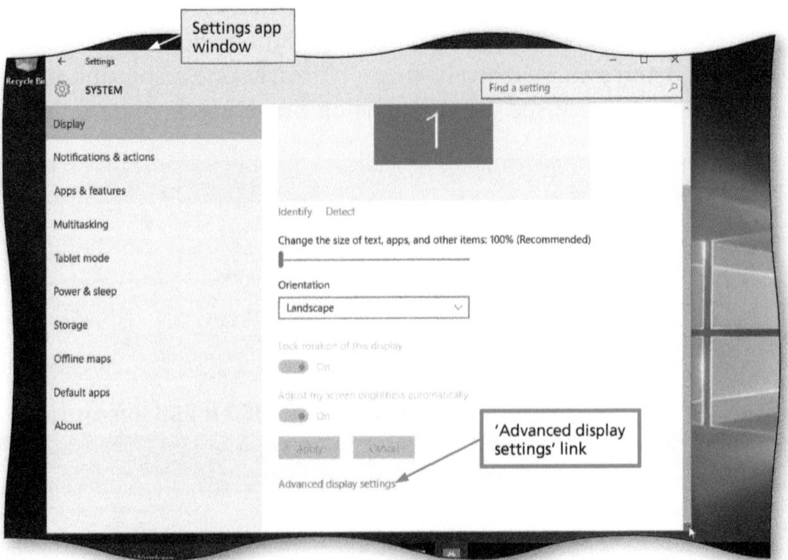

Figure 59

- Click 'Advanced display settings' in the Settings app window to display the advanced display settings.
- If necessary, scroll to display the Resolution box (Figure 60).

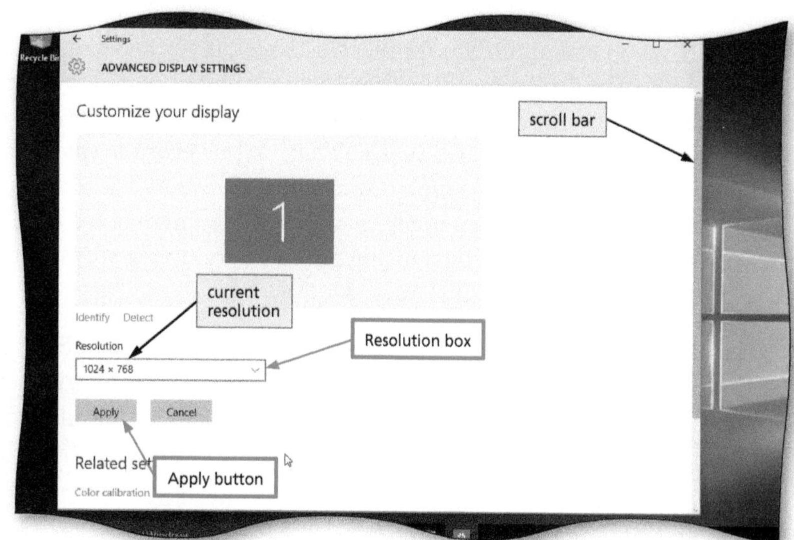

Figure 60

- Click the Resolution box to display a list of available screen resolutions (Figure 61).
- If necessary, scroll to and then click 1366 × 768 to select the screen resolution. If your screen resolution already is set to 1366 × 768, click the Close button to close the Settings app window and then skip Step 5.

Q&A What if my computer does not support the 1366 × 768 resolution?
If your computer does not support the recommended resolution, select a resolution that is close to 1366 × 768.

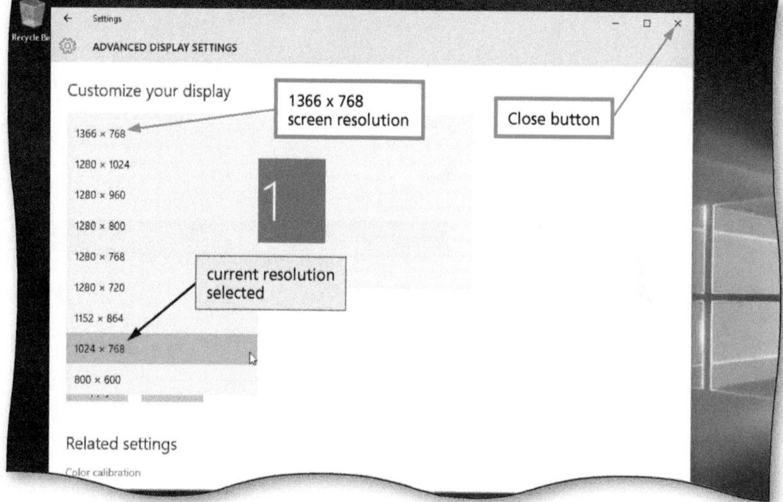

Figure 61

5

- Click the Apply button (shown in Figure 60) to change the screen resolution and display a confirmation message (Figure 62).
- Click the Keep changes button to accept the new screen resolution.
- Click the Close button (shown in Figure 61) to close the Settings app window.

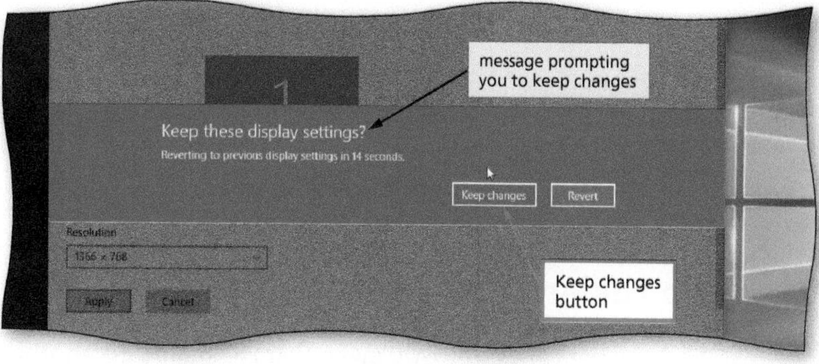

Figure 62

Other Ways

1. Click Start button, click Settings, click System, click Display (if necessary), click 'Advanced display settings,' select desired resolution in Resolution box, click Apply button, click Keep changes button
2. Type **screen resolution** in search box, click 'Change the screen resolution,' select desired resolution in Resolution box, click Apply, click Keep changes

To Exit an App with One Document Open

When you exit an Office app, such as Excel, if you have made changes to a file since the last time the file was saved, the app displays a dialog box asking if you want to save the changes you made to the file before it closes the app window. ***Why?*** *The dialog box contains three buttons with these resulting actions: the Save button saves the changes and then exits the app, the Don't Save button exits the app without saving changes, and the Cancel button closes the dialog box and redisplays the file without exiting the app.*

If no changes have been made to an open document since the last time the file was saved, the app will close the window without displaying a dialog box. The following steps exit Excel. You would follow similar steps in other Office apps.

- If necessary, click the Excel app button on the taskbar to display the Excel window on the desktop. If the Backstage view is displayed, click the Back button to return to the worksheet (Figure 63).

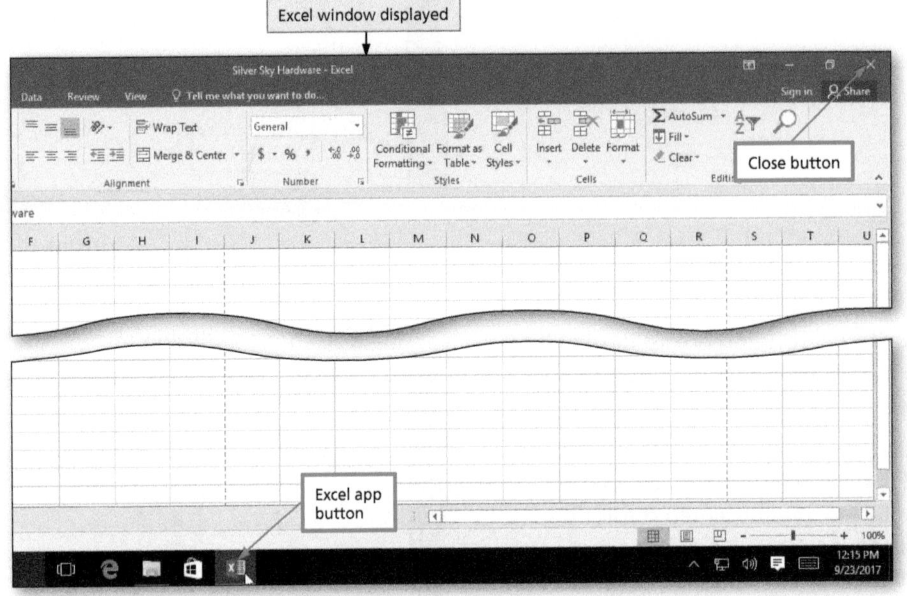

Figure 63

- Click the Close button on the right side of the Excel window title bar to close the document and exit Excel. If a Microsoft Excel dialog box appears, click the Save button to save any changes made to the document since the last save.

Q&A What if I have more than one document open in Excel?
You could click the Close button for each open document. When you click the last open document's Close button, you also exit Excel. As an alternative that is more efficient, you could right-click the Excel app button on the taskbar and then click 'Close all windows' on the shortcut menu to close all open documents and exit Excel.

Other Ways

1. Right-click Excel app button on Windows taskbar, click 'Close window' on shortcut menu
2. Press ALT+F4

To Copy a Folder to OneDrive

To back up your files or easily make them available on another computer or mobile device, you can copy them to OneDrive. The following steps copy your CIS 101 folder to OneDrive. If you do not have access to a OneDrive account, read the following steps without performing them. ***Why?*** *It often is good practice to have a backup of your files so that they are available in case something happens to your original copies.*

1

- Click the File Explorer button on the taskbar to make the folder window the active window.
- Navigate to the CIS 101 folder [or your class folder] in the Documents folder.
- Click Documents in the This PC area of the navigation pane to display the CIS 101 folder in the file list.

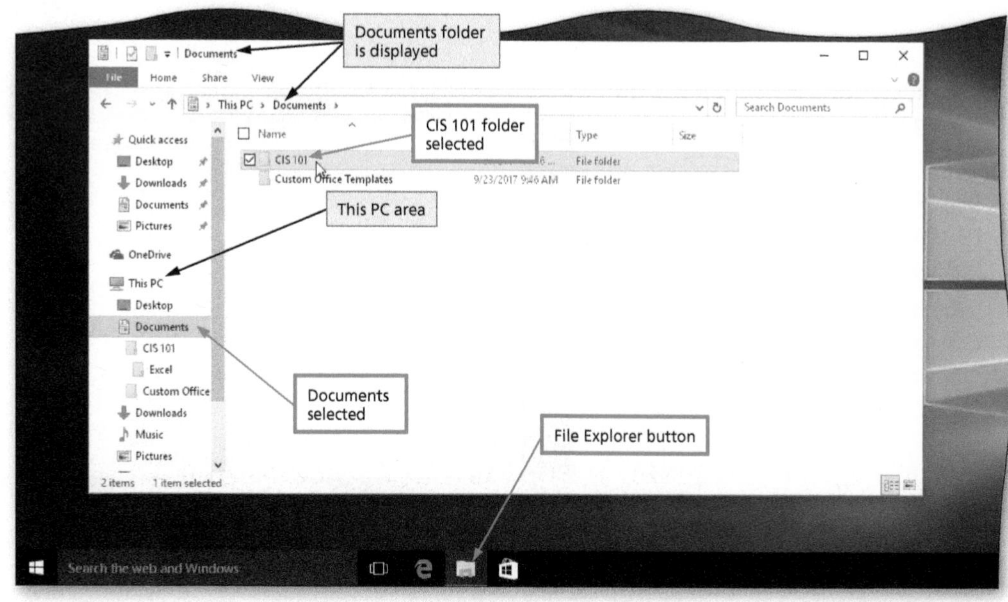

Figure 64

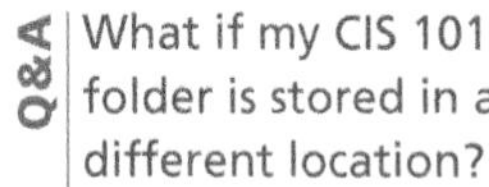

What if my CIS 101 folder is stored in a different location?

Use the navigation pane to navigate to the location of your CIS 101 folder. The CIS 101 folder should be displayed in the file list once you have located it.

- Click the CIS 101 folder in the file list to select it (Figure 64).

2

- Click Home on the ribbon to display the Home tab.
- Click the Copy to button (Home tab | Organize group) to display the Copy to menu (Figure 65).

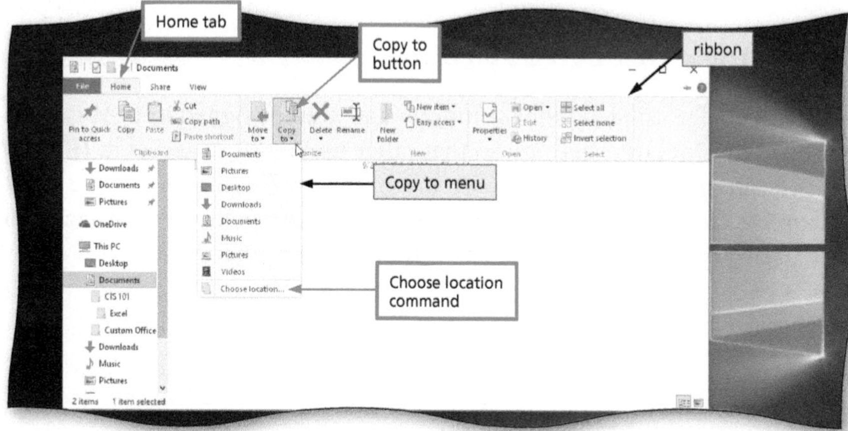

Figure 65

3

- Click Choose location on the Copy to menu to display the Copy Items dialog box.
- Click OneDrive (Copy Items dialog box) to select it (Figure 66).

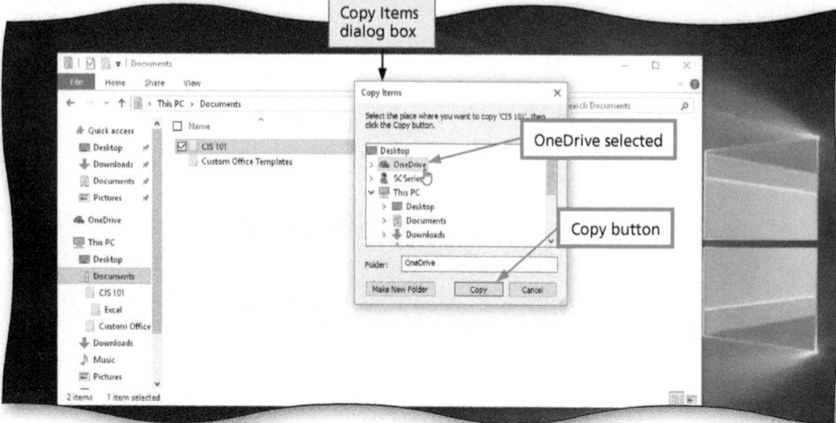

Figure 66

- Click the Copy button (Copy Items dialog box) to copy the selected folder to OneDrive.
- Click OneDrive in the navigation pane to verify the CIS 101 folder displays in the file list (Figure 67).

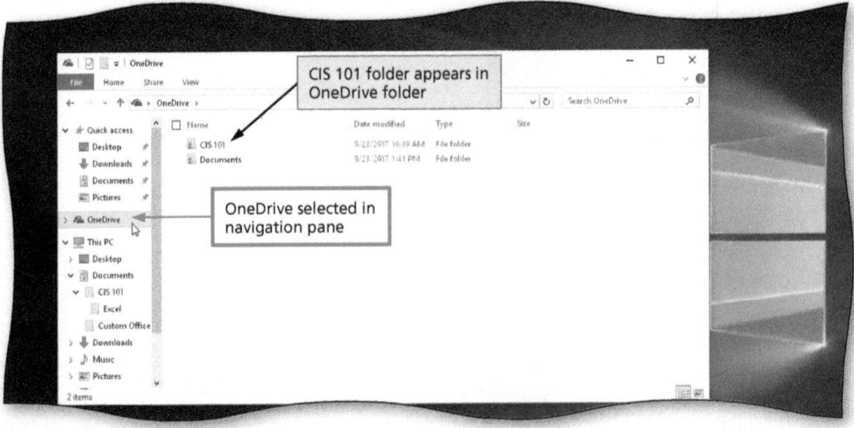

Figure 67

Q&A Why does a Microsoft OneDrive dialog box display when I click OneDrive in the navigation pane?
If you are not currently signed in to Windows using a Microsoft account, you will manually need to sign in to a Microsoft account to save files to OneDrive. Follow the instructions on the screen to sign in to your Microsoft account. If the Microsoft Excel window indicates you are signed in to your Microsoft account, that does not necessarily mean you are signed in to Windows with a Microsoft account.

Other Ways

1. In File Explorer, select folder to copy, click Copy button (Home tab | Clipboard group), display contents of OneDrive in file list, click Paste button (Home tab | Clipboard group)
2. In File Explorer, select folder to copy, press CTRL+C, display contents of OneDrive in file list, press CTRL+V
3. Drag folder to copy to OneDrive in navigation pane

To Unlink a OneDrive Account

1 SIGN IN | 2 USE WINDOWS | 3 USE APPS | 4 FILE MANAGEMENT | 5 SWITCH APPS | 6 SAVE FILES
7 CHANGE SCREEN RESOLUTION | 8 EXIT APPS | 9 USE ADDITIONAL APP FEATURES | 10 USE HELP

If you are using a public computer and are not signed in to Windows with a Microsoft account, you should unlink your OneDrive account so that other users cannot access it. ***Why?*** *If you do not unlink your OneDrive account, other people accessing the same user account on the computer will be able to view, remove, and add to files stored in your OneDrive account.* The following steps unlink your OneDrive account. If you do not wish to unlink your OneDrive account, read these steps without performing them.

- Click the 'Show hidden icons' button on the Windows taskbar to show a menu of hidden icons (Figure 68).

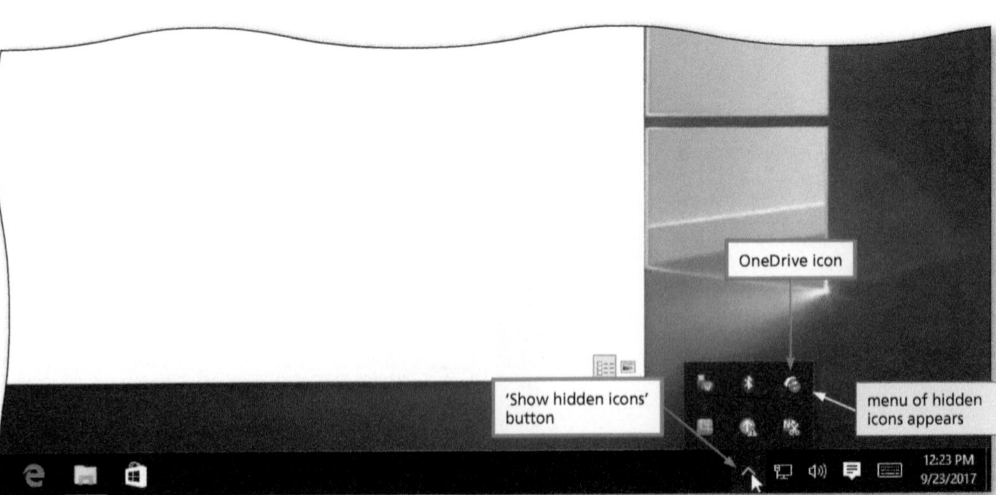

Figure 68

2

- Right click the OneDrive icon (shown in Figure 68) to display a shortcut menu (Figure 69).

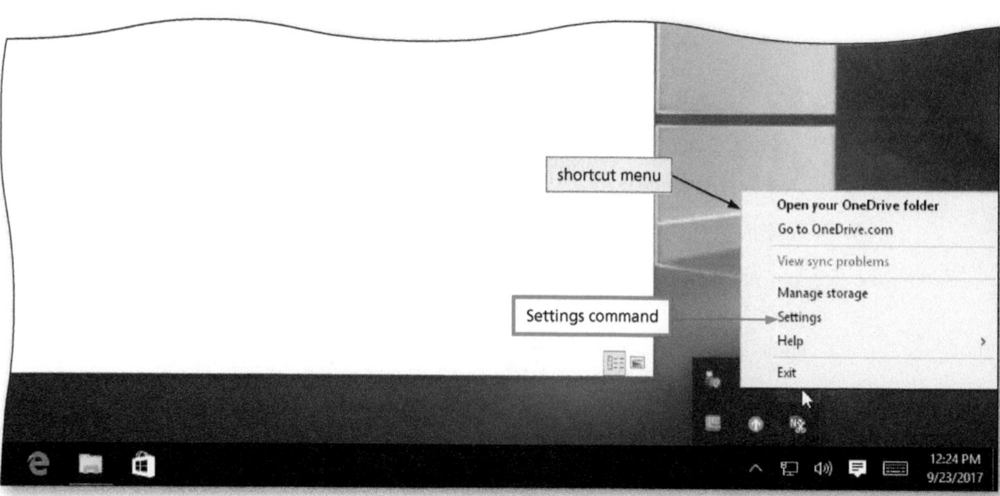

Figure 69

3

- Click Settings on the shortcut menu to display the Microsoft OneDrive dialog box (Figure 70).

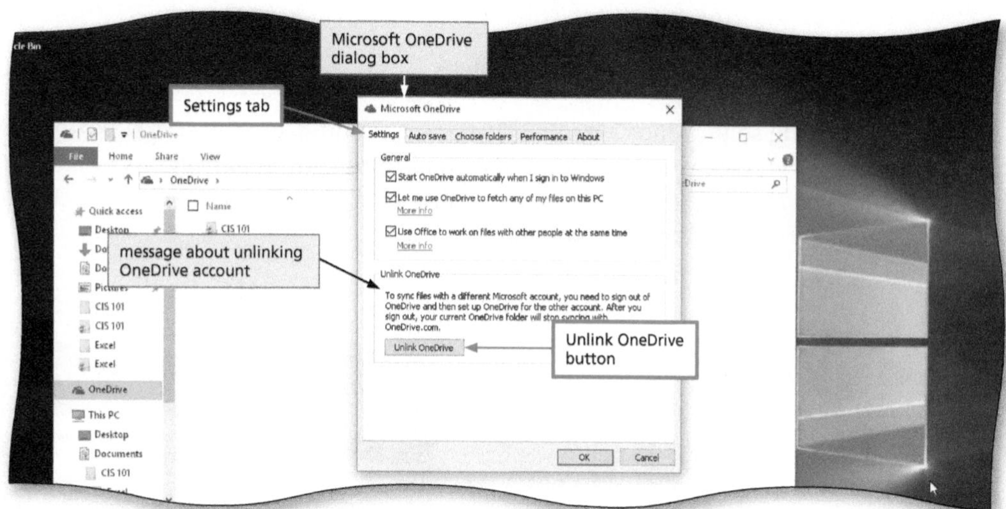

Figure 70

4

- If necessary, click the Settings tab.
- Click the Unlink OneDrive button (Microsoft OneDrive dialog box) to unlink the OneDrive account (Figure 71).
- When the Microsoft OneDrive dialog box appears with a Welcome to OneDrive message, click the Close button.
- Minimize the File Explorer window.

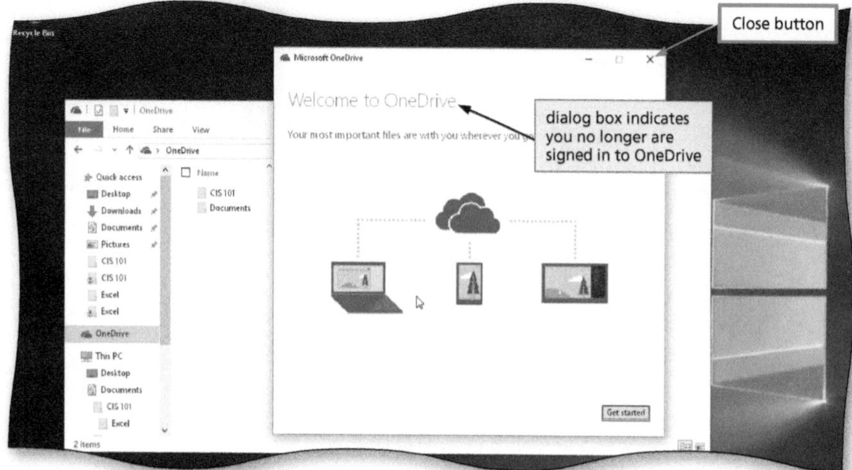

Figure 71

Break Point: If you wish to take a break, this is a good place to do so. To resume at a later time, continue to follow the steps from this location forward.

Additional Common Features of Office Apps

The previous section used Excel to illustrate common features of Office and some basic elements unique to Excel. The following sections continue to use Excel to present additional common features of Office.

In the following pages, you will learn how to do the following:

1. Run Excel using the search box.
2. Open a document in Excel.
3. Close the document.
4. Reopen the document just closed.
5. Create a blank Excel document from File Explorer and then open the file.
6. Save a document with a new file name.

To Run an App Using the Search Box

The following steps, which assume Windows is running, use the search box to run Excel based on a typical installation; however, you would follow similar steps to run any app. ***Why?*** *Some people prefer to use the search box to locate and run an app, as opposed to searching through a list of all apps on the Start menu.* You may need to ask your instructor how to run Excel on your computer.

- Type **Excel 2016** as the search text in the search box and watch the search results appear in the search results (Figure 72).

Q&A

Do I need to type the complete app name or use correct capitalization?
No, you need to type just enough characters of the app name for it to appear in the search results. For example, you may be able to type Excel or excel, instead of Excel 2016.

What if the search does not locate the Excel app on my computer?
You may need to adjust the Windows search settings. Search for the word, index; click 'Indexing Options Control Panel'; click the Modify button (Indexing Options dialog box); expand the Local Disk, if necessary; place a check mark beside all Program Files entries; and then click the OK button. It may take a few minutes for the index to rebuild. If it still does not work, you may need to click the Advanced button (Indexing Options dialog box) and then click the Rebuild button (Advanced Options dialog box).

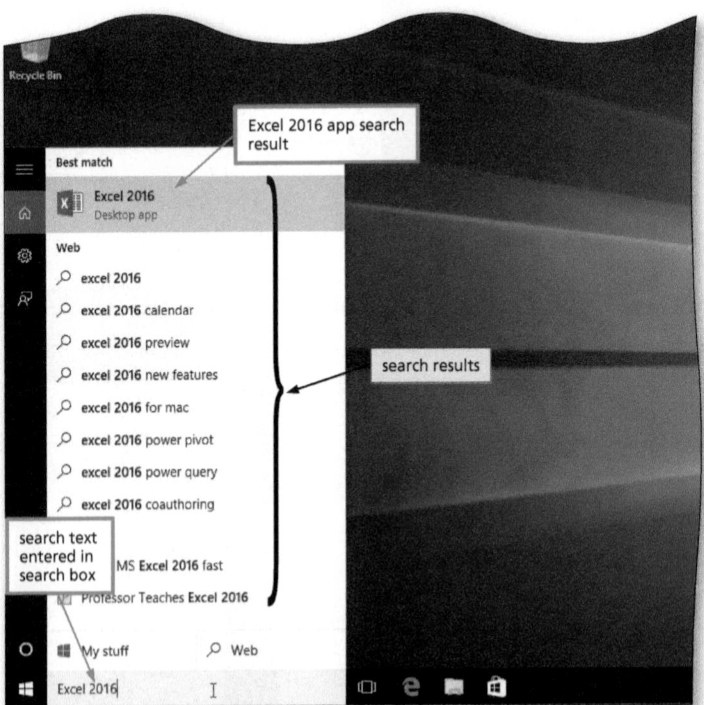

Figure 72

2

- Click the app name, Excel 2016, in the search results to run Excel and display the Excel start screen.
- Click the Blank workbook thumbnail on the Excel start screen (shown earlier in this module in Figure 9) to create a blank workbook and display it in the Excel window.
- If the Excel window is not maximized, click the Maximize button on its title bar to maximize the window (Figure 73).

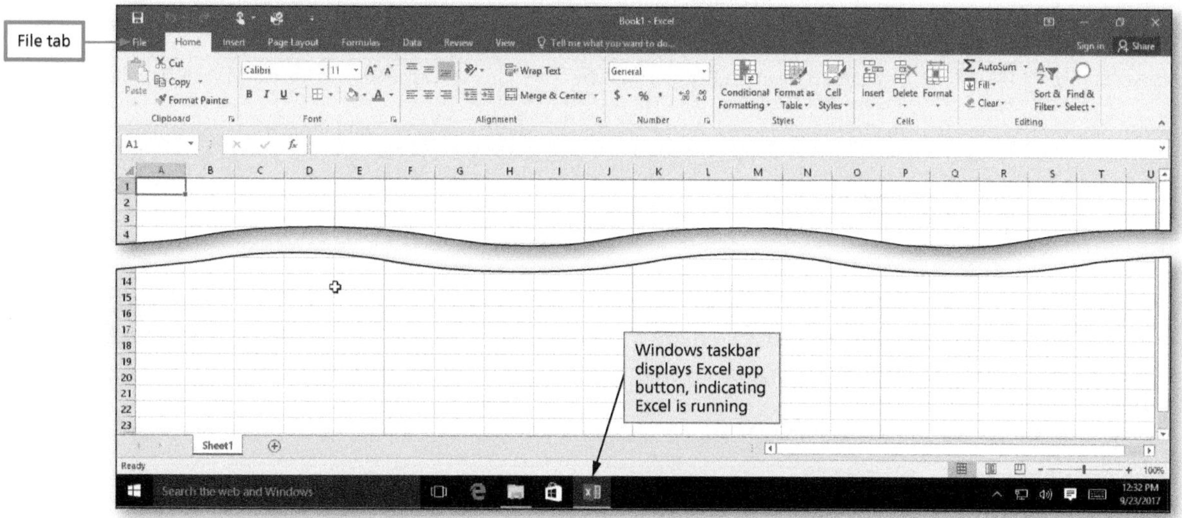

Figure 73

To Open an Existing File

1 SIGN IN | 2 USE WINDOWS | 3 USE APPS | 4 FILE MANAGEMENT | 5 SWITCH APPS | 6 SAVE FILES
7 CHANGE SCREEN RESOLUTION | 8 EXIT APPS | 9 USE ADDITIONAL APP FEATURES | 10 USE HELP

As discussed earlier, the Backstage view contains a set of commands that enable you to manage documents and data about the documents. ***Why?*** *From the Backstage view in Excel, for example, you can create, open, print, and save documents. You also can share documents, manage versions, set permissions, and modify document properties. In other Office apps, the Backstage view may contain features specific to those apps.* The following steps open a saved file, specifically the Silver Sky Hardware file.

1

- Click File on the ribbon (shown in Figure 73) to open the Backstage view and then if necessary, click the Open tab in the Backstage view to display the Open gallery in the Backstage view.
- Click the Browse button in the right pane to display the Open dialog box.
- If necessary, navigate to the location of the file to open (Excel folder in the CIS 101 folder).
- Click the file to open, Silver Sky Hardware in this case, to select the file (Figure 74).

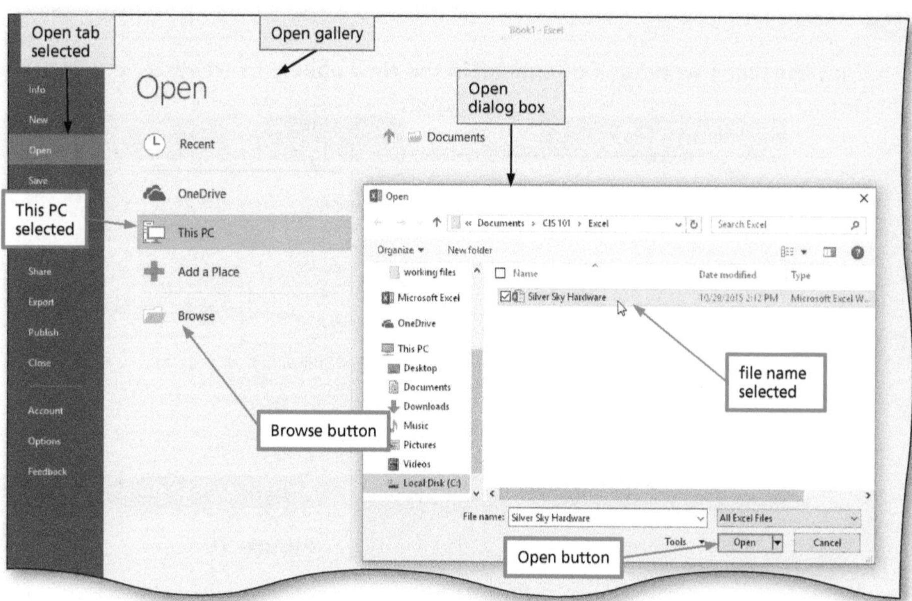

Figure 74

- Click the Open button (Open dialog box) to open the file (shown earlier in the module in Figure 50). If necessary, click the Enable Content button.

Q&A Why did a Security Warning appear?
The Security Warning appears when you open an Office file that might contain harmful content. The files you create in this module are not harmful, but you should be cautious when opening files from other people.

Other Ways

1. Press CTRL+O, browse for file
2. Navigate to file in File Explorer window, double-click file name
3. Click Recent in Backstage view, click file name

To Create a New Document from the Backstage View

You can open multiple documents in an Office program, such as Excel, so that you can work on the documents at the same time. The following steps create a file, a blank workbook in this case, from the Backstage view. ***Why?** You want to create a new document while keeping the current document open.*

- Click File on the ribbon to open the Backstage view.
- Click the New tab in the Backstage view to display the New gallery (Figure 75).

Q&A Can I create documents through the Backstage view in other Office apps?
Yes. If the Office app has a New tab in the Backstage view, the New gallery displays various options for creating a new file.

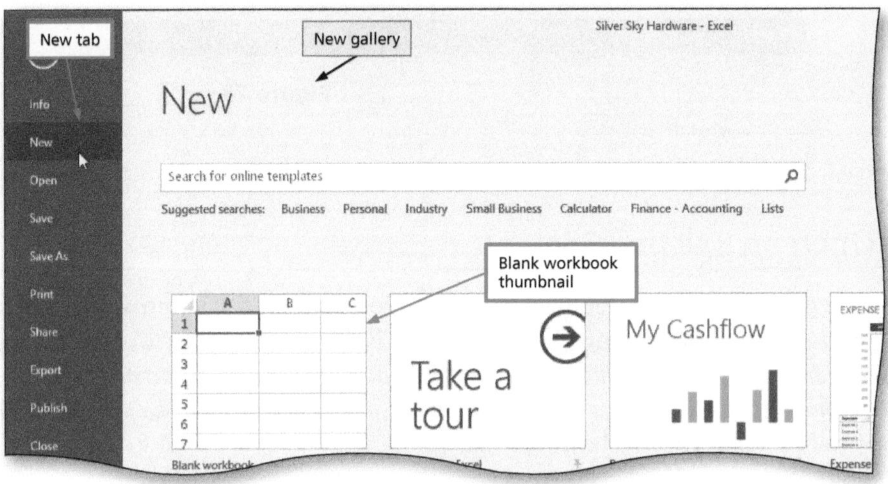

Figure 75

- Click the Blank workbook thumbnail in the New gallery to create a new document (Figure 76).

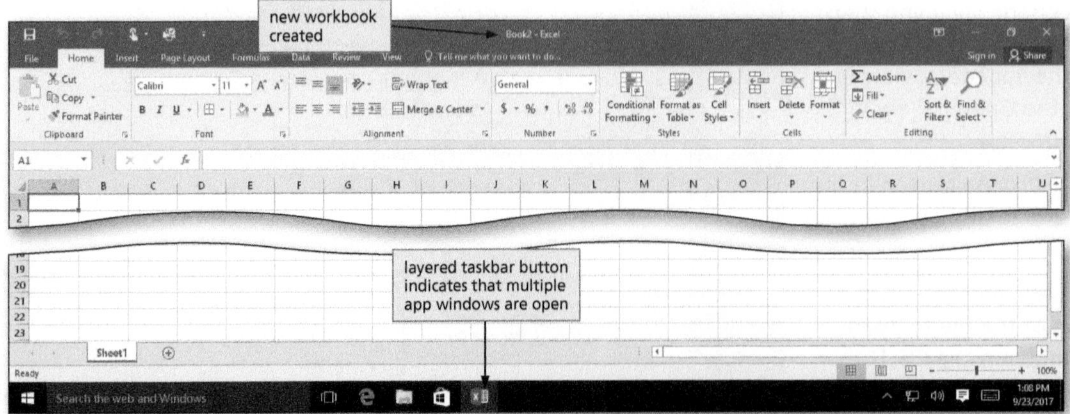

Figure 76

Other Ways

1. Press CTRL+N

To Enter a Worksheet Title

The new Excel workbook will contain a sales analysis. The following steps enter a worksheet title.

1. If it is not already the active cell, click cell A1 to make it the active cell.
2. Type **Silver Sky Hardware Sales Analysis** in cell A1.
3. Click the Enter button to complete the entry and enter the worksheet title in cell A1 (Figure 77).

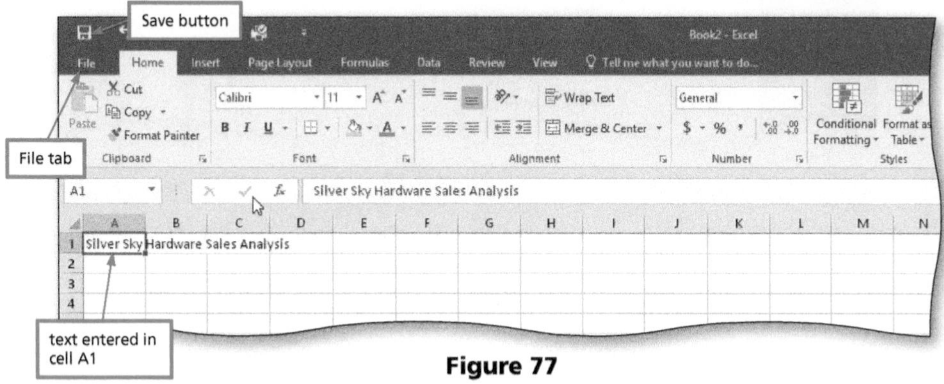

Figure 77

To Save a File

The following steps save the second document in the Excel folder in the class folder (CIS 101, in this case) in the Documents folder using the file name, SSH Sales Analysis.

1. Click the Save button on the Quick Access Toolbar, which depending on settings will display either the Save As gallery in the Backstage view or the Save As dialog box.
2. If your screen displays the Backstage view, click the Browse button in the right pane to display the Save As dialog box.
3. If necessary, type **SSH Sales Analysis** in the File name box (Save As dialog box) to change the file name. Do not press the ENTER key after typing the file name because you do not want to close the dialog box at this time.
4. If necessary, navigate to the desired save location (in this case, the Excel folder in the CIS 101 folder [or your class folder] in the Documents folder). For specific instructions, perform the tasks in Steps 4a and 4b in the previous section in this module titled To Save a File in a Folder.
5. Click the Save button (Save As dialog box) to save the document in the selected folder on the selected drive with the entered file name.

To Close a File Using the Backstage View

Sometimes, you may want to close an Office file, such as an Excel workbook, and start over with a new file. ***Why?*** *You should close a file when you are done working with it so that you do not make inadvertent changes to it.* The following steps close the current active Excel file, that is, the SSH Sales Analysis document, without exiting Excel.

1

- Click File on the ribbon to open the Backstage view (Figure 78).

2

- Click Close in the Backstage view to close the open file (SSH Sales Analysis, in this case) without exiting the active app (Excel).

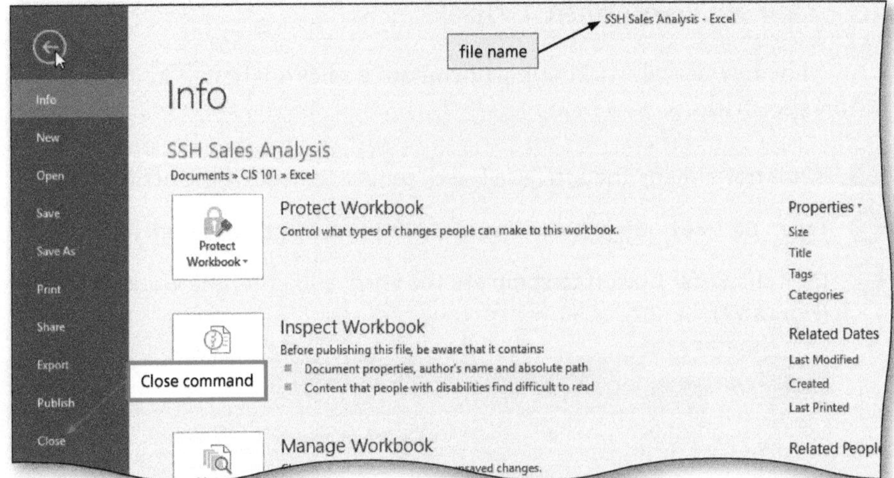

Figure 78

Q&A What if Excel displays a dialog box about saving?
Click the Save button if you want to save the changes, click the Don't Save button if you want to ignore the changes since the last time you saved, and click the Cancel button if you do not want to close the workbook.

Can I use the Backstage view to close an open file in other Office apps, such as Word and PowerPoint?
Yes.

Other Ways

1. Press CTRL+F4

To Open a Recent File Using the Backstage View

1 SIGN IN | 2 USE WINDOWS | 3 USE APPS | 4 FILE MANAGEMENT | 5 SWITCH APPS | 6 SAVE FILES
7 CHANGE SCREEN RESOLUTION | 8 EXIT APPS | 9 USE ADDITIONAL APP FEATURES | **10 USE HELP**

You sometimes need to open a file that you recently modified. ***Why?*** *You may have more changes to make, such as adding more content or correcting errors.* The Backstage view allows you to access recent files easily. The following steps reopen the SSH Sales Analysis file just closed.

1

- Click File on the ribbon to open the Backstage view.
- If necessary, click the Open tab in the Backstage view to display the Open gallery (Figure 79).

2

- Click the desired file name in the Recent list, SSH Sales Analysis in this case, to open the file.

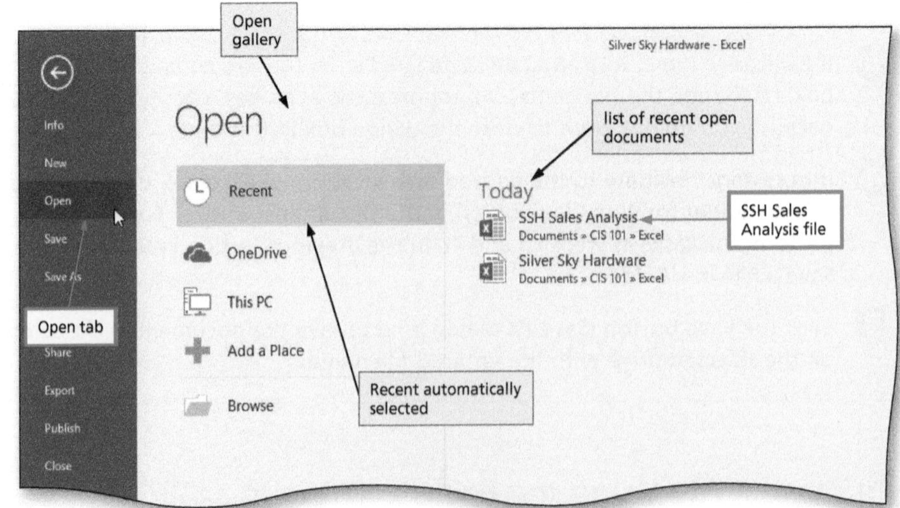

Figure 79

Q&A Can I use the Backstage view to open a recent file in other Office apps, such as Word and PowerPoint?
Yes, as long as the file name appears in the list of recent files.

Other Ways

1. Click File on ribbon, click Open in Backstage view, click Browse button, navigate to file (Open dialog box), click Open button

To Create a New Blank Workbook from File Explorer

1 SIGN IN | 2 USE WINDOWS | 3 USE APPS | 4 FILE MANAGEMENT | 5 SWITCH APPS | 6 SAVE FILES
7 CHANGE SCREEN RESOLUTION | 8 EXIT APPS | 9 USE ADDITIONAL APP FEATURES | 10 USE HELP

File Explorer provides a means to create a blank Office document without first running an Office app. The following steps use File Explorer to create a blank Excel workbook. ***Why?*** *Sometimes you might need to create a blank workbook and then return to it later for editing.*

1

- Click the File Explorer button on the taskbar to make the folder window the active window.
- If necessary, double-click the Documents folder in the navigation pane to expand the Documents folder.
- If necessary, double-click your class folder (CIS 101, in this case) in the navigation pane to expand the folder.
- Click the Excel folder in the navigation pane to display its contents in the file list.
- With the Excel folder selected, right-click an open area in the file list to display a shortcut menu.
- Point to New on the shortcut menu to display the New submenu (Figure 80).

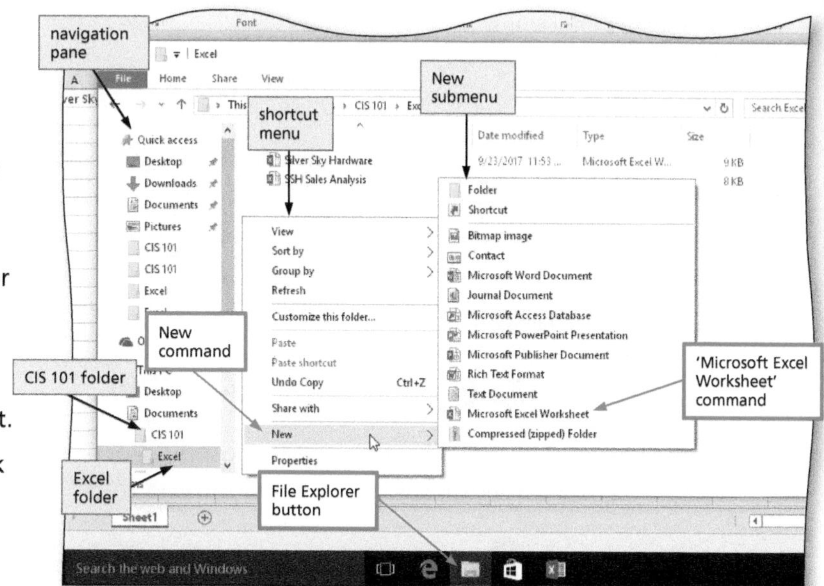

Figure 80

- Click 'Microsoft Excel Worksheet' on the New submenu to display an icon and text box for a new file in the current folder window with the file name, New Microsoft Excel Worksheet, selected (Figure 81).

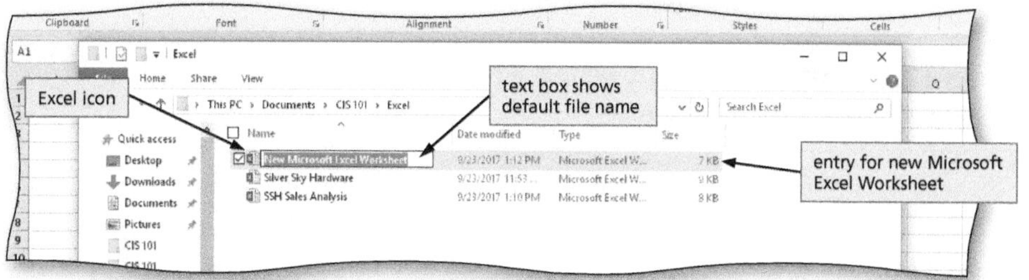

Figure 81

3

- Type **SSH Expenditures** in the text box and then press the ENTER key to assign a new file name to the new file in the current folder (Figure 82).

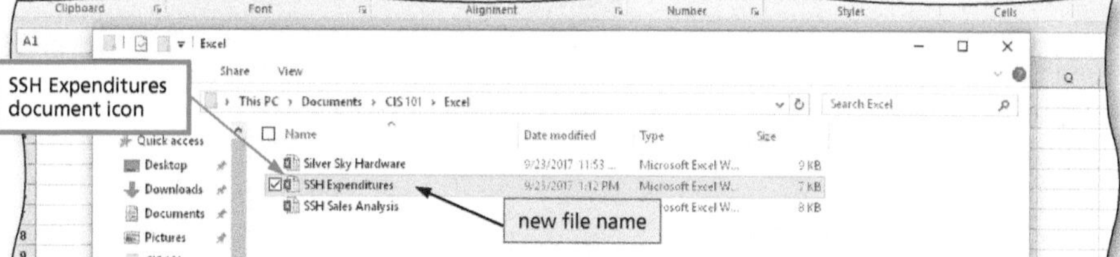

Figure 82

To Open a File Using File Explorer

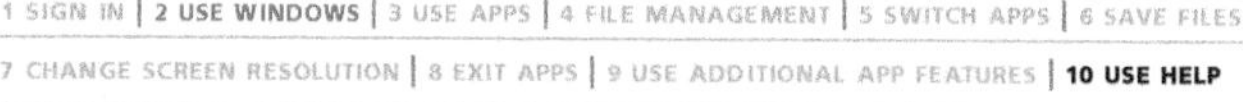

Previously in this module, you learned how to run Excel using the Start menu and the search box. The following steps, which assume Windows is running, open a file using File Explorer. If the app you used to create the file (Microsoft Excel, in this case) is not running, Windows will run the app and open the file. ***Why?*** *Another way to open a file is from File Explorer, which causes the app in which the file was created to run, if necessary, and then open the selected file.*

- If necessary, display the file to open in the folder window in File Explorer (shown in Figure 82).
- Right-click the file icon or file name you want to open (SSH Expenditures, in this case) to display a shortcut menu (Figure 83).

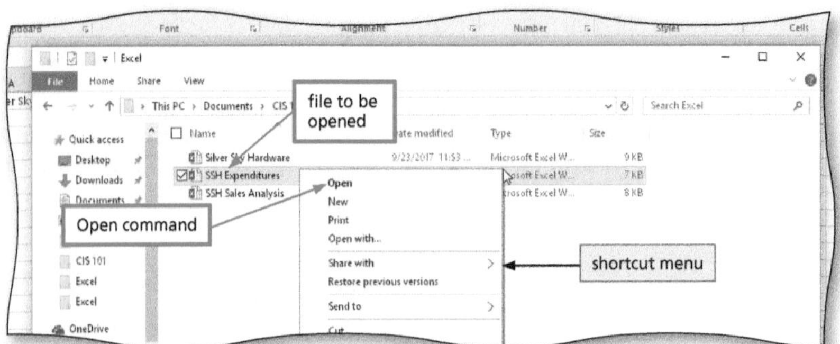

Figure 83

2

- Click Open on the shortcut menu to open the selected file in the app used to create the file, Excel in this case (shown in Figure 84).
- If the window is not maximized, click the Maximize button on the title bar to maximize the window.

Other Ways

1. Double-click file name in file list

To Enter a Worksheet Title

The next step is to enter a worksheet title in the blank Excel worksheet. The following steps enter a worksheet title.

1. If it is not already the active cell, click cell A1 to make it the active cell.
2. Type **`Silver Sky Hardware Expenditures`** in cell A1.
3. Click the Enter button to complete the entry and enter the worksheet title in cell A1.

To Save an Existing Office File with the Same File Name

1 SIGN IN | 2 USE WINDOWS | 3 USE APPS | 4 FILE MANAGEMENT | 5 SWITCH APPS | 6 SAVE FILES
7 CHANGE SCREEN RESOLUTION | 8 EXIT APPS | 9 USE ADDITIONAL APP FEATURES | **10 USE HELP**

Saving frequently cannot be overemphasized. ***Why?*** *You have made modifications to the file since you created it. Thus, you should save again. Similarly, you should continue saving files frequently so that you do not lose the changes you have made since the time you last saved the file.* You can use the same file name, such as SSH Expenditures, to save the changes made to the workbook. The following step saves a file again with the same file name.

- Click the Save button on the Quick Access Toolbar to overwrite the previously saved file (SSH Expenditures, in this case) in the Excel folder (Figure 84).

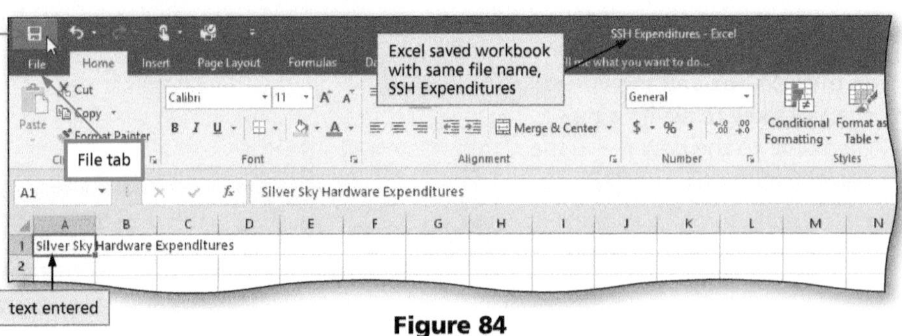

Figure 84

Other Ways

1. Press CTRL+S
2. Press SHIFT+F12

To Save a File with a New File Name

You might want to save a file with a different file name or to a different location. For example, you might start a homework assignment with a data file and then save it with a final file name for submission to your instructor, saving it to a location designated by your instructor. The following steps save a file with a different file name.

1 Click the File tab to open the Backstage view.

2 Click the Save As tab to display the Save As gallery.

3 Click the Browse button in the left pane to display the Save As dialog box.

4 Type **SSH Income and Expenses** in the File name box (Save As dialog box) to change the file name. Do not press the ENTER key after typing the file name because you do not want to close the dialog box at this time.

5 If necessary, navigate to the desired save location (in this case, the Excel folder in the CIS 101 folder [or your class folder] in the Documents folder). For specific instructions, perform the tasks in Steps 4a and 4b in the previous section titled To Save a File in a Folder.

6 Click the Save button (Save As dialog box) to save the document in the selected folder on the selected drive with the entered file name.

To Exit an Office App

You are finished using Excel. The following steps exit Excel.

1 Because you have multiple Excel workbooks open, right-click the Excel app button on the taskbar and then click 'Close all windows' on the shortcut menu to close all open workbooks and exit Excel.

2 If a dialog box appears, click the Save button to save any changes made to the file since the last save.

Renaming, Moving, and Deleting Files

Earlier in this module, you learned how to organize files in folders, which is part of a process known as **file management**. The following sections cover additional file management topics including renaming, moving, and deleting files.

To Rename a File

1 SIGN IN | 2 USE WINDOWS | 3 USE APPS | 4 FILE MANAGEMENT | 5 SWITCH APPS | 6 SAVE FILES
7 CHANGE SCREEN RESOLUTION | 8 EXIT APPS | 9 USE ADDITIONAL APP FEATURES | 10 USE HELP

In some circumstances, you may want to change the name of, or rename, a file or a folder. ***Why?*** *You may want to distinguish a file in one folder or drive from a copy of a similar file, or you may decide to rename a file to better identify its contents.* The following steps change the name of the Silver Sky Hardware file in the Excel folder to Silver Sky Hardware Workbook.

1

- If necessary, click the File Explorer button on the taskbar to make the folder window the active window.
- If necessary, navigate to the location of the file to be renamed (in this case, the Excel folder in the CIS 101 [or your class folder] folder in the Documents folder) to display the file(s) it contains in the file list.
- Click the file to be renamed, the Silver Sky Hardware icon or file name in the file list in this case, to select it.
- Right-click the selected file to display a shortcut menu that presents a list of commands related to files (Figure 85).

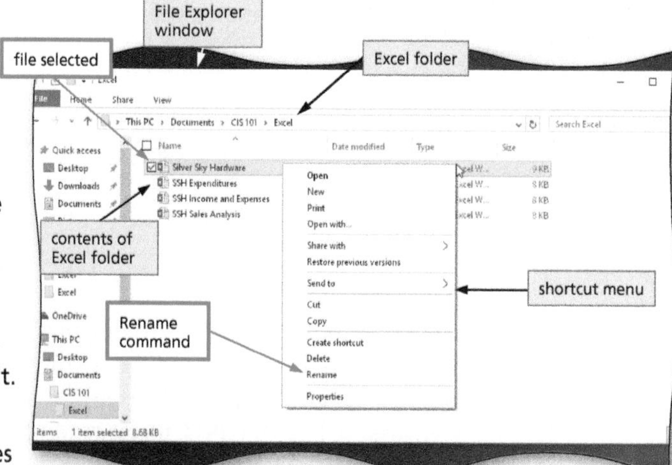

Figure 85

- Click Rename on the shortcut menu to place the current file name in a text box.
- Type **Silver Sky Hardware Workbook** in the text box and then press the ENTER key (Figure 86).

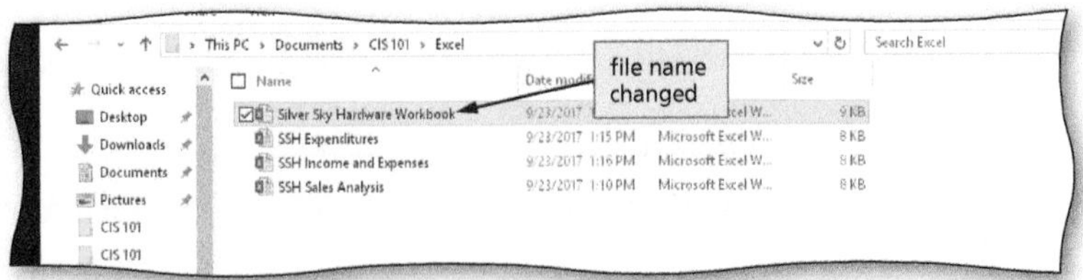

Figure 86

Q&A Are any risks involved in renaming files that are located on a hard drive?
If you inadvertently change a file extension (the three letter or four letters following the period) while renaming a file, the app that created the file might not be able to recognize and open the file.

Can I rename a file when it is open?
No, a file must be closed to change the file name.

Other Ways

1. Select file, press F2, type new file name, press ENTER
2. Select file, click Rename (Home tab | Organize group), type new file name, press ENTER

1 SIGN IN | 2 USE WINDOWS | 3 USE APPS | 4 FILE MANAGEMENT | 5 SWITCH APPS | 6 SAVE FILES
7 CHANGE SCREEN RESOLUTION | 8 EXIT APPS | 9 USE ADDITIONAL APP FEATURES | 10 USE HELP

To Move a File

***Why?** You may want to move a file from one folder, called the source folder, to another, called the destination folder.* When you move a file, it no longer appears in the original folder. If the destination and the source folders are on the same media, you can move a file by dragging it. If the folders are on different media, you will need to right-drag the file and then click Move here on the shortcut menu. The following step moves the SSH Income and Expenses file from the Excel folder to the CIS 101 folder.

- If necessary, in File Explorer, navigate to the location of the file to be moved (in this case, the Excel folder in the CIS 101 folder [or your class folder] in the Documents folder).
- If necessary, click the Excel folder in the navigation pane to display the files it contains in the right pane.
- Drag the file to be moved, the SSH Income and Expenses file in the right pane, to the CIS 101 folder in the navigation pane (Figure 87).

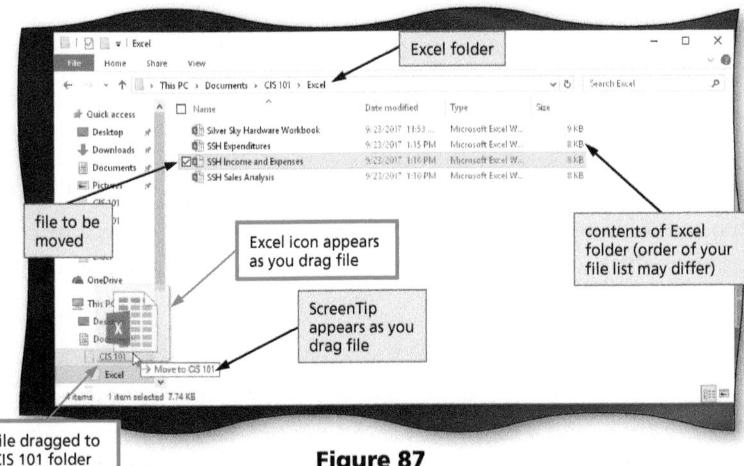

Figure 87

Experiment

- Click the CIS 101 folder in the navigation pane to verify that the file was moved. When you have finished, return to the Excel folder.

Other Ways

1. Right-click file to move, click Cut on shortcut menu, right-click destination folder, click Paste on shortcut menu
2. Select file to move, press CTRL+X, select destination folder, press CTRL+V

1 SIGN IN | 2 USE WINDOWS | 3 USE APPS | 4 FILE MANAGEMENT | 5 SWITCH APPS | 6 SAVE FILES
7 CHANGE SCREEN RESOLUTION | 8 EXIT APPS | 9 USE ADDITIONAL APP FEATURES | 10 USE HELP

To Delete a File

A final task you may want to perform is to delete a file. Exercise caution when deleting a file or files. When you delete a file from a hard drive, the deleted file is stored in the Recycle Bin where you can recover it until you empty the Recycle Bin. If you delete a file from removable media, such as a USB flash drive, the file is deleted permanently. The next steps delete the SSH Income and Expenses file from the CIS 101 folder. ***Why?** When a file no longer is needed, you can delete it to conserve space on your storage location.*

- If necessary, in File Explorer, navigate to the location of the file to be deleted (in this case, the CIS 101 folder [or your class folder] in the Documents folder).
- Click the file to be deleted, the SSH Income and Expenses icon or file name in the right pane in this case, to select the file.
- Right-click the selected file to display a shortcut menu (Figure 88).

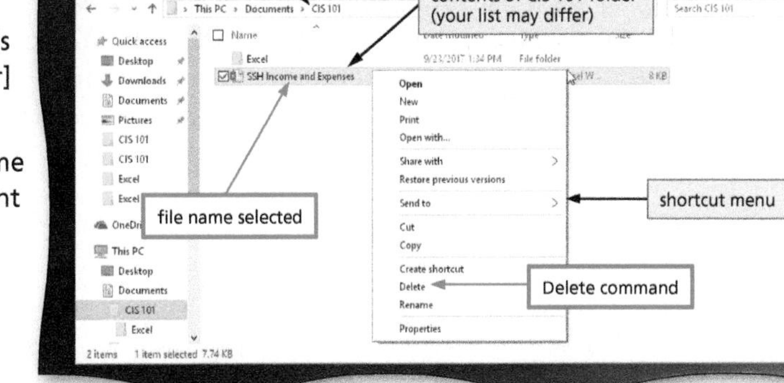

Figure 88

- Click Delete on the shortcut menu to delete the file.
- If a dialog box appears, click the Yes button to delete the file.

Q&A Can I use this same technique to delete a folder?
Yes. Right-click the folder and then click Delete on the shortcut menu. When you delete a folder, all of the files and folders contained in the folder are deleted as well. For example, if you delete the CIS 101 folder, you will delete all folders and files inside the CIS 101 folder.

Other Ways

1. Select file, press DELETE

Microsoft Office and Windows Help

At any time while you are using one of the Office apps, such as Excel, you can use Office Help to display information about all topics associated with the app. Help in other Office apps operates in a similar fashion.

In Office, Help is presented in a window that has browser-style navigation buttons. Each Office app has its own Help home page, which is the starting Help page that is displayed in the Help window. If your computer is connected to the Internet, the contents of the Help page reflect both the local help files installed on the computer and material from Microsoft's website.

To Open the Help Window in an Office App

1 SIGN IN | 2 USE WINDOWS | 3 USE APPS | 4 FILE MANAGEMENT | 5 SWITCH APPS | 6 SAVE FILES
7 CHANGE SCREEN RESOLUTION | 8 EXIT APPS | 9 USE ADDITIONAL APP FEATURES | 10 USE HELP

The following step opens the Excel 2016 Help window. ***Why?*** *You might not understand how certain commands or operations work in Excel, so you can obtain the necessary information using help.*

- Run Excel.
- Click the Blank workbook thumbnail to display a blank workbook.
- Press F1 to open the Excel 2016 Help window (Figure 89).

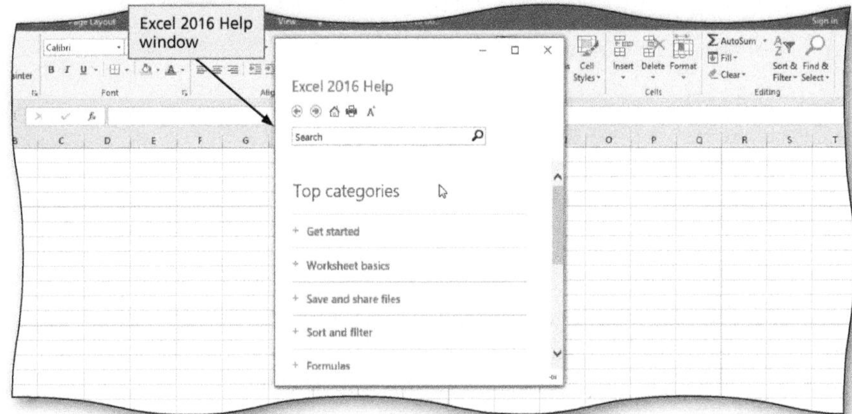

Figure 89

Moving and Resizing Windows

At times, it is useful, or even necessary, to have more than one window open and visible on the screen at the same time. You can resize and move these open windows so that you can view different areas of and elements in the window. In the case of the Help window, for example, it could be covering document text in the Excel window that you need to see.

To Move a Window by Dragging

You can move any open window that is not maximized to another location on the desktop by dragging the title bar of the window. ***Why?*** *You might need to have a better view of what is behind the window or just want to move the window so that you can see it better.* The following step drags the Excel 2016 Help window to the upper-left corner of the desktop.

- Drag the window title bar (the Excel 2016 Help window title bar, in this case) so that the window moves to the upper-left corner of the desktop, as shown in Figure 90.

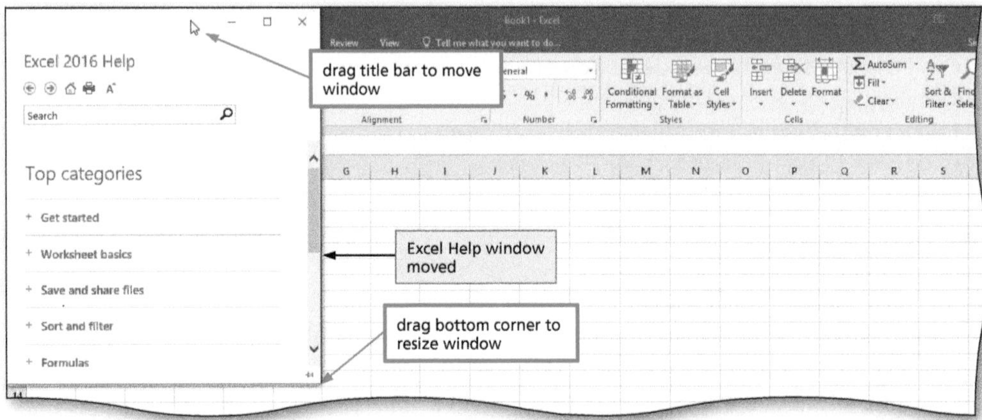

Figure 90

To Resize a Window by Dragging

A method used to change the size of the window is to drag the window borders. The following step changes the size of the Excel 2016 Help window by dragging its borders. ***Why?*** *Sometimes, information is not visible completely in a window, and you want to increase the size of the window.*

- Point to the lower-right corner of the window (the Excel 2016 Help window, in this case) until the pointer changes to a two-headed arrow.
- Drag the bottom border downward to display more of the active window (Figure 91).

Q&A

Can I drag other borders on the window to enlarge or shrink the window?

Yes, you can drag the left, right, and top borders and any window corner to resize a window.

Will Windows remember the new size of the window after I close it?

Yes. When you reopen the window, Windows will display it at the same size it was when you closed it.

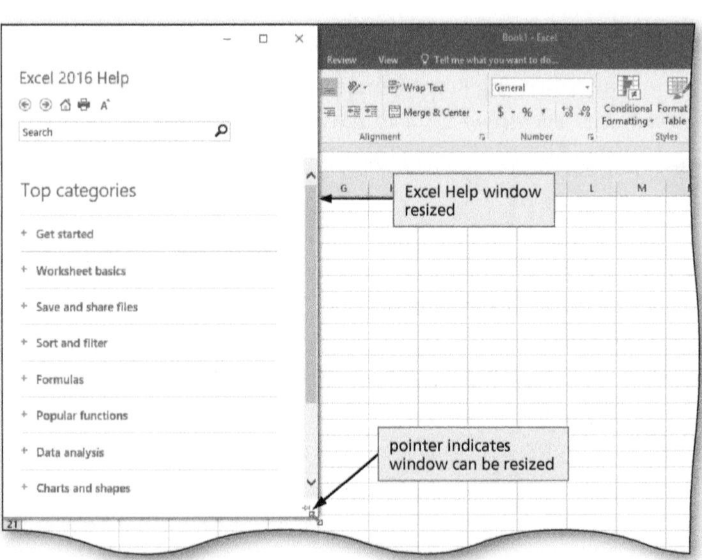

Figure 91

Using Office Help

Once an Office app's Help window is open, several methods exist for navigating Help. You can search for help by entering search text in the Search text box or by clicking the links in the Help window.

To Obtain Help Using the Search Text Box

Assume for the following example that you want to know more about fonts. The following steps use the Search text box to obtain useful information about fonts by entering the word, fonts, as search text. ***Why?*** *You may not know the exact help topic you are looking to find, so using keywords can help narrow your search.*

- Type **fonts** in the Search text box at the top of the Excel 2016 Help window to enter the search text.
- Press the ENTER key to display the search results (Figure 92).

Q&A Why do my search results differ?
If you do not have an Internet connection, your results will reflect only the content of the Help files on your computer. When searching for help online, results also can change as content is added, deleted, and updated on the online Help webpages maintained by Microsoft.

Why were my search results not very helpful?
When initiating a search, be sure to check the spelling of the search text; also, keep your search specific to return the most accurate results.

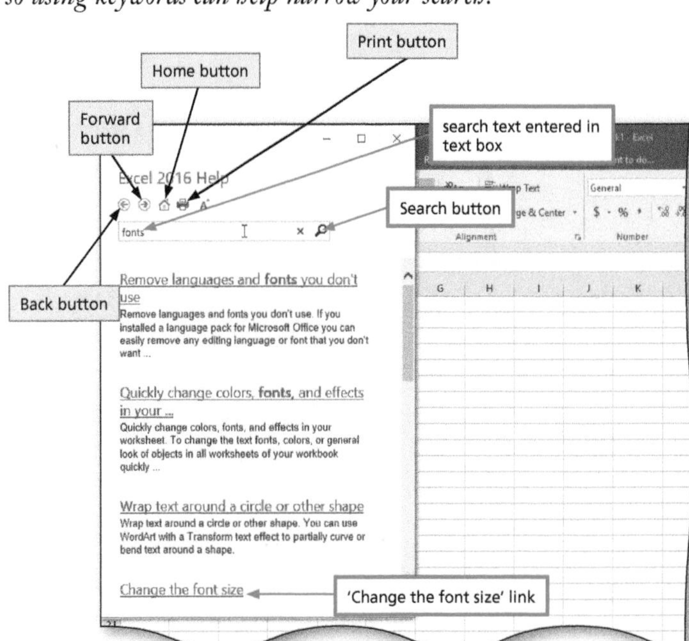

Figure 92

- Click the 'Change the font size', or similar, link to display the Help information associated with the selected topic (Figure 93).

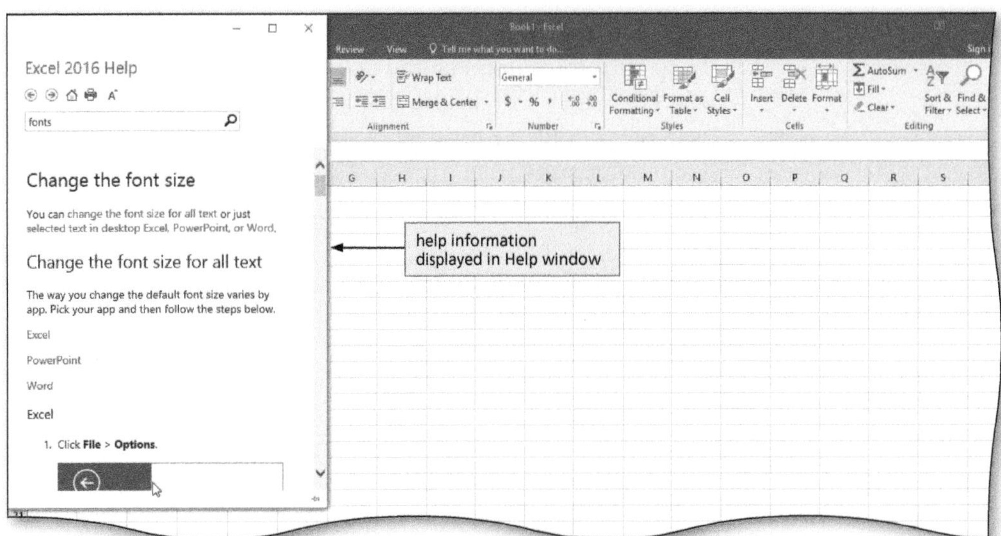

Figure 93

- Click the Home button in the Help window to clear the search results and redisplay the Help home page (Figure 94).
- Click the Close button in the Excel 2016 Help window to close the window.

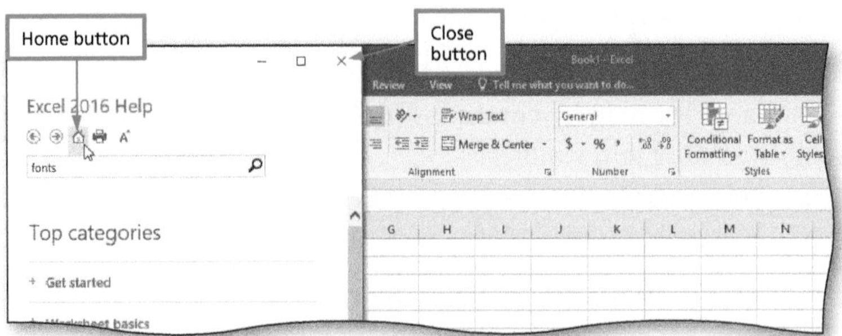

Figure 94

Obtaining Help while Working in an Office App

You also can access the Help functionality without first opening the Help window and initiating a search. For example, you may be confused about how a particular command works, or you may be presented with a dialog box that you are not sure how to use.

If you want to learn more about a command, point to its button and wait for the ScreenTip to appear, as shown in Figure 95. If the Help icon and 'Tell me more' link appear in the ScreenTip, click the 'Tell me more' link (or press the F1 key while pointing to the button) to open the Help window associated with that command.

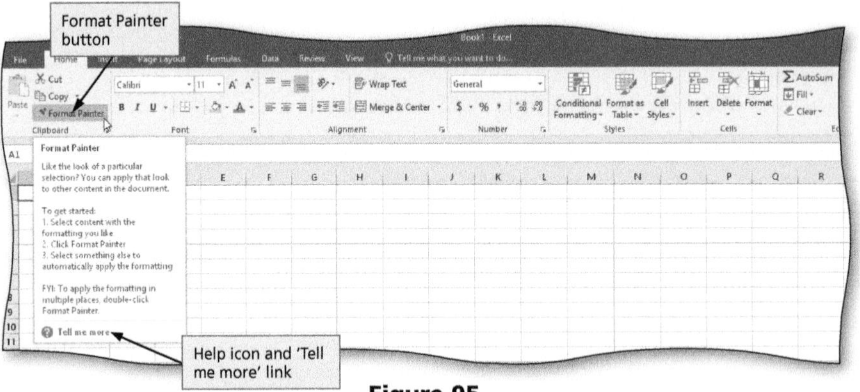

Figure 95

Dialog boxes also contain Help buttons, as shown in Figure 96. Clicking the Help button (or pressing the F1 key) while the dialog box is displayed opens a Help window, which will display help contents specific to the dialog box, if available. If no help file is available for that particular dialog box, then the window will display the Help home page.

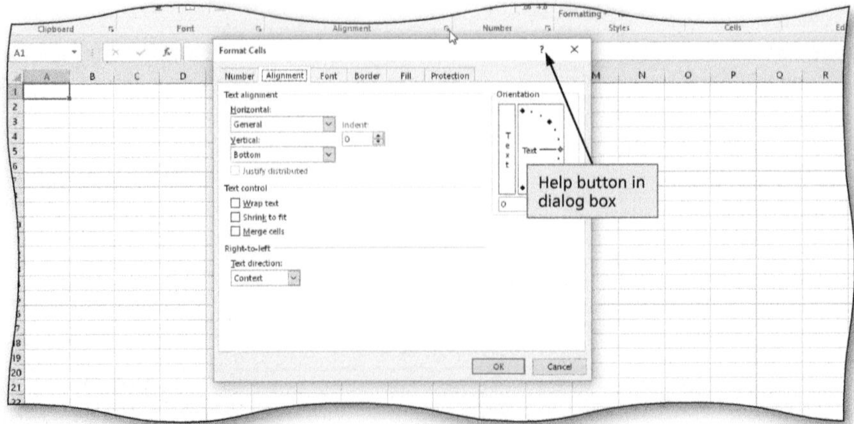

Figure 96

As mentioned previously, the Tell Me box is integrated into the ribbon in most Office apps and can perform a variety of functions, including providing easy access to commands and help content as you type.

To Obtain Help Using the Tell Me Box

1 SIGN IN | 2 USE WINDOWS | 3 USE APPS | 4 FILE MANAGEMENT | 5 SWITCH APPS | 6 SAVE FILES
7 CHANGE SCREEN RESOLUTION | 8 EXIT APPS | 9 USE ADDITIONAL APP FEATURES | 10 USE HELP

If you are having trouble finding a command in an Office app, you can use the Tell Me box to search for the function you are trying to perform. As you type, the Tell Me box will suggest commands that match the search text you are entering. ***Why?*** *You can use the Tell Me box to access commands quickly you otherwise may be unable to find on the ribbon.* The following steps find information about margins.

- Type **margins** in the Tell Me box and watch the search results appear.
- Click Adjust Margins, or another active link, to display a submenu displaying the various margin settings (Figure 97).
- Click an empty area of the document window to close the search results.

- Exit Microsoft Excel.

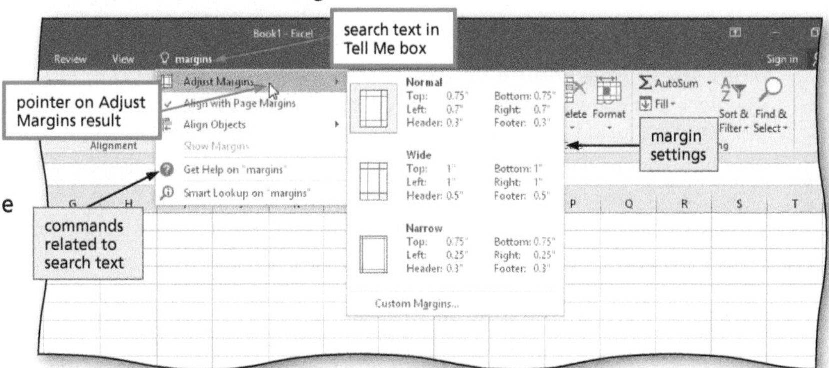

Figure 97

Using the Windows Search Box

One of the more powerful Windows features is the Windows search box. The search box is a central location from where you can enter search text and quickly access related Windows commands or web search results. In addition, **Cortana** is a new search tool in Windows that you can access using the search box. It can act as a personal assistant by performing functions such as providing ideas; searching for apps, files, and folders; and setting reminders. In addition to typing search text in the search box, you also can use your computer or mobile device's microphone to give verbal commands.

To Use the Windows Search Box

1 SIGN IN | 2 USE WINDOWS | 3 USE APPS | 4 FILE MANAGEMENT | 5 SWITCH APPS | 6 SAVE FILES
7 CHANGE SCREEN RESOLUTION | 8 EXIT APPS | 9 USE ADDITIONAL APP FEATURES | 10 USE HELP

The following step uses the Windows search box to search for a Windows command. ***Why?*** *Using the search box to locate apps, settings, folders, and files can be faster than navigating windows and dialog boxes to search for the desired content.*

- Type **notification** in the search box in the Windows taskbar to display the search results. The search results include related Windows settings, Windows Store apps, and web search results (Figure 98).
- Click an empty area of the desktop to close the search results.
- Close the File Explorer window.

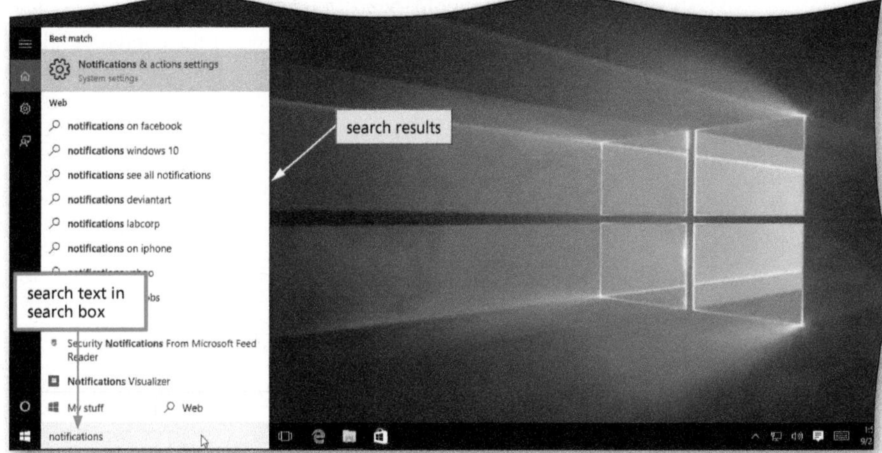

Figure 98

Summary

In this module, you learned how to use the Windows interface, several touch screen and mouse operations, and file and folder management. You also learned some basic features of Excel and discovered the common elements that exist among Microsoft Office apps. Topics covered included signing in, using Windows, using apps, file management, switching between apps, saving files, changing screen resolution, exiting apps, using additional app features, and using help.

CONSIDER THIS: PLAN AHEAD

What guidelines should you follow to plan your projects?

The process of communicating specific information is a learned, rational skill. Computers and software, especially Microsoft Office 2016, can help you develop ideas and present detailed information to a particular audience and minimize much of the laborious work of drafting and revising projects. No matter what method you use to plan a project, it is beneficial to follow some specific guidelines from the onset to arrive at a final product that is informative, relevant, and effective. Use some aspects of these guidelines every time you undertake a project, and others as needed in specific instances.

1. Determine the project's purpose.
   a) Clearly define why you are undertaking this assignment.
   b) Begin to draft ideas of how best to communicate information by handwriting ideas on paper; composing directly on a laptop, tablet, or mobile device; or developing a strategy that fits your particular thinking and writing style.
2. Analyze your audience.
   a) Learn about the people who will read, analyze, or view your work.
   b) Determine their interests and needs so that you can present the information they need to know and omit the information they already possess.
   c) Form a mental picture of these people or find photos of people who fit this profile so that you can develop a project with the audience in mind.
3. Gather possible content.
   a) Locate existing information that may reside in spreadsheets, databases, or other files.
   b) Conduct a web search to find relevant websites.
   c) Read pamphlets, magazine and newspaper articles, and books to gain insights of how others have approached your topic.
4. Determine what content to present to your audience.
   a) Write three or four major ideas you want audience members to remember after reading or viewing your project.
   b) Envision your project's endpoint, the key fact you wish to emphasize, so that all project elements lead to this final element.
   c) Determine relevant time factors, such as the length of time necessary to develop the project, how long readers will spend reviewing your project, or the amount of time allocated for your speaking engagement.
   d) Decide whether a graph, photo, or artistic element can express or enhance a particular concept.
   e) Be mindful of the order in which you plan to present the content, and place the most important material at the top of the worksheet. Readers and audience members generally remember the first and last pieces of information they see and hear.

How should you submit solutions to questions in the assignments identified with a ✻ symbol?

Every assignment in this book contains one or more questions with a ✻ symbol. These questions require you to think beyond the assigned file. Present your solutions to the question in the format required by your instructor. Possible formats may include one or more of these options: write the answer; create a document that contains the answer; present your answer to the class; discuss your answer in a group; record the answer as audio or video using a webcam, smartphone, or portable media player; or post answers on a blog, wiki, or website.

Apply Your Knowledge

Reinforce the skills and apply the concepts you learned in this module.

Creating a Folder and a Workbook

Instructions: You will create an Excel Assignments folder and then create an Excel workbook and save it in the folder.

Perform the following tasks:

1. Open the File Explorer window and then double-click to open the Documents folder.
2. Click the New folder button on the Quick Access Toolbar to display a new folder icon and text box for the folder name.
3. Type **Excel Assignments** in the text box to name the folder. Press the ENTER key to create the folder in the Documents folder.
4. Run Excel and create a new blank workbook.
5. Enter the text shown in Figure 99.

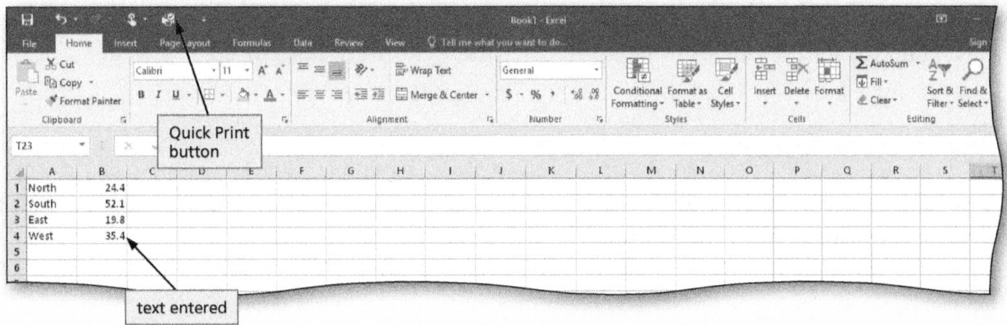

Figure 99

6. If requested by your instructor, enter your name in the Excel workbook.
7. Click the Save button on the Quick Access Toolbar. Navigate to the Excel Assignments folder in the Documents folder and then save the document using the file name, Apply 1 Workbook.
8. If your Quick Access Toolbar does not show the Quick Print button, add the Quick Print button to the Quick Access Toolbar. Print the document using the Quick Print button on the Quick Access Toolbar. When you are finished printing, remove the Quick Print button from the Quick Access Toolbar.
9. Submit the printout to your instructor.
10. Close the File Explorer window.
11. Exit Excel.
12. ✻ What other commands might you find useful to include on the Quick Access Toolbar?

Extend Your Knowledge

Extend the skills you learned in this module and experiment with new skills. You will use Help to complete the assignment.

Using Help

Instructions: Use Excel Help to perform the following tasks.

Perform the following tasks:

1. Run Excel.
2. Press F1 to open the Excel 2016 Help window (shown in Figure 89).
3. Search Excel Help to answer the following questions and type the answers in a new blank Excel workbook.
   a. What are three new features to Excel 2016?
   b. What type of training is available through Excel Help for Excel 2016?
   c. What are the steps to customize the ribbon?
   d. What is the purpose of the Office Clipboard?
   e. What is the Name box?
   f. What is a sparkline?
   g. How do you insert charts?
   h. How do you change the size of text?
   i. What are the steps to zoom in and out of a workbook?
   j. What is the purpose of the Insights pane? How do you display it?
4. If requested by your instructor, enter your name it the Excel workbook.
5. Save the workbook with a new file name and then submit it in the format specified by your instructor.
6. Exit Excel.
7. What search text did you use to perform the searches above? Did it take multiple attempts to search and locate the exact information for which you were searching?

Expand Your World

Create a solution that uses cloud or web technologies by learning and investigating on your own from general guidance.

Creating Folders on OneDrive and Using the Excel Online App

Instructions: You will create the folders shown in Figure 100 on OneDrive. Then, you will use the Excel Online app to create a small file and save it in a folder on OneDrive.

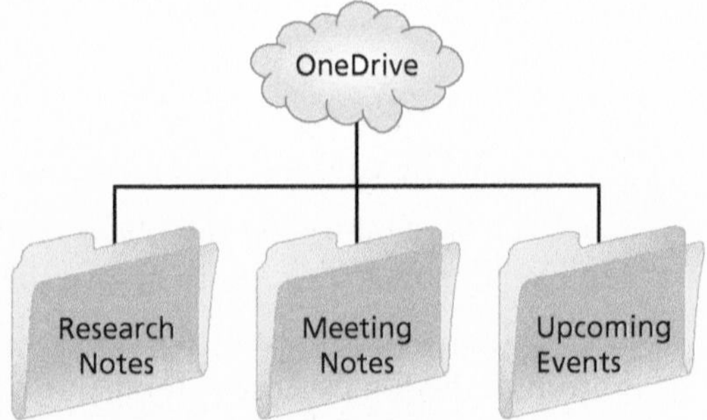

Figure 100

Perform the following tasks:

1. Sign in to OneDrive in your browser.
2. Use the New button to create the folder structure shown in Figure 100.
3. In the Upcoming Events folder, create an Excel workbook with the file name, Extend 1 Task List, that contains the text, Prepare itinerary for upcoming trip, in cell A1.
4. If requested by your instructor, add your name to the Excel workbook.
5. Save the workbook in the Upcoming Events folder and then exit the Excel Online app.

6. Submit the assignment in the format specified by your instructor.
7. Based on your current knowledge of OneDrive, do you think you will use it? What about the Excel Online app?

In the Labs

Design, create, modify, and/or use files following the guidelines, concepts, and skills presented in this module. Labs 1 and 2, which increase in difficulty, require you to create solutions based on what you learned in the module; Lab 3 requires you to apply your creative thinking and problem-solving skills to design and implement a solution.

Lab 1: Creating Folders for a Bookstore

Problem: Your friend works for a local bookstore. He would like to organize his files in relation to the types of books available in the store. He has seven main categories: fiction, biography, children, humor, social science, nonfiction, and medical. You are to create a folder structure similar to Figure 101.

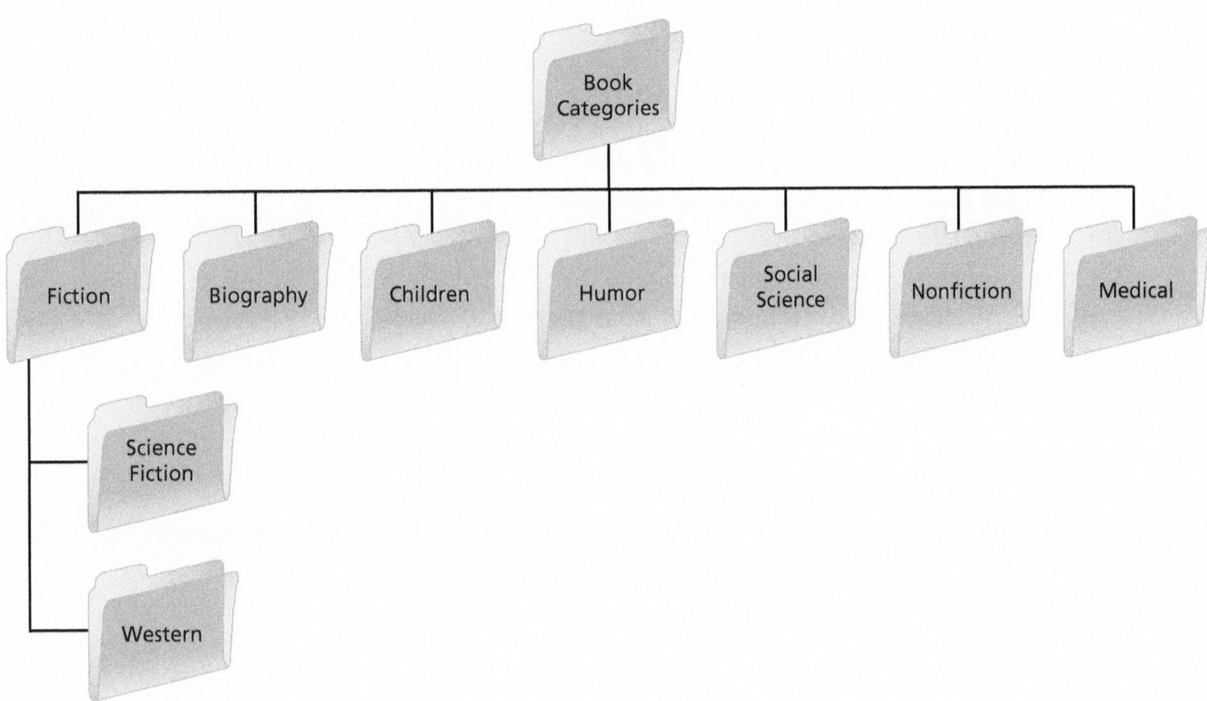

Figure 101

Perform the following tasks:

1. Click the File Explorer button on the taskbar and display the contents of the Documents folder.
2. In the Documents folder, create the main folder and name it Book Categories.
3. Navigate to the Book Categories folder.
4. Within the Book Categories folder, create a folder for each of the following: Fiction, Biography, Children, Humor, Social Science, Nonfiction, and Medical.
5. Within the Fiction folder, create two additional folders, one for Science Fiction and the second for Western.

Continued >

In the Labs *continued*

6. If requested by your instructor, add another folder using your last name as the folder name.
7. Submit the assignment in the format specified by your instructor.
8. Think about how you use your computer for various tasks (consider personal, professional, and academic reasons). What folders do you think will be required on your computer to store the files you save?

Lab 2: Creating Excel Workbooks and Saving Them in Appropriate Folders

Problem: You are taking a class that requires you to complete three Excel modules. You will save the work completed in each module in a different folder (Figure 102).

Perform the following tasks:

1. Create the folders shown in Figure 102.
2. Create an Excel workbook containing the text, Module 1 Notes, in cell A1.
3. In the Backstage view, click Save As.
4. Click the Browse button to display the Save As dialog box. Click Documents to open the Documents folder. Navigate to the Module 1 folder and then save the file using the file name, Lab 2 Module 1 Notes.

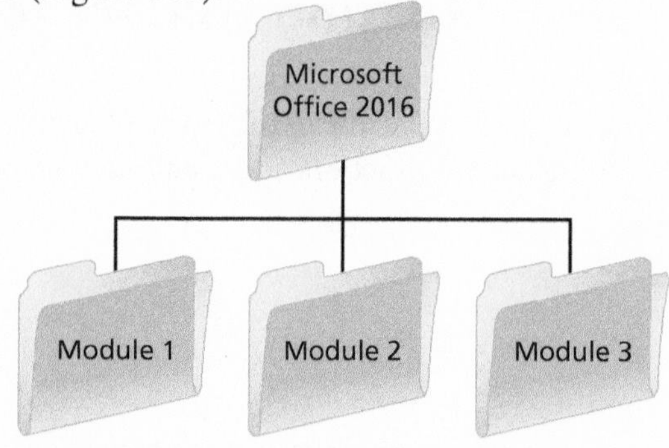

Figure 102

5. Create another Excel workbook containing the text, Module 2 Notes, in cell A1, and then save it in the Module 2 folder using the file name, Lab 2 Module 2 Notes.
6. Create a third Excel workbook containing the text, Module 3 Notes, in cell A1, and then save it in the Module 3 folder using the file name, Lab 2 Module 3 Notes.
7. If requested by your instructor, add your name to each of the three Excel workbooks.
8. Submit the assignment in the format specified by your instructor.
9. Based on your current knowledge of Windows and Excel, how will you organize folders for assignments in this class? Why?

Lab 3: Consider This: Your Turn

Researching Malware

Problem: You have just purchased a new computer running the Windows operating system. Because you want to be sure that it is protected from malware, you decide to research malware, malware protection, and removing malware.

Part 1: Research the following three topics: malware, malware protection, and removing malware. Use the concepts and techniques presented in this module to use the search box on the Windows taskbar to find information regarding these topics. Create an Excel workbook that contains steps to safeguard a computer properly from malware, three ways to prevent malware, as well as at least two different methods to remove malware or a virus should your computer become infected (include one tip per row). Submit your assignment and the answers to the following critical thinking questions in the format specified by your instructor.

Part 2: What decisions did you make while researching malware for this assignment? What was the rationale behind these decisions? How did you locate the required information about malware?

1 Creating a Worksheet and a Chart

Objectives

You will have mastered the material in this module when you can:

- Describe the Excel worksheet
- Enter text and numbers
- Use the Sum button to sum a range of cells
- Enter a simple function
- Copy the contents of a cell to a range of cells using the fill handle
- Apply cell styles
- Format cells in a worksheet
- Create a 3-D pie chart
- Change a worksheet name and sheet tab color
- Change document properties
- Preview and print a worksheet
- Use the AutoCalculate area to display statistics
- Correct errors on a worksheet

Introduction

Almost every organization collects vast amounts of data. Often, data is consolidated into a summary so that people in the organization better understand the meaning of the data. An Excel worksheet allows data to be summarized and charted easily. A **chart** conveys a visual representation of data. In this module, you will create a worksheet that includes a chart. The data in the worksheet and chart comprise a personal budget that contains monthly estimates for each income and expense category.

Project — Personal Budget Worksheet and Chart

The project in this module follows proper design guidelines and uses Excel to create the worksheet and chart shown in Figure 1–1a and Figure 1–1b. The worksheet contains budget data for Linda Fox. She has compiled a list of her expenses and sources of income and wants to use this information to create an easy-to-read worksheet to see how much she will be ahead or behind each month. In addition, she would like a 3-D pie chart to show her estimated expenses by category for each of the 12 months.

Personal Budget Worksheet

Monthly Estimates

Income	January	February	March	April	May	June	July	August	September	October	November	December	Total
Wages	$1,417.12	$ 1,417.12	$1,417.12	$1,417.12	$1,417.12	$1,417.12	$1,417.12	$ 1,417.12	$ 1,417.12	$ 1,417.12	$ 1,417.12	$ 1,417.12	$17,005.44
Dividends	4,029.71	-	-	-	-	-	4,029.71	-	-	-	-	-	8,059.42
Total	$5,446.83	$ 1,417.12	$1,417.12	$1,417.12	$1,417.12	$1,417.12	$5,446.83	$ 1,417.12	$ 1,417.12	$ 1,417.12	$ 1,417.12	$ 1,417.12	$25,064.86
Expenses	**January**	**February**	**March**	**April**	**May**	**June**	**July**	**August**	**September**	**October**	**November**	**December**	**Total**
Rent	$ 410.00	$ 410.00	$ 410.00	$ 410.00	$ 410.00	$ 410.00	$ 410.00	$ 410.00	$ 410.00	$ 410.00	$ 410.00	$ 410.00	$ 4,920.00
Food	280.00	280.00	280.00	280.00	280.00	280.00	280.00	280.00	280.00	280.00	280.00	280.00	3,360.00
Tuition	1,500.00	-	-	-	300.00	-	-	1,500.00	-	-	-	-	3,300.00
Books	500.00	-	-	-	100.00	-	-	500.00	-	-	-	-	1,100.00
Entertainment	100.00	100.00	100.00	100.00	100.00	100.00	100.00	100.00	100.00	100.00	100.00	100.00	1,200.00
Car Payment	215.47	215.47	215.47	215.47	215.47	215.47	215.47	215.47	215.47	215.47	215.47	215.47	2,585.64
Gas	100.00	100.00	100.00	100.00	100.00	100.00	100.00	100.00	100.00	100.00	100.00	100.00	1,200.00
Miscellaneous	100.00	100.00	100.00	100.00	100.00	100.00	100.00	100.00	100.00	100.00	100.00	100.00	1,200.00
Total	$3,205.47	$ 1,205.47	$1,205.47	$1,205.47	$1,605.47	$1,205.47	$1,205.47	$ 3,205.47	$ 1,205.47	$ 1,205.47	$ 1,205.47	$ 1,205.47	$18,865.64
Net	$2,241.36	$ 211.65	$ 211.65	$ 211.65	$ (188.35)	$ 211.65	$4,241.36	$(1,788.35)	$ 211.65	$ 211.65	$ 211.65	$ 211.65	$ 6,199.22

Monthly Expense Chart | Monthly Finances

Figure 1–1(a) Personal Budget Worksheet

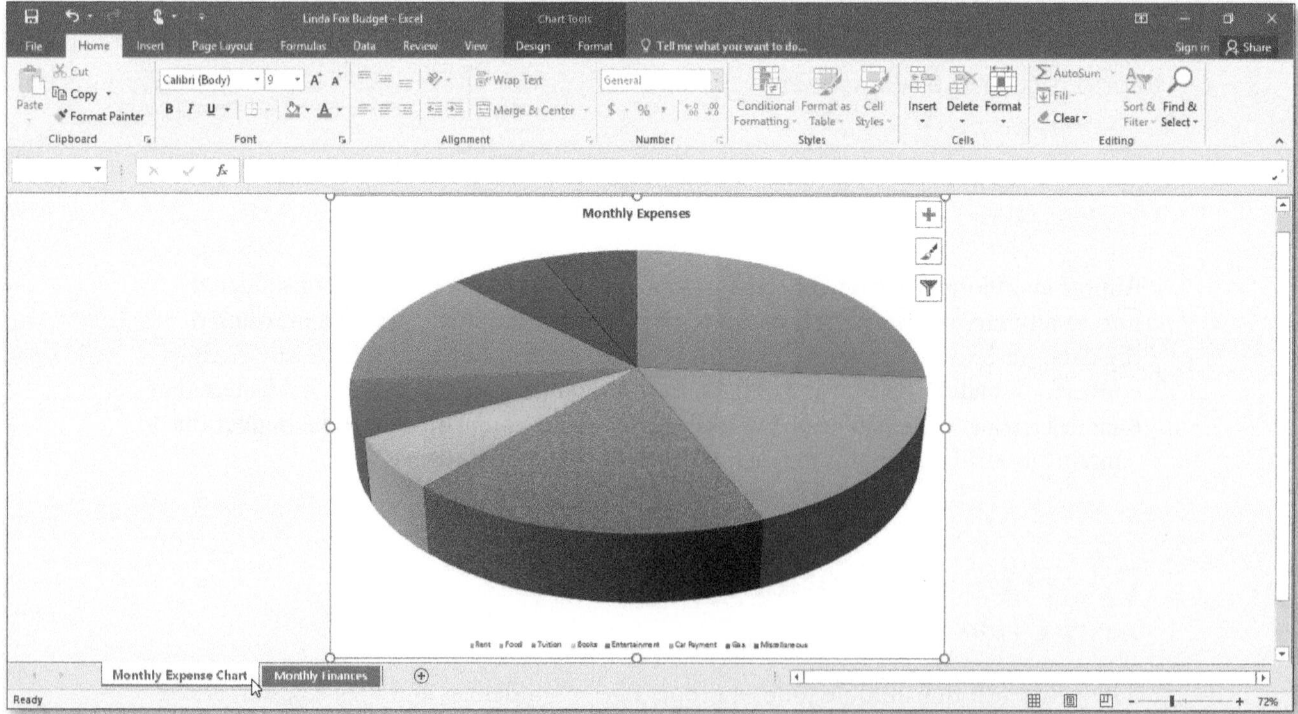

Figure 1–1(b) Pie Chart Showing Monthly Expenses by Category

The first step in creating an effective worksheet is to make sure you understand what is required. The person or persons requesting the worksheet may supply their requirements in a requirements document, or you can create one. A requirements document includes a needs statement, a source of data, a summary of calculations, and any other special requirements for the worksheet, such as charting and web support. Figure 1–2 shows the requirements document for the new workbook to be created in this module.

Worksheet Title	Personal Budget Worksheet
Word	A yearly projection of Linda Fox's personal budget
Source of data	Data supplied by Linda Fox includes monthly estimates for income and expenses
Calculations	The following calculations must be made: 1. For each month, a total for income and expenses 2. For each budget item, a total for the item 3. For the year, total all income and expenses 4. Net = income – expenses

Figure 1–2

For an introduction to Windows and instructions about how to perform basic Windows tasks, read the Office and Windows module at the beginning of this book, where you can learn how to resize windows, change screen resolution, create folders, move and rename files, use Windows Help, and much more.

In this module, you will learn how to perform basic workbook tasks using Excel. The following roadmap identifies general activities you will perform as you progress through this module:

1. ENTER TEXT in a blank worksheet.
2. CALCULATE SUMS AND USE FORMULAS in the worksheet.
3. FORMAT TEXT in the worksheet.
4. INSERT a pie CHART into the worksheet.
5. Assign a NAME to the sheet TAB.
6. PREVIEW AND PRINT the WORKSHEET.

CONSIDER THIS

Why is it important to plan a worksheet?

The key to developing a useful worksheet is careful planning. Careful planning can reduce your effort significantly and result in a worksheet that is accurate, easy to read, flexible, and useful. When analyzing a problem and designing a worksheet solution, what steps should you follow?

- Define the problem, including need, source of data, calculations, charting, and web or special requirements.
- Design the worksheet.
- Enter the data and formulas.
- Test the worksheet.

After carefully reviewing the requirements document (Figure 1–2) and making the necessary decisions, the next step is to design a solution or draw a sketch of the worksheet based on the requirements, including titles, column and row headings, the location of data values, and the 3-D pie chart, as shown in Figure 1–3. The dollar signs and commas that you see in the sketch of the worksheet indicate formatted numeric values.

sketch of worksheet and chart

Personal Budget Worksheet

Income	January	December	Total
Wages	$99,999.99	$99,999.99	$99,999.99
Dividend			
Total	$99,999.99	$99,999.99	$99,999.99

Expenses	January	December	Total
Rent	$99,999.99	$99,999.99	$99,999.99
Food			
Tuition			
Books			
Entertainment			
Car payment			
Gas			
Miscellaneous			
Total	$99,999.99	$99,999.99	$99,999.99
Net	$99,999.99	$99,999.99	$99,999.99

Monthly Expenses

Legend of Expenses

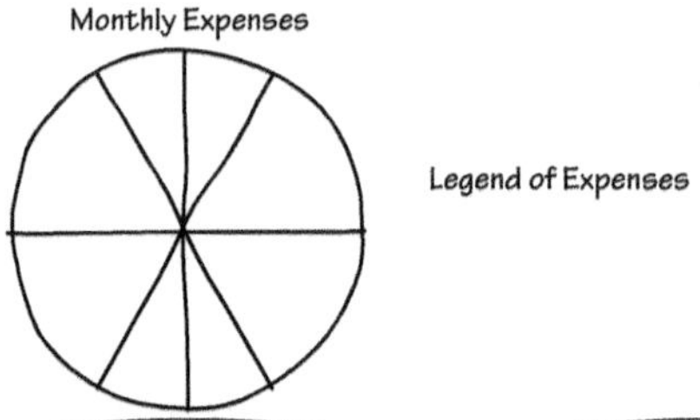

Figure 1–3

For an introduction to Office and instructions about how to perform basic tasks in Office apps, read the Office and Windows module at the beginning of this book, where you can learn how to run an application, use the ribbon, save a file, open a file, print a file, exit an application, use Help, and much more.

With a good understanding of the requirements document, an understanding of the necessary decisions, and a sketch of the worksheet, the next step is to use Excel to create the worksheet and chart.

Selecting a Cell

To enter data into a cell, you first must select it. The easiest way to **select** a cell (make it active) is to use the mouse to move the block plus sign pointer to the cell and then click.

An alternative method is to use the arrow keys that are located just to the right of the alphanumeric keys on a standard keyboard. An arrow key selects the cell adjacent to the active cell in the direction of the arrow on the key.

You know a cell is selected, or active, when a heavy border surrounds the cell and the active cell reference appears in the Name box on the left side of the formula bar. Excel also changes the color of the active cell's column and row headings to a darker shade.

BTW
Touch Screen Differences
The Office and Windows interfaces may vary if you are using a touch screen. For this reason, you might notice that the function or appearance of your touch screen differs slightly from this module's presentation.

Entering Text

In Excel, any set of characters containing a letter, hyphen (as in a telephone number), or space is considered **text**. Text is used for titles, such as column and row titles, on the worksheet.

Worksheet titles and subtitles should be as brief and meaningful as possible. A worksheet title could include the name of the organization, department, or a description of the content of the worksheet. A worksheet subtitle, if included, could include a more detailed description of the content of the worksheet. Examples of worksheet titles are January 2018 Payroll and Year 2018 Projected Budget, and examples of subtitles are Finance Department and Monthly Projections, respectively.

As shown in Figure 1–4, data in a worksheet is identified by row and column titles so that the meaning of each entry is clear. Rows typically contain information such as categories of data. Columns typically describe how data is grouped in the worksheet, such as by month or by department.

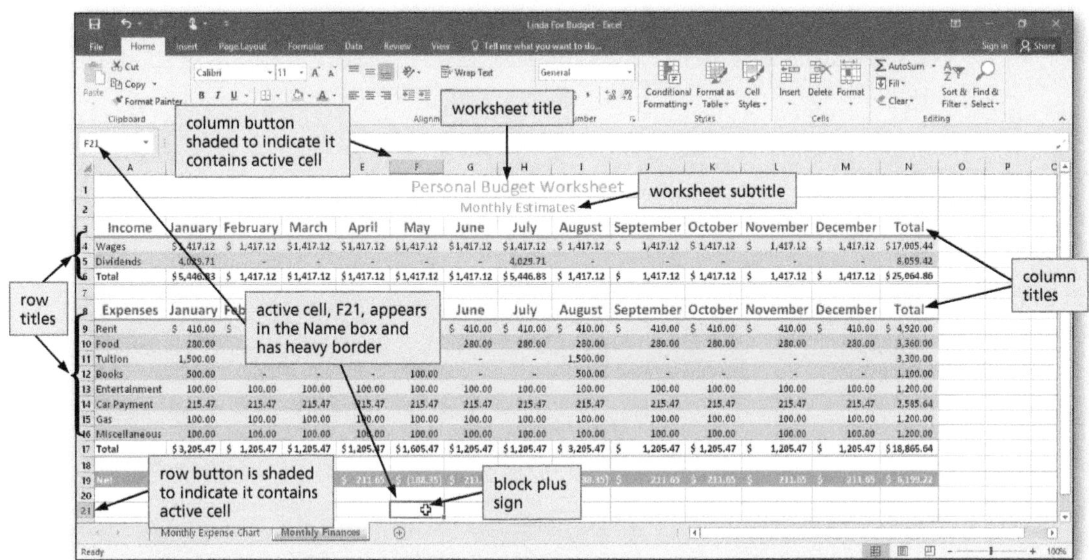

Figure 1–4

BTW

Excel Screen Resolution

If you are using a computer to step through the project in this module and you want your screens to match the figures in this book, you should change your screen's resolution to 1366 x 768. For information about how to change a computer's resolution, refer to the Office and Windows module at the beginning of this book.

To Enter the Worksheet Titles

1 ENTER TEXT | 2 CALCULATE SUMS & USE FORMULAS | 3 FORMAT TEXT
4 INSERT CHART | 5 NAME TAB | 6 PREVIEW & PRINT WORKSHEET

As shown in Figure 1–4, the worksheet title, Personal Budget Worksheet, identifies the purpose of the worksheet. The worksheet subtitle, Monthly Estimates, identifies the type of data contained in the worksheet. ***Why?*** *A title and subtitle help the reader to understand clearly what the worksheet contains.* The following steps enter the worksheet titles in cells A1 and A2. Later in this module, the worksheet titles will be formatted so that they appear as shown in Figure 1–4.

- Run Excel and create a blank workbook in the Excel window.
- If necessary, click cell A1 to make cell A1 the active cell (Figure 1–5).

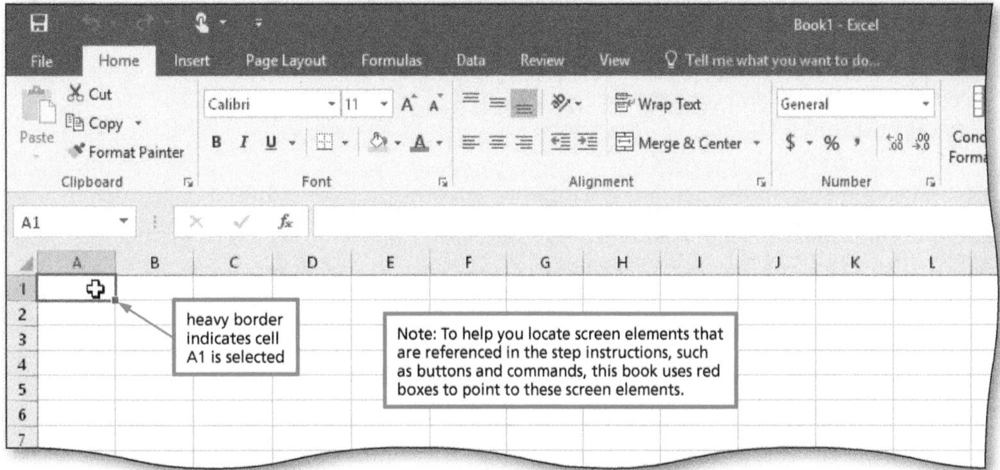

Figure 1–5

2

- Type **`Personal Budget Worksheet`** in cell A1 (Figure 1–6).

Q&A Why did the appearance of the formula bar change?
Excel displays the title in the formula bar and in cell A1. When you begin typing a cell entry, Excel enables two additional boxes in the formula bar: the Cancel button and the Enter button. Clicking the Enter button completes an entry. Clicking the Cancel button cancels an entry.

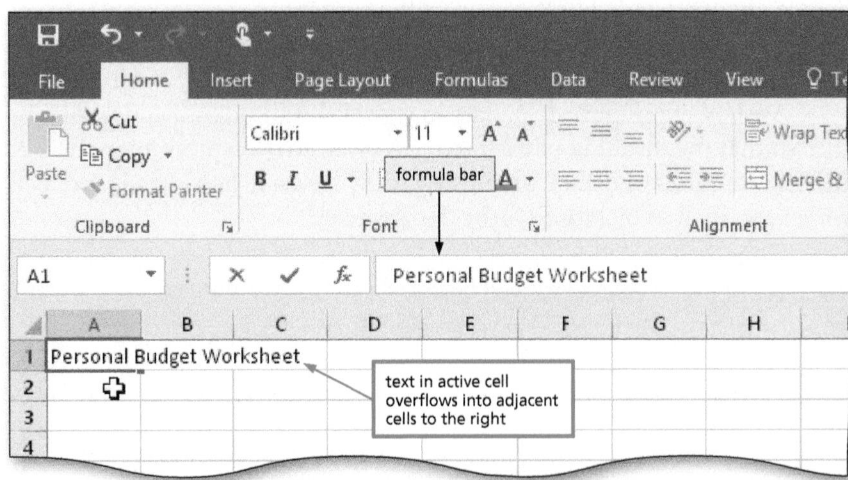

Figure 1–6

- Click the Enter button to complete the entry and enter the worksheet title (Figure 1–7).

Q&A Why does the entered text appear in three cells?
When the text is longer than the width of a cell, Excel displays the overflow characters in adjacent cells to the right as long as those adjacent cells contain no data. If the adjacent cells contain data, Excel hides the overflow characters. The overflow characters are visible in the formula bar whenever that cell is active.

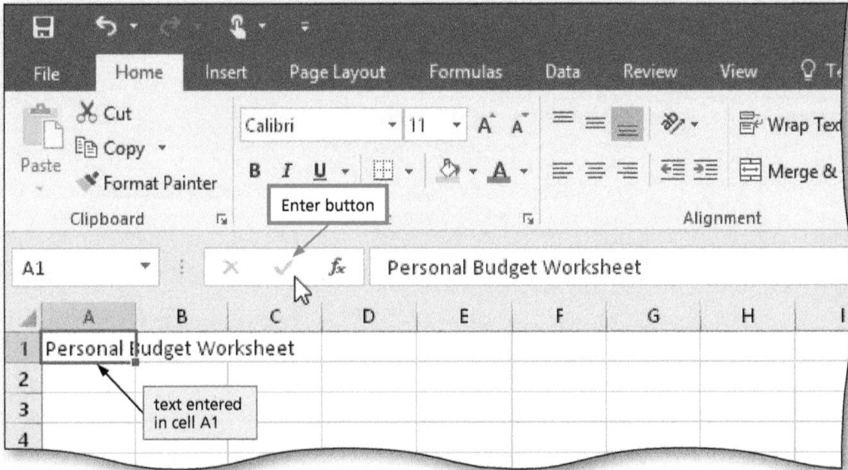

Figure 1–7

- Click cell A2 to select it.
- Type **`Monthly Estimates`** as the cell entry.
- Click the Enter button to complete the entry and enter the worksheet subtitle (Figure 1–8).

Q&A What happens when I click the Enter button?
When you complete an entry by clicking the Enter button, the insertion point disappears and the cell in which the text is entered remains the active cell.

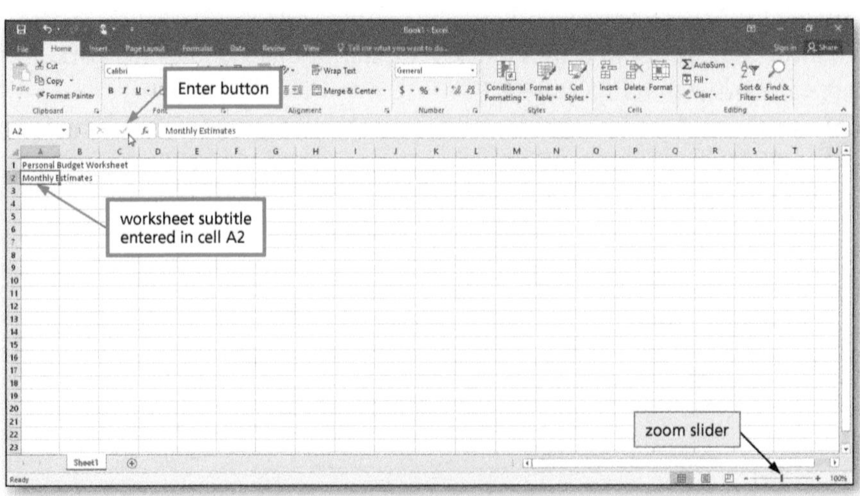

Figure 1–8

Other Ways

1. To complete entry, click any cell other than active cell
2. To complete entry, press ENTER
3. To complete entry, press HOME, PAGE UP, PAGE DOWN, END, UP ARROW, DOWN ARROW, LEFT ARROW, or RIGHT ARROW

CONSIDER THIS

Why is it difficult to read the text on my screen?
If you are having trouble reading the cell values in your spreadsheet, you can zoom in to make the cells larger. When you zoom in, fewer columns and rows display on your screen, and you might have to scroll more often. To zoom in, drag the zoom slider on the right of the status bar, or click the plus button on the zoom slider, until you reach your desired zoom level. In addition to the zoom slider, you also can zoom by clicking the Zoom button (View tab | Zoom group), selecting a desired zoom percentage (Zoom dialog box), and then clicking the OK button (Zoom dialog box).

AutoCorrect

The **AutoCorrect** feature of Excel works behind the scenes, correcting common mistakes when you complete a text entry in a cell. AutoCorrect makes three types of corrections for you:

1. Corrects two initial uppercase letters by changing the second letter to lowercase.
2. Capitalizes the first letter in the names of days.
3. Replaces commonly misspelled words with their correct spelling. For example, it will change the misspelled word *recieve* to *receive* when you complete the entry. AutoCorrect will correct the spelling of hundreds of commonly misspelled words automatically.

BTW
The Ribbon and Screen Resolution
Excel may change how the groups and buttons within the groups appear on the ribbon, depending on the computer's screen resolution. Thus, your ribbon may look different from the ones in this book if you are using a screen resolution other than 1366 x 768.

To Enter Column Titles

1 ENTER TEXT | 2 CALCULATE SUMS & USE FORMULAS | 3 FORMAT TEXT
4 INSERT CHART | 5 NAME TAB | 6 PREVIEW & PRINT WORKSHEET

The worksheet is divided into two parts, income and expense, as shown in Figure 1–4. Grouping income and expense data by month is a common method for organizing budget data. The column titles shown in row 3 identify the income section of the worksheet and indicate that the income values will be grouped by month. Likewise, row 8 is clearly identified as the expense section and similarly indicates that the expense values will be estimated on a per month basis. The following steps enter the column titles in row 3. ***Why?*** *Data entered in columns should be identified using column titles to identify what the column contains.*

- Click cell A3 to make it the active cell.
- Type **Income** to begin entry of a column title in the active cell (Figure 1–9).

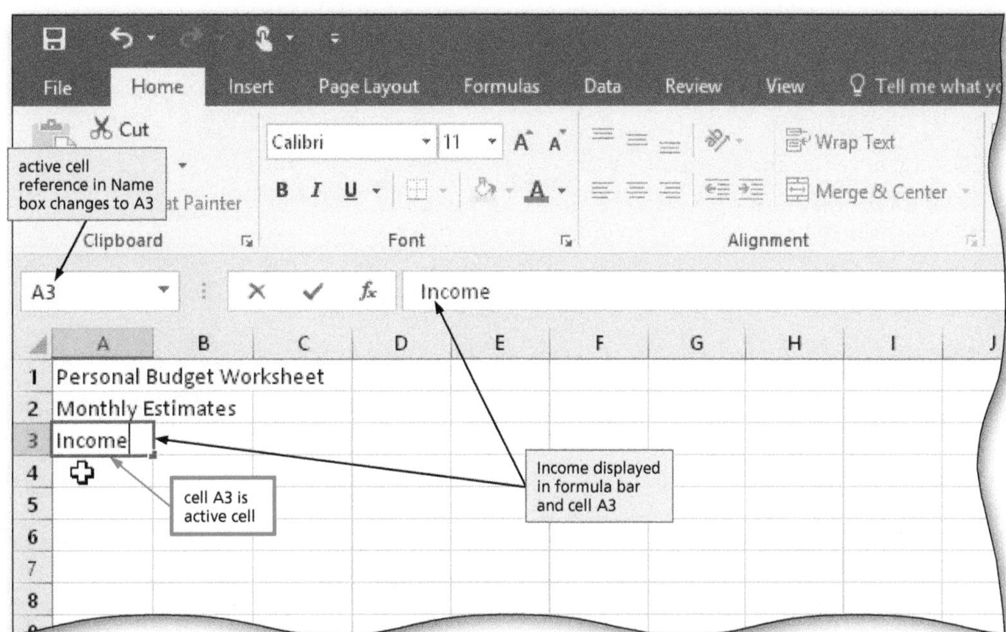

Figure 1–9

2

- Press the RIGHT ARROW key to enter the column title and make the cell to the right the active cell (Figure 1–10).

Q&A Why is the RIGHT ARROW key used to complete the entry in the cell?
Pressing an arrow key to complete an entry makes the adjacent cell in the direction of the arrow (up, down, left, or right) the next active cell. However, if your next entry is in a nonadjacent cell, you can complete your current entry by clicking the next cell in which you plan to enter data. You also can press the ENTER key and then click the appropriate cell for the next entry.

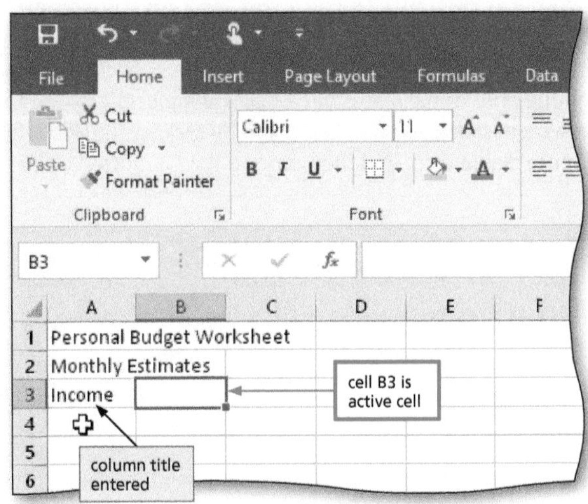

Figure 1–10

3

- Repeat Steps 1 and 2 to enter the remaining column titles; that is, enter **January** in cell B3, **February** in cell C3, **March** in cell D3, **April** in cell E3, **May** in cell F3, **June** in cell G3, **July** in cell H3, **August** in cell I3, **September** in cell J3, **October** in cell K3, **November** in cell L3, **December** in cell M3, and **Total** in cell N3 (complete the last entry in cell N3 by clicking the Enter button in the formula bar).
- Click cell A8 to select it.
- Repeat Steps 1 and 2 to enter the remaining column titles; that is, enter **Expenses** in cell A8, **January** in cell B8, **February** in cell C8, **March** in cell D8, **April** in cell E8, **May** in cell F8, **June** in cell G8, **July** in cell H8, **August** in cell I8, **September** in cell J8, **October** in cell K8, **November** in cell L8, **December** in cell M8, and **Total** in cell N8 (complete the last entry in cell N8 by clicking the Enter button in the formula bar) (Figure 1–11).

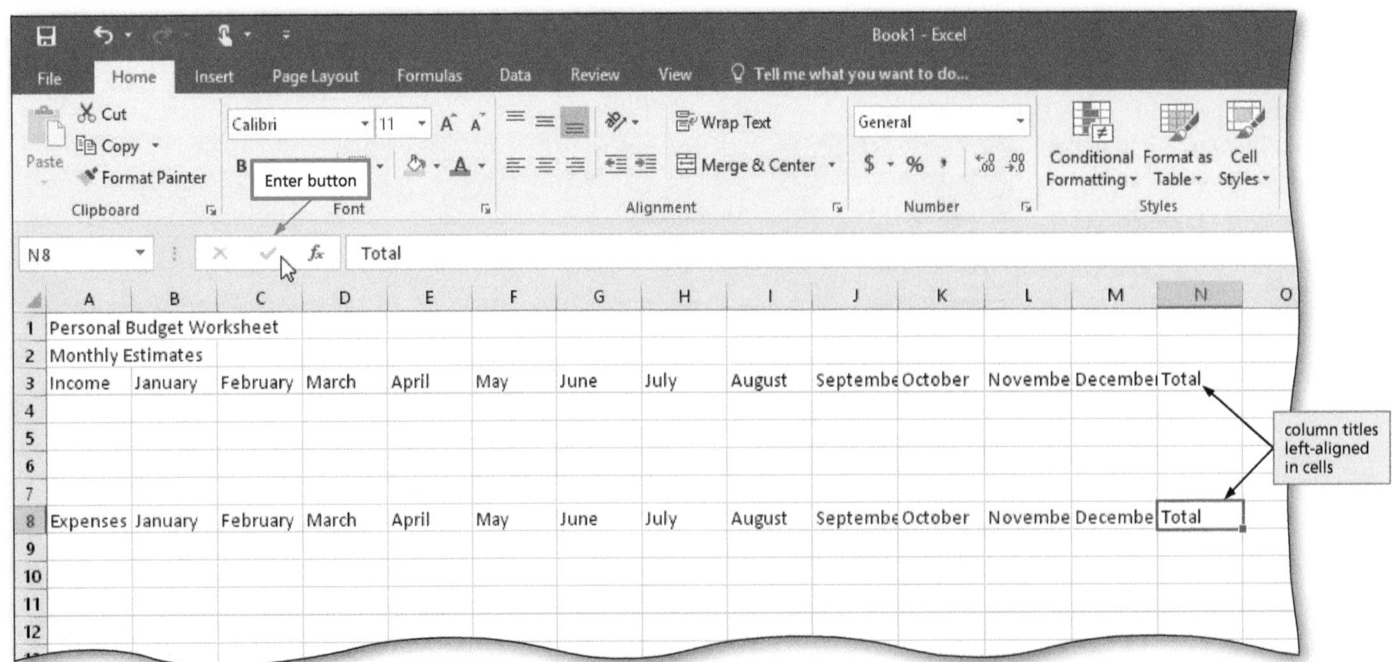

Figure 1–11

To Enter Row Titles

The next step in developing the worksheet for this project is to enter the row titles in column A. For the Personal Budget Worksheet data, the row titles contain a list of income types and expense types. Each income or expense item should be placed in its own row. ***Why?*** *Entering one item per row allows for maximum flexibility, in case more income or expense items are added in the future.* The following steps enter the row titles in the worksheet.

1

- Click cell A4 to select it.
- Type **Wages** and then click cell A5 or press the DOWN ARROW key to enter a row title (Figure 1–12).

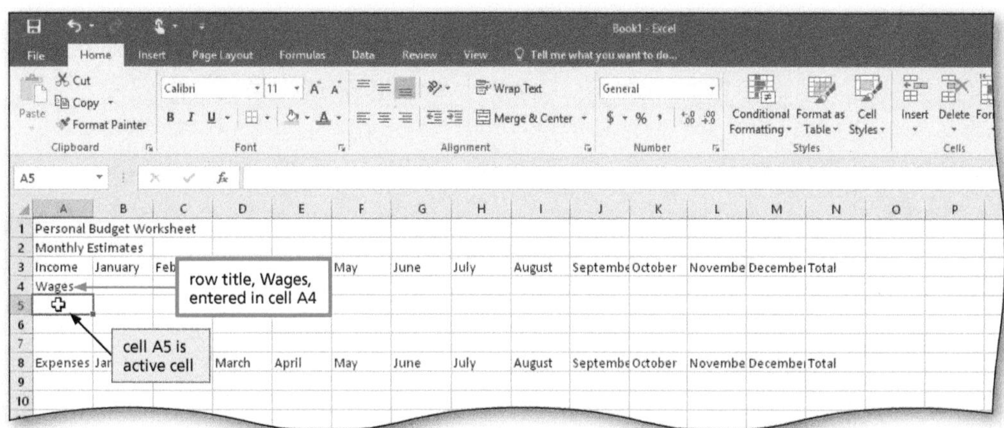

Figure 1–12

2

- Repeat Step 1 to enter the remaining row titles in column A; that is, enter **Dividends** in cell A5, **Total** in cell A6, **Rent** in cell A9, **Food** in cell A10, **Tuition** in cell A11, **Books** in cell A12, **Entertainment** in cell A13, **Car Payment** in cell A14, **Gas** in cell A15, **Miscellaneous** in cell A16, **Total** in cell A17, and **Net** in cell A19 (Figure 1–13).

Q&A Why is the text left-aligned in the cells?
Excel automatically left-aligns the text in the cell. Excel treats any combination of numbers, spaces, and nonnumeric characters as text. For example, Excel would recognize the following entries as text: 401AX21, 921–231, 619 321, 883XTY. How to change the text alignment in a cell is discussed later in this module.

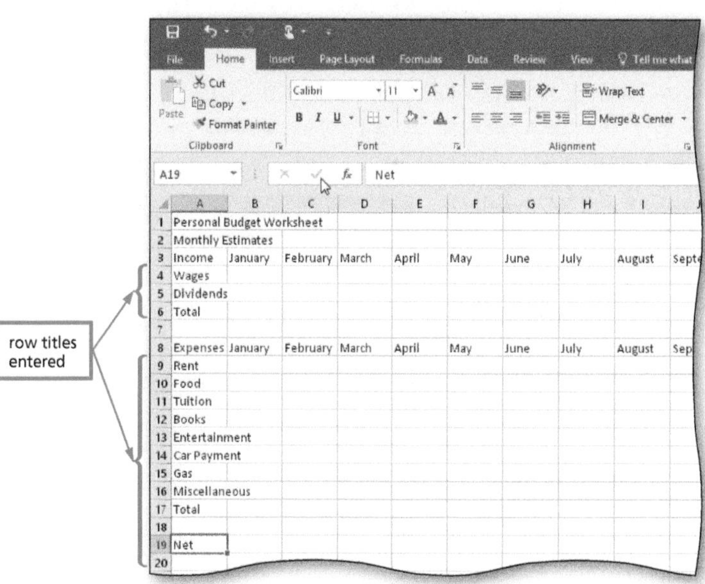

Figure 1–13

Entering Numbers

In Excel, you enter a **number** into a cell to represent an amount or value. A number can contain only the following characters:

0 1 2 3 4 5 6 7 8 9 + – ( ) , / . $ % E e

If a cell entry contains any other keyboard character (including spaces), Excel interprets the entry as text and treats it accordingly. The use of special characters is explained when they are used in this book.

To Enter Numbers

1 ENTER TEXT | 2 CALCULATE SUMS & USE FORMULAS | 3 FORMAT TEXT
4 INSERT CHART | 5 NAME TAB | 6 PREVIEW & PRINT WORKSHEET

The Personal Budget Worksheet numbers used in Module 1 are summarized in Table 1–1. These numbers, which represent yearly income and expense amounts, are entered in rows 4–5 and 9–16. ***Why?*** *One of the most powerful features of Excel is the ability to perform calculations on numeric data. Before you can perform calculations, you first must enter the data.* The following steps enter the numbers in Table 1–1 one row at a time.

Table 1–1 Personal Budget Worksheet

Income	January	February	March	April	May	June	July	August	September	October	November	December
Wages	1417.12	1417.12	1417.12	1417.12	1417.12	1417.12	1417.12	1417.12	1417.12	1417.12	1417.12	1417.12
Dividends	4029.71	0	0	0	0	0	4029.71	0	0	0	0	0

Expenses	January	February	March	April	May	June	July	August	September	October	November	December
Rent	410	410	410	410	410	410	410	410	410	410	410	410
Food	280	280	280	280	280	280	280	280	280	280	280	280
Tuition	1500	0	0	0	300	0	0	1500	0	0	0	0
Books	500	0	0	0	100	0	0	500	0	0	0	0
Entertainment	100	100	100	100	100	100	100	100	100	100	100	100
Car Payment	215.47	215.47	215.47	215.47	215.47	215.47	215.47	215.47	215.47	215.47	215.47	215.47
Gas	100	100	100	100	100	100	100	100	100	100	100	100
Miscellaneous	100	100	100	100	100	100	100	100	100	100	100	100

1

- Click cell B4 to select it.
- Type **1417.12** and then press the RIGHT ARROW key to enter the data in the selected cell and make the cell to the right (cell C4) the active cell (Figure 1–14).

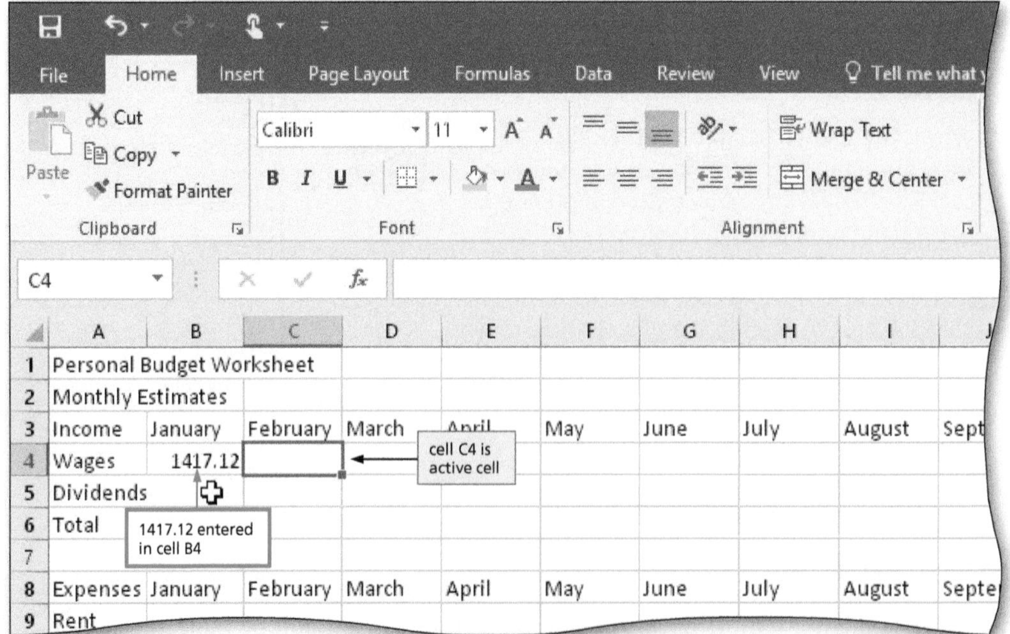

Figure 1–14

Q&A Do I need to enter dollar signs, commas, or trailing zeros for the amounts?

You are not required to type dollar signs, commas, or trailing zeros. When you enter a dollar value that has cents, however, you must add the decimal point and the numbers representing the cents. Later in this module, you will learn how to format numbers with dollar signs, commas, and trailing zeros to improve their appearance and readability.

2

- Enter **1417.12** in cells C4, D4, E4, F4, G4, H4, I4, J4, K4, L4, and M4 to complete the first row of numbers in the worksheet (Figure 1–15).

Q&A Why are the numbers right-aligned?
When you enter numeric data in a cell, Excel recognizes the values as numbers and automatically right-aligns the values in order to vertically align decimal and integer values.

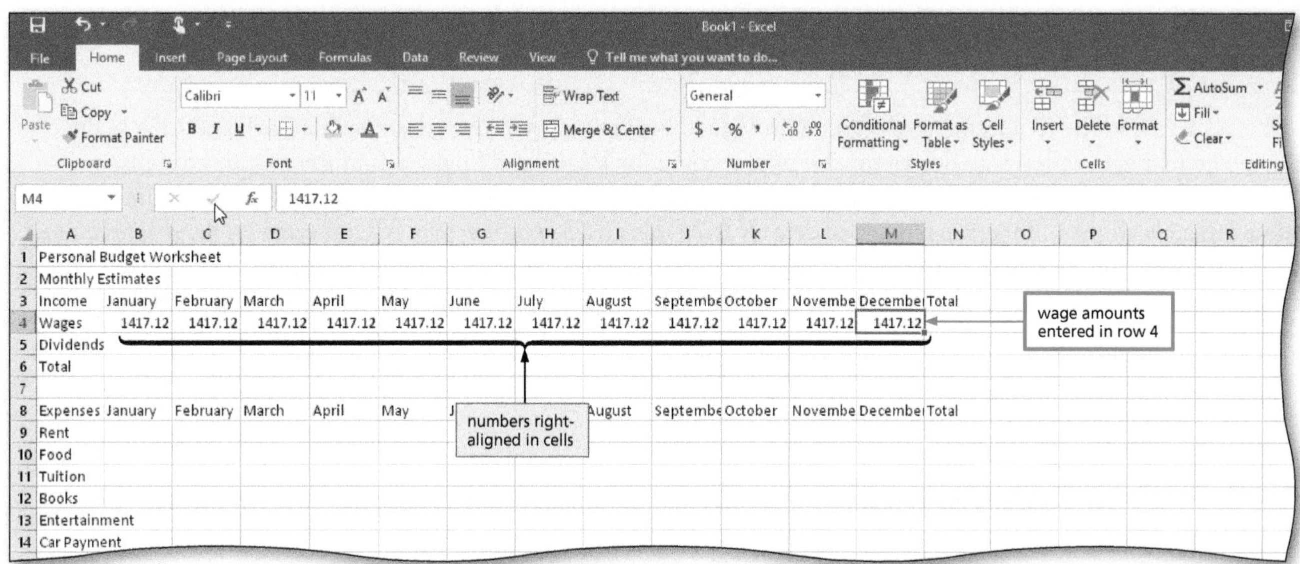

Figure 1–15

3

- Click cell B5 to select it and complete the entry in the previously selected cell.
- Enter the remaining numbers provided in Table 1–1 for each of the nine remaining budget items in row 5 and rows 9–16 (Figure 1–16).

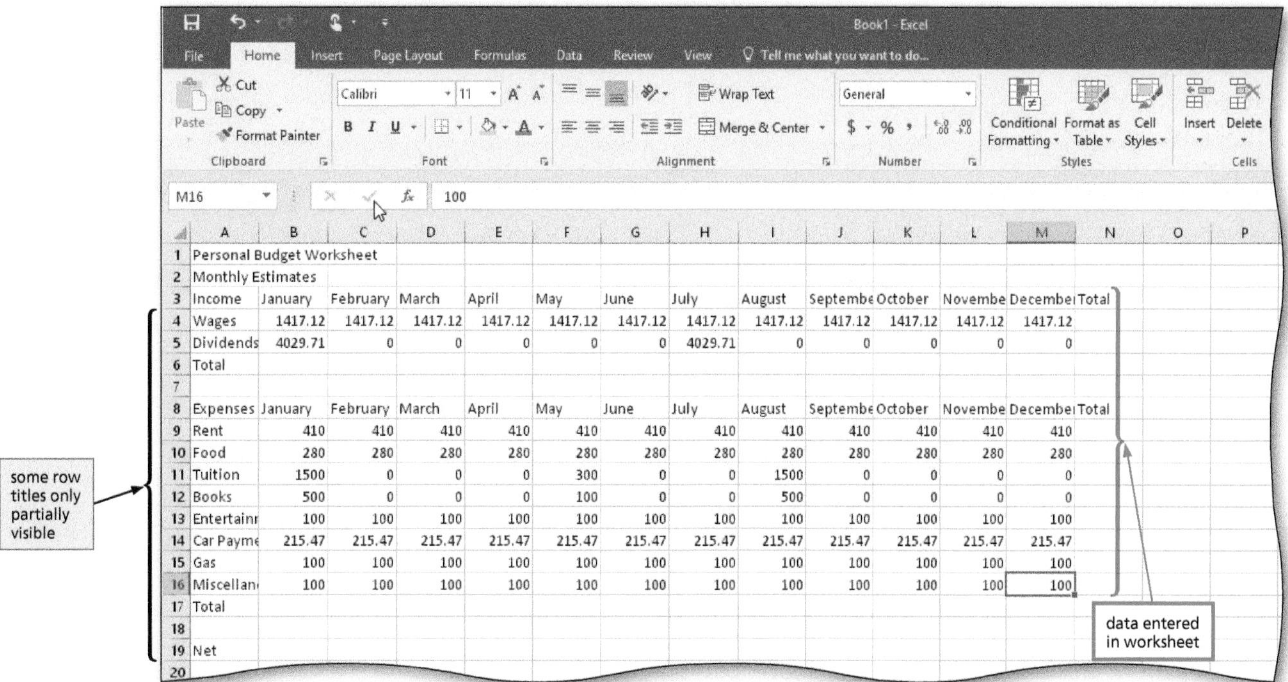

Figure 1–16

Calculating a Sum

The next step in creating the worksheet is to perform any necessary calculations, such as calculating the column and row totals. In Excel, you easily can perform calculations using a **function**, or a predefined formula. When you use functions, Excel performs the calculations for you, which helps to prevent errors and allows you to work more efficiently.

To Sum a Column of Numbers

As stated in the requirements document in Figure 1–2, totals are required for each month and each budget item. The first calculation is to determine the total income for Wages and Dividends in the month of January (column B). To calculate this value in cell B6, Excel must add, or sum, the numbers in cells B4 and B5. The **SUM function** adds all the numbers in a range of cells. ***Why?*** *Excel's SUM function is an efficient means to accomplish this task.*

A **range** is a series of two or more adjacent cells in a column, row or rectangular group of cells. For example, the group of adjacent cells B4 and B5 is a range. Many Excel operations are performed on a range of cells.

After calculating the total income for January, the monthly totals for income and expenses and the yearly total for each budget item will be calculated. The following steps sum the numbers in column B.

- Click cell B6 to make it the active cell.
- Click the Sum button (Home tab | Editing group) to enter a formula in the formula bar and in the active cell (Figure 1–17).

Q&A

What if my screen displays the Sum menu?
If you are using a touch screen, you may not have a separate Sum button and Sum arrow. In this case, select the desired option (Sum) on the Sum menu.

How does Excel know which cells to sum?
Excel automatically selects what it considers to be your choice of the range to sum. When proposing the range, Excel first looks for a range of cells with numbers above the active cell and then to the left. If Excel proposes the wrong range, you can correct it by dragging through the correct range before pressing the ENTER key. You also can enter the correct range by typing the beginning cell reference, a colon (:), and the ending cell reference.

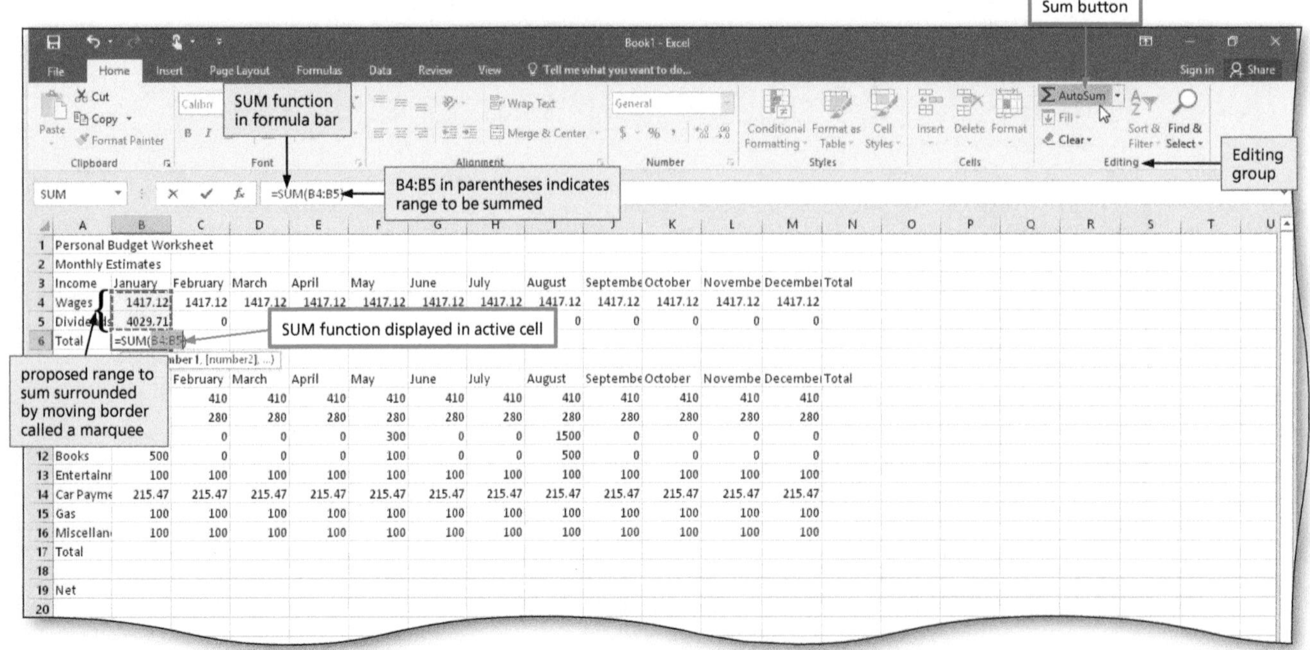

Figure 1–17

2

- Click the Enter button in the formula bar to enter the sum in the active cell.

Q&A What is the purpose of the arrow next to the Sum button on the ribbon?
The Sum arrow (shown in Figure 1–17) displays a list of functions that allow you to easily determine the average of a range of numbers, the number of items in a selected range, or the maximum or minimum value of a range.

3

- Repeat Steps 1 and 2 to enter the SUM function in cell B17 (Figure 1–18).

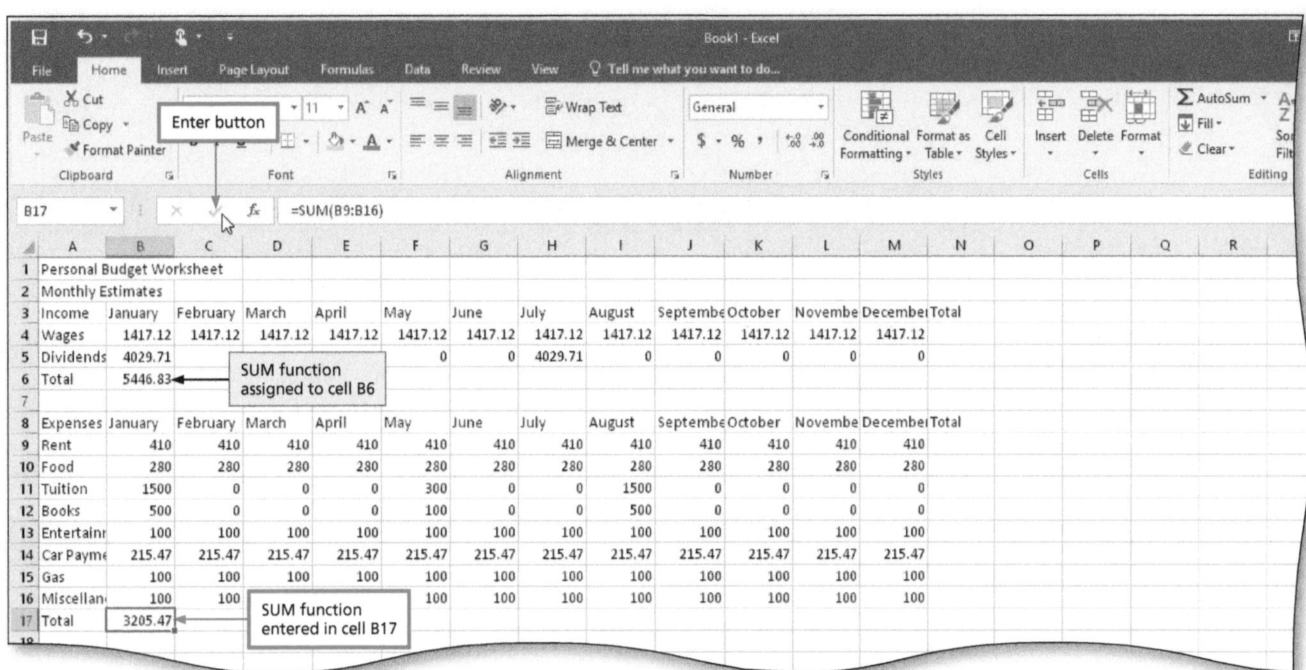

Figure 1–18

Other Ways

1. Click Insert Function button in formula bar, select SUM in Select a function list, click OK button (Insert Function dialog box), click OK button (Function Arguments dialog box)
2. Click Sum arrow (Home tab | Editing group), click More Functions in list, scroll to and then click SUM (Insert Function dialog box), click OK button, select range (Function Arguments dialog box), click OK button
3. Type **=S** in cell, select SUM in list, select range, click Enter button
4. Press ALT+EQUAL SIGN (=) twice

Using the Fill Handle to Copy a Cell to Adjacent Cells

You want to calculate the totals for income during each month in cells C6:M6. Table 1–2 illustrates the similarities between the function and range used in cell B6 and the function and ranges required to sum the totals in cells C6, D6, E6, F6, G6, H6, I6, J6, K6, L6, and M6.

To calculate each total for each range across the worksheet, you could follow the same steps shown previously in Figure 1–17 and Figure 1–18. A more efficient method, however, would be to copy the SUM function from cell B6 to the range C6:M6. The cell being copied is called the **source area** or **copy area**. The range of cells receiving the copy is called the **destination area** or **paste area**.

Table 1–2 Sum Function Entries in Row 6

Cell	SUM Function Entries	Result
B6	=SUM(B4:B5)	Sums cells B4 and B5
C6	=SUM(C4:C5)	Sums cells C4 and C5
D6	=SUM(D4:D5)	Sums cells D4 and D5
E6	=SUM(E4:E5)	Sums cells E4 and E5
F6	=SUM(F4:F5)	Sums cells F4 and F5
G6	=SUM(G4:G5)	Sums cells G4 and G5
H6	=SUM(H4:H5)	Sums cells H4 and H5
I6	=SUM(I4:I5)	Sums cells I4 and I5
J6	=SUM(J4:J5)	Sums cells J4 and J5
K6	=SUM(K4:K5)	Sums cells K4 and K5
L6	=SUM(L4:L5)	Sums cells L4 and L5
M6	=SUM(M4:M5)	Sums cells M4 and M5

Although the SUM function entries in Table 1–2 are similar to each other, they are not exact copies. The range in each SUM function entry uses cell references that are one column to the right of the previous column. When you copy formulas that include cell references, Excel automatically adjusts them for each new position, resulting in the SUM function entries illustrated in Table 1–2. Each adjusted cell reference is called a **relative reference.**

To Copy a Cell to Adjacent Cells in a Row

1 ENTER TEXT | 2 CALCULATE SUMS & USE FORMULAS | 3 FORMAT TEXT
4 INSERT CHART | 5 NAME TAB | 6 PREVIEW & PRINT WORKSHEET

The easiest way to copy the SUM formula from cell B6 to cells C6:M6 is to use the fill handle. ***Why?*** *Using the fill handle copies content to adjacent cells more efficiently.* The **fill handle** is the small green square located in the lower-right corner of the heavy border around the active cell. The following steps use the fill handle to copy cell B6 to the adjacent cells C6:M6.

1

- With cell B6 active, point to the fill handle to activate it. Your pointer changes to a crosshair (Figure 1–19).

Q&A Why is my fill handle not a green square?
If you are using a touch screen, the fill handle appears as a black and white rectangle with a blue down arrow in it.

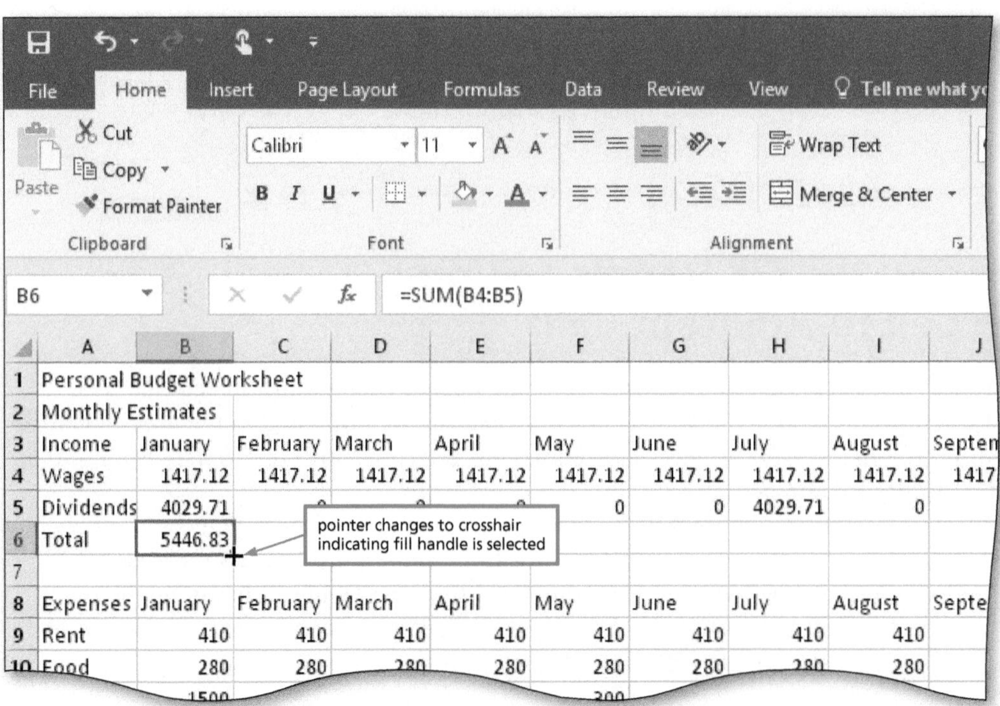

Figure 1–19

- Drag the fill handle to select the destination area, range C6:M6, which will draw a heavy green border around the source area and the destination area (Figure 1–20). Do not release the mouse button.

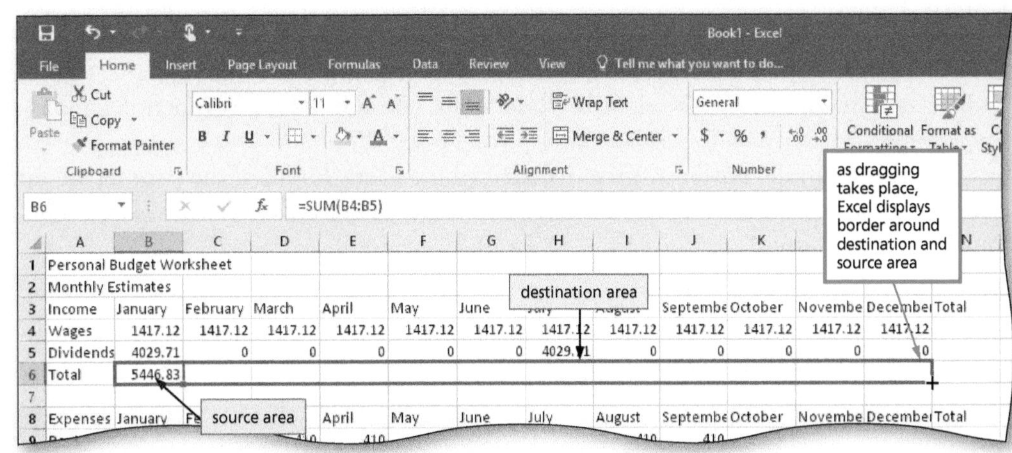

Figure 1–20

- Release the mouse button to copy the SUM function from the active cell to the destination area and calculate the sums (Figure 1–21).

Q&A What is the purpose of the 'Auto Fill Options' button?
The 'Auto Fill Options' button allows you to choose whether you want to copy the values from the source area to the destination area with the existing formatting, without the formatting, or with the formatting but without the functions.

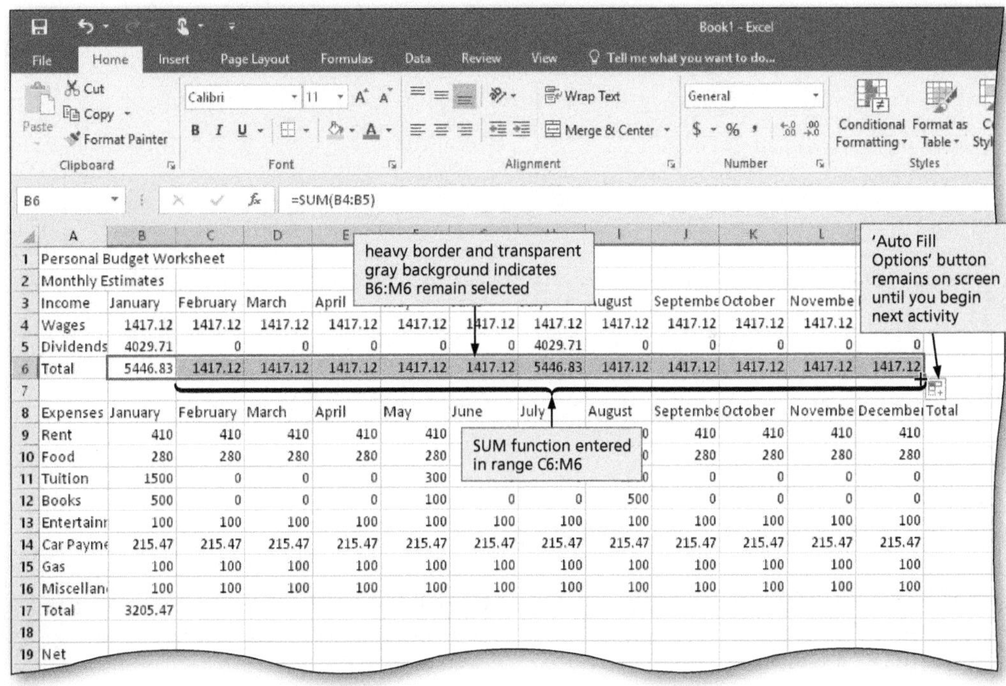

Figure 1–21

- Repeat Steps 1–3 to copy the SUM function from cell B17 to the range C17:M17 (Figure 1–22).

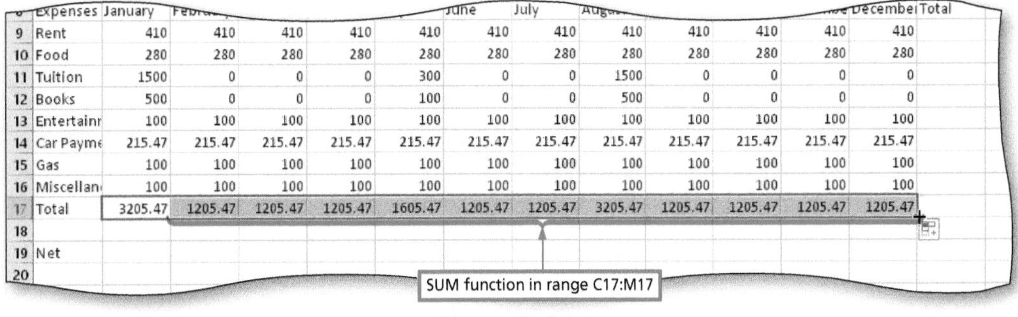

Figure 1–22

Other Ways

1. Select source area, click Copy button (Home tab | Clipboard group), select destination area, click Paste button (Home tab | Clipboard group)
2. Right-click source area, click Copy on shortcut menu, select and right-click destination area, click Paste on shortcut menu

To Calculate Multiple Totals at the Same Time

The next step in building the worksheet is to determine the total income, total expenses, and total for each budget item in column N. To calculate these totals, you use the SUM function similar to how you used it to total the income and expenses for each month in rows 6 and 17.

In this example, however, Excel will determine totals for all of the rows at the same time. ***Why?*** *By determining multiple totals at the same time, the number of steps to add totals is reduced.* The following steps sum multiple totals at once.

- Click cell N4 to make it the active cell (Figure 1–23).

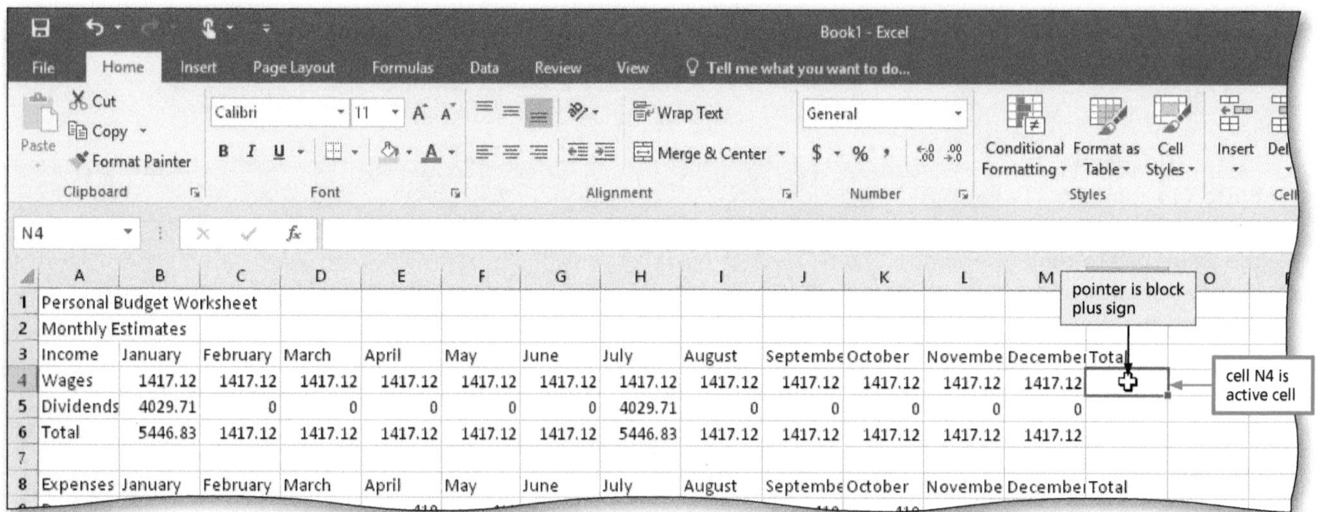

Figure 1–23

2

- With the pointer in cell N4 and in the shape of a block plus sign, drag the pointer down to cell N6 to highlight the range with a transparent view (Figure 1–24).

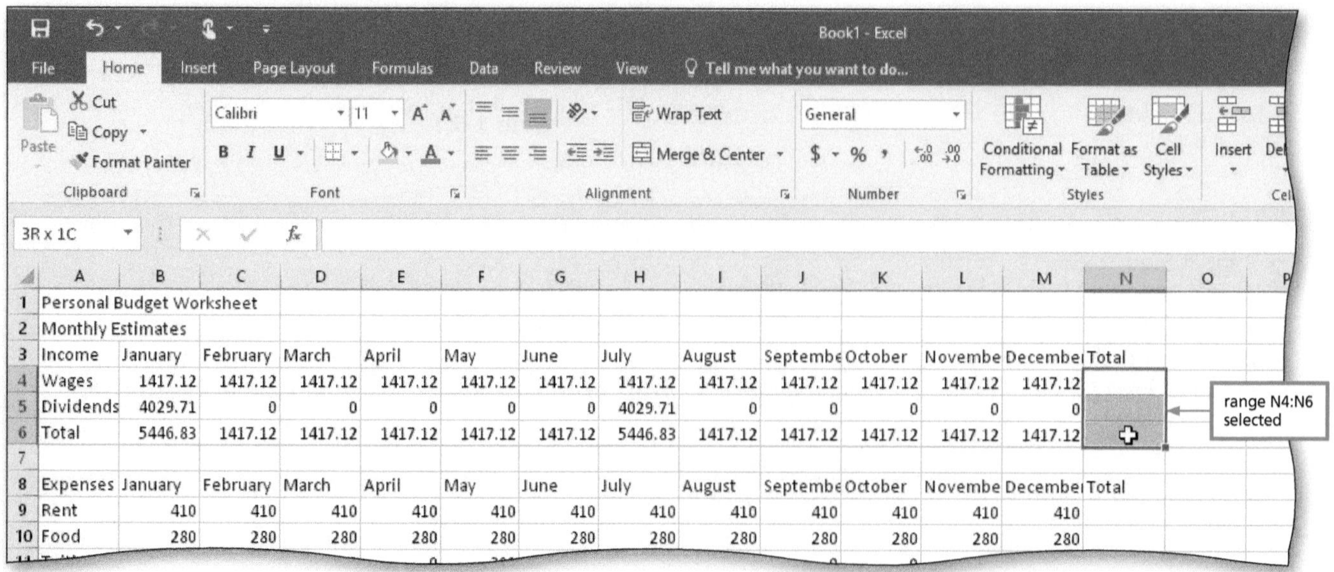

Figure 1–24

3

- Click the Sum button (Home tab | Editing group) to calculate the sums of the corresponding rows (Figure 1–25).

Q&A How does Excel create unique totals for each row?
If each cell in a selected range is adjacent to a row of numbers, Excel assigns the SUM function to each cell when you click the Sum button.

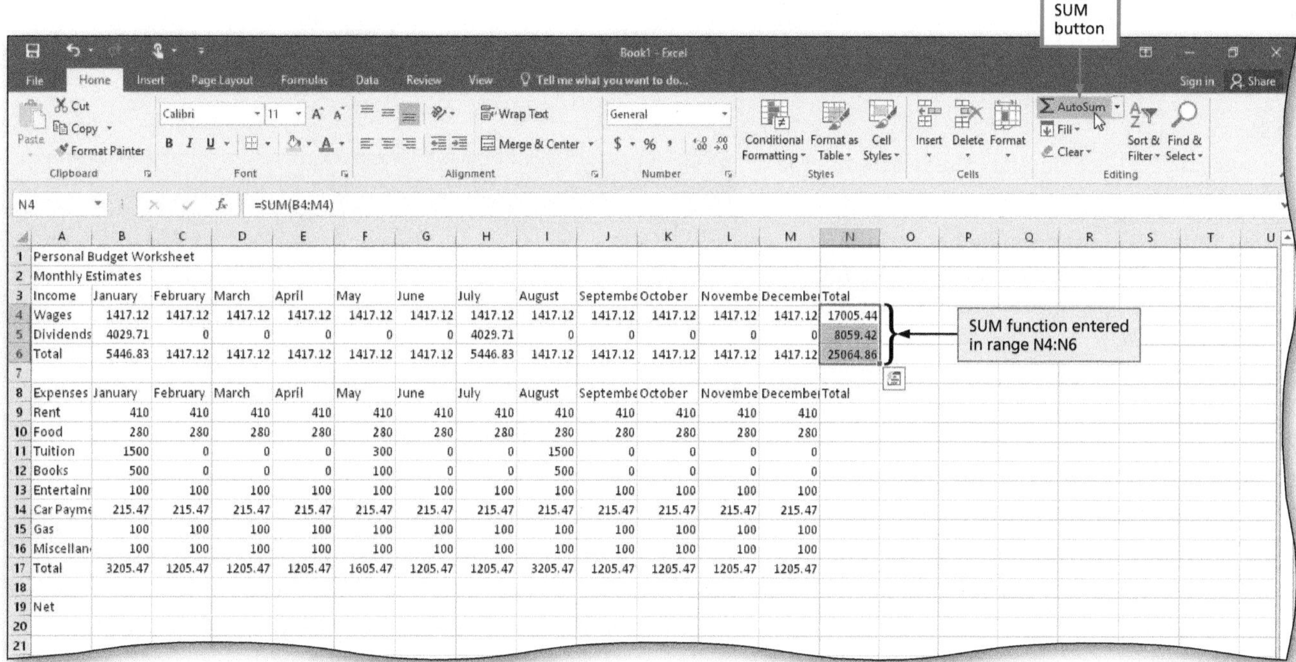

	A	B	C	D	E	F	G	H	I	J	K	L	M	N
1	Personal Budget Worksheet													
2	Monthly Estimates													
3	Income	January	February	March	April	May	June	July	August	Septembe	October	Novembe	Decembe	Total
4	Wages	1417.12	1417.12	1417.12	1417.12	1417.12	1417.12	1417.12	1417.12	1417.12	1417.12	1417.12	1417.12	17005.44
5	Dividends	4029.71	0	0	0	0	0	4029.71	0	0	0	0	0	8059.42
6	Total	5446.83	1417.12	1417.12	1417.12	1417.12	1417.12	5446.83	1417.12	1417.12	1417.12	1417.12	1417.12	25064.86
7														
8	Expenses	January	February	March	April	May	June	July	August	Septembe	October	Novembe	Decembe	Total
9	Rent	410	410	410	410	410	410	410	410	410	410	410	410	
10	Food	280	280	280	280	280	280	280	280	280	280	280	280	
11	Tuition	1500	0	0	0	300	0	0	1500	0	0	0	0	
12	Books	500	0	0	0	100	0	0	500	0	0	0	0	
13	Entertainr	100	100	100	100	100	100	100	100	100	100	100	100	
14	Car Payme	215.47	215.47	215.47	215.47	215.47	215.47	215.47	215.47	215.47	215.47	215.47	215.47	
15	Gas	100	100	100	100	100	100	100	100	100	100	100	100	
16	Miscellan	100	100	100	100	100	100	100	100	100	100	100	100	
17	Total	3205.47	1205.47	1205.47	1205.47	1605.47	1205.47	1205.47	3205.47	1205.47	1205.47	1205.47	1205.47	
18														
19	Net													

Figure 1–25

4

- Repeat Steps 1–3 to select cells N9 to N17 and calculate the sums of the corresponding rows (Figure 1–26).

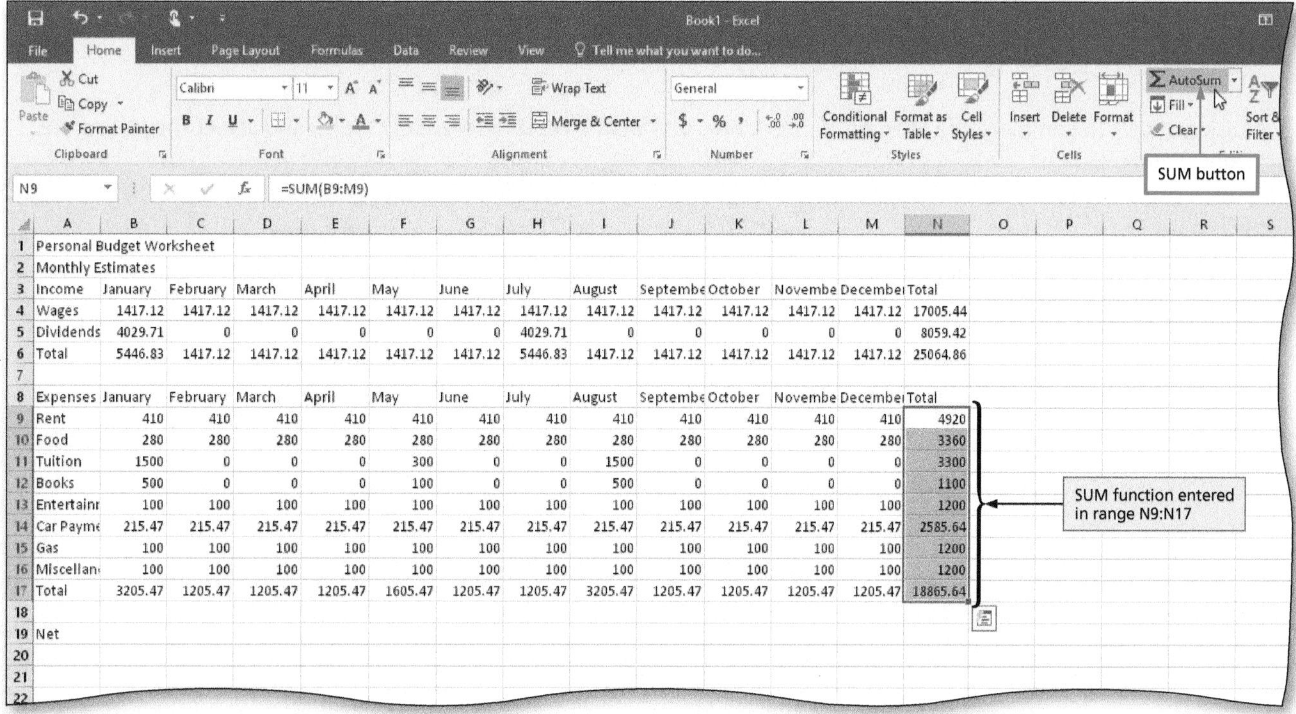

	A	B	C	D	E	F	G	H	I	J	K	L	M	N
1	Personal Budget Worksheet													
2	Monthly Estimates													
3	Income	January	February	March	April	May	June	July	August	Septembe	October	Novembe	Decembe	Total
4	Wages	1417.12	1417.12	1417.12	1417.12	1417.12	1417.12	1417.12	1417.12	1417.12	1417.12	1417.12	1417.12	17005.44
5	Dividends	4029.71	0	0	0	0	0	4029.71	0	0	0	0	0	8059.42
6	Total	5446.83	1417.12	1417.12	1417.12	1417.12	1417.12	5446.83	1417.12	1417.12	1417.12	1417.12	1417.12	25064.86
7														
8	Expenses	January	February	March	April	May	June	July	August	Septembe	October	Novembe	Decembe	Total
9	Rent	410	410	410	410	410	410	410	410	410	410	410	410	4920
10	Food	280	280	280	280	280	280	280	280	280	280	280	280	3360
11	Tuition	1500	0	0	0	300	0	0	1500	0	0	0	0	3300
12	Books	500	0	0	0	100	0	0	500	0	0	0	0	1100
13	Entertainr	100	100	100	100	100	100	100	100	100	100	100	100	1200
14	Car Payme	215.47	215.47	215.47	215.47	215.47	215.47	215.47	215.47	215.47	215.47	215.47	215.47	2585.64
15	Gas	100	100	100	100	100	100	100	100	100	100	100	100	1200
16	Miscellan	100	100	100	100	100	100	100	100	100	100	100	100	1200
17	Total	3205.47	1205.47	1205.47	1205.47	1605.47	1205.47	1205.47	3205.47	1205.47	1205.47	1205.47	1205.47	18865.64
18														
19	Net													

Figure 1–26

To Enter a Formula Using the Keyboard

The net for each month, which will appear in row 19, is equal to the income total in row 6 minus the expense total in row 17. The formula needed in the worksheet is noted in the requirements document as follows:

Net (row 19) = Income (row 6) – Expenses (row 17)

The following steps enter the net formula in cell B19 using the keyboard. ***Why?*** *Sometimes a predefined function does not fit your needs; therefore, you enter a formula of your own.*

1

- Select cell B19 to deselect the selected range.
- Type **=b6-b17** in the cell. The formula is displayed in the formula bar and the current cell, and colored borders are drawn around the cells referenced in the formula (Figure 1–27).

Q&A What occurs on the worksheet as I enter the formula?

The equal sign (=) preceding b6–b17 in the formula alerts Excel that you are entering a formula or function and not text. Because the most common error when entering a formula is to reference the wrong cell, Excel highlights the cell references in the formula in color, and uses same colors to highlight the borders of the cells to help you ensure that your cell references are correct. The minus sign (–) following b6 in the formula is the arithmetic operator that directs Excel to perform the subtraction operation.

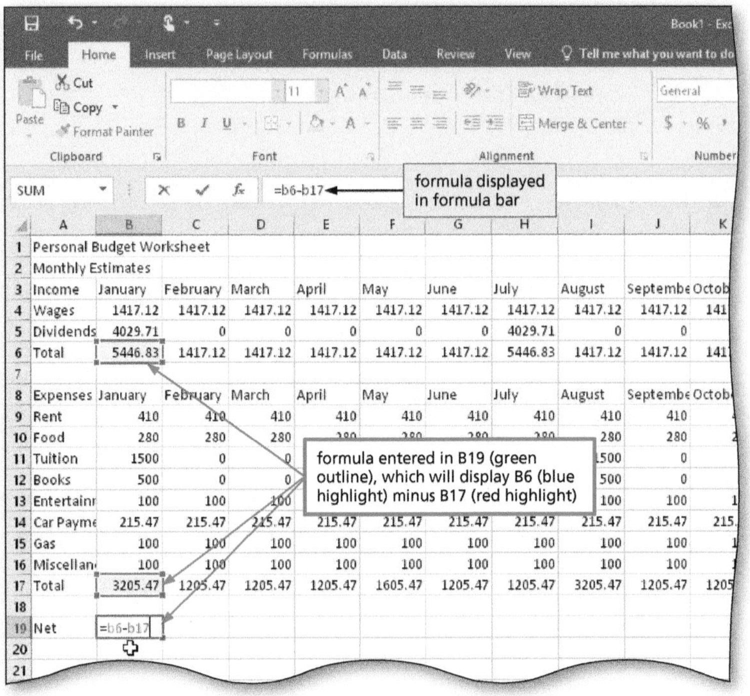

Figure 1–27

2

- Click cell C19 to complete the arithmetic operation, display the result in the worksheet, and select the cell to the right (Figure 1–28).

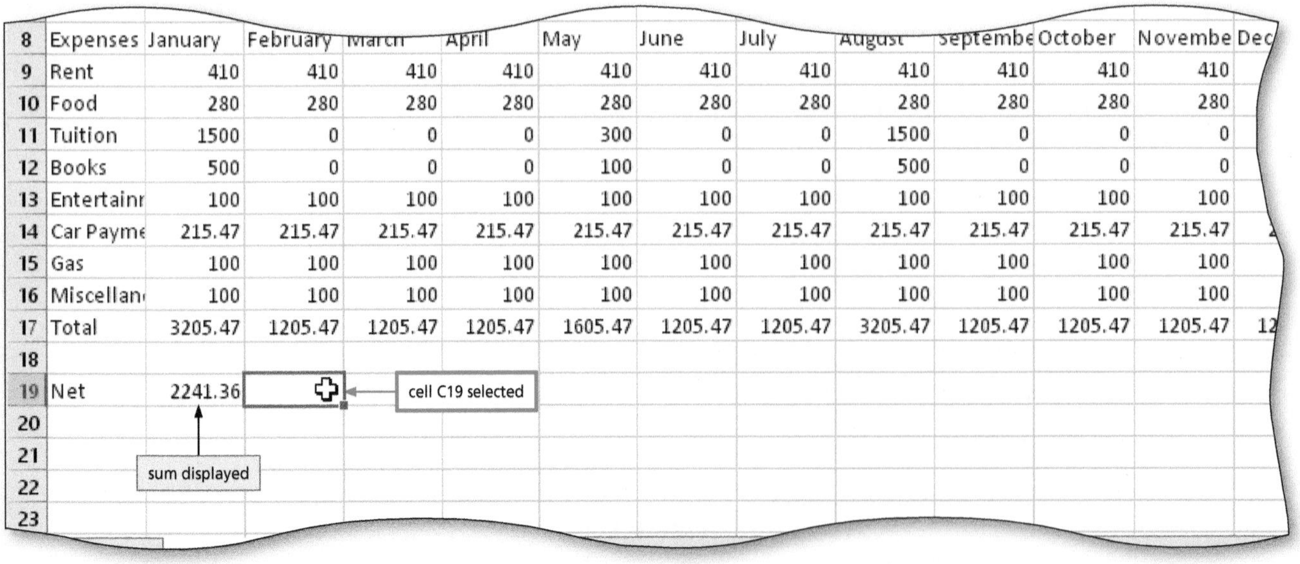

	A	B	C	D	E	F	G	H	I	J	K	L	M
8	Expenses	January	February	March	April	May	June	July	August	Septembe	October	Novembe	Dec
9	Rent	410	410	410	410	410	410	410	410	410	410	410	
10	Food	280	280	280	280	280	280	280	280	280	280	280	
11	Tuition	1500	0	0	0	300	0	0	1500	0	0	0	
12	Books	500	0	0	0	100	0	0	500	0	0	0	
13	Entertainr	100	100	100	100	100	100	100	100	100	100	100	
14	Car Payme	215.47	215.47	215.47	215.47	215.47	215.47	215.47	215.47	215.47	215.47	215.47	
15	Gas	100	100	100	100	100	100	100	100	100	100	100	
16	Miscellan	100	100	100	100	100	100	100	100	100	100	100	
17	Total	3205.47	1205.47	1205.47	1205.47	1605.47	1205.47	1205.47	3205.47	1205.47	1205.47	1205.47	12
18													
19	Net	2241.36											
20													
21													
22													
23													

Figure 1–28

To Copy a Cell to Adjacent Cells in a Row

The easiest way to copy the SUM formula from cell B19 to cells C19, D19, E19, F19, G19, H19, I19, J19, K19, L19, M19, and N19 is to use the fill handle. The following steps use the fill handle to copy the formula in cell B19 to the adjacent cells C19:N19.

1. Select cell B19.
2. Drag the fill handle to select the destination area, range C19:N19, which draws a shaded border around the source area and the destination area. Release the mouse button to copy the simple formula function from the active cell to the destination area and calculate the results.
3. Save the worksheet on your hard drive, OneDrive, or other storage location using Linda Fox Budget as the file name.

Q&A
Why should I save the workbook at this time?
You have performed many tasks while creating this workbook and do not want to risk losing work completed thus far.

Break Point: If you wish to take a break, this is a good place to do so. You can exit Excel. To resume at a later time, run Excel, open the file called Linda Fox Budget, and continue following the steps from this location forward.

Formatting the Worksheet

The text, numeric entries, and functions for the worksheet now are complete. The next step is to format the worksheet. You **format** a worksheet to emphasize certain entries and make the worksheet easier to read and understand.

Figure 1–29a shows the worksheet before formatting. Figure 1–29b shows the worksheet after formatting. As you can see from the two figures, a worksheet that is formatted not only is easier to read but also looks more professional.

To change the unformatted worksheet in Figure 1–29a so that it looks like the formatted worksheet in Figure 1–29b, the following tasks must be completed:

BTW
Organizing Files and Folders
You should organize and store files in folders so that you easily can find the files later. For example, if you are taking an introductory technology class called CIS 101, a good practice would be to save all Excel files in an Excel folder in a CIS 101 folder. For a discussion of folders and detailed examples of creating folders, refer to the Office and Windows module at the beginning of this book.

What steps should I consider when formatting a worksheet?
The key to formatting a worksheet is to consider the ways you can enhance the worksheet so that it appears professional. When formatting a worksheet, consider the following steps:

- Identify in what ways you want to emphasize various elements of the worksheet.
- Increase the font size of cells.
- Change the font color of cells.
- Center the worksheet titles, subtitles, and column headings.
- Modify column widths to best fit text in cells.
- Change the font style of cells.

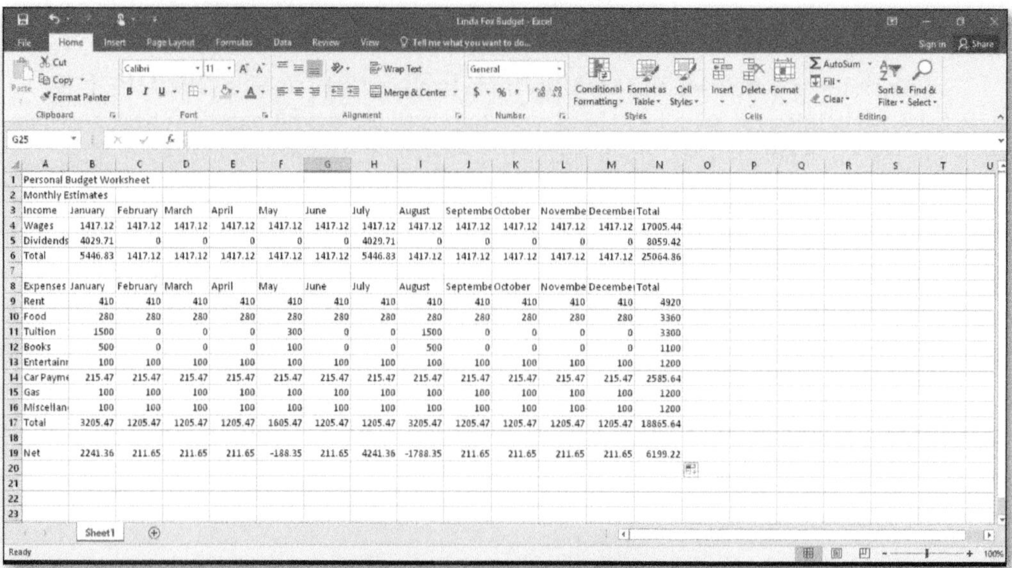

(a) Unformatted Worksheet

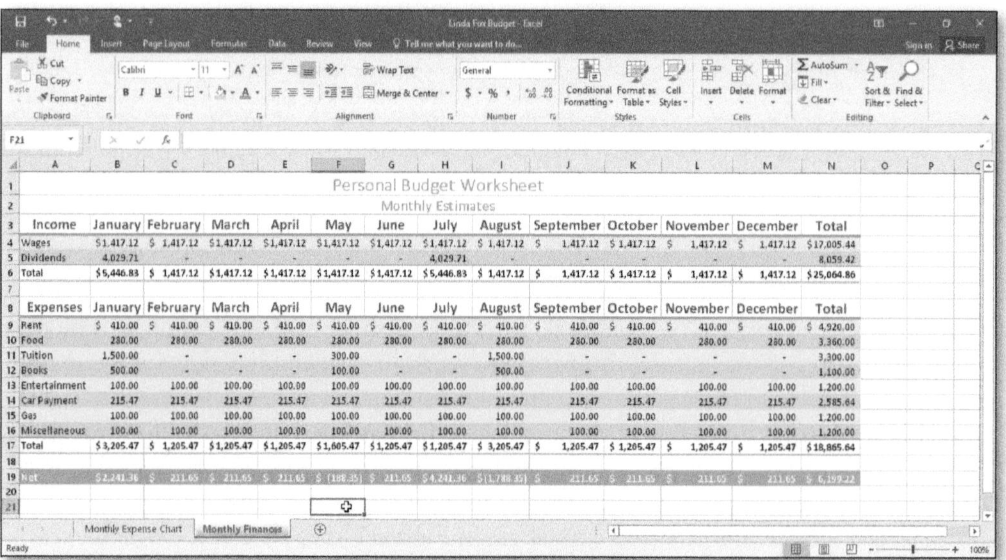

(b) Formatted Worksheet

Figure 1–29

1. Change the font, change the font style, increase the font size, and change the font color of the worksheet titles in cells A1 and A2.
2. Center the worksheet titles in cells A1 and A2 across columns A through N.
3. Format the body of the worksheet. The body of the worksheet, range A3:N19, includes the column titles, row titles, and numbers. Formatting the body of the worksheet changes the numbers to use a dollars-and-cents format, with dollar signs in rows 4 and 9 and in the total rows (row 6 and 17); changes the styles of some rows; adds underlining that emphasizes portions of the worksheet; and modifies the column widths to fit the text in the columns and make the text and numbers readable.

Although the formatting procedures are explained in the order described above, you could make these format changes in any order. Modifying the column widths, however, usually is done last because other formatting changes may affect the size of data in the cells in the column.

Font Style, Size, and Color

The characters that Excel displays on the screen are a specific font, style, size, and color. The **font**, or font face, defines the appearance and shape of the letters, numbers, and special characters. Examples of fonts include Calibri, Cambria, Times New Roman, Arial, and Courier. **Font style** indicates how the characters are emphasized. Common font styles include regular, bold, underline, and italic. The **font size** specifies the size of the characters. Font size is gauged by a measurement system called points. A single point is 1/72 of one inch in height. Thus, a character with a **point size** of 10 is 10/72 of one inch in height. Finally, Excel has a wide variety of **font colors** from which to choose to define the color of the characters.

When Excel first runs, the default font for the entire workbook is Calibri, with a font size, font style, and font color of 11-point regular black. You can change the font characteristics in a single cell, a range of cells, the entire worksheet, or the entire workbook.

To Change a Cell Style

1 ENTER TEXT | 2 CALCULATE SUMS & USE FORMULAS | 3 FORMAT TEXT
4 INSERT CHART | 5 NAME TAB | 6 PREVIEW & PRINT WORKSHEET

You can change several characteristics of a cell, such as the font, font size, and font color, all at once by assigning a predefined cell style to a cell. A **cell style** is a predefined font, font size, and font color that you can apply to a cell. ***Why?*** *Using the predefined styles provides a consistent appearance to common portions of your worksheets, such as worksheet titles, worksheet subtitles, column headings, and total rows.* The following steps assign the Title cell style to the worksheet title in cell A1.

- Click cell A1 to make cell A1 the active cell.
- Click the Cell Styles button (Home tab | Styles group) to display the Cell Styles gallery (Figure 1–30).

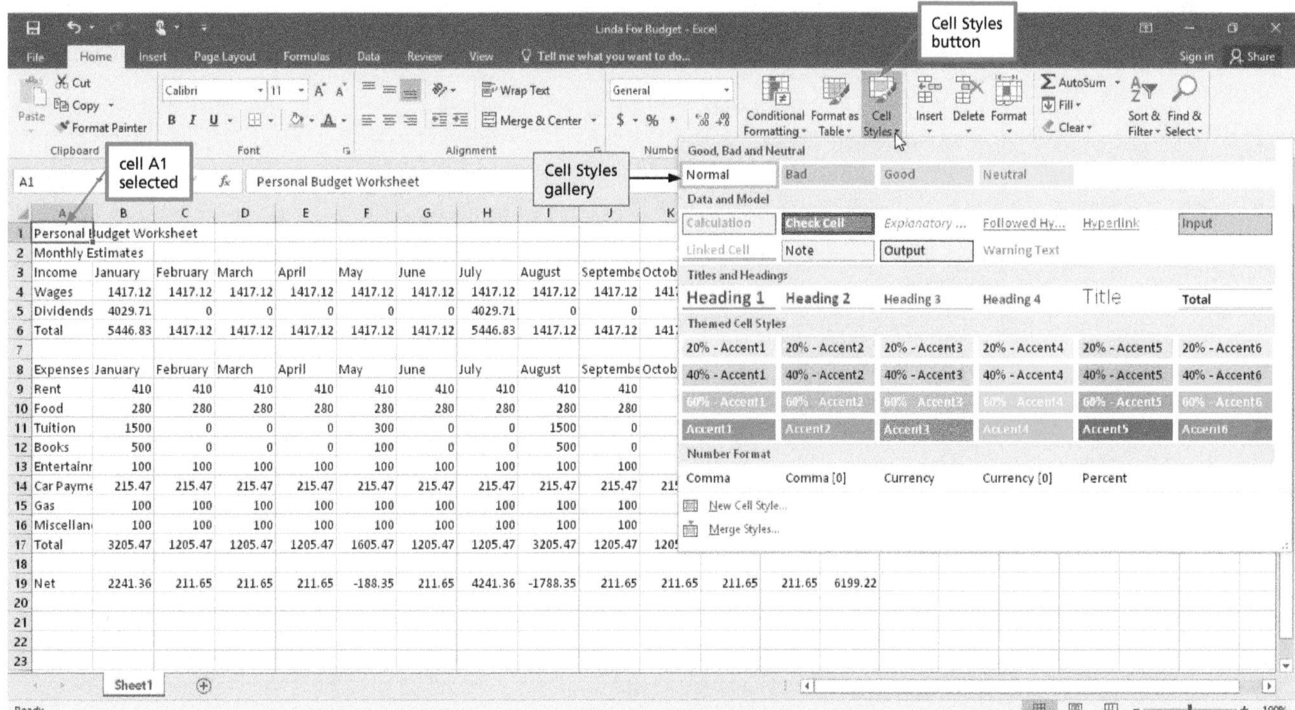

Figure 1–30

2

- Point to the Title cell style in the Titles and Headings area of the Cell Styles gallery to see a live preview of the cell style in the active cell (Figure 1–31).

Q&A Can I use live preview on a touch screen?
Live preview is not available on a touch screen.

Experiment

- Point to other cell styles in the Cell Styles gallery to see a live preview of those cell styles in cell A1.

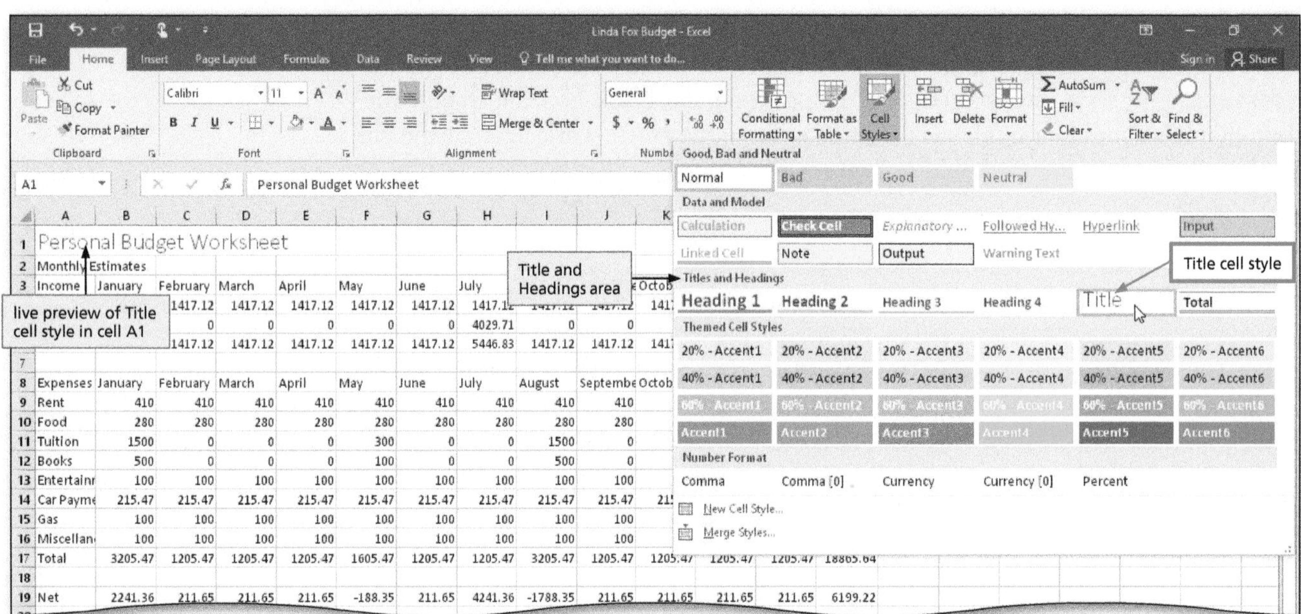

Figure 1–31

3

- Click the Title cell style to apply the cell style to the active cell (Figure 1–32).

Q&A Why do settings in the Font group on the ribbon change?
The font and font size change to reflect the font changes applied to the active cell, cell A1, as a result of applying the Title cell style.

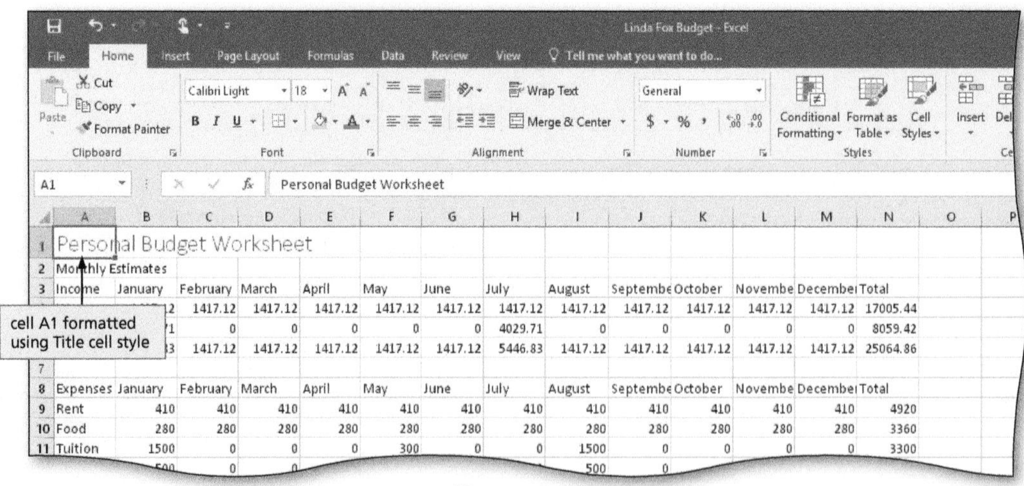

Figure 1–32

To Change the Font

1 ENTER TEXT | 2 CALCULATE SUMS & USE FORMULAS | 3 FORMAT TEXT
4 INSERT CHART | 5 NAME TAB | 6 PREVIEW & PRINT WORKSHEET

Why? Different fonts often are used in a worksheet to make it more appealing to the reader and to relate or distinguish data in the worksheet. The following steps change the worksheet subtitle's font to Calibri Light.

1

- Click cell A2 to make it the active cell.
- Click the Font arrow (Home tab | Font group) to display the Font gallery. If necessary, scroll to Calibri Light.
- Point to Calibri Light in the Font gallery to see a live preview of the selected font in the active cell (Figure 1–33).

Experiment

- Point to several other fonts in the Font gallery to see a live preview of the other fonts in the selected cell.

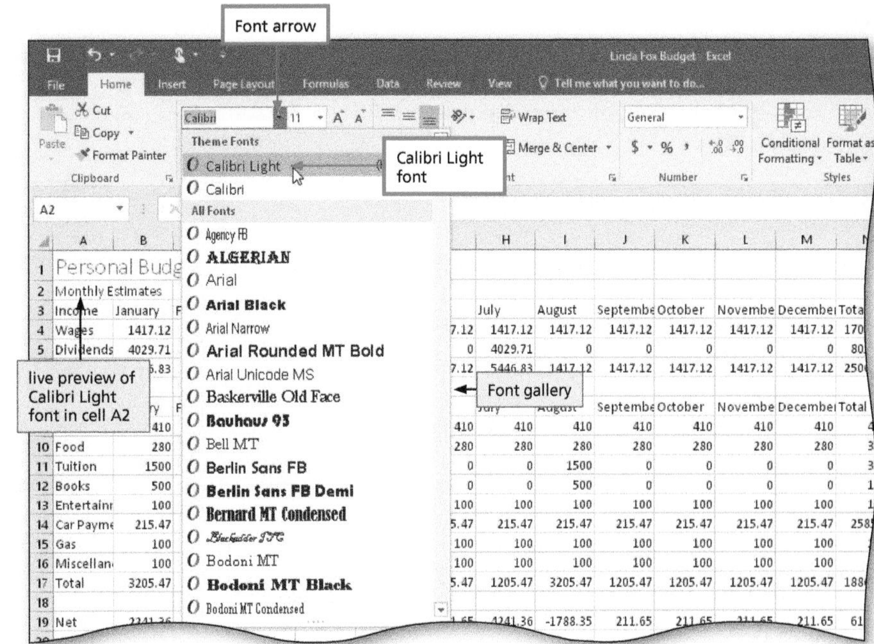

Figure 1–33

2

- Click Calibri Light in the Font gallery to change the font of the worksheet subtitle to Calibri Light (Figure 1–34).

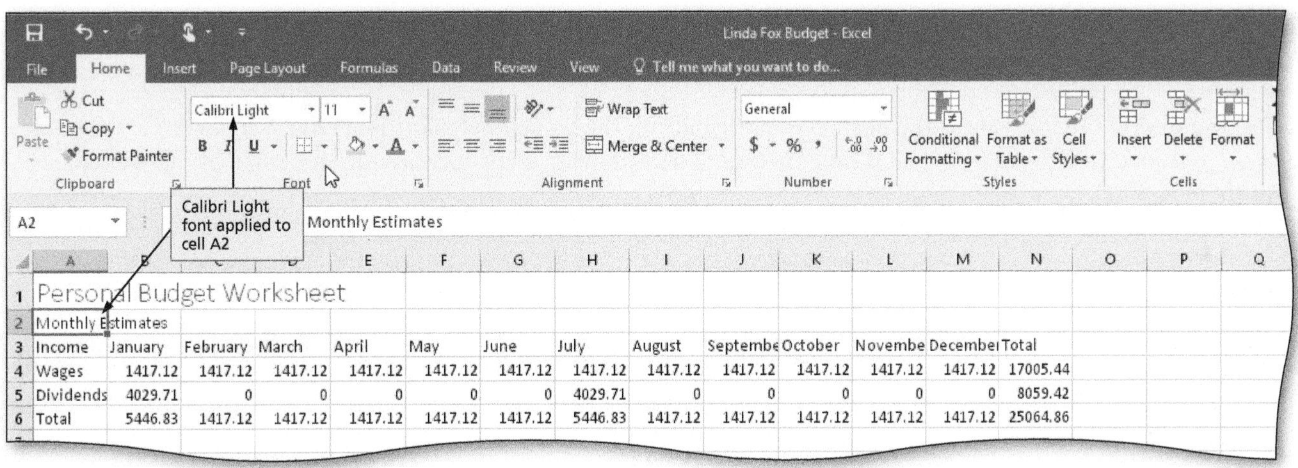

Figure 1–34

Other Ways

1. Click Font Settings Dialog Box Launcher, click Font tab (Format Cells dialog box), click desired font in Font list, click OK button
2. Right-click cell to display mini toolbar, click Font box arrow on mini toolbar, click desired font in Font gallery
3. Right-click selected cell, click Format Cells on shortcut menu, click Font tab (Format Cells dialog box), click desired font, click OK button

1 ENTER TEXT | 2 CALCULATE SUMS & USE FORMULAS | **3 FORMAT TEXT**
4 INSERT CHART | 5 NAME TAB | 6 PREVIEW & PRINT WORKSHEET

To Apply Bold Style to a Cell

Bold, or boldface, text has a darker appearance than normal text. ***Why?*** *You apply bold style to a cell to emphasize it or make it stand out from the rest of the worksheet.* The following steps apply bold style to the worksheet title and subtitle.

1

- Click cell A1 to make it active and then click the Bold button (Home tab | Font group) to change the font style of the active cell to bold (Figure 1–35).

Q&A What if a cell already has the bold style applied?
If the active cell contains bold text, then Excel displays the Bold button with a darker gray background.

How do I remove the bold style from a cell?
Clicking the Bold button (Home tab | Font group) a second time removes the bold style.

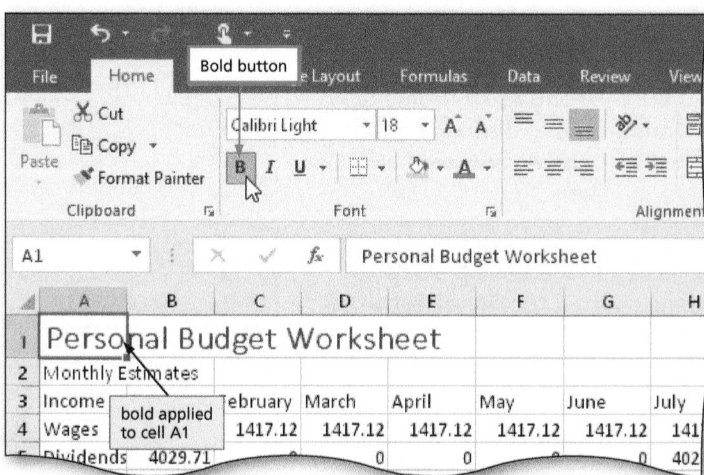

Figure 1–35

2

- Repeat Step 1 to bold cell A2.

Other Ways

1. Click Font Settings Dialog Box Launcher, click Font tab (Format Cells dialog box), click Bold in Font style list, click OK button
2. Right-click selected cell, click Bold button on mini toolbar
3. Right-click selected cell, click Format Cells on shortcut menu, click Font tab (Format Cells dialog box), click Bold, click OK button
4. Press CTRL+B

To Increase the Font Size of a Cell Entry

1 ENTER TEXT | 2 CALCULATE SUMS & USE FORMULAS | 3 FORMAT TEXT
4 INSERT CHART | 5 NAME TAB | 6 PREVIEW & PRINT WORKSHEET

Increasing the font size is the next step in formatting the worksheet subtitle. ***Why?*** *You increase the font size of a cell so that the entry stands out and is easier to read.* The following steps increase the font size of the worksheet subtitle in cell A2.

1

- With cell A2 selected, click the Font Size arrow (Home tab | Font group) to display the Font Size gallery.
- Point to 14 in the Font Size gallery to see a live preview of the active cell with the selected font size (Figure 1–36).

Experiment

- If you are using a mouse, point to several other font sizes in the Font Size list to see a live preview of those font sizes in the selected cell.

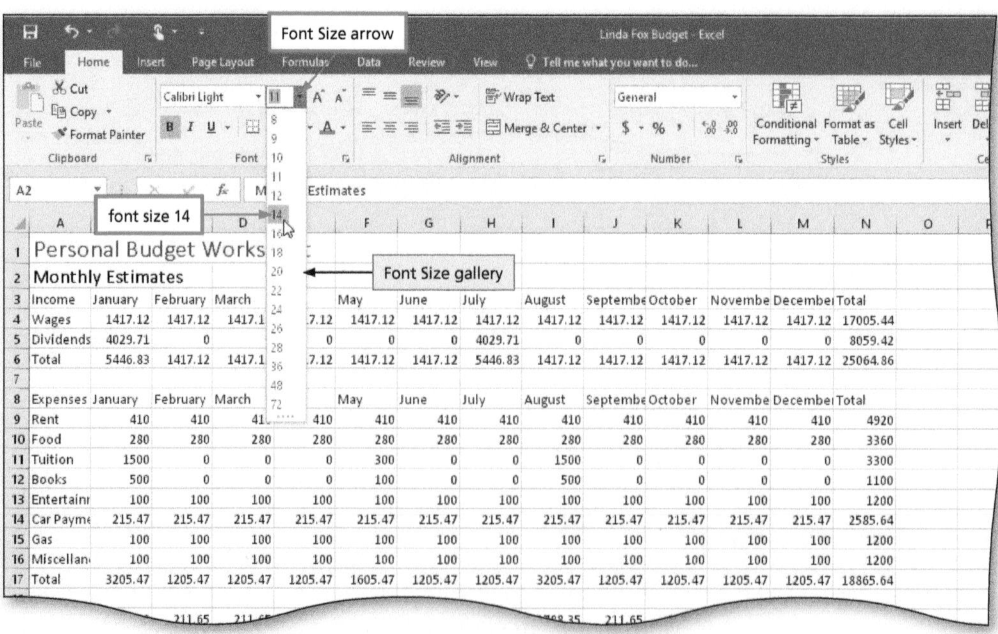

Figure 1–36

1

- Click 14 in the Font Size gallery to change the font size in the active cell (Figure 1–37).

Q&A Can I choose a font size that is not in the Font Size gallery?
Yes. An alternative to selecting a font size in the Font Size gallery is to click the Font Size box (Home tab | Font group), type the font size you want, and then press the ENTER key.

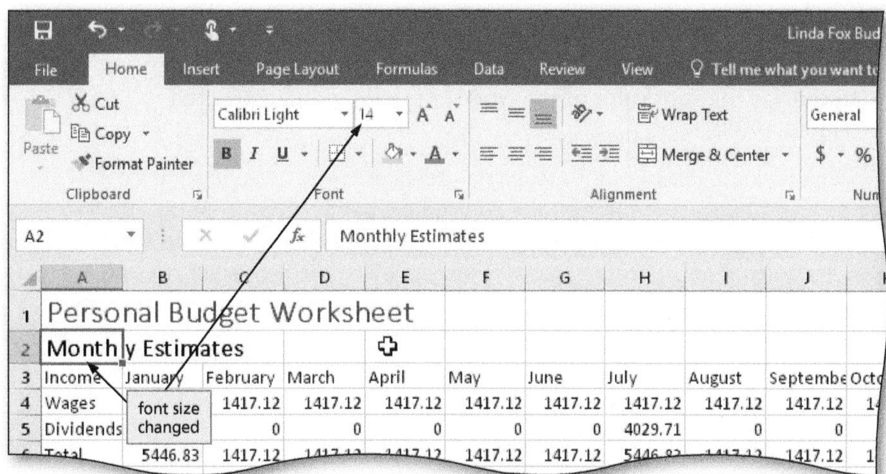

Figure 1–37

Other Ways

1. Click 'Increase Font Size' button (Home tab | Font group) or 'Decrease Font Size' button (Home tab | Font group)
2. Click Font Settings Dialog box Launcher, click Font tab (Format Cells dialog box), click desired size in Size list, click OK button
3. Right-click cell to display mini toolbar, click Font Size arrow on mini toolbar, click desired font size in Font Size gallery
4. Right-click selected cell, click Format Cells on shortcut menu, click Font tab (Format Cells dialog box), select font size in Size box, click OK button

To Change the Font Color of a Cell Entry

1 ENTER TEXT | 2 CALCULATE SUMS & USE FORMULAS | 3 FORMAT TEXT
4 INSERT CHART | 5 NAME TAB | 6 PREVIEW & PRINT WORKSHEET

The next step is to change the color of the font in cells A1 and A2 to orange. ***Why?*** *Changing the font color of cell entries can help the text stand out more. You also can change the font colors to match the company or product's brand colors.* The following steps change the font color of a cell entry.

1

- Click cell A1 and then click the Font Color arrow (Home tab | Font group) to display the Font Color gallery.
- Point to 'Orange, Accent 2' (column 6, row 1) in the Theme Colors area of the Font Color gallery to see a live preview of the font color in the active cell (Figure 1–38).

Experiment

- Point to several other colors in the Font Color gallery to see a live preview of other font colors in the active cell.

Q&A How many colors are in the Font Color gallery?
You can choose from approximately 70 different font colors in the Font Color gallery. Your Font Color gallery may have more or fewer colors, depending on the color settings of your operating system. The Theme Colors area contains colors that are included in the current workbook's theme.

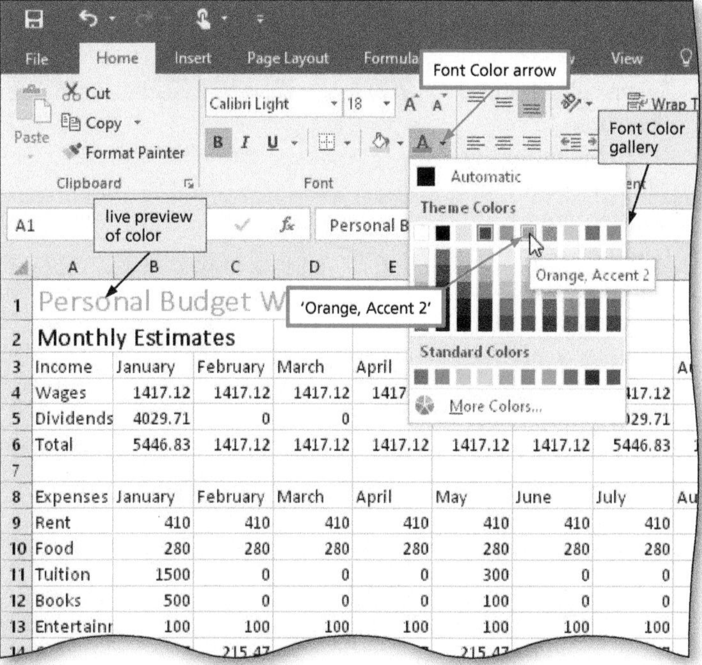

Figure 1–38

2

- Click 'Orange, Accent 2' (column 6, row 1) in the Font Color gallery to change the font color of the worksheet title in the active cell (Figure 1–39).

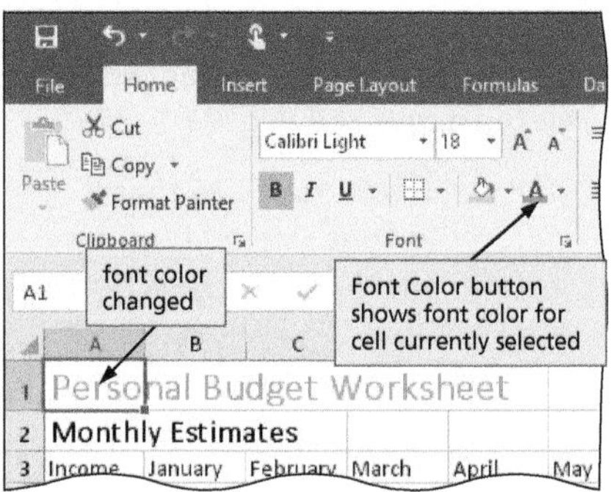

Figure 1–39

Q&A Why does the Font Color button change after I select the new font color?
When you choose a color on the Font Color gallery, Excel changes the Font Color button (Home tab | Font group) to your chosen color. Then when you want to change the font color of another cell to the same color, you need only to select the cell and then click the Font Color button (Home tab | Font group).

3

- Click the Font Color button to apply Orange, Accent 2 (column 6, row 1) to cell A2.

Other Ways

1. Click Font Settings Dialog Box Launcher, click Font tab (Format Cells dialog box), click desired color in Color list, click OK button
2. Right-click the cell to display mini toolbar, click Font Color arrow on mini toolbar, click desired font color in Font Color gallery
3. Right-click selected cell, click Format Cells on shortcut menu, click Font tab (Format Cells dialog box), select color in Font Color gallery, click OK button

To Center Cell Entries across Columns by Merging Cells

1 ENTER TEXT | 2 CALCULATE SUMS & USE FORMULAS | 3 FORMAT TEXT
4 INSERT CHART | 5 NAME TAB | 6 PREVIEW & PRINT WORKSHEET

The final step in formatting the worksheet title and subtitle is to center them across columns A through N. ***Why?*** *Centering a title across the columns used in the body of the worksheet improves the worksheet's appearance.* To do this, the 14 cells in the range A1:N1 are combined, or merged, into a single cell that is the width of the columns in the body of the worksheet. The 14 cells in the range A2:N2 are merged in a similar manner. **Merging cells** involves creating a single cell by combining two or more selected cells. The following steps center the worksheet title and subtitle across columns by merging cells.

1

- Select cell A1 and then drag to cell N1 to highlight the range to be merged and centered (Figure 1–40).

Q&A What if a cell in the range B1:N1 contains data?
For the 'Merge & Center' button (Home tab | Alignment group) to work properly, all the cells except the leftmost cell in the selected range must be empty.

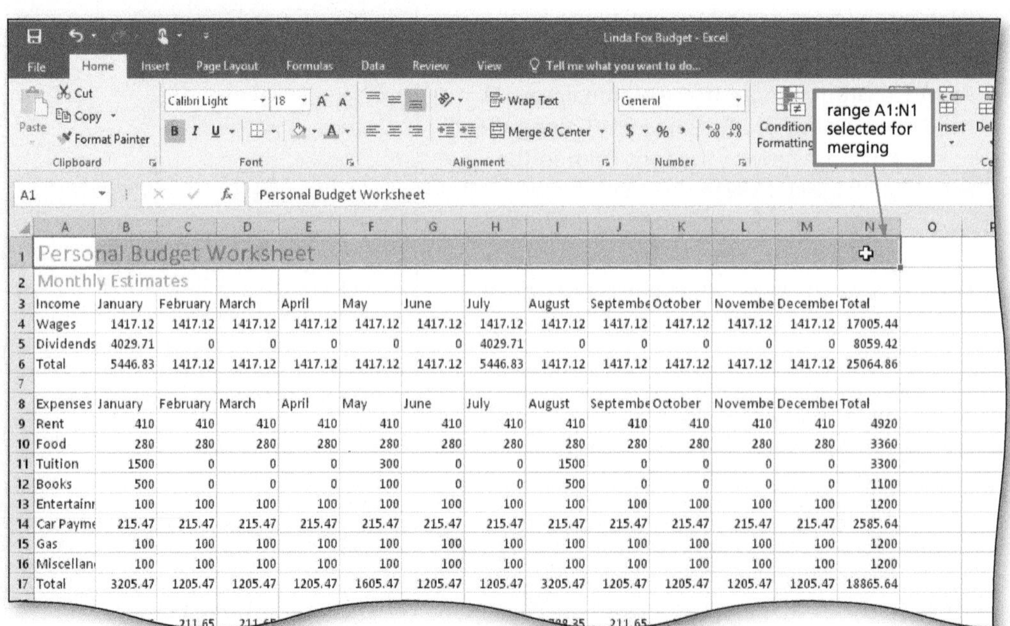

Income	January	February	March	April	May	June	July	August	Septembe	October	Novembe	Decembei	Total
Wages	1417.12	1417.12	1417.12	1417.12	1417.12	1417.12	1417.12	1417.12	1417.12	1417.12	1417.12	1417.12	17005.44
Dividends	4029.71	0	0	0	0	0	4029.71	0	0	0	0	0	8059.42
Total	5446.83	1417.12	1417.12	1417.12	1417.12	1417.12	5446.83	1417.12	1417.12	1417.12	1417.12	1417.12	25064.86
Expenses	January	February	March	April	May	June	July	August	Septembe	October	Novembe	Decembei	Total
Rent	410	410	410	410	410	410	410	410	410	410	410	410	4920
Food	280	280	280	280	280	280	280	280	280	280	280	280	3360
Tuition	1500	0	0	0	300	0	0	1500	0	0	0	0	3300
Books	500	0	0	0	100	0	0	500	0	0	0	0	1100
Entertainr	100	100	100	100	100	100	100	100	100	100	100	100	1200
Car Payme	215.47	215.47	215.47	215.47	215.47	215.47	215.47	215.47	215.47	215.47	215.47	215.47	2585.64
Gas	100	100	100	100	100	100	100	100	100	100	100	100	1200
Miscellan	100	100	100	100	100	100	100	100	100	100	100	100	1200
Total	3205.47	1205.47	1205.47	1205.47	1605.47	1205.47	1205.47	3205.47	1205.47	1205.47	1205.47	1205.47	18865.64

Figure 1–40

2

- Click the 'Merge & Center' button (Home tab | Alignment group) to merge cells A1 through N1 and center the contents of the leftmost cell across the selected columns (Figure 1–41).

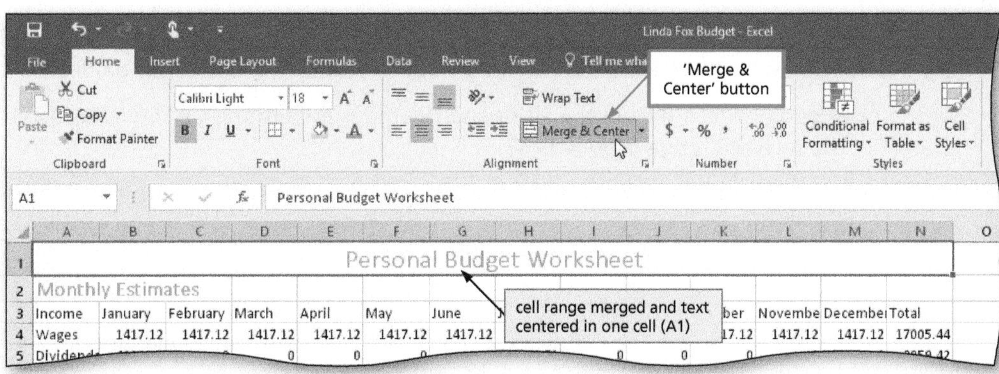

Figure 1–41

Q&A What if my screen displays a Merge & Center menu?
Select the desired option on the Merge & Center menu if you do not have a separate 'Merge & Center' button and 'Merge & Center' arrow.

What happened to cells B1 through N1?
After the merge, cells B1 through N1 no longer exist. The new cell A1 now extends across columns A through N.

3

- Repeat Steps 1 and 2 to merge and center the worksheet subtitle across cells A2 through N2 (Figure 1–42).

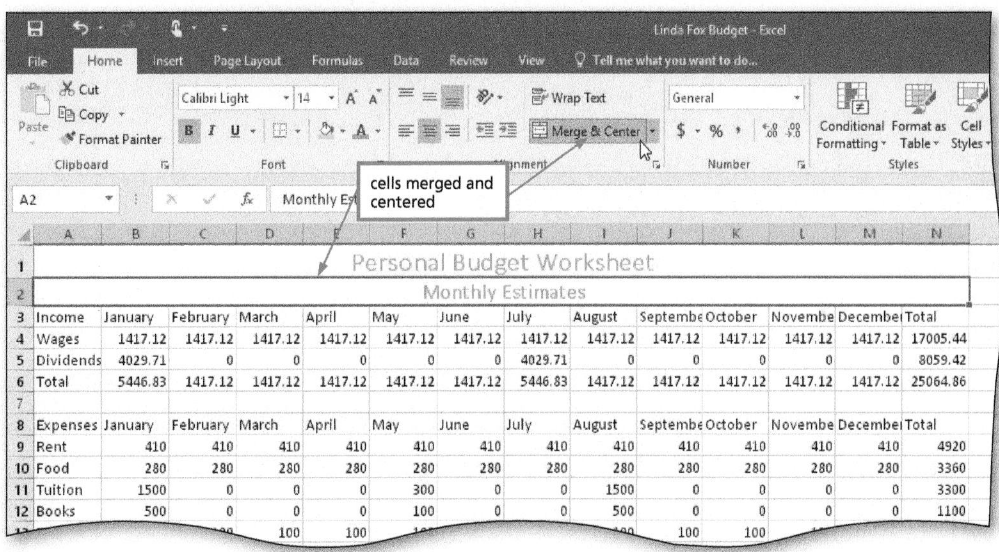

Figure 1–42

Q&A Are cells B1 through N1 and B2 through N2 lost forever?
No. The opposite of merging cells is **splitting** a merged cell. After you have merged multiple cells into one cell, you can unmerge, or split, the cell to display the original range of cells. You split a merged cell by selecting it and clicking the 'Merge & Center' button. For example, if you click the 'Merge & Center' button a second time in Step 2, it will split the merged cell A1 into cells A1, B1, C1, D1, E1, F1, G1, H1, I1, J1, K1, L1, M1, and N1, and move the title to it's original location in cell A1.

Other Ways

1. Right-click selection, click 'Merge & Center' button on mini toolbar
2. Right-click selected cell, click Format Cells on shortcut menu, click Alignment tab (Format Cells dialog box), select 'Center Across Selection' in Horizontal list, click OK button

To Format Rows Using Cell Styles

1 ENTER TEXT | 2 CALCULATE SUMS & USE FORMULAS | 3 FORMAT TEXT
4 INSERT CHART | 5 NAME TAB | 6 PREVIEW & PRINT WORKSHEET

The next step to format the worksheet is to format the rows. ***Why?*** *Row titles and the total row should be formatted so that the column titles and total row can be distinguished from the data in the body of the worksheet. Data rows can be formatted to make them easier to read as well.* The following steps format the column titles and total row using cell styles in the default worksheet theme.

- Click cell A3 and then drag to cell N3 to select the range.
- Click the Cell Styles button (Home tab | Styles group) to display the Cell Styles gallery.
- Point to the Heading 1 cell style in the Titles and Headings area of the Cell Styles gallery to see a live preview of the cell style in the selected range (Figure 1–43).

Experiment

- Point to other cell styles in the Titles and Headings area of the Cell Styles gallery to see a live preview of other styles.

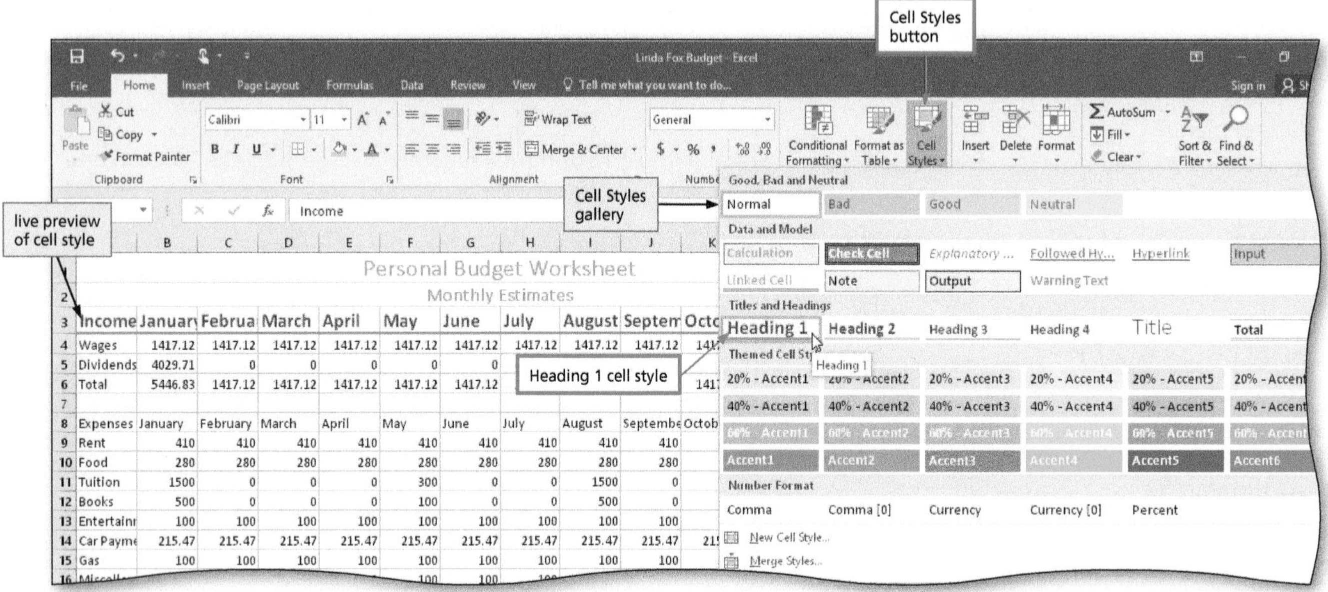

Figure 1–43

- Click the Heading 1 cell style to apply the cell style to the selected range.
- Click the Center button (Home tab | Alignment group) to center the column headings in the selected range.
- Select the range A8 to N8 (Figure 1–44).

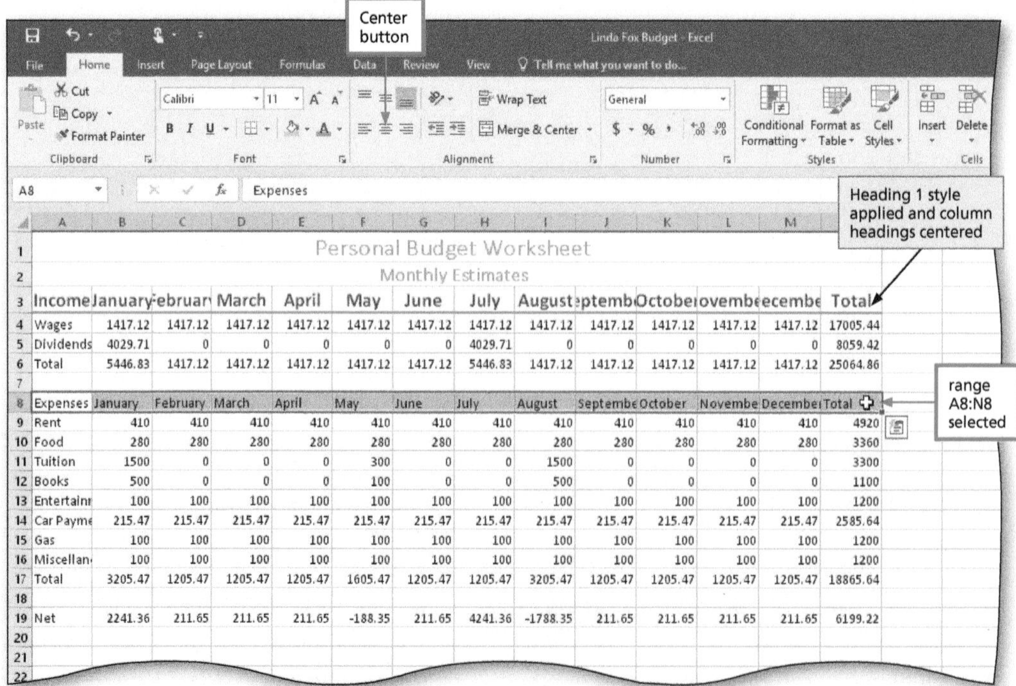

Figure 1–44

3

- Apply the Heading 1 cell style format and then center the headings (Figure 1–45).

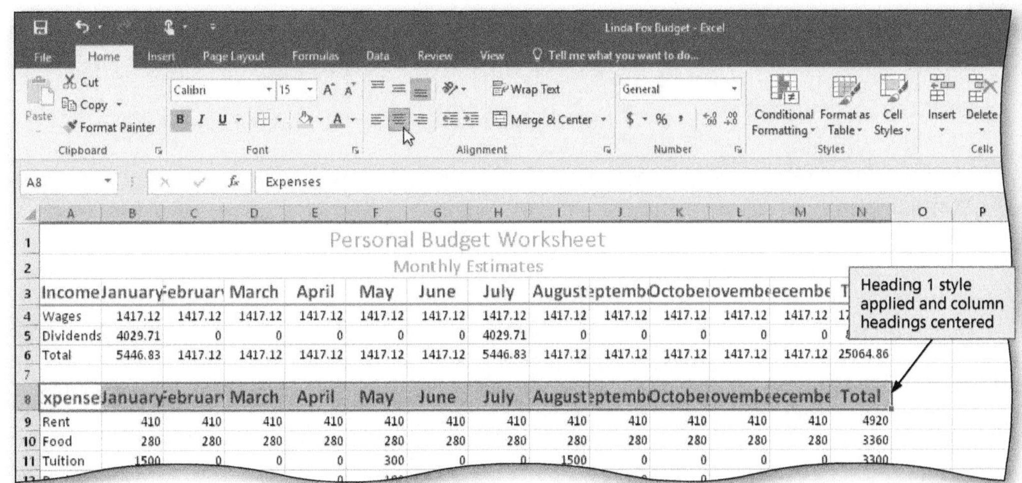

Figure 1–45

4

- Format the range A6:N6 and A17:N17 with the Total cell style format.
- Format the range A19:N19 with the Accent2 cell style format.
- Format the range A4:N4, A9:N9, A11:N11, A13:N13, A15:N15 with the 20% - Accent2 cell style format.
- Format the range A5:N5, A10:N10, A12:N12, A14:N14, A16:N16 with the 40% - Accent2 cell style format. Deselect the selected ranges

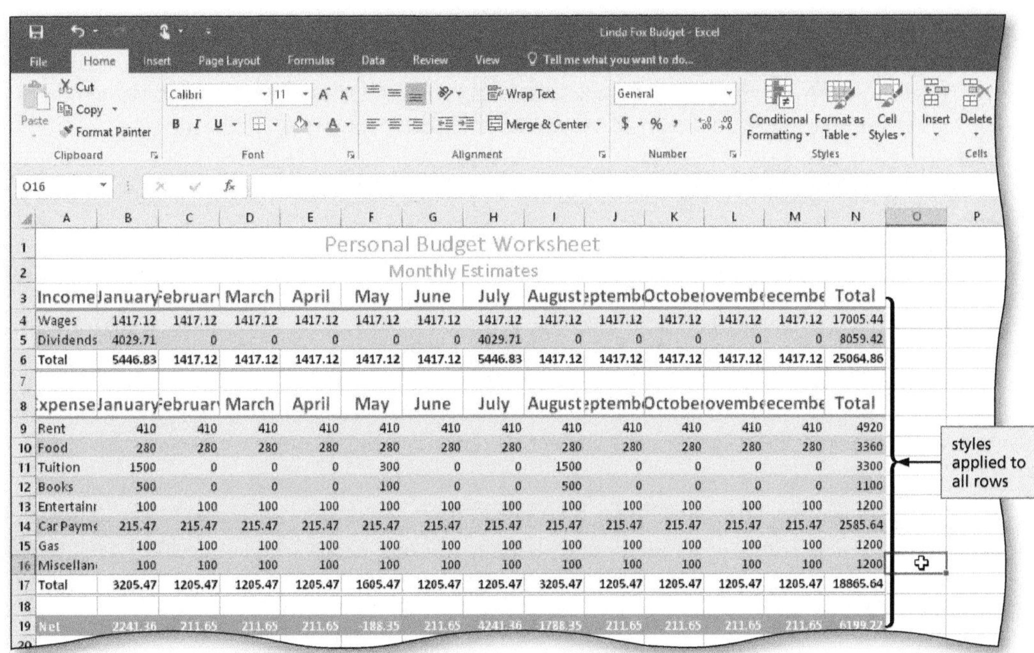

Figure 1–46

1 ENTER TEXT | 2 CALCULATE SUMS & USE FORMULAS | 3 FORMAT TEXT
4 INSERT CHART | 5 NAME TAB | 6 PREVIEW & PRINT WORKSHEET

To Format Numbers in the Worksheet

The requirements document requested that numbers in the first row and last row of each section should be formatted to use a dollar-and-cents format, while other numbers receive a comma format. ***Why?*** *Using a dollar-and-cents format for selected cells makes it clear to users of the worksheet that the numbers represent dollar values without cluttering the entire worksheet with dollar signs, and applying the comma format makes larger numbers easier to read.* Excel allows you to apply various number formats, many of which are discussed in later modules. The following steps use buttons on the ribbon to format the numbers in the worksheet.

- Select the range B4:N4.
- Click the 'Accounting Number Format' button (Home tab | Number group) to apply the accounting number format to the cells in the selected range.

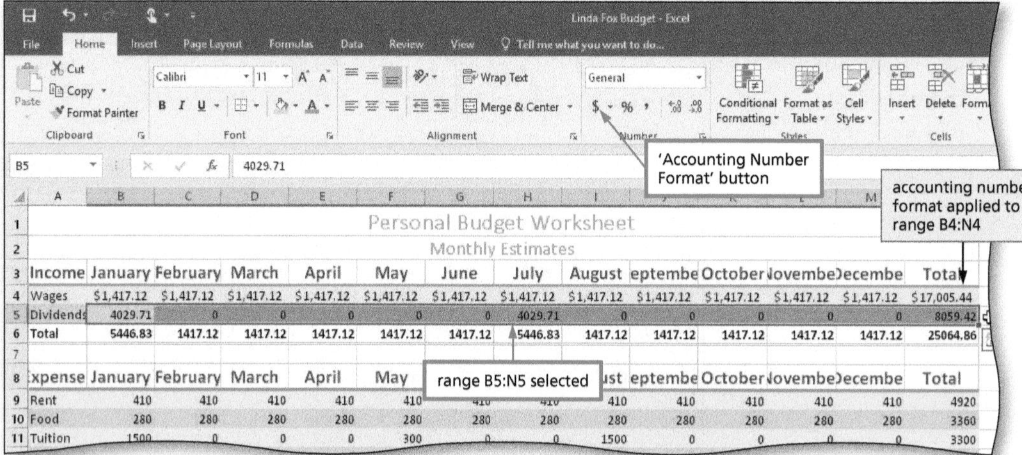

Figure 1–47

Q&A What if my screen displays an Accounting Number Format menu?
If you are using a touch screen, you may not have a separate 'Accounting Number Format' button and 'Accounting Number Format' arrow. In this case, select the desired option on the Accounting Number Format menu.

What effect does the accounting number format have on the selected cells?
The accounting number format causes numbers to be displayed with two decimal places and to align vertically. Cell widths are adjusted automatically to accommodate the new formatting.

- Select the range B5:N5 (Figure 1–47).

- Click the Comma Style button (Home tab | Number group) to apply the comma style format to the selected range.

Q&A What effect does the comma style format have on the selected cells?
The comma style format formats numbers to have two decimal places and commas as thousands separators.

- Select the range B6:N6 to make it the active range (Figure 1–48).

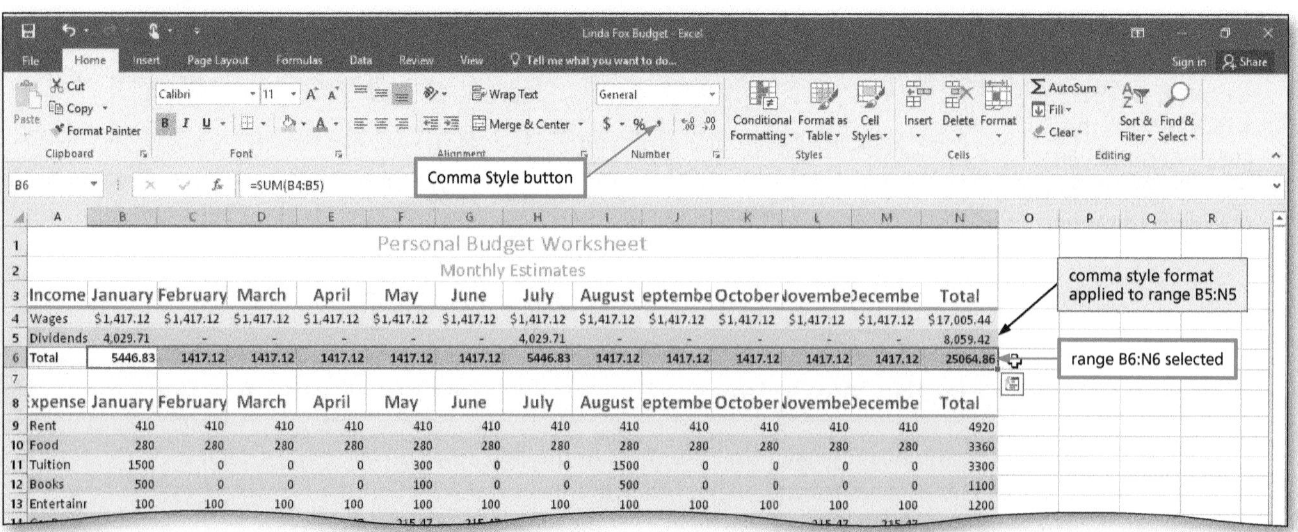

Figure 1–48

- Click the 'Accounting Number Format' button (Home tab | Number group) to apply the accounting number format to the cells in the selected range.

4

- Format the ranges B9:N9, B17:N17, and B19:N19 with the accounting number format.
- Format the range B10:N16 with the comma style format. Click cell A1 to deselect the selected ranges (Figure 1–49).

Q&A How do I select the range B10:N16?
Select this range the same way as you select a range of cells in a column or row; that is, click the first cell in the range (B10, in this case) and drag to the last cell in the range (N16, in this case).

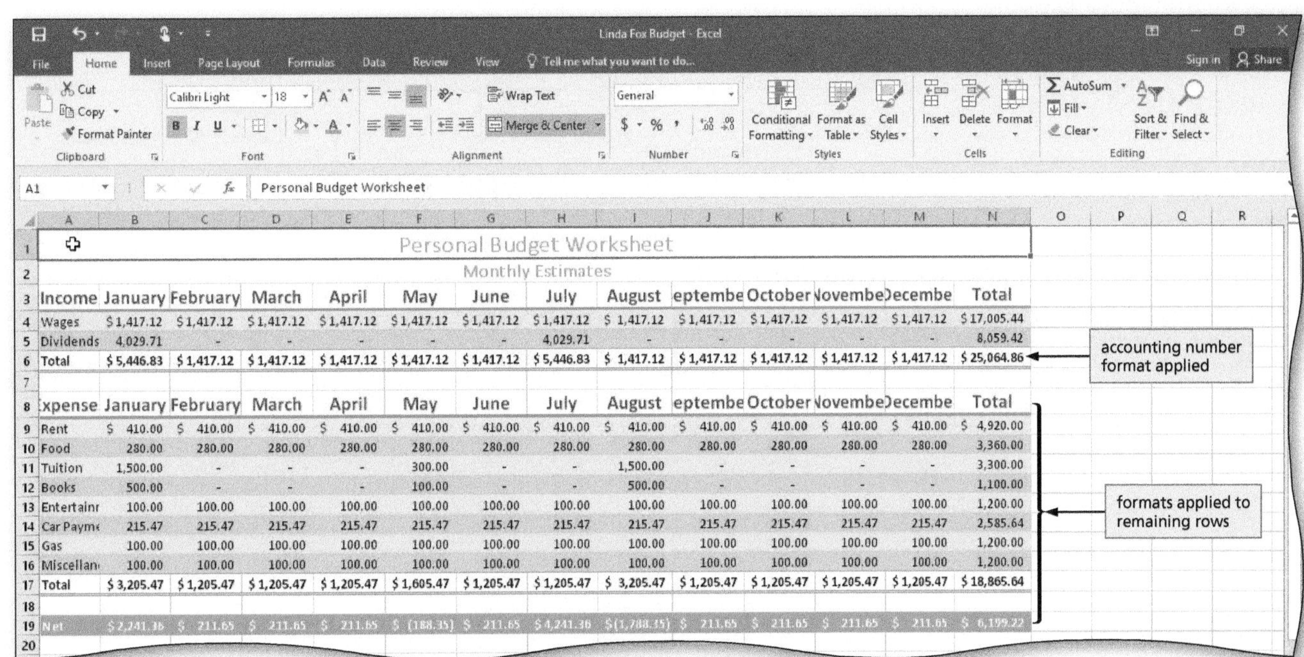

Figure 1–49

Other Ways

1. Click 'Accounting Number Format' or Comma Style button on mini toolbar
2. Right-click selected cell, click Format Cells on shortcut menu, click Number tab (Format Cells dialog box), select Accounting in Category list or select Number and click 'Use 1000 Separator', click OK button

1 ENTER TEXT | 2 CALCULATE SUMS & USE FORMULAS | 3 FORMAT TEXT
4 INSERT CHART | 5 NAME TAB | 6 PREVIEW & PRINT WORKSHEET

To Adjust the Column Width

The last step in formatting the worksheet is to adjust the width of the columns so that each title is visible. ***Why?*** *To make a worksheet easy to read, the column widths should be adjusted appropriately.* Excel offers other methods for adjusting cell widths and row heights, which are discussed later in this book. The following steps adjust the width of columns A through N so that the contents of the columns are visible.

- Point to the boundary on the right side of the column A heading above row 1 to change the pointer to a split double arrow (Figure 1–50).

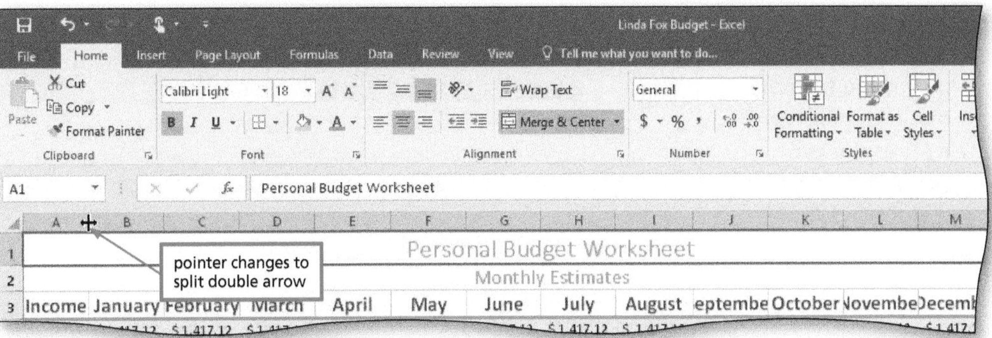

Figure 1–50

2

- Double-click the boundary to adjust the width of the column to accommodate the width of the longest item in the column (Figure 1–51).

Q&A What if all of the items in the column are already visible?
If all of the items are shorter in length than the width of the column and you double-click the column boundary, Excel will reduce the width of the column.

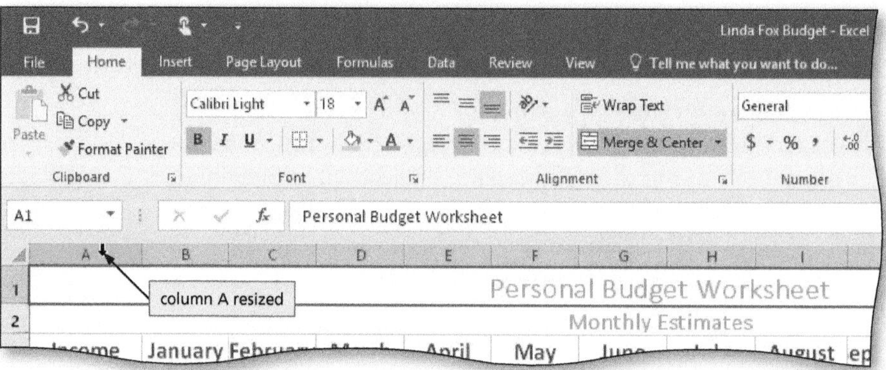

Figure 1–51

3

- Repeat Steps 1 and 2 to adjust the column width of columns B through N (Figure 1–52).

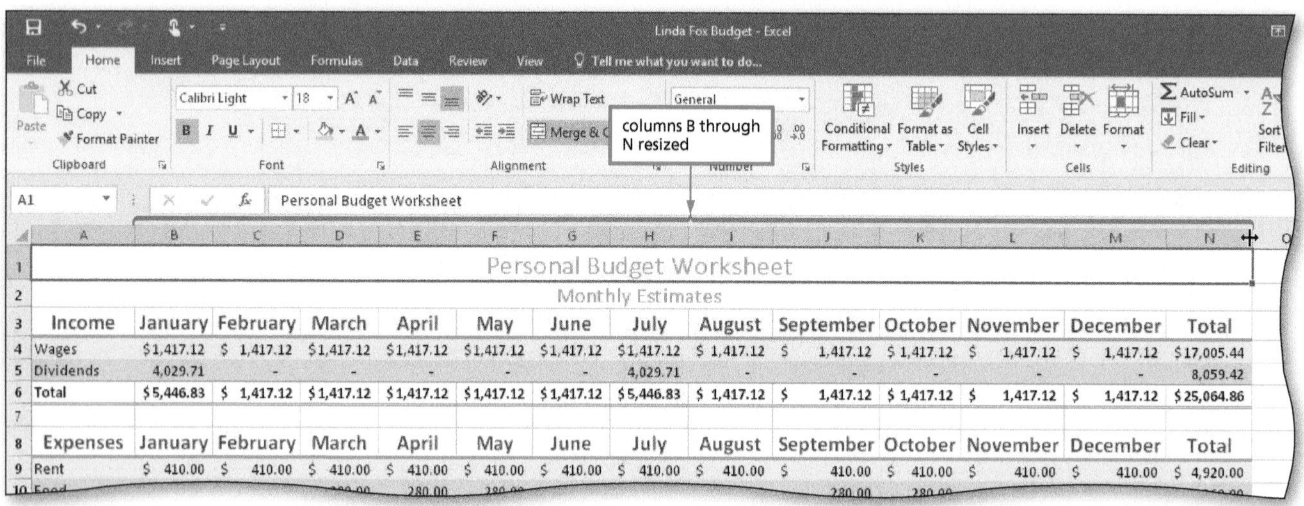

Figure 1–52

1 ENTER TEXT | 2 CALCULATE SUMS & USE FORMULAS | 3 FORMAT TEXT
4 INSERT CHART | 5 NAME TAB | 6 PREVIEW & PRINT WORKSHEET

To Use the Name Box to Select a Cell

The next step is to chart the monthly expenses. To create the chart, you need to identify the range of the data you want to feature on the chart and then select it. In this case you want to start with cell A3. Rather than clicking cell A3 to select it, you will select the cell by using the Name box, which is located to the left of the formula bar. ***Why?*** *You might want to use the Name box to select a cell if you are working with a large worksheet and it is faster to type the cell name rather than scrolling to and clicking it.* The following steps select cell A3 using the Name box.

- Click the Name box in the formula bar and then type **a3** as the cell you want to select (Figure 1–53).

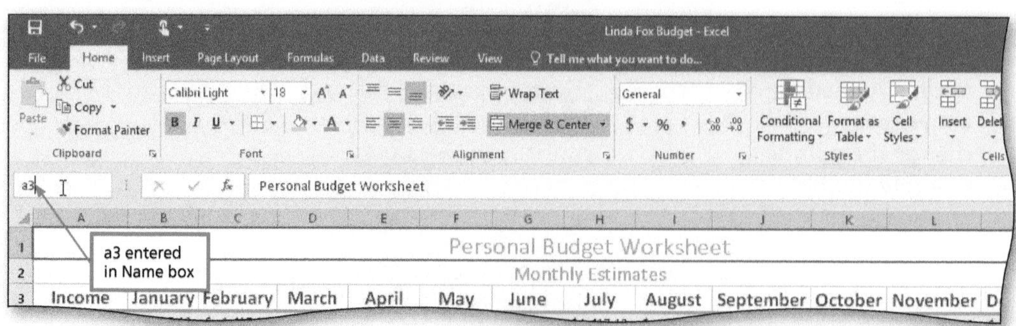

Figure 1–53

2

- Press the ENTER key to change the active cell in the Name box and make cell A3 the active cell (Figure 1–54).

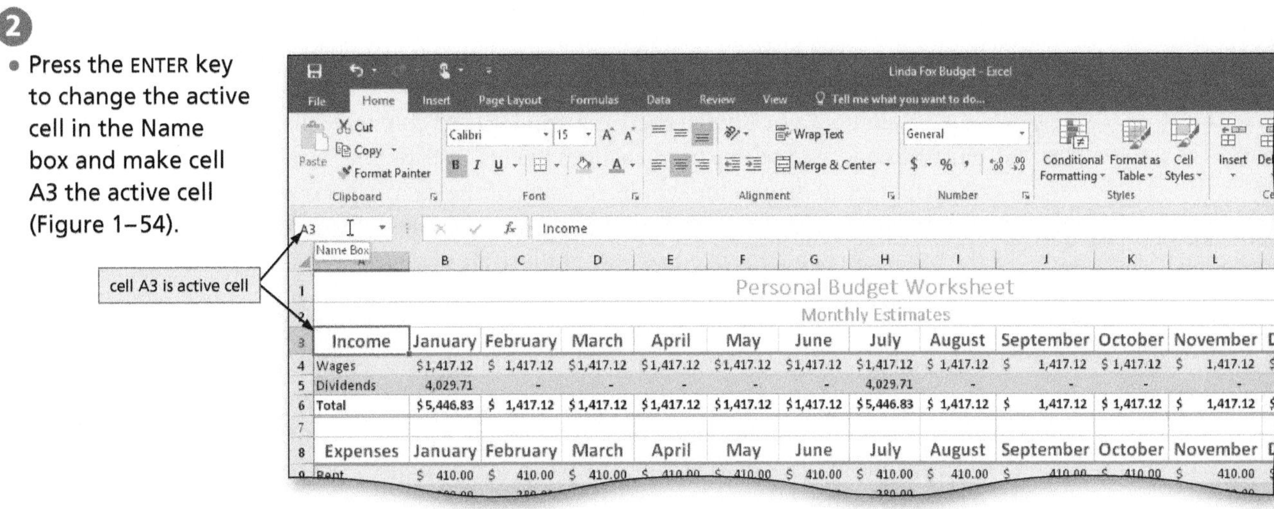

Figure 1–54

Other Ways to Select Cells

As you will see in later modules, in addition to using the Name box to select any cell in a worksheet, you also can use it to assign names to a cell or range of cells. Excel supports several additional ways to select a cell, as summarized in Table 1–3.

Table 1–3 Selecting Cells in Excel

Key, Box, or Command	Function
ALT+PAGE DOWN	Selects the cell one worksheet window to the right and moves the worksheet window accordingly.
ALT+PAGE UP	Selects the cell one worksheet window to the left and moves the worksheet window accordingly.
ARROW	Selects the adjacent cell in the direction of the arrow on the key.
CTRL+ARROW	Selects the border cell of the worksheet in combination with the arrow keys and moves the worksheet window accordingly. For example, to select the rightmost cell in the row that contains the active cell, press CTRL+RIGHT ARROW. You also can press the END key, release it, and then press the appropriate arrow key to accomplish the same task.
CTRL+HOME	Selects cell A1 or the cell one column and one row below and to the right of frozen titles and moves the worksheet window accordingly.
Find command on Find & Select menu (Home tab | Editing group) or SHIFT+F5	Finds and selects a cell that contains specific contents that you enter in the Find and Replace dialog box. If necessary, Excel moves the worksheet window to display the cell. You also can press CTRL+F to display the Find and Replace dialog box.
Go To command on Find & Select menu (Home tab | Editing group) or F5	Selects the cell that corresponds to the cell reference you enter in the Go To dialog box and moves the worksheet window accordingly. You also can press CTRL+G to display the Go To dialog box.
HOME	Selects the cell at the beginning of the row that contains the active cell and moves the worksheet window accordingly.
Name box	Selects the cell in the workbook that corresponds to the cell reference you enter in the Name box.
PAGE DOWN	Selects the cell down one worksheet window from the active cell and moves the worksheet window accordingly.
PAGE UP	Selects the cell up one worksheet window from the active cell and moves the worksheet window accordingly.

Break Point: If you wish to take a break, this is a good place to do so. Be sure to save the Linda Fox Budget file again and then you can exit Excel. To resume at a later time, run Excel, open the file called Linda Fox Budget, and continue following the steps from this location forward.

Adding a Pie Chart to the Worksheet

Excel includes 15 chart types from which you can choose, including column, line, pie, bar, area, X Y (scatter), stock, surface, radar, treemap, sunburst,

BTW

Excel Help

At any time while using Excel, you can find answers to questions and display information about various topics through Excel Help. Used properly, this form of assistance can increase your productivity and reduce your frustrations by minimizing the time you spend learning how to use Excel. For instructions about Excel Help and exercises that will help you gain confidence in using it, read the Office and Windows module at the beginning of this book.

histogram, box & whisker, waterfall, and combo. The type of chart you choose depends on the type and quantity of data you have and the message or analysis you want to convey.

A column or cylinder chart is a good way to compare values side by side. A line chart often is used to illustrate changes in data over time. Pie charts show the contribution of each piece of data to the whole, or total, of the data. A pie chart can go even further in comparing values across categories by showing each pie piece in comparison with the others. Area charts, like line charts, illustrate changes over time, but often are used to compare more than one set of data, and the area below the lines is filled in with a different color for each set of data. An X Y (scatter) chart is used much like a line chart, but each piece of data is represented by a dot and is not connected with a line. Scatter charts are typically used for viewing scientific, statistical, and engineering data. A stock chart provides a number of methods commonly used in the financial industry to show fluctuations in stock market data. A surface chart compares data from three columns and/or rows in a 3-D manner. A radar chart can compare aggregate values of several sets of data in a manner that resembles a radar screen, with each set of data represented by a different color. A combo chart allows you to combine multiple types of charts.

Excel 2016 includes five new charts. Treemap and sunburst charts are hierarchy charts, used to compare parts to a whole. A treemap chart uses nested rectangles to show data in a hierarchy. A sunburst chart stacks multiple pie charts on one another to illustrate related data. New statistical charts include histogram and box & whisker charts. A histogram chart shows the distribution of data. A box & whisker chart, or box plot, is used to display variation within a set of data. The new waterfall chart is used to visualize increases and decreases within a set of data and is grouped with stock charts.

As outlined in the requirements document in Figure 1–2, the budget worksheet should include a pie chart to graphically represent the yearly expense totals for each item in Linda Fox's budget. The pie chart shown in Figure 1–55 is on its own sheet in the workbook. The pie chart resides on a separate sheet, called a **chart sheet**, which contains only the chart.

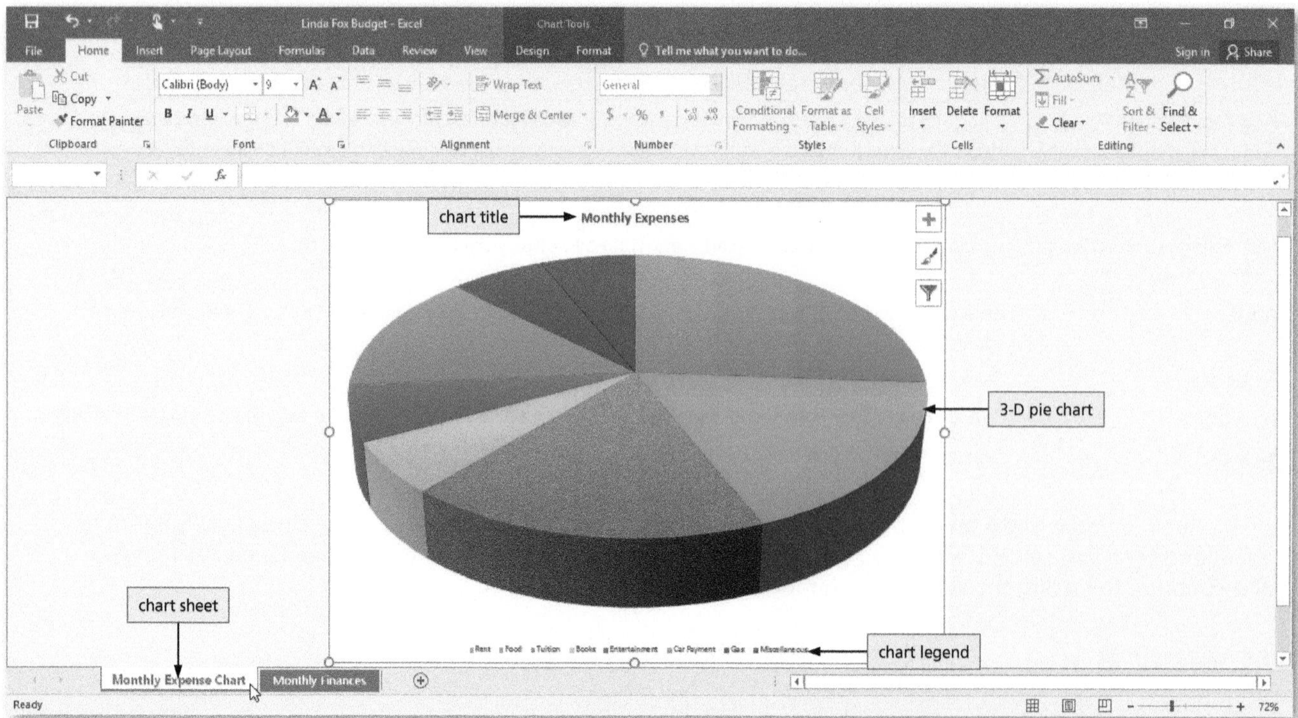

Figure 1–55

In this worksheet, the ranges you want to chart are the nonadjacent ranges A9:A16 (expense titles) and N9:N16 (yearly expense totals). The expense titles in the range A9:A16 will identify the slices of the pie chart; these entries are called category names. The range N9:N16 contains the data that determines the size of the slices in the pie; these entries are called the **data series.** Because eight budget items are being charted, the 3-D pie chart contains eight slices.

To Add a 3-D Pie Chart

1 ENTER TEXT | 2 CALCULATE SUMS & USE FORMULAS | 3 FORMAT TEXT
4 INSERT CHART | 5 NAME TAB | 6 PREVIEW & PRINT WORKSHEET

Why? *When you want to see how each part relates to the whole, you use a pie chart.* The following steps draw the 3-D pie chart.

- Select the range A9:A16 to identify the range of the category names for the 3-D pie chart.
- While holding down the CTRL key, select the nonadjacent range N9:N16.
- Click Insert on the ribbon to display the Insert tab.
- Click the 'Insert Pie or Doughnut Chart' button (Insert tab | Charts group) to display the Insert Pie or Doughnut Chart gallery (Figure 1–56).

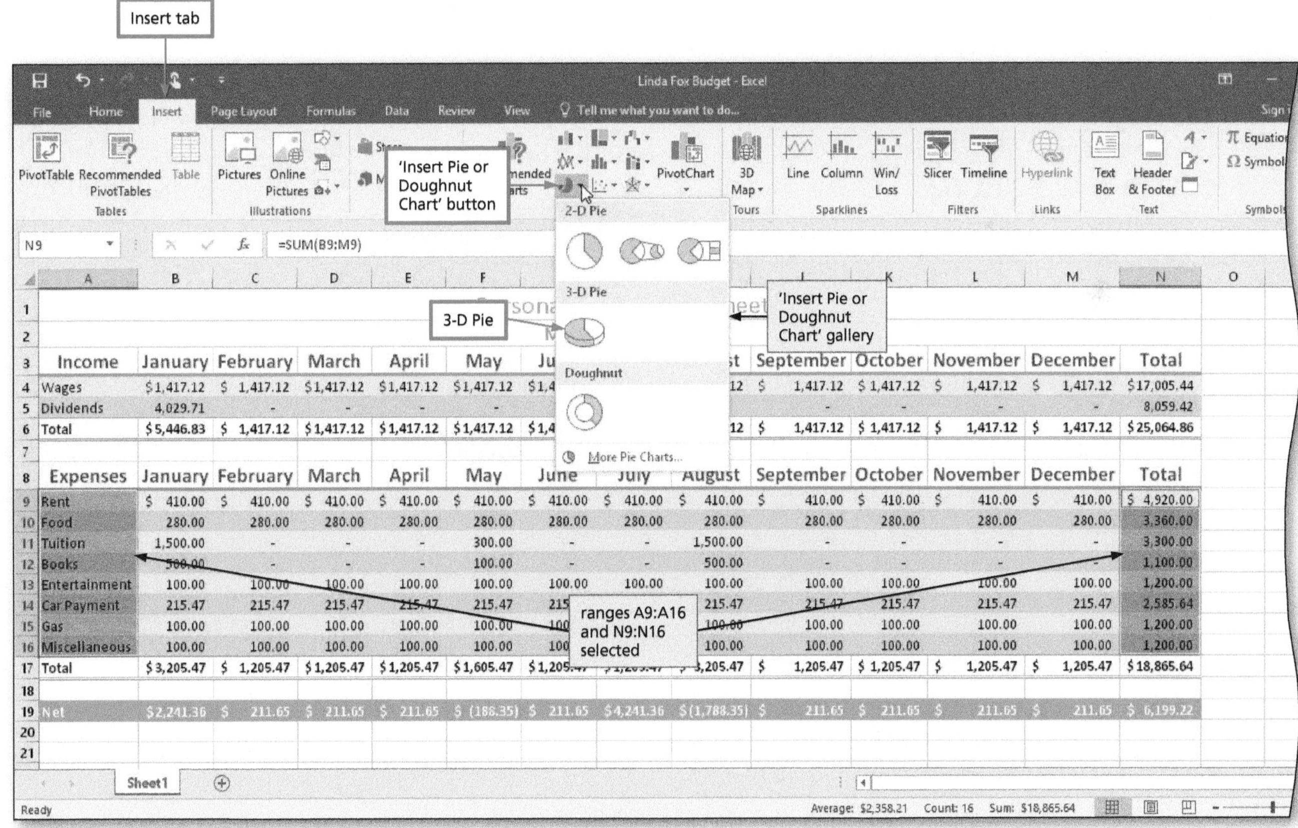

Figure 1–56

2

- Click 3-D Pie in the Insert Pie or Doughnut Chart gallery to insert the chart in the worksheet (Figure 1–57).

Q&A Why have new tabs appeared on the ribbon?

The new tabs provide additional options and functionality when you are working with certain objects, such as charts, and only display when you are working with those objects.

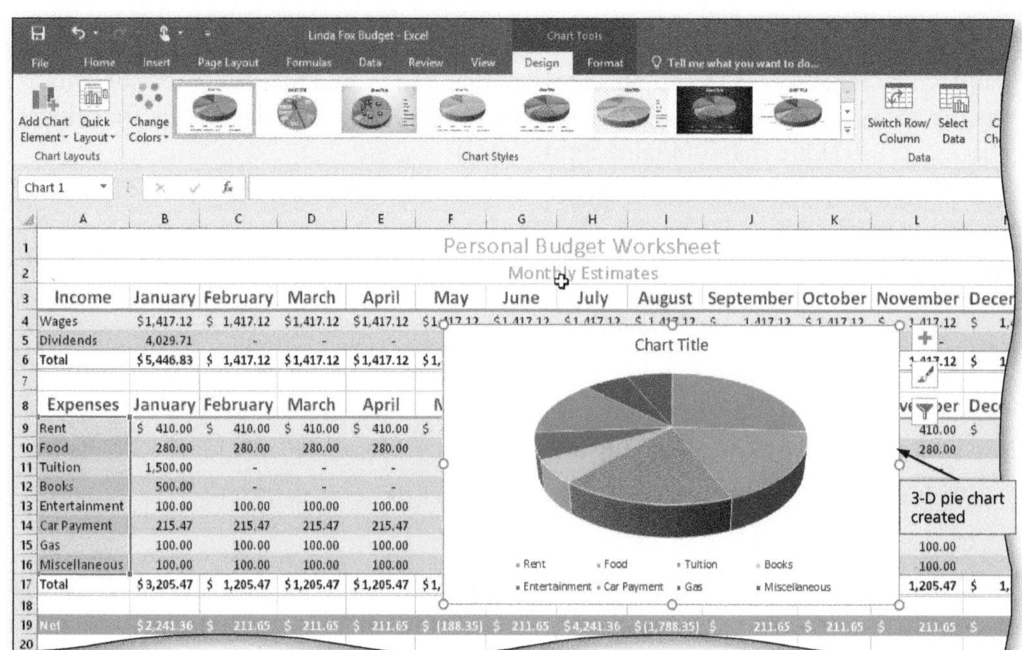

Figure 1–57

3

- Click and drag to select all the text in the chart title.
- Type `Monthly Expenses` to specify the title.
- Deselect the chart title to view the new title (Figure 1–58).

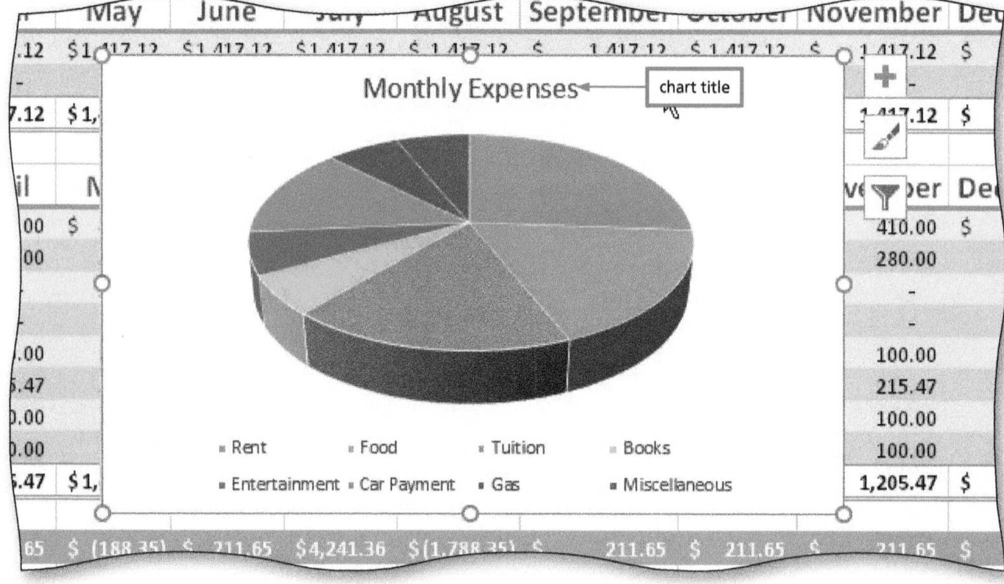

Figure 1–58

To Apply a Style to a Chart

1 ENTER TEXT | 2 CALCULATE SUMS & USE FORMULAS | 3 FORMAT TEXT
4 INSERT CHART | 5 NAME TAB | 6 PREVIEW & PRINT WORKSHEET

Why? *If you want to enhance the appearance of a chart, you can apply a chart style.* The following steps apply Style 5 to the 3-D pie chart.

1

- Click the Chart Styles button to display the Chart Styles gallery.
- Scroll in the Chart Style gallery to display the Style 5 chart style (Figure 1–59).

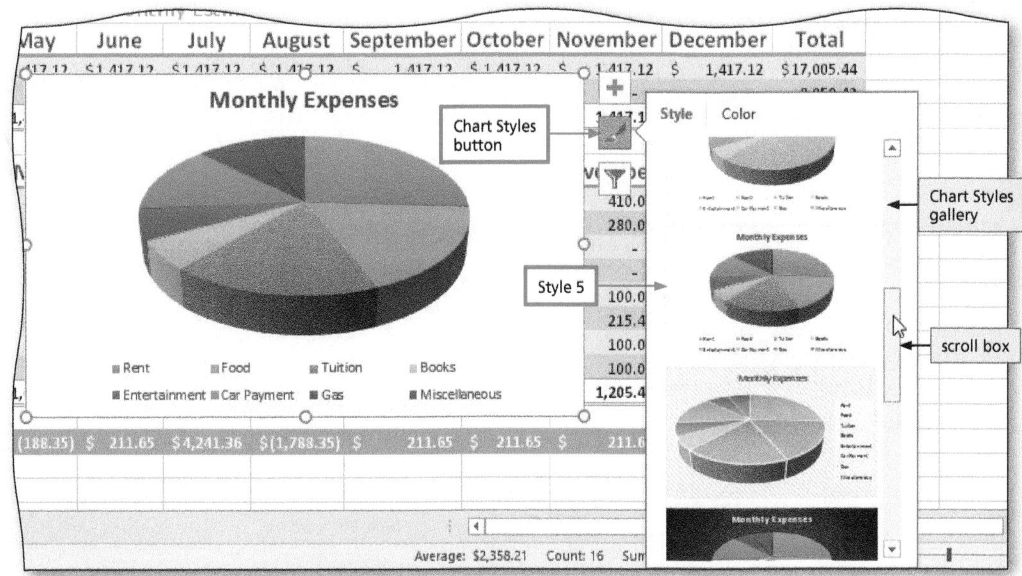

Figure 1–59

2

- Click Style 5 in the Chart Styles gallery to change the chart style to Style 5 (Figure 1–60).

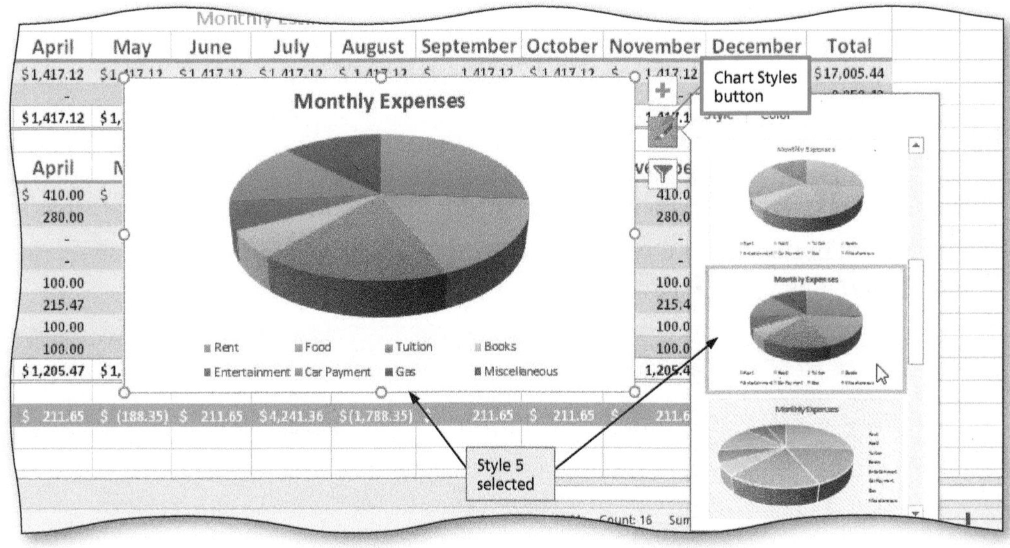

Figure 1–60

- Click the Chart Styles button to close the Chart Styles gallery.

Changing the Sheet Tab Names

The sheet tabs at the bottom of the window allow you to navigate between any worksheet in the workbook. You click the sheet tab of the worksheet you want to view in the Excel window. By default, the worksheets are named Sheet1, Sheet2, and so on. The worksheet names become increasingly important as you move toward more sophisticated workbooks, especially workbooks in which you reference cells between worksheets.

BTW

Exploding a Pie Chart

If you want to draw attention to a particular slice in a pie chart, you can offset the slice so that it stands out from the rest. A pie chart with one or more slices offset is referred to as an exploded pie chart. To offset a slice, click the slice two times to select it (do not double-click) and then drag the slice outward.

To Move a Chart to a New Sheet

Why? By moving a chart to its own sheet, the size of the chart will increase, which can improve readability. The following steps move the 3-D pie chart to a chart sheet named, Monthly Expenses.

1

- Click the Move Chart button (Chart Tools Design tab | Location group) to display the Move Chart dialog box (Figure 1–61).

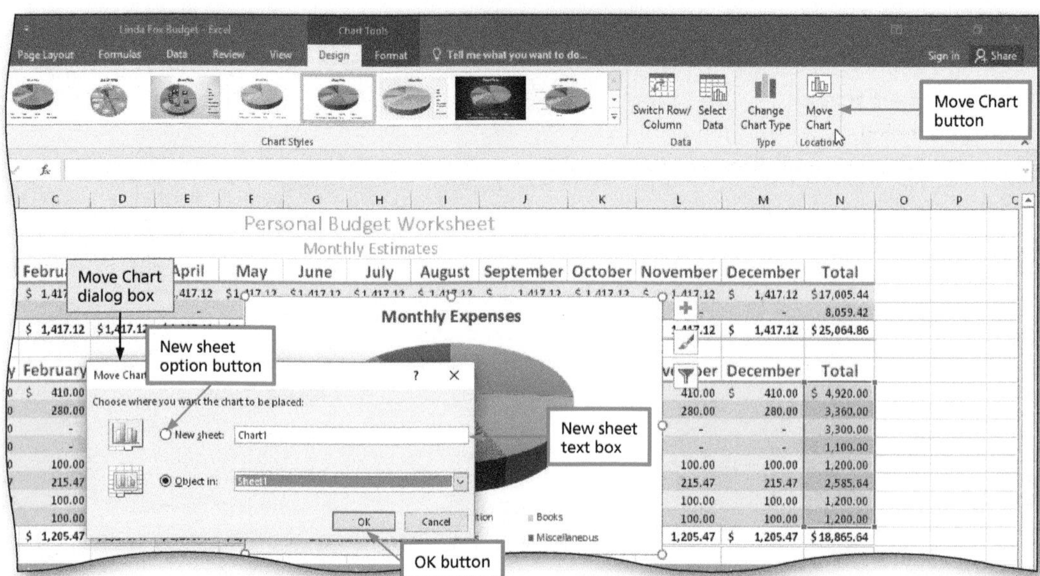

Figure 1–61

2

- Click New sheet to select it (Move Chart dialog box) and then type `Monthly Expense Chart` in the New sheet text box to enter a sheet tab name for the worksheet that will contain the chart.
- Click the OK button (Move Chart dialog box) to move the chart to a new chart sheet with the sheet tab name, Monthly Expense Chart (Figure 1–62).

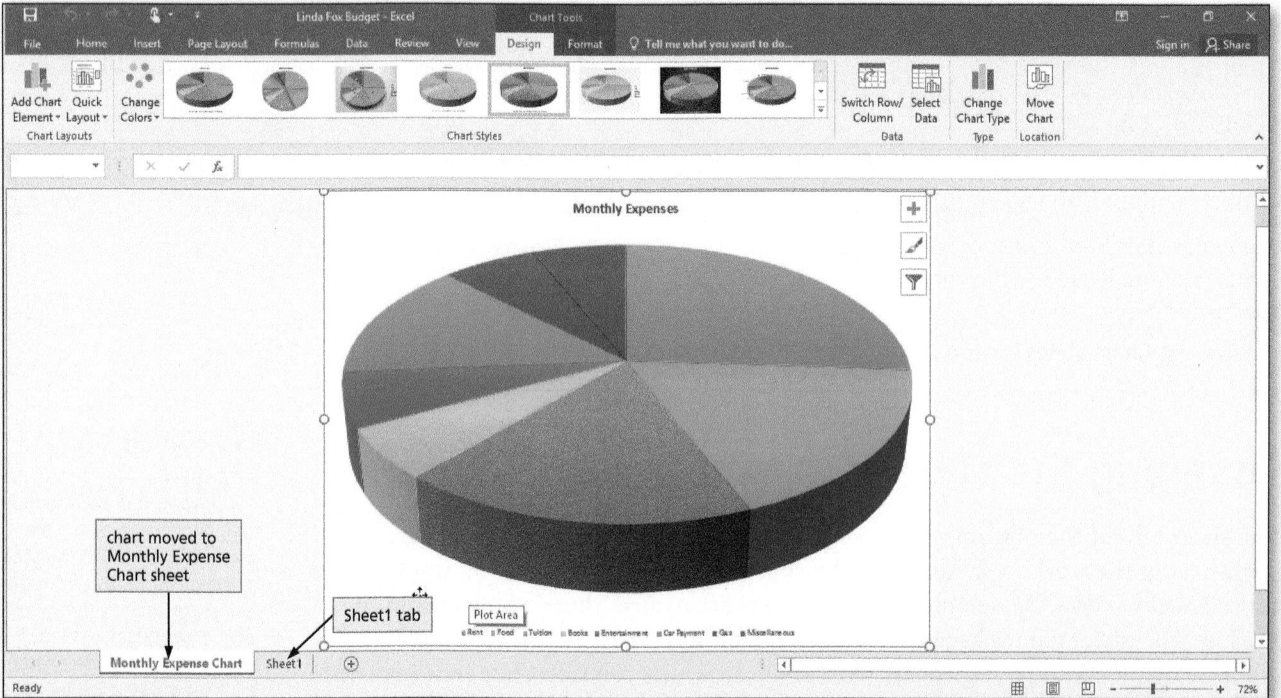

Figure 1–62

To Change the Sheet Tab Name

You decide to change the name of the Sheet1 tab to Monthly Finances. ***Why?** Use simple, meaningful names for each sheet tab. Sheet tab names often match the worksheet title. If a worksheet includes multiple titles in multiple sections of the worksheet, use a sheet tab name that encompasses the meaning of all of the sections.* The following steps rename the sheet tab.

1

- Double-click the sheet tab labeled Sheet1 in the lower-left corner of the window.
- Type `Monthly Finances` as the sheet tab name and then press the ENTER key to assign the new name to the sheet tab (Figure 1–63).

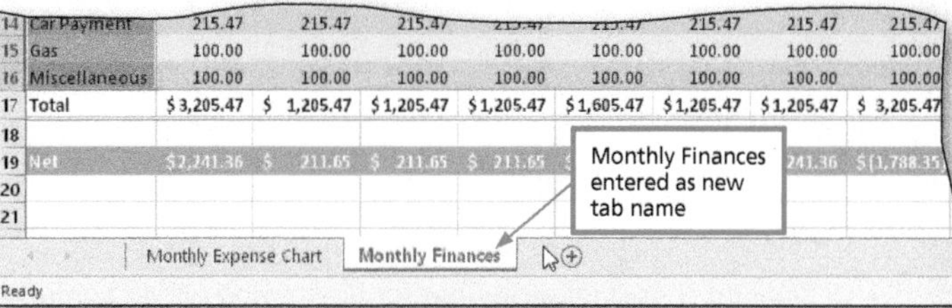

Figure 1–63

Q&A What is the maximum length for a sheet tab name?
Sheet tab names can be up to 31 characters (including spaces) in length. Longer worksheet names, however, mean that fewer sheet tabs will display on your screen. If you have multiple worksheets with long sheet tab names, you may have to scroll through sheet tabs.

2

- Right-click the sheet tab labeled, Monthly Finances, in the lower-left corner of the window to display a shortcut menu.
- Point to Tab Color on the shortcut menu to display the Tab Color gallery (Figure 1–64).

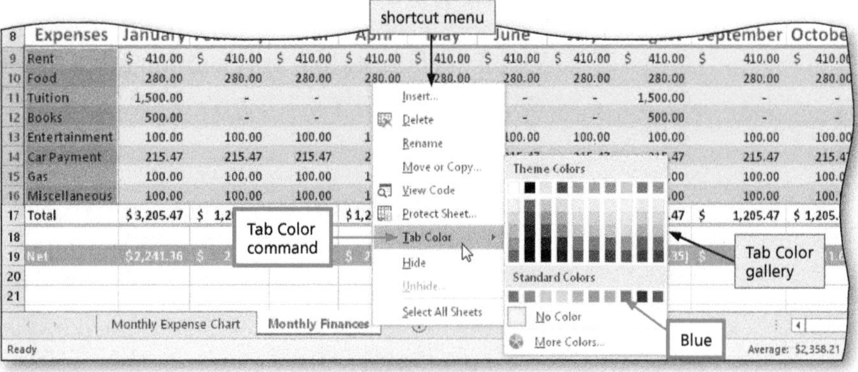

Figure 1–64

3

- Click a color that matches your shirt in the Theme Colors area to change the color of the tab (Figure 1–65).
- If necessary, click Home on the ribbon to display the Home tab.
- Save the workbook again on the same storage location with the same file name.

Q&A Why should I save the workbook again?
You have made several modifications to the workbook since you last saved it. Thus, you should save it again.

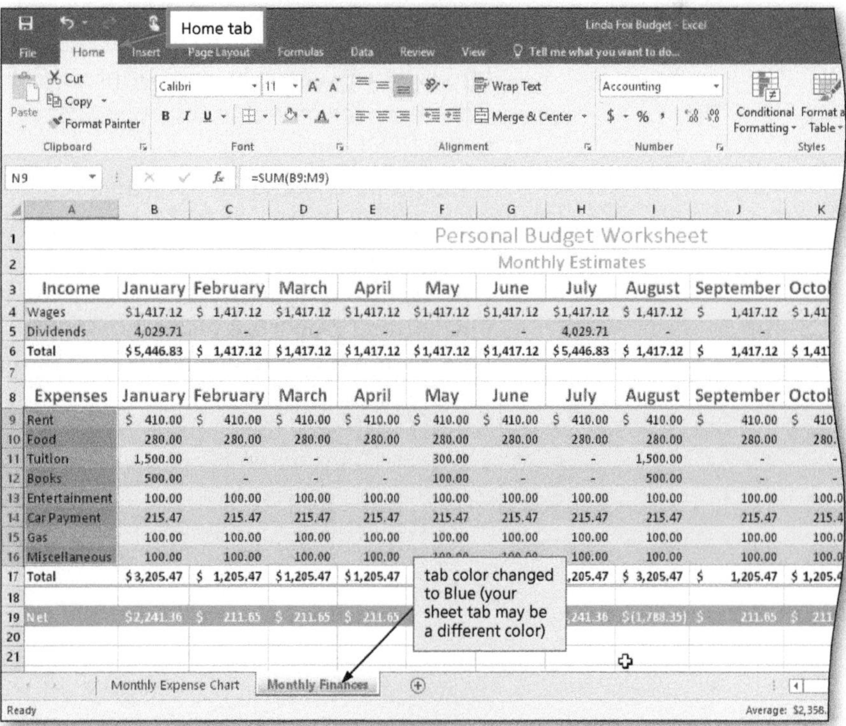

Figure 1–65

Document Properties

Excel helps you organize and identify your files by using **document properties,** which are the details about a file such as the project author, title, and subject. For example, you could use the class name or topic to describe the workbook's purpose or content in the document properties.

CONSIDER THIS

Why would you want to assign document properties to a workbook?
Document properties are valuable for a variety of reasons:

- Users can save time locating a particular file because they can view a file's document properties without opening the workbook.
- By creating consistent properties for files having similar content, users can better organize their workbooks.
- Some organizations require Excel users to add document properties so that other employees can view details about these files.

Common document properties include standard properties and those that are automatically updated. **Standard properties** are associated with all Microsoft Office files and include author, title, and subject. **Automatically updated properties** include file system properties, such as the date you create or change a file, and statistics, such as the file size.

To Change Document Properties

To change document properties, you would follow these steps.

1. Click File on the ribbon to open the Backstage view and then, if necessary, click the Info tab in the Backstage view to display the Info gallery. The Properties list is found in the right pane of the Info gallery.
2. If the property you wish to change is in the Properties list, click to the right of the property category to display a text box. (Note that not all properties are editable.) Type the desired text for the property and then click anywhere in the Info gallery to enter the data, or press TAB to navigate to the next property. Click the Back button in the upper-left corner of the Backstage view to return to the Excel window.
3. If the property you wish to change is not in the Properties list or you cannot edit it, click the Properties button to display the Properties menu, and then click Advanced Properties to display the Summary tab in the Properties dialog box. Type your desired text in the appropriate property text boxes. Click the OK button (Properties dialog box) to close the dialog box and then click the Back button in the upper-left corner of the Backstage view to return to the workbook.

Q&A

Why do some of the document properties in my Properties dialog box contain data?
Depending on where you are using Office 2016, your school, university, or place of employment may have customized the properties.

Printing a Worksheet

After creating a worksheet, you may want to print it. Printing a worksheet enables you to distribute the worksheet to others in a form that can be read or viewed but not edited. It is a good practice to save a workbook before printing a worksheet, in the event you experience difficulties printing.

CONSIDER THIS

What is the best method for distributing a workbook?

The traditional method of distributing a workbook uses a printer to produce a hard copy. A **hard copy** or **printout** is information that exists on paper. Hard copies can be useful for the following reasons:

- Some people prefer proofreading a hard copy of a workbook rather than viewing it on the screen to check for errors and readability.
- Hard copies can serve as a backup reference if your storage medium is lost or becomes corrupted and you need to recreate the workbook.

Instead of distributing a hard copy of a workbook, users can distribute the workbook as an electronic image that mirrors the original workbook's appearance. An electronic image of a workbook is not an editable file; it simply displays a picture of the workbook. The electronic image of the workbook can be sent as an email attachment, posted on a website, or copied to a portable storage medium such as a USB flash drive. Two popular electronic image formats, sometimes called fixed formats, are PDF by Adobe Systems and XPS by Microsoft. In Excel, you can create electronic image files through the Save As dialog box and the Export, Share, and Print tabs in the Backstage view. Electronic images of workbooks, such as PDF and XPS, can be useful for the following reasons:

- Users can view electronic images of workbooks without the software that created the original workbook (e.g., Excel). Specifically, to view a PDF file, you use a program called Adobe Reader, which can be downloaded free from Adobe's website. Similarly, to view an XPS file, you use a program called XPS Viewer, which is included in the latest version of Windows.
- Sending electronic workbooks saves paper and printer supplies. Society encourages users to contribute to **green computing**, which involves reducing the electricity consumed and environmental waste generated when using computers, mobile devices, and related technologies.

To Preview and Print a Worksheet in Landscape Orientation

1 ENTER TEXT | 2 CALCULATE SUMS & USE FORMULAS | 3 FORMAT TEXT
4 INSERT CHART | 5 NAME TAB | **6 PREVIEW & PRINT WORKSHEET**

Pages printed in **portrait orientation** have the short (8½") edge at the top of the printout; the printed page is taller than it is wide. **Landscape orientation** prints the long (11") edge at the top of the paper; the printed page is wider than it is tall. With the completed workbook saved, you may want to print it. ***Why?*** *Because the worksheet is included in a report delivered in person, you will print a hard copy on a printer.* The following steps print a hard copy of the contents of the worksheet.

- Click File on the ribbon to open the Backstage view.
- Click the Print tab in the Backstage view to display the Print gallery (Figure 1–66).

Q&A

How can I print multiple copies of my worksheet?
Increase the number in the Copies box in the Print gallery.

What if I decide not to print the worksheet at this time?
Click the Back button in the upper-left corner of the Backstage view to return to the workbook window.

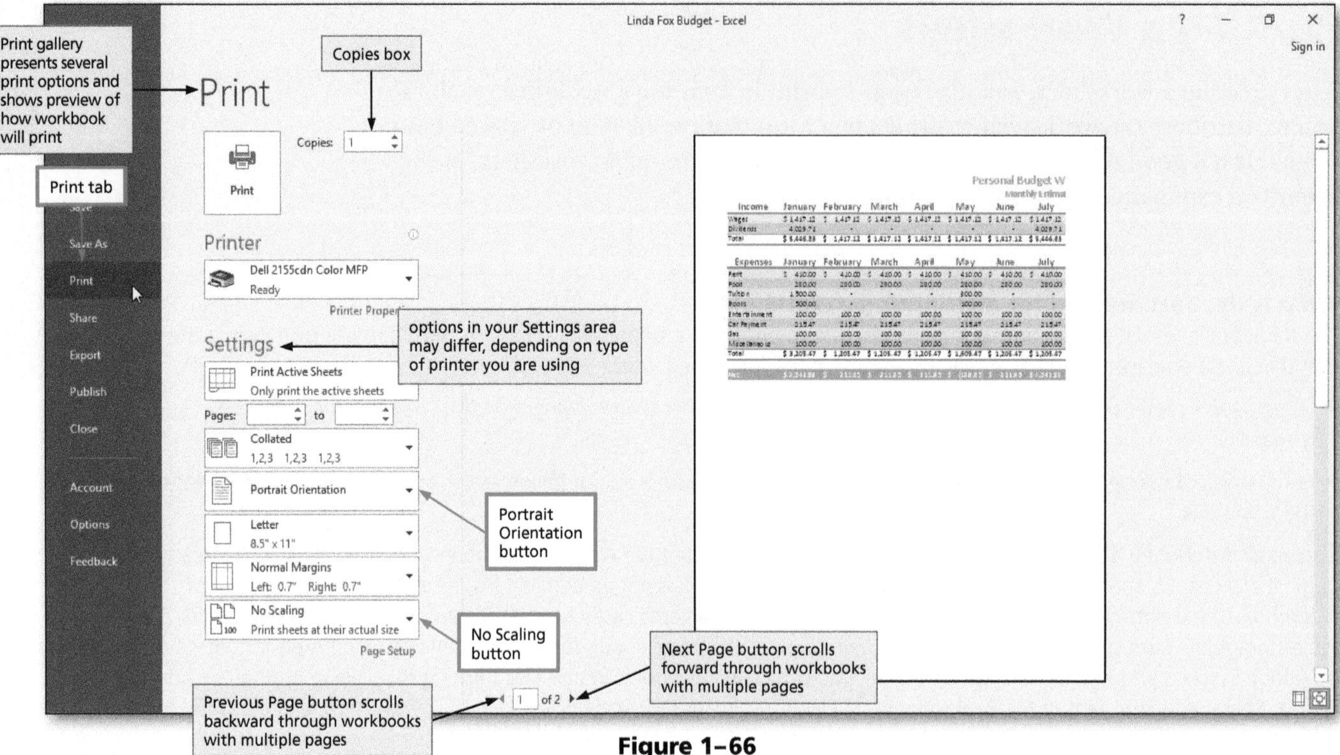

Figure 1–66

2

- Verify that the printer listed on the Printer Status button will print a hard copy of the workbook. If necessary, click the Printer Status button to display a list of available printer options and then click the desired printer to change the currently selected printer.

3

- Click the Portrait Orientation button in the Settings area and then select Landscape Orientation to change the orientation of the page to landscape.
- Click the No Scaling button and then select 'Fit Sheet on One Page' to print the entire worksheet on one page (Figure 1–67).

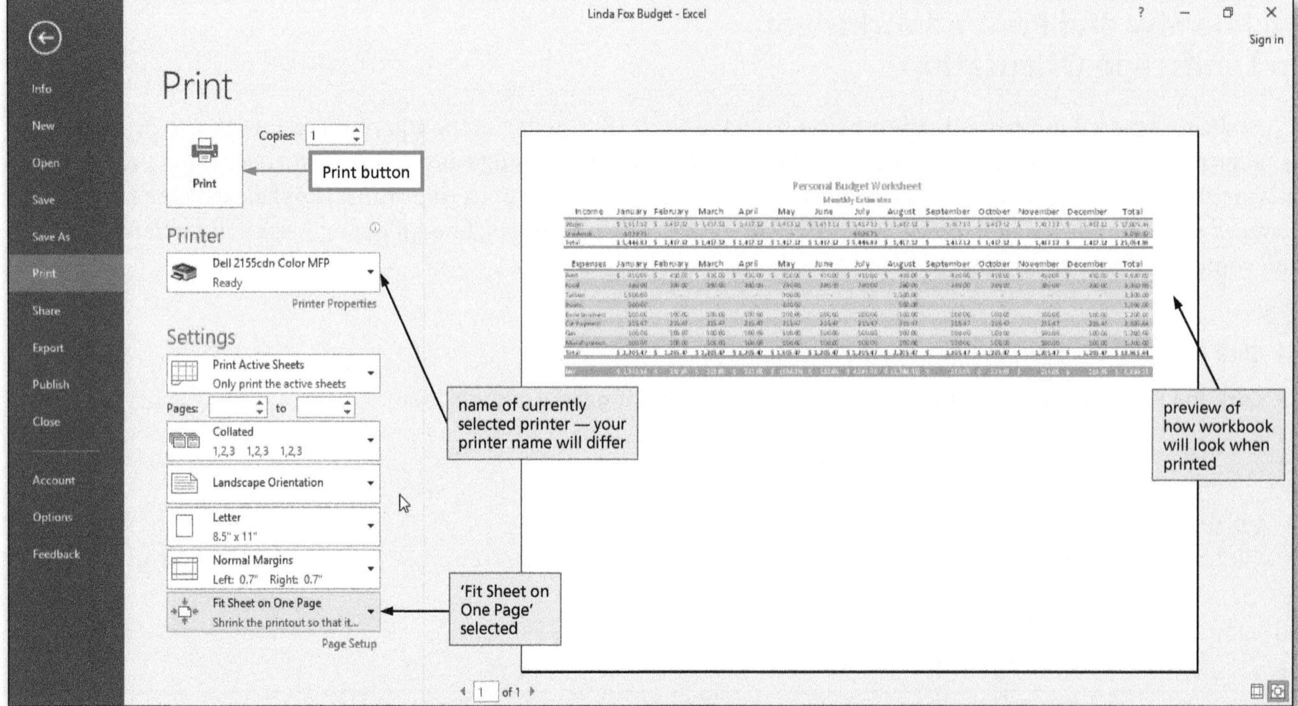

Figure 1–67

4

- Click the Print button in the Print gallery to print the worksheet in landscape orientation on the currently selected printer.
- When the printer stops, retrieve the hard copy (Figure 1–68).

Q&A
Do I have to wait until my worksheet is complete to print it?
No, you can print a document at any time while you are creating it.

Personal Budget Worksheet

Monthly Estimates

Income	January	February	March	April	May	June	July	August	September	October	November	December	Total
Wages	$ 1,417.12	$ 1,417.12	$ 1,417.12	$ 1,417.12	$ 1,417.12	$ 1,417.12	$ 1,417.12	$ 1,417.12	$ 1,417.12	$ 1,417.12	$ 1,417.12	$ 1,417.12	$ 17,005.44
Dividends	4,029.71	-	-	-	-	-	4,029.71	-	-	-	-	-	8,059.42
Total	**$ 5,446.83**	**$ 1,417.12**	**$ 1,417.12**	**$ 1,417.12**	**$ 1,417.12**	**$ 1,417.12**	**$ 5,446.83**	**$ 1,417.12**	**$ 1,417.12**	**$ 1,417.12**	**$ 1,417.12**	**$ 1,417.12**	**$ 25,064.86**

Expenses	January	February	March	April	May	June	July	August	September	October	November	December	Total
Rent	$ 410.00	$ 410.00	$ 410.00	$ 410.00	$ 410.00	$ 410.00	$ 410.00	$ 410.00	$ 410.00	$ 410.00	$ 410.00	$ 410.00	$ 4,920.00
Food	280.00	280.00	280.00	280.00	280.00	280.00	280.00	280.00	280.00	280.00	280.00	280.00	3,360.00
Tuition	1,500.00	-	-	-	300.00	-	-	1,500.00	-	-	-	-	3,300.00
Books	500.00	-	-	-	100.00	-	-	500.00	-	-	-	-	1,100.00
Entertainment	100.00	100.00	100.00	100.00	100.00	100.00	100.00	100.00	100.00	100.00	100.00	100.00	1,200.00
Car Payment	215.47	215.47	215.47	215.47	215.47	215.47	215.47	215.47	215.47	215.47	215.47	215.47	2,585.64
Gas	100.00	100.00	100.00	100.00	100.00	100.00	100.00	100.00	100.00	100.00	100.00	100.00	1,200.00
Miscellaneous	100.00	100.00	100.00	100.00	100.00	100.00	100.00	100.00	100.00	100.00	100.00	100.00	1,200.00
Total	**$ 3,205.47**	**$ 1,205.47**	**$ 1,205.47**	**$ 1,205.47**	**$ 1,605.47**	**$ 1,205.47**	**$ 1,205.47**	**$ 3,205.47**	**$ 1,205.47**	**$ 1,205.47**	**$ 1,205.47**	**$ 1,205.47**	**$ 18,865.64**
Net	$ 2,241.36	$ 211.65	$ 211.65	$ 211.65	$ (188.35)	$ 211.65	$ 4,241.36	$ (1,788.35)	$ 211.65	$ 211.65	$ 211.65	$ 211.65	$ 6,199.22

Figure 1–68

Other Ways

1. Press CTRL+P to open Print Gallery, press ENTER

Autocalculate

You easily can obtain a total, an average, or other information about the numbers in a range by using the **AutoCalculate area** on the status bar. First, select the range of cells containing the numbers you want to check. Next, right-click the AutoCalculate area to display the Customize Status Bar shortcut menu (Figure 1–69). The check marks indicate that the calculations are displayed in the status bar; more than one may be selected. The functions of the AutoCalculate commands on the Customize Status Bar shortcut menu are described in Table 1–4.

Table 1–4 Commonly Used Status Bar Commands

Command	Function
Average	AutoCalculate area displays the average of the numbers in the selected range
Count	AutoCalculate area displays the number of non-empty cells in the selected range
Numerical Count	AutoCalculate area displays the number of cells containing numbers in the selected range
Minimum	AutoCalculate area displays the lowest value in the selected range
Maximum	AutoCalculate area displays the highest value in the selected range
Sum	AutoCalculate area displays the sum of the numbers in the selected range

BTW

Distributing a Workbook

Instead of printing and distributing a hard copy of a workbook, you can distribute the workbook electronically. Options include sending the workbook via email; posting it on cloud storage (such as OneDrive) and sharing the file with others; posting it on social media, a blog, or other website; and sharing a link associated with an online location of the workbook. You also can create and share a PDF or XPS image of the workbook, so that users can view the file in Acrobat Reader or XPS Viewer instead of in Excel.

To Use the AutoCalculate Area to Determine a Maximum

The following steps determine the largest monthly total in the budget. ***Why?*** *Sometimes, you want a quick analysis, which can be especially helpful when your worksheet contains a lot of data.*

- Select the range B19:M19. Right-click the status bar to display the Customize Status Bar shortcut menu (Figure 1–69).

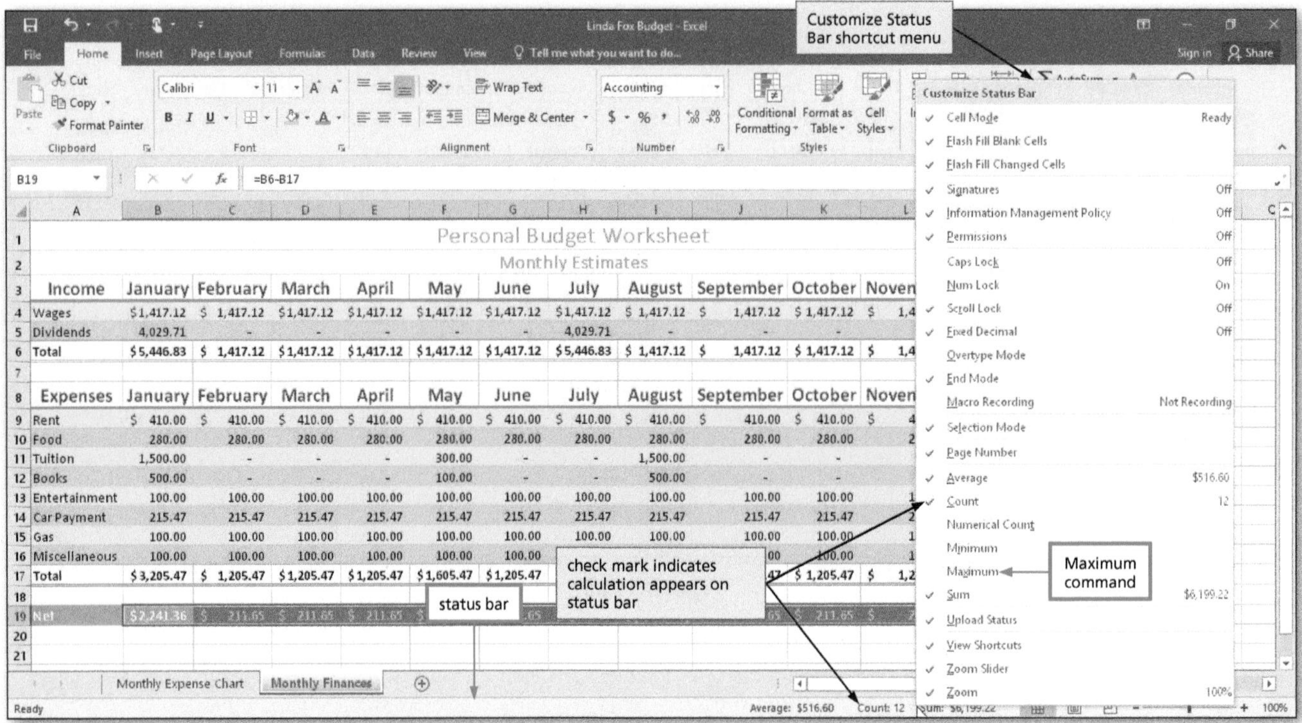

Figure 1–69

- Click Maximum on the shortcut menu to display the Maximum value in the range B19:M19 in the AutoCalculate area of the status bar.
- Click anywhere on the worksheet to close the shortcut menu (Figure 1–70).

maximum value displayed in AutoCalculate area

Figure 1–70

- Right-click the AutoCalculate area and then click Maximum on the shortcut menu to deselect it. The Maximum value will no longer appear on the status bar.
- Close the shortcut menu.

4

- Save the workbook using the same file name in the same storage location.
- If desired, sign out of your Microsoft account.
- Exit Excel.

Correcting Errors

You can correct data entry errors on a worksheet using one of several methods. The method you choose will depend on the extent of the error and whether you notice it while entering the data or after you have entered the incorrect data into the cell.

Correcting Errors while Entering Data into a Cell

If you notice an error while you are entering data into a cell, press the BACKSPACE key to erase the incorrect character(s) and then enter the correct character(s). If the error is a major one, click the Cancel box in the formula bar or press the ESC key to erase the entire entry and then reenter the data.

Correcting Errors after Entering Data into a Cell

If you find an error in the worksheet after entering the data, you can correct the error in one of two ways:

1. If the entry is short, select the cell, retype the entry correctly, and then click the Enter button or press the ENTER key. The new entry will replace the old entry.
2. If the entry in the cell is long and the errors are minor, using Edit mode may be a better choice than retyping the cell entry. In **Edit mode**, Excel displays the active cell entry in the formula bar and a flashing insertion point in the active cell, and you can edit the contents directly in the cell — a procedure called **in-cell editing.**
   a. Double-click the cell containing the error to switch Excel to Edit mode (Figure 1–71).
   b. Make corrections using the following in-cell editing methods.
      (1) To insert new characters between two characters, place the insertion point between the two characters and begin typing. Excel inserts the new characters to the left of the insertion point.

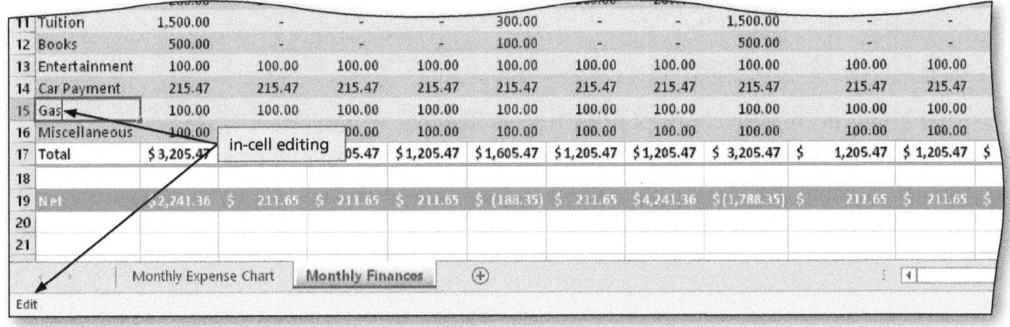

Figure 1–71

(2) To delete a character in the cell, move the insertion point to the left of the character you want to delete and then press the DELETE key, or place the insertion point to the right of the character you want to delete and then press the BACKSPACE key. You also can drag to select the character or adjacent characters you want to delete and then press the DELETE key or CTRL+X, or click the Cut button (Home tab | Clipboard group).

(3) When you are finished editing an entry, click the Enter button or press the ENTER key.

There are two ways for entering data in Edit mode: Insert mode and Overtype mode. In the default **Insert mode**, as you type a character, Excel inserts the character and moves all characters to the right of the typed character one position to the right. You can change to Overtype mode by pressing the INSERT key. In **Overtype mode**, Excel replaces, or overtypes, the character to the right of the insertion point. The INSERT key toggles the keyboard between Insert mode and Overtype mode.

While in Edit mode, you may have reason to move the insertion point to various points in the cell, select portions of the data in the cell, or switch from inserting characters to overtyping characters. Table 1–5 summarizes the more common tasks performed during in-cell editing.

Table 1–5 Summary of In-Cell Editing Tasks

	Task	Mouse Operation	Keyboard
1.	Move the insertion point to the beginning of data in a cell.	Point to the left of the first character and click.	Press HOME
2.	Move the insertion point to the end of data in a cell.	Point to the right of the last character and click.	Press END
3.	Move the insertion point anywhere in a cell.	Point to the appropriate position and click the character.	Press RIGHT ARROW or LEFT ARROW
4.	Highlight one or more adjacent characters.	Drag through adjacent characters.	Press SHIFT+RIGHT ARROW or SHIFT+LEFT ARROW
5.	Select all data in a cell.	Double-click the cell with the insertion point in the cell if the data in the cell contains no spaces.	
6.	Delete selected characters.	Click the Cut button (Home tab | Clipboard group).	Press DELETE
7.	Delete characters to the left of the insertion point.		Press BACKSPACE
8.	Delete characters to the right of the insertion point.		Press DELETE
9.	Toggle between Insert and Overtype modes.		Press INSERT

Undoing the Last Cell Entry

The Undo button on the Quick Access Toolbar (Figure 1–72) allows you to erase recent cell entries. Thus, if you enter incorrect data in a cell and notice it immediately, click the Undo button and Excel changes the cell entry to what it was prior to the incorrect data entry.

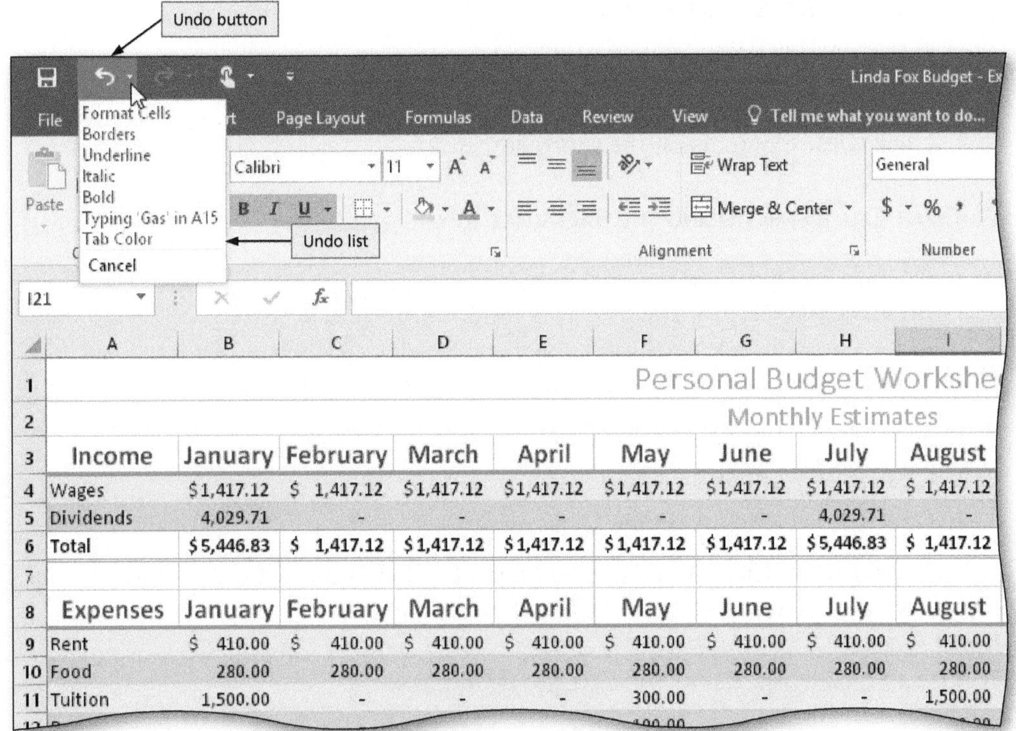

Figure 1–72

Excel remembers the last 100 actions you have completed. Thus, you can undo up to 100 previous actions by clicking the Undo arrow to display the Undo list and then clicking the action to be undone (Figure 1–72). You can drag through several actions in the Undo list to undo all of them at once. If no actions are available for Excel to undo, then the dimmed appearance of the Undo button indicates that it is unavailable.

The Redo button, next to the Undo button on the Quick Access Toolbar, allows you to repeat previous actions; that is, if you accidentally undo an action, you can use the Redo button to perform the action again.

Clearing a Cell or Range of Cells

If you enter data into the wrong cell or range of cells, you can erase, or clear, the data using one of the first four methods listed below. The fifth method clears the formatting from the selected cells. To clear a cell or range of cells, you would perform the following steps:

To Clear Cell Entries Using the Fill Handle

1. Select the cell or range of cells and then point to the fill handle so that the pointer changes to a crosshair.
2. Drag the fill handle back into the selected cell or range until a shadow covers the cell or cells you want to erase.

To Clear Cell Entries Using the Shortcut Menu

1. Select the cell or range of cells to be cleared.
2. Right-click the selection.
3. Click Clear Contents on the shortcut menu.

To Clear Cell Entries Using the Backspace Key

1. Select the cell or range of cells to be cleared.
2. Press the BACKSPACE key.

To Clear Cell Entries and Formatting Using the Clear Button

1. Select the cell or range of cells to be cleared.
2. Click the Clear button (Home tab | Editing group).
3. Click Clear Contents on the Clear menu.

Note that the Clear All command on the Clear menu is the only command that clears both the cell entry and the cell formatting.

To Clear Formatting Using the Cell Styles Button

1. Select the cell or range of cells from which you want to remove the formatting.
2. Click the Cell Styles button (Home tab | Styles group) and then click Normal in the Cell Styles gallery.

As you are clearing cell entries, always remember that you should *never press the SPACEBAR to clear a cell.* Pressing the SPACEBAR enters a blank character. A blank character is interpreted by Excel as text and is different from an empty cell, even though the cell may appear empty.

Clearing the Entire Worksheet

If the required worksheet edits are extremely extensive or if the requirements drastically change, you may want to clear the entire worksheet and start over. To clear the worksheet or delete an embedded chart, you would use the following steps.

To Clear the Entire Worksheet

1. Click the Select All button on the worksheet. The Select All button is located above the row 1 identifier and to the left of the column A heading.
2. Click the Clear button (Home tab | Editing group) and then click Clear All on the menu to delete both the entries and formats.

The Select All button selects the entire worksheet. Instead of clicking the Select All button, you can press CTRL+A. To clear an unsaved workbook, click the Close Window button on the workbook's title bar or click the Close button in the Backstage view. Click the No button if the Microsoft Excel dialog box asks if you want to save changes. To start a new, blank workbook, click the New button in the Backstage view.

Summary

In this module you have learned how to create a personal budget worksheet and chart. Topics covered included selecting a cell, entering text, entering numbers, calculating a sum, using the fill handle, formatting a worksheet, adding a pie chart, changing sheet tab names, printing a worksheet, AutoCalculate, and correcting errors.

CONSIDER THIS: PLAN AHEAD

What decisions will you need to make when creating workbooks and charts in the future?

1. Determine the workbook structure.
   a) Determine the data you will need for your workbook.
   b) Sketch a layout of your data and your chart.
2. Create the worksheet.
   a) Enter titles, subtitles, and headings.
   b) Enter data, functions, and formulas.
3. Format the worksheet.
   a) Format the titles, subtitles, and headings using styles.
   b) Format the totals.
   c) Format the numbers.
   d) Format the text.
   e) Adjust column widths.
4. Create the chart.
   a) Determine the type of chart to use.
   b) Determine the chart title and data.
   c) Format the chart.

Apply Your Knowledge

Reinforce the skills and apply the concepts you learned in this module.

Changing the Values in a Worksheet

Note: To complete this assignment, you will be required to use the Data Files. Please contact your instructor for information about accessing the required files.

Instructions: Run Excel. Open the workbook Apply 1–1 Lima Wholesale (Figure 1–73a). The workbook you open contains sales data for Lima Wholesale. You are to apply formatting to the worksheet and move the chart to a new sheet tab.

Table 1–6 New Worksheet Data

Cell	Change Cell Contents To
A2	Monthly Departmental Sales
B5	15242.36
C7	114538.23
D5	25747.85
E6	39851.44
F7	29663.77
G6	19885.41

Perform the following tasks:

1. Make the changes to the worksheet described in Table 1–6 so that the worksheet appears as shown in Figure 1–73b. As you edit the values in the cells containing numeric data, watch the totals in row 8, the totals in column H, and the chart change.
2. Change the worksheet title in cell A1 to the Title cell style and then merge and center it across columns A through H.
3. Use buttons in the Font group on the Home tab on the ribbon to change the worksheet subtitle in cell A2 to 16-point font and then center it across columns A through H. Change the font color of cell A2 to Dark Blue, Text 2, Darker 25%.
4. Apply the worksheet name, Monthly Sales, and the Dark Blue, Text 2, Darker 25% color to the sheet tab.
5. Move the chart to a new sheet called Sales Analysis Chart (Figure 1–73c). Change the chart title to SALES TOTALS.
6. If requested by your instructor, replace Lima in cell A1 with your last name.
7. Save the workbook using the file name, Apply 1–1 Lima Wholesale Sales Analysis.
8. Submit the revised workbook as specified by your instructor and exit Excel.
9. Besides the styles used in the worksheet, what other changes could you make to enhance the worksheet?

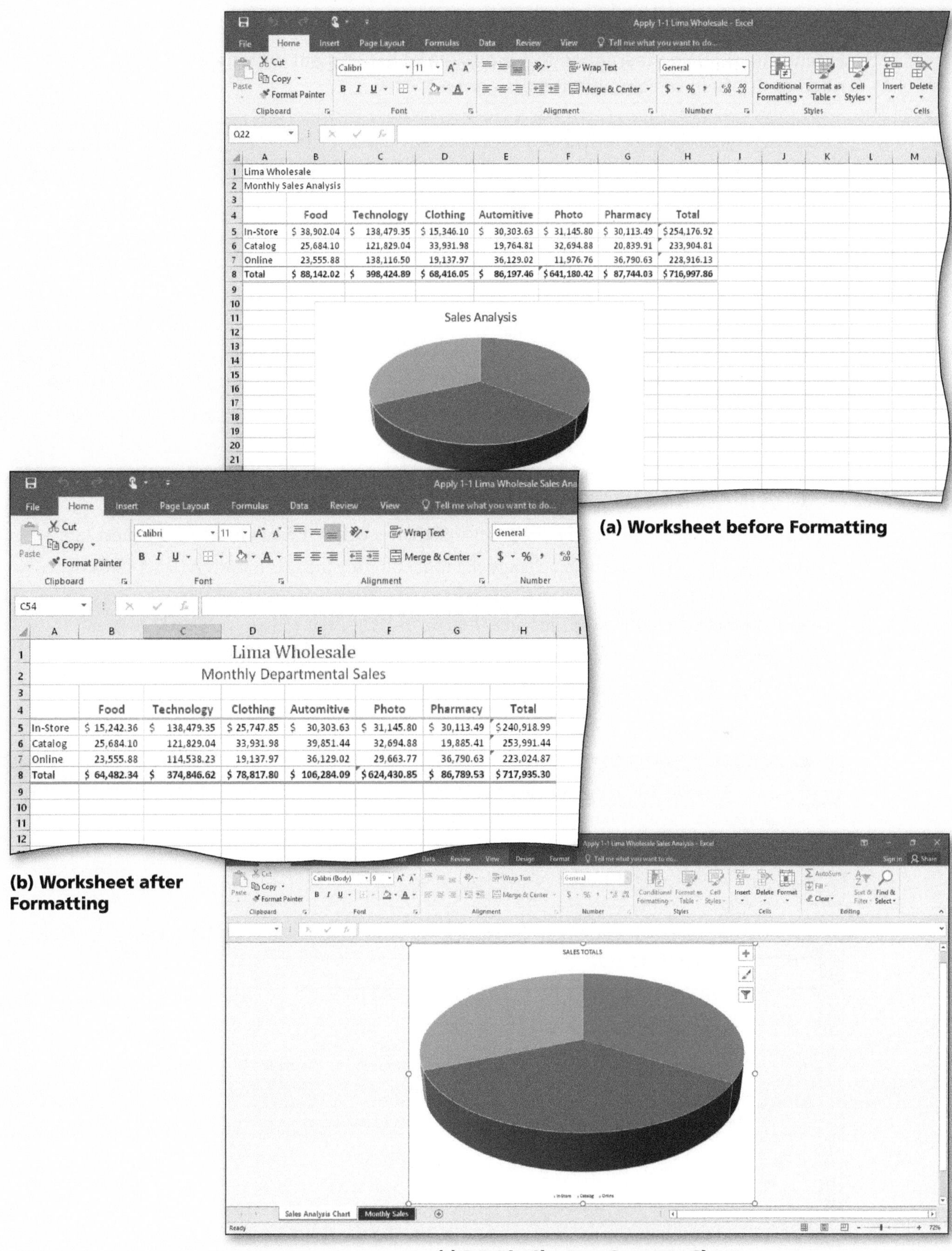

(a) Worksheet before Formatting

(b) Worksheet after Formatting

(c) 3-D Pie Chart on Separate Sheet

Figure 1–73

Extend Your Knowledge

Extend the skills you learned in this module and experiment with new skills. You may need to use Help to complete the assignment.

Creating Styles and Formatting a Worksheet

Note: To complete this assignment, you will be required to use the Data Files. Please contact your instructor for information about accessing the required files.

Instructions: Run Excel. Open the workbook Extend 1–1 Dasminne Grocery (Figure 1–74). The workbook you open contains sales data for Dasminne Grocery. You are to create styles and format a worksheet using them.

Perform the following tasks:

1. Select cell A4. Use the New Cell Style command in the Cell Styles gallery to create a style that uses the Blue, Accent 1, Darker 50% font color (row 6, column 5). Name the style, MyHeadings.
2. Select cell A5. Use the New Cell style dialog box to create a style that uses the Blue, Accent 1, Darker 25% (row 5, column 5) font color. Name the style, MyRows.
3. Select cell ranges B4:G4 and A5:A8. Apply the MyHeadings style to the cell ranges.
4. Select the cell range B5:G7. Apply the MyRows style to the cell range.
5. Apply a worksheet name to the sheet tab and apply a color of your choice to the sheet tab.
6. If requested by your instructor, change the font color for the text in cells A1 and A2 to the color of your eyes, if available.
7. Save the workbook using the file name, Extend 1–1 Dasminne Grocery Third Quarter.
8. Submit the revised workbook as specified by your instructor and exit Excel.
9. What other styles would you create to improve the worksheet's appearance?

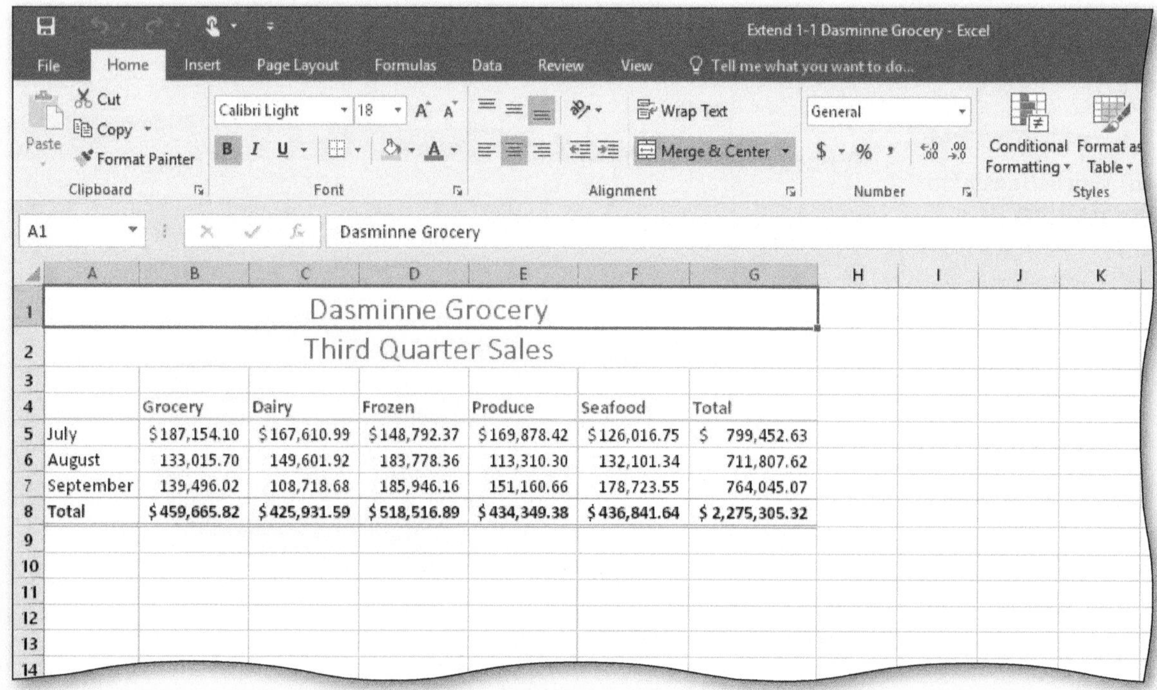

	A	B	C	D	E	F	G
1	Dasminne Grocery						
2	Third Quarter Sales						
3							
4		Grocery	Dairy	Frozen	Produce	Seafood	Total
5	July	$187,154.10	$167,610.99	$148,792.37	$169,878.42	$126,016.75	$ 799,452.63
6	August	133,015.70	149,601.92	183,778.36	113,310.30	132,101.34	711,807.62
7	September	139,496.02	108,718.68	185,946.16	151,160.66	178,723.55	764,045.07
8	Total	$459,665.82	$425,931.59	$518,516.89	$434,349.38	$436,841.64	$ 2,275,305.32

Figure 1–74

Expand Your World

Create a solution that uses cloud or web technologies by learning and investigating on your own from general guidance.

College Loan Calculator

Instructions: You are tasked with determining how long it will take you to pay back your college loans. You decide to download and use one of Excel's templates to create your worksheet.

Perform the following tasks:

1. Click the New tab in the Backstage view and then search for and click the College loan calculator template to download it.
2. Enter data for your estimated salary after graduation, the date you will begin paying back loans, as well as fictitious (but realistic) information for four loans, including loan number, lender, loan amount, annual interest rate, beginning date, and length (in years).
3. Save the file as Expand 1-1: College Loans. Print the worksheet.
4. Submit the assignment as specified by your instructor.
5. Which template would you use if you wanted to plan and keep track of a budget for a wedding?

In the Labs

Design, create, modify, and/or use a workbook following the guidelines, concepts, and skills presented in this module. Labs 1 and 2, which increase in difficulty, require you to create solutions based on what you learned in the module; Lab 3 requires you to apply your creative thinking and problem-solving skills to design and implement a solution.

Lab 1: First Quarter Revenue Analysis Worksheet

Problem: You work as a spreadsheet specialist for Katie's Kicks, which has four regional shops in the state of Florida. Your manager has asked you to develop a first quarter revenue analysis similar to the one shown in Figure 1–75.

Perform the following tasks:

1. Run Excel and create a new blank workbook. Enter the worksheet title, Katie's Kicks, in cell A1 and the worksheet subtitle, First Quarter Revenue Analysis, in cell A2. Beginning in row 4, enter the region data shown in Table 1–7.

Table 1–7 Katie's Kicks

	North	South	East	West
Sneakers	72714.58	77627.29	76607.31	49008.32
Shoes	45052.23	69165.66	76243.41	84844.01
Sandals	77630.94	78684.24	56601.25	72716.68
Accessories	65423.73	77690.69	58383.67	54433.07
Miscellaneous	55666.92	78618.97	47317.09	68594.40

2. Create totals for each region, product, and company grand total.
3. Format the worksheet title with the Title cell style. Center the title across columns A through F.

Continued >

In the Labs *continued*

4. Format the worksheet subtitle to 16-point Calibri Light, and change the font color to Blue-Gray, Text 2. Center the subtitle across columns A through F.
5. Use Cell Styles to format the range A4:F4 with the Heading 3 cell style, the range B4:F4 with the Accent1 cell style, and the range A10:F10 with the Total cell style.
6. Center the column titles in row 4. Apply the accounting number format to the ranges B5:F5 and B10:F10. Apply the comma style format to the range B6:F9. Adjust any column widths to the widest text entry in each column.
7. Select the ranges B4:E4 and B10:E10 and then insert a 3-D pie chart. Apply the Style 3 chart style to the chart. Move the chart to a new worksheet named Revenue Analysis Chart. Change the chart title to First Quarter Revenue Analysis.
8. Rename the Sheet1 tab, First Quarter, and apply the Green color to the sheet tab.
9. If requested by your instructor, change the font color of the text in cells A1 and A2 to the color of the shirt you currently are wearing.
10. Save the workbook using the file name, Lab 1-1 Katie's Kicks.
11. Preview and print the worksheet in landscape orientation.
12. If you wanted to chart the item totals instead of the regions, which ranges would you use to create the chart?
13. Submit the assignment as specified by your instructor.

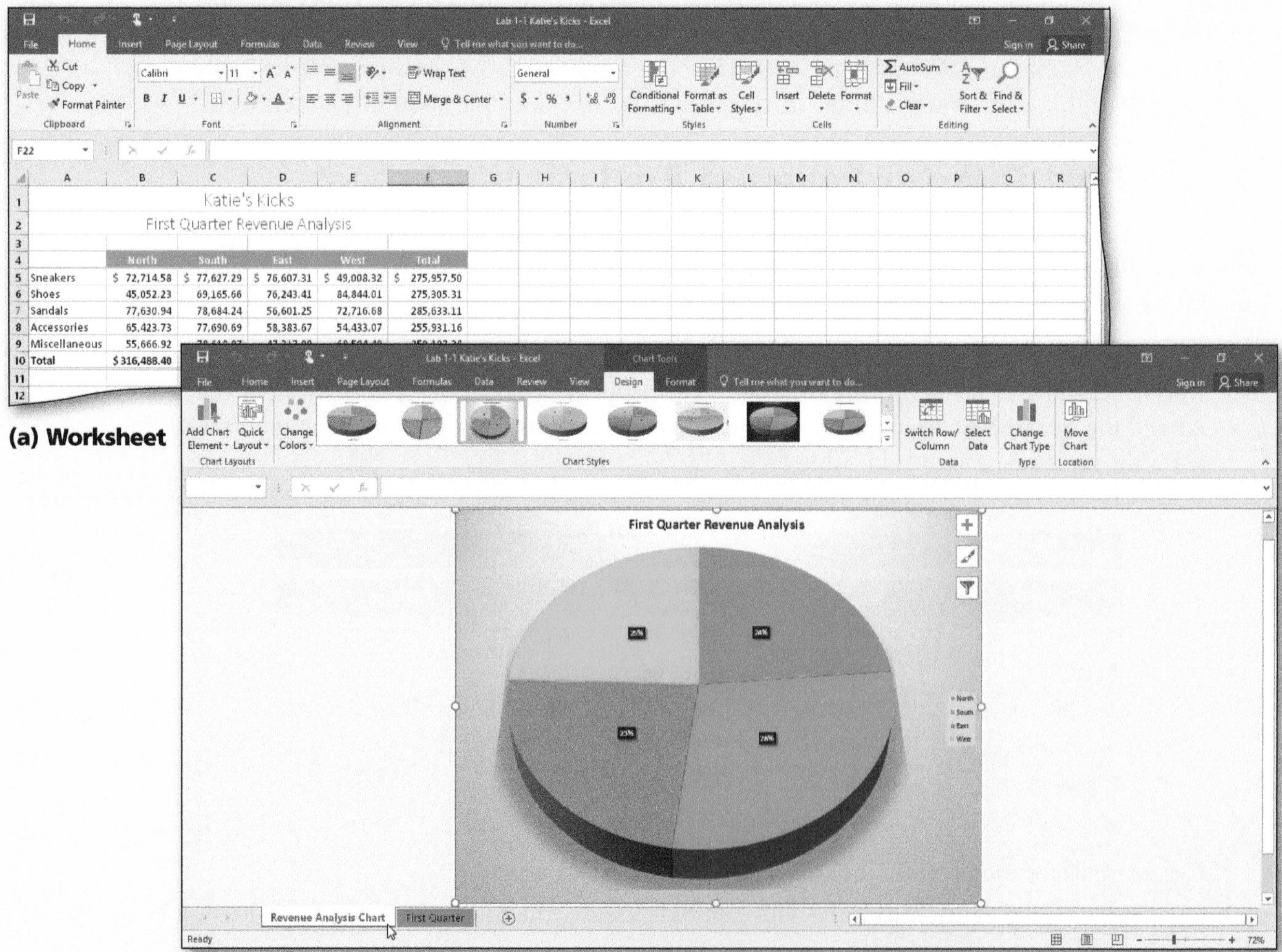

(a) Worksheet

(b) Pie Chart

Figure 1–75

Lab 2: Sales Analysis Worksheet

Problem: As the chief accountant for Davis Mobile Concepts, a leading car audio dealer serving four states, you have been asked by the vice president to create a worksheet to analyze the yearly sales for each state (Figure 1–76). The packages and corresponding sales by state for the year are shown in Table 1–8.

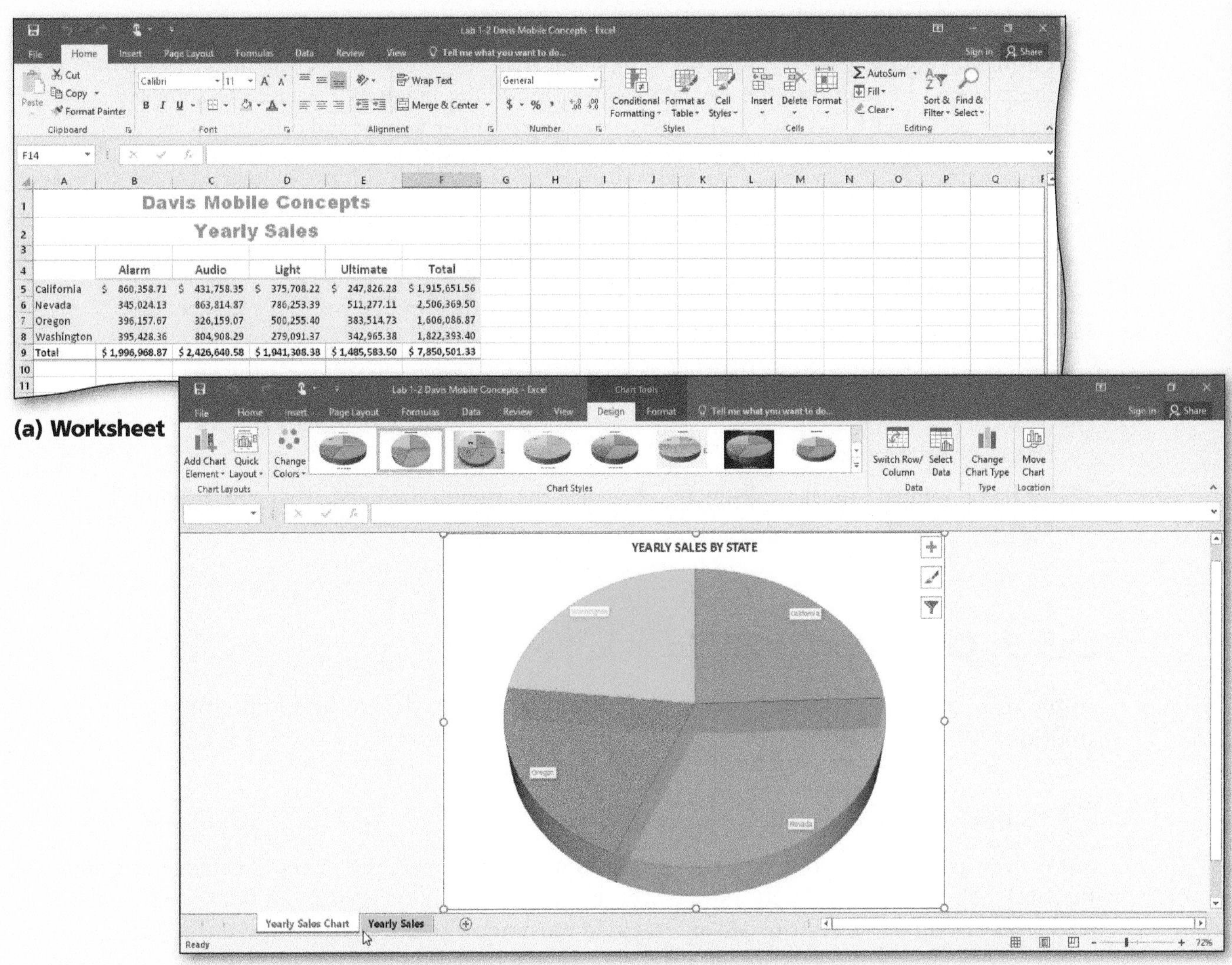

(a) Worksheet

(b) Pie Chart

Figure 1–76

Perform the following tasks:

1. Create the worksheet shown in Figure 1–76a using the data in Table 1–8.

Table 1–8 Davis Mobile Concepts				
	Alarm	Audio	Light	Ultimate
California	860358.71	431758.35	375708.22	247826.28
Nevada	345024.13	863814.87	786253.39	511277.11
Oregon	396157.67	326159.07	500255.40	383514.73
Washington	395428.36	804908.29	279091.37	342965.38

Continued >

In the Labs *continued*

2. Use the SUM function to determine total revenue for each of the four packages, the totals for each state, and the company total. Add column and row headings for the totals row and totals column, as appropriate.
3. Format the worksheet title and subtitle with the Title cell style and center them across columns A through F. Use the Font group on the ribbon to format the worksheet title and subtitle as 18-point Arial Black. Format the title and subtitle with Green, Accent 6 font color. Center the titles across columns A through F.
4. Format the range B4:F4 with the Heading 2 cell style and center the text in the cells. Format the range A5:F8 with the 20% - Accent6 cell style and the range A9:F9 with the Total cell style. Format cells B5:F5 and B9:F9 with the accounting number format and cells B6:F8 with the comma style format. If necessary, resize all columns to fit the data.
5. Create a 3-D pie chart on its own sheet that shows the total sales contributions of each state. Chart the state names (A5:A8) and corresponding totals (F5:F8). Use the sheet tab name, Yearly Sales Chart. Apply a chart style of your choosing. Change the chart title to Yearly Sales by State.
6. Change the Sheet1 tab name to Yearly Sales and apply the Orange color to the sheet tab.
7. If requested by your instructor, change the state in cell A8 to the state in which you were born. If your state already is listed in the spreadsheet, choose a different state.
8. Save the workbook using the file name, Lab 1-2 Davis Mobile Concepts. Print the worksheet in landscape orientation.
9. If you wanted to make a distinction between the rows in the table, what could you do?
10. Submit the assignment as specified by your instructor.

Lab 3: Consider This: Your Turn

Apply your creative thinking and problem-solving skills to design and implement a solution.

Comparing Televisions

Part 1: You are shopping for a new television and want to compare the prices of three televisions. Research new televisions. Create a worksheet that compares the type, size, and the price for each television, as well as the costs to add an extended warranty. Use the concepts and techniques presented in this module to calculate the average price of a television and average cost of an extended warranty and to format the worksheet. Submit your assignment in the format specified by your instructor.

Part 2: Based upon the data you found, how could you chart the information to show the comparisons? Which chart would be the best to use? Include a chart to compare the different television costs.

2 Formulas, Functions, and Formatting

Objectives

You will have mastered the material in this module when you can:

- Use Flash Fill
- Enter formulas using the keyboard
- Enter formulas using Point mode
- Apply the MAX, MIN, and AVERAGE functions
- Verify a formula using Range Finder
- Apply a theme to a workbook
- Apply a date format to a cell or range
- Add conditional formatting to cells
- Change column width and row height
- Check the spelling on a worksheet
- Change margins and headers in Page Layout view
- Preview and print versions and sections of a worksheet

Introduction

In Module 1, you learned how to enter data, sum values, format a worksheet to make it easier to read, and draw a chart. This module continues to illustrate these topics and presents some new ones.

The new topics covered in this module include using formulas and functions to create a worksheet. Recall from Module 1 that a function is a prewritten formula that is built into Excel. Other new topics include using option buttons, verifying formulas, applying a theme to a worksheet, adding borders, formatting numbers and text, using conditional formatting, changing the widths of columns and heights of rows, checking spelling, generating alternative worksheet displays and printouts, and adding page headers and footers to a worksheet. One alternative worksheet display and printout shows the formulas in the worksheet instead of the values. When you display the formulas in the worksheet, you see exactly what text, data, formulas, and functions you have entered into it.

Project — Worksheet with Formulas and Functions

The project in this module follows proper design guidelines and uses Excel to create the worksheet shown in Figure 2–1. Every two weeks, the owners of Olivia's Art Supply create a salary report by hand, where they keep track of employee payroll data. Before paying employees, the owners must summarize the hours worked, pay rate, and tax information for each employee to ensure that the business properly compensates its employees. This report also includes the following information for each employee: name, email address, number of dependents, hours worked, hourly pay rate, tax information, net pay, and hire date. As the complexity of creating the salary report increases, the owners want to use Excel to make the process easier.

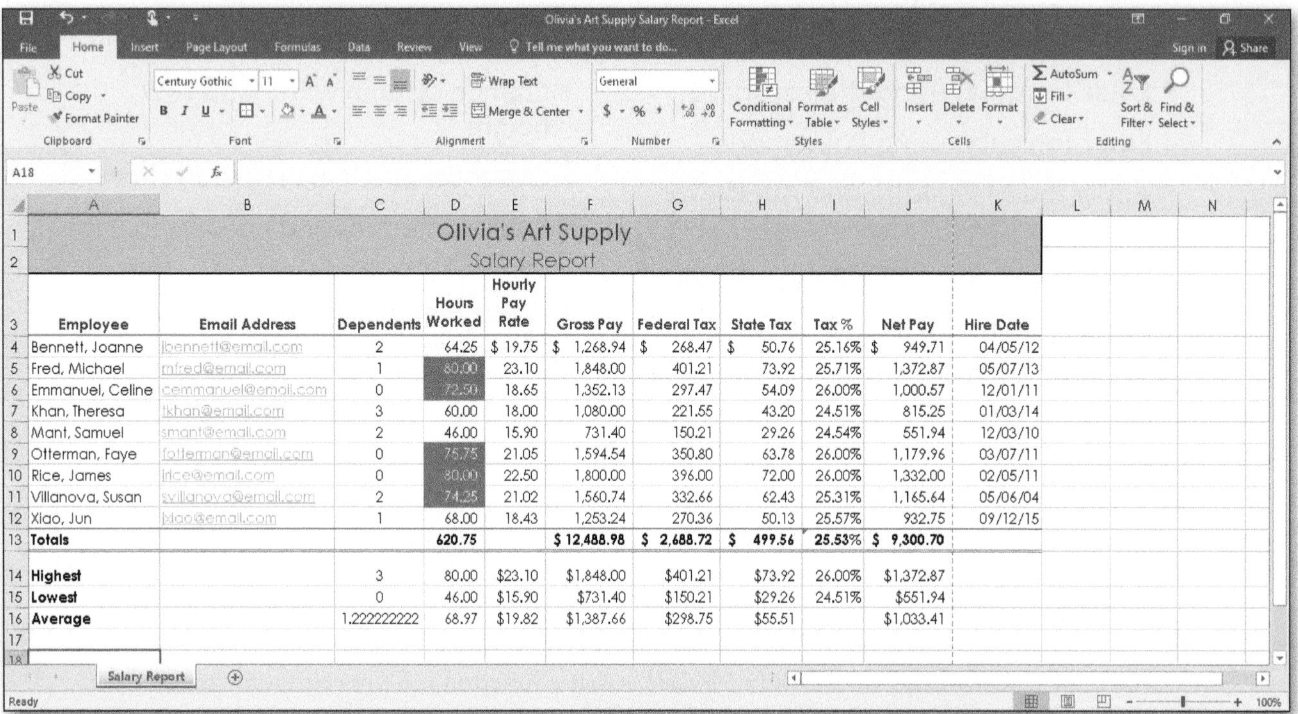

Olivia's Art Supply — Salary Report										
Employee	Email Address	Dependents	Hours Worked	Hourly Pay Rate	Gross Pay	Federal Tax	State Tax	Tax %	Net Pay	Hire Date
Bennett, Joanne	jbennett@email.com	2	64.25	$ 19.75	$ 1,268.94	$ 268.47	$ 50.76	25.16%	$ 949.71	04/05/12
Fred, Michael	mfred@email.com	1	80.00	23.10	1,848.00	401.21	73.92	25.71%	1,372.87	05/07/13
Emmanuel, Celine	cemmanuel@email.com	0	72.50	18.65	1,352.13	297.47	54.09	26.00%	1,000.57	12/01/11
Khan, Theresa	tkhan@email.com	3	60.00	18.00	1,080.00	221.55	43.20	24.51%	815.25	01/03/14
Mant, Samuel	smant@email.com	2	46.00	15.90	731.40	150.21	29.26	24.54%	551.94	12/03/10
Otterman, Faye	fotterman@email.com	0	75.75	21.05	1,594.54	350.80	63.78	26.00%	1,179.96	03/07/11
Rice, James	jrice@email.com	0	80.00	22.50	1,800.00	396.00	72.00	26.00%	1,332.00	02/05/11
Villanova, Susan	svillanova@email.com	2	74.25	21.02	1,560.74	332.66	62.43	25.31%	1,165.64	05/06/04
Xiao, Jun	jxiao@email.com	1	68.00	18.43	1,253.24	270.36	50.13	25.57%	932.75	09/12/15
Totals			**620.75**		**$ 12,488.98**	**$ 2,688.72**	**$ 499.56**	**25.53%**	**$ 9,300.70**	
Highest		3	80.00	$23.10	$1,848.00	$401.21	$73.92	26.00%	$1,372.87	
Lowest		0	46.00	$15.90	$731.40	$150.21	$29.26	24.51%	$551.94	
Average		1.222222222	68.97	$19.82	$1,387.66	$298.75	$55.51		$1,033.41	

Figure 2–1

Recall that the first step in creating an effective worksheet is to make sure you understand what is required. The people who request the worksheet usually provide the requirements. The requirements document for the Olivia's Art Supply Salary Report worksheet includes the following needs: source of data, summary of calculations, and other facts about its development (Figure 2–2).

Worksheet Title	Olivia's Art Supply Salary Report
Needs	An easy-to-read worksheet that summarizes the company's salary report (Figure 2–3). For each employee, the worksheet is to include the employee's name, email address, number of dependents, hours worked, hourly pay rate, gross pay, federal tax, state tax, total tax percent, net pay, and hire date. The worksheet also should include the total pay for all employees, as well as the highest value, lowest value, and average for each category of data.
Source of Data	Supplied data includes employee names, number of dependents, hours worked, hourly pay rate, and hire dates.
Calculations	The following calculations must be made for each of the employees: 1. Gross Pay = Hours Worked * Hourly Pay Rate 2. Federal Tax = 0.22 * (Gross Pay * Number of Dependents * 24.32) 3. State Tax = 0.04 * Gross Pay 4. Tax % = (Federal Tax + State Tax) / Gross Pay 5. Net Pay = Gross Pay * (Federal Tax + State Tax) 6. Compute the totals for hours worked, gross pay, federal tax, state tax, and net pay 7. Compute the total tax percent 8. Use the MAX and MIN functions to determine the highest and lowest values for number of dependents, hours worked, hourly pay rate, gross pay, federal tax, state tax, total tax percent, and net pay 9. Use the AVERAGE function to determine the average for hours worked, number of dependents, hourly pay rate, gross pay, federal tax, state tax, and net pay

Figure 2–2

In addition, using a sketch of the worksheet can help you visualize its design. The sketch for the Olivia's Art Supply Salary Report worksheet includes a title, a subtitle, column and row headings, and the location of data values (Figure 2–3). It also uses specific characters to define the desired formatting for the worksheet, as follows:

1. The row of Xs below the leftmost column heading defines the cell entries as text, such as employee names.

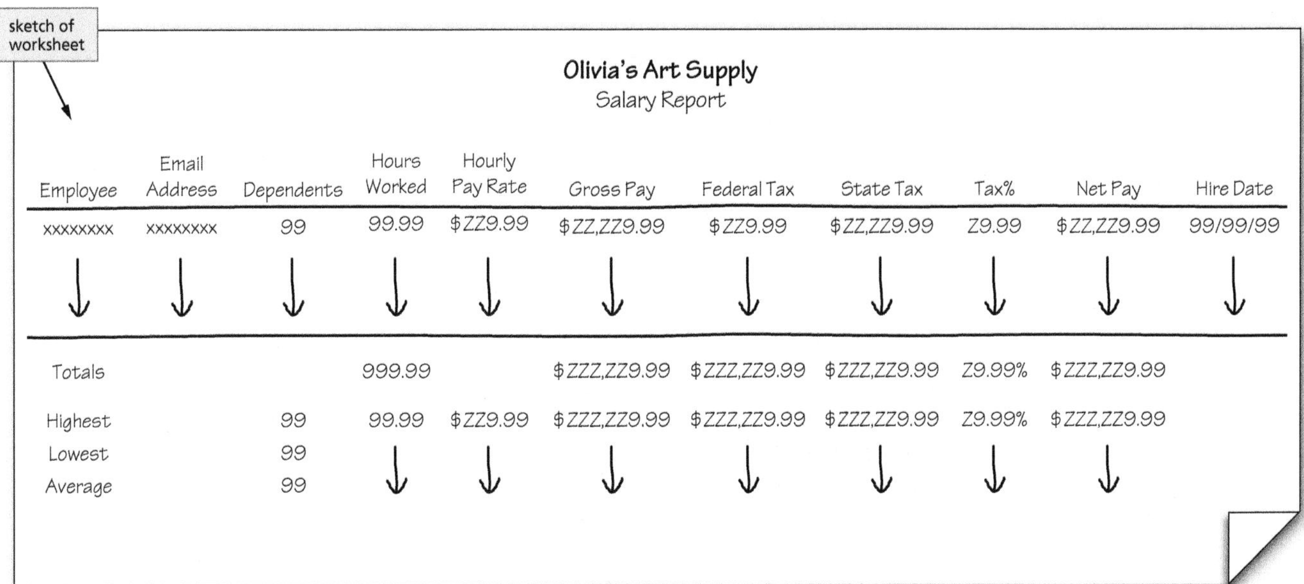

Figure 2–3

For an introduction to Windows and instructions about how to perform basic Windows tasks, read the Office and Windows module at the beginning of this book, where you can learn how to resize windows, change screen resolution, create folders, move and rename files, use Windows Help, and much more.

For an introduction to Office and instructions about how to perform basic tasks in Office apps, read the Office and Windows module at the beginning of this book, where you can learn how to run an application, use the ribbon, save a file, open a file, print a file, exit an application, use Help, and much more.

2. The rows of Zs and 9s with slashes, dollar signs, decimal points, commas, and percent signs in the remaining columns define the cell entries as numbers. The Zs indicate that the selected format should instruct Excel to suppress leading 0s. The 9s indicate that the selected format should instruct Excel to display any digits, including 0s.
3. The decimal point means that a decimal point should appear in the cell entry and indicates the number of decimal places to use.
4. The slashes in the last column identify the cell entry as a date.
5. The dollar signs that are adjacent to the Zs below the totals row signify a floating dollar sign, or one that appears next to the first significant digit.
6. The commas indicate that the selected format should instruct Excel to display a comma separator only if the number has sufficient digits (values in the thousandths) to the left of the decimal point.
7. The percent sign (%) in the Tax % column indicates a percent sign should appear after the number.

In this module, you will learn how to use functions and create formulas. The following roadmap identifies general activities you will perform as you progress through this module:

1. ENTER FORMULAS in the worksheet.
2. ENTER FUNCTIONS in the worksheet.
3. VERIFY FORMULAS in the worksheet.
4. FORMAT the WORKSHEET.
5. CHECK SPELLING.
6. PRINT the WORKSHEET.

CONSIDER THIS

What is the function of an Excel worksheet?

The function, or purpose, of a worksheet is to provide a user with direct ways to accomplish tasks. In designing a worksheet, functional considerations should supersede visual aesthetics. Consider the following when designing your worksheet:

- Avoid the temptation to use flashy or confusing visual elements within the worksheet.
- Understand the requirements document.
- Choose the proper functions and formulas.
- Build the worksheet.

BTW

Touch Screen Differences

The Office and Windows interfaces may vary if you are using a touch screen. For this reason, you might notice that the function or appearance of your touch screen differs slightly from this module's presentation.

Entering the Titles and Numbers into the Worksheet

The first step in creating the worksheet is to enter the titles and numbers into the worksheet. The following sets of steps enter the worksheet title and subtitle and then the salary report data shown in Table 2–1.

To Enter the Worksheet Title and Subtitle

With a good comprehension of the requirements document, an understanding of the necessary decisions, and a sketch of the worksheet, the next step is to use Excel to create the worksheet. The following steps enter the worksheet title and subtitle into cells A1 and A2.

1. Run Excel and create a blank workbook in the Excel window.
2. If necessary, select cell A1. Type **`Olivia's Art Supply`** in the selected cell and then press the DOWN ARROW key to enter the worksheet title.
3. Type **`Salary Report`** in cell A2 and then press the DOWN ARROW key to enter the worksheet subtitle.

BTW

Screen Resolution
If you are using a computer or mobile device to step through the project in this module and you want your screens to match the figures in this book, you should change your screen's resolution to 1366 x 768. For information about how to change a computer's resolution, refer to the Office and Windows module at the beginning of this book.

To Enter the Column Titles

The column titles in row 3 begin in cell A3 and extend through cell K3. The employee names and the row titles begin in cell A4 and continue down to cell A16. The employee data is entered into rows 4 through 12 of the worksheet. The remainder of this section explains the steps required to enter the column titles, payroll data, and row titles, as shown in Figure 2–4, and then to save the workbook. The following steps enter the column titles.

1. With cell A3 selected, type **`Employee`** and then press the RIGHT ARROW key to enter the column heading.
2. Type **`Email Address`** in cell B3 and then press the RIGHT ARROW key.
3. In cell C3, type **`Dependents`** and then press the RIGHT ARROW key.
4. In cell D3, type **`Hours`** and then press the ALT+ENTER keys to enter the first line of the column heading. Type **`Worked`** and then press the RIGHT ARROW key to enter the column heading.

Q&A Why do I use the ALT+ENTER keys?
You press ALT+ENTER in order to start a new line in a cell. The final line can be completed by clicking the Enter button, pressing the ENTER key, or pressing one of the arrow keys. When you see ALT+ENTER in a step, press the ENTER key while holding down the ALT key and then release both keys.

5. Type **`Hourly`** in cell E3, press the ALT+ENTER keys, type **`Pay Rate,`** and then press the RIGHT ARROW key.
6. Type **`Gross Pay`** in cell F3 and then press the RIGHT ARROW key.
7. Type **`Federal Tax`** in cell G3 and then press the RIGHT ARROW key.
8. Type **`State Tax`** in cell H3 and then press the RIGHT ARROW key.
9. Type **`Tax %`** in cell I3 and then press the RIGHT ARROW key.
10. Type **`Net Pay`** in cell J3 and then press the RIGHT ARROW key.
11. Type **`Hire Date`** in cell K3 and then press the RIGHT ARROW key.

BTW

Wrapping Text
If you have a long text entry, such as a paragraph, you can instruct Excel to wrap the text in a cell. This method is easier than your pressing ALT+ENTER to end each line of text within the paragraph. To wrap text, right-click in the cell, click Format Cells on a shortcut menu, click the Alignment tab, and then click Wrap text. Excel will increase the height of the cell automatically so that the additional lines will fit. If you want to control where each line ends in the cell, rather than letting Excel wrap the text based on the cell width, you must end each line with ALT+ENTER.

To Enter the Salary Data

The salary data in Table 2-1 includes a hire date for each employee. Excel considers a date to be a number and, therefore, it displays the date right-aligned in the cell. The following steps enter the data for each employee, except their email addresses, which will be entered later in this module.

BTW

Two-Digit Years

When you enter a two-digit year value (xx) that is less than 30, Excel changes that value to 20xx; when you enter a value that is 30 or greater (zz), Excel changes the value to 19zz. Use four-digit years, if necessary, to ensure that Excel interprets year values the way you intend.

1. Select cell A4. Type `Bennett, Joanne` and then press the RIGHT ARROW key two times to enter the employee name and make cell C4 the active cell.
2. Type `2` in cell C4 and then press the RIGHT ARROW key.
3. Type `64.25` in cell D4 and then press the RIGHT ARROW key.
4. Type `19.75` in cell E4.
5. Click cell K4 and then type `4/5/12`.
6. Enter the payroll data in Table 2–1 for the eight remaining employees in rows 5 through 12.

Q&A

In Step 5, why did the date change from 4/5/12 to 4/5/2012?

When Excel recognizes a date in mm/dd/yy format, it formats the date as mm/dd/yyyy. Most professionals prefer to view dates in mm/dd/yyyy format as opposed to mm/dd/yy format to avoid confusion regarding the intended year. For example, a date displayed as 3/3/50 could imply a date of 3/3/1950 or 3/3/2050.

Table 2–1 Olivia's Art Supply Salary Report Data

Employee	Email Address	Dependents	Hours Worked	Hourly Pay Rate	Hire Date
Bennett, Joanne		2	64.25	19.75	4/5/12
Fred, Michael		1	80.00	23.10	5/7/13
Emmanuel, Celine		0	72.50	18.65	12/1/11
Khan, Theresa		3	60.00	18.00	1/3/14
Mant, Samuel		2	46.00	15.90	12/3/10
Otterman, Faye		0	75.75	21.05	3/7/11
Rice, James		0	80.00	22.50	2/5/11
Villanova, Susan		2	74.25	21.02	5/6/04
Xiao, Jun		1	68.00	18.43	9/12/15

BTW

The Ribbon and Screen Resolution

Excel may change how the groups and buttons within the groups appear on the ribbon, depending on the computer or mobile device's screen resolution. Thus, your ribbon may look different from the ones in this book if you are using a screen resolution other than 1366 x 768.

Flash Fill

When you are entering data in a spreadsheet, occasionally Excel will recognize a pattern in the data you are entering. **Flash Fill** is an Excel feature that looks for patterns in the data and automatically fills or formats data in remaining cells. For example if column A contains a list of 10 phone numbers without parentheses around the area code or dashes after the prefix, Flash Fill can help create formatted phone numbers with relative ease. To use Flash Fill, simply start entering formatted phone numbers in cells next to the unformatted numbers. After entering a few formatted phone numbers, Flash Fill will suggest similarly formatted phone numbers for the remaining cells in the column. If you do not want to wait for Excel to offer suggestions, type one or two examples and then click the Flash Fill button (Data tab | Data Tools group). Flash fill will autocomplete the remaining cells. If Flash Fill makes a mistake, simply click the Undo button, enter a few more examples, and try again. In addition to formatting data, Flash Fill can perform tasks such as concatenating data from multiple cells and separating data from one cell into multiple cells.

To Use Flash Fill

In the Olivia's Art Supply Salary Report worksheet, you can use Flash Fill to generate email addresses using first and last names from another column in the worksheet. ***Why?*** *The Flash Fill feature is a convenient way to avoid entering a lot of data manually.* The following steps use Flash Fill to generate employee email addresses using the names entered in column A.

- Click cell B4 to select it.
- Type **`jbennett@email.com`** and then press the DOWN ARROW key to select cell B5.
- Type **`mfred@email.com`** and then click the Enter button to enter Michael Fred's email address in cell B5 (Figure 2–4).

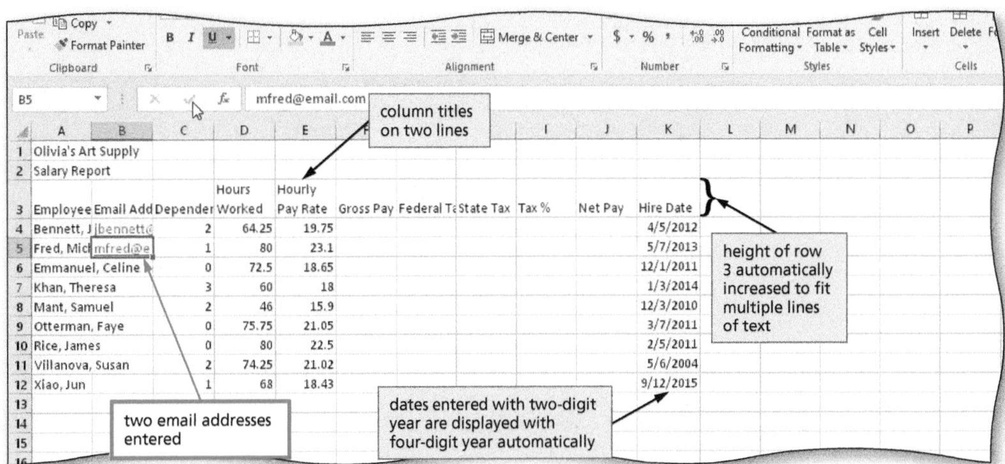

Figure 2–4

- Click Data on the ribbon to select the Data tab.
- Click Flash Fill (Data tab | Data Tools group) to enter similarly formatted email addresses in the range B6:B12.
- Remove the entries from cells B1 and B2 (Figure 2–5).

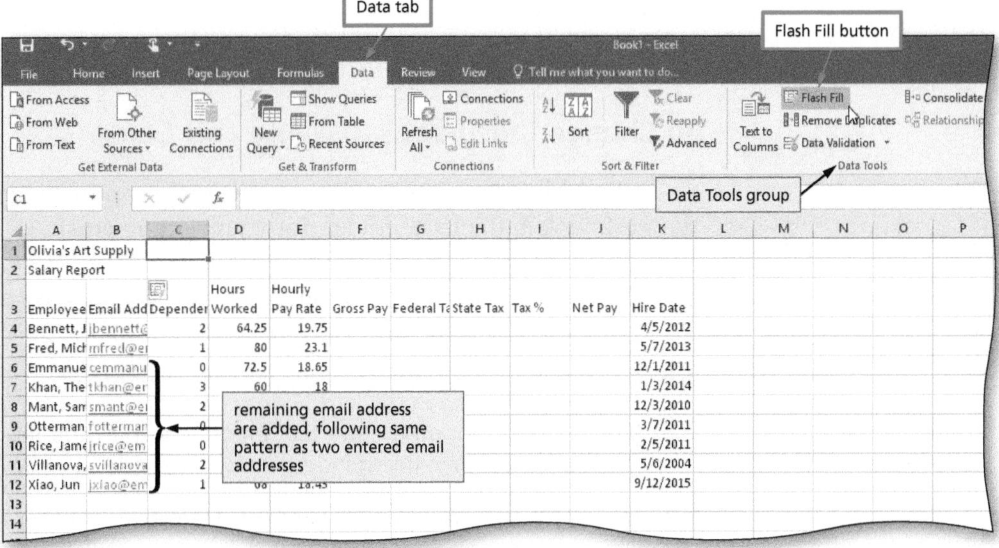

Figure 2–5

Q&A

Why was I unable to click the Flash Fill button after entering the first email address?

One entry might not have been enough for Excel to recognize a pattern. For instance, Flash Fill might have used the letter *j* before each last name in the email address, instead of using the first initial and last name.

What would have happened if I kept typing examples without clicking the Flash Fill button?

As soon as Excel recognized a pattern, it would have displayed suggestions for the remaining cells. Pressing the ENTER key when the suggestions appear will populate the remaining cells.

BTW
Formatting Worksheets
With early worksheet programs, users often skipped rows to improve the appearance of the worksheet. With Excel it is not necessary to skip rows because you can increase row heights to add white space between information.

To Enter the Row Titles

The following steps add row titles for the rows that will contain the totals, highest, lowest, and average amounts.

1. Select cell A13. Type **Totals** and then press the DOWN ARROW key to enter a row header.
2. Type **Highest** in cell A14 and then press the DOWN ARROW key.
3. Type **Lowest** in cell A15 and then press the DOWN ARROW key.
4. Type **Average** in cell A16 and then press the DOWN ARROW key (Figure 2–6).

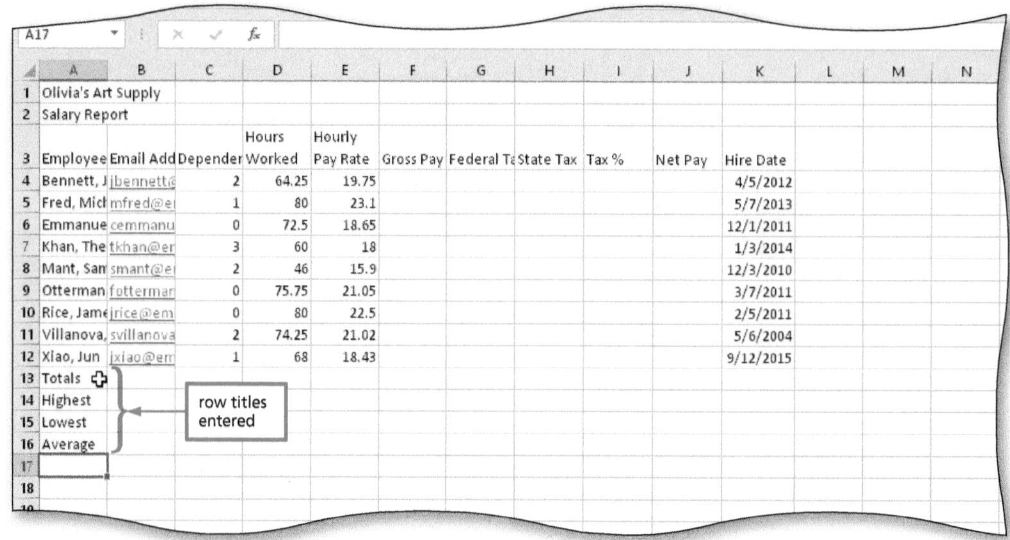

Figure 2–6

BTW
Organizing Files and Folders
You should organize and store files in folders so that you easily can find the files later. For example, if you are taking an introductory technology class called CIS 101, a good practice would be to save all Excel files in an Excel folder in a CIS 101 folder. For a discussion of folders and detailed examples of creating folders, refer to the Office and Windows module at the beginning of this book.

To Change the Sheet Tab Name and Color

The following steps change the sheet tab name, change the tab color, and save the workbook in the Excel folder (for your assignments).

1. Double-click the Sheet1 tab and then enter **Salary Report** as the sheet tab name and then press the ENTER key.
2. Right-click the sheet tab to display the shortcut menu.
3. Point to Tab Color on the shortcut menu to display the Tab Color gallery. Click Green (column 6, row 7) in the Standard Colors area to apply the color to the sheet tab.
4. Save the workbook in your hard drive, OneDrive, or other storage location using Olivia's Art Supply Salary Report as the file name.

Q&A
Why should I save the workbook at this time?
You have performed many tasks while creating this workbook and do not want to risk losing work completed thus far.

Entering Formulas

One of the reasons Excel is such a valuable tool is that you can assign a formula to a cell, and Excel will calculate the result. A **formula** consists of cell references, numbers, and arithmetic operators that instruct Excel to perform a calculation. Consider, for example, what would happen if you had to multiply 64.25 by 19.75 and then manually enter the product for Gross Pay, 1,268.94, in cell F4. Every time the values in cells D4 or E4 changed, you would have to recalculate the product and enter the new value in cell F4. By contrast, if you enter a formula in cell F4 to multiply the values in cells D4 and E4, Excel recalculates the product whenever new values are entered into those cells and displays the result in cell F4.

A formula in a cell that contains a reference back to itself is called a **circular reference.** Excel warns you when you create circular references. In almost all cases, circular references are the result of an incorrect formula. A circular reference can be direct or indirect. For example, placing the formula =A1 in cell A1 results in a direct circular reference. A **direct circular reference** occurs when a formula refers to the same cell in which it is entered. An **indirect circular reference** occurs when a formula in a cell refers to another cell or cells that include a formula that refers back to the original cell.

BTW

Entering Numbers in a Range

An efficient way to enter data into a range of cells is to select a range and then enter the first number in the upper-left cell of the range. Excel responds by accepting the value and moving the active cell selection down one cell. When you enter the last value in the first column, Excel moves the active cell selection to the top of the next column.

To Enter a Formula Using the Keyboard

1 ENTER FORMULAS | **2 ENTER FUNCTIONS** | **3 VERIFY FORMULAS**
4 FORMAT WORKSHEET | **5 CHECK SPELLING** | **6 PRINT WORKSHEET**

The formulas needed in the worksheet are noted in the requirements document as follows:

1. Gross Pay (column F) = Hours Worked × Hourly Pay Rate
2. Federal Tax (column G) = 0.22 × (Gross Pay – Dependents × 24.32)
3. State Tax (column H) = 0.04 × Gross Pay
4. Tax % (column I) = (Federal Tax + State Tax) / Gross Pay
5. Net Pay (column J) = Gross Pay – (Federal Tax + State Tax)

The gross pay for each employee, which appears in column F, is equal to hours worked in column D times hourly pay rate in column E. Thus, the gross pay for Joanne Bennett in cell F4 is obtained by multiplying 64.25 (cell D4) by 19.75 (cell E4) or = D4 × E4. The following steps enter the initial gross pay formula in cell F4 using the keyboard. ***Why?** In order for Excel to perform the calculations, you must first enter the formulas.*

1

- With cell F4 selected, type **=d4*e4** in the cell to display the formula in the formula bar and the current cell and to display colored borders around the cells referenced in the formula (Figure 2–7).

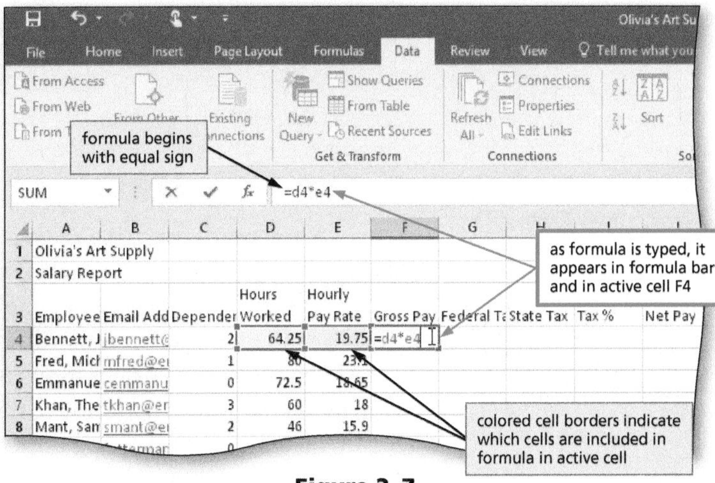

Figure 2–7

Q&A

What happens when I enter the formula?
The **equal sign** (=) preceding d4*e4 alerts Excel that you are entering a formula or function — not text. Because the most common error when entering a formula is to reference the wrong cell, Excel colors the cells referenced in the formula. The colored cells help you determine whether the cell references are correct. The asterisk (*) following d4 is the arithmetic operator for multiplication.

Is there a function, similar to the SUM function, that calculates the product of two or more numbers?
Yes. The **PRODUCT function** calculates the product of two or more numbers. For example, the function, =PRODUCT(D4,E4) will calculate the product of cells D4 and E4.

2

- Press the RIGHT ARROW key to complete the arithmetic operation indicated by the formula, display the result in the worksheet, and select the cell to the right (Figure 2–8). The number of decimal places on your screen may be different than shown in Figure 2–8, but these values will be adjusted later in this module.

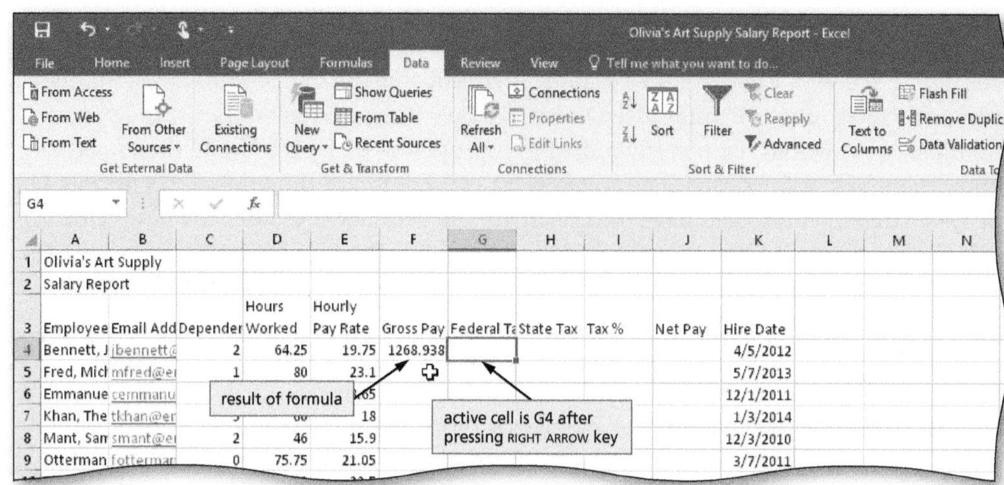

Figure 2–8

BTW
Automatic Recalculation
Every time you enter a value into a cell in the worksheet, Excel automatically recalculates all formulas. You can change to manual recalculation by clicking the Calculation Options button (Formulas tab | Calculation group) and then clicking Manual. In manual calculation mode, pressing the F9 key instructs Excel to recalculate all formulas.

Arithmetic Operations

Excel provides powerful functions and capabilities that allow you to perform arithmetic operations easily and efficiently. Table 2–2 describes multiplication and other valid Excel arithmetic operators.

Table 2–2 Arithmetic Operations Listed in Order of Operations

Arithmetic Operator	Meaning	Example of Usage	Result
-	Negation	-78	Negative 78
%	Percentage	=23%	Multiplies 23 by 0.01
^	Exponentiation	=3 ^ 4	Raises 3 to the fourth power
*	Multiplication	=61.5 * C5	Multiplies the contents of cell C5 by 61.5
/	Division	=H3 / H11	Divides the contents of cell H3 by the contents of cell H11
+	Addition	=11 + 9	Adds 11 and 9
–	Subtraction	=22 – F15	Subtracts the contents of cell F15 from 22

BTW
Troubling Formulas
If Excel does not accept a formula, remove the equal sign from the left side and complete the entry as text. Later, after you have entered additional data in the cells reliant on the formula or determined the error, reinsert the equal sign to change the text back to a formula and edit the formula as needed.

Order of Operations

When more than one arithmetic operator is involved in a formula, Excel follows the same basic order of operations that you use in algebra. The **order of operations** is the collection of rules that define which mathematical operations take precedence over the others in expressions with multiple operations. Moving from left to right in a formula, the order of operations is as follows: first negation (–), then all percentages (%), then all exponentiations (^), then all multiplications (*) and divisions (/), and, finally, all additions (+) and subtractions (–).

As in algebra, you can use parentheses to override the order of operations. For example, if Excel follows the order of operations, 8 * 3 + 2 equals 26. If you use parentheses, however, to change the formula to 8 * (3 + 2), the result is 40, because the parentheses instruct Excel to add 3 and 2 before multiplying by 8. Table 2–3 illustrates several examples of valid Excel formulas and explains the order of operations.

Table 2–3 Examples of Excel Formulas

Formula	Result
=G15	Assigns the value in cell G15 to the active cell.
=2^4 + 7	Assigns the sum of 16 + 7 (or 23) to the active cell.
=100 + D2 or =D2 +100 or =(100 + D2)	Assigns 100 plus the contents of cell D2 to the active cell.
=25% * 40	Assigns the product of 0.25 times 40 (or 10) to the active cell.
– (K15 * X45)	Assigns the negative value of the product of the values contained in cells K15 and X45 to the active cell. *Tip:* You do not need to type an equal sign before an expression that begins with a minus sign, which indicates a negation.
=(U8 – B8) * 6	Assigns the difference between the values contained in cells U8 and B8 times 6 to the active cell.
=J7 / A5 + G9 * M6 – Z2 ^ L7	Completes the following operations, from left to right: exponentiation (Z2 ^ L7), then division (J7 / A5), then multiplication (G9 * M6), then addition (J7 / A5) + (G9 * M6), and finally subtraction (J7 / A5 + G9 * M6) – (Z2 ^ L7). If cells A5 = 6, G9 = 2, J7 = 6, L7 = 4, M6 = 5, and Z2 = 2, then Excel assigns the active cell the value –5; that is, 6 / 6 + 2 * 5 – 2 ^ 4 = –5.

BTW

Parentheses

Remember that you can use parentheses to override the order of operations. You cannot use brackets or braces in place of parentheses in arithmetic operations.

1 ENTER FORMULAS | **2 ENTER FUNCTIONS** | **3 VERIFY FORMULAS**
4 FORMAT WORKSHEET | **5 CHECK SPELLING** | **6 PRINT WORKSHEET**

To Enter Formulas Using Point Mode

The sketch of the worksheet in Figure 2–3 calls for the federal tax, state tax, tax percentage, and net pay for each employee to appear in columns G, H, I, and J, respectively. All four of these values are calculated using formulas in row 4:

Federal Tax (cell G4) = 0.22 × (Gross Pay – Dependents × 24.32) or = 0.22 * (F4 – C4 * 24.32)
State Tax (cell H4) = 0.04 × Gross Pay or = 0.04 * F4
Tax % (cell I4) = (Federal Tax + State Tax) / Gross Pay or = (G4 + H4) / F4
Net Pay (cell J4) = Gross Pay – (Federal Tax + State Tax) or = F4 – (G4 + H4)

An alternative to entering the formulas in cells G4, H4, I4, and J4 using the keyboard is to enter the formulas using the pointer and Point mode. **Point mode** allows you to select cells for use in a formula by using the pointer. The following steps enter formulas using Point mode. ***Why?*** *Using Point mode makes it easier to create formulas without worrying about typographical errors when entering cell references.*

1

- With cell G4 selected, type **=0.22*(** to begin the formula and then click cell F4 to add a cell reference in the formula (Figure 2–9).

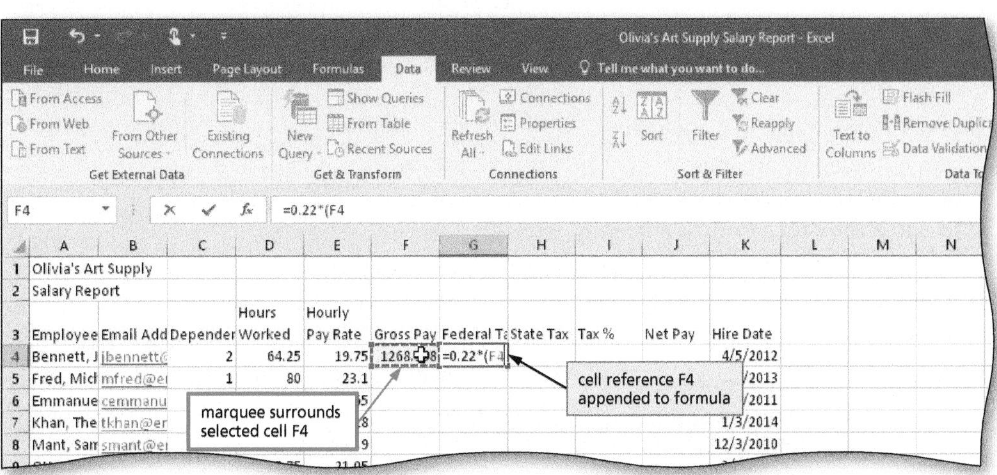

Figure 2–9

- Type **-** (minus sign) and then click cell C4 to add a subtraction operator and a reference to another cell to the formula.
- Type ***24.32)** to complete the formula (Figure 2–10).

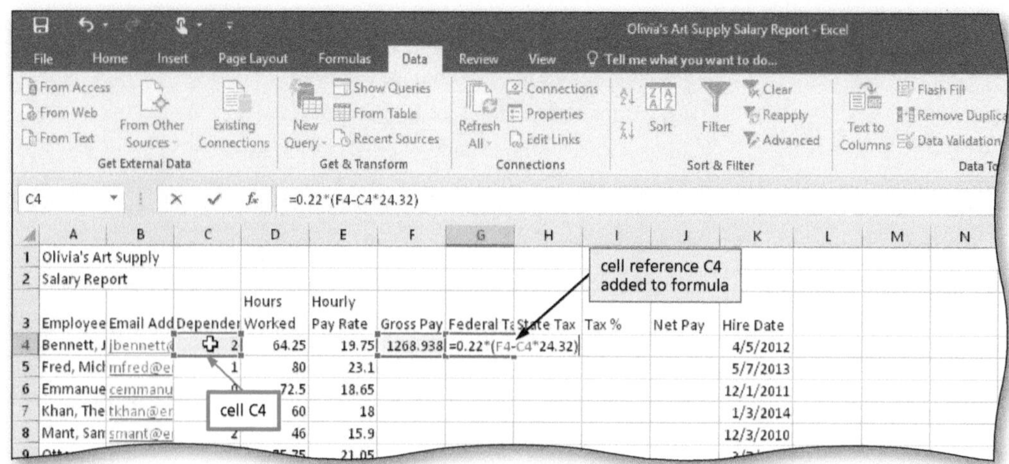

Figure 2–10

3

- Click the Enter button in the formula bar and then select cell H4 to prepare to enter the next formula.
- Type **=0.04*** and then click cell F4 to add a cell reference to the formula (Figure 2–11).

Q&A Why should I use Point mode to enter formulas?

Using Point mode to enter formulas often is faster and more accurate than using the keyboard, but only when the cell you want to select does not require you to scroll. In many instances, as in these steps, you may want to use both the keyboard and pointer when entering a formula in a cell. You can use the keyboard to begin the formula, for example, and then use the pointer to select a range of cells.

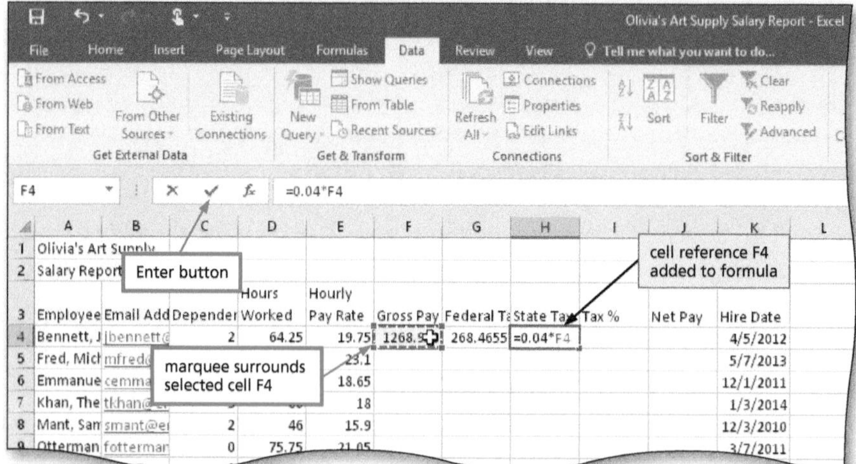

Figure 2–11

4

- Click the Enter button in the formula bar to enter the formula in cell H4.
- Select cell I4. Type **=(** (equal sign followed by an open parenthesis) and then click cell G4 to add a reference to the formula.
- Type **+** (plus sign) and then click cell H4 to add a cell reference to the formula.
- Type **)/** (close parenthesis followed by a forward slash), and then click cell F4 to add a cell reference to the formula.
- Click the Enter button in the formula bar to enter the formula in cell I4 (Figure 2–12).

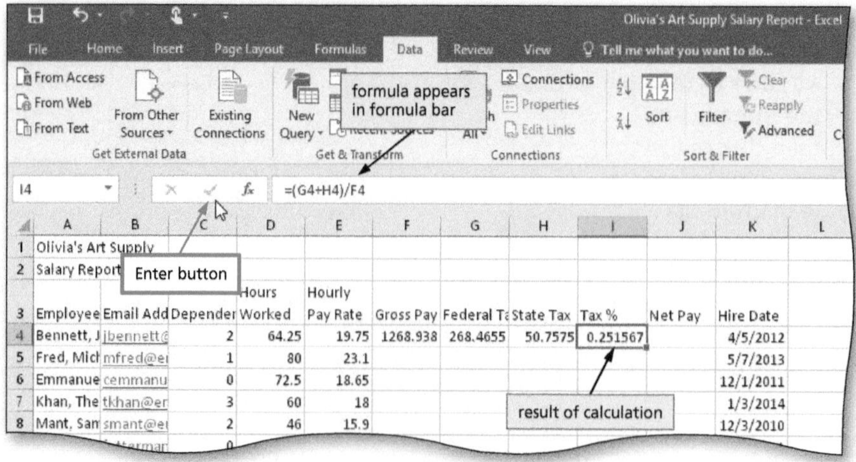

Figure 2–12

5

- Click cell J4, type = (equal sign) and then click cell F4.
- Type -((minus sign followed by an open parenthesis) and then click cell G4.
- Type + (plus sign), click cell H4, and then type) (close parenthesis) to complete the formula (Figure 2–13).
- Click the Enter button.

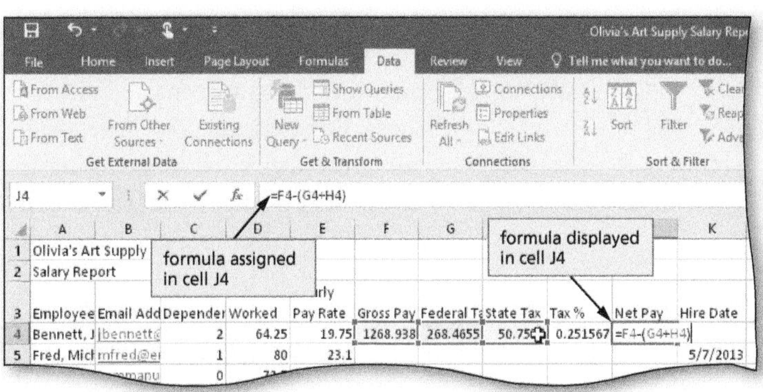

Figure 2–13

To Copy Formulas Using the Fill Handle

The five formulas for Joanne Bennett in cells F4, G4, H4, I4, and J4 now are complete. The next step is to copy them to the range F5:J12. When copying formulas in Excel, the source area is the cell, or range, from which data or formulas are being copied. When a range is used as a source, it sometimes is called the **source range**. The destination area is the cell, or range, to which data or formulas are being copied. When a range is used as a destination, it sometimes is called the **destination range**. Recall from Module 1 that the fill handle is a small square in the lower-right corner of the active cell or active range. The following steps copy the formulas using the fill handle.

1 Select the source range, F4:J4 in this case, activate the fill handle, drag the fill handle down through cell J12, and then continue to hold the mouse button to select the destination range.

2 Release the mouse button to copy the formulas to the destination range (Figure 2–14).

Q&A How does Excel adjust the cell references in the formulas in the destination area?
Recall that when you copy a formula, Excel adjusts the cell references so that the new formulas contain new cell references corresponding to the new locations and perform calculations using the appropriate values. Thus, if you copy downward, Excel adjusts the row portion of cell references relative to the source cell. If you copy across, then Excel adjusts the column portion of cell references relative to the source cell. Cell references that adjust relative to the location of the source cell are called **relative cell references**.

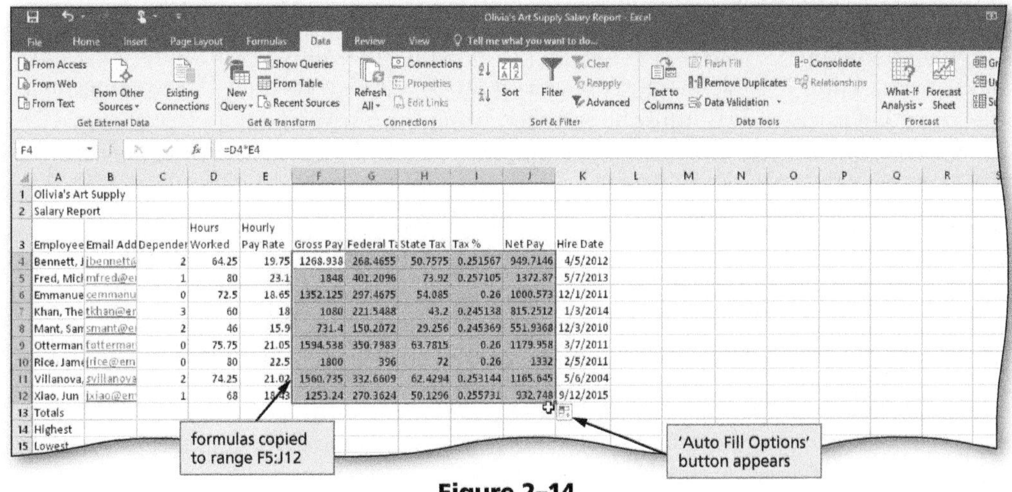

Figure 2–14

Option Buttons

Excel displays option buttons in a worksheet to indicate that you can complete an operation using automatic features such as AutoCorrect, Auto Fill, error checking, and others. For example, the 'Auto Fill Options' button shown in Figure 2 – 14 appears after a fill operation, such as dragging the fill handle. When an error occurs in a formula in a cell, Excel displays the Trace Error button next to the cell and identifies the cell with the error by placing a green triangle in the upper left of the cell.

Table 2–4 summarizes the option buttons available in Excel. When one of these buttons appears on your worksheet, click its arrow to produce the list of options for modifying the operation or to obtain additional information.

Table 2 – 4 Option Buttons in Excel

Name	Menu Function
Auto Fill Options	Provides options for how to fill cells following a fill operation, such as dragging the fill handle
AutoCorrect Options	Undoes an automatic correction, stops future automatic corrections of this type, or causes Excel to display the AutoCorrect Options dialog box
Insert Options	Lists formatting options following an insertion of cells, rows, or columns
Paste Options	Specifies how moved or pasted items should appear (for example, with original formatting, without formatting, or with different formatting)
Trace Error	Lists error-checking options following the assignment of an invalid formula to a cell

CONSIDER THIS

Why is the Paste Options button important?

The Paste Options button provides powerful functionality. When performing copy and paste operations, the button allows you great freedom in specifying what it is you want to paste. You can choose from the following options:

- Paste an exact copy of what you copied, including the cell contents and formatting.
- Copy only formulas.
- Copy only formatting.
- Copy only values.
- Copy a combination of these options.
- Copy a picture of what you copied.

BTW
Selecting a Range
You can select a range using the keyboard. Press the F8 key and then use the arrow keys to select the desired range. After you are finished, make sure to press the F8 key to turn off the selection process or you will continue to select ranges.

To Determine Totals Using the Sum Button

The next step is to determine the totals in row 13 for the hours worked in column D, gross pay in column F, federal tax in column G, state tax in column H, and net pay in column J. To determine the total hours worked in column D, the values in the range D4 through D12 must be summed using the SUM function. Recall that a function is a prewritten formula that is built into Excel. Similar SUM functions can be used in cells F13, G13, H13, and J13 to total gross pay, federal tax, state tax, and net pay, respectively. The following steps determine totals in cell D13, the range F13:H13, and cell J13.

1. Select the cell to contain the sum, cell D13 in this case. Click the Sum button (Home tab | Editing group) to sum the contents of the range D4:D12 in cell D13 and then click the Enter button to display a total in the selected cell.
2. Select the range to contain the sums, range F13:H13 in this case. Click the Sum button (Home tab | Editing group) to display totals in the selected range.

3 Select the cell to contain the sum, cell J13 in this case. Click the Sum button (Home tab | Editing group) to sum the contents of the range J4:J12 in cell J13 and then click the Enter button to display a total in the selected cell (Figure 2–15).

Q&A Why did I have to click the Enter button?
When calculating a sum for a single column, you click the Enter button. If you are calculating the sum for multiple ranges, you click the Sum button.

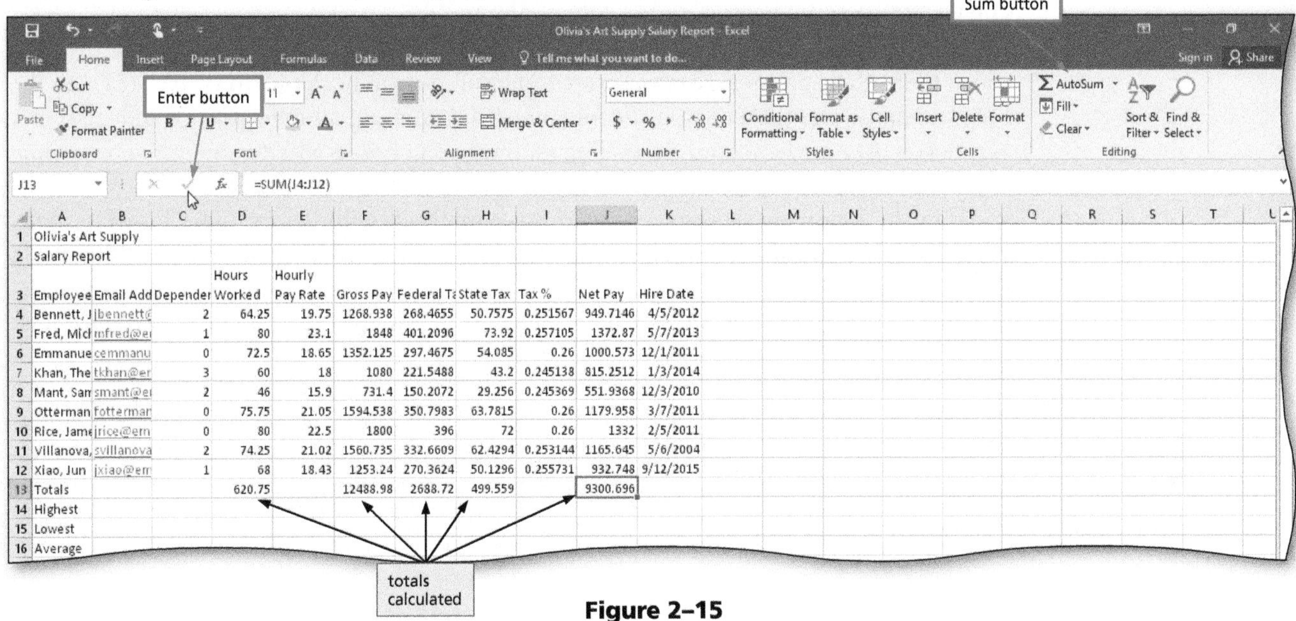

Figure 2–15

To Determine the Total Tax Percentage

With the totals in row 13 determined, the next step is to copy the tax percentage formula in cell I12 to cell I13. The following step copies the tax percentage formula.

1 Select the cell to be copied, I12 in this case, and then drag the fill handle down through cell I13 to copy the formula (Figure 2–16).

Q&A Why was the SUM function not used for tax percentage in I13?
The total tax percentage is calculated using the totals of the Gross Pay, Federal Tax and State Tax columns, not by summing the tax percentage column.

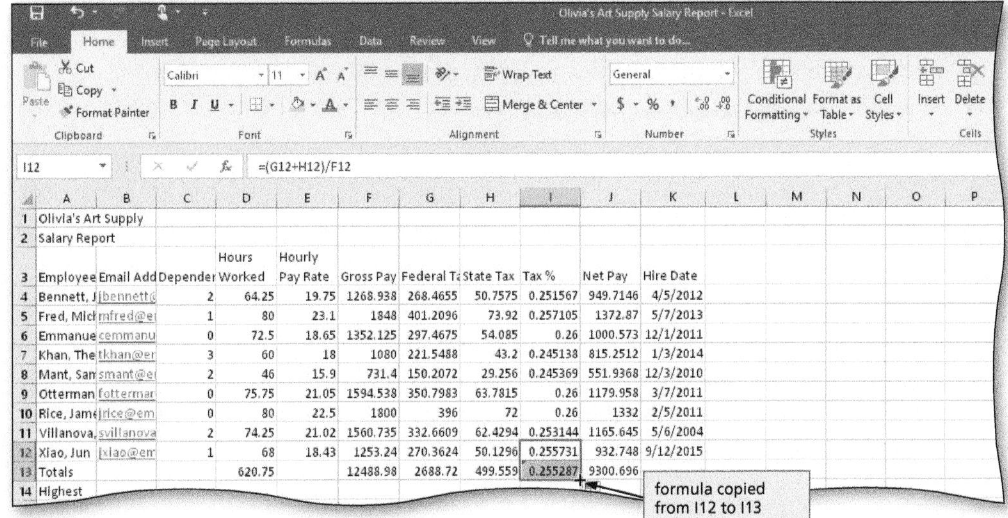

Figure 2–16

BTW
Statistical Functions
Excel usually considers a blank cell to be equal to 0. The statistical functions, however, ignore blank cells. Excel thus calculates the average of three cells with values of 10, blank, and 8 to be 9 [(10 + 8) / 2] and not 6 [(10 + 0 + 8) / 3].

Using the AVERAGE, MAX, and MIN Functions

The next step in creating the Olivia's Art Supply Salary Report worksheet is to compute the highest value, lowest value, and average value for the number of dependents listed in the range C4:C12 using the MAX, MIN, and AVERAGE functions in the range C14:C16. Once the values are determined for column C, the entries can be copied across to the other columns.

With Excel, you can enter functions using one of five methods: (1) keyboard, touch gesture, or pointer; (2) the Insert Function button in the formula bar; (3) the Sum menu; (4) the Sum button (Formulas tab | Function Library group); and (5) the Name box area in the formula bar. The method you choose will depend on your typing skills and whether you can recall the function name and required arguments.

In the following sections, three of these methods will be used. The Insert Function button in the formula bar method will be used to determine the highest number of dependents (cell C14). The Sum menu will be used to determine the lowest number of dependents (cell C15). The keyboard and pointer will be used to determine the average number of dependents (cell C16).

To Determine the Highest Number in a Range of Numbers Using the Insert Function Dialog Box

1 ENTER FORMULAS | 2 ENTER FUNCTIONS | 3 VERIFY FORMULAS
4 FORMAT WORKSHEET | 5 CHECK SPELLING | 6 PRINT WORKSHEET

The next step is to select cell C14 and determine the highest (maximum) number in the range C4:C12. Excel includes a function called the **MAX function** that displays the highest value in a range. The following steps use the Insert Function dialog box to enter the MAX function. ***Why?*** *Although you could enter the MAX function using the keyboard and Point mode as described previously, an alternative method to entering the function is to use the Insert Function button in the formula bar to open the Insert Function dialog box. The Insert Function dialog box is helpful if you do not remember the name of a function or need to search for a particular function by what it does.*

- Select the cell to contain the maximum number, cell C14 in this case.
- Click the Insert Function button in the formula bar to display the Insert Function dialog box.
- Click MAX in the Select a function list (Insert Function dialog box; Figure 2–17). You may need to scroll.

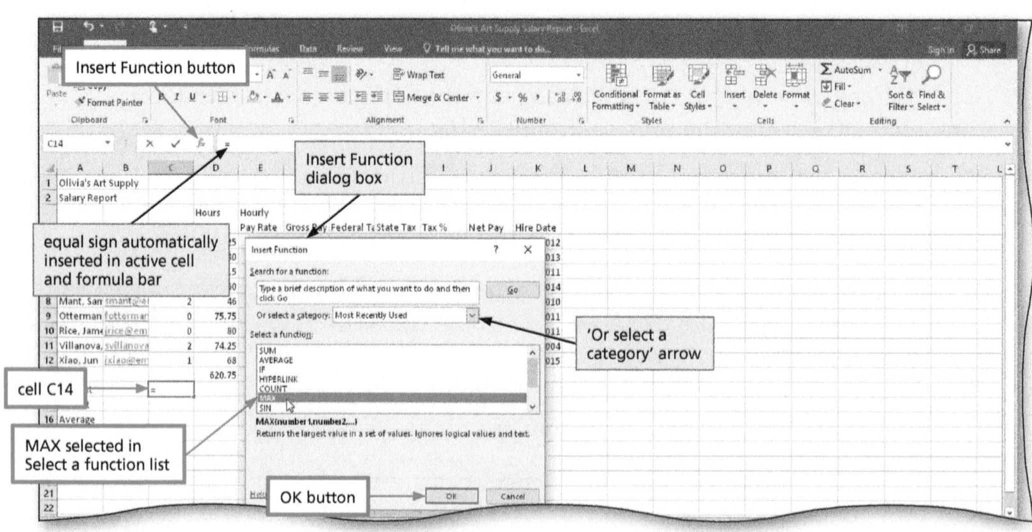

Figure 2–17

Q&A

What if the MAX function is not in the Select a function list?
Click the 'Or select a category' arrow to display the list of function categories, select All, and then scroll down and select the MAX function in the Select a function list.

How can I learn about other functions?
Excel has more than 400 functions that perform nearly every type of calculation you can imagine. These functions are categorized in the Insert Function dialog box shown in Figure 2–17. To view the categories, click the 'Or select a category' arrow. Click the name of a function in the Select a function list to display a description of the function.

2

- Click the OK button (Insert Function dialog box) to display the Function Arguments dialog box.
- Replace the text in the Number1 box with the text, `c4:c12` (Function Arguments dialog box) to enter the first argument of the function (Figure 2–18).

Q&A What are the numbers that appear to the right of the Number1 box in the Function Arguments dialog box?
The numbers shown to the right of the Number1 box are the values in the selected range (or if the range is large, the first few numbers only). Excel also displays the value the MAX function will return to cell C14 in the Function Arguments dialog box, shown in Figure 2–18.

Figure 2–18

3

- Click the OK button (Function Arguments dialog box) to display the highest value in the chosen range in cell C14 (Figure 2–19).

Q&A Why should I not just enter the highest value that I see in the range C4:C12 in cell C14?
In this example, rather than entering the MAX function, you could examine the range C4:C12, determine that the highest number of dependents is 3, and manually enter the number 3 as a constant in cell C14. Excel would display the number similar to how it appears in Figure 2–19. However, because C14 would then contain a constant, Excel would continue to display 3 in cell C14 even if the values in the range change. If you use the MAX function, Excel will recalculate the highest value in the range each time a new value is entered.

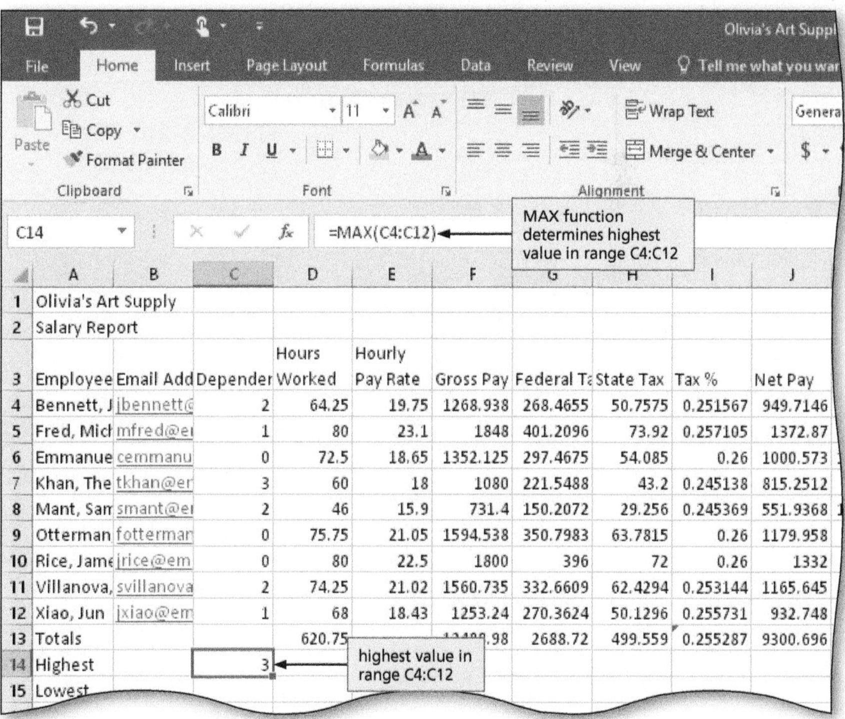

Figure 2–19

Other Ways

1. Click Sum arrow (Home tab | Editing group), click Max
2. Click Sum arrow (Formulas tab | Function Library group), click Max
3. Type **=MAX(** in cell, specify range, type)

To Determine the Lowest Number in a Range of Numbers Using the Sum Menu

1 ENTER FORMULAS | 2 ENTER FUNCTIONS | 3 VERIFY FORMULAS
4 FORMAT WORKSHEET | 5 CHECK SPELLING | 6 PRINT WORKSHEET

The next step is to enter the **MIN function** in cell C15 to determine the lowest (minimum) number in the range C4:C12. Although you can enter the MIN function using the method used to enter the MAX function, the following steps illustrate an alternative method using the Sum button (Home tab | Editing group). ***Why?*** *Using the Sum menu allows you quick access to five commonly used functions, without having to memorize their names or required arguments.*

- Select cell C15 and then click the Sum arrow (Home tab | Editing group) to display the Sum menu (Figure 2–20).

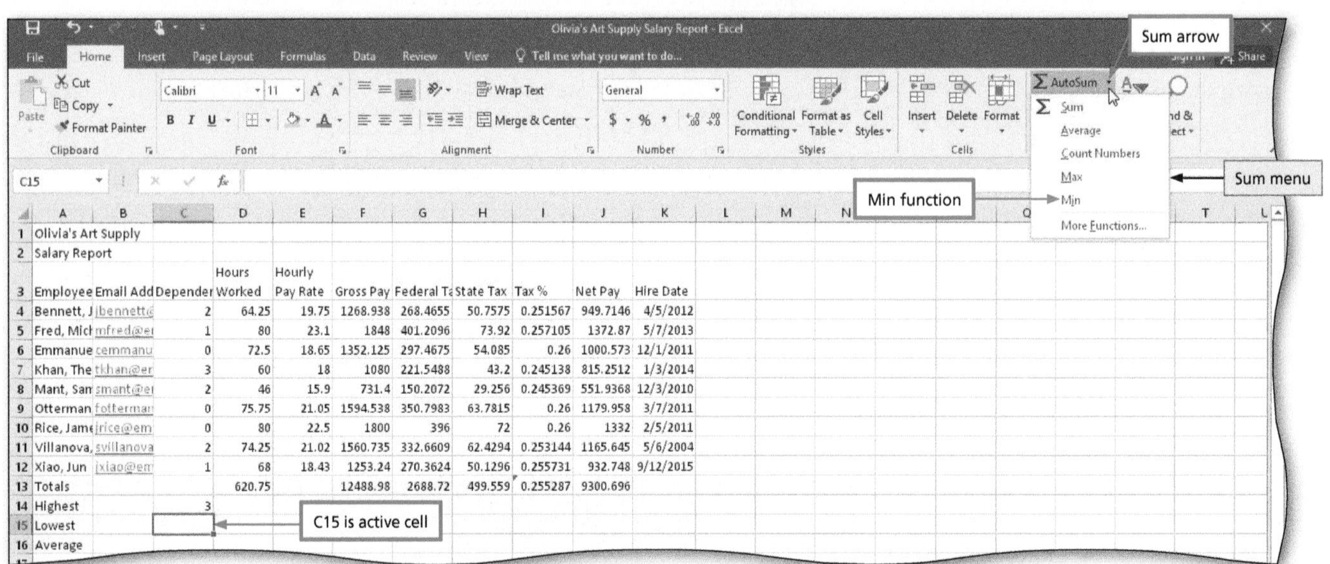

Figure 2–20

- Click Min to display the MIN function in the formula bar and in the active cell (Figure 2–21).

Q&A Why does Excel select the incorrect range?
The range selected by Excel is not always the right one. Excel attempts to guess which cells you want to include in the function by looking for ranges containing numeric data that are adjacent to the selected cell.

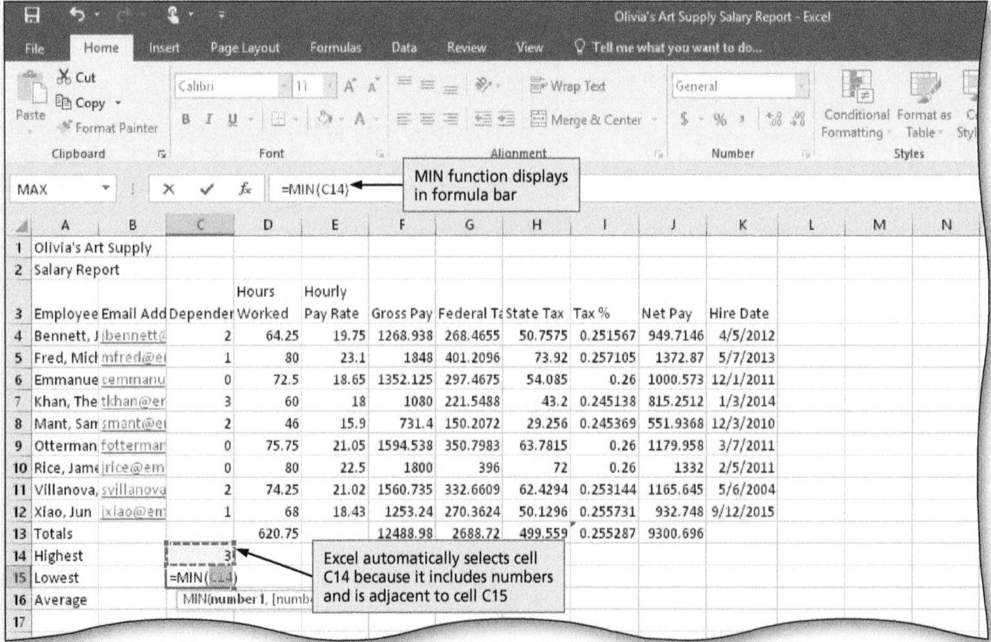

Figure 2–21

3

- Click cell C4 and then drag through cell C12 to update the function with the new range (Figure 2–22).

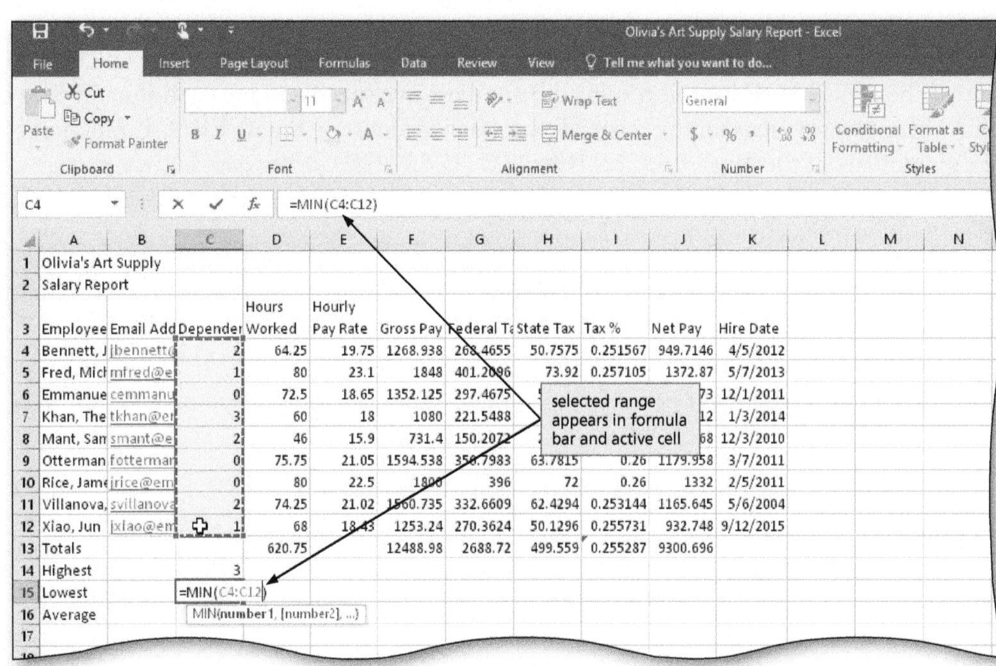

Figure 2–22

4

- Click the Enter button to determine the lowest value in the range C4:C12 and display the result in cell C15 (Figure 2–23).

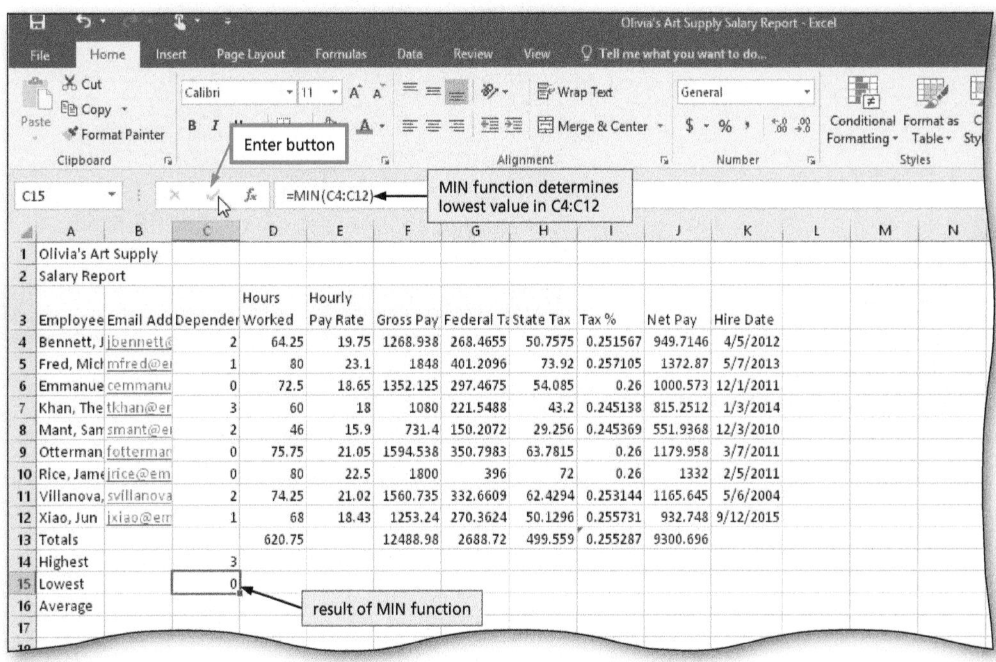

Figure 2–23

Other Ways

1. Click Insert Function button in formula bar, select Statistical category if necessary, click MIN, specify arguments
2. Click Sum arrow (Formulas tab | Function Library group), click Min
3. Type `=MIN(` in cell, fill in arguments, type `)`

To Determine the Average of a Range of Numbers Using the Keyboard

The **AVERAGE function** sums the numbers in a specified range and then divides the sum by the number of cells with numeric values in the range. The following steps use the AVERAGE function to determine the average of the numbers in the range C4:C12. ***Why?*** *The AVERAGE function calculates the average of a range of numbers.*

- Select the cell to contain the average, cell C16 in this case.
- Type **=av** in the cell to display the Formula AutoComplete list. Press the DOWN ARROW key to highlight the AVERAGE function (Figure 2–24).

Q&A What is happening as I type?
As you type the equal sign followed by the characters in the name of a function, Excel displays the Formula AutoComplete list. This list contains those functions whose names match the letters you have typed.

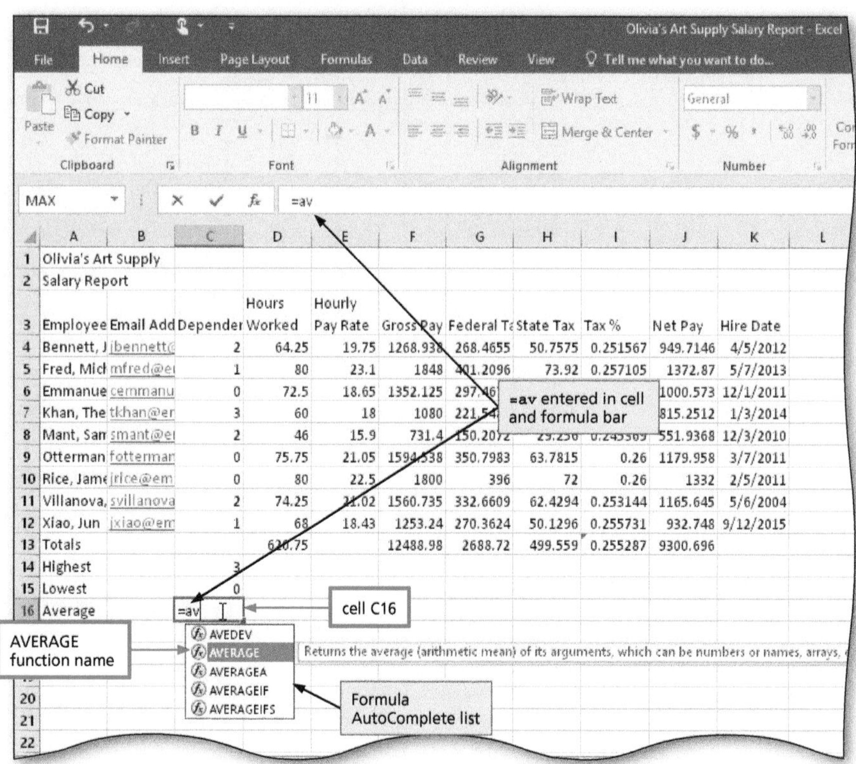

Figure 2–24

- Double-click AVERAGE in the Formula AutoComplete list to select the function.
- Select the range to be averaged, C4:C12 in this case, to insert the range as the argument to the function (Figure 2–25).

Q&A As I drag, why does the function in cell C16 change?
When you click cell C4, Excel surrounds cell C4 with a marquee and appends C4 to the left parenthesis in the formula bar. When you begin dragging, Excel appends to the argument a colon (:) and the cell reference of the cell where the pointer is located.

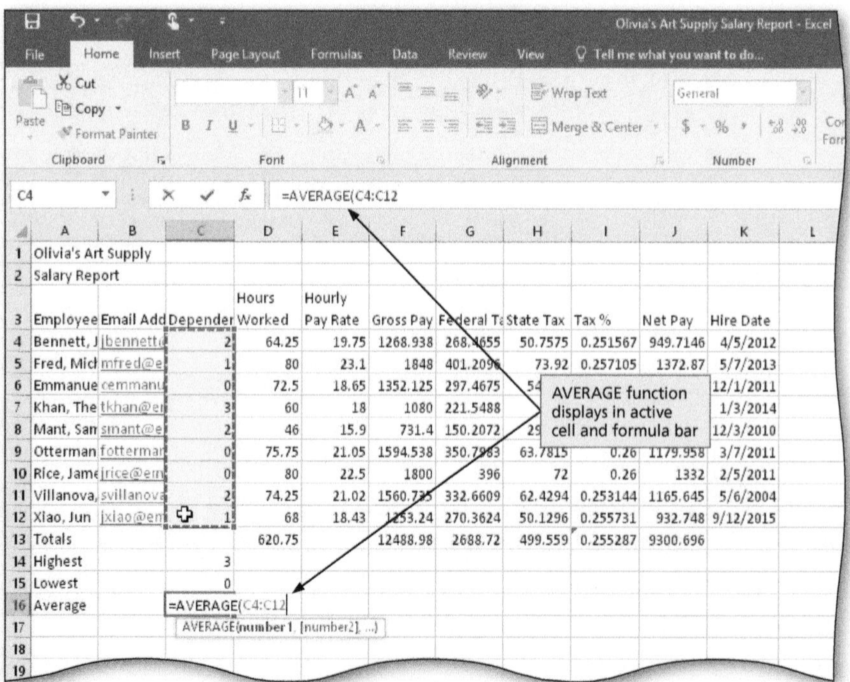

Figure 2–25

3

- Click the Enter button to compute the average of the numbers in the selected range and display the result in the selected cell (Figure 2–26).

Q&A Can I use the arrow keys to complete the entry instead?

No. While in Point mode, the arrow keys change the selected cell reference in the range you are selecting instead of completing the entry.

What is the purpose of the parentheses in the function?

Most Excel functions require that the argument (in this case, the range C4:C12) be included within parentheses following the function name. In this case, Excel appended the right parenthesis to complete the AVERAGE function when you clicked the Enter button.

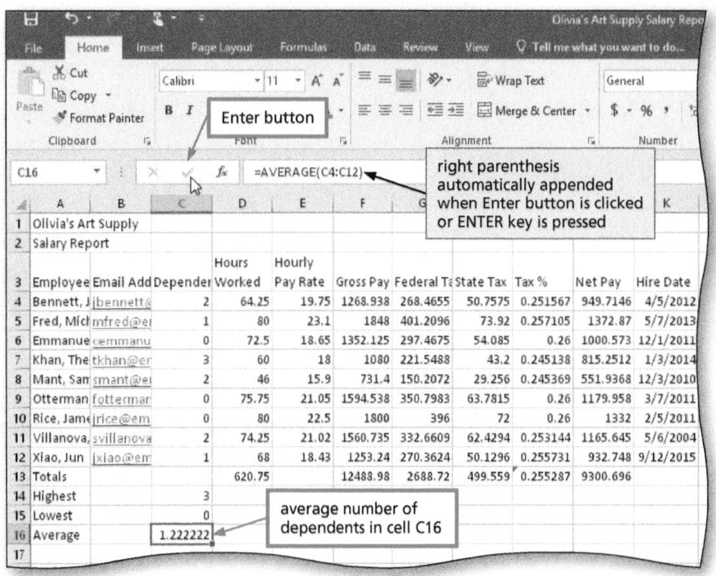

Figure 2–26

To Copy a Range of Cells across Columns to an Adjacent Range Using the Fill Handle

The next step is to copy the AVERAGE, MAX, and MIN functions in the range C14:C16 to the adjacent range D14:J16. The following steps use the fill handle to copy the functions.

1. Select the source range from which to copy the functions, in this case C14:C16.
2. Drag the fill handle in the lower-right corner of the selected range through cell J16 to copy the three functions to the selected range.
3. Select cell I16 and then press the DELETE key to delete the average of the Tax % (Figure 2–27).

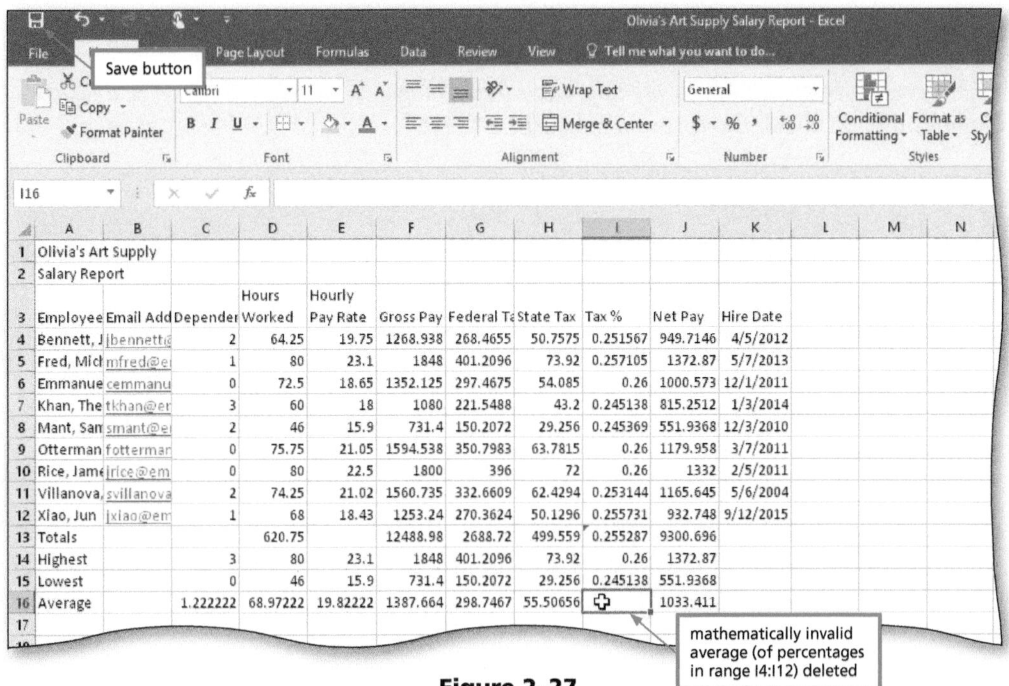

Figure 2–27

4 Save the workbook again on the same storage location with the same file name.

Q&A

Why delete the formula in cell I16?
You deleted the average in cell I16 because averaging this type of percentage is mathematically invalid.

How can I be sure that the function arguments are correct for the cells in range D14:J16?
Remember that Excel adjusts the cell references in the copied functions so that each function refers to the range of numbers above it in the same column. Review the functions in rows 14 through 16 by clicking on individual cells and examining the function as it appears in the formula bar. You should see that the functions in each column reference the appropriate ranges.

Other Ways

1. Select source area, click Copy button (Home tab | Clipboard group), select destination area, click Paste button (Home tab | Clipboard group)
2. Right-click source area, click Copy on shortcut menu; right-click destination area, click Paste icon on shortcut menu
3. Select source area and then point to border of range; while holding down CTRL, drag source area to destination area
4. Select source area, press CTRL+C, select destination area, press CTRL+V

Break Point: If you wish to take a break, this is a good place to do so. You can exit Excel now. To resume at a later time, run Excel, open the file called Olivia's Art Supply Salary Report, and continue following the steps from this location forward.

Verifying Formulas Using Range Finder

One of the more common mistakes made with Excel is to include an incorrect cell reference in a formula. An easy way to verify that a formula references the cells you want it to reference is to use Range Finder. **Range Finder** checks which cells are referenced in the formula assigned to the active cell.

To use Range Finder to verify that a formula contains the intended cell references, double-click the cell with the formula you want to check. Excel responds by highlighting the cells referenced in the formula so that you can verify that the cell references are correct.

To Verify a Formula Using Range Finder

1 ENTER FORMULAS | 2 ENTER FUNCTIONS | 3 VERIFY FORMULAS
4 FORMAT WORKSHEET | 5 CHECK SPELLING | 6 PRINT WORKSHEET

Why? Range Finder allows you to correct mistakes by making immediate changes to the cells referenced in a formula. The following steps use Range Finder to check the formula in cell I4.

- Double-click cell I4 to activate Range Finder (Figure 2–28).

- Press the ESC key to quit Range Finder and then click anywhere in the worksheet, such as cell A18, to deselect the current cell.

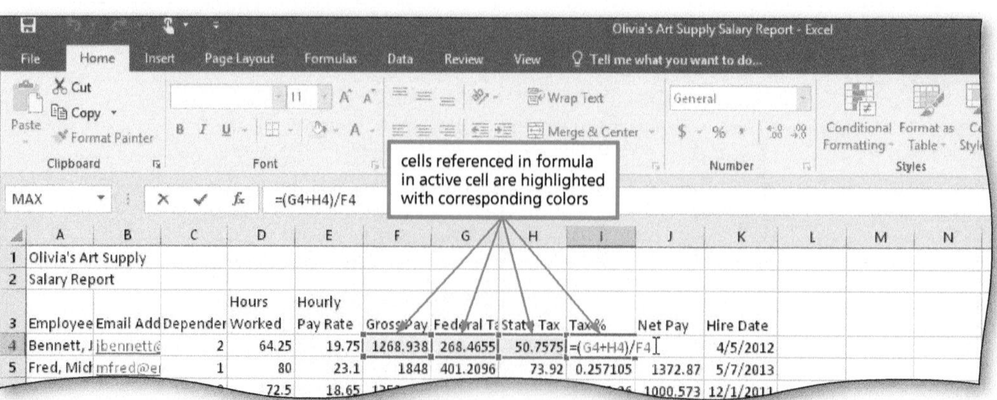

Figure 2–28

Formatting the Worksheet

Although the worksheet contains the appropriate data, formulas, and functions, the text and numbers need to be formatted to improve their appearance and readability.

In Module 1, cell styles were used to format much of the worksheet. This section describes how to change the unformatted worksheet in Figure 2–29a to the formatted worksheet in Figure 2–29b using a theme and other commands on the ribbon. A **theme** formats a worksheet by applying a collection of fonts, font styles, colors, and effects to give it a consistent appearance.

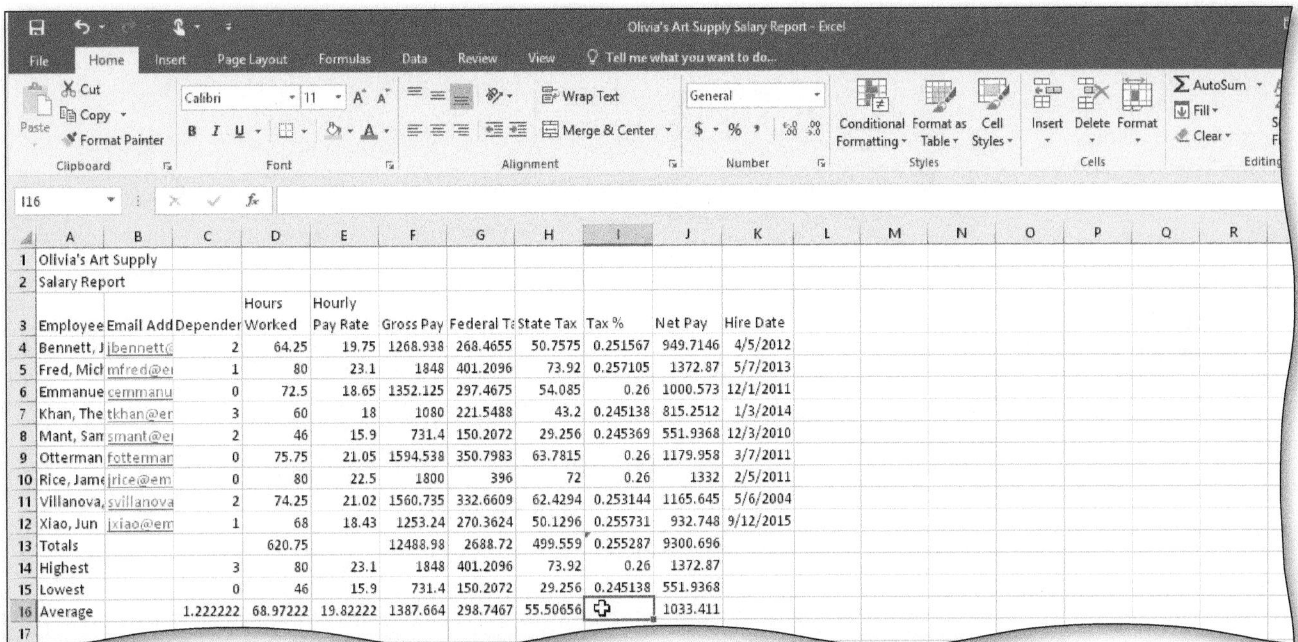

	A	B	C	D	E	F	G	H	I	J	K
1	Olivia's Art Supply										
2	Salary Report										
3	Employee	Email Add	Depender	Hours Worked	Hourly Pay Rate	Gross Pay	Federal Ta	State Tax	Tax %	Net Pay	Hire Date
4	Bennett, J	jbennett@	2	64.25	19.75	1268.938	268.4655	50.7575	0.251567	949.7146	4/5/2012
5	Fred, Mich	mfred@e	1	80	23.1	1848	401.2096	73.92	0.257105	1372.87	5/7/2013
6	Emmanue	cemmanu	0	72.5	18.65	1352.125	297.4675	54.085	0.26	1000.573	12/1/2011
7	Khan, The	tkhan@er	3	60	18	1080	221.5488	43.2	0.245138	815.2512	1/3/2014
8	Mant, Sam	smant@e	2	46	15.9	731.4	150.2072	29.256	0.245369	551.9368	12/3/2010
9	Otterman	fotterman	0	75.75	21.05	1594.538	350.7983	63.7815	0.26	1179.958	3/7/2011
10	Rice, Jame	jrice@em	0	80	22.5	1800	396	72	0.26	1332	2/5/2011
11	Villanova,	svillanova	2	74.25	21.02	1560.735	332.6609	62.4294	0.253144	1165.645	5/6/2004
12	Xiao, Jun	jxiao@em	1	68	18.43	1253.24	270.3624	50.1296	0.255731	932.748	9/12/2015
13	Totals			620.75		12488.98	2688.72	499.559	0.255287	9300.696	
14	Highest		3	80	23.1	1848	401.2096	73.92	0.26	1372.87	
15	Lowest		0	46	15.9	731.4	150.2072	29.256	0.245138	551.9368	
16	Average		1.222222	68.97222	19.82222	1387.664	298.7467	55.50656		1033.411	
17											

(a) Unformatted Worksheet

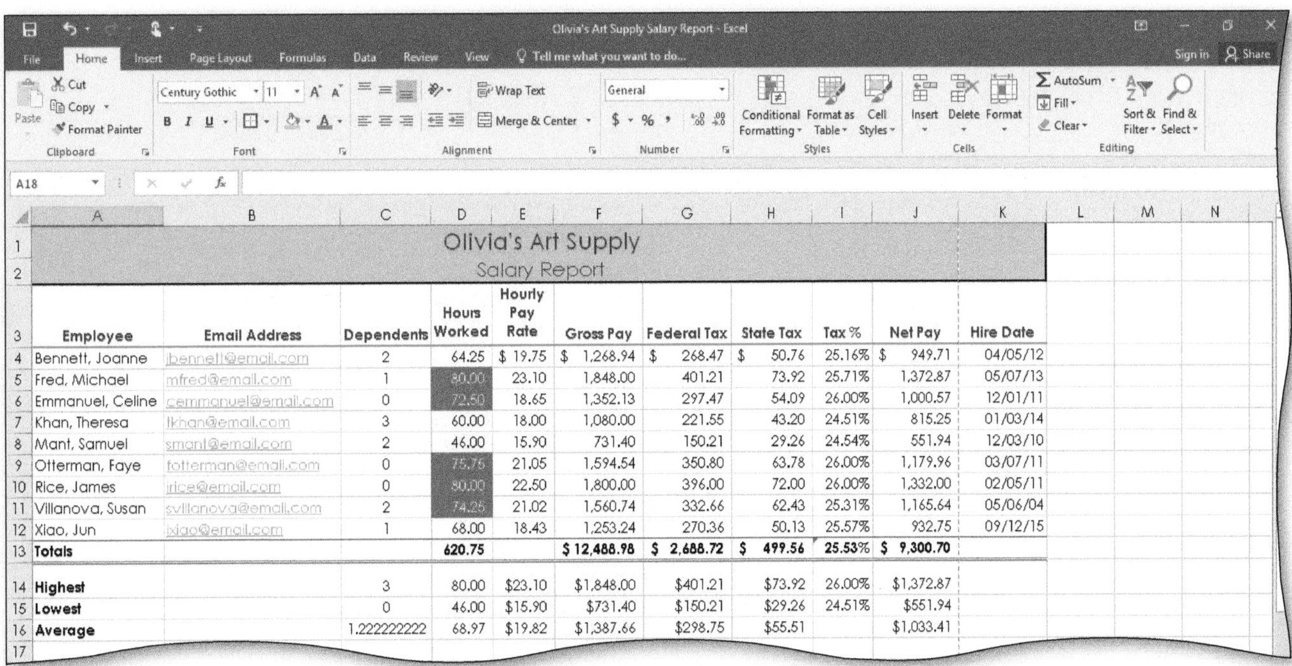

	A	B	C	D	E	F	G	H	I	J	K
1	Olivia's Art Supply										
2	Salary Report										
3	Employee	Email Address	Dependents	Hours Worked	Hourly Pay Rate	Gross Pay	Federal Tax	State Tax	Tax %	Net Pay	Hire Date
4	Bennett, Joanne	jbennett@email.com	2	64.25	$ 19.75	$ 1,268.94	$ 268.47	$ 50.76	25.16%	$ 949.71	04/05/12
5	Fred, Michael	mfred@email.com	1	80.00	23.10	1,848.00	401.21	73.92	25.71%	1,372.87	05/07/13
6	Emmanuel, Celine	cemmanuel@email.com	0	72.50	18.65	1,352.13	297.47	54.09	26.00%	1,000.57	12/01/11
7	Khan, Theresa	tkhan@email.com	3	60.00	18.00	1,080.00	221.55	43.20	24.51%	815.25	01/03/14
8	Mant, Samuel	smant@email.com	2	46.00	15.90	731.40	150.21	29.26	24.54%	551.94	12/03/10
9	Otterman, Faye	fotterman@email.com	0	75.75	21.05	1,594.54	350.80	63.78	26.00%	1,179.96	03/07/11
10	Rice, James	jrice@email.com	0	80.00	22.50	1,800.00	396.00	72.00	26.00%	1,332.00	02/05/11
11	Villanova, Susan	svillanova@email.com	2	74.25	21.02	1,560.74	332.66	62.43	25.31%	1,165.64	05/06/04
12	Xiao, Jun	jxiao@email.com	1	68.00	18.43	1,253.24	270.36	50.13	25.57%	932.75	09/12/15
13	**Totals**			620.75		$ 12,488.98	$ 2,688.72	$ 499.56	25.53%	$ 9,300.70	
14	**Highest**		3	80.00	$23.10	$1,848.00	$401.21	$73.92	26.00%	$1,372.87	
15	**Lowest**		0	46.00	$15.90	$731.40	$150.21	$29.26	24.51%	$551.94	
16	**Average**		1.222222222	68.97	$19.82	$1,387.66	$298.75	$55.51		$1,033.41	
17											

(b) Formatted Worksheet

Figure 2–29

To Change the Workbook Theme

***Why?** A company or department may choose a specific theme as their standard theme so that all of their documents have a similar appearance. Similarly, you may want to have a theme that sets your work apart from the work of others. Other Office programs, such as Word and PowerPoint, include the same themes so that all of your Microsoft Office documents can share a common look.* The following steps change the workbook theme to the Ion theme.

1

- Click Page Layout to display the Page Layout tab.
- Click the Themes button (Page Layout tab | Themes group) to display the Themes gallery (Figure 2–30).

Experiment

- Point to several themes in the Themes gallery to preview the themes.

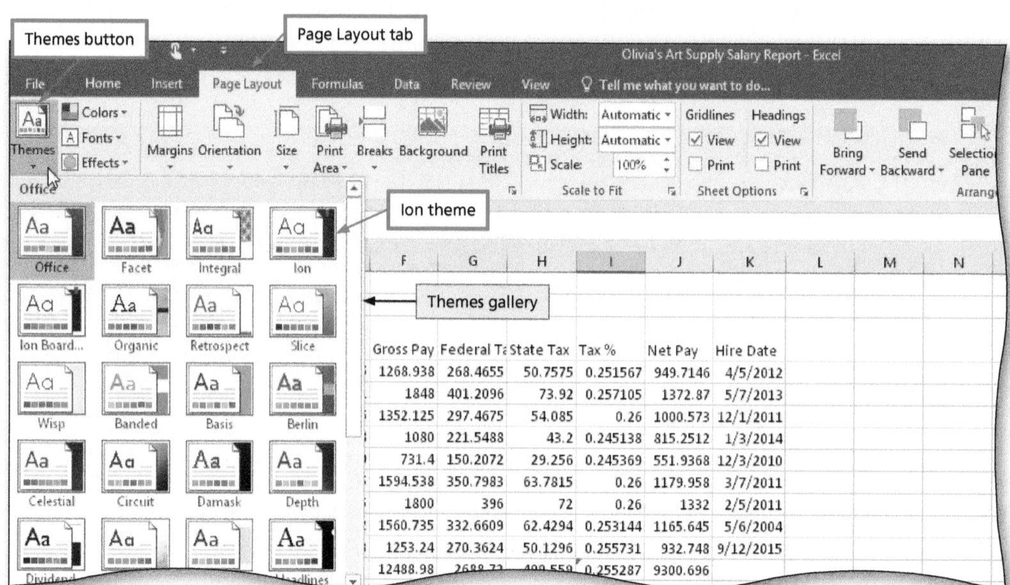

Figure 2–30

2

- Click Ion in the Themes gallery to change the workbook theme (Figure 2–31).

Q&A Why did the cells in the worksheet change?
Originally, the cells in the worksheet were formatted with the default font of the default Office theme. The Ion theme has a different default font than the Office theme, so when you changed the theme, the font changed. If you had modified the font for any cells, those cells would not have changed to the default font of the Ion theme.

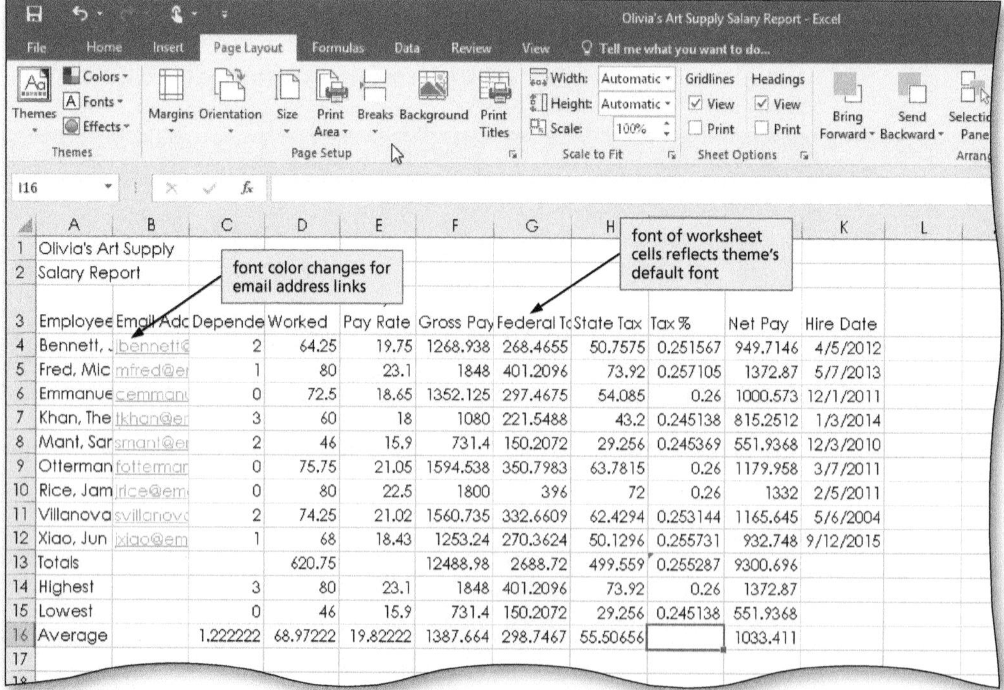

Figure 2–31

To Format the Worksheet Titles

The following steps merge and center the worksheet titles, apply the Title cells style to the worksheet titles, and decrease the font of the worksheet subtitle.

1. Display the Home tab.

2. Select the range to be merged, A1:K1 in this case, and then click the 'Merge & Center' button (Home tab | Alignment group) to merge and center the text in the selected range.

3. Select the range A2:K2 and then click the 'Merge & Center' button (Home tab | Alignment group) to merge and center the text.

4. Select the range to contain the Title cell style, in this case A1:A2, click the Cell Styles button (Home tab | Styles group) to display the Cell Styles gallery, and then click the Title cell style in the Cell Styles gallery to apply the Title cell style to the selected range.

5. Select cell A2 and then click the 'Decrease Font Size' button (Home tab | Font group) to decrease the font size of the selected cell to the next lower font size (Figure 2–32).

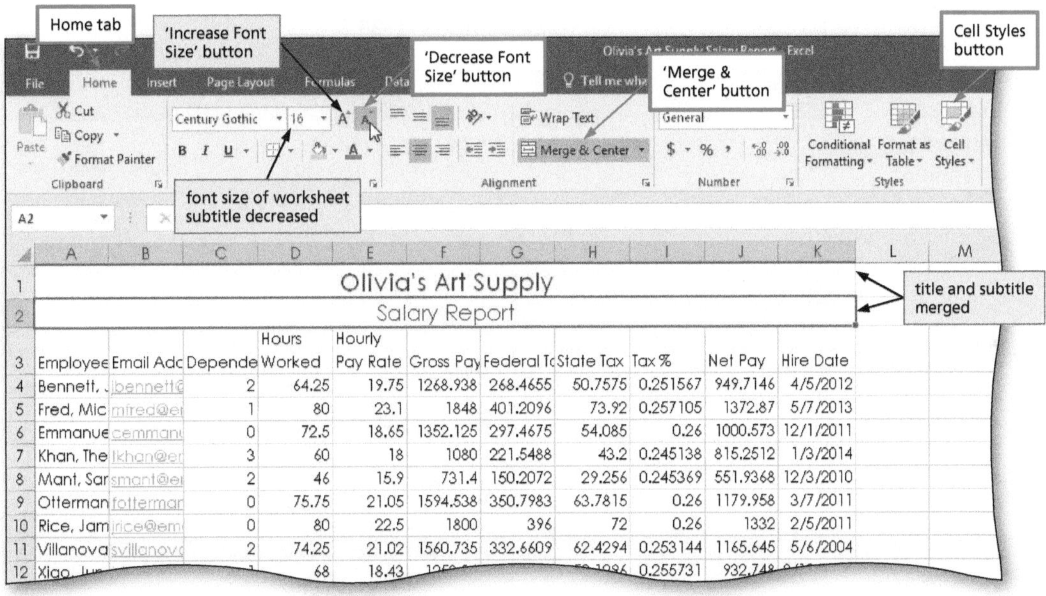

Figure 2–32

Q&A What happens when I click the 'Decrease Font Size' button?
When you click the 'Decrease Font Size' button, Excel assigns the next smaller font size in the Font Size gallery to the selected range. The 'Increase Font Size' button works in a similar manner, assigning the next larger font size in the Font Size gallery to the selected range.

CONSIDER THIS

Which colors work best when formatting your worksheet?
Knowing how people perceive colors can help you focus attention on parts of your worksheet. Warmer colors (red and orange) tend to reach toward the reader. Cooler colors (blue, green, and violet) tend to pull away from the reader.

To Change the Background Color and Apply a Box Border to the Worksheet Title and Subtitle

1 ENTER FORMULAS | 2 ENTER FUNCTIONS | 3 VERIFY FORMULAS
4 FORMAT WORKSHEET | 5 CHECK SPELLING | 6 PRINT WORKSHEET

Why? A background color and border can draw attention to the title of a worksheet. The final formats assigned to the worksheet title and subtitle are the blue-gray background color and thick outside border. The following steps complete the formatting of the worksheet titles.

- Select the range A1:A2 and then click the Fill Color arrow (Home tab | Font group) to display the Fill Color gallery (Figure 2–33).

Experiment

- Point to a variety of colors in the Fill Color gallery to preview the selected colors in the range A1:A2.

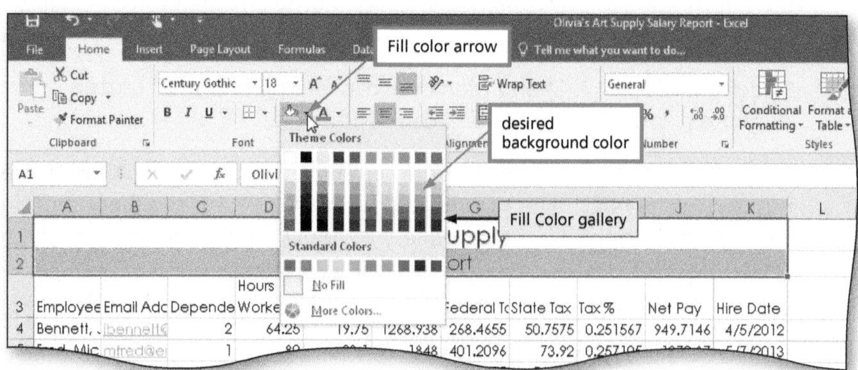

Figure 2–33

2

- Click Blue-Gray, Accent 5, Lighter 60% (column 9, row 3) in the Theme Colors area to change the background color of the range of cells (Figure 2–34).

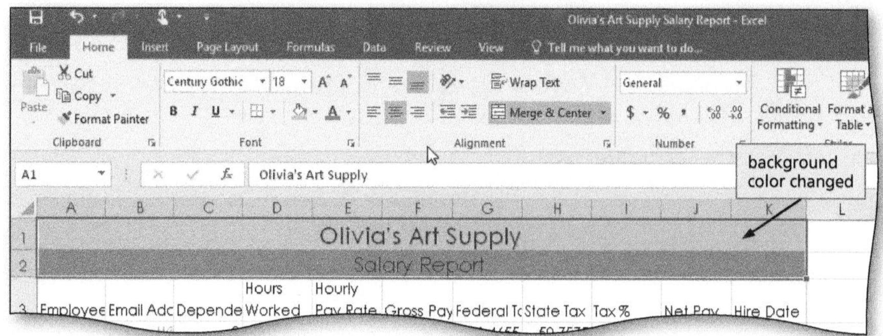

Figure 2–34

3

- Click the Borders arrow (Home tab | Font group) to display the Borders gallery (Figure 2–35).

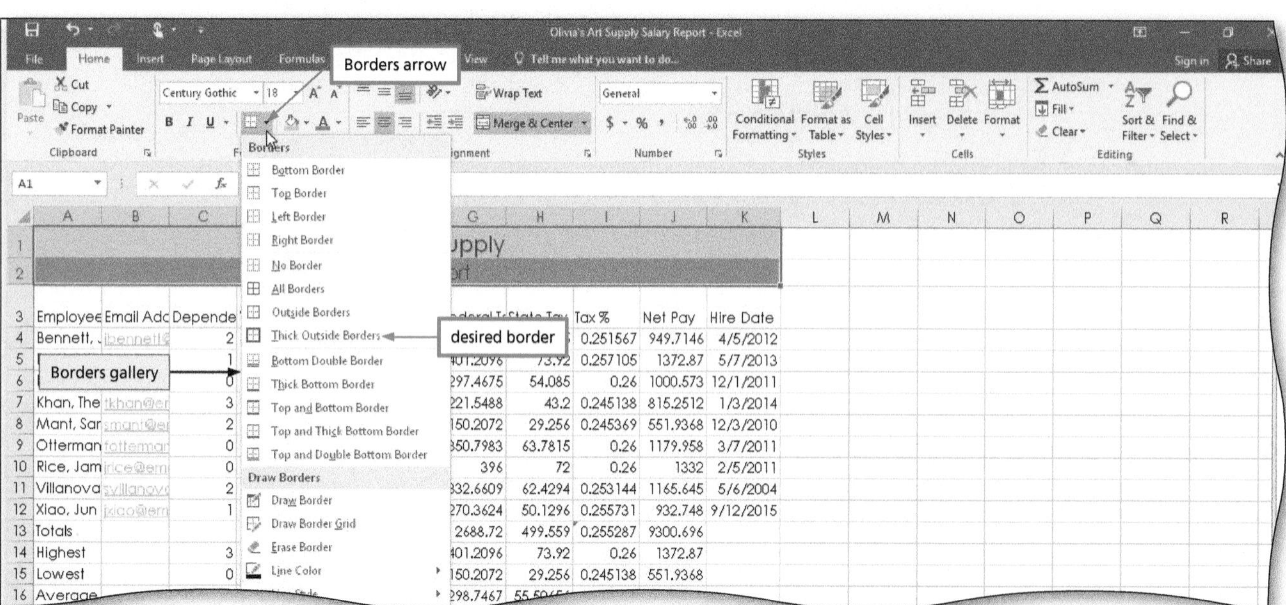

Figure 2–35

4

- Click 'Thick Outside Borders' in the Borders gallery to create a thick outside border around the selected range.
- Click anywhere in the worksheet, such as cell A18, to deselect the current range (Figure 2–36).

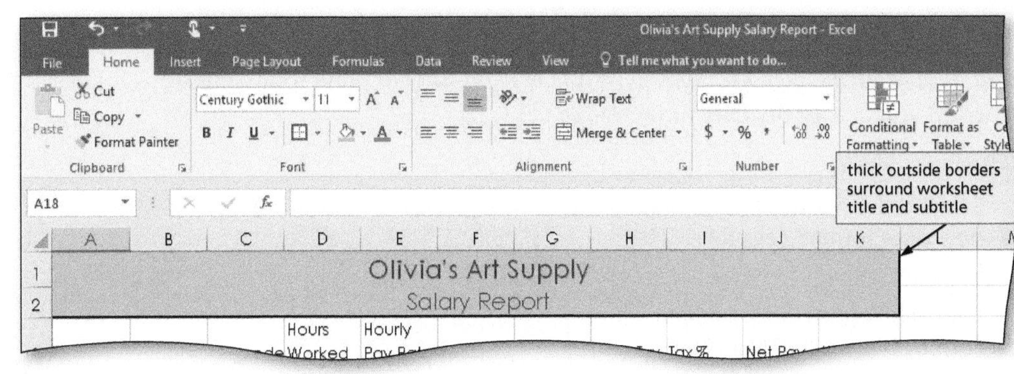

Figure 2–36

Other Ways

1. Click Font Settings Dialog Box Launcher (Home tab | Font group), click Fill tab (Format Cells dialog box), click desired fill, click OK button
2. Right-click range, click Format Cells on shortcut menu, click Fill tab (Format Cells dialog box), click desired fill, click OK button
3. Press CTRL+1, click Fill tab (Format Cells dialog box), click desired fill, click OK button

To Apply a Cell Style to the Column Headings and Format the Total Rows

As shown in Figure 2–29b, the column titles (row 3) should have the Heading 3 cell style and the totals row (row 13) should have the Total cell style. The headings in the range A14:A16 should be bold. The following steps assign these styles and formats to row 3, row 13, and the range A14:A16.

BTW

Color Selection

Bright colors jump out of a dark background and are easiest to see. White or yellow text on a dark blue, green, purple, or black background is ideal for highlighting.

1. Select the range to be formatted, cells A3:K3 in this case.
2. Use the Cell Styles gallery to apply the Heading 3 cell style to the range A3:K3.
3. Click the Center button (Home tab | Alignment group) to center the column headings.
4. Apply the Total cell style to the range A13:K13.
5. Bold the range A14:A16 (Figure 2–37).

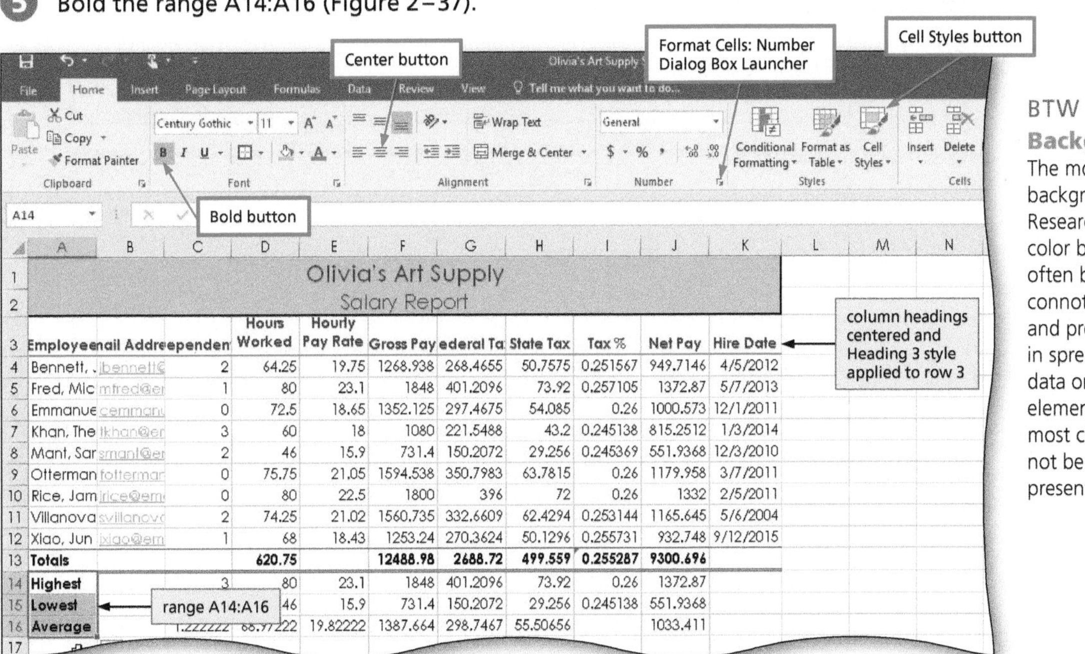

Figure 2–37

BTW

Background Colors

The most popular background color is blue. Research shows that the color blue is used most often because this color connotes serenity, reflection, and proficiency. Use color in spreadsheets to highlight data or to format worksheet elements such as titles. In most cases, colors should not be used for data presentation.

To Format Dates and Center Data in Cells

Why? You may want to change the format of the dates to better suit your needs. In addition, numbers that are not used in calculations often are centered instead of right-aligned. The following steps format the dates in the range K4:K12 and center the data in the range C4:C16.

1

- Select the range to contain the new date format, cells K4:K12 in this case.
- Click the Format Cells: Number Format Dialog Box Launcher (Home tab | Number group) (shown in Figure 2–37) to display the Format Cells dialog box.
- If necessary, click the Number tab (Format Cells dialog box), click Date in the Category list, and then click 03/14/12 in the Type list to choose the format for the selected range (Figure 2–38).

- Click the OK button (Format Cells dialog box) to format the dates in the current column using the selected date format style.

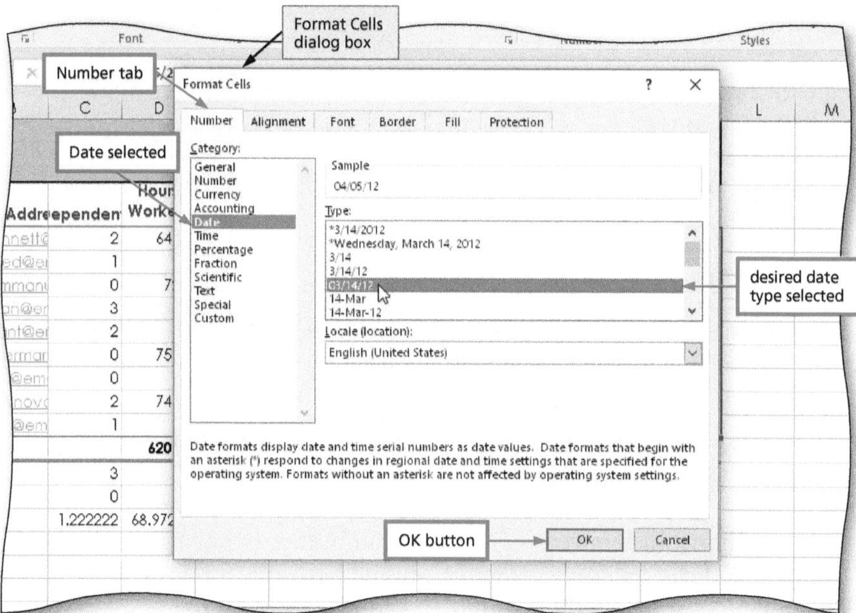

Figure 2–38

- Select the range C4:C16 and then click the Center button (Home tab | Alignment group) to center the data in the selected range.
- Select cell E4 to deselect the selected range (Figure 2–39).

Q&A How can I format an entire column at once?
Instead of selecting the range C4:C16 in Step 3, you could have clicked the column C heading immediately above cell C1, and then clicked the Center button (Home tab | Alignment group). In this case, all cells in column C down to the last cell in the worksheet would have been formatted to use center alignment. This same procedure could have been used to format the dates in column K.

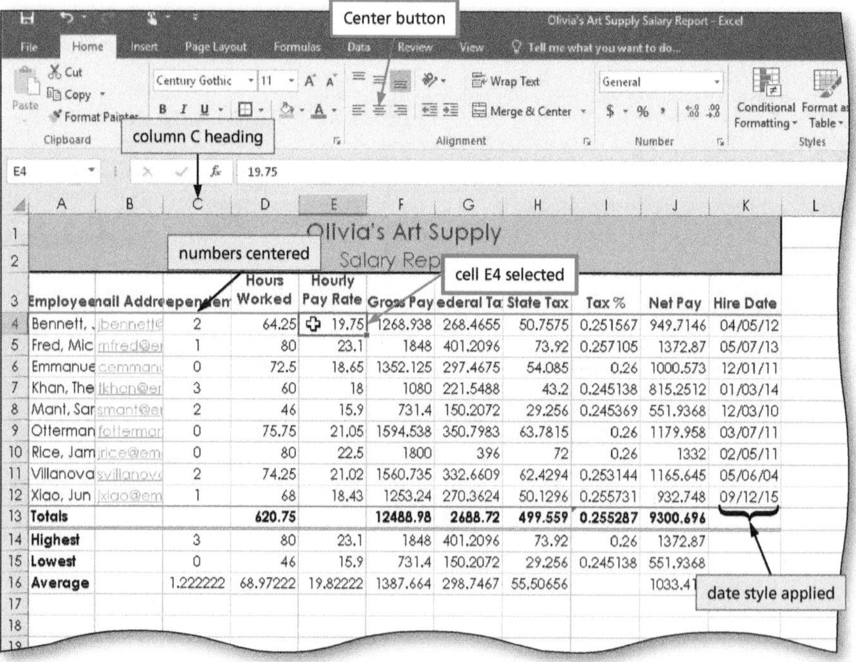

Figure 2–39

Other Ways

1. Right-click range, click Format Cells on shortcut menu, click Number tab (Format Cells dialog box), click desired number format, click OK button
2. Press CTRL+1, click Number tab (Format Cells dialog box), click desired number format, click OK button

To Apply an Accounting Number Format and Comma Style Format Using the Ribbon

As shown in Figure 2–29b, the worksheet is formatted to resemble an accounting report. In columns E through H and J, the numbers in the first row (row 4), the totals row (row 13), and the rows below the totals (rows 14 through 16) have dollar signs, while the remaining numbers (rows 5 through 12) in columns E through H and column J do not. The following steps assign formats using the 'Accounting Number Format' button and the Comma Style button. ***Why?*** *This gives the worksheet a more professional look.*

1. Select the range to contain the accounting number format, cells E4:H4 in this case.
2. While holding down the CTRL key, select cell J4, the range F13:H13, and cell J13 to select the nonadjacent ranges and cells.
3. Click the 'Accounting Number Format' button (Home tab | Number group) to apply the accounting number format with fixed dollar signs to the selected nonadjacent ranges.

Q&A What is the effect of applying the accounting number format?
The 'Accounting Number Format' button assigns a fixed dollar sign to the numbers in the ranges and rounds the figure to the nearest 100th. A fixed dollar sign is one that appears to the far left of the cell, with multiple spaces between it and the first digit in the cell.

4. Select the ranges to contain the comma style format, cells E5:H12 and J5:J12 in this case.
5. Click the Comma Style button (Home tab | Number group) to assign the comma style format to the selected ranges.
6. Select the range D4:D16 and then click the Comma Style button (Home tab | Number group) to assign the comma style format to the selected range (Figure 2–40).

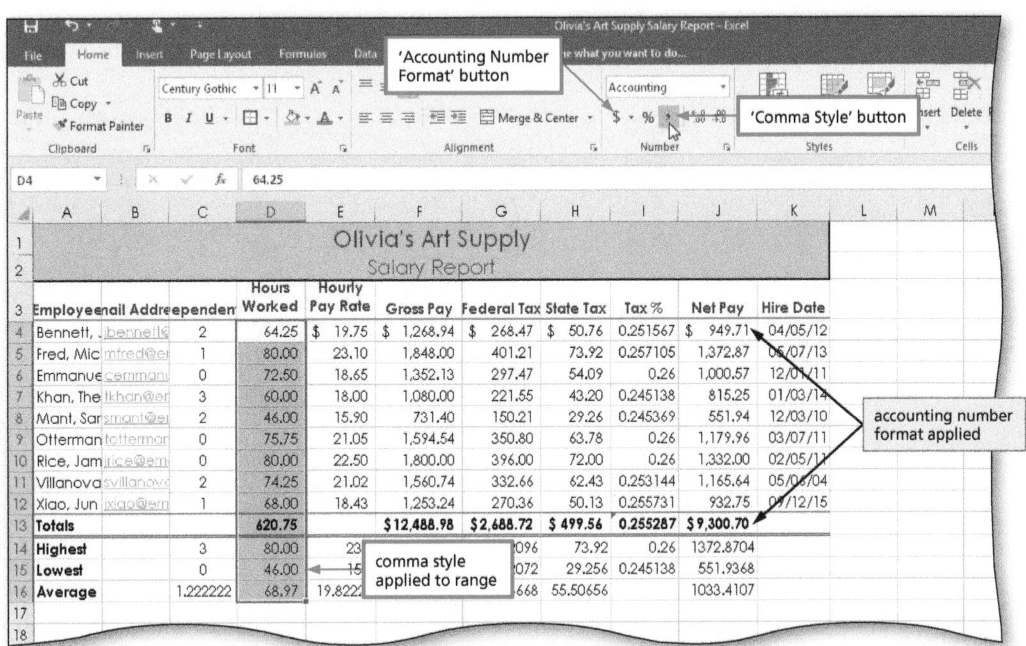

Figure 2–40

To Apply a Currency Style Format with a Floating Dollar Sign Using the Format Cells Dialog Box

***Why?** The Currency format places dollar signs immediately to the left of the number (known as floating dollar signs, as they change position depending on the number of digits in the cell) and displays a zero for cells that have a value of zero.* The following steps use the Format Cells dialog box to apply the currency style format with a floating dollar sign to the numbers in the ranges E14:H16 and J14:J16.

1

- Select the ranges (E14:H16 and J14:J16) and then click the Number Format Dialog Box Launcher (Home tab | Number group) to display the Format Cells dialog box.
- If necessary, click the Number tab to display the Number sheet (Format Cells dialog box).
- Click Currency in the Category list to select the necessary number format category and then click the third style ($1,234.10) in the Negative numbers list to select the desired currency format for negative numbers (Figure 2–41).

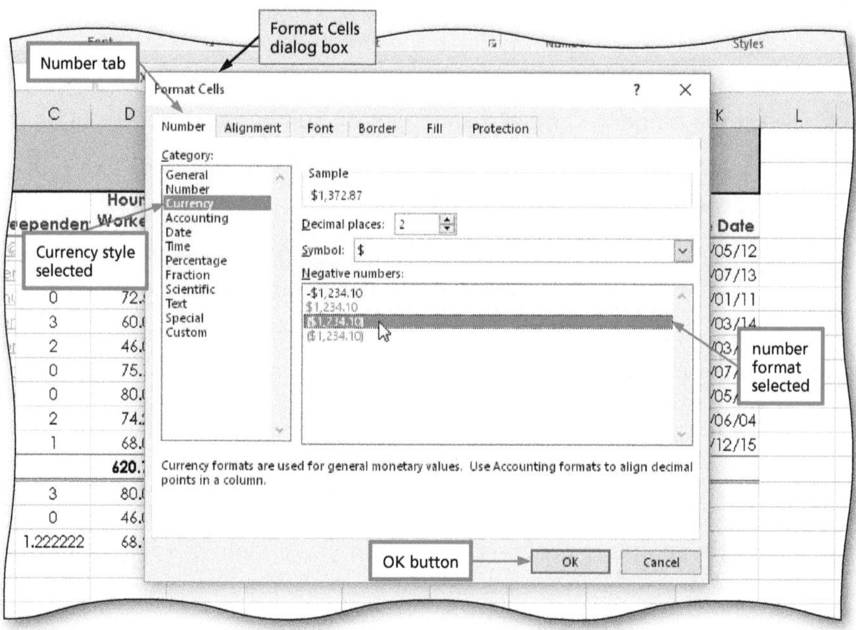

Figure 2–41

Q&A How do I decide which number format to use?
Excel offers many ways to format numbers. Once you select a number category, you can select the number of decimal places, whether to include a dollar sign (or a symbol of another currency), and how negative numbers should appear. Selecting the appropriate negative numbers format is important, because some formats add a space to the right of the number in order to align numbers in the worksheet on the decimal points and some do not.

2

- Click the OK button (Format Cells dialog box) to assign the currency style format with a floating dollar sign to the selected ranges (Figure 2–42).

5	Fred, Mic	mfred@e	1	80.00	23.10	1,848.00	401.21	73.92	0.257105	1,372.87	05/07/13
6	Emmanue	cemman	0	72.50	18.65	1,352.13	297.47	54.09	0.26	1,000.57	12/01/11
7	Khan, The	tkhan@e	3	60.00	18.00	1,080.00	221.55	43.20	0.245138	815.25	01/03/14
8	Mant, Sar	smant@e	2	46.00	15.90	731.40	150.21	29.26	0.245369	551.94	12/03/10
9	Otterman	fotterman	0	75.75	21.05	1,594.54	350.80	63.78	0.26	1,179.96	03/07/11
10	Rice, Jam	jrice@em	0	80.00	22.50	1,800.00	396.00	72.00	0.26	1,332.00	02/05/11
11	Villanova	svillanov	2	74.25	21.02	1,560.74	332.66	62.43	0.253144	1,165.64	05/06/04
12	Xiao, Jun	jxiao@em	1	68.00	18.43	1,253.24	270.36	50.13	0.255731	932.75	09/12/15
13	**Totals**			**620.75**		**$12,488.98**	**$2,688.72**	**$ 499.56**	**0.255287**	**$9,300.70**	
14	**Highest**		3	80.00	$23.10	$1,848.00	$401.21	$73.92	0.26	$1,372.87	
15	**Lowest**		0	46.00	$15.90	$731.40	$150.21	$29.26	0.245138	$551.94	
16	**Average**		1.222222	68.97	$19.82	$1,387.66	$298.75	$55.51		$1,033.41	
17											
18											
19											

Salary Report

Ready — Average: $532.86

currency style applied to selected ranges

Figure 2–42

Q&A What is the difference between using the accounting number style and currency style?
When using the currency style, recall that a floating dollar sign always appears immediately to the left of the first digit. With the accounting number style, the fixed dollar sign always appears on the left side of the cell.

Other Ways

1. Press CTRL+1, click Number tab (Format Cells dialog box), click Currency in Category list, select format, click OK button
2. Press CTRL+SHIFT+DOLLAR SIGN ($)

To Apply a Percent Style Format and Use the Increase Decimal Button

The next step is to format the tax percentage in column I. ***Why?*** *Currently, Excel displays the numbers as decimal fractions when they should appear as percentages.* The following steps format the range I4:I15 to the percent style format with two decimal places.

1

- Select the range to format, cells I4:I15 in this case.
- Click the Percent Style button (Home tab | Number group) to display the numbers in the selected range as a rounded whole percent.

Q&A What is the result of clicking the Percent Style button?
The Percent Style button instructs Excel to display a value as a percentage, which is determined by multiplying the cell entry by 100, rounding the result to the nearest percentage, and adding a percent sign. For example, when cell I4 is formatted using the Percent Style buttons, Excel displays the actual value 0.251567 as 25%.

- Click the Increase Decimal button (Home tab | Number group) two times to display the numbers in the selected range with two decimal places (Figure 2–43).

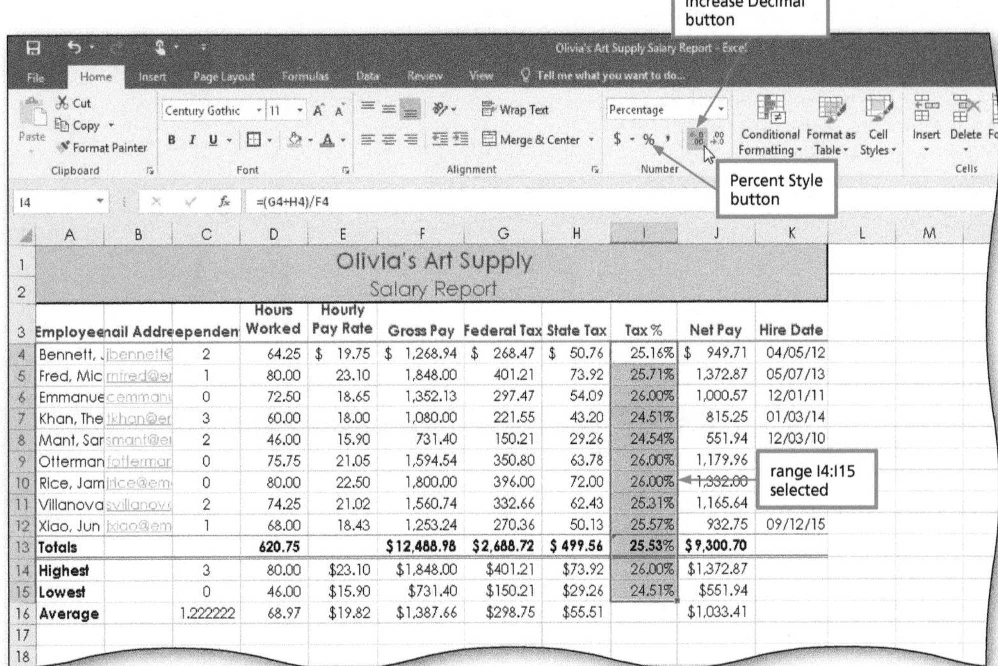

Figure 2–43

Other Ways

1. Right-click selected range, click Format Cells on shortcut menu, click Number tab (Format Cells dialog box), click Percentage in Category list, select format, click OK button
2. Press CTRL+1, click Number tab (Format Cells dialog box), click Percentage in Category list, select format, click OK button
3. Press CTRL+SHIFT+PERCENT SIGN (%)

Conditional Formatting

Conditional formatting offers you the ability to automatically change how a cell appears — the font, font color, background fill, and other options — based on the value in the cell. Excel offers a variety of commonly used conditional formatting rules, along with the ability to create your own custom rules and formatting. The next step is to emphasize the values greater than 72 in column D by formatting them to appear with a blue background and white font color (Figure 2–44).

BTW
Conditional Formatting
You can assign any format to a cell, a range of cells, a worksheet, or an entire workbook conditionally. If the value of the cell changes and no longer meets the specified condition, Excel suppresses the conditional formatting.

To Apply Conditional Formatting

The following steps assign conditional formatting to the range D4:D12. ***Why?*** *After formatting, any cell with a value greater than 72 in column D will appear with a blue background and a white font.*

1

- Select the range D4:D12.
- Click the Conditional Formatting button (Home tab | Styles group) to display the Conditional Formatting menu (Figure 2–44).

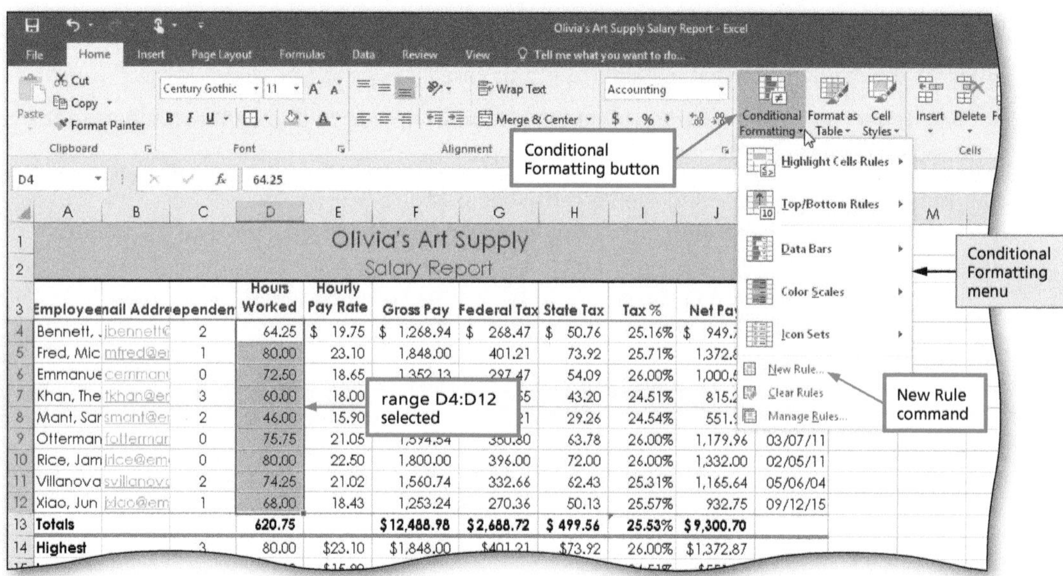

Figure 2–44

2

- Click New Rule on the Conditional Formatting menu to display the New Formatting Rule dialog box.
- Click 'Format only cells that contain' in the Select a Rule Type area (New Formatting Rule dialog box) to change the Edit the Rule Description area.
- In the Edit the Rule Description area, click the arrow in the relational operator box (second box) to display a list of relational operators, and then select greater than to select the desired operator.
- Select the rightmost box, and then type 72 to enter the value of the rule description (Figure 2–45).

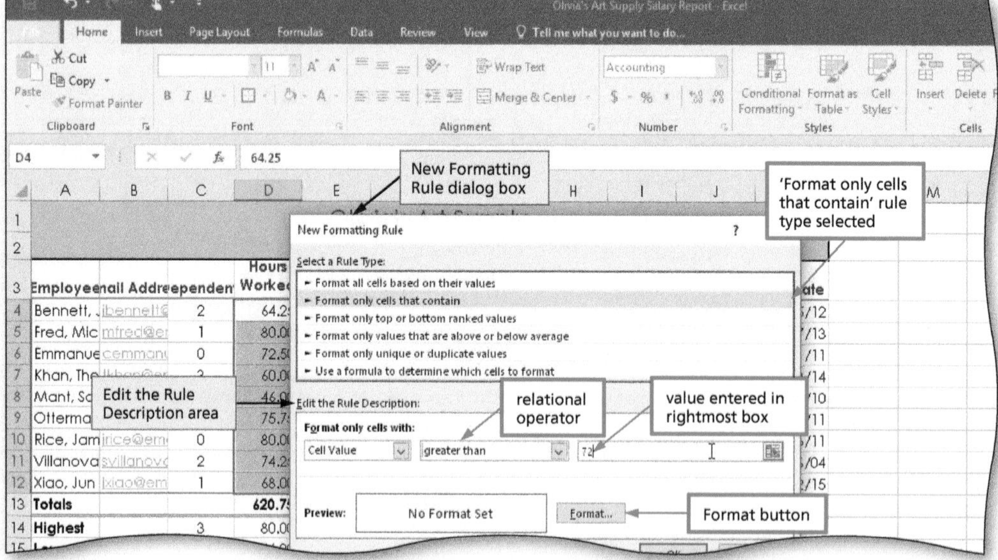

Figure 2–45

What do the changes in the Edit the Rule Description area indicate?

The Edit the Rule Description area allows you to view and edit the rules for the conditional format. In this case, the rule indicates that Excel should format only those cells with cell values greater than 72.

3

- Click the Format button (New Formatting Rule dialog box) to display the Format Cells dialog box.
- If necessary, click the Font tab (Format Cells dialog box) to display the Font sheet. Click the Color arrow to display the Color gallery and then click White, Background 1 (column 1, row 1) in the Color gallery to select the font color (Figure 2–46).

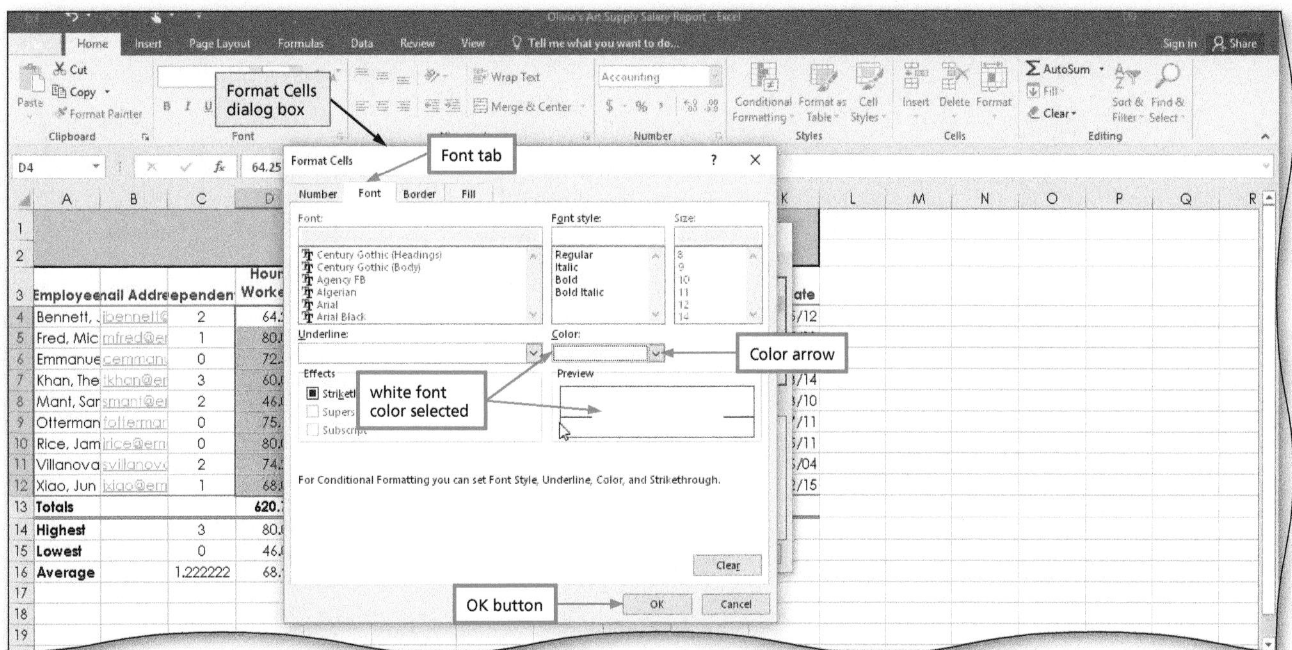

Figure 2–46

4

- Click the Fill tab (Format Cells dialog box) to display the Fill sheet and then click the blue color in column 9, row 1 to select the background color (Figure 2–47).

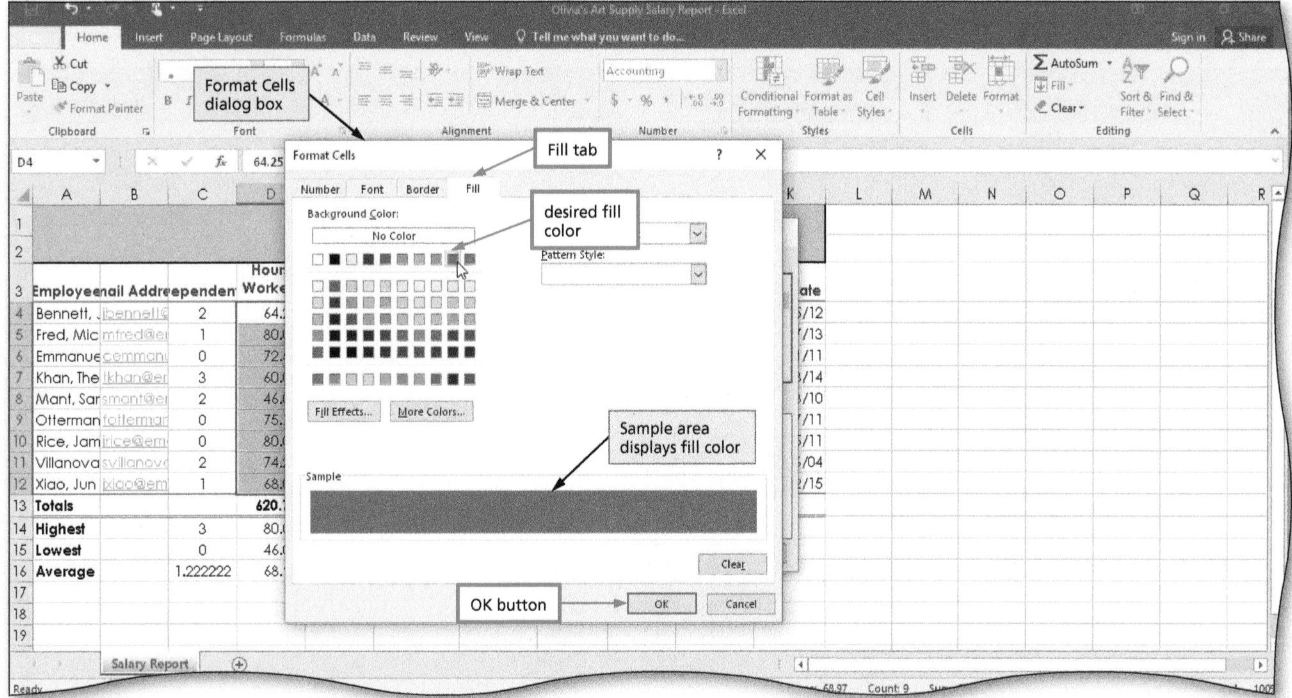

Figure 2–47

- Click the OK button (Format Cells dialog box) to close the Format Cells dialog box and display the New Formatting Rule dialog box with the desired font and background colors displayed in the Preview area (Figure 2–48).

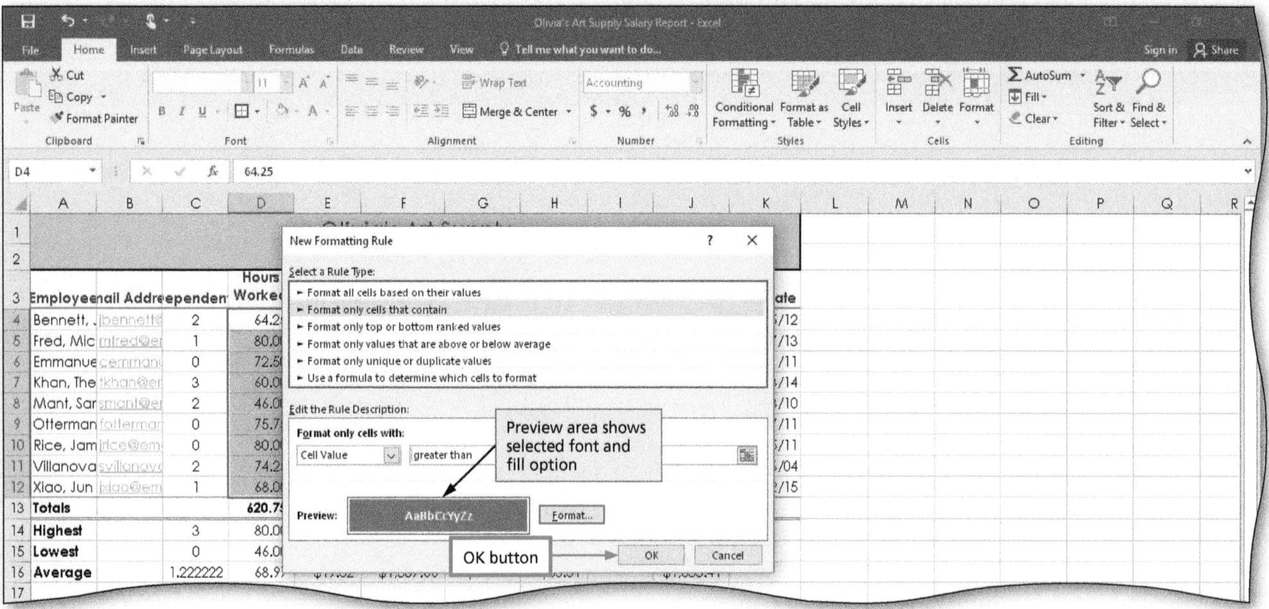

Figure 2–48

6

- Click the OK button (New Formatting Rule dialog box) to assign the conditional format to the selected range.
- Click anywhere in the worksheet, such as cell A18, to deselect the current range (Figure 2–49).

Q&A

What should I do if I make a mistake setting up a rule?

If after you have applied the conditional formatting you realize you made a mistake when creating a rule, select the cell(s) with the rule you want to edit, click the Conditional Formatting button (Home tab | Styles group), select the rule you want to edit, and then click either the Edit Rule button (to edit the selected rule) or the Delete Rule button (to delete the selected rule).

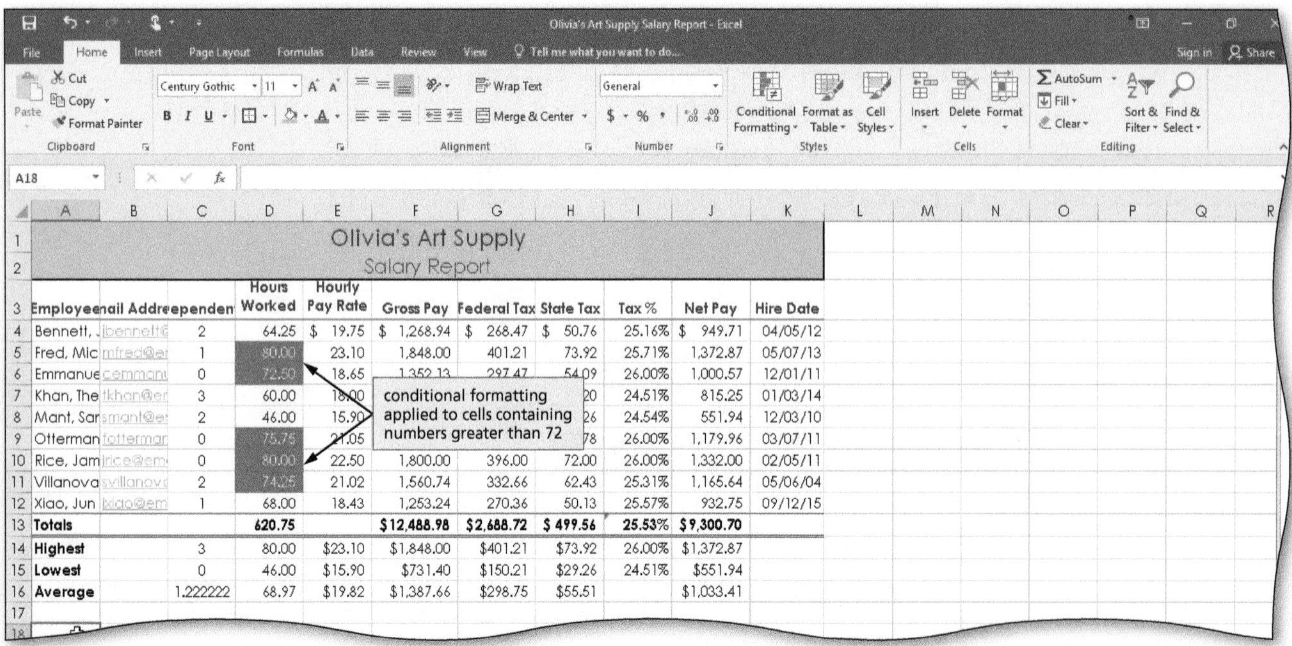

Figure 2–49

Conditional Formatting Operators

As shown in the New Formatting Rule dialog box, when the selected rule type is "Format only the cells that contain," the second text box in the Edit the Rule Description area allows you to select a relational operator, such as greater than, to use in the condition. The eight different relational operators from which you can choose for conditional formatting are summarized in Table 2–5.

Table 2–5 Summary of Conditional Formatting Relational Operators

Relational Operator	Formatting will be applied if...
between	cell value is between two numbers
not between	cell value is not between two numbers
equal to	cell value is equal to a number
not equal to	cell value is not equal to a number
greater than	cell value is greater than a number
less than	cell value is less than a number
greater than or equal to	cell value is greater than or equal to a number
less than or equal to	cell value is less than or equal to a number

BTW

Excel Help

At any time while using Excel, you can find answers to questions and display information about various topics through Excel Help. Used properly, this form of assistance can increase your productivity and reduce your frustrations by minimizing the time you spend learning how to use Excel. For instructions about Excel Help and exercises that will help you gain confidence in using it, read the Office and Windows module at the beginning of this book.

Changing Column Width and Row Height

You can change the width of the columns or height of the rows at any time to make the worksheet easier to read or to ensure that an entry fits properly in a cell. By default, all of the columns in a blank worksheet have a width of 8.43 characters, or 64 pixels. This value may change depending on the theme applied to the workbook. For example, when the Ion theme was applied to the workbook in this module, the default width of the columns changed to 8.38 characters. A **character** is defined as a letter, number, symbol, or punctuation mark. An average of 8.43 characters in 11-point Calibri font (the default font used by Excel) will fit in a cell.

The default row height in a blank worksheet is 15 points (or 20 pixels), which easily fits the 11-point default font. Recall from Module 1 that a point is equal to 1/72 of an inch. Thus, 15 points is equal to about 1/5 of an inch.

Another measure of the height and width of cells is pixels. A **pixel**, which is short for picture element, is a dot on the screen that contains a color. The size of the dot is based on your screen's resolution. At the resolution of 1366 × 768 used in this book, 1366 pixels appear across the screen and 768 pixels appear down the screen for a total of 1,049,088 pixels. It is these 1,049,088 pixels that form the font and other items you see on the screen.

BTW

Hidden Rows and Columns

For some people, trying to unhide a range of columns using the mouse can be frustrating. An alternative is to use the keyboard: select the columns to the right and left of the hidden columns and then press CTRL+SHIFT+) (RIGHT PARENTHESIS). To use the keyboard to hide a range of columns, press CTRL+0 (zero). You also can use the keyboard to unhide a range of rows by selecting the rows immediately above and below the hidden rows and then pressing CTRL+SHIFT+((LEFT PARENTHESIS). To use the keyboard to hide a range of rows, press CTRL+9.

To Change Column Width

When changing the column width, you can set the width manually or you can instruct Excel to size the column to best fit. **Best fit** means that the width of the column will be increased or decreased so that the widest entry will fit in the column. ***Why?*** *Sometimes, you may prefer more or less white space in a column than best fit provides. To change the white space, Excel allows you to change column widths manually.*

When the format you assign to a cell causes the entry to exceed the width of a column, Excel changes the column width to best fit. If you do not assign a format to a cell or cells in a column, the column width will remain 8.43 characters. Recall from Module 1 that to set a column width to best fit, double-click the right boundary of the column heading above row 1. The following steps change the column widths.

1

- Drag through column headings A, B, and C above row 1 to select the columns.
- Point to the boundary on the right side of column heading C to cause the pointer to become a split double arrow (Figure 2–50).

Q&A What if I want to make a large change to the column width?
If you want to increase or decrease column width significantly, you can right-click a column heading and then use the Column Width command on the shortcut menu to change the column's width. To use this command, however, you must select one or more entire columns.

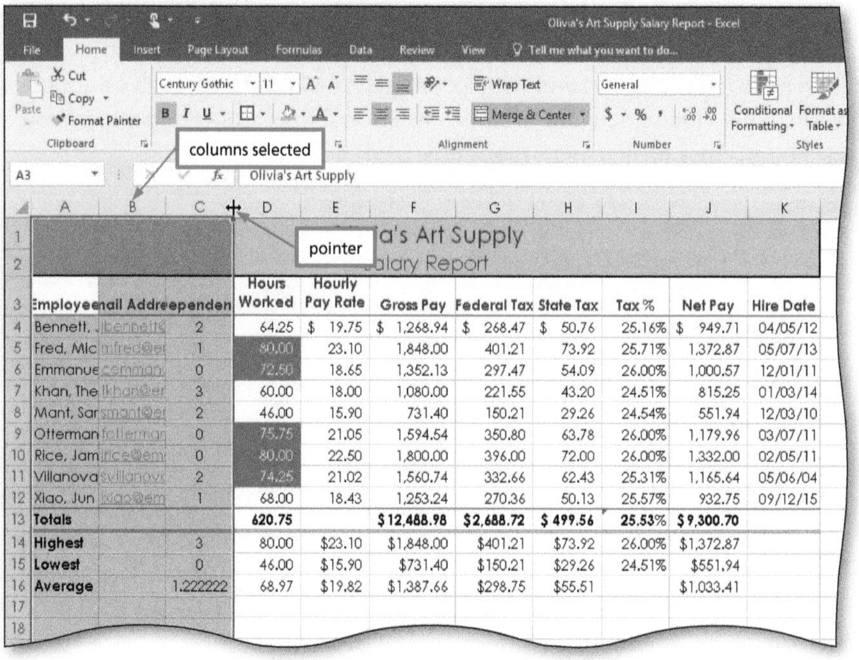

Figure 2–50

2

- Double-click the right boundary of column heading C to change the width of the selected columns to best fit.
- Point to the right boundary of the column H heading above row 1.
- When the pointer changes to a split double arrow, drag until the ScreenTip indicates Width: 10.25 (87 pixels). Do not release the mouse button (Figure 2–51).

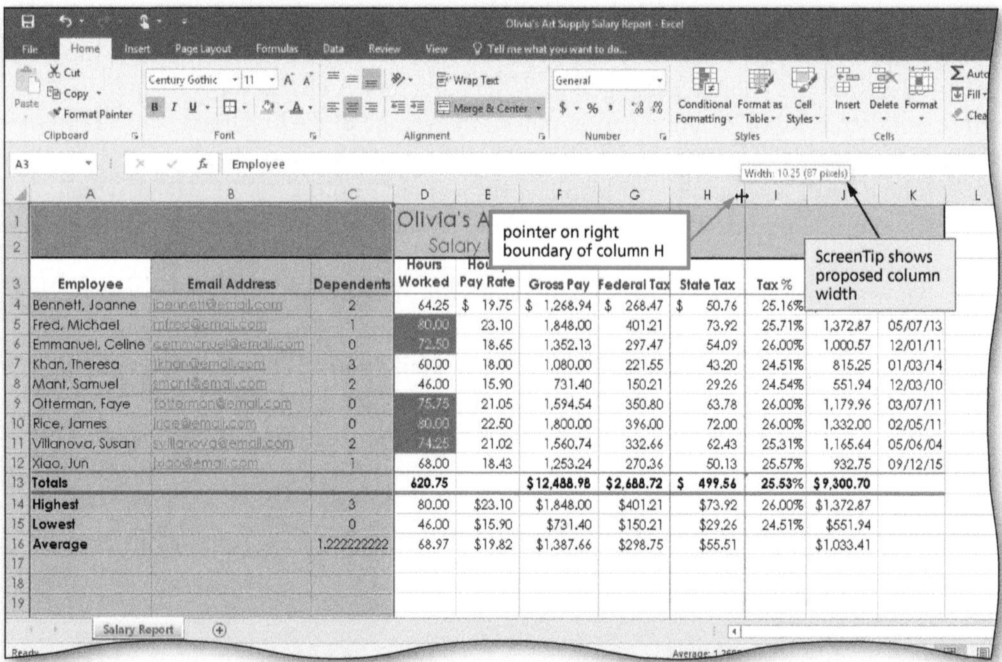

Figure 2–51

Q&A What happens if I change the column width to zero (0)?
If you decrease the column width to 0, the column is hidden. Hiding cells is a technique you can use to hide data that might not be relevant to a particular report. To instruct Excel to display a hidden column, position the mouse pointer to the right of the column heading boundary where the hidden column is located and then drag to the right.

3

- Release the mouse button to change the column width.
- Click the column D heading above row 1 to select the column.
- While holding down the CTRL key, click the column E heading and then the column I heading above row 1 so that nonadjacent columns are selected.
- Point to the boundary on the right side of the column I heading above row 1.
- Drag until the ScreenTip indicates Width: 7.50 (65 pixels). Do not release the mouse button (Figure 2–52).

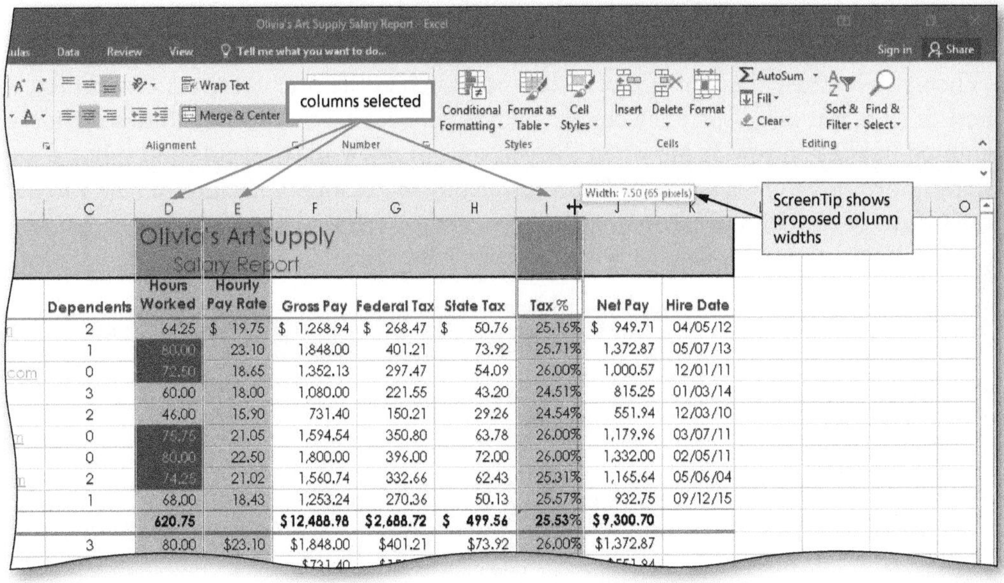

Figure 2–52

4

- Release the mouse button to change the column widths.
- Click the column F heading and drag to select the column G heading.
- While holding down the CTRL key, click the column J heading and drag to select the column K heading above row 1 so that nonadjacent columns are selected.
- Drag the right boundary of column G until the ScreenTip indicates Width: 11.00 (93 pixels). Release the mouse button to change the column widths.
- Click anywhere in the worksheet, such as cell A18, to deselect the columns (Figure 2–53).

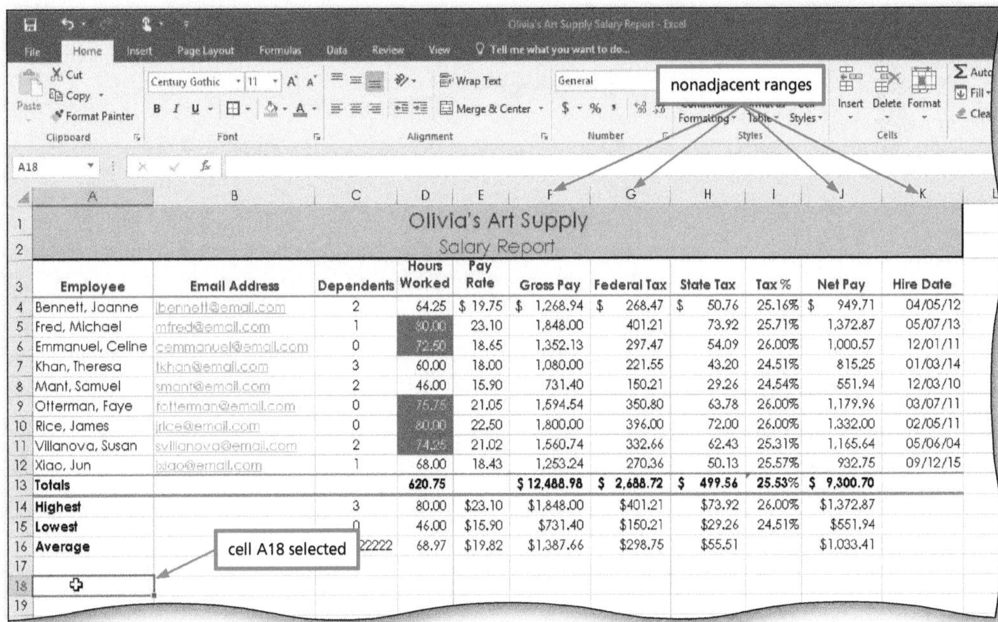

Figure 2–53

Other Ways

1. Click column heading or drag through multiple column headings, right-click selected column, click Column Width on shortcut menu, enter desired column width, click OK button

To Change Row Height

***Why?** You also can increase or decrease the height of a row manually to improve the appearance of the worksheet.* When you increase the font size of a cell entry, such as the title in cell A1, Excel increases the row height to best fit so that it can display the characters properly. Recall that Excel did this earlier when multiple lines were entered in a cell in row 3, and when the cell style of the worksheet title and subtitle was changed. The following steps improve the appearance of the worksheet by increasing the height of row 3 to 48.00 points and increasing the height of row 14 to 27.00 points.

1

- Point to the boundary below row heading 3 until the pointer becomes a split double arrow.
- Drag down until the ScreenTip indicates Height: 48.00 (64 pixels). Do not release the mouse button (Figure 2–54).

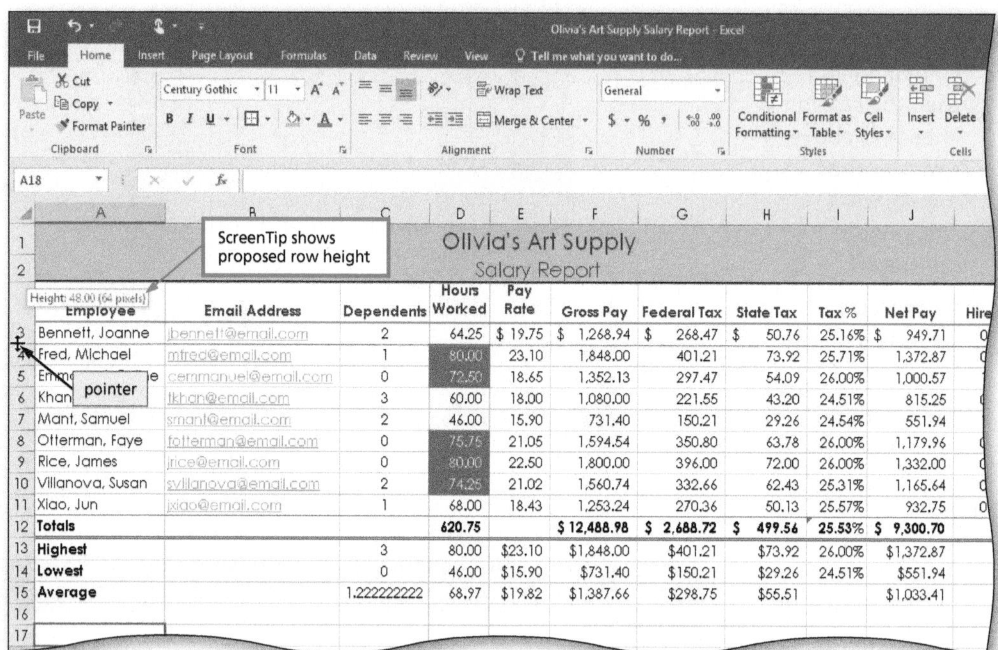

Figure 2–54

2

- Release the mouse button to change the row height.
- Point to the boundary below row heading 14 until the pointer becomes a split double arrow and then drag downward until the ScreenTip indicates Height: 27.00 (36 pixels). Do not release the mouse button (Figure 2–55).

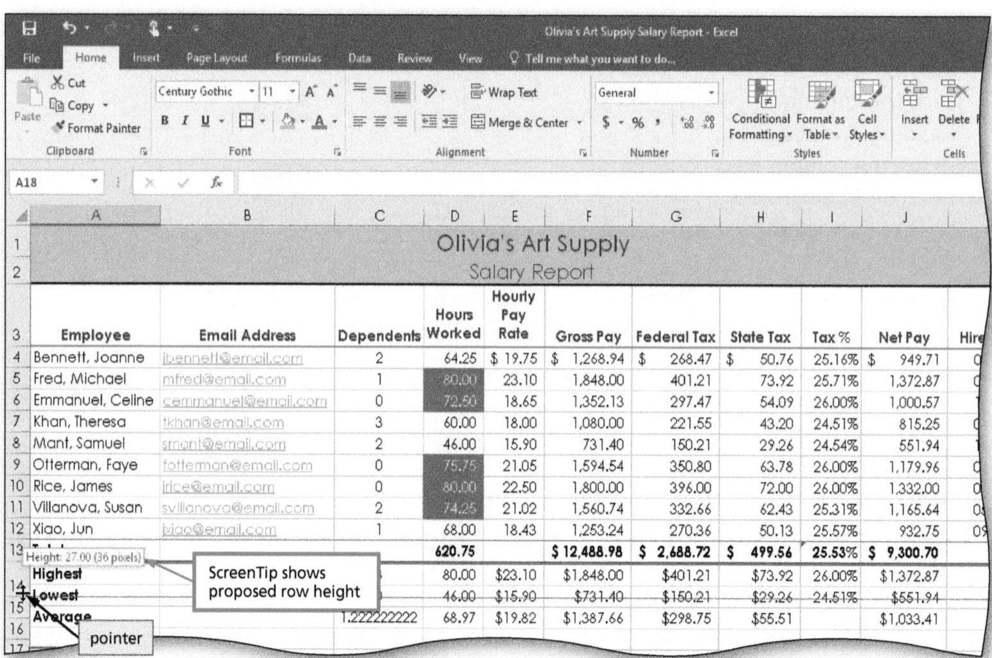

Figure 2–55

3

- Release the mouse button to change the row height.
- Click anywhere in the worksheet, such as cell A18, to deselect the current cell (Figure 2–56).

Q&A Can I hide a row?

Yes. As with column widths, when you decrease the row height to 0, the row is hidden. To instruct Excel to display a hidden row, position the pointer just below the row heading boundary where the row is hidden and then drag downward. To set a row height to best fit, double-click the bottom boundary of the row heading. You also can hide and unhide rows by right-clicking the row or column heading and selecting the option to hide or unhide the cells.

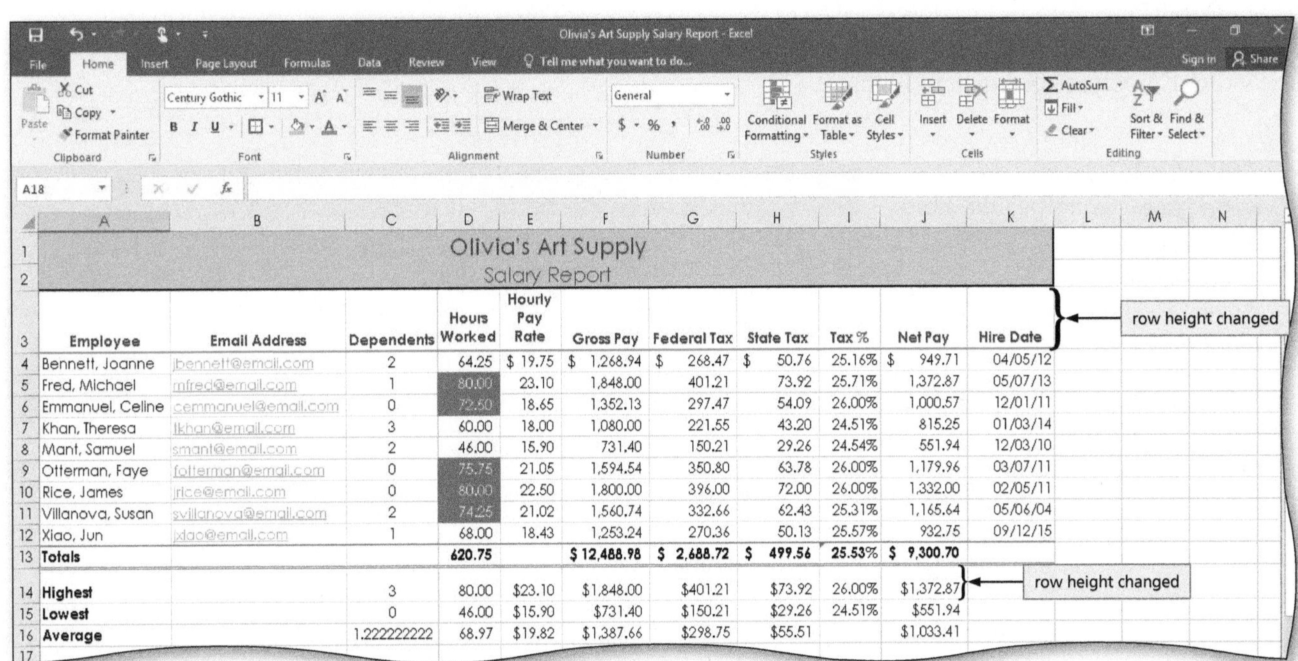

	Employee	Email Address	Dependents	Hours Worked	Hourly Pay Rate	Gross Pay	Federal Tax	State Tax	Tax %	Net Pay	Hire Date
1	Olivia's Art Supply										
2	Salary Report										
4	Bennett, Joanne	jbennett@email.com	2	64.25	$ 19.75	$ 1,268.94	$ 268.47	$ 50.76	25.16%	$ 949.71	04/05/12
5	Fred, Michael	mfred@email.com	1	80.00	23.10	1,848.00	401.21	73.92	25.71%	1,372.87	05/07/13
6	Emmanuel, Celine	cemmanuel@email.com	0	72.50	18.65	1,352.13	297.47	54.09	26.00%	1,000.57	12/01/11
7	Khan, Theresa	tkhan@email.com	3	60.00	18.00	1,080.00	221.55	43.20	24.51%	815.25	01/03/14
8	Mant, Samuel	smant@email.com	2	46.00	15.90	731.40	150.21	29.26	24.54%	551.94	12/03/10
9	Otterman, Faye	fotterman@email.com	0	75.75	21.05	1,594.54	350.80	63.78	26.00%	1,179.96	03/07/11
10	Rice, James	jrice@email.com	0	80.00	22.50	1,800.00	396.00	72.00	26.00%	1,332.00	02/05/11
11	Villanova, Susan	svillanova@email.com	2	74.25	21.02	1,560.74	332.66	62.43	25.31%	1,165.64	05/06/04
12	Xiao, Jun	jxiao@email.com	1	68.00	18.43	1,253.24	270.36	50.13	25.57%	932.75	09/12/15
13	Totals			620.75		$ 12,488.98	$ 2,688.72	$ 499.56	25.53%	$ 9,300.70	
14	Highest		3	80.00	$23.10	$1,848.00	$401.21	$73.92	26.00%	$1,372.87	
15	Lowest		0	46.00	$15.90	$731.40	$150.21	$29.26	24.51%	$551.94	
16	Average		1.222222222	68.97	$19.82	$1,387.66	$298.75	$55.51		$1,033.41	

Figure 2–56

Other Ways

1. Right-click row heading or drag through multiple row headings, right-click selected heading, click Row Height on shortcut menu, enter desired row height, click OK button

Break Point: If you wish to take a break, this is a good place to do so. Be sure to save the Olivia's Art Supply Salary Report file again and then you can exit Excel. To resume at a later time, run Excel, open the file called Olivia's Art Supply Salary Report, and continue following the steps from this location forward.

Checking Spelling

Excel includes a **spelling checker** you can use to check a worksheet for spelling errors. The spelling checker looks for spelling errors by comparing words on the worksheet against words contained in its standard dictionary. If you often use specialized terms that are not in the standard dictionary, you may want to add them to a custom dictionary using the Spelling dialog box. When the spelling checker finds a word that is not in either dictionary, it displays the word in the Spelling dialog box. You then can correct it if it is misspelled.

BTW

Spell Checking

While Excel's spell checker is a valuable tool, it is not infallible. You should proofread your workbook carefully by pointing to each word and saying it aloud as you point to it. Be mindful of misused words such as its and it's, through and though, and to and too. Nothing undermines a good impression more than a professional looking report with misspelled words.

CONSIDER THIS

Does the spelling checker catch all spelling mistakes?
While Excel's spelling checker is a valuable tool, it is not infallible. You should proofread your workbook carefully by pointing to each word and saying it aloud as you point to it. Be mindful of misused words such as its and it's, through and though, your and you're, and to and too. Nothing undermines a good impression more than a professional report with misspelled words.

To Check Spelling on the Worksheet

Why? *Everything in a worksheet should be checked to make sure there are no spelling errors.* To illustrate how Excel responds to a misspelled word, the following steps purposely misspell the word, Employee, in cell A3 as the word, Empolyee, as shown in Figure 2–57.

1

- Click cell A3 and then type **`Empolyee`** to misspell the word, Employee.
- Select cell A2 so that the spelling checker begins checking at the selected cell.
- Click Review on the ribbon to display the Review tab.
- Click the Spelling button (Review tab | Proofing group) to use the spelling checker to display the misspelled word in the Spelling dialog box (Figure 2–57).

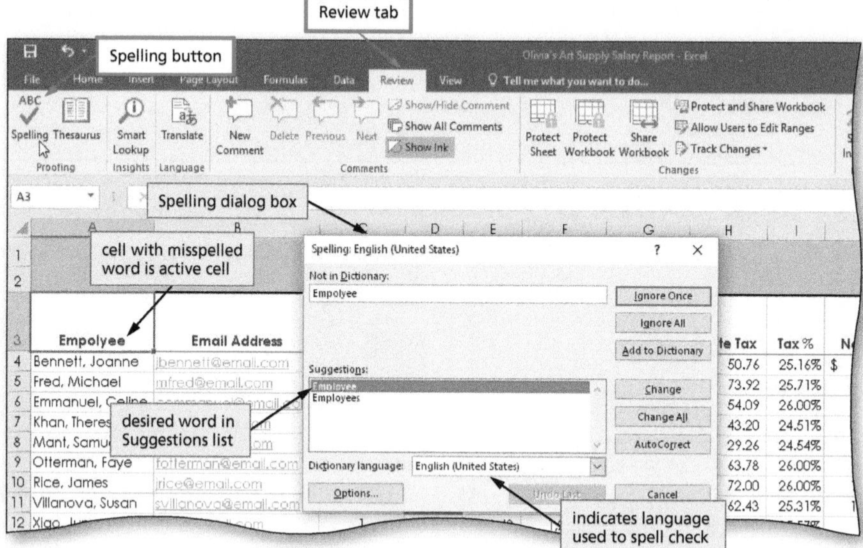

Figure 2–57

Q&A What happens when the spelling checker finds a misspelled word?
When the spelling checker identifies that a cell contains a word not in its standard or custom dictionary, it selects that cell as the active cell and displays the Spelling dialog box. The Spelling dialog box displays the word that was not found in the dictionary and offers a list of suggested corrections (Figure 2–58).

2

- Verify that the word highlighted in the Suggestion area is correct.
- Click the Change button (Spelling dialog box) to change the misspelled word to the correct word (Figure 2–58).
- Click the Close button to close the Spelling dialog box.
- If a Microsoft Excel dialog box is displayed, click the OK button.

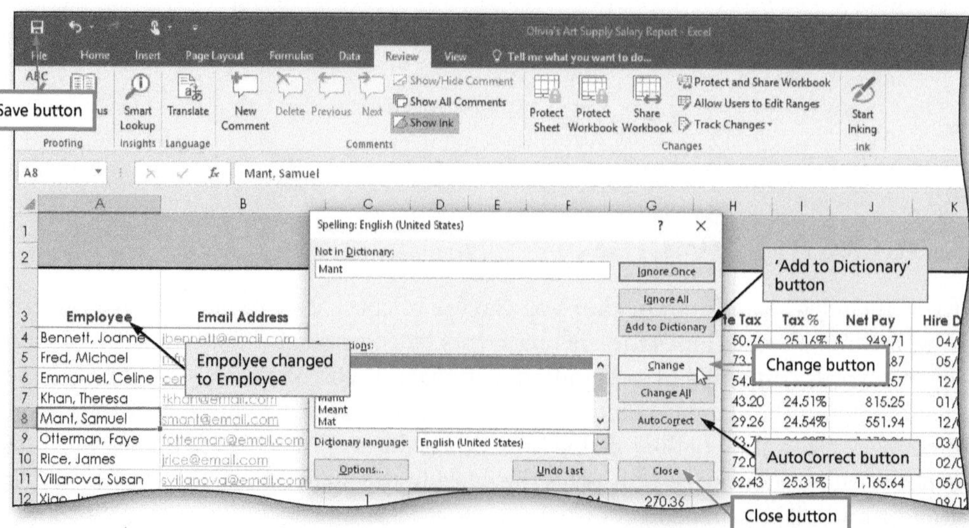

Figure 2–58

3

- Click anywhere in the worksheet, such as cell A18, to deselect the current cell.
- Display the Home tab.
- Save the workbook again on the same storage location with the same file name.

Q&A What other actions can I take in the Spelling dialog box?
If one of the words in the Suggestions list is correct, select it and then click the Change button. If none of the suggested words are correct, type the correct word in the 'Not in Dictionary' text box and then click the Change button. To change the word throughout the worksheet, click the Change All button instead of the Change button. To skip correcting the word, click the Ignore Once button. To have Excel ignore the word for the remainder of the worksheet, click the Ignore All button.

Other Ways

1. Press F7

Additional Spelling Checker Considerations

Consider these additional guidelines when using the spelling checker:

- To check the spelling of the text in a single cell, double-click the cell to make the formula bar active and then click the Spelling button (Review tab | Proofing group).
- If you select a single cell so that the formula bar is not active and then start the spelling checker, Excel checks the remainder of the worksheet, including notes and embedded charts.
- If you select a cell other than cell A1 before you start the spelling checker, Excel will display a dialog box when the spelling checker reaches the end of the worksheet, asking if you want to continue checking at the beginning.
- If you select a range of cells before starting the spelling checker, Excel checks the spelling of the words only in the selected range.
- To check the spelling of all the sheets in a workbook, right-click any sheet tab, click 'Select All Sheets' on the sheet tab shortcut menu, and then start the spelling checker.
- To add words to the dictionary, such as your last name, click the 'Add to Dictionary' button in the Spelling dialog box (shown in Figure 2–58) when Excel flags the word as not being in the dictionary.
- Click the AutoCorrect button (shown in Figure 2–58) to add the misspelled word and the correct version of the word to the AutoCorrect list. For example, suppose that you misspell the word, do, as the word, dox. When the spelling checker displays the Spelling dialog box with the correct word, do, in the Suggestions list, click the AutoCorrect button. Then, anytime in the future that you type the word, dox, Excel will change it to the word, do.

BTW

Error Checking

Always take the time to check the formulas of a worksheet before submitting it to your supervisor. You can check formulas by clicking the Error Checking button (Formulas tab | Formula Auditing group). You also should test the formulas by employing data that tests the limits of formulas. Experienced spreadsheet specialists spend as much time testing a workbook as they do creating it, and they do so before placing the workbook into production.

BTW

Distributing a Workbook

Instead of printing and distributing a hard copy of a workbook, you can distribute the workbook electronically. Options include sending the workbook via email; posting it on cloud storage (such as OneDrive) and sharing the file with others; posting it on social media, a blog, or other website; and sharing a link associated with an online location of the workbook. You also can create and share a PDF or XPS image of the workbook, so that users can view the file in Acrobat Reader or XPS Viewer instead of in Excel.

Printing the Worksheet

Excel allows for a great deal of customization in how a worksheet appears when printed. For example, the margins on the page can be adjusted. A header or footer can be added to each printed page as well. A **header** is text and graphics that print at the top of each page. Similarly, a **footer** is text and graphics that print at the bottom of each page. Excel also has the capability to alter the worksheet in Page Layout view. Page Layout view allows you to create or modify a worksheet while viewing how it will look in printed format. The default view that you have worked in up until this point in the book is called Normal view.

To Change the Worksheet's Margins, Header, and Orientation in Page Layout View

1 ENTER FORMULAS | 2 ENTER FUNCTIONS | 3 VERIFY FORMULAS
4 FORMAT WORKSHEET | 5 CHECK SPELLING | 6 PRINT WORKSHEET

The following steps change to Page Layout view, narrow the margins of the worksheet, change the header of the worksheet, and set the orientation of the worksheet to landscape. ***Why?*** *You may want the printed worksheet to fit on one page. You can do that by reducing the page margins and changing the page orientation to fit wider printouts across a sheet of paper. You can use the header to identify the content on each page.* **Margins** are those portions of a printed page outside the main body of the printed document and always are blank when printed. The current worksheet is too wide for a single page and requires landscape orientation to fit on one page in a readable manner.

- Click the Page Layout button on the status bar to view the worksheet in Page Layout view (Figure 2–59).

Q&A What are the features of Page Layout view?

Page Layout view shows the worksheet divided into pages. A gray background separates each page. The white areas surrounding each page indicate the print margins. The top of each page includes a Header area, and the bottom of each page includes a Footer area. Page Layout view also includes rulers at the top and left margin of the page that assists you in placing objects on the page, such as charts and pictures.

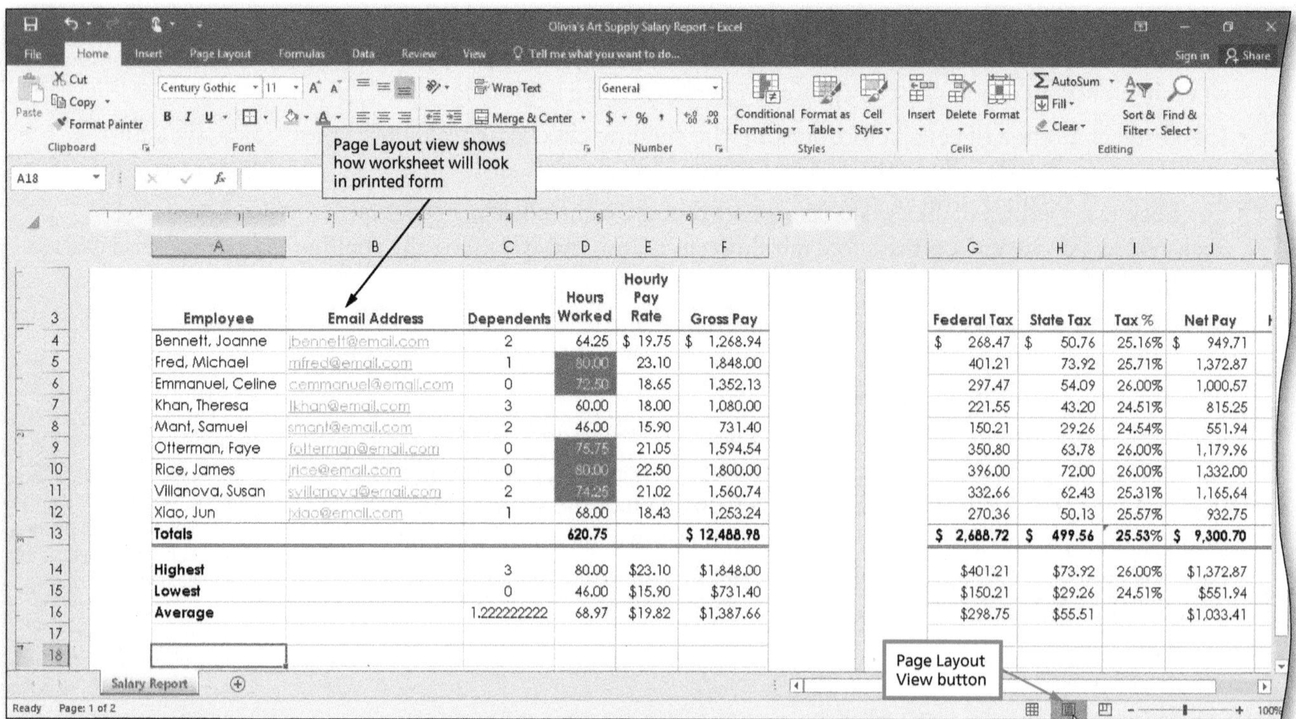

Figure 2–59

2

- Display the Page Layout tab.
- Click the Adjust Margins button (Page Layout tab | Page Setup group) to display the Margins gallery (Figure 2–60).

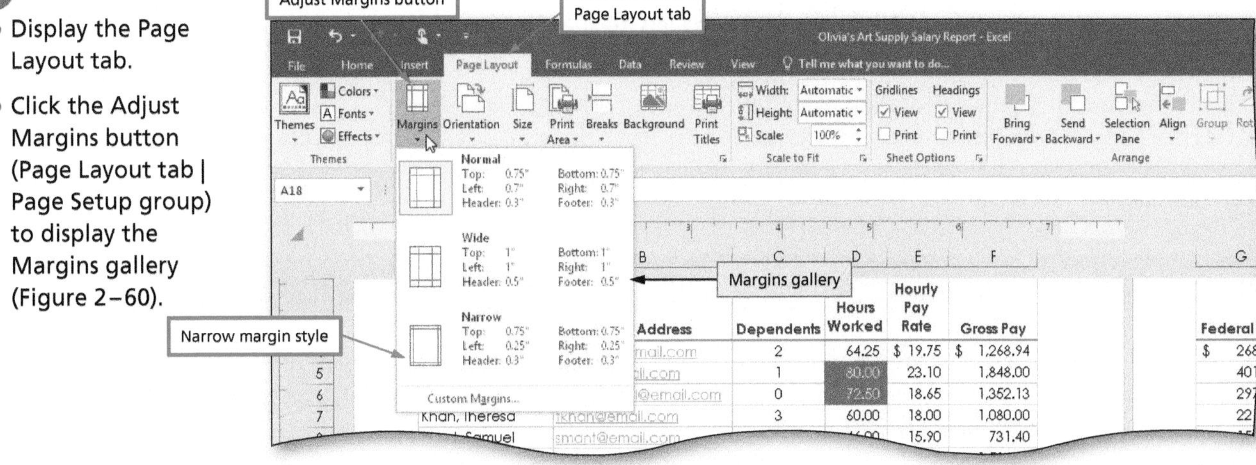

Figure 2–60

3

- Click Narrow in the Margins gallery to change the worksheet margins to the Narrow margin style.
- Click the center of the Header area above the worksheet title.
- Type **`Jayne Smith`** and then press the ENTER key. Type **`Chief Financial Officer`** to complete the worksheet header (Figure 2–61).
- If requested by your instructor, type your name instead of Jayne Smith.
- Select cell A6 to deselect the header.

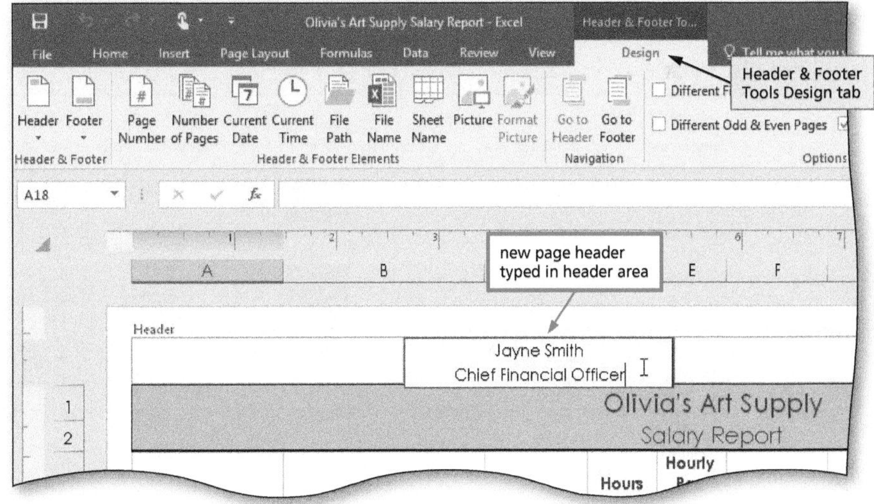

Figure 2–61

Q&A What else can I place in a header?
You can add additional text, page number information, date and time information, the file path of the workbook, the file name of the workbook, the sheet name of the workbook, and pictures to a header.

4

- Display the Page Layout tab.
- Click the 'Change Page Orientation' button (Page Layout tab | Page Setup group) to display the Change Page Orientation gallery (Figure 2–62).

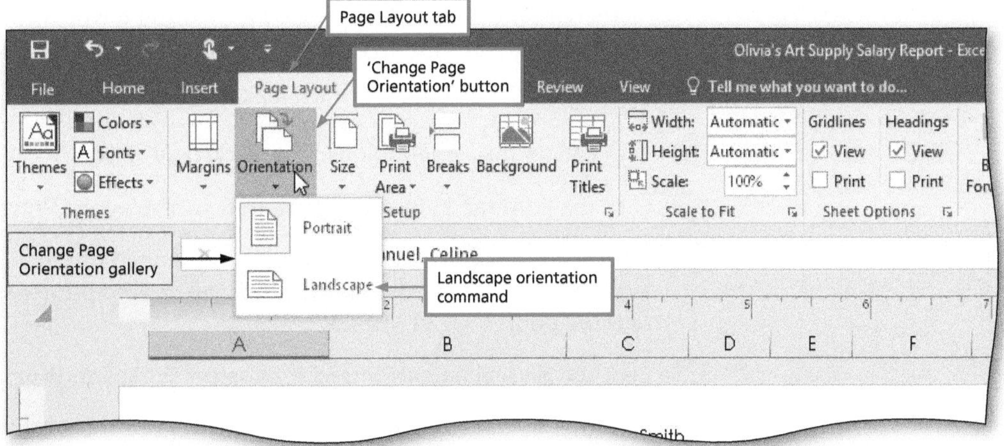

Figure 2–62

5

- Click Landscape in the Change Page Orientation gallery to change the worksheet's orientation to landscape (Figure 2–63).

Q&A Do I need to change the orientation every time I want to print the worksheet?
No. Once you change the orientation and save the workbook, Excel will save the orientation setting for that workbook until you change it. When you open a new workbook, Excel sets the orientation to portrait.

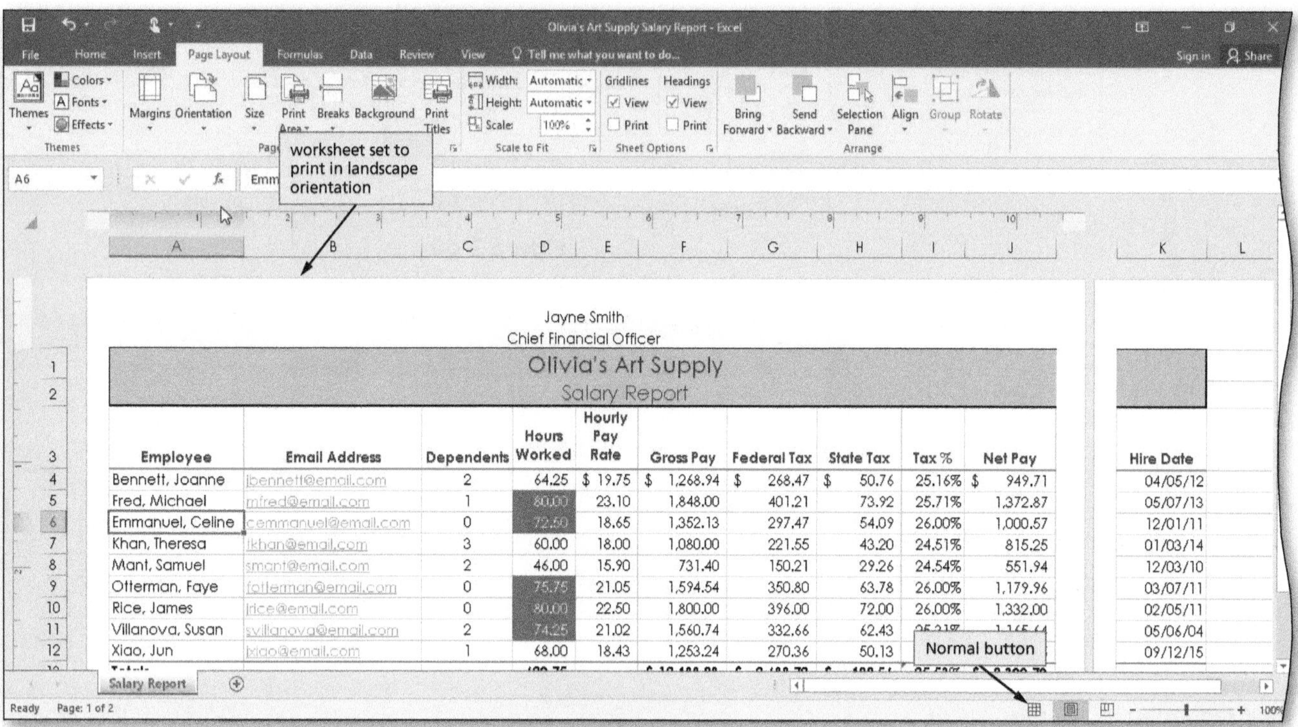

Figure 2–63

Other Ways

1. Click Page Setup Dialog Box Launcher (Page Layout tab | Page Setup group), click Page tab (Page Setup dialog box), click Portrait or Landscape, click OK button

To Print a Worksheet

Excel provides multiple options for printing a worksheet. In the following sections, you first print the worksheet and then print a section of the worksheet. The following steps print the worksheet.

1. Click File on the ribbon to open the Backstage view.
2. Click the Print tab in the Backstage view to display the Print gallery.
3. If necessary, click the Printer Status button in the Print gallery to display a list of available Printer options and then click the desired printer to change the currently selected printer.
4. Click the No Scaling button and then select 'Fit Sheet on One Page' to select it.
5. Click the Print button in the Print gallery to print the worksheet in landscape orientation on the currently selected printer.

6 When the printer stops, retrieve the hard copy (Figure 2–64).

Jayne Smith
Chief Financial Officer

Olivia's Art Supply
Salary Report

Employee	Email Address	Dependents	Hours Worked	Hourly Pay Rate	Gross Pay	Federal Tax	State Tax	Tax %	Net Pay	Hire Date
Bennett, Joanne	jbennett@email.com	2	64.25	$ 19.75	$ 1,268.94	$ 268.47	$ 50.76	25.16%	$ 949.71	04/05/12
Fred, Michael	mfred@email.com	1	80.00	23.10	1,848.00	401.21	73.92	25.71%	1,372.87	05/07/13
Emmanuel, Celine	cemmanuel@email.com	0	72.50	18.65	1,352.13	297.47	54.09	26.00%	1,000.57	12/01/11
Khan, Theresa	tkhan@email.com	3	60.00	18.00	1,080.00	221.55	43.20	24.51%	815.25	01/03/14
Mant, Samuel	smant@email.com	2	46.00	15.90	731.40	150.21	29.26	24.54%	551.94	12/03/10
Otterman, Faye	fotterman@email.com	0	75.75	21.05	1,594.54	350.80	63.78	26.00%	1,179.96	03/07/11
Rice, James	jrice@email.com	0	80.00	22.50	1,800.00	396.00	72.00	26.00%	1,332.00	02/05/11
Villanova, Susan	svillanova@email.com	2	74.25	21.02	1,560.74	332.66	62.43	25.31%	1,165.64	05/06/04
Xiao, Jun	jxiao@email.com	1	68.00	18.43	1,253.24	270.36	50.13	25.57%	932.75	09/12/15
Totals			**620.75**		**$ 12,488.98**	**$ 2,688.72**	**$ 499.56**	**25.53%**	**$ 9,300.70**	
Highest		3	80.00	$23.10	$1,848.00	$401.21	$73.92	26.00%	$1,372.87	
Lowest		0	46.00	$15.90	$731.40	$150.21	$29.26	24.51%	$551.94	
Average		1.222222222	68.97	$19.82	$1,387.66	$298.75	$55.51		$1,033.41	

Figure 2–64

To Print a Section of the Worksheet

You can print portions of the worksheet by selecting the range of cells to print and then clicking the Selection option button in the Print what area in the Print dialog box. ***Why?*** *To save paper, you only want to print the portion of the worksheet you need, instead of printing the entire worksheet.* The following steps print the range A3:F16.

1

- Select the range to print, cells A3:F16 in this case.
- Click File on the ribbon to open the Backstage view.
- Click the Print tab to display the Print gallery.
- Click 'Print Active Sheets' in the Settings area (Print tab | Print gallery) to display a list of options that determine what Excel should print (Figure 2–65).

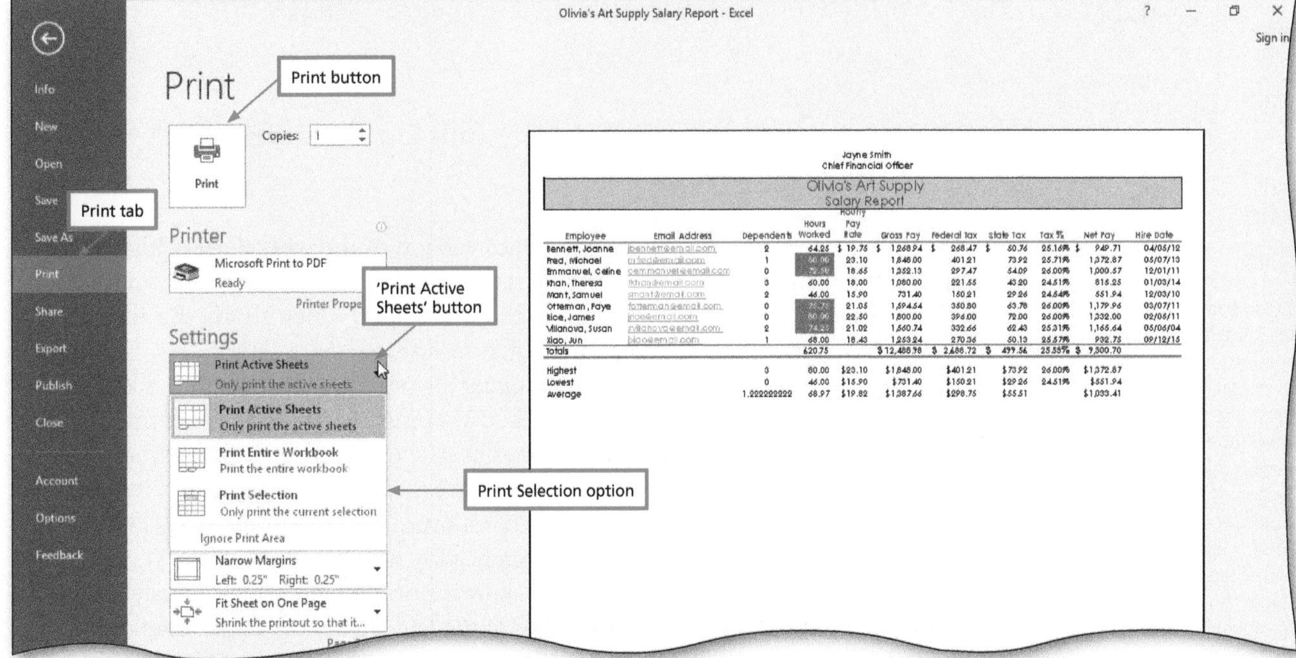

Figure 2–65

2

- Click Print Selection to instruct Excel to print only the selected range.
- Click the Print button in the Print gallery to print the selected range of the worksheet on the currently selected printer (Figure 2–66).
- Click the Normal button on the status bar to return to Normal view.
- Click anywhere in the worksheet, such as cell A18, to deselect the range A3:F16.

Q&A What can I print?
Excel includes three options for selecting what to print (Figure 2–65). As shown in the previous steps, the Print Selection option instructs Excel to print the selected range. The 'Print Active Sheets' option instructs Excel to print the active worksheet (the worksheet currently on the screen) or selected worksheets. Finally, the 'Print Entire Workbook' option instructs Excel to print all of the worksheets in the workbook.

Jayne Smith
Chief Financial Officer

Employee	Email Address	Dependents	Hours Worked	Hourly Pay Rate	Gross Pay
Bennett, Joanne	jbennett@email.com	2	64.25	$ 19.75	$ 1,268.94
Fred, Michael	mfred@email.com	1	80.00	23.10	1,848.00
Emmanuel, Celine	cemmanuel@email.com	0	72.50	18.65	1,352.13
Khan, Theresa	tkhan@email.com	3	60.00	18.00	1,080.00
Mant, Samuel	smant@email.com	2	46.00	15.90	731.40
Otterman, Faye	fotterman@email.com	0	75.75	21.05	1,594.54
Rice, James	jrice@email.com	0	80.00	22.50	1,800.00
Villanova, Susan	svillanova@email.com	2	74.25	21.02	1,560.74
Xiao, Jun	jxiao@email.com	1	68.00	18.43	1,253.24
Totals			**620.75**		**$ 12,488.98**
Highest		3	80.00	$23.10	$1,848.00
Lowest		0	46.00	$15.90	$731.40
Average		1.222222222	68.97	$19.82	$1,387.66

Figure 2–66

Other Ways

1. Select range, click Print Area button (Page Layout tab | Page Setup group), click 'Set Print Area', click File tab to open Backstage view, click Print tab, click Print button

Displaying and Printing the Formulas Version of the Worksheet

BTW
Values versus Formulas
When completing class assignments, do not enter numbers in cells that require formulas. Most instructors will check both the values version and formulas version of your worksheets. The formulas version verifies that you entered formulas, rather than numbers, in formula-based cells.

Thus far, you have been working with the values version of the worksheet, which shows the results of the formulas you have entered, rather than the actual formulas. Excel also can display and print the formulas version of the worksheet, which shows the actual formulas you have entered, rather than the resulting values.

The formulas version is useful for debugging a worksheet. **Debugging** is the process of finding and correcting errors in the worksheet. Viewing and printing the formulas version instead of the values version makes it easier to see any mistakes in the formulas.

When you change from the values version to the formulas version, Excel increases the width of the columns so that the formulas do not overflow into adjacent cells, which makes the formulas version of the worksheet significantly wider than the values version. To fit the wide printout on one page, you can use landscape orientation, which already has been selected for the workbook, and the Fit to option in the Page tab in the Page Setup dialog box.

To Display the Formulas in the Worksheet and Fit the Printout on One Page

The following steps change the view of the worksheet from the values version to the formulas version of the worksheet and then print the formulas version on one page. ***Why?*** *Printing the formulas in the worksheet can help you verify that your formulas are correct and that the worksheet displays the correct calculations.*

1

- Press CTRL+ACCENT MARK (`) to display the worksheet with formulas.
- Click the right horizontal scroll arrow until column K appears (Figure 2–67).

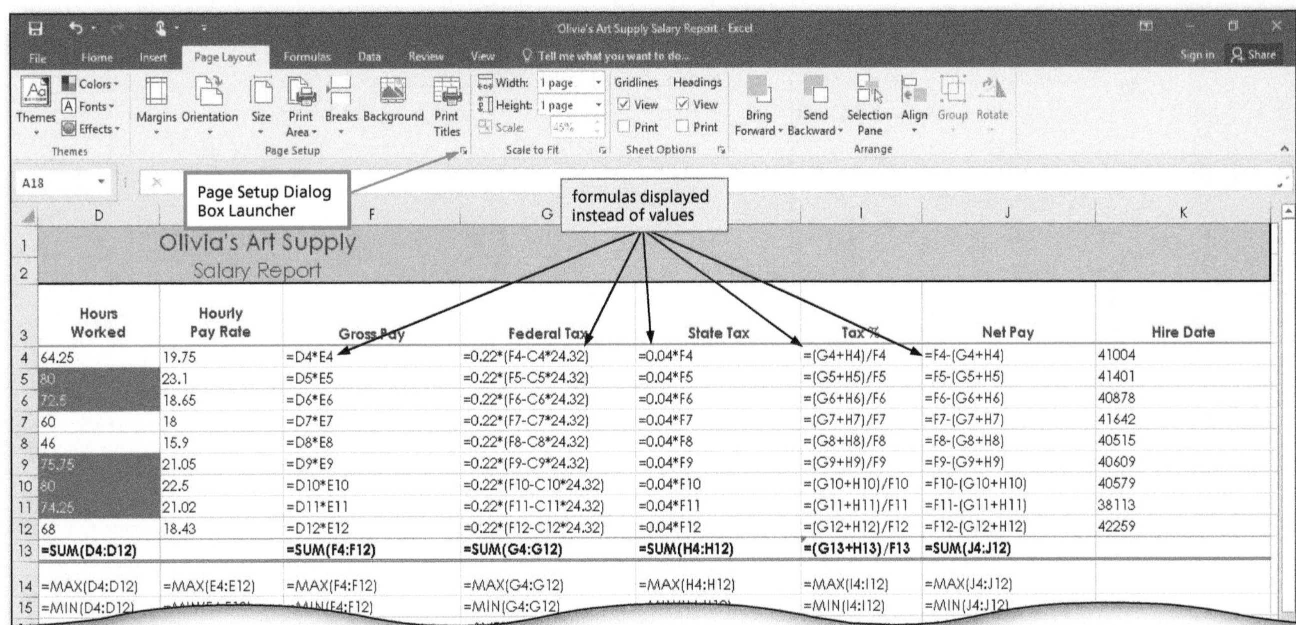

Figure 2–67

2

- Click the Page Setup Dialog Box Launcher (Page Layout tab | Page Setup group) to display the Page Setup dialog box (Figure 2–68).
- If necessary, click Landscape in the Orientation area in the Page tab to select it.
- If necessary, click the Fit to option button in the Scaling area to select it.

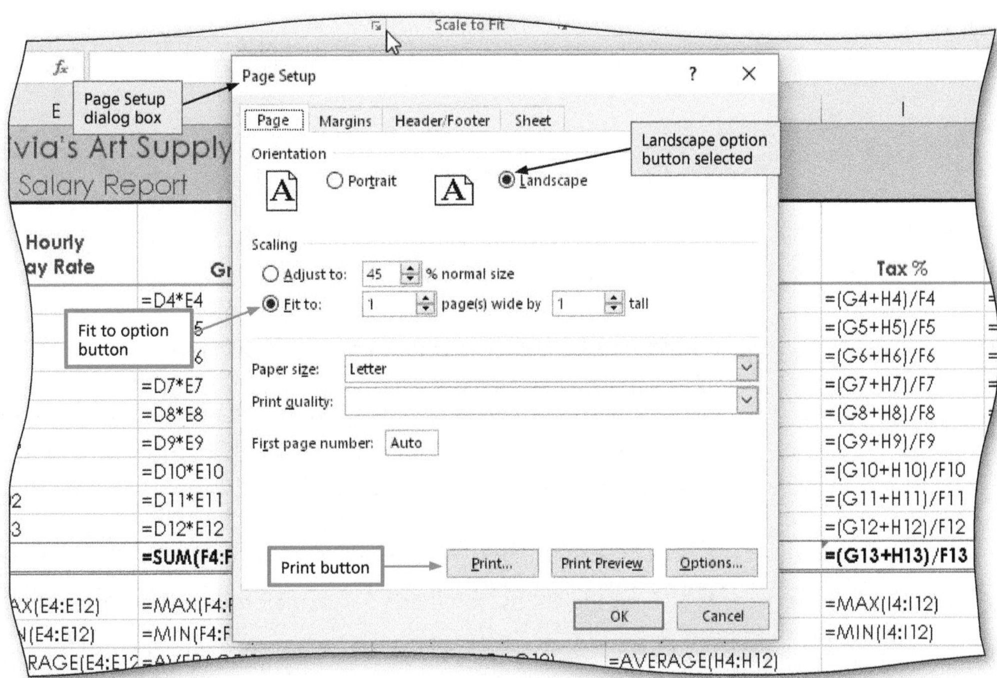

Figure 2–68

- Click the Print button (Page Setup dialog box) to open the Print tab in the Backstage view. In the Backstage view, select the Print Active Sheets option in the Settings area of the Print gallery (Figure 2–69).
- Click the Print button to print the worksheet.

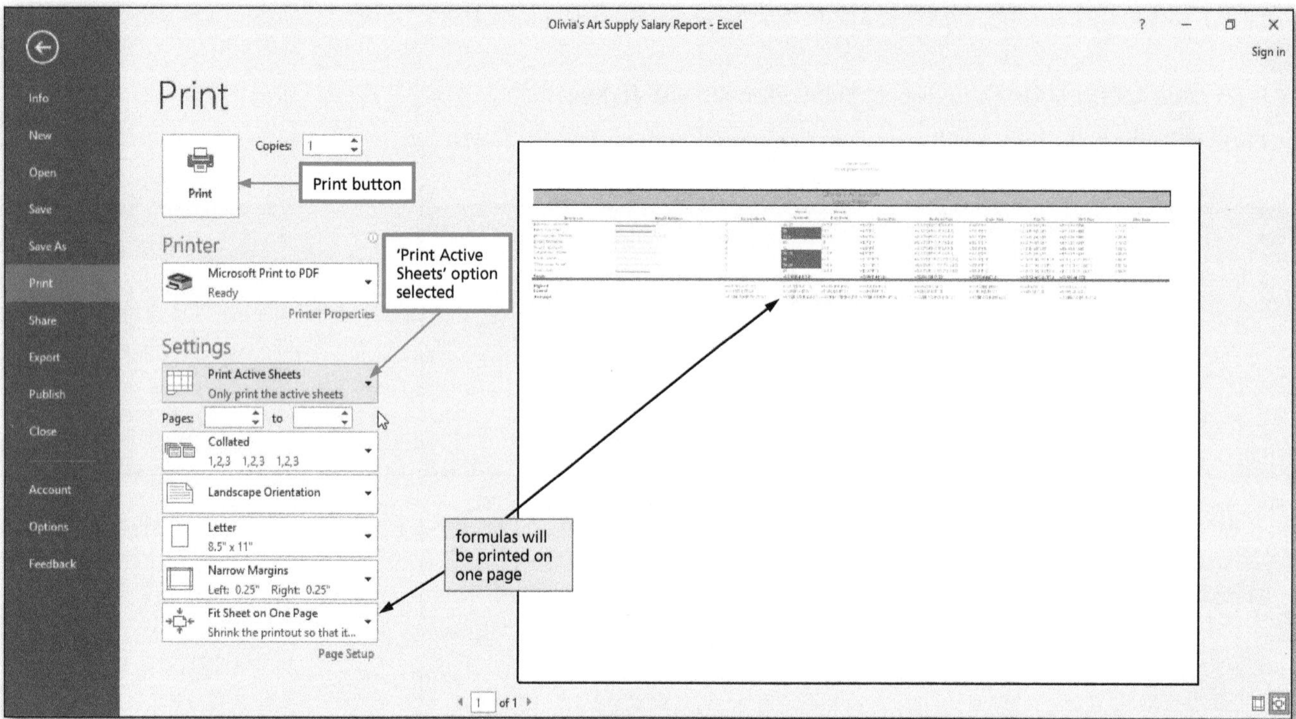

Figure 2–69

- After viewing and printing the formulas version, press CTRL+ACCENT MARK (`) to instruct Excel to display the values version.
- Click the left horizontal scroll arrow until column A appears.

To Change the Print Scaling Option Back to 100%

Depending on your printer, you may have to change the Print Scaling option back to 100% after using the Fit to option. Doing so will cause the worksheet to print at the default print scaling of 100%. The following steps reset the Print Scaling option so that future worksheets print at 100%, instead of being resized to print on one page.

1. If necessary, display the Page Layout tab and then click the Page Setup Dialog Box Launcher (Page Layout tab | Page Setup group) to display the Page Setup dialog box.
2. Click the Adjust to option button in the Scaling area to select the Adjust to setting.
3. If necessary, type `100` in the Adjust to box to adjust the print scaling to 100%.
4. Click the OK button (Page Setup dialog box) to set the print scaling to normal.

5 Display the Home tab.

6 Save the workbook again on the same storage location with the same file name.

7 If desired, sign out of your Microsoft account.

8 Exit Excel.

Q&A What is the purpose of the Adjust to box in the Page Setup dialog box?
The Adjust to box allows you to specify the percentage of reduction or enlargement in the printout of a worksheet. The default percentage is 100%. When you click the Fit to option button, this percentage changes to the percentage required to fit the printout on one page.

Summary

In this module you have learned how to enter formulas, calculate an average, find the highest and lowest numbers in a range, verify formulas using Range Finder, add borders, align text, format numbers, change column widths and row heights, and add conditional formatting to a range of numbers. In addition, you learned how to use the spelling checker to identify misspelled words in a worksheet, print a section of a worksheet, and display and print the formulas version of the worksheet using the Fit to option.

CONSIDER THIS: PLAN AHEAD

What decisions will you need to make when creating workbooks in the future?

1. Determine the workbook structure.
   a) Determine the formulas and functions you will need for your workbook.
   b) Sketch a layout of your data and functions.
2. Create the worksheet.
   a) Enter the titles, subtitles, and headings.
   b) Enter the data, desired functions, and formulas.
3. Format the worksheet.
   a) Determine the theme for the worksheet.
   b) Format the titles, subtitles, and headings using styles.
   c) Format the totals, minimums, maximums, and averages.
   d) Format the numbers and text.
   e) Resize columns and rows.

Apply Your Knowledge

Reinforce the skills and apply the concepts you learned in this module.

Cost Analysis Worksheet

Note: To complete this assignment, you will be required to use the Data Files. Please contact your instructor for information about accessing the required files.

Instructions: Run Excel. Open the workbook Apply 2-1 Proximity Bus. You will enter and copy formulas and functions and apply formatting to the worksheet in order to analyze the costs associated with a bus company's fleet of vehicles, as shown in Figure 2–70.

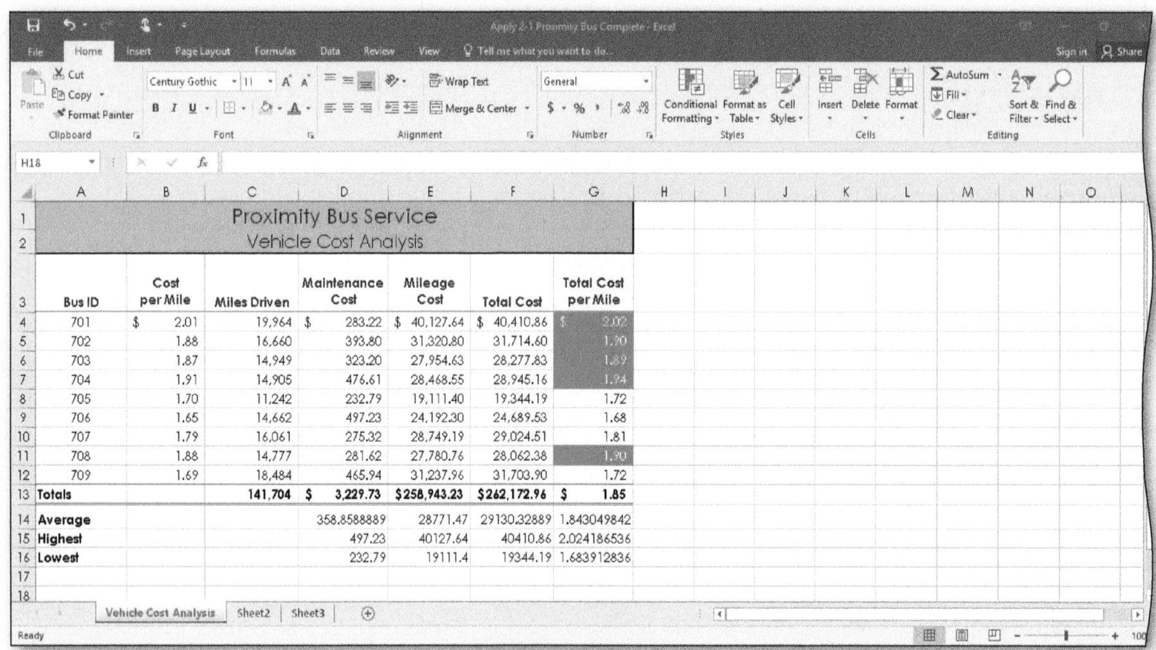

	Proximity Bus Service Vehicle Cost Analysis						
	Bus ID	**Cost per Mile**	**Miles Driven**	**Maintenance Cost**	**Mileage Cost**	**Total Cost**	**Total Cost per Mile**
4	701	$ 2.01	19,964	$ 283.22	$ 40,127.64	$ 40,410.86	$ 2.02
5	702	1.88	16,660	393.80	31,320.80	31,714.60	1.90
6	703	1.87	14,949	323.20	27,954.63	28,277.83	1.89
7	704	1.91	14,905	476.61	28,468.55	28,945.16	1.94
8	705	1.70	11,242	232.79	19,111.40	19,344.19	1.72
9	706	1.65	14,662	497.23	24,192.30	24,689.53	1.68
10	707	1.79	16,061	275.32	28,749.19	29,024.51	1.81
11	708	1.88	14,777	281.62	27,780.76	28,062.38	1.90
12	709	1.69	18,484	465.94	31,237.96	31,703.90	1.72
13	**Totals**		**141,704**	**$ 3,229.73**	**$258,943.23**	**$262,172.96**	**$ 1.85**
14	**Average**			358.8588889	28771.47	29130.32889	1.843049842
15	**Highest**			497.23	40127.64	40410.86	2.024186536
16	**Lowest**			232.79	19111.4	19344.19	1.683912836

Figure 2–70

Perform the following tasks:

1. Use the following formulas in cells E4, F4, and G4:
   Mileage Cost (cell E4) = Cost per Mile * Miles Driven or = B4 * C4
   Total Cost (cell F4) = Maintenance Cost + Mileage Cost or = D4 + E4
   Total Cost per Mile (cell G4) = Total Cost / Miles Driven or = F4 / C4
   Use the fill handle to copy the three formulas in the range E4:G4 to the range E5:G12.
2. Determine totals for the miles driven, maintenance cost, mileage cost, and total cost in row 13. Copy the formula in cell G12 to G13 to assign the formula in cell G12 to G13 in the total line. If necessary, reapply the Total cell style to cell G13.
3. In the range D14:D16, determine the average value, highest value, and lowest value, respectively, for the values in the range D4:D12. Use the fill handle to copy the three functions to the range E14:G16.
4. Format the worksheet as follows:
   a. Change the workbook theme to Vapor Trail by using the Themes button (Page Layout tab | Themes group)
   b. Cell A1 — change to Title cell style
   c. Cell A2 — change to a font size of 16
   d. Cells A1:A2 — Red, Accent 1, Lighter 60% fill color and a thick outside borders
   e. Cells B4, D4:G4, and D13:G13 — accounting number format with two decimal places and fixed dollar signs by using the 'Accounting Number Format' button (Home tab | Number group)

f. Cells B5:B12, and D5:G12 — comma style format with two decimal places by using the Comma Style button (Home tab | Number group)
g. Cells C4:C13 — comma style format with no decimal places.
h. Cells G4:G12 — apply conditional formatting so that cells with a value greater than 1.85 appear with a red background color and white font

5. If necessary increase the size of any columns that do not properly display data.
6. Switch to Page Layout view. Enter your name, course, laboratory assignment number, and any other information, as specified by your instructor, in the Header area.
7. Preview and print the worksheet in landscape orientation. Save the workbook using the file name, Apply 2-1 Proximity Bus Complete.
8. Use Range Finder to verify the formula in cell G13.
9. Print the range A3:D16. Press CTRL+ACCENT MARK (`) to change the display from the values version of the worksheet to the formulas version. Print the formulas version in landscape orientation on one page by using the Fit to option in the Page tab in the Page Setup dialog box. Press CTRL+ACCENT MARK (`) to change the display of the worksheet back to the values version. Close the workbook without saving it.
10. Besides adding a header to your document, can you think of anything else that could be added when printing the worksheet?
11. Submit the workbook as specified by your instructor.

Extend Your Knowledge

Extend the skills you learned in this module and experiment with new skills. You may need to use Help to complete the assignment.

Creating a Customer Tracking Worksheet for Jonee's Animal Supply

Note: To complete this assignment, you will be required to use the Data Files. Please contact your instructor for information about accessing the required files.

Instructions: Run Excel. Open the workbook Extend 2–1 Jonee's Animal Supply. You are to apply Flash Fill and four types of conditional formatting to cells in a worksheet (Figure 2–71).

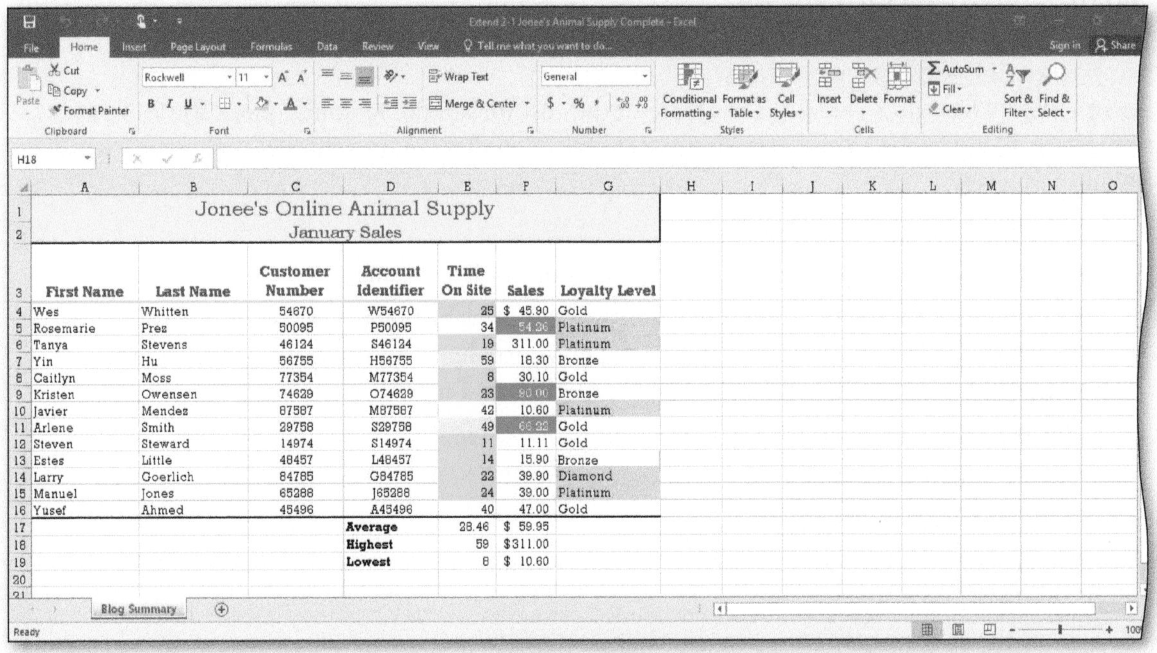

Jonee's Online Animal Supply
January Sales

First Name	Last Name	Customer Number	Account Identifier	Time On Site	Sales	Loyalty Level
Wes	Whitten	54670	W54670	25	$ 45.90	Gold
Rosemarie	Prez	50095	P50095	34	[illegible]	Platinum
Tanya	Stevens	46124	S46124	19	311.00	Platinum
Yin	Hu	56755	H56755	59	18.30	Bronze
Caitlyn	Moss	77354	M77354	8	30.10	Gold
Kristen	Owensen	74629	O74629	23	90.00	Bronze
Javier	Mendez	87587	M87587	42	10.60	Platinum
Arlene	Smith	29758	S29758	49	[illegible]	Gold
Steven	Steward	14974	S14974	11	11.11	Gold
Estes	Little	48457	L48457	14	15.90	Bronze
Larry	Goerlich	84785	G84785	22	39.90	Diamond
Manuel	Jones	65288	J65288	24	39.00	Platinum
Yusef	Ahmed	45496	A45496	40	47.00	Gold
			Average	28.46	$ 59.95	
			Highest	59	$311.00	
			Lowest	8	$ 10.60	

Blog Summary

Figure 2–71

Continued >

Extend Your Knowledge *continued*

Perform the following tasks:

1. Add the account identifiers to the cells in the range D4:D16. The account identifier is determined by taking the first initial of the customer's last name followed by the entire customer number. For example, the account identifier for Wes Whitten is W54670. Continue entering two or three account identifiers, then use Flash Fill to complete the remaining cells. If necessary, add the thick bottom border back to cell D16.
2. Select the range E4:E16. Click the Conditional Formatting button (Home tab | Styles group) and then click New Rule on the Conditional Formatting menu. Select 'Format only top or bottom ranked values' in the Select a Rule Type area (New Formatting Rule dialog box).
3. If requested by your instructor, enter any value between 10 and 30 in the text box, (otherwise enter 20) in the Edit the Rule Description (New Formatting Rule dialog box) area, and then click the '% of the selected range' check box to select it.
4. Click the Format button, and choose a light purple background in the Fill sheet to assign this conditional format. Click the OK button in each dialog box and view the worksheet.
5. With range E4:E16 selected, apply a conditional format to the range that uses a yellow background color to highlight cells with scores that are below average. *Hint:* Explore some of the preset conditional rules to assist with formatting this range of cells.
6. With range F4:F16 selected, apply a conditional format to the range that uses a white font and green background to highlight cells that contain a value between 50 and 150.
7. With range G4:G16 selected, apply a conditional format to the range that uses a light gray background color to highlight cells that contain Platinum or Diamond. (*Hint:* You need to apply two separate formats, one for Platinum and one for Diamond.)
8. When might you want to look for values above the average in a worksheet?
9. Save the workbook using the file name, Extend 2–1 Jonee's Animal Supply Complete. Submit the revised workbook as specified by your instructor.

Expand Your World

Create a solution that uses cloud or web technologies by learning and investigating on your own from general guidance.

Four-Year College Cost Calculator

Instructions: You want to create an estimate of the cost for attending your college for four years. You decide to create the worksheet using Excel Online so that you can share it with your friends online.

Perform the following tasks:

1. Sign in to your Microsoft account on the web and run Excel Online.
2. Create a blank workbook. In the first worksheet, use row headings for each year of college (Freshman, Sophomore, Junior, and Senior). For the column headings, use your current expenses (such as car payment, rent, utilities, tuition, and food).
3. Enter expenses for each year based upon estimates you find by searching the web.
4. Calculate the total for each column. Also determine highest, lowest, and average values for each column.
5. Using the techniques taught in this module, create appropriate titles and format the worksheet accordingly.
6. Submit the assignment as specified by your instructor.

In the Labs

Design, create, modify, and/or use a workbook following the guidelines, concepts, and skills presented in this module. Labs 1 and 2, which increase in difficulty, require you to create solutions based on what you learned in the module; Lab 3 requires you to apply your creative thinking and problem-solving skills to design and implement a solution.

Lab 1: Insurance Premium Worksheet

Problem: You are a part-time assistant in the accounting department at Aylin Insurance, an Orlando-based insurance company. You have been asked to use Excel to generate a report that summarizes the existing balances on annual premiums, similar to the one shown in Figure 2–72. Include the three columns of customer data in Table 2-6 in the report, plus two additional columns to compute a monthly fee and a current balance for each customer. Assume no negative unpaid monthly balances.

Perform the following tasks:

1. Enter and format the worksheet title **Aylin Insurance** and worksheet subtitle **Premium Analysis** in cells A1 and A2. Change the theme of the worksheet to the Berlin theme. Apply the Title cell style to cells A1 and A2. Change the font size in cell A1 to 26 points, and change the font size in cell A2 to 18 points. Merge and center the worksheet title and subtitle across columns A through E. Draw a thick outside border around the range A1:A2.
2. Change the width of column A to 20.00 points. Change the widths of columns B through E to 14.00 points. Change the heights of row 3 to 36.00 points and row 14 to 25.50 points.

Table 2–6 Aylin Insurance Premium Data

Customer	Previous Balance	Payments
Albasco, Robin	1600.72	72.15
Deon, Jade	1518.62	382.3
Goodman, Brad	679.29	80.69
Hill, Raine	1060.42	107.6
Klonde, Albert	1178.83	125.63
Lang, Rose	1280.2	79.85
Moore, Jeffrey	1253.88	389.79
Piper, Taylor	477.11	278.52
Sothens, Mary	821.31	153.14

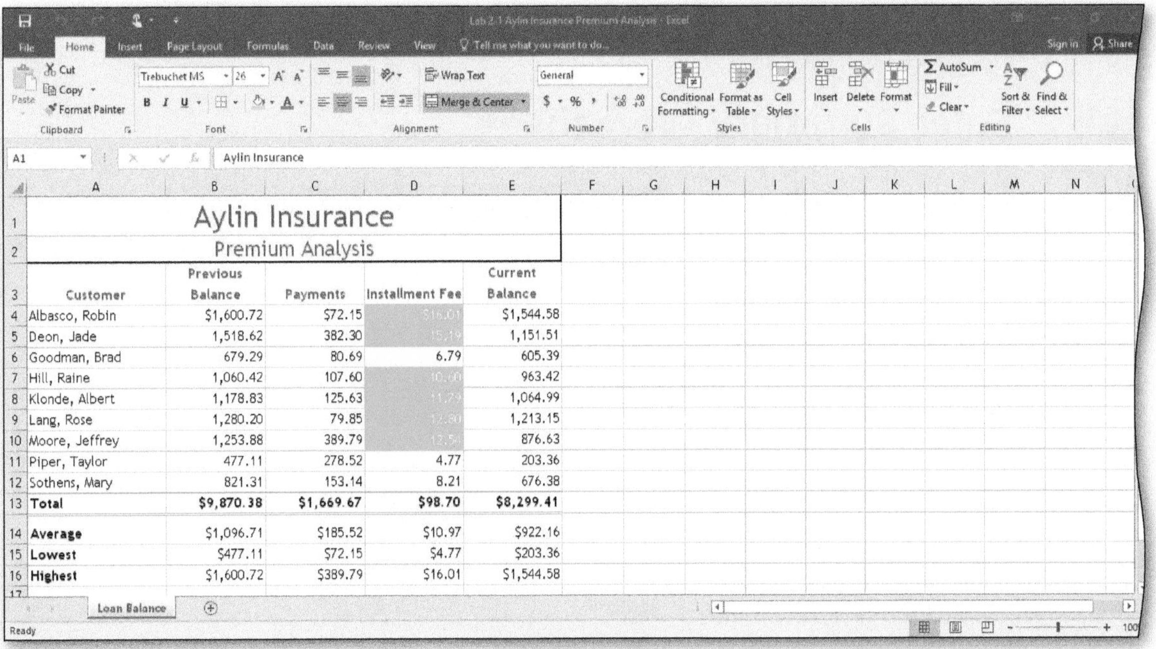

Figure 2–72

Continued >

In the Labs *continued*

3. Enter the column titles in row 3 and row titles in the range A13:A16, as shown in Figure 2–72. Center the column titles in the range A3:E3. Apply the Heading 4 cell style to the range A3:E3. Apply the Total cell style to the range A13:E13. Bold the titles in the range A13:A16. Change the font size in the range A3:E16 to 12 points.
4. Enter the data in Table 2-6 in the range A4:C12.
5. Use the following formulas to determine the installment fee in column D and the current balance in column E for the first customer. Copy the two formulas down through the remaining customers.

   a. Installment Fee (cell D4) = 1% * Previous Balance

   b. Current Balance (E4) = Previous Balance – Payments + Installment Fee
6. Determine the totals in row 13.
7. Determine the average, minimum, and maximum values in cells B14:B16 for the range B4:B12, and then copy the range B14:B16 to C14:E16.
8. Format the numbers as follows: (a) assign the currency style with a floating dollar sign to the cells containing numeric data in the ranges B4:E4 and B13:E16, and (b) assign a number style with two decimal places and a thousand's separator (currency with no dollar sign) to the range B5:E12.
9. Use conditional formatting to change the formatting to white font on an orange background in any cell in the range D4:D12 that contains a value greater than 10.
10. Change the worksheet name from Sheet1 to Loan Balance and the sheet tab color to the Orange standard color.
11. Change the worksheet header with your name, course number, and other information as specified by your instructor.
12. Use the spelling checker to check the spelling in the worksheet. Preview and then print the worksheet in landscape orientation. Save the workbook using the file name, Lab 2-1 Aylin Insurance Premium Analysis.
13. When you created the formula for the installment fee, you used 1%. What would you have to do if the rate changed today to 2% to update the formulas?

Lab 2: Sales Summary Worksheet

Problem: You have been asked to build a worksheet for International Moving Company that analyzes the financing needs for the company's first year in business. The company plans to begin operations in January with an initial investment of $750,000.00. The expected revenue and costs for the company's first year are shown in Table 2–7. The desired worksheet is shown in Figure 2–73. The initial investment is shown as the starting balance for January (cell B4). The amount of financing required by the company is shown as the lowest ending balance (cell F18).

Table 2–7 International Moving Company Financing Needs Data

Month	Incomes	Expenses
January	1209081	1262911
February	1163811	1381881
March	1300660	1250143
April	1229207	1209498
May	1248369	1355232
June	1196118	1260888
July	1162970	1242599
August	1195824	1368955
September	1305669	1235604
October	1224741	1383254
November	1159644	1411768
December	1210000	1540000

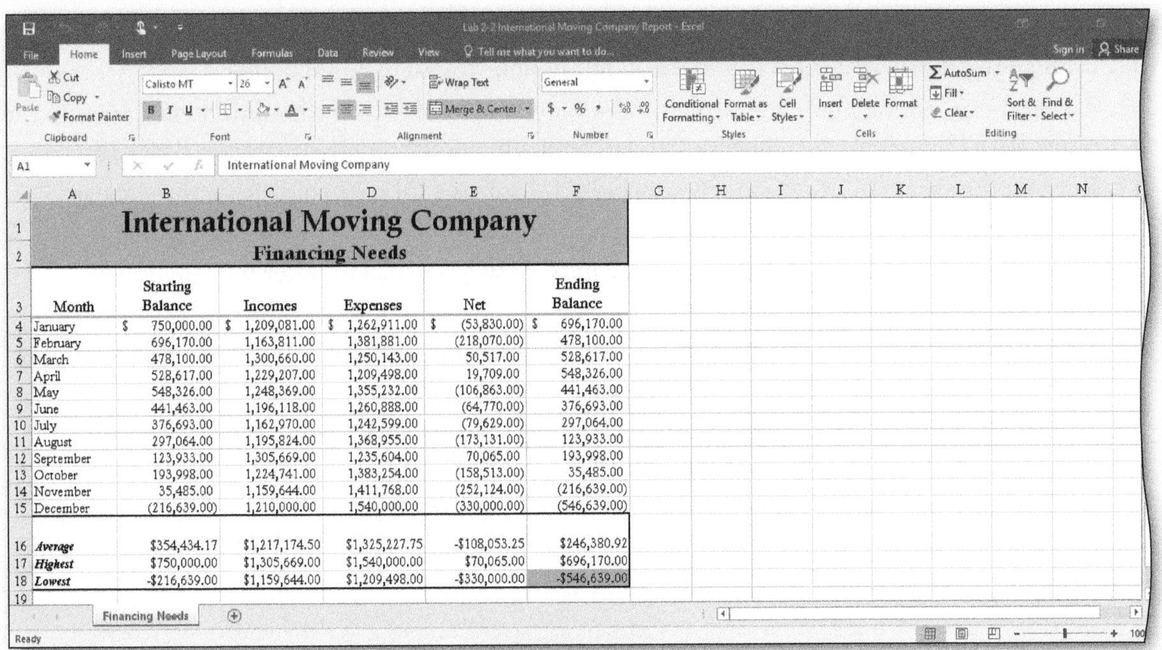

International Moving Company

Financing Needs

Month	Starting Balance	Incomes	Expenses	Net	Ending Balance
January	$ 750,000.00	$ 1,209,081.00	$ 1,262,911.00	$ (53,830.00)	$ 696,170.00
February	696,170.00	1,163,811.00	1,381,881.00	(218,070.00)	478,100.00
March	478,100.00	1,300,660.00	1,250,143.00	50,517.00	528,617.00
April	528,617.00	1,229,207.00	1,209,498.00	19,709.00	548,326.00
May	548,326.00	1,248,369.00	1,355,232.00	(106,863.00)	441,463.00
June	441,463.00	1,196,118.00	1,260,888.00	(64,770.00)	376,693.00
July	376,693.00	1,162,970.00	1,242,599.00	(79,629.00)	297,064.00
August	297,064.00	1,195,824.00	1,368,955.00	(173,131.00)	123,933.00
September	123,933.00	1,305,669.00	1,235,604.00	70,065.00	193,998.00
October	193,998.00	1,224,741.00	1,383,254.00	(158,513.00)	35,485.00
November	35,485.00	1,159,644.00	1,411,768.00	(252,124.00)	(216,639.00)
December	(216,639.00)	1,210,000.00	1,540,000.00	(330,000.00)	(546,639.00)
Average	$354,434.17	$1,217,174.50	$1,325,227.75	-$108,053.25	$246,380.92
Highest	$750,000.00	$1,305,669.00	$1,540,000.00	$70,065.00	$696,170.00
Lowest	-$216,639.00	$1,159,644.00	$1,209,498.00	-$330,000.00	-$546,639.00

Figure 2–73

Perform the following tasks:

1. Apply the Slate theme to a new workbook.
2. Increase the width of column A to 12.00 and the width of columns B through F to 14.50.
3. Enter the worksheet title **`International Moving Company`** in cell A1 and the worksheet subtitle **`Financing Needs`** in cell A2. Enter the column titles in row 3, as shown in Figure 2–73. In row 3, use ALT+ENTER to start a new line in a cell.
4. Enter the financing needs data described in Table 2-7 in columns A, C, and D in rows 4 through 15. Enter the initial starting balance (cell B4) of 750000.00. Enter the row titles in the range A16:A18, as shown in Figure 2–73.
5. For the months of February through December, the starting balance is equal to the previous month's ending balance. Obtain the starting balance for February by setting the starting balance of February to the ending balance of January. Use a cell reference rather than typing in the data. Copy the formula for February to the remaining months.
6. Obtain the net amounts in column E by subtracting the expenses in column D from the incomes in column C. Enter the formula in cell E4 and copy it to the range E5:E15. Obtain the ending balance amounts in column F by adding the starting balance in column B to the net in column E. Enter the formula in cell F4 and copy it to the range F5:F15.
7. In the range B16:B18, use the AVERAGE, MAX, and MIN functions to determine the average value, highest value, and lowest value in the range B4:B15. Copy the range B16:B18 to the range C16:F18.
8. One at a time, merge and center the worksheet title and subtitle across columns A through F. Select cells A1 and A2 and change the background color to Tan, Accent 2 from the theme colors (column 6, row 1). Apply the Title cell style to cells A1 and A2. Change the worksheet title in cell A1 to 26-point. Bold both the title and subtitle. Draw a thick outside border around the range A1:A2.
9. Center the titles in row 3, columns A through F. Apply the Heading 2 cell style to the range A3:F3. Italicize and bold the row titles in the range A16:A18.
10. Draw a thick outside border around the range A16:F18. Change the background color for cell F18 to the same colors applied to the worksheet title in Step 8.

Continued >

In the Labs *continued*

11. Change the row heights of row 3 to 42.00 points and row 16 to 33.00 points.
12. Assign the accounting number format to the range B4:F4. Assign the comma style format to the range B5:F15. Assign a currency format with a floating dollar sign to the range B16:F18.
13. Rename the sheet tab as `Financing Needs`. Apply the Orange color from the standard colors (column 3) to the sheet tab.
14. Change the worksheet header with your name, course number, and other information as specified by your instructor.
15. Save the workbook using the file name, Lab 2-2 International Moving Company Report. Print the entire worksheet in landscape orientation. Next, print only the range A3:B15.
16. Display the formulas version by pressing CTRL+ACCENT MARK (`). Print the formulas version using the Fit to option in the Scaling area in the Page tab (Page Setup dialog box). After printing the worksheet, reset the Scaling option by selecting the Adjust to option in the Page tab (Page Setup dialog box) and changing the percent value to 100%. Change the display from the formulas version to the values version by pressing CTRL+ACCENT MARK (`). Do not save the workbook.
17. Submit the revised workbook as requested by your instructor.
18. In reviewing the worksheet you created, how do you think the company could obtain a positive result without increasing income or decreasing expenses?

Lab 3: Consider This: Your Turn

Apply your creative thinking and problem-solving skills to design and implement a solution.

Internet Service Summary

Instructions Part 1: You and your friends have decided to subscribe to a new Internet service provider. You would like to maximize services while keeping costs low. Research and find three Internet service providers in your area. If you cannot find three service providers in your area, you can research three service providers in another area of your choosing. For each company, find the best service package as well as the basic service package. Using the cost figures you find, calculate the cost per month for each service for a year. Include totals, minimum, maximum, and average values. Use the concepts and techniques presented in this module to create and format the worksheet.

Instructions Part 2: Which companies did you choose for your report? Which services offered the best deals that you would be willing to use?

3 Working with Large Worksheets, Charting, and What-If Analysis

Objectives

You will have mastered the material in this module when you can:

- Rotate text in a cell
- Create a series of month names
- Copy, paste, insert, and delete cells
- Format numbers using format symbols
- Enter and format the system date
- Use absolute and mixed cell references in a formula
- Use the IF function to perform a logical test
- Create and format sparkline charts
- Change sparkline chart types and styles
- Use the Format Painter button to format cells
- Create a clustered column chart on a separate chart sheet
- Use chart filters to display a subset of data in a chart
- Change the chart type and style
- Reorder sheet tabs
- Change the worksheet view
- Freeze and unfreeze rows and columns
- Answer what-if questions
- Goal seek to answer what-if questions
- Use the Smart Lookup Insight
- Understand accessibility features

Introduction

This module introduces you to techniques that will enhance your ability to create worksheets and draw charts. This module also covers other methods for entering values in cells, such as allowing Excel to automatically enter and format values based on a perceived pattern in the existing values. In addition, you will learn how to use absolute cell references and how to use the IF function to assign a value to a cell based on a logical test.

When you set up a worksheet, you should use cell references in formulas whenever possible, rather than constant values. The use of a cell reference allows you to change a value in multiple formulas by changing the value in a single cell. The cell references in a formula are called assumptions. **Assumptions** are values in cells that you can change to determine new values for formulas. This module emphasizes the use of assumptions and shows how to use assumptions to answer what-if questions, such as what happens to the six-month operating income if you decrease the Equipment

Repair and Maintenance expenses assumption by 1%. Being able to analyze the effect of changing values in a worksheet is an important skill in making business decisions.

Worksheets are normally much larger than those you created in the previous modules, often extending beyond the size of the Excel window. When you cannot view the entire worksheet on the screen at once, working with a large worksheet can be frustrating. This module introduces several Excel commands that allow you to control what is displayed on the screen so that you can focus on critical parts of a large worksheet. One command allows you to freeze rows and columns so that they remain visible, even when you scroll. Another command splits the worksheet into separate panes so that you can view different parts of a worksheet on the screen at once. Another changes the magnification to allow you to see more content, albeit at a smaller size. This is useful for reviewing the general layout of content on the worksheet.

From your work in Module 1, you know how easily you can create charts in Excel. This module covers additional charting techniques that allow you to convey meaning visually, such as by using sparkline charts or clustered column charts. This module also introduces the Accessibility checker.

For an introduction to Windows and instructions about how to perform basic Windows tasks, read the Office and Windows module at the beginning of this book, where you can learn how to resize windows, change screen resolution, create folders, move and rename files, use Windows Help, and much more.

Project — Financial Projection Worksheet with What-If Analysis and Chart

The project in this module uses Excel to create the worksheet and clustered column chart shown in Figures 3-1a and 3-1b. Kaitlyn's Ice Cream Shoppe operates kiosks at colleges and universities and serves both hard and soft serve ice cream. Each December and June, the chief executive officer projects monthly sales revenues, costs of goods sold, gross margin, expenses, and operating income for the upcoming six-month period, based on figures from the previous six months. The CEO requires an easy-to-read worksheet that shows financial projections for the upcoming six months to use for procuring partial financing and for determining staffing needs. The worksheet should allow for quick analysis, if projections for certain numbers change, such as the percentage of expenses

For an introduction to Office and instructions about how to perform basic tasks in Office apps, read the Office and Windows module at the beginning of this book, where you can learn how to run an application, use the ribbon, save a file, open a file, print a file, exit an application, use Help, and much more.

BTW
Excel Screen Resolution
If you are using a computer or mobile device to step through the project in this module and you want your screens to match the figures in this book, you should change your screen's resolution to 1366 x 768. For information about how to change a computer's resolution, refer to the Office and Windows module at the beginning of this book.

	A	B	C	D	E	F	G	H	I
1	Kaitlyn's Ice Cream Shoppe							9/29/2017	
2	Six-Month Financial Projection								
3		January	February	March	April	May	June	Total	Chart
4	Revenue	$55,000.00	$62,500.00	$67,000.00	$90,250.00	$77,500.00	$74,750.00	$427,000.00	
5	Cost of Goods Sold	11,687.50	13,281.25	14,237.50	19,178.13	16,468.75	15,884.38	90,737.50	
6	Gross Margin	$43,312.50	$49,218.75	$52,762.50	$71,071.88	$61,031.25	$58,865.63	$336,262.50	
7									
8	Expenses								
9	Bonus	$0.00	$0.00	$5,000.00	$5,000.00	$5,000.00	$5,000.00	$20,000.00	
10	Commission	12,375.00	14,062.50	15,075.00	20,306.25	17,437.50	16,818.75	96,075.00	
11	Site Rental	5,500.00	6,250.00	6,700.00	9,025.00	7,750.00	7,475.00	42,700.00	
12	Marketing	2,750.00	3,125.00	3,350.00	4,512.50	3,875.00	3,737.50	21,350.00	
13	Equipment Repair and Maintenance	2,200.00	2,500.00	2,680.00	3,610.00	3,100.00	2,990.00	17,080.00	
14	Total Expenses	$22,825.00	$25,937.50	$32,805.00	$42,453.75	$37,162.50	$36,021.25	$197,205.00	
15									
16	Operating Income	$20,487.50	$23,281.25	$19,957.50	$28,618.13	$23,868.75	$22,844.38	$139,057.50	
17									

Six-Month Financial Projection | Expense Chart

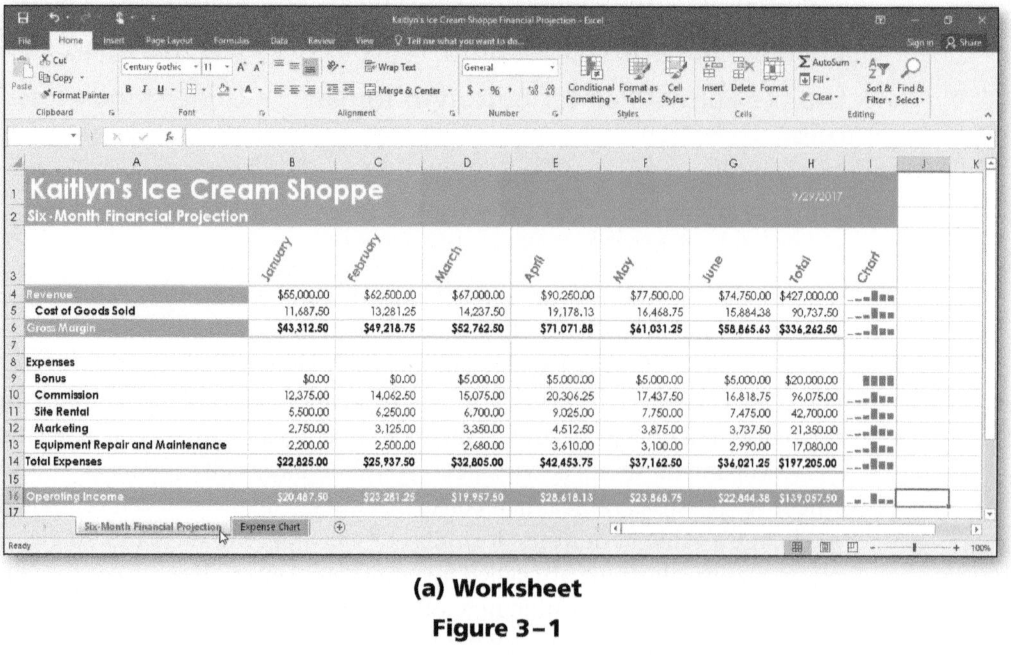

(a) Worksheet

Figure 3–1

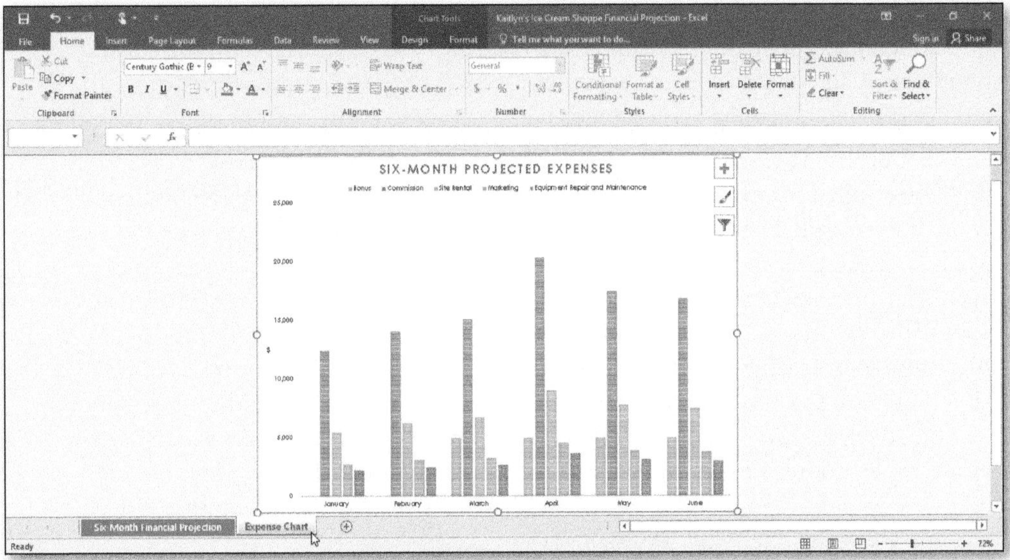

(b) Clustered Column Chart

Figure 3–1 (Continued)

allocated to commission or the cost of the kiosk rentals. In addition, you need to create a column chart that shows the breakdown of expenses for each month in the period.

The requirements document for the Kaitlyn's Ice Cream Shoppe Six-Month Financial Projection worksheet is shown in Figure 3–2. It includes the needs, source of data, summary of calculations, and chart requirements.

> BTW
> **Touch Screen Differences**
> The Office and Windows interfaces may vary if you are using a touch screen. For this reason, you might notice that the function or appearance of your touch screen differs slightly from this module's presentation.

Worksheet Title	Kaitlyn's Ice Cream Shoppe Six-Month Financial Projection
Needs	• A woksheet that shows Kaitlyn's Ice Cream Shoppe projected monthly sales revenue, cost of goods sold, gross margin, expenses, and operating income for a six-month period. • A clustered column chart that shows the expected contribution of each expense category to total expenses.
Source of Data	Data supplied by the business owner includes projections of the monthly sales and expenses based on prior year figures (see Table 3–1). Remaining numbers in the worksheet are based on formulas.
Calculations	The following calculations are needed for each month: • Cost of Goods Sold = Revenue * (1 – Margin) • Gross Margin = Revenue – Cost of Goods Sold • Bonus expense = Predetermined bonus amount if Revenue exceeds the Revenue for Bonus, otherwise Bonus = 0 • Commission expense = Commission percentage × Revenue • Site Rental expense = Kiosk Rental Percentage × Revenue • Marketing expense = Marketing percentage × Revenue • Equipment Repair and Maintenance expense = Equipment Repair and Maintenance percentage × Revenue • Total expenses = sum of all expenses • Operating Income = Gross Margin – Total expenses
Chart Requirements	• Show sparkline charts for revenue and each of the items noted in the calculations area above. • Show a clustered column chart that shows the contributions of each month's expense categories to the total monthly expense figure.

Figure 3–2

Using a sketch of the worksheet can help you visualize its design. The sketch of the worksheet consists of titles, column and row headings, location of data values, calculations, and a rough idea of the desired formatting (Figure 3–3a). The sketch of the clustered column chart shows the expected expenses for each of the six months (Figure 3–3b). The assumptions about income and expenses will be entered at the bottom of the worksheet (Figure 3–3a). The projected monthly sales revenue will be entered in row 4 of the worksheet. The projected monthly sales revenue and the assumptions shown in Table 3–1 will be used to calculate the remaining numbers in the worksheet.

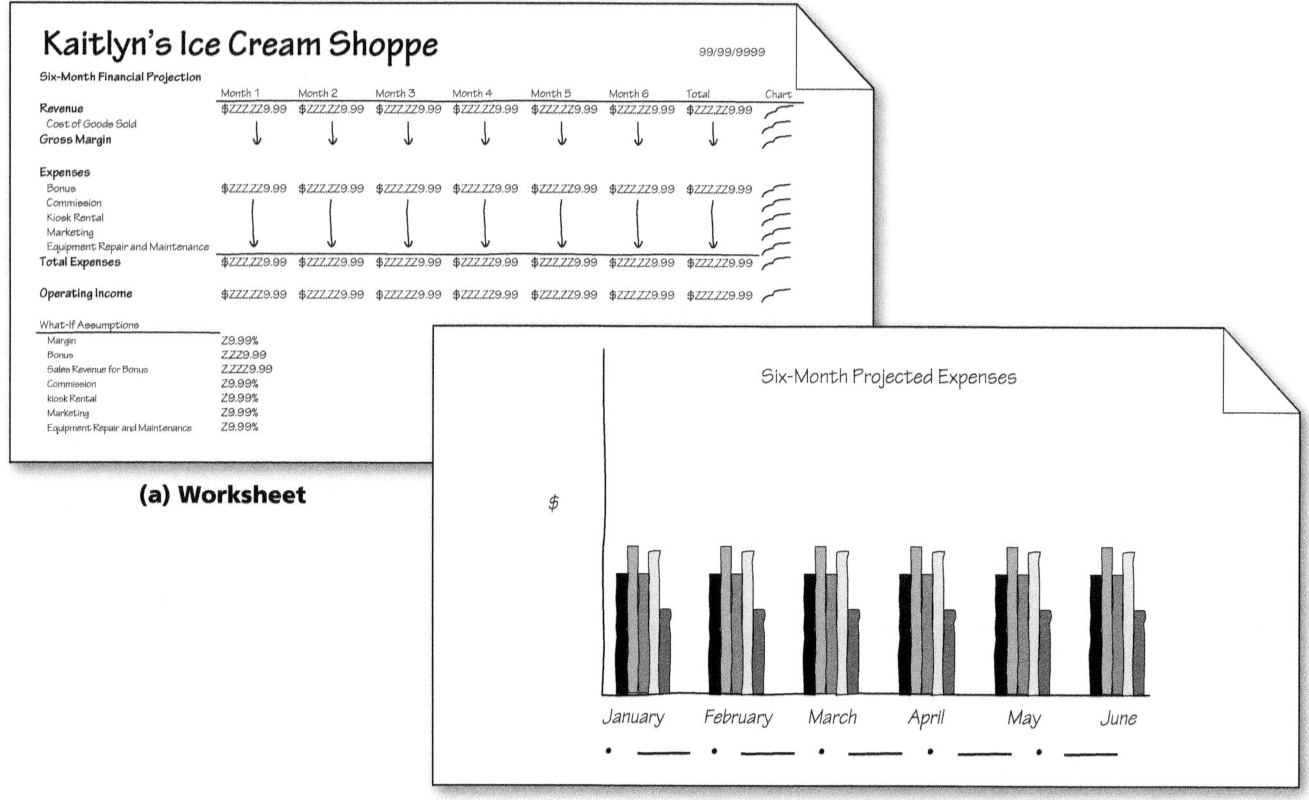

(a) Worksheet

(b) Clustered Column Chart

Figure 3–3

Table 3–1 Kaitlyn's Ice Cream Shoppe Six-Month Financial Projections Data and What-If Assumptions	
Projected Monthly Total Sales Revenues	
January	55,000.00
February	62,500.00
March	67,000.00
April	90,250.00
May	77,500.00
June	74,750.00
What-If Assumptions	
Margin	78.75%
Bonus	$3,500.00
Sales Revenue for Bonus	65,000.00
Commission	25.00%
Site Rental	10.00%
Marketing	5.00%
Equipment Repair and Maintenance	3.50%

With a solid understanding of the requirements document, an understanding of the necessary decisions, and a sketch of the worksheet, the next step is to use Excel to create the worksheet.

In this module, you will learn how to create and use the workbook shown in Figure 3–1. The following roadmap identifies general activities you will perform as you progress through this module:

1. ENTER the HEADINGS and DATA in the worksheet.
2. ENTER FORMULAS and FUNCTIONS in the worksheet.
3. CREATE SPARKLINE CHARTS in a range of cells.
4. FORMAT the WORKSHEET.
5. CREATE a COLUMN CHART on a separate chart sheet.
6. CHANGE VIEWS of the worksheet.
7. ASK WHAT-IF QUESTIONS.

BTW

Excel Help

At any time while using Excel, you can find answers to questions and display information about various topics through Excel Help. Used properly, this form of assistance can increase your productivity and reduce your frustrations by minimizing the time you spend learning how to use Excel. For instructions about Excel Help and exercises that will help you gain confidence in using it, read the Office and Windows module at the beginning of this book.

To Enter the Worksheet Titles and Apply a Theme

The worksheet contains two titles in cells A1 and A2. In the previous modules, titles were centered across the worksheet. With large worksheets that extend beyond the size of a window, it is best to leave titles left-aligned, as shown in the sketch of the worksheet in Figure 3–3a, so that the worksheet will print the title on the first page if the worksheet requires multiple pages. This allows the user to easily find the worksheet title when necessary. The following steps enter the worksheet titles and change the workbook theme to Savon.

1. Run Excel and create a blank workbook in the Excel window.
2. Select cell A1 and then type `Kaitlyn's Ice Cream Shoppe` as the worksheet title.
3. Select cell A2, type `Six-Month Financial Projection` as the worksheet subtitle, and then press the ENTER key to enter the worksheet subtitle.
4. Apply the Savon theme to the workbook.

BTW

The Ribbon and Screen Resolution

Excel may change how the groups and buttons within the groups appear on the ribbon, depending on the computer or mobile device's screen resolution. Thus, your ribbon may look different from the ones in this book if you are using a screen resolution other than 1366 x 768.

BTW

Rotating Text in a Cell

In Excel, you use the Alignment sheet in the Format Cells dialog box (shown in Figure 3–5) to position data in a cell by centering, left-aligning, or right-aligning; indenting; aligning at the top, bottom, or center; and rotating. If you enter 90 in the Degrees box in the Orientation area, the text will appear vertically and read from bottom to top in the cell.

Rotating Text and Using the Fill Handle to Create a Series

The data on the worksheet, including month names and the What-If Assumptions section, now can be added to the worksheet.

CONSIDER THIS

What should you take into account when planning a worksheet layout?

Using Excel, you can change text and number formatting in many ways, which affects the visual impact of the worksheet. Rotated text often provides a strong visual appeal. Rotated text also allows you to fit more text into a smaller column width. When laying out a worksheet, keep in mind the content you want to emphasize and the length of the cell titles relative to the numbers.

To Rotate Text in a Cell

The design of the worksheet calls specifically for data for the six months of the selling season. Because there always will be only six months of data in the worksheet, place the months across the top of the worksheet as column headings rather than as row headings. Place the income and expense categories in rows, as they are more numerous than the number of months. This layout allows you to easily navigate the worksheet. Ideally, a proper layout will create a worksheet that is longer than it is wide.

When you first enter text, its angle is zero degrees (0°), and it reads from left to right in a cell. Excel allows you to rotate text in a cell counterclockwise by entering a number between 1° and 90°. ***Why?*** *Rotating text is one method of making column headings visually distinct.* The following steps enter the month name, January, in cell B3 and format cell B3 by rotating the text.

1

- If necessary, click the Home tab and then select cell B3 because this cell will include the first month name in the series of month names.
- Type **January** as the cell entry and then click the Enter button.
- Click the Alignment Settings Dialog Box Launcher (Home tab | Alignment group) to display the Format Cells dialog box (Figure 3–4).

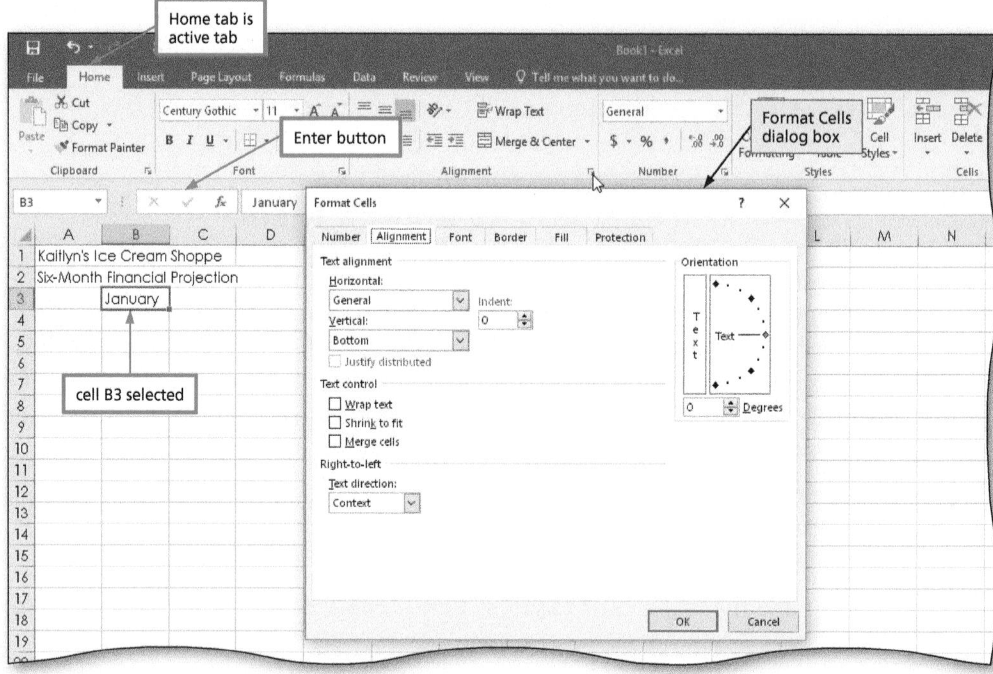

Figure 3–4

- Click the 60° point in the Orientation area (Format Cells dialog box) to move the indicator in the Orientation area to the 60° point and display a new orientation in the Degrees box (Figure 3–5).

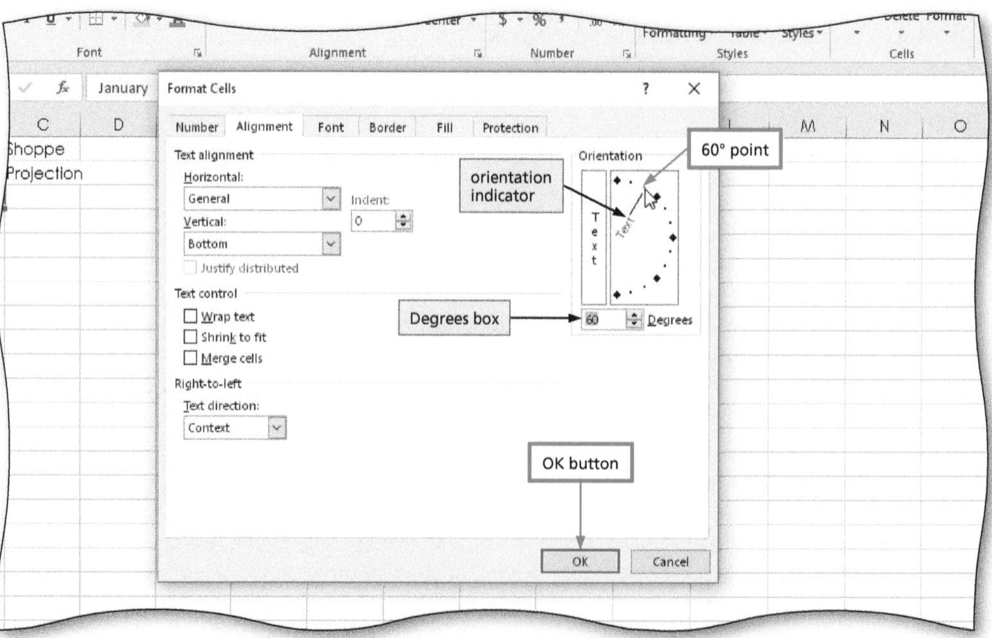

Figure 3–5

- Click the OK button (Format Cells dialog box) to rotate the text in the active cell and increase the height of the current row to best fit the rotated text (Figure 3–6).

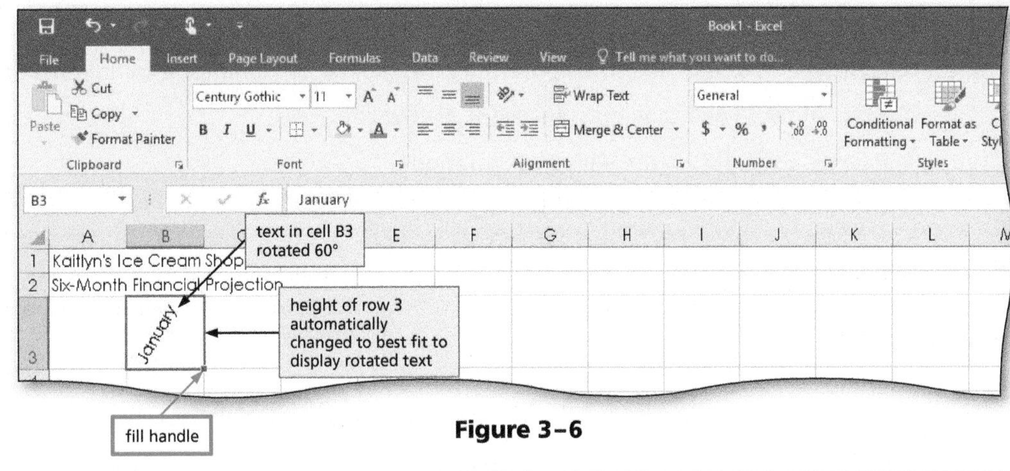

Figure 3–6

Other Ways

1. Right-click selected cell, click Format Cells on shortcut menu, click Alignment tab (Format Cells dialog box), click 60° point, click OK button

To Use the Fill Handle to Create a Series of Month Names

1 ENTER HEADINGS & DATA | 2 ENTER FORMULAS & FUNCTIONS | 3 CREATE SPARKLINE CHARTS
4 FORMAT WORKSHEET | 5 CREATE COLUMN CHART | 6 CHANGE VIEWS | 7 ASK WHAT-IF QUESTIONS

***Why?** Once the first month in the series has been entered and formatted, you can complete the data series using the fill handle rather than typing and formatting all the entries.* The following steps use the fill handle and the entry in cell B3 to create a series of month names in cells C3:G3.

- Drag the fill handle on the lower-right corner of cell B3 to the right to select the range to fill, C3:G3 in this case. Do not release the mouse button (Figure 3–7).

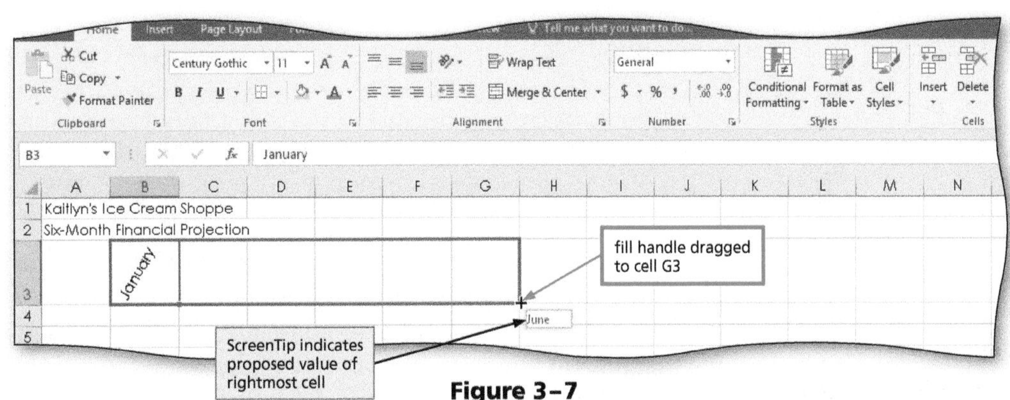

Figure 3–7

- Release the mouse button to create a month name series in the selected range and copy the format of the selected cell to the selected range.
- Click the 'Auto Fill Options' button below the lower-right corner of the fill area to display the Auto Fill Options menu (Figure 3–8).

Q&A What if I do not want to copy the format of cell B3 during the auto fill operation?

In addition to creating a series of values, dragging the fill handle instructs Excel to copy the format of cell B3 to the range C3:G3. With some fill operations, you may not want to copy the formats of the source cell or range to the destination cell or range. If this is the case, click the 'Auto Fill Options' button after the range fills and then select the desired option on the Auto Fill Options menu (Figure 3–8).

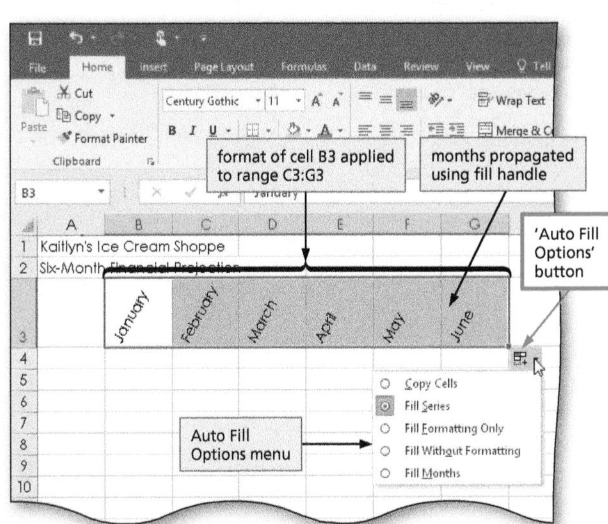

Figure 3–8

3

- Click the 'Auto Fill Options' button to hide the Auto Fill Options menu.
- Select cell H3, type `Total`, and then press the RIGHT ARROW key to enter a column heading.
- Type `Chart` in cell I3 and then press the RIGHT ARROW key.

Q&A

Why is the word, Total, formatted with a 60° rotation?

Excel tries to save you time by recognizing the format in adjacent cell G3 and applying it to cell H3. Such behavior also occurs when typing the column heading in cell I3.

Other Ways

1. Type text in cell, apply formatting, right-drag fill handle in direction to fill, click Fill Months on shortcut menu
2. Type text in cell, apply formatting, select range, click Fill button (Home tab | Editing group), click Series, click AutoFill (Series dialog box), click OK button

BTW

The Fill Handle

If you drag the fill handle up or to the left, Excel will decrement the series rather than increment the series. To copy a word, such as January or Monday, which Excel might interpret as the start of a series, hold down the CTRL key while you drag the fill handle to a destination area. If you drag the fill handle back into the middle of a cell, Excel erases the contents of the cell.

Using the Auto Fill Options Menu

As shown in Figure 3–8, Fill Series is the default option that Excel uses to fill an area, which means it fills the destination area with a series, using the same formatting as the source area. If you choose another option on the Auto Fill Options menu, Excel changes the contents of the destination range. Following the use of the fill handle, the 'Auto Fill Options' button remains active until you begin the next Excel operation. Table 3–2 summarizes the options on the Auto Fill Options menu.

Table 3–2 Options Available on the Auto Fill Options Menu

Auto Fill Option	Description
Copy Cells	Fill destination area with contents using format of source area. Do not create a series.
Fill Series	Fill destination area with series using format of source area. This option is the default.
Fill Formatting Only	Fill destination area using format of source area. No content is copied unless fill is series.
Fill Without Formatting	Fill destination area with contents, without applying the formatting of source area.
Fill Months	Fill destination area with series of months using format of source area. Same as Fill Series and shows as an option only if source area contains the name of a month.

You can create several different types of series using the fill handle. Table 3–3 illustrates several examples. Notice in examples 4 through 7, 9, and 11 that, if you use the fill handle to create a series of nonsequential numbers or months, you must enter the first item in the series in one cell and the second item in the series in an adjacent cell, and then select both cells and drag the fill handle through the destination area.

BTW

Custom Fill Sequences

You can create your own custom fill sequences for use with the fill handle. For example, if you often type the same list of products or names in Excel, you can create a custom fill sequence. You then can type the first product or name and then use the fill handle automatically to fill in the remaining products or names. To create a custom fill sequence, display the Excel Options dialog box by clicking Options in the Backstage view. Click the Advanced tab (Excel Options dialog box) and then click the 'Edit Custom Lists' button in the General section (Excel Options dialog box).

Table 3–3 Examples of Series Using the Fill Handle

Example	Contents of Cell(s) Copied Using the Fill Handle	Next Three Values of Extended Series
1	4:00	5:00, 6:00, 7:00
2	Qtr2	Qtr3, Qtr4, Qtr1
3	Quarter 1	Quarter 2, Quarter 3, Quarter 4
4	22-Jul, 22-Sep	22-Nov, 22-Jan, 22-Mar
5	2017, 2018	2019, 2020, 2021
6	1, 2	3, 4, 5
7	625, 575	525, 475, 425
8	Mon	Tue, Wed, Thu
9	Sunday, Tuesday	Thursday, Saturday, Monday
10	4th Section	5th Section, 6th Section, 7th Section
11	2205, 2208	2211, 2214, 2217

To Increase Column Widths

***Why?** In Module 2, you increased column widths after the values were entered into the worksheet. Sometimes, you may want to increase the column widths before you enter values and, if necessary, adjust them later.* The following steps increase the column widths.

- Move the pointer to the boundary between column heading A and column heading B so that the pointer changes to a split double arrow in preparation of adjusting the column widths.
- Drag the pointer to the right until the ScreenTip displays the desired column width, Width: 38.00 (309 pixels) in this case. Do not release the mouse button (Figure 3–9).

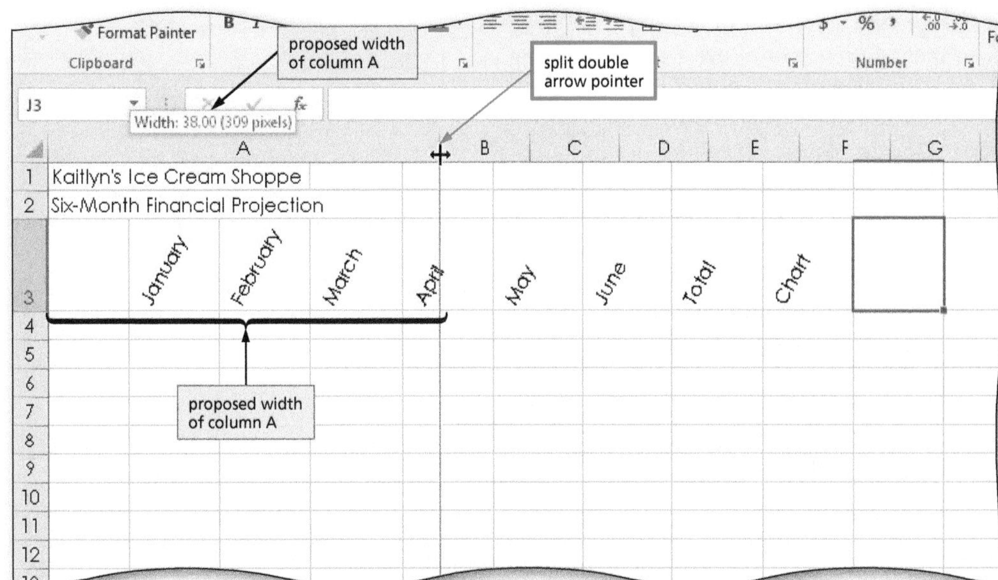

Figure 3–9

- Release the mouse button to change the width of the column.
- Click column heading B to select the column and then drag through column heading G to select the range in which to change the widths.
- Move the pointer to the boundary between column headings B and C in preparation of resizing column B and then drag the pointer to the right until the ScreenTip displays the desired width, Width: 14.50 (121 pixels) in this case. Do not lift your finger or release the mouse button (Figure 3–10).

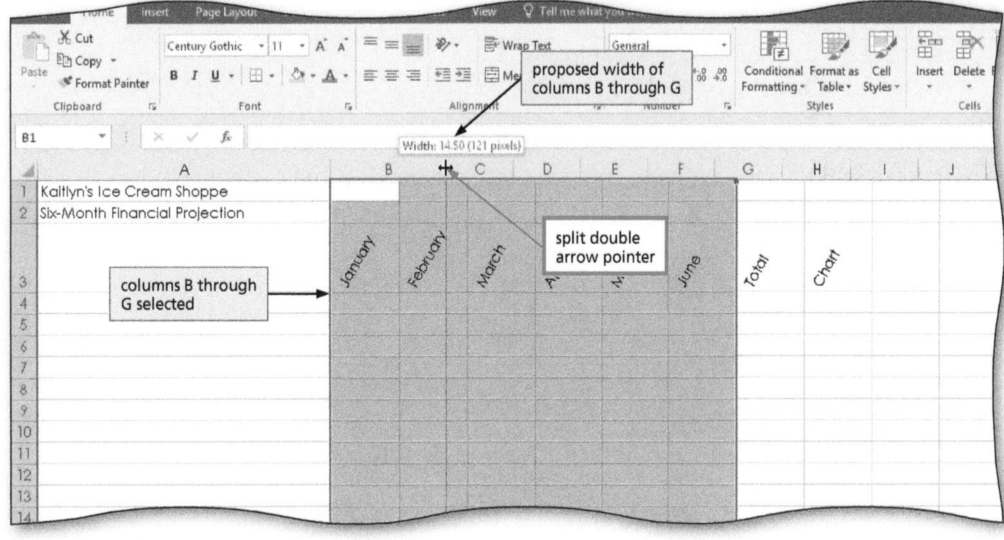

Figure 3–10

3

- Release the mouse button to change the width of the selected columns.
- If necessary, scroll the worksheet so that column H is visible and then use the technique described in Step 1 to increase the width of column H to 18.00 (149 pixels).

To Enter and Indent Row Titles

Excel allows you to indent text in cells. The following steps enter the row titles in column A and indent several of the row titles to create a visual hierarchy. ***Why?*** *You can create a hierarchy by indenting some of the row titles, like in an outline or table of contents.*

- If necessary, scroll the worksheet so that column A and row 4 are visible and then enter **`Revenue`** in cell A4, **`Cost of Goods Sold`** in cell A5, **`Gross Margin`** in cell A6, **`Expenses`** in cell A8, **`Bonus`** in cell A9, **`Commission`** in cell A10, **`Site Rental`** in cell A11, **`Marketing`** in cell A12, **`Equipment Repair and Maintenance`** in cell A13, **`Total Expenses`** in cell A14, and **`Operating Income`** in cell A16.
- Select cell A5 and then click the Increase Indent button (Home tab | Alignment group) to increase the indentation of the text in the selected cell.
- Select the range A9:A13 and then click the Increase Indent button (Home tab | Alignment group) to increase the indentation of the text in the selected range (Figure 3–11).

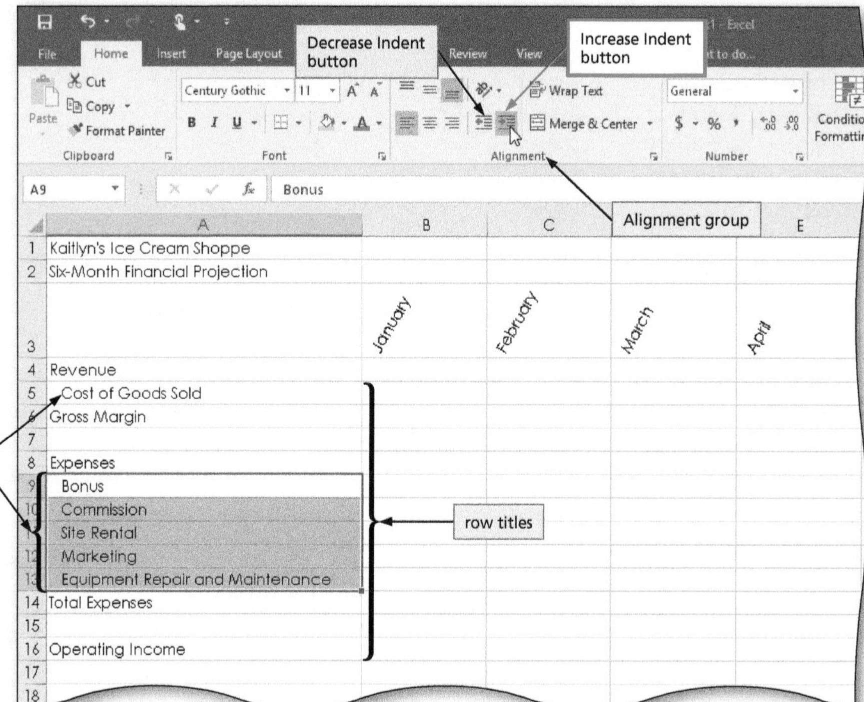

Figure 3–11

- Select cell A18 to finish entering the row titles and deselect the current cell.

Q&A What happens when I click the Increase Indent button?
The Increase Indent button (Home tab | Alignment group) indents the contents of a cell two spaces to the right each time you click it. The Decrease Indent button decreases the indent by two spaces each time you click it.

Other Ways

1. Right-click range, click Format Cells on shortcut menu, click Alignment tab (Format Cells dialog box), click Left (Indent) in Horizontal list, type number of spaces to indent in Indent box, click OK button (Format Cells dialog box)

Copying a Range of Cells to a Nonadjacent Destination Area

The What-If Assumptions section should be placed in an area of the worksheet that is accessible yet does not impair the view of the main section of the worksheet. As shown in Figure 3–3a, the What-If Assumptions will be placed below the calculations in the worksheet. This will allow the reader to see the main section of the worksheet when first opening the workbook. Additionally, the row titles in the Expenses area are the same as the row titles in the What-If Assumptions table, with the exception of the two additional entries in cells A19 (Margin) and A21 (Sales Revenue for Bonus). Hence, the row titles in the What-If Assumptions table can be created by copying the range A9:A13 to the range A19:A23 and then inserting two rows for the additional entries in cells A19 and A21. You cannot use the fill handle to copy the range because the source area (range A9:A13) is not adjacent to the destination area (range A19:A23).

A more versatile method of copying a source area is to use the Copy button and Paste button (Home tab | Clipboard group). You can use these two buttons to copy a source area to an adjacent or nonadjacent destination area.

BTW
Fitting Entries in a Cell
An alternative to increasing column widths or row heights is to shrink the characters in a cell to fit the current width of the column. To shrink to fit, click Format Cells Alignment Dialog Box Button Launcher (Home tab | Alignment group) and then place a check mark in the 'Shrink to fit' check box in the Text control area (Format Cells dialog box).

To Copy a Range of Cells to a Nonadjacent Destination Area

1 ENTER HEADINGS & DATA | 2 ENTER FORMULAS & FUNCTIONS | 3 CREATE SPARKLINE CHARTS
4 FORMAT WORKSHEET | 5 CREATE COLUMN CHART | 6 CHANGE VIEWS | 7 ASK WHAT-IF QUESTIONS

The Copy button copies the contents and format of the source area to the **Office Clipboard**, a temporary storage area in the computer's memory that allows you to collect text and graphics from any Office document and then paste them into almost any other type of document. The Paste button pastes a copy of the contents of the Office Clipboard in the destination area. ***Why?*** *Copying the range of cells rather than reentering the content assures consistency within the worksheet.* The following steps enter the What-If Assumptions row heading and then use the Copy and Paste buttons to copy the range A9:A13 to the nonadjacent range A19:A23.

- With cell A18 selected, type **`What-If Assumptions`** as the new row title and then click the Enter button.
- Select the range A9:A13 and then click the Copy button (Home tab | Clipboard group) to copy the values and formats of the selected range, A9:A13 in this case, to the Office Clipboard.
- Select cell A19, the top cell in the destination area (Figure 3–12).

Q&A
Why do I not select the entire destination area?
You are not required to select the entire destination area (A19:A23) because Excel only needs to know the upper-left cell of the destination area. In the case of a single column range, such as A19:A23, the top cell of the destination area (cell A19) also is the upper-left cell of the destination area.

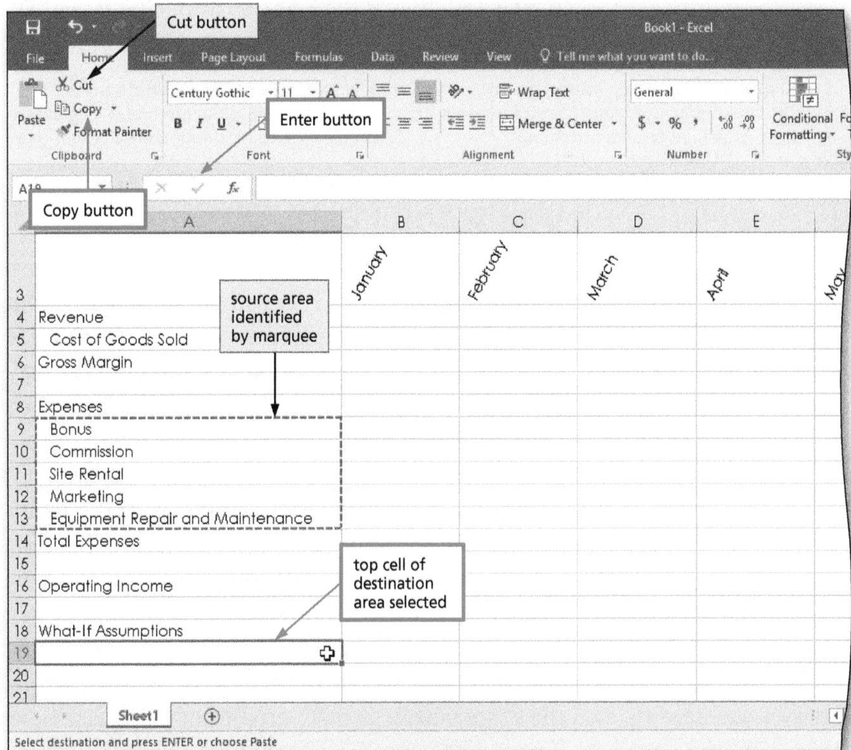

Figure 3–12

- Click the Paste button (Home tab | Clipboard group) to copy the values and formats of the last item placed on the Office Clipboard, range A9:A13, to the destination area, A19:A23. If necessary, scroll down to see the complete destination area (Figure 3–13).

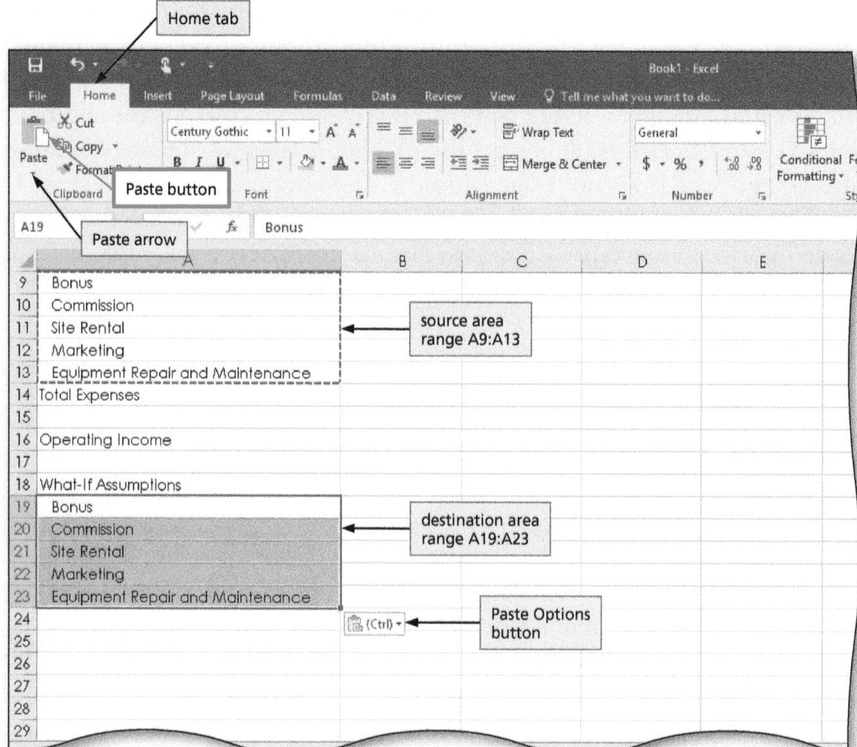

Figure 3–13

Q&A What if there was data in the destination area before I clicked the Paste button?

Any data contained in the destination area prior to the copy and paste is lost. When you complete a copy, the values and formats in the destination area are replaced with the values and formats of the source area. If you accidentally delete valuable data, click the Undo button on the Quick Access Toolbar or press CTRL+Z.

3

- Press the ESC key to remove the marquee from the source area and disable the Paste button (Home tab | Clipboard group).

Other Ways

1. Right-click source area, click Copy on shortcut menu, right-click destination area, click Paste icon on shortcut menu
2. Select source area and point to border of range; while holding down CTRL key, drag source area to destination area
3. Select source area, press CTRL+C, select destination area, press CTRL+V

BTW

Copying and Pasting from Other Programs

If you need data in Excel that is stored in another program, copying and pasting likely will help you. You might need to experiment before you are successful, because Excel might attempt to copy formatting or other information that you did not intend to paste from the other program. Trying various Paste Option buttons will solve most of such problems.

BTW

Move It or Copy It

Contrary to popular belief, move and copy operations are not the same. When you move a cell, the data in the original location is cleared and the format of the cell is reset to the default. When you copy a cell, the data and format of the copy area remains intact. In short, you should copy cells to duplicate entries and move cells to rearrange entries.

Using the Paste Options Menu

After you click the Paste button, Excel displays the Paste Options button, as shown in Figure 3–13. If you click the Paste Options arrow and select an option in the Paste Options gallery, Excel modifies the most recent paste operation based on your selection. Table 3–4 summarizes the options available in the Paste Options gallery. When the Paste Options button is visible, you can use keyboard shortcuts to access the paste commands available in the Paste Options gallery. Additionally, you can use combinations of the options in the Paste Options gallery to customize your paste operation. That is, after clicking one of the icons in the Paste Options gallery, you can display the gallery again to further adjust your paste operation. The Paste button (Home tab | Clipboard group) includes an arrow that, when clicked, displays the same options as the Paste Options button.

An alternative to clicking the Paste button is to press the ENTER key. The ENTER key completes the paste operation, removes the marquee from the source area, and disables the Paste button so that you cannot paste the copied source area to other destination areas. The ENTER key was not used in the previous set of steps so that the capabilities of the Paste Options button could be discussed. The Paste Options button does not appear on the screen when you use the ENTER key to complete the paste operation.

Using Drag and Drop to Move or Copy Cells

You also can use the mouse to move or copy cells. First, you select the source area and point to the border of the cell or range. You know you are pointing to the

Table 3–4 Paste Gallery Commands

Paste Option Icon	Paste Option	Description
	Paste	Copy contents and format of source area. This option is the default.
	Formulas	Copy formulas from the source area, but not the contents and format.
	Formulas & Number Formatting	Copy formulas and format for numbers and formulas of source area, but not the contents.
	Keep Source Formatting	Copy contents, format, and styles of source area.
	No Borders	Copy contents and format of source area, but not any borders.
	Keep Source Column Widths	Copy contents and format of source area. Change destination column widths to source column widths.
	Transpose	Copy the contents and format of the source area, but transpose, or swap, the rows and columns.
123	Values	Copy contents of source area but not the formatting for formulas.
% 123	Values & Number Formatting	Copy contents and format of source area for numbers or formulas, but use format of destination area for text.
123	Values & Source Formatting	Copy contents and formatting of source area but not the formula.
	Formatting	Copy format of source area but not the contents.
	Paste Link	Copy contents and format and link cells so that a change to the cells in source area updates the corresponding cells in destination area.
	Picture	Copy an image of the source area as a picture.
	Linked Picture	Copy an image of the source area as a picture so that a change to the cells in source area updates the picture in destination area.

border of the cell or range when the pointer changes to a four-headed arrow. To move the selected cell or cells, drag the selection to the destination area. To copy a selection, hold down the CTRL key while dragging the selection to the destination area. You know Excel is in Copy mode when a small plus sign appears next to the pointer. Be sure to release the mouse button before you release the CTRL key. Using the mouse to move or copy cells is called **drag and drop.**

BTW

Cutting

When you cut a cell or range of cells using the Cut command on a shortcut menu or Cut button (Home tab | Clipboard group), Excel copies the cells to the Office Clipboard; it does not remove the cells from the source area until you paste the cells in the destination area by either clicking the Paste button (Home tab | Clipboard group) or pressing the ENTER key. When you complete the paste, Excel clears the cell's or range of cell's entries and their formats from the source area.

Using Cut and Paste to Move Cells

Another way to move cells is to select them, click the Cut button (Home tab | Clipboard group) (Figure 3–12) to remove the cells from the worksheet and copy them to the Office Clipboard, select the destination area, and then click the Paste button (Home tab | Clipboard group) or press the ENTER key. You also can use the Cut command on the shortcut menu, instead of the Cut button on the ribbon.

Inserting and Deleting Cells in a Worksheet

At any time while the worksheet is on the screen, you can insert cells to enter new data or delete cells to remove unwanted data. You can insert or delete individual cells; a range of cells, rows, or columns; or entire worksheets.

To Insert a Row

Why? According to the sketch of the worksheet in Figure 3–3a, two rows must be inserted in the What-If Assumptions table, one above Bonus for the Margin assumption and another between Bonus and Commission for the Sales Revenue for Bonus assumption. The following steps insert the new rows into the worksheet.

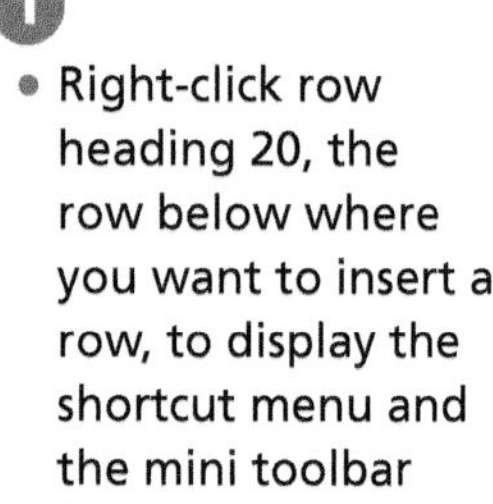

1

- Right-click row heading 20, the row below where you want to insert a row, to display the shortcut menu and the mini toolbar (Figure 3–14).

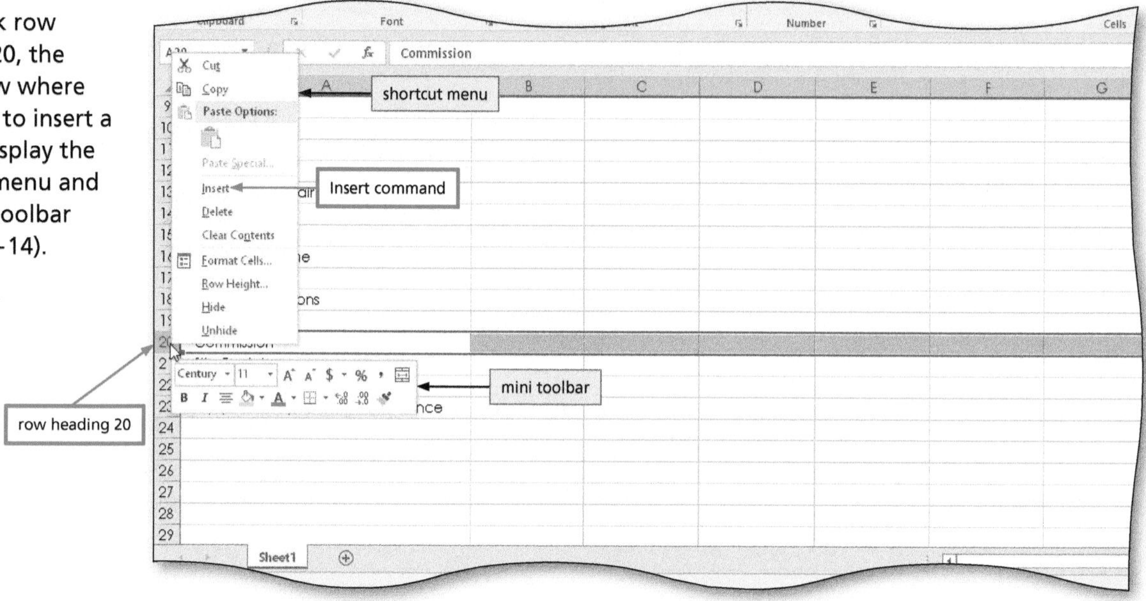

Figure 3–14

2

- Click Insert on the shortcut menu to insert a new row in the worksheet by shifting the selected row and all rows below it down one row.
- Select cell A20 in the new row and then type `Sales Revenue for Bonus` to enter a new row title (Figure 3–15).

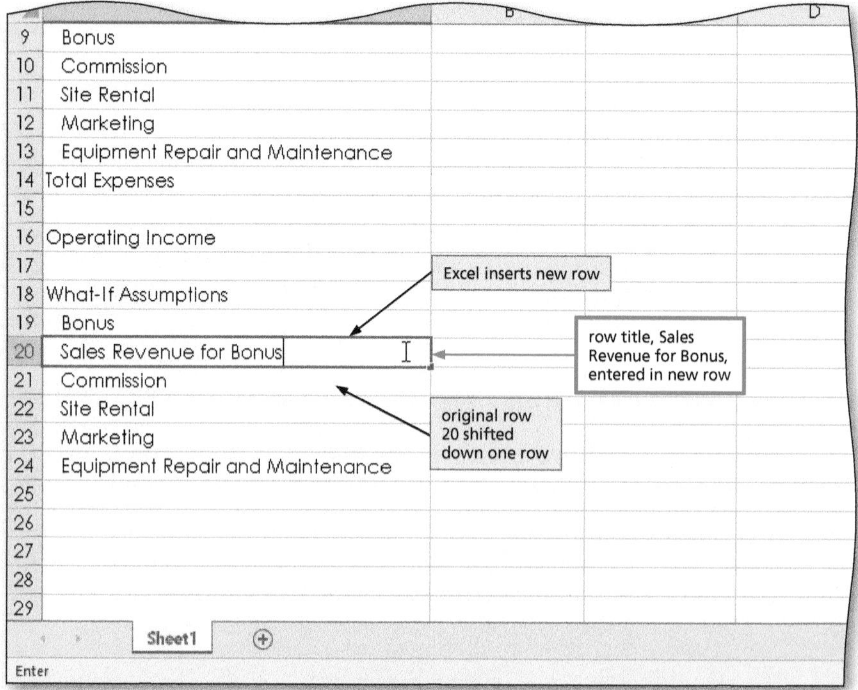

Figure 3–15

Q&A What is the resulting format of the new row?

The cells in the new row inherit the formats of the cells in the row above them. You can change this behavior by clicking the Insert Options button that appears below the inserted row. Following the insertion of a row, the Insert Options button allows you to select from the following options: (1) 'Format Same As Above', (2) 'Format Same As Below', and (3) Clear Formatting. The 'Format Same as Above' option is the default. The Insert Options button remains active until you begin the next Excel operation. Excel does not display the Insert Options button if the initial row does not contain any formatted data.

3

- Right-click row heading 19, the row below where you want to insert a row, to display the shortcut menu and the mini toolbar.
- Click Insert on the shortcut menu to insert a new row in the worksheet.
- Click the Insert Options button below row 19 (Figure 3–16).
- Click 'Format Same As Below' on the menu.
- Select cell A19 in the new row and then type **`Margin`** to enter a new row title.

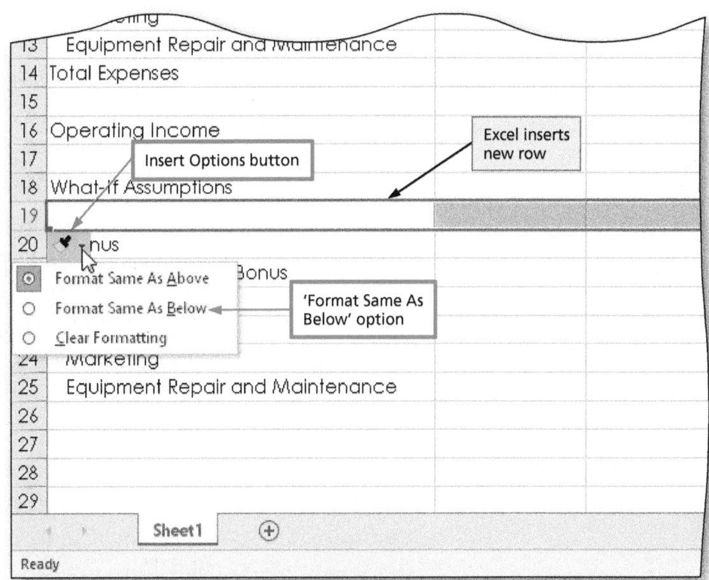

Figure 3–16

Q&A What would happen if cells in the shifted rows were included in formulas?
If the rows that shift down included cell references in formulas located in the worksheet, Excel would automatically adjust the cell references in the formulas to their new locations. Thus, in Step 2, if a formula in the worksheet referenced a cell in row 19 before the insert, then Excel would adjust the cell reference in the formula to row 20 after the insert.

4

- Save the workbook on your hard drive, OneDrive, or other storage location using **`Kaitlyn's Ice Cream Shoppe Financial Projection`** as the file name.

Other Ways

1. Click Insert Cells arrow (Home tab | Cells group), click 'Insert Sheet Rows'
2. Press CTRL+SHIFT+PLUS SIGN, click Entire row (Insert dialog box), click OK button

Inserting Columns

You insert columns into a worksheet in the same way you insert rows. To insert columns, select one or more columns immediately to the right of where you want Excel to insert the new column or columns. Select the number of columns you want to insert, click the Insert arrow (Home tab | Cells group), and then click 'Insert Sheet Columns' in the Insert list; or right-click the selected column(s) and then click Insert on the shortcut menu. The Insert command on the shortcut menu requires that you select an entire column (or columns) to insert a column (or columns). Following the insertion of a column, Excel displays the Insert Options button, which allows you to modify the insertion in a fashion similar to that discussed earlier when inserting rows.

Inserting Single Cells or a Range of Cells

You can use the Insert command on the shortcut menu or the Insert Cells command on the Insert menu — produced by clicking the Insert button (Home tab | Cells group) — to insert a single cell or a range of cells. You should be aware that if you shift a single cell or a range of cells, however, it no longer lines up with its associated cells. To ensure that the values in the worksheet do not get out of order,

BTW
Inserting Multiple Rows
If you want to insert multiple rows, you have two choices. You can insert a single row by using the Insert command on the shortcut menu and then repeatedly press the F4 key to continue inserting rows. Alternatively, you can select a number of existing rows equal to the number of rows that you want to insert. For instance, if you want to insert five rows, select five existing rows in the worksheet, right-click the selected rows, and then click Insert on the shortcut menu.

BTW
Dragging Ranges
You can move and insert a selected cell or range between existing cells by holding down the SHIFT key while you drag the selection to the gridline where you want to insert the selected cell or range. You also can copy and insert by holding down the CTRL+SHIFT keys while you drag the selection to the desired gridline.

BTW

Ranges and Undo

The incorrect use of copying, deleting, inserting, and moving ranges of cells have the potential to render a worksheet useless. Carefully review the results of these actions before continuing on to the next task. If you are not sure the result of the action is correct, click the Undo button on the Quick Access Toolbar.

BTW

Organizing Files and Folders

You should organize and store files in folders so that you easily can find the files later. For example, if you are taking an introductory technology class called CIS 101, a good practice would be to save all Excel files in an Excel folder in a CIS 101 folder. For a discussion of folders and detailed examples of creating folders, refer to the Office and Windows module at the beginning of this book.

spreadsheet experts recommend that you insert only entire rows or entire columns. When you insert a single cell or a range of cells, Excel displays the Insert Options button so that you can change the format of the inserted cell, using options similar to those for inserting rows and columns.

Deleting Columns and Rows

The Delete button (Home tab | Cells group) or the Delete command on the shortcut menu removes cells (including the data and format) from the worksheet. Deleting cells is not the same as clearing cells. The Clear Contents command, described in Module 1, clears the data from the cells, but the cells remain in the worksheet. The Delete command removes the cells from the worksheet and shifts the remaining rows up (when you delete rows) or shifts the remaining columns to the left (when you delete columns). If formulas located in other cells reference cells in the deleted row or column, Excel does not adjust these cell references. Excel displays the error message **#REF!** in those cells to indicate a cell reference error. For example, if cell A7 contains the formula =A4+A5 and you delete row 5, Excel assigns the formula =A4+#REF! to cell A6 (originally cell A7) and displays the error message, #REF!, in cell A6. Excel also displays an Error Options button when you select the cell containing the error message, #REF!, which allows you to select options to determine the nature of the problem.

To Enter Numbers with Format Symbols

1 ENTER HEADINGS & DATA | **2 ENTER FORMULAS & FUNCTIONS** | **3 CREATE SPARKLINE CHARTS**
4 FORMAT WORKSHEET | **5 CREATE COLUMN CHART** | **6 CHANGE VIEWS** | **7 ASK WHAT-IF QUESTIONS**

The next step in creating the Financial Projection worksheet is to enter the what-if assumptions values in the range B19:B25. The numbers in the table can be entered and then formatted using techniques from Modules 1 and 2, or each number can be entered with **format symbols**, which assign a format to numbers as they are entered. When a number is entered with a format symbol, Excel displays it with the assigned format. Valid format symbols include the dollar sign ($), comma (,), and percent sign (%).

If you enter a whole number, it appears without any decimal places. If you enter a number with one or more decimal places and a format symbol, Excel displays the number with two decimal places. Table 3–5 illustrates several examples of numbers entered with format symbols. The number in parentheses in column 4 indicates the number of decimal places.

Table 3–5 Numbers Entered with Format Symbols

Format Symbol	Typed in Formula Bar	Displays in Cell	Comparable Format
,	374,149	374,149	Comma(0)
	5,833.6	5,833.60	Comma(2)
$	$58917	$58,917	Currency(0)
	$842.51	$842.51	Currency(2)
	$63,574.9	$63,574.90	Currency(2)
%	85%	85%	Percent(0)
	12.80%	12.80%	Percent(2)
	68.2242%	68.2242%	Percent(4)

Why? *In some cases, using a format symbol is the most efficient method for entering and formatting data.* The following step enters the numbers in the What-If Assumptions table with format symbols.

1

- Enter the following values, using format symbols to apply number formatting: `78.75%` in cell B19, `3,500.00` in cell B20, `65,000.00` in cell B21, `25.00%` in cell B22, `10.00%` in cell B23, `5.00%` in cell B24, and `3.50%` in cell B25 (Figure 3–17).

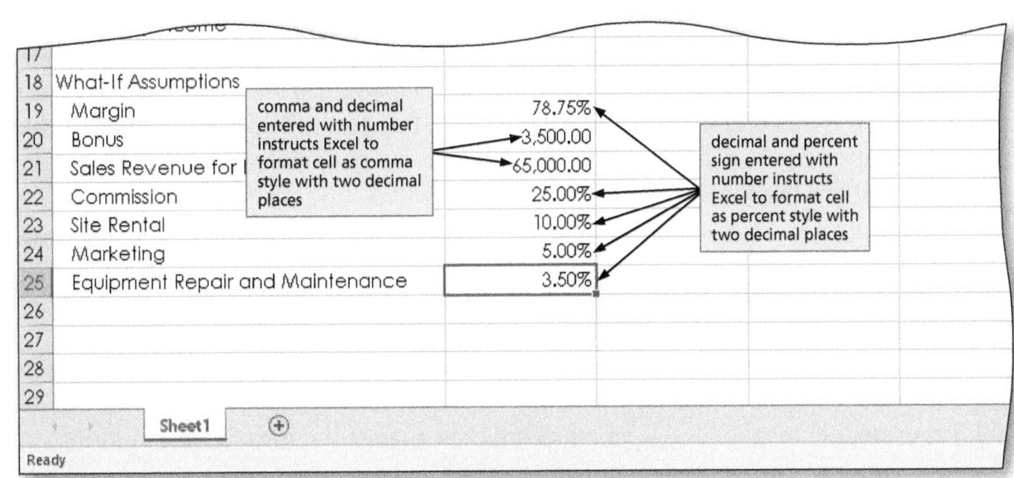

Figure 3–17

Other Ways

1. Right-click range, click Format Cells on shortcut menu, click Number tab (Format Cells dialog box), click category in Category list, select desired format, click OK button
2. Press CTRL+1, click Number tab (Format Cells dialog box), click category in Category list, select desired format, click OK button

To Enter the Projected Monthly Sales

The following steps enter the projected revenue, listed previously in Table 3–1, in row 4 and compute the projected six-month revenue in cell H4.

1. If necessary, display the Home tab.
2. Enter `55,000.00` in cell B4, `62,500.00` in cell C4, `67,000.00` in cell D4, `90,250.00` in cell E4, `77,500.00` in cell F4, and `74,750.00` in cell G4.
3. Select cell H4 and then click the Sum button (Home tab | Editing group) twice to create a sum in the selected cell (Figure 3–18).

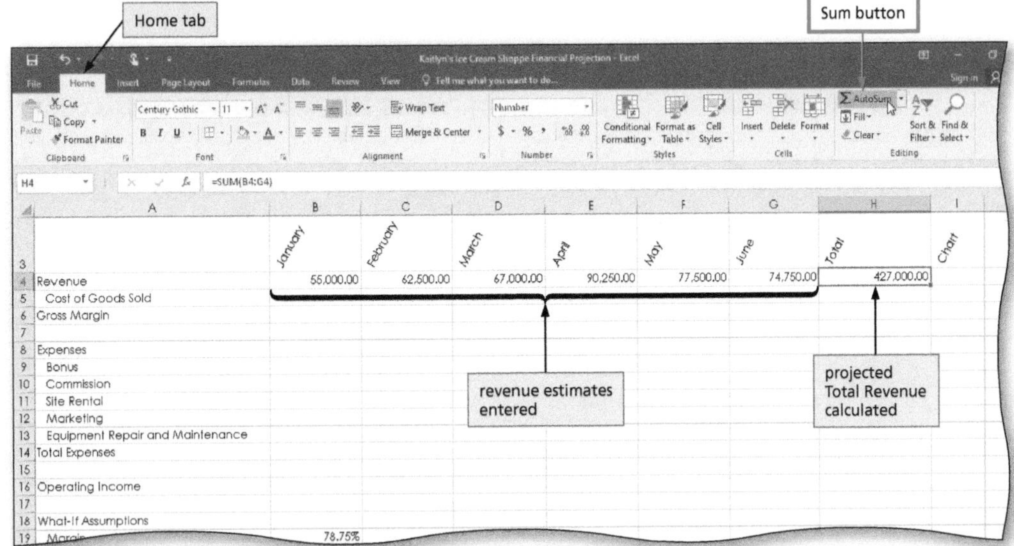

Figure 3–18

To Enter and Format the System Date

Why? *The sketch of the worksheet in Figure 3–3a includes a date stamp on the right side of the heading section. A date stamp shows the date a workbook, report, or other document was created or the time period it represents.* In business, a report often is meaningless without a date stamp. For example, if a printout of the worksheet in this module were distributed to the company's analysts, the date stamp would show when the six-month projections were made, as well as what time period the report represents.

A simple way to create a date stamp is to use the NOW function to enter the system date tracked by your computer in a cell in the worksheet. The **NOW function** is one of 24 date and time functions available in Excel. When assigned to a cell, the NOW function returns a number that corresponds to the system date and time beginning with December 31, 1899. For example, January 1, 1900 equals 1, January 2, 1900 equals 2, and so on. Noon equals .5. Thus, noon on January 1, 1900 equals 1.5 and 6:00 p.m. on January 1, 1900 equals 1.75. If the computer's system date is set to the current date, then the date stamp is equivalent to the current date. The following steps enter the NOW function and then change the format from mm/dd/yyyy hh:mm to mm/dd/yyyy.

1

- Select cell H1 and then click the Insert Function button in the formula bar to display the Insert Function dialog box.
- Click the 'Or select a category' arrow (Insert Function dialog box) and then select 'Date & Time' to populate the 'Select a function' list with data and time functions.
- Scroll down in the 'Select a function' list and then click NOW to select the required function (Figure 3–19).

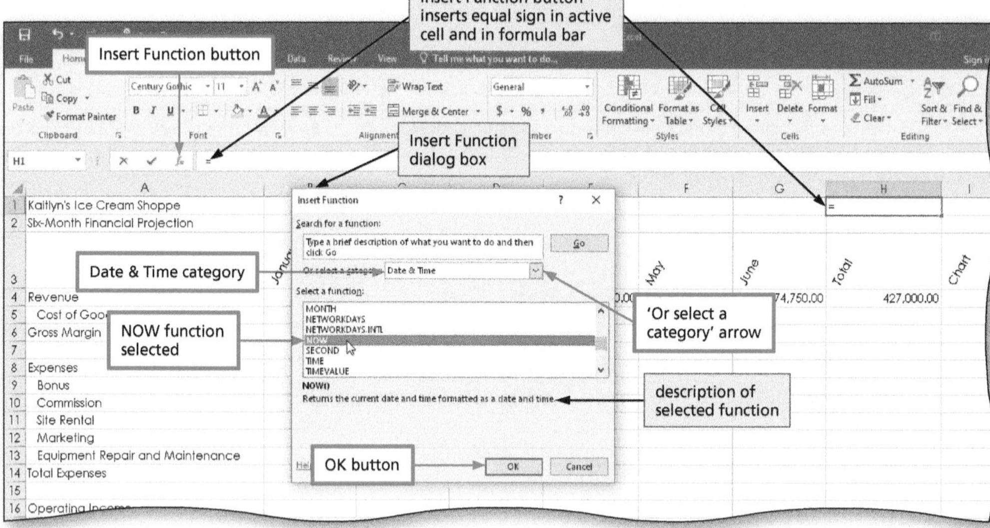

Figure 3–19

2

- Click the OK button (Insert Function dialog box) to close the Insert Function dialog box and display the Function Arguments dialog box (Figure 3–20).

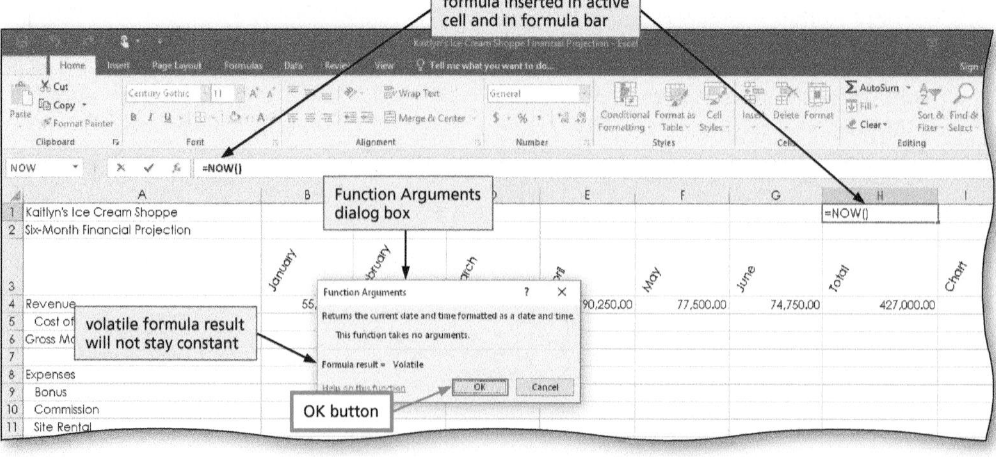

Figure 3–20

What is meant by 'Formula result = Volatile' in the Function Arguments dialog box?
The NOW function is an example of a volatile function. A **volatile function** is one where the number that the function returns is not constant but changes each time the worksheet is opened. As a result, any formula using the NOW function will have a variable result.

3

- Click the OK button (Function Arguments dialog box) to display the system date and time in the selected cell, using the default date and time format, which is mm/dd/yyyy hh:mm.

Q&A What does the mm/dd/yyyy hh:mm format represent?
The mm/dd/yyyy hh:mm format can be explained as follows: the first mm is the month, dd is the day of the month, yyyy is the year, hh is the hour of the day, and the second mm is the minutes past the hour. Excel applies this date and time format to the result of the NOW function.

- Right-click cell H1 to display a shortcut menu and mini toolbar.
- Click Format Cells on the shortcut menu to display the Format Cells dialog box.
- If necessary, click the Number tab (Format Cells dialog box) to display the Number sheet.
- Click Date in the Category list (Format Cells dialog box) to display the date format options in the Type list. Scroll down in the Type list and then click 3/14/2012 to display a sample of the data in the Sample area in the dialog box (Figure 3–21).

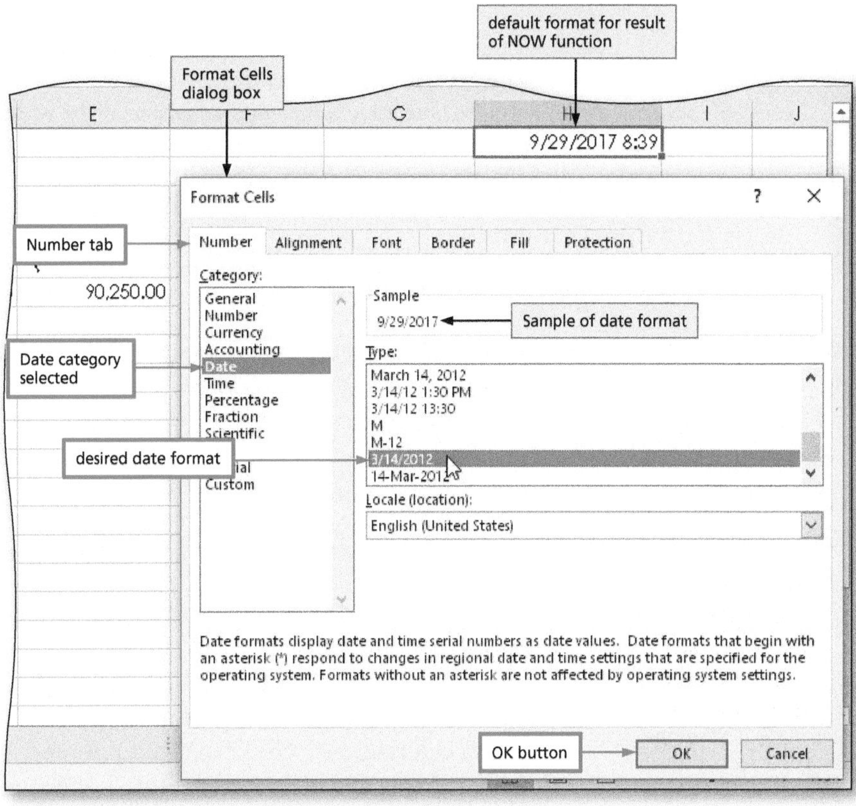

Figure 3–21

Q&A Why do the dates in the Type box show March 14, 2012 instead of the current date?
March 14, 2012 is just used as a sample date in this version of Office.

4

- Click the OK button (Format Cells dialog box) to display the system date (the result of the NOW function) in the format mm/dd/yyyy.
- Double-click the border between columns H and I to change the width of the column to best fit (Figure 3–22).

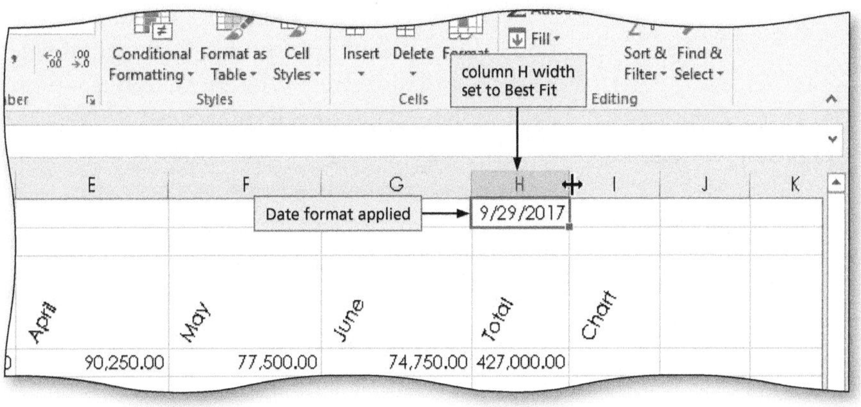

Experiment

- If instructed by your professor, select cell H2 and enter the place of your birth.
- Save the workbook again on the same storage location with the same file name.

Figure 3–22

Q&A Why should I save the workbook again?
You have made several modifications to the workbook since you last saved it. Thus, you should save it again.

Other Ways

1. Click 'Date & Time' button (Formulas tab | Function Library group), click NOW
2. Press CTRL+SEMICOLON (this enters the date as a static value, meaning the date will not change when the workbook is opened at a later date)
3. Press CTRL+SHIFT+# to format date as day-month-year

CONSIDER THIS

When would you not want to use the system date?
Using the system date results in the date value being updated whenever the worksheet is opened. Think carefully about whether or not this is the result you want. If you want the date to reflect the current date, using the system date is appropriate. If you want to record when the worksheet was created, using a hard-coded date makes more sense. If both pieces of information may be important, consider two date entries in the worksheet: a fixed entry identifying the date the worksheet was created and the volatile system date.

Break Point: If you wish to take a break, this is a good place to do so. You can exit Excel now. To resume at a later time, run Excel, open the file called Kaitlyn's Ice Cream Shoppe Financial Projection, and continue following the steps from this location forward.

BTW
Absolute Referencing
Absolute referencing is one of the more difficult worksheet concepts to understand. One point to keep in mind is that the paste operation is the only operation affected by an absolute cell reference. An absolute cell reference instructs the paste operation to use the same cell reference as it copies a formula from one cell to another.

Absolute Versus Relative Addressing

The next sections describe the formulas and functions needed to complete the calculations in the worksheet.

As you learned in Modules 1 and 2, Excel modifies cell references when copying formulas. However, sometimes while copying formulas you do not want Excel to change a cell reference. To keep a cell reference constant when copying a formula or function (that is, the cell references do not change relative to where you are copying the formula), Excel uses a technique called **absolute cell referencing.** To specify an absolute cell reference in a formula, enter a dollar sign ($) before any column letters or row numbers you want to keep constant in formulas you plan to copy. For example, B4 is an absolute cell reference, whereas B4 is a relative cell reference. Both reference the same cell. The difference becomes apparent when they are copied to a destination area. A formula using the absolute cell reference B4 instructs Excel to keep the cell reference B4 constant (absolute) in the formula as it is copied to the destination area. A formula using the **relative cell reference** B4 instructs Excel to adjust the cell reference as it is copied to the destination area. A cell reference where one factor remains constant and the other one varies is called a **mixed cell reference.** A mixed cell reference includes a dollar sign before the column or the row, not before both. When planning formulas, be aware of when you might need to use absolute, relative, and mixed cell references. Table 3–6 provides some additional examples of each of these types of cell references.

Table 3–6 Examples of Absolute, Relative, and Mixed Cell References

Cell Reference	Type of Reference	Meaning
B4	Absolute cell reference	Both column and row references remain the same when you copy this cell, because the cell references are absolute.
B4	Relative cell reference	Both column and row references are relative. When copied to another cell, both the column and row in the cell reference are adjusted to reflect the new location.
B$4	Mixed reference	This cell reference is mixed. The column reference changes when you copy this cell to another column because it is relative. The row reference does not change because it is absolute.
$B4	Mixed reference	This cell reference is mixed. The column reference does not change because it is absolute. The row reference changes when you copy this cell reference to another row because it is relative.

Figure 3–23 illustrates how the type of cell reference used affects the results of copying a formula to a new place in a worksheet. In Figure 3–23a, cells D6:D9 contain formulas. Each formula multiplies the content of cell A2 by 2; the difference between formulas lies in how cell A2 is referenced. Cells C6:C9 identify the type of reference: absolute, relative, or mixed.

Figure 3–23b shows the values that result from copying the formulas in cells D6:D9 to ranges E6:E9, F7:F10, and G11:G14. Figure 3–23c shows the formulas that result from copying the formulas. While all formulas initially multiplied the content of cell A2 by 2, the values and formulas in the destination ranges illustrate how Excel adjusts cell references according to how you reference those cells in original formulas.

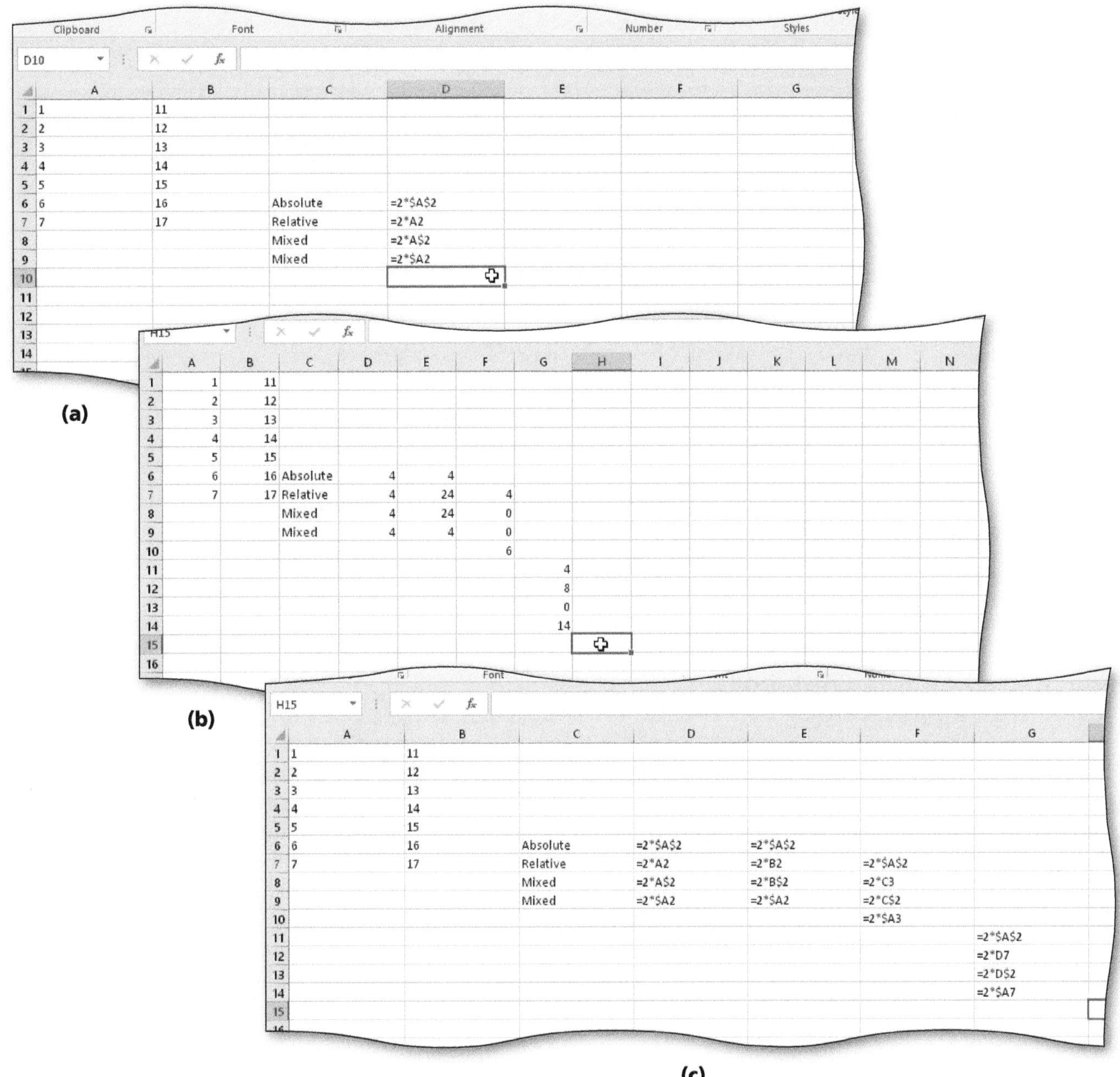

Figure 3–23

In the worksheet, you need to enter formulas that calculate the following values for January: cost of goods sold (cell B5), gross margin (cell B6), expenses (range B9:B13), total expenses (cell B14), and operating income (cell B16). The formulas are based on the projected monthly revenue in cell B4 and the assumptions in the range B19:B25.

The calculations for each column (month) are the same, except for the reference to the projected monthly revenue in row 4, which varies according to the month (B4 for January, C4 for February, and so on). Thus, the formulas for January can be entered in column B and then copied to columns C through G. Table 3–7 shows the formulas for determining the January cost of goods sold, gross margin, expenses, total expenses, and operating income in column B.

Table 3–7 Formulas for Determining Cost of Goods Sold, Gross Margin, Expenses, Total Expenses, and Operating Income for January

Cell	Row Title	Calculation	Formula
B5	Cost of Goods Sold	Revenue times (1 minus Margin %)	=B4 * (1 – B19)
B6	Gross Margin	Revenue minus Cost of Goods Sold	=B4 – B5
B9	Bonus	Bonus equals value in B20 or 0	=IF(B4 >= B21, B20, 0)
B10	Commission	Revenue times Commission %	=B4 * B22
B11	Site Rental	Revenue times Site Rental %	=B4 * B23
B12	Marketing	Revenue times Marketing %	=B4 * B24
B13	Equipment Repair and Maintenance	Revenue times Equipment Repair and Maintenance %	=B4 * B25
B14	Total Expenses	Sum of April Expenses	=SUM(B9:B13)
B16	Operating Income	Gross Margin minus Total Expenses	=B6 – B14

To Enter a Formula Containing Absolute Cell References

1 ENTER HEADINGS & DATA | 2 ENTER FORMULAS & FUNCTIONS | 3 CREATE SPARKLINE CHARTS
4 FORMAT WORKSHEET | 5 CREATE COLUMN CHART | 6 CHANGE VIEWS | 7 ASK WHAT-IF QUESTIONS

Why? *As the formulas are entered in column B for January, as shown in Table 3–7, and then copied to columns C through G (February through June) in the worksheet, Excel will adjust the cell references for each column.* After the copy, the February Commission expense in cell C10 would be =C4 * C22. While the cell reference C4 (February Revenue) is correct, the cell reference C22 references an empty cell. The formula for cell C10 should read =C4 * B22, rather than =C4 * C22, because B22 references the Commission % value in the What-If Assumptions table. In this instance, you must use an absolute cell reference to keep the cell reference in the formula the same, or constant, when it is copied. To enter an absolute cell reference, you can type the dollar sign ($) as part of the cell reference or enter it by pressing the F4 key with the insertion point in or to the right of the cell reference to change it to absolute. The following steps enter the cost of goods sold formula =B4 * (1 – B19) in cell B5 using Point mode.

1

- Click cell B5 to select the cell in which to enter the first formula.
- Type = (equal sign), select cell B4, type **`*(1-B19`** to continue entering the formula, and then press the F4 key to change the cell reference from a relative cell reference to an absolute cell reference. Type) (closing parenthesis) to complete the formula (Figure 3–24).

Q&A Is an absolute reference required in this formula?

No, a mixed cell reference also could have been used. The formula in cell B5 will be copied across columns, rather than down rows. So, the formula entered in cell B5 in Step 1 could have been entered as =B4*(1–$B19) using a mixed cell reference, rather than =B4*(1–B19), because when you copy a formula across columns, the row does not change. The key is to ensure that column B remains constant as you copy the formula across columns. To change the absolute cell reference to a mixed cell reference, continue to press the F4 key until you achieve the desired cell reference.

Enter button
=B4*(1-B19)
formula appears in formula bar
cell B4 is relative
cell B19 is absolute

Figure 3–24

- Click the Enter button in the formula bar to display the result, 11687.5, instead of the formula in cell B5 (Figure 3–25).

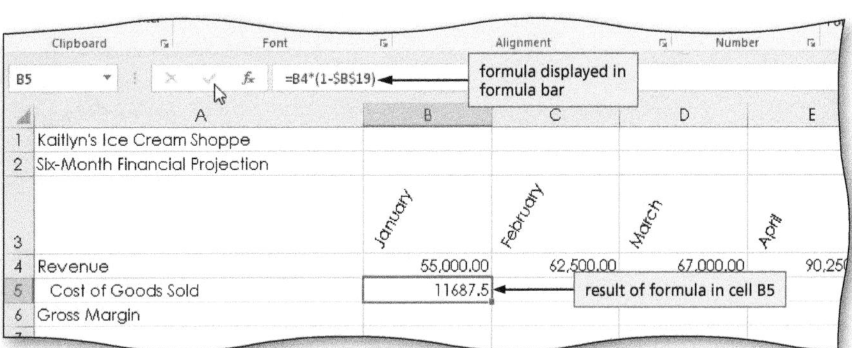

Figure 3–25

3

- Click cell B6 to select the cell in which to enter the next formula, type = (equal sign), click cell B4, type – (minus sign), and then click cell B5 to add a reference to the cell to the formula.
- Click the Enter button in the formula bar to display the result in the selected cell, in this case gross margin for January, 43,312.50, in cell B6 (Figure 3–26).

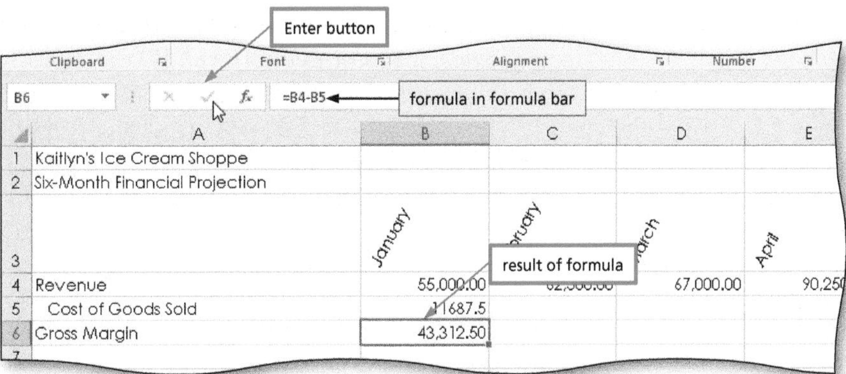

Figure 3–26

BTW
Logical Operators in IF Functions
IF functions can use logical operators, such as AND, OR, and NOT. For example, the three IF functions =IF(AND(A1>C1, B1<C2), "OK", "Not OK") and =IF(OR(K5>J5, C3<K6), "OK", "Not OK") and =IF(NOT(B10<C10), "OK", "Not OK") use logical operators. In the first example, both logical tests must be true for the value_if_true OK to be assigned to the cell. In the second example, one or the other logical tests must be true for the value_if_ true OK to be assigned to the cell. In the third example, the logical test B10<C10 must be false for the value_if_true OK to be assigned to the cell.

Making Decisions — The IF Function

In addition to calculations that are constant across all categories, you may need to make calculations that will differ depending on whether a particular condition or set of conditions are met. For this project, you need to vary compensation according to how much revenue is generated in any particular month. According to the requirements document in Figure 3–2, a bonus will be paid in any month where revenue is greater than the sales revenue for bonus value. If the projected January revenue in cell B4 is greater than or equal to the sales revenue for bonus in cell B21 (65,000.00), then the projected January bonus value in cell B9 is equal to the bonus value in cell B20 (3,500.00); otherwise, the value in cell B9 is equal to 0. One way to assign the projected January bonus value in cell B9 is to manually check to see if the projected revenue in cell B4 equals or exceeds the sales revenue for the bonus amount in cell B21 and, if so, then to enter 3,500.00 in cell B9. You can use this manual process for all six months by checking the values for the each month.

Because the data in the worksheet changes each time a report is prepared or the figures are adjusted, however, it is preferable to have Excel calculate the monthly bonus. To do so, cell B9 must include a formula or function that compares the projected revenue with the sales revenue for bonus value, and displays 3,500.00 or 0.00 (zero), depending on whether the projected January revenue in cell B4 is greater than, equal to, or less than the sales revenue for bonus value in cell B21. This decision-making process is a **logical test**. It can be represented in diagram form, as shown in Figure 3–27.

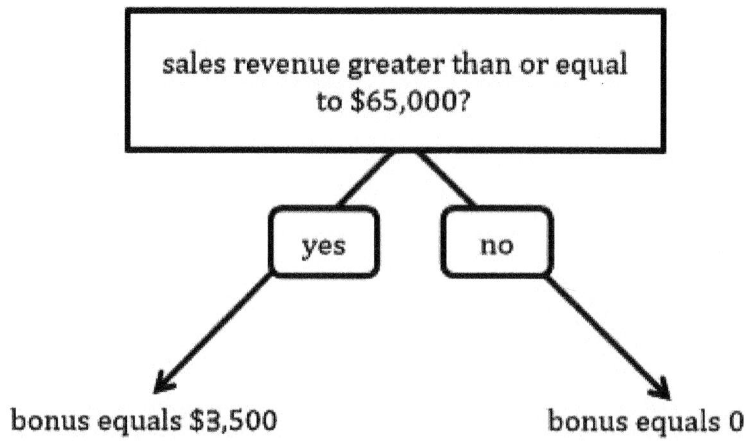

Figure 3–27

In Excel, you use the **IF function** when you want to assign a value to a cell based on a logical test. For example, cell B9 can be assigned the following IF function:

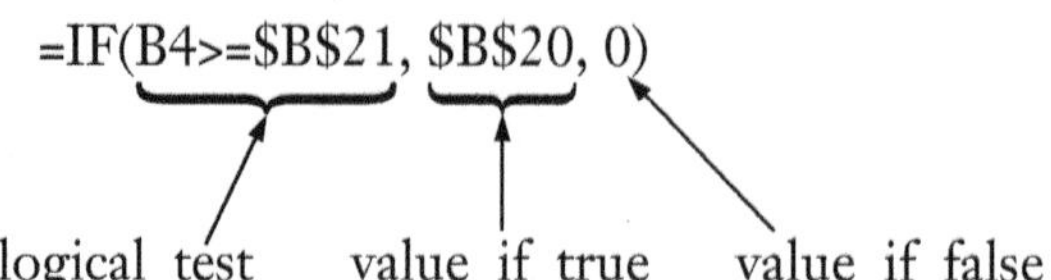

This IF function instructs Excel that if the projected January revenue in cell B4 is greater than or equal to the sales revenue for bonus value in cell B21, then Excel should display the bonus value found in cell B20 in cell B9. If the projected January revenue in cell B4 is not greater than or equal to the sales revenue for bonus value in cell B21, then Excel should display a 0 (zero) in cell B9.

The general form of the IF function is:

=IF(logical_test, value_if_true, value_if_false)

The argument, logical_test, is made up of two expressions and a comparison operator. Each expression can be a cell reference, a number, text, a function, or a formula. In this example, the logical test compares the projected revenue with the sales revenue for bonus, using the comparison operator greater than or equal to. Valid comparison operators, their meanings, and examples of their use in IF functions are shown in Table 3–8. The argument, value_if_true, is the value you want Excel to display in the cell when the logical test is true. The argument, value_if_false, is the value you want Excel to display in the cell when the logical test is false.

Table 3–8 Comparison Operators

Comparison Operator	Meaning	Example
=	Equal to	=IF(A1=A2, "True", "False")
<	Less than	=IF(A1<A2, "True", "False")
>	Greater than	=IF(A1>A2, "True", "False")
>=	Greater than or equal to	=IF(A1>=A2, "True", "False")
<=	Less than or equal to	=IF(A1<=A2, "True", "False")
<>	Not equal to	=IF(A1<>A2, "True", "False")

1 ENTER HEADINGS & DATA | 2 ENTER FORMULAS & FUNCTIONS | **3 CREATE SPARKLINE CHARTS**
4 FORMAT WORKSHEET | 5 CREATE COLUMN CHART | 6 CHANGE VIEWS | 7 ASK WHAT-IF QUESTIONS

To Enter an IF Function

Why? *Use an IF function to determine the value for a cell based on a logical test.* The following steps assign the IF function =IF(B4>=B21,B20,0) to cell B9. This IF function determines whether or not the worksheet assigns a bonus for January.

1

- Click cell B9 to select the cell for the next formula.
- Click the Insert Function button in the formula bar to display the Insert Function dialog box.
- Click the 'Or select a category' arrow (Insert Function dialog box) and then select Logical in the list to populate the 'Select a function' list with logic functions.
- Click IF in the 'Select a function' list to select the required function (Figure 3–28).

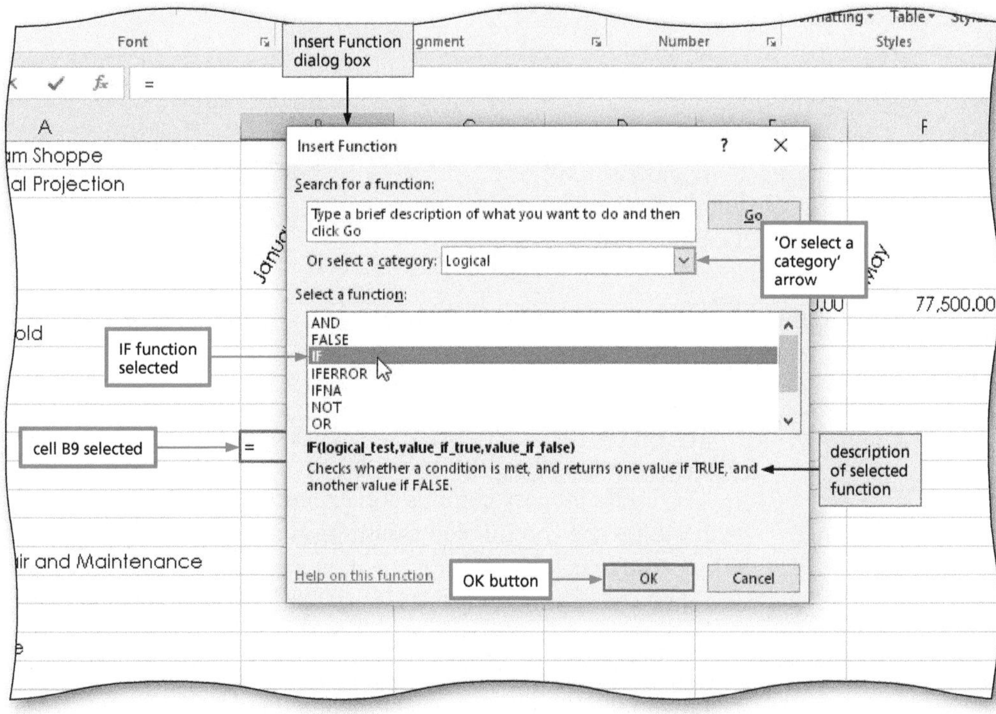

Figure 3–28

- Click the OK button (Insert Function dialog box) to display the Function Arguments dialog box.
- Type **b4>=b21** in the Logical_test box to enter a logical test for the IF function.
- Type **b20** in the Value_if_true box to enter the result of the IF function if the logical test is true.
- Type **0** (zero) in the Value_if_false box to enter the result of the IF function if the logical test is false (Figure 3–29).

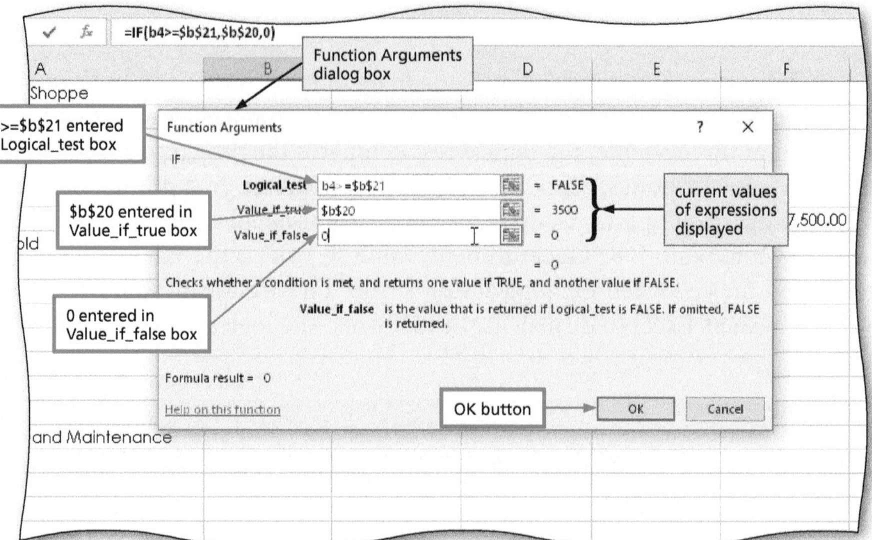

Figure 3–29

- Click the OK button (Function Arguments dialog box) to insert the IF function in the selected cell (Figure 3–30).

Q&A Why does cell B9 contain the value 0 (zero)?

The value that Excel displays in cell B9 depends on the values assigned to cells B4, B20, and B21. For example, if the value for January revenue in cell B4 is increased to 65,000.00 or higher, then the IF function in cell B9 will display 3,500.00. If you change the sales revenue for bonus in cell B21 from 65,000.00 to another number and the value in cell B4 is greater than or equal to the value in cell B21, it also will change the results in cell B9.

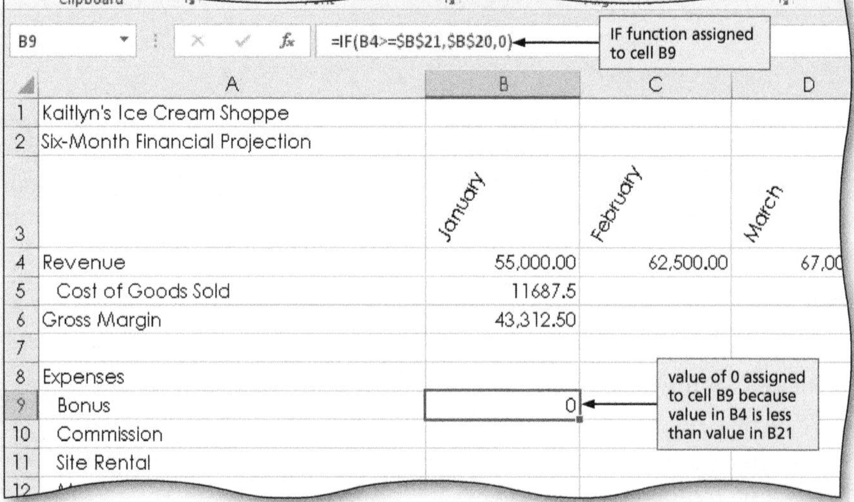

Figure 3–30

Other Ways

1. Click Logical button (Formulas tab | Function Library group), click IF

To Enter the Remaining Formulas for January

The January commission expense in cell B10 is equal to the revenue in cell B4 times the commission assumption in cell B22 (25.00%). The January site rental expense in cell B11 is equal to the projected January revenue in cell B4 times the site rental assumption in cell B23 (10.00%). Similar formulas determine the remaining January expenses in cells B12 and B13.

The total expenses value in cell B14 is equal to the sum of the expenses in the range B9:B13. The operating income in cell B16 is equal to the gross margin in cell B6 minus the total expenses in cell B14. Because the formulas are short, they are typed in the following steps, rather than entered using Point mode.

1. Select cell B10. Type **=b4*b22** and then press the DOWN ARROW key to enter the formula in the selected cell. Type **=b4*b23** and then press the DOWN ARROW key to enter the formula in cell B11. Type **=b4*b24**, press the DOWN ARROW key, type **=b4*b25**, and then press the DOWN ARROW key again.

2. With cell B14 selected, click the Sum button (Home tab | Editing group) twice to insert a SUM function in the selected cell. Select cell B16 to prepare to enter the next formula. Type **=b6-b14** and then press the ENTER key to enter the formula in the selected cell.

3. Press CTRL+ACCENT MARK (`) to display the formulas version of the worksheet (Figure 3–31).

4. When you are finished viewing the formulas version, press CTRL+ACCENT MARK (`) again to return to the values version of the worksheet.

Q&A Why should I view the formulas version of the worksheet?
Viewing the formulas version (Figure 3–31) of the worksheet allows you to check the formulas you entered in the range B5:B16. Recall that formulas were entered in lowercase. You can see that Excel converts all the formulas from lowercase to uppercase.

BTW
Replacing a Formula with a Constant
Using the following steps, you can replace a formula with its result so that the cell value remains constant: (1) click the cell with the formula; (2) press the F2 key or click in the formula bar; (3) press the F9 key to display the value in the formula bar; and (4) press the ENTER key.

BTW
Error Messages
When Excel cannot calculate a formula, it displays an error message in a cell. These error messages always begin with a number sign (#). The more commonly occurring error messages are as follows: #DIV/0! (tries to divide by zero); #NAME? (uses a name Excel does not recognize); #N/A (refers to a value not available); #NULL! (specifies an invalid intersection of two areas); #NUM! (uses a number incorrectly); #REF (refers to a cell that is not valid); #VALUE! (uses an incorrect argument or operand); and ##### (refers to cells not wide enough to display entire entry).

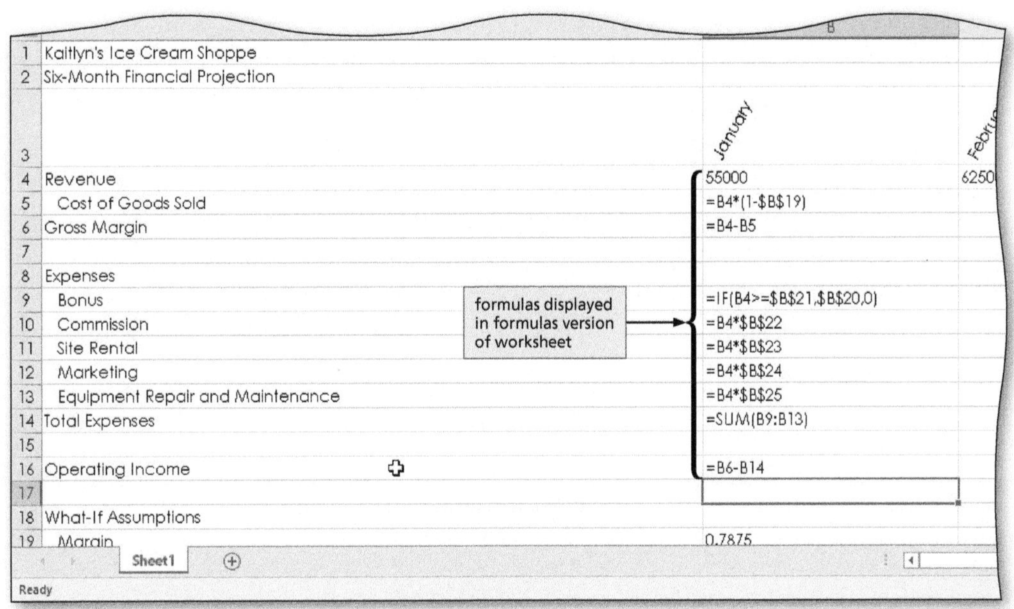

Figure 3–31

To Copy Formulas with Absolute Cell References Using the Fill Handle

1 ENTER HEADINGS & DATA | 2 ENTER FORMULAS & FUNCTIONS | 3 CREATE SPARKLINE CHARTS
4 FORMAT WORKSHEET | 5 CREATE COLUMN CHART | 6 CHANGE VIEWS | 7 ASK WHAT-IF QUESTIONS

***Why?** Using the fill handle ensures a quick, accurate copy of the formulas.* The following steps use the fill handle to copy the January formulas in column B to the other five months in columns C through G.

- Select the range B5:B16 and then point to the fill handle in the lower-right corner of the selected cell, B16 in this case, to display the crosshair pointer (Figure 3–32).

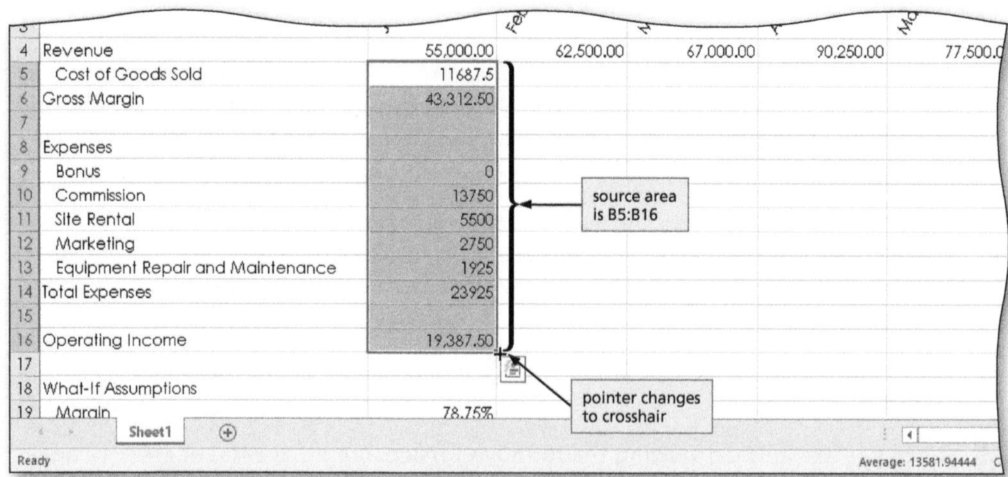

Figure 3–32

2

- Drag the fill handle to the right to copy the formulas from the source area, B5:B16 in this case, to the destination area, C5:G16 in this case, and display the calculated amounts (Figure 3–33).

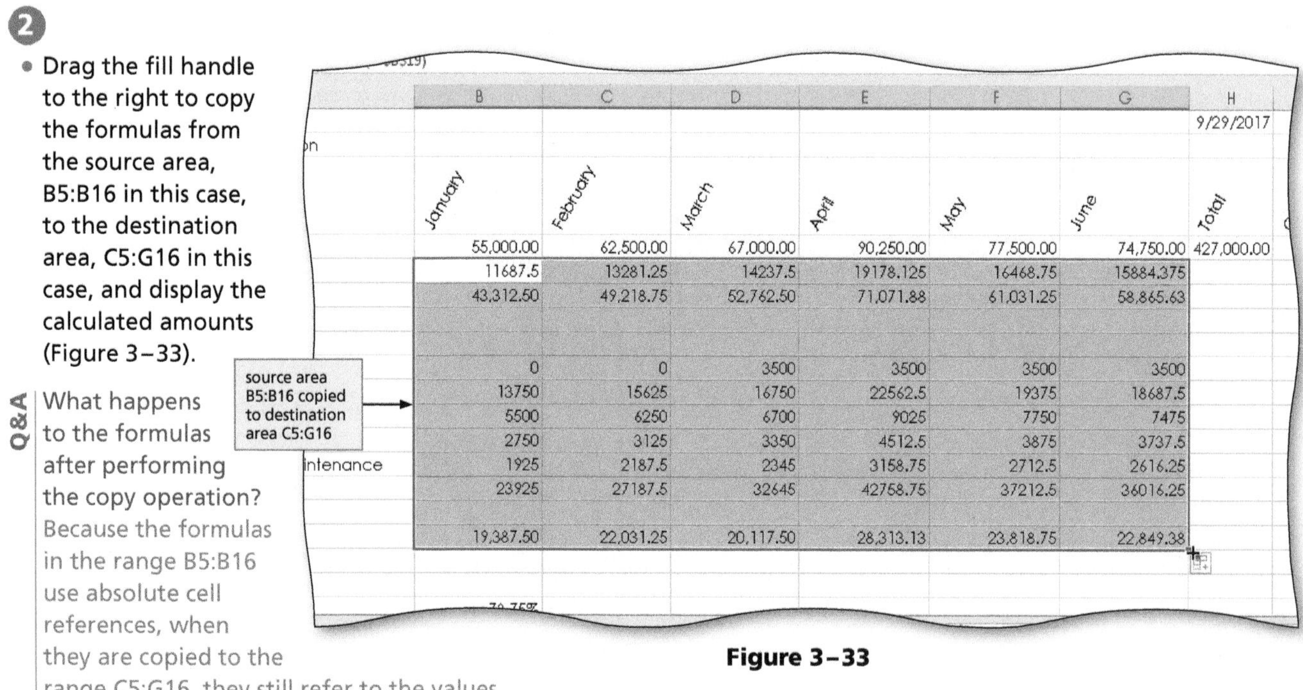

Figure 3–33

Q&A What happens to the formulas after performing the copy operation?

Because the formulas in the range B5:B16 use absolute cell references, when they are copied to the range C5:G16, they still refer to the values in the What-If Assumptions table.

To Determine Row Totals in Nonadjacent Cells

The following steps determine the row totals in column H. To determine the row totals using the Sum button, select only the cells in column H containing numbers in adjacent cells to the left. If, for example, you select the range H5:H16, Excel will display 0s as the sum of empty rows in cells H7, H8, and H15.

1 Select the range H5:H6. While holding down the CTRL key, select the range H9:H14 and cell H16, as shown in Figure 3–34.

2 Click the Sum button (Home tab | Editing group) to display the row totals in the selected ranges (Figure 3–34).

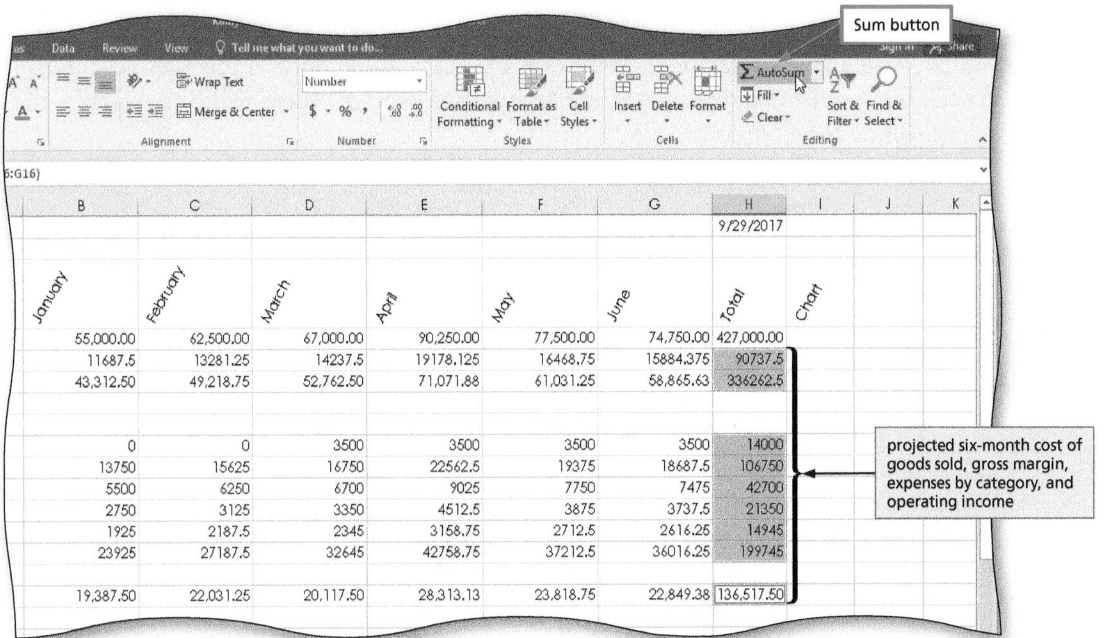

Figure 3–34

3 Save the workbook again on the same storage location with the same file name.

Nested Forms of the IF Function

A **nested IF function** is one in which the action to be taken for the true or false case includes yet another IF function. The second IF function is considered to be nested, or layered, within the first. You can use a nested IF function to add another condition to the decision-making process. Study the nested IF function below, which would add another level of bonus to the compensation at Kaitlyn's Ice Cream Shoppe. In this case, Kaitlyn's Ice Cream Shoppe assigns a bonus for sales of $65,000 and above. For months where sales make that level, additional bonus money is available for sales of $80,000 and above. In this case, three outcomes are possible, two of which involve paying a bonus. Figure 3–35 depicts a decision tree for this logical test.

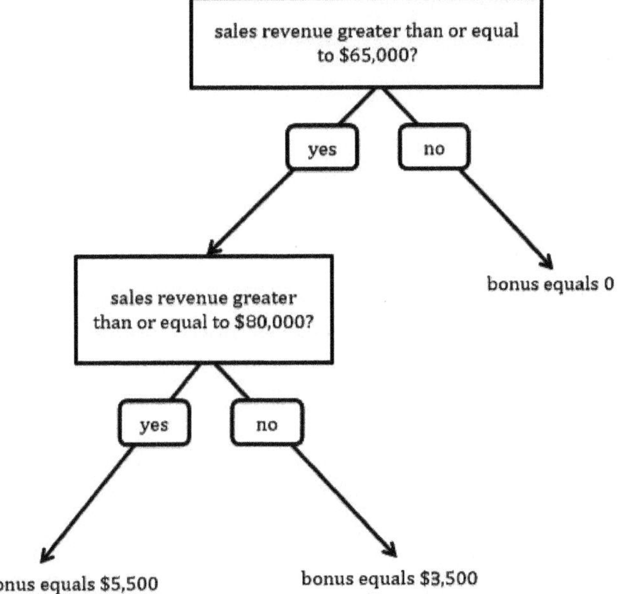

Figure 3–35

BTW
Using IFERROR
Similar to the IF function, the IFERROR function checks a formula for correctness. For example, =IFERROR(formula, "Error Message") examines the formula argument. If an error appears (such as #N/A), Excel displays the Error Message text in the cell instead of the Excel #N/A error.

Assume the following in this example: (1) the nested IF function is assigned to cell B9, which will display one of three values; (2) cell B4 contains the sales revenue; (3) cell B21 contains the sales revenue for a bonus of $3,500; and cell B22 contains the sales revenue for a bonus of $5,500.

=IF(B4>=B21, IF(B4>=B22,5500,3500),0)

The nested IF function instructs Excel to display one, and only one, of the following three values in cell B9: (1) 5,500, (2) 3,500, or (3) 0.

You can nest IF functions as deep as you want, but after you get beyond three IF functions, the logic becomes difficult to follow, and alternative solutions, such as the use of multiple cells and simple IF functions, should be considered.

Adding and Formatting Sparkline Charts

Sometimes you may want to condense a range of data into a small chart in order to show a trend or variation in the range, and Excel's standard charts may be too large or extensive for your needs. A sparkline chart provides a simple way to show trends and variations in a range of data within a single cell. Excel includes three types of sparkline charts: line, column, and win/loss. Because sparkline charts appear in a single cell, you can use them to convey succinct, eye-catching summaries of the data they represent.

To Add a Sparkline Chart to the Worksheet

1 ENTER HEADINGS & DATA | 2 ENTER FORMULAS & FUNCTIONS | **3 CREATE SPARKLINE CHARTS**
4 FORMAT WORKSHEET | 5 CREATE COLUMN CHART | 6 CHANGE VIEWS | 7 ASK WHAT-IF QUESTIONS

Each row of monthly data, including those containing formulas, provides useful information that can be summarized by a line sparkline chart. ***Why?*** *A line sparkline chart is a good choice because it shows trends over the six-month period for each row of data.* The following steps add a line sparkline chart to cell I4 and then use the fill handle to create line sparkline charts in the range I5:I16 to represent the monthly data shown in rows 4 through 16.

- If necessary, scroll the worksheet so that both columns B and I and row 3 are visible on the screen.
- Select cell I4 to prepare to insert a sparkline chart in the cell.
- Display the Insert tab and then click the Line Sparkline button (Insert tab | Sparklines group) to display the Create Sparklines dialog box (Figure 3–36).

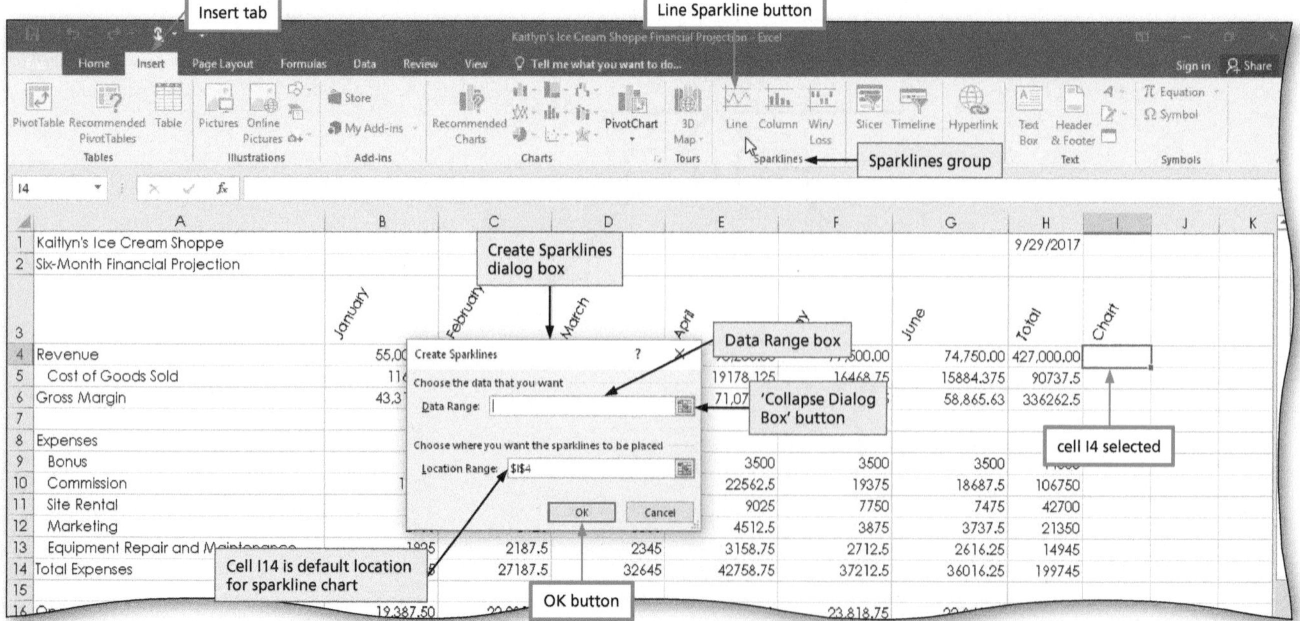

Figure 3–36

2

- Drag through the range B4:G4 to select the range. Do not release the mouse button (Figure 3–37).

Figure 3–37

Q&A What happened to the Create Sparklines dialog box?
When a dialog box includes a 'Collapse Dialog Box' button (Figure 3–36), selecting cells or a range collapses the dialog box so that only the current text box is visible. This allows you to select your desired range without the dialog box getting in the way. Once the selection is made, the dialog box expands back to its original size. You also can click the 'Collapse Dialog Box' button to make your selection and then click the 'Expand Dialog Box' button (Figure 3–37) to expand the dialog box.

3

- Release the mouse button to insert the selected range, B4:G4 in this case, in the Data Range box.
- Click the OK button shown in Figure 3–36 (Create Sparklines dialog box) to insert a line sparkline chart in the selected cell and display the Sparkline Tools Design tab (Figure 3–38).

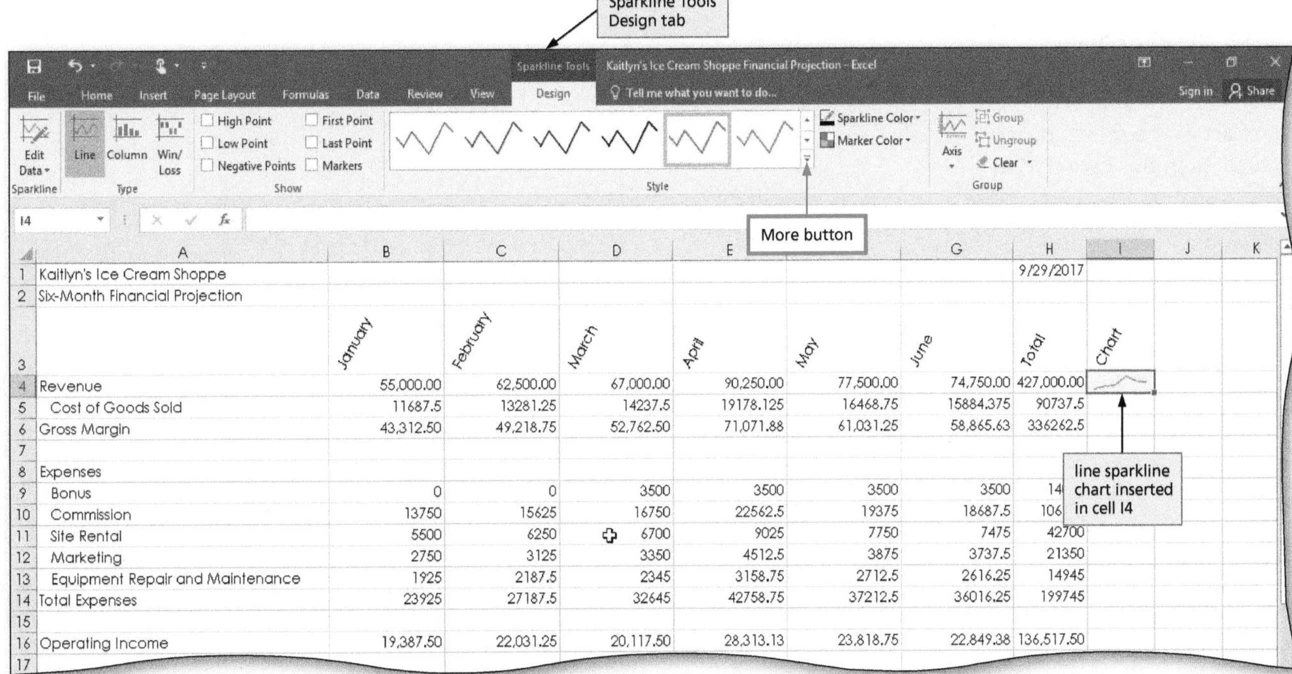

Figure 3–38

To Change the Sparkline Style and Copy the Sparkline Chart

Why? *The default style option may not provide the visual impact you seek. Changing the sparkline style allows you to alter how the sparkline chart appears.* The following steps change the sparkline chart style.

- Click the More button (Sparkline Tools Design tab | Style group) to display the Sparkline Style gallery (Figure 3–39).

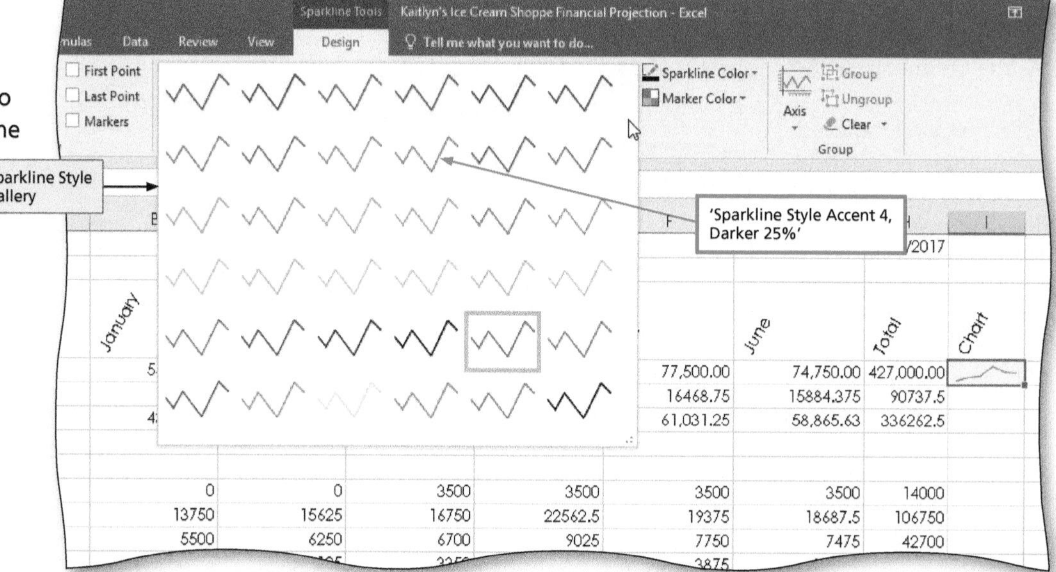

Figure 3–39

2

- Click 'Sparkline Style Accent 4, Darker 25%' in the Sparkline Style gallery to apply the style to the sparkline chart in the selected cell, I4 in this case.
- Point to the fill handle in cell I4 and then drag through cell I16 to copy the line sparkline chart.
- Select cell I18 (Figure 3–40).

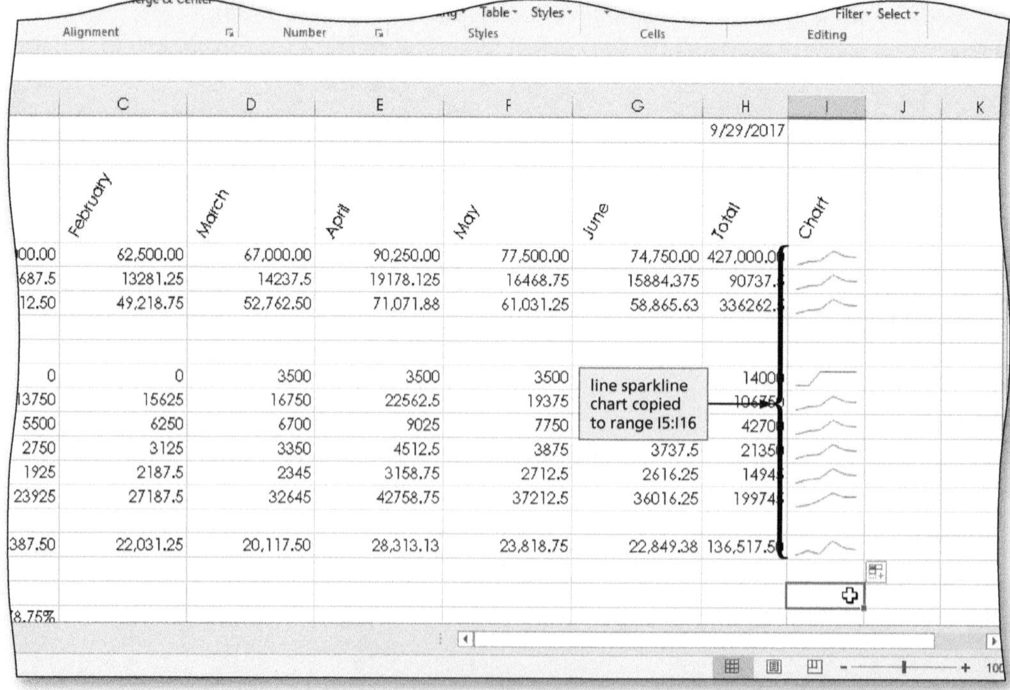

Figure 3–40

Q&A Why do sparkline charts not appear in cells I7, I8, and I15?
There is no data in the ranges B7:G7, B8:G8, and B15:G15, so Excel cannot draw sparkline charts. If you added data to cells in those ranges, Excel would then generate line sparkline charts for those rows, because the drag operation defined sparkline charts for cells I7, I8, and I15.

To Change the Sparkline Type

In addition to changing the sparkline chart style, you also can change the sparkline chart type. ***Why?*** *You may decide that a different chart type will better illustrate the characteristics of your data.* As shown in Figure 3–40, most of the sparkline charts look similar. Changing the sparkline chart type allows you to decide if a different chart type will better present your data to the reader. The following steps change the line sparkline charts to column sparkline charts.

1

- Select the range I4:I16 to select the sparkline charts.
- Click the Sparkline Tools Design tab to make it the active tab.
- Click the 'Convert to Column Sparkline' button (Sparkline Tools Design tab | Type group) to change the sparkline charts in the selected range to the column type (Figure 3–41).

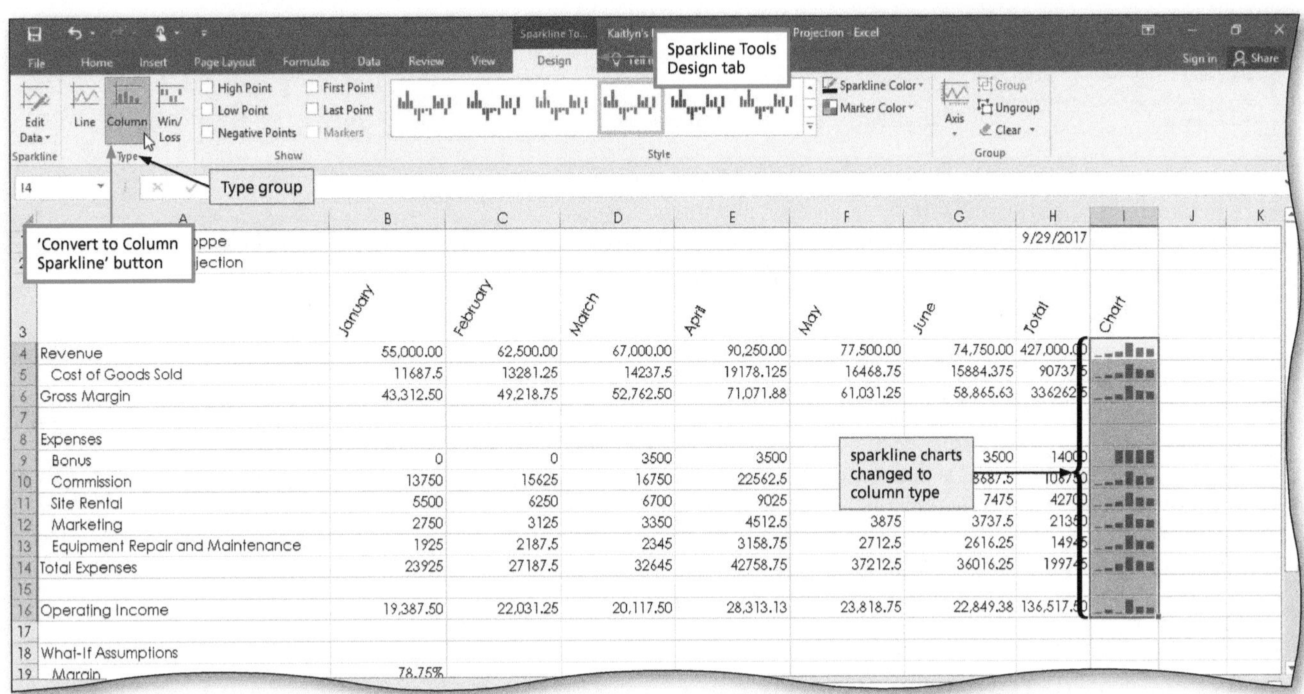

Figure 3–41

- Select cell I18.
- Save the workbook again on the same storage location with the same file name.

BTW

Customizing Sparkline Charts

You can customize sparkline charts in a number of ways on the Sparkline Tools Design tab. In the Show group (Sparkline Tools Design tab), you can specify values to show as markers on the chart, such as the highest value, lowest value, any negative numbers, the first point, and the last point. You can change the color of the sparkline and markers in the Style group (Sparkline Tools Design tab).

Formatting the Worksheet

The worksheet created thus far shows the financial projections for the six-month period, from January to June. Its appearance is uninteresting, however, even though some minimal formatting (formatting assumptions numbers, changing the column widths, formatting the date, and formatting the sparkline chart) was performed earlier. This section completes the formatting of the worksheet by making the numbers easier to read and emphasizing the titles, assumptions, categories, and totals, as shown in Figure 3–42.

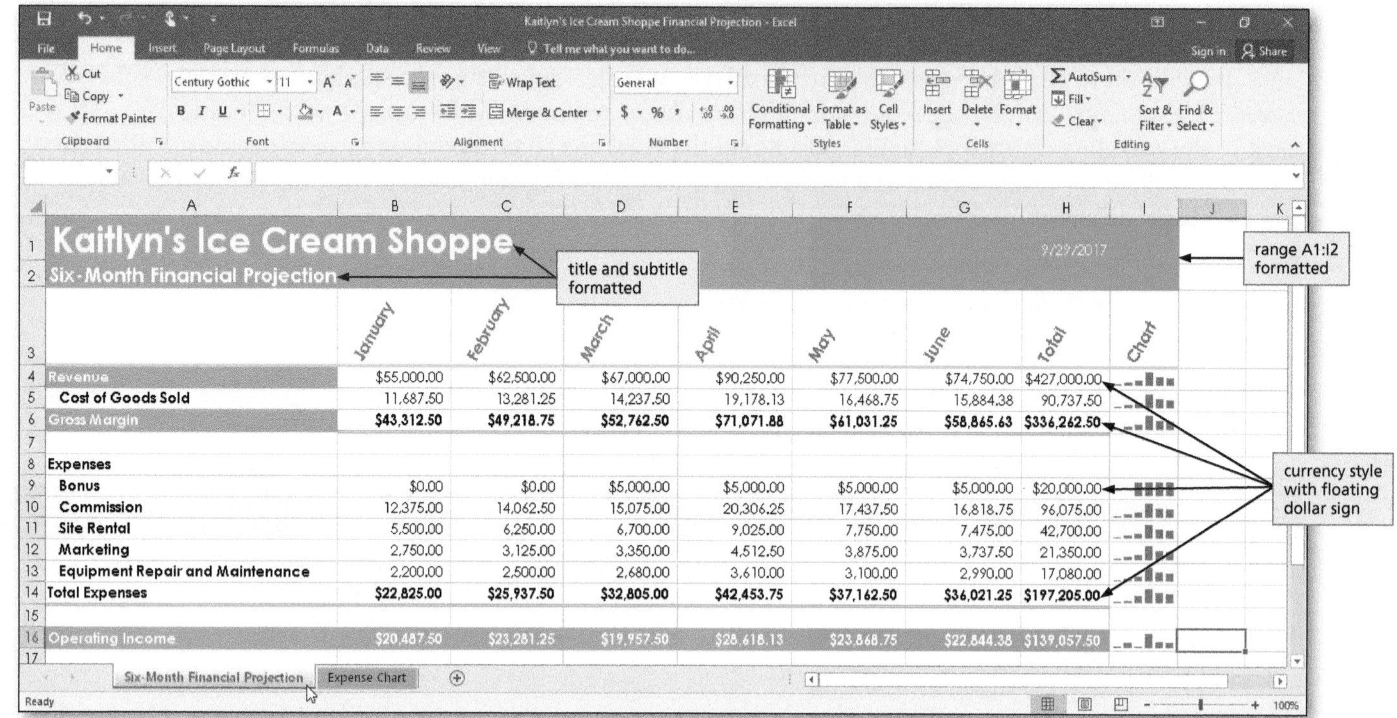

Figure 3–42

CONSIDER THIS

How should you format various elements of the worksheet?

A worksheet, such as the one presented in this module, should be formatted in the following manner: (1) format the numbers; (2) format the worksheet title, column titles, row titles, and total rows; and (3) format the assumptions table. Numbers in heading rows and total rows should be formatted with a currency symbol. Other dollar amounts should be formatted with a comma style. The assumptions table should be diminished in its formatting so that it does not distract from the main data and calculations in the worksheet. Assigning a smaller font size to the data in the assumptions table would set it apart from other data formatted with a larger font size.

To Assign Formats to Nonadjacent Ranges

1 ENTER HEADINGS & DATA | 2 ENTER FORMULAS & FUNCTIONS | 3 CREATE SPARKLINE CHARTS
4 FORMAT WORKSHEET | **5 CREATE COLUMN CHART** | **6 CHANGE VIEWS** | **7 ASK WHAT-IF QUESTIONS**

The following steps assign formats to the numbers in rows 4 through 16. ***Why?*** *These formats increase the readability of the data.*

1

- Select the range B4:H4 as the first range to format.
- While holding down the CTRL key, select the nonadjacent ranges B6:H6, B9:H9, B14:H14, and B16:H16, and then release the CTRL key to select nonadjacent ranges.
- Click the Number Format Dialog Box Launcher (Home tab | Number group) to display the Format Cells dialog box.
- Click Currency in the Category list (Format Cells dialog box), if necessary select 2 in the Decimal places box and then select $ in the Symbol list to ensure a dollar sign shows in the cells to be formatted, and select the black font color ($1,234.10) in the Negative numbers list to specify the desired currency style for the selected ranges (Figure 3–43).

Q&A

Why was this particular style chosen for the negative numbers?

In accounting, negative numbers often are shown with parentheses surrounding the value rather than with a negative sign preceding the value. Although the data being used in this module contains no negative numbers, you still must select a negative number format. It is important to be consistent when selecting negative number formats if you are applying different formats in a column; otherwise, the decimal points may not line up.

Q&A Why is the Format Cells dialog box used to create the format for the ranges in this step?
The requirements for this worksheet call for a floating dollar sign. You can use the Format Cells dialog box to assign a currency style with a floating dollar sign, instead of using the 'Accounting Number Format' button (Home tab | Number group), which assigns a fixed dollar sign.

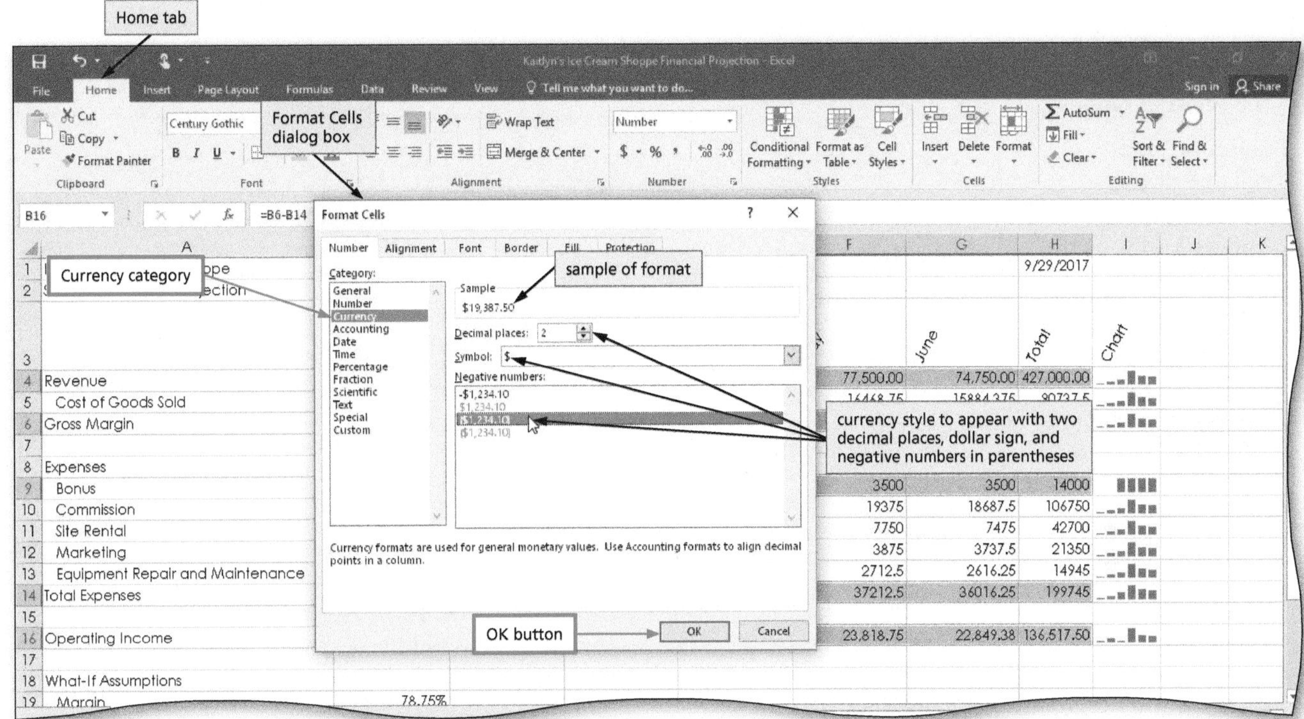

Figure 3–43

2

- Click the OK button (Format Cells dialog box) to close the Format Cells dialog box and apply the desired format to the selected ranges.
- Select the range B5:H5 as the next range to format.
- While holding down the CTRL key, select the range B10:H13, and then release the CTRL key to select nonadjacent ranges.
- Click the Number Format Dialog Box Launcher (Home tab | Number group) to display the Format Cells dialog box.
- Click Currency in the Category list (Format Cells dialog box), if necessary select 2 in the Decimal places box, select None in the Symbol list so that a dollar sign does not show in the cells to be formatted, and select the black font color (1,234.10) in the Negative numbers list (Figure 3–44).

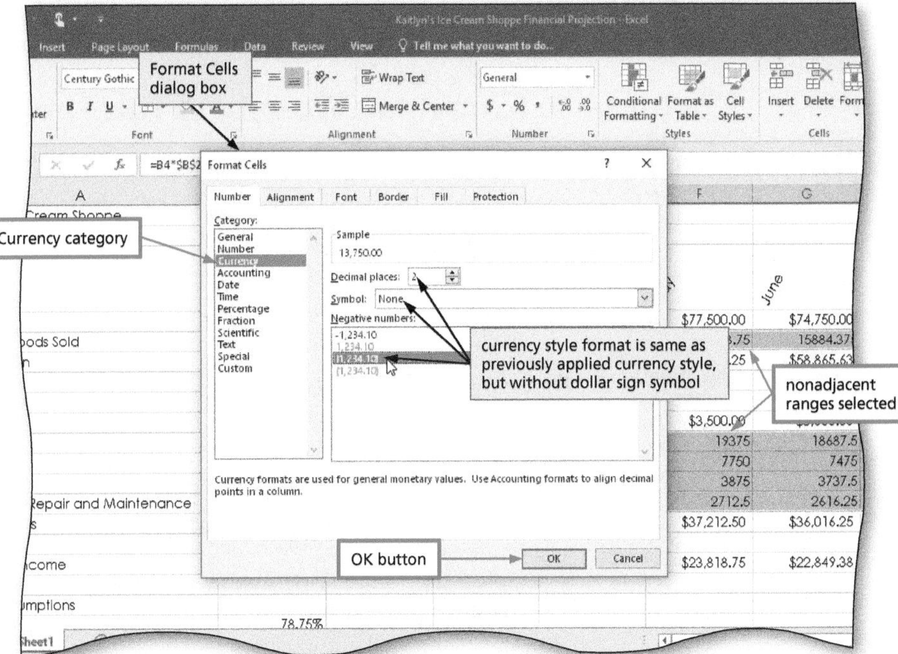

Figure 3–44

3

- Click the OK button (Format Cells dialog box) to close the Format Cells dialog box and apply the desired format to the selected ranges.
- Select an empty cell and display the formatted numbers, as shown in Figure 3–45.

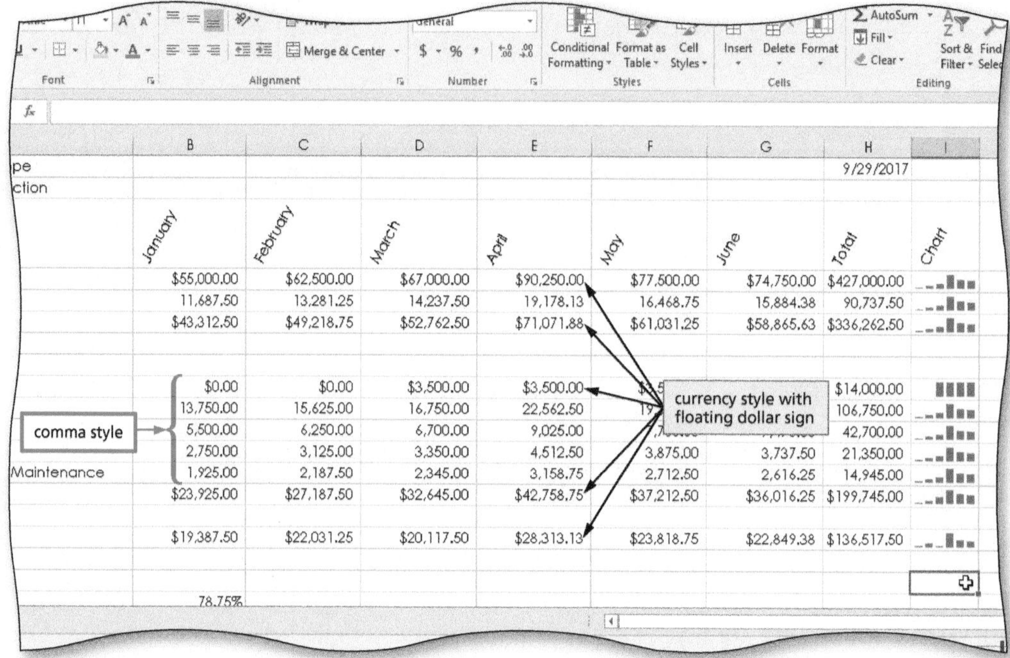

Figure 3–45

Q&A Why is the Format Cells dialog box used to create the style for the ranges in Steps 2 and 3?
The Format Cells dialog box is used to assign the comma style instead of the Comma Style button (Home tab | Number group), because the Comma Style button assigns a format that displays a dash (–) when a cell has a value of 0. The specifications for this worksheet call for displaying a value of 0 as 0.00 (see cell B9 in Figure 3–45) rather than as a dash. To create a comma style using the Format Cells dialog box, you use a currency style with no dollar sign.

Other Ways

1. Right-click range, click Format Cells on shortcut menu, click Number tab (Format Cells dialog box), click category in Category list, select format, click OK button (Format Cells dialog box)
2. Press CTRL+1, click Number tab (Format Cells dialog box), click category in Category list, select format, click OK button (Format Cells dialog box)

BTW
Toggle Commands
Many of the commands on the ribbon, in galleries, and as shortcut keys function as toggles. For example, if you click Freeze Panes in the Freeze Panes gallery, the command changes to Unfreeze Panes the next time you view the gallery. These types of commands work like on-off switches, or toggles.

To Format the Worksheet Titles

The following steps emphasize the worksheet titles in cells A1 and A2 by changing the font and font size. The steps also format all of the row headers in column A with a bold font style.

1. Press CTRL+HOME to select cell A1 and then click the column A heading to select the column.
2. Click the Bold button (Home tab | Font group) to bold all of the data in the selected column.
3. Increase the font size in cell A1 to 28 point.
4. Increase the font size in cell A2 to 16 point.
5. Select the range A1:I2 and change the fill color to Green, Accent 4 to add a background color to the selected range.
6. With A1:I2 selected, change the font color to White, Background 1.
7. Click an empty cell to deselect the range (Figure 3–46).

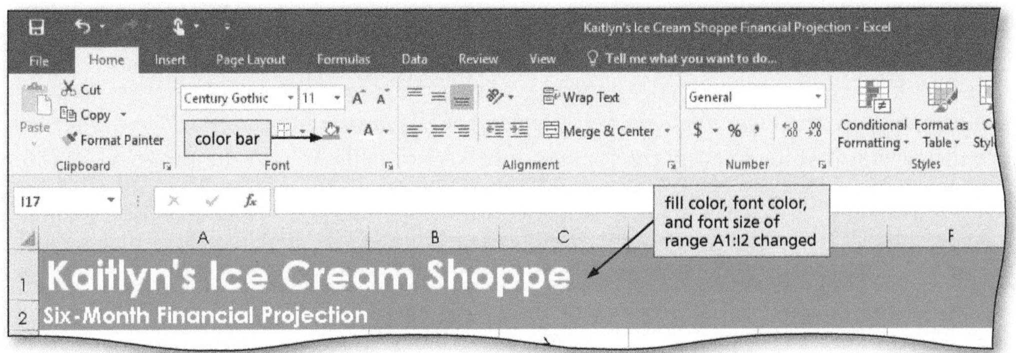

Figure 3–46

Other Ways

1. Right-click range, click Format Cells on shortcut menu, click Fill tab (Format Cells dialog box) to color background (or click Font tab to color font), click OK button
2. Press CTRL+1, click Fill tab (Format Cells dialog box) to color background (or click Font tab to color font), click OK button

To Assign Cell Styles to Nonadjacent Rows and Colors to a Cell

The following steps improve the appearance of the worksheet by formatting the headings in row 3 and the totals in rows 6, 14, and 16. Cell A4 also is formatted with a background color and font color.

1. Select the range A3:I3 and apply the Heading 2 cell style.
2. Select the range A6:H6 and while holding down the CTRL key, select the ranges A14:H14 and A16:H16.
3. Apply the Total cell style to the selected nonadjacent ranges.
4. Select cell A4 and click the Fill Color button (Home tab | Font group) to apply the last fill color used (Green, Accent 4) to the cell contents.
5. Click the Font Color button (Home tab | Font group) to apply the last font color used (White, Background 1) to the cell contents (Figure 3–47).

BTW

The Fill and Font Color Buttons

You may have noticed that the color bar at the bottom of the Fill Color and Font Color buttons (Home tab | Font group) (Figure 3–46) changes to the most recently selected color. To apply this same color to a cell background or text, select a cell and then click the Fill Color button to use the color as a background or click the Font Color button to use the color as a font color.

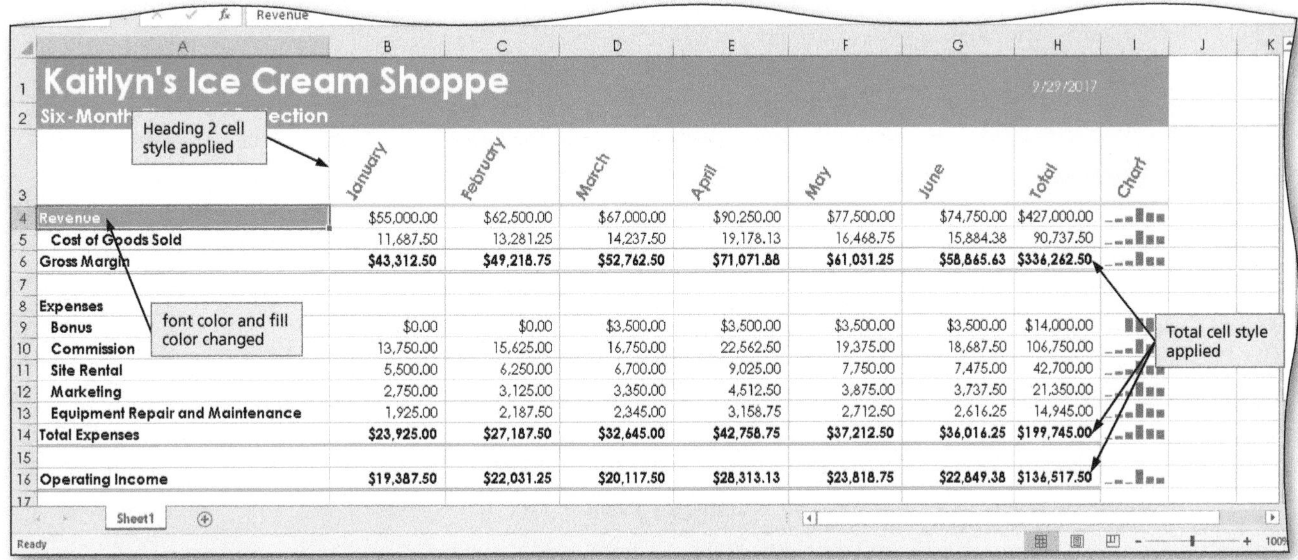

	January	February	March	April	May	June	Total	Chart
Revenue	$55,000.00	$62,500.00	$67,000.00	$90,250.00	$77,500.00	$74,750.00	$427,000.00	
Cost of Goods Sold	11,687.50	13,281.25	14,237.50	19,178.13	16,468.75	15,884.38	90,737.50	
Gross Margin	$43,312.50	$49,218.75	$52,762.50	$71,071.88	$61,031.25	$58,865.63	$336,262.50	
Expenses								
Bonus	$0.00	$0.00	$3,500.00	$3,500.00	$3,500.00	$3,500.00	$14,000.00	
Commission	13,750.00	15,625.00	16,750.00	22,562.50	19,375.00	18,687.50	106,750.00	
Site Rental	5,500.00	6,250.00	6,700.00	9,025.00	7,750.00	7,475.00	42,700.00	
Marketing	2,750.00	3,125.00	3,350.00	4,512.50	3,875.00	3,737.50	21,350.00	
Equipment Repair and Maintenance	1,925.00	2,187.50	2,345.00	3,158.75	2,712.50	2,616.25	14,945.00	
Total Expenses	$23,925.00	$27,187.50	$32,645.00	$42,758.75	$37,212.50	$36,016.25	$199,745.00	
Operating Income	$19,387.50	$22,031.25	$20,117.50	$28,313.13	$23,818.75	$22,849.38	$136,517.50	

Figure 3–47

To Copy a Cell's Format Using the Format Painter Button

1 ENTER HEADINGS & DATA | 2 ENTER FORMULAS & FUNCTIONS | 3 CREATE SPARKLINE CHARTS
4 FORMAT WORKSHEET | 5 CREATE COLUMN CHART | 6 CHANGE VIEWS | 7 ASK WHAT-IF QUESTIONS

Why? Using the format painter, you can format a cell quickly by copying a cell's format to another cell or a range of cells. The following steps use the format painter to copy the format of cell A4 to cells A6 and the range A16:H16.

1

- If necessary, click cell A4 to select a source cell for the format to paint.
- Double-click the Format Painter button (Home tab | Clipboard group) and then move the pointer onto the worksheet to cause the pointer to change to a block plus sign with a paintbrush (Figure 3–48).

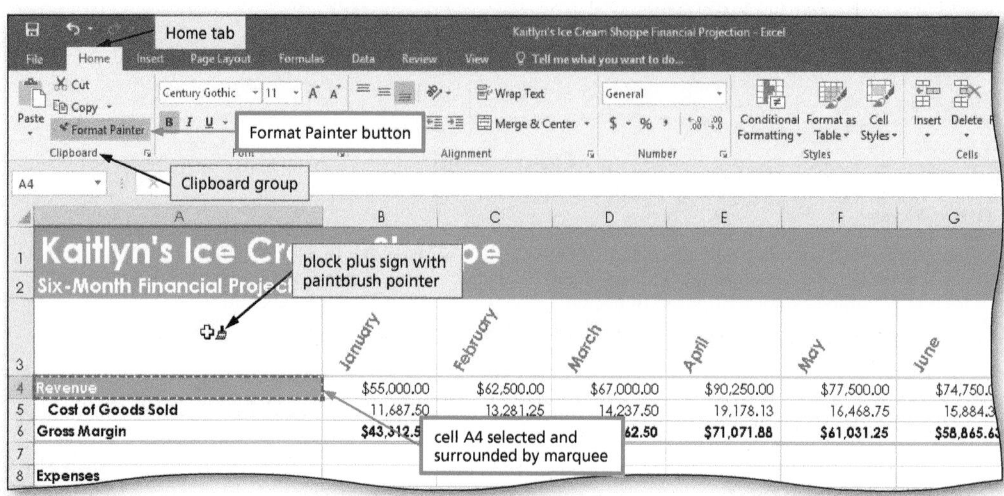

Figure 3–48

2

- Click cell A6 to assign the format of the source cell, A4 in this case, to the destination cell, A6 in this case.
- With the pointer still a block plus sign with a paintbrush, drag through the range A16:H16 to assign the format of the source cell, A4 in this case, to the destination range, A16:H16 in this case.
- Click the Format Painter button or press the ESC key to turn off the format painter.
- Apply the currency style to the range B16:H16 to cause the cells in the range to appear with a floating dollar sign and two decimal places (Figure 3–49).

Q&A Why does the currency style need to be reapplied to the range B16:H16?
Sometimes, the use of the format painter results in unintended outcomes. In this case, changing the background fill color and font color for the range B16:H16 resulted in the loss of the currency style because the format being copied did not include the currency style. Reapplying the currency style to the range results in the proper number style, fill color, and font color.

		Janu	Fe	M	Apr	May	Ju	To	Ch
4	Revenue	$55,000.00	$62,500.00	$67,000.00	$90,250.00	$77,500.00	$74,750.00	$427,000.00	
5	Cost of Goods Sold	11,687.50	13,281.25	14,237.50	19,178.13	16,468.75	15,884.38	90,737.50	
6	Gross Margin	$43,312.50	$49,218.75	$52,762.50	$71,071.88	$61,031.25	$58,865.63	$336,262.50	
7									
8	Expenses								
9	Bonus	$0.00	$0.00	$3,500.00	$3,500.00	$3,500.00	$3,500.00	$14,000.00	
10	Commission			16,750.00	22,562.50	19,375.00	18,687.50	106,750.00	
11	Site Rental			6,700.00	9,025.00	7,750.00	7,475.00	42,700.00	
12	Marketing			3,350.00	4,512.50	3,875.00	3,737.50	21,350.00	
13	Equipment Repair and Maintenance	1,925.00	2,187.50	2,345.00	3,158.75	2,712.50	2,616.25	14,945.00	
14	Total Expenses	$23,925.00	$27,187.50	$32,645.00	$42,758.75	$37,212.50	$36,016.25	$199,745.00	
15									
16	Operating Income	$19,387.50	$22,031.25	$20,117.50	$28,313.13	$23,818.75	$22,849.38	$134,517.50	

format of cell A4 applied to cells A6 and A16:H16 and currency style reapplied to B16:H16

Sheet1 — Ready — Average: $39,005.00 Count: 7 Sum: $273,035.00 — 100%

Figure 3–49

Other Ways

1. Click Copy button (Home tab | Clipboard group), select cell, click Paste arrow (Home tab | Clipboard group), click Formatting button in Paste gallery
2. Right-click cell, click Copy on shortcut menu, right-click cell, click Formatting icon on shortcut menu

To Format the What-If Assumptions Table

The following steps format the What-If Assumptions table, the final step in improving the appearance of the worksheet.

1. Select cell A18.
2. Change the font size to 8 pt.
3. Italicize and underline the text in cell A18.
4. Select the range A19:B25, and change the font size to 8 pt.
5. Select the range A18:B25 and then click the Fill Color button (Home tab | Font group) to apply the most recently used background color to the selected range.
6. Click the Font Color button (Home tab | Font group) to apply the most recently used font color to the selected range.
7. Deselect the range A18:B25 and display the What-If Assumptions table, as shown in Figure 3–50.
8. Save the workbook on the same storage location with the same file name.

Q&A What happens when I click the Italic and Underline buttons?
When you assign the italic font style to a cell, Excel slants the characters slightly to the right, as shown in cell A18 in Figure 3–50. The underline format underlines only the characters in the cell, rather than the entire cell, as is the case when you assign a cell a bottom border.

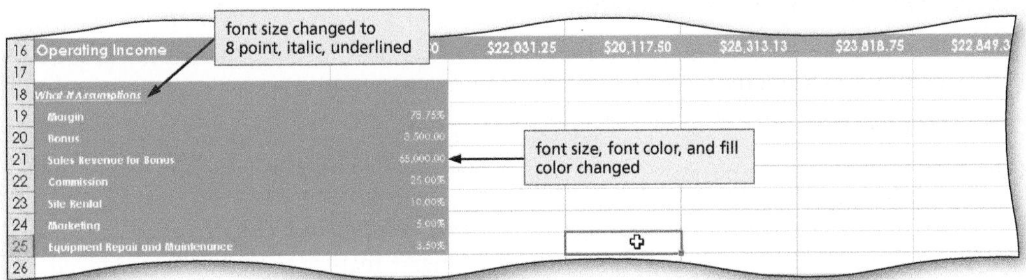

Figure 3–50

BTW
Painting a Format to Nonadjacent Ranges
Double-click the Format Painter button (Home tab | Clipboard group) and then drag through the nonadjacent ranges to paint the formats to the ranges. Click the Format Painter button again to deactivate it.

BTW
Selecting Nonadjacent Ranges
One of the more difficult tasks to learn is selecting nonadjacent ranges. To complete this task, do not hold down the CTRL key when you select the first range because Excel will consider the current active cell to be the first selection, and you may not want the current active cell in the selection. Once the first range is selected, hold down the CTRL key and drag through the nonadjacent ranges. If a desired range is not visible in the window, use the scroll arrows to view the range. You need not hold down the CTRL key while you scroll.

Break Point: If you wish to take a break, this is a good place to do so. You can exit Excel now. To resume at a later time, run Excel, open the file called Kaitlyn's Ice Cream Shoppe Financial Projection, and continue following the steps from this location forward.

Adding a Clustered Column Chart to the Workbook

The next step in the module is to create a clustered column chart on a separate sheet in the workbook, as shown in Figure 3–51. Use a clustered column chart to compare values side by side, broken down by category. Each column shows the value for a particular category, by month in this case.

The clustered column chart in Figure 3–51 shows the projected expense amounts, by category, for each of the six months. The clustered column chart allows the user to see how the various expense categories compare with each other each month, and across months.

Recall that charts can either be embedded in a worksheet or placed on a separate chart sheet. The clustered column chart will reside on its own sheet, because if placed on the worksheet, it would not be visible when the worksheet first opens and could be missed.

BTW
Charts
When you change a value on which a chart is dependent, Excel immediately redraws the chart based on the new value. With bar charts, you can drag the bar in the chart in one direction or another to change the corresponding value in the worksheet.

BTW
Chart Items
When you rest the pointer over a chart item, such as a legend, bar, or axis, Excel displays a chart tip containing the name of the item.

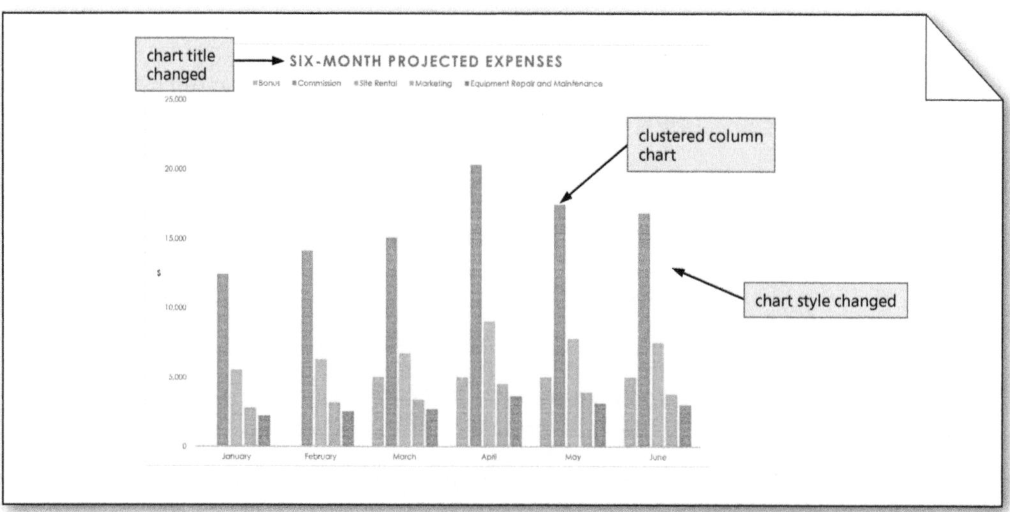

Figure 3–51

In this worksheet, the ranges to chart are the nonadjacent ranges B3:G3 (month names) and A9:G13 (monthly projected expenses, by category). The month names in the range B3:G3 will identify the major groups for the chart; these entries are called **category names.** The range A9:G13 contains the data that determines the individual columns in each month cluster, along with the names that identify each column; these entries are called the **data series.** Because six months of five expense categories are being charted, the chart will contain six clusters of five columns each, unless a category has the value of zero for a given month.

To Draw a Clustered Column Chart on a Separate Chart Sheet Using the Recommended Charts Feature

1 ENTER HEADINGS & DATA | 2 ENTER FORMULAS & FUNCTIONS | 3 CREATE SPARKLINE CHARTS
4 FORMAT WORKSHEET | 5 CREATE COLUMN CHART | **6 CHANGE VIEWS** | **7 ASK WHAT-IF QUESTIONS**

Why? *This Excel feature evaluates the selected data and makes suggestions regarding which chart types will provide the most suitable representation.* The following steps use the Recommended Charts feature to draw the clustered column chart on a separate chart sheet.

1

- Select the range A3:G3 to identify the range of the categories.
- Hold down the CTRL key and select the data range A9:G13.
- Display the Insert tab.
- Click the Recommended Charts button (Insert tab | Charts group) to display the Insert Chart dialog box with the Recommended Charts tab active (Figure 3–52).

Experiment

- Click the various recommended chart types, reading the description for each of its best use and examining the chart preview.

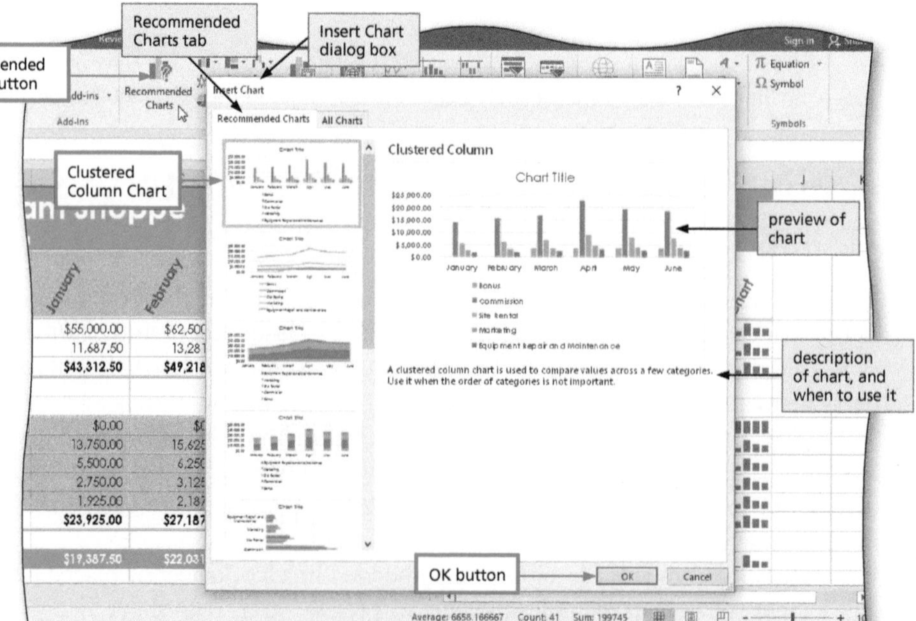

Figure 3–52

- Click the first Clustered Column recommended chart to select it and then click the OK button (Insert Chart dialog box).
- When Excel draws the chart, click the Move Chart button (Chart Tools Design tab | Location group) to display the Move Chart dialog box.
- Click New sheet (Move Chart dialog box) and then type **Expense Chart** in the New sheet text box to enter a sheet tab name for the chart sheet (Figure 3–53).

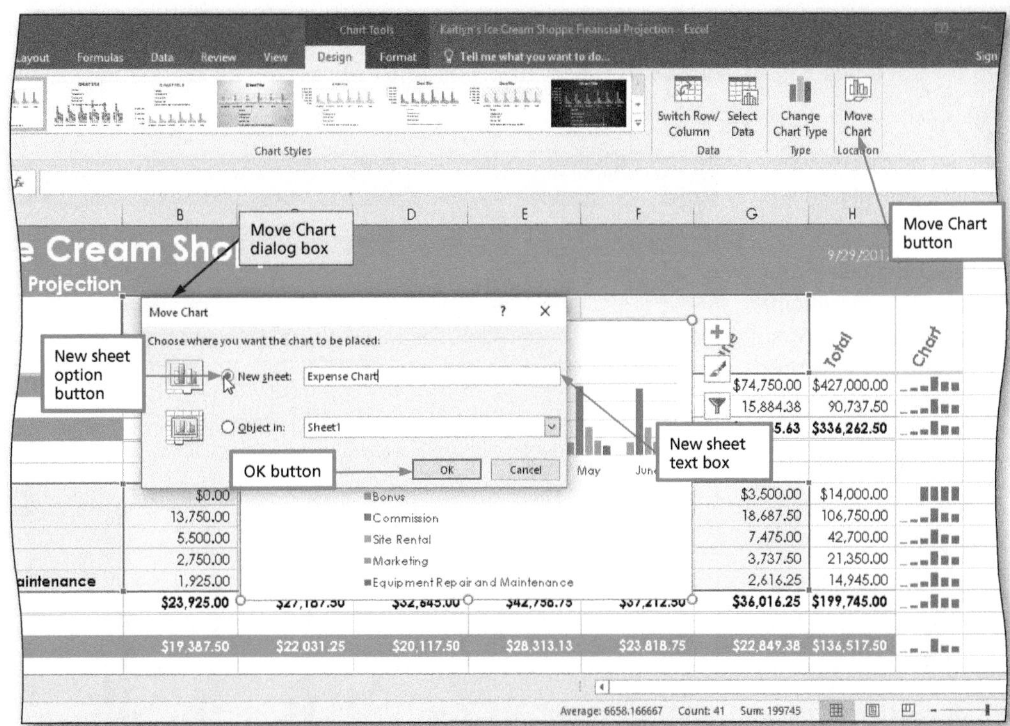

Figure 3–53

- Click the OK button (Move Chart dialog box) to move the chart to a new chart sheet with a new sheet tab name, Expense Chart (Figure 3–54).

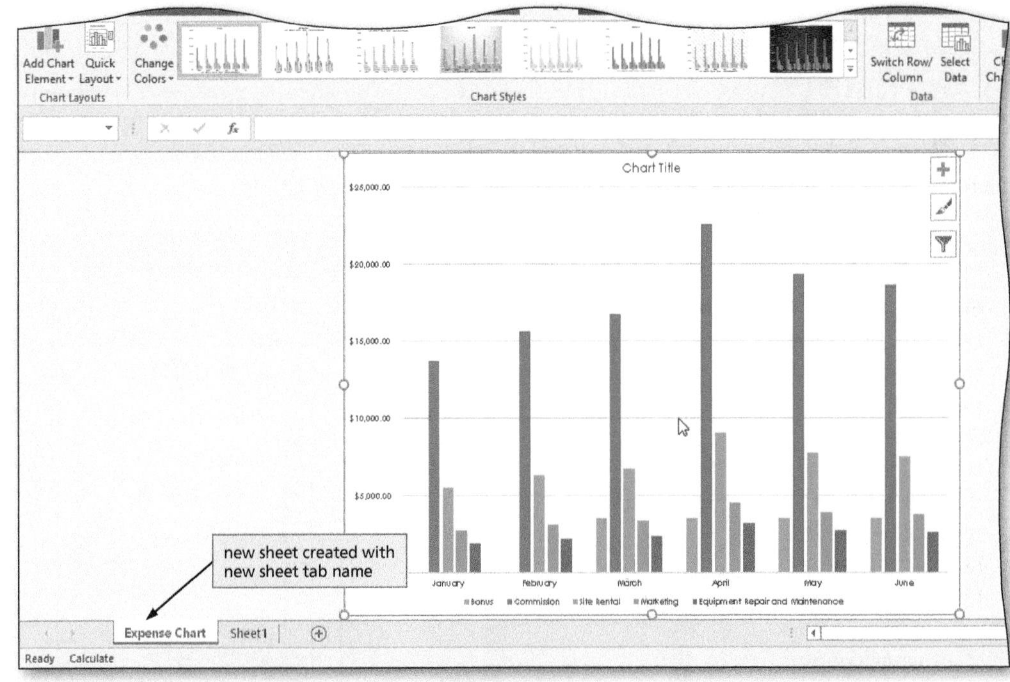

Figure 3–54

Q&A Why do January and February have only four columns charted?

Both January and February have a value of $0 for the Bonus category. Values of zero are not charted in a column chart, so these two months have one fewer column than the other months.

Other Ways

1. Select range to chart, PRESS F11

To Insert a Chart Title

1 ENTER HEADINGS & DATA | 2 ENTER FORMULAS & FUNCTIONS | 3 CREATE SPARKLINE CHARTS
4 FORMAT WORKSHEET | 5 CREATE COLUMN CHART | 6 CHANGE VIEWS | 7 ASK WHAT-IF QUESTIONS

The next step is to insert a chart title. ***Why?*** *A chart title identifies the chart content for the viewer.* Before you can format a chart item, such as the chart title, you must select it. The following step inserts a chart title.

1

- Click anywhere in the chart title placeholder to select it.
- Select the text in the chart title placeholder and then type `Six-Month Projected Expenses` to add a new chart title.
- Select the text in the new title and then display the Home tab.
- Click the Underline button (Home tab | Font group) to assign an underline format to the chart title (Figure 3–55).
- Click anywhere outside of the chart title to deselect it.

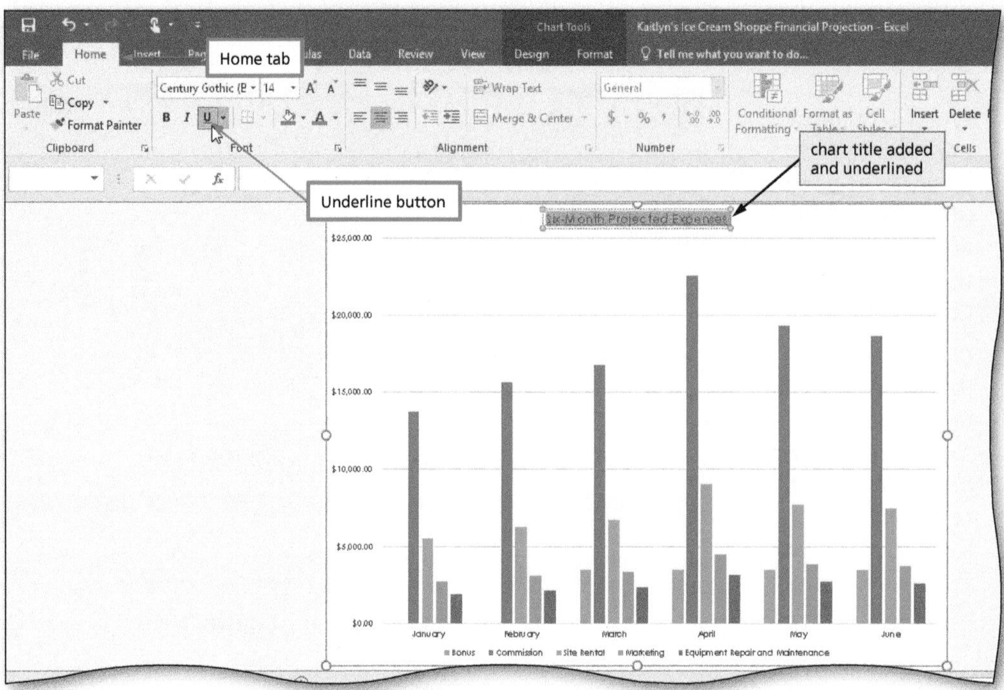

Figure 3–55

To Add Data Labels

1 ENTER HEADINGS & DATA | 2 ENTER FORMULAS & FUNCTIONS | 3 CREATE SPARKLINE CHARTS
4 FORMAT WORKSHEET | 5 CREATE COLUMN CHART | 6 CHANGE VIEWS | 7 ASK WHAT-IF QUESTIONS

The next step is to add data labels. ***Why?*** *Data labels can make a chart more easily understood. You can remove them if they do not accomplish that.* The following steps add data labels.

1

- Click the Chart Elements button (on the chart) to display the Chart Elements gallery. Point to Data Labels to display an arrow and then click the arrow to display the Data Labels fly-out menu (Figure 3–56).

 **Experiment**

- If you are using a mouse, point to each option on the Data Labels fly-out menu to see a live preview of the data labels.

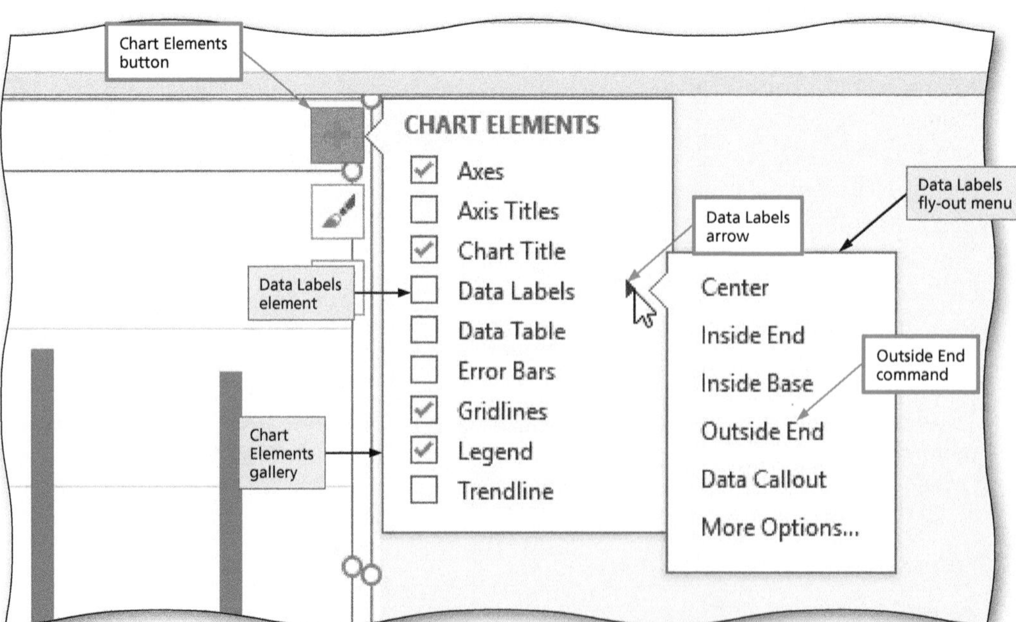

Figure 3–56

2

- Click Outside End on the Data Labels fly-out menu so that data labels are displayed outside the chart at the end of each column.
- Click the Chart Elements button to close the gallery (Figure 3–57).

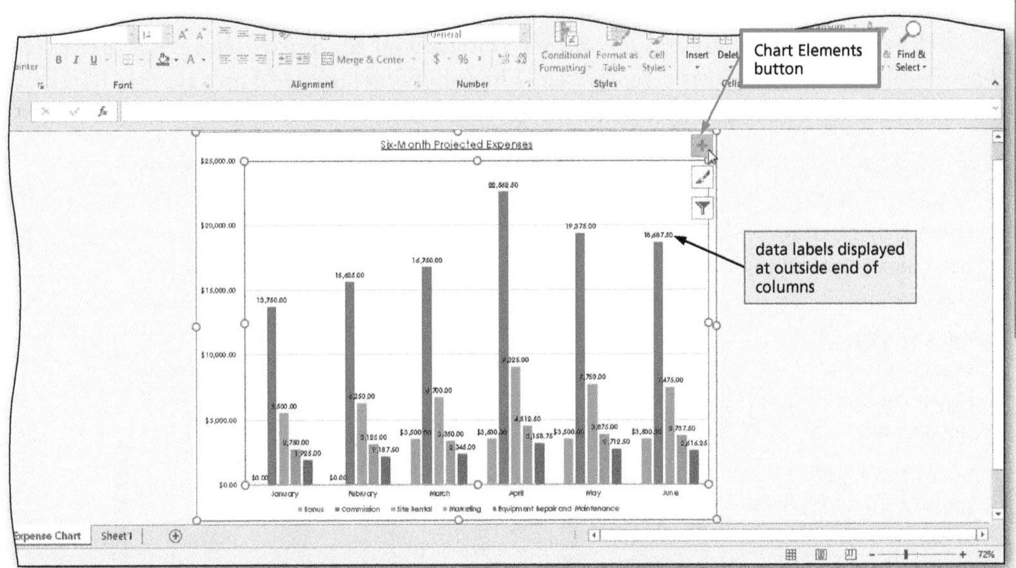

Figure 3–57

To Apply Chart Filters

1 ENTER HEADINGS & DATA | 2 ENTER FORMULAS & FUNCTIONS | 3 CREATE SPARKLINE CHARTS
4 FORMAT WORKSHEET | 5 CREATE COLUMN CHART | 6 CHANGE VIEWS | 7 ASK WHAT-IF QUESTIONS

Why? With some data, you may find that certain data series or categories make it difficult to examine differences and patterns between other series or categories. Excel allows you to easily filter data series and categories to allow more in-depth examinations of subsets of data. In this case, filters can be used to temporarily remove the compensation categories Bonus and Commission from the chart, to allow a comparison across the non-compensation expenses. The following steps apply filters to the clustered column chart.

1

- Click the Chart Filters button (on the chart) to display the Chart Filters gallery.
- In the Series section, click the Bonus and Commission check boxes to remove their check marks and then click the Apply button to filter these series from the chart (Figure 3–58).

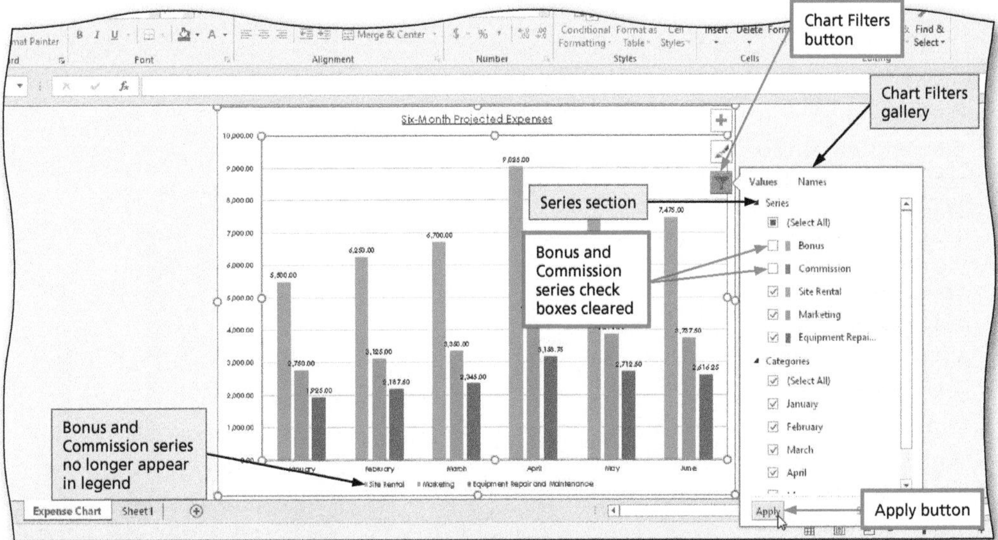

Figure 3–58

Q&A What happens when I remove the check marks from Bonus and Commission?

When you remove the check marks from Bonus and Commission, Excel filters the Bonus and Commission series out and redraws the chart without them.

2

- Click the Chart Filters button to close the gallery.

To Add an Axis Title to the Chart

***Why?** Often the unit of measurement or categories for the charted data is not obvious. You can add an axis title, or titles for both axes, for clarity or completeness.* The following steps add an axis title for the vertical axis.

- If necessary, click anywhere in the chart area outside the chart to select the chart.
- Click the Chart Elements button to display the Chart Elements gallery. Point to Axis Titles to display an arrow and then click the arrow to display the Axis Titles fly-out menu.

- Point to each option on the fly-out menu to see a live preview of the axes' titles.

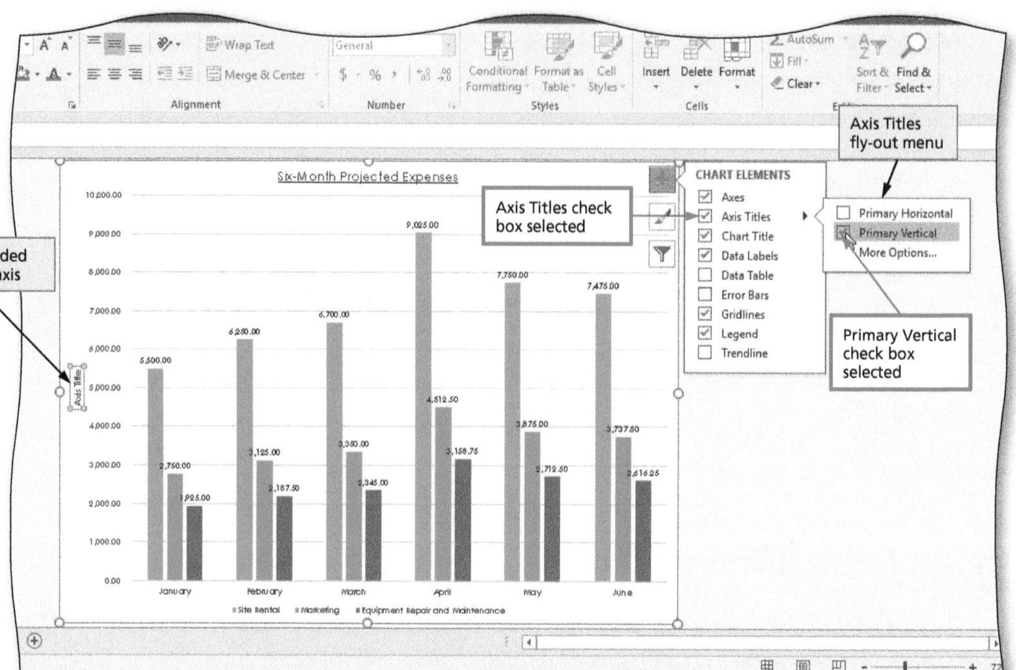

Figure 3–59

- Click Primary Vertical on the Axis Titles fly-out menu to add an axis title to the vertical axis (Figure 3–59).

- Click the Chart Elements button to remove the Chart Elements gallery from the window.
- Select the placeholder text in the vertical axis title and replace it with $ (a dollar sign).
- Right-click the axis title to display a shortcut menu (Figure 3–60).

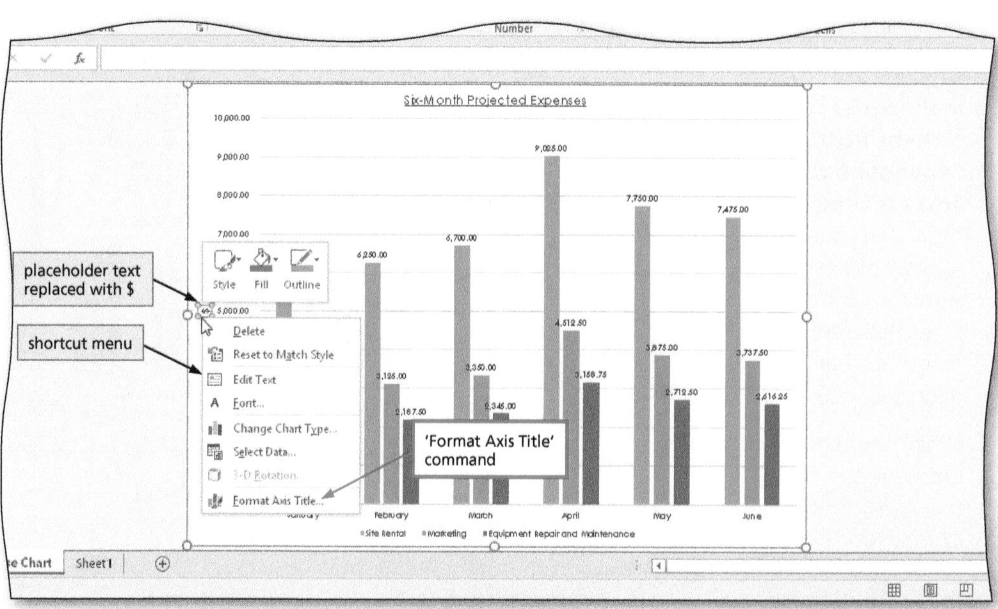

Figure 3–60

3

- Click 'Format Axis Title' on the shortcut menu to open the Format Axis Title task pane.
- If necessary, click the Title Options tab, click the 'Size & Properties' button, and then, if necessary, click the Alignment arrow to expand the Alignment section.
- Click the Text direction arrow to display the Text direction list (Figure 3–61).

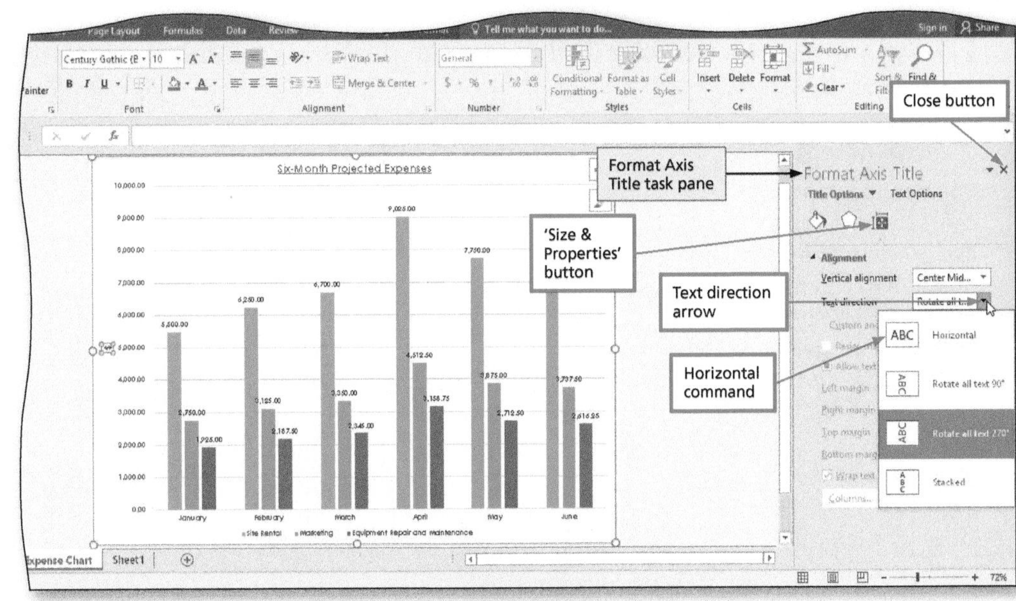

Figure 3–61

- Click Horizontal in the Text direction list to change the orientation of the vertical axis title.
- Click the Close button (shown in Figure 3–61) on the task pane to close the Format Axis Title task pane.

To Change the Chart Style

1 ENTER HEADINGS & DATA | 2 ENTER FORMULAS & FUNCTIONS | 3 CREATE SPARKLINE CHARTS
4 FORMAT WORKSHEET | 5 CREATE COLUMN CHART | **6 CHANGE VIEWS** | 7 ASK WHAT-IF QUESTIONS

***Why?** You decide that a chart with a different look would better convey meaning to viewers.* The following steps change the chart style.

1

- Click the More button (Chart Tools Design tab | Chart Styles group) (shown in Figure 3–61) to display the Chart Styles gallery (Figure 3–62).

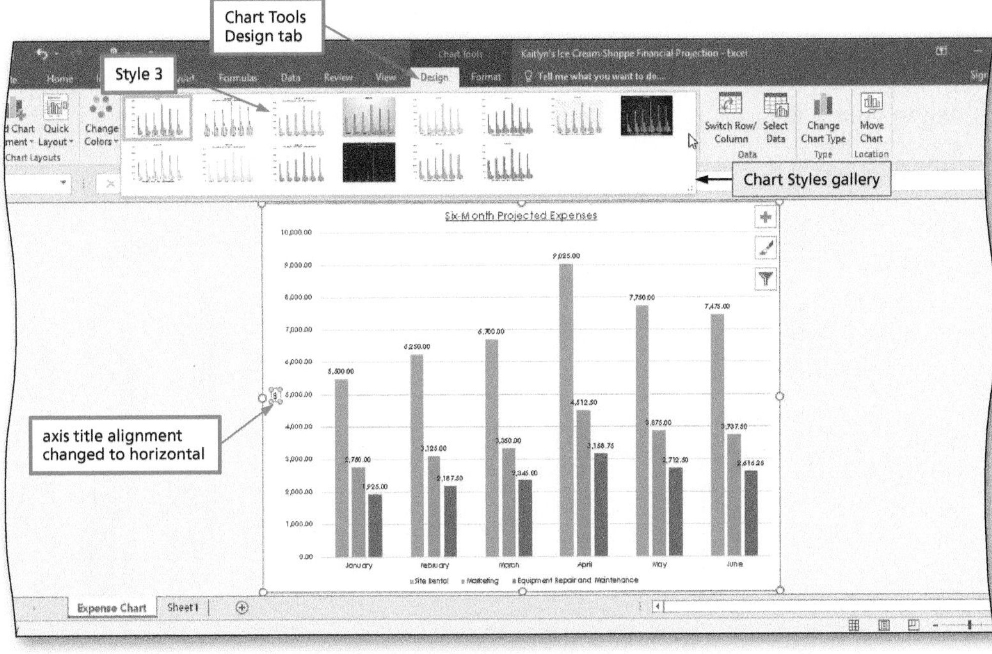

Figure 3–62

- Click Style 3 to apply a new style to the chart (Figure 3–63).

Experiment

- Point to the various chart styles to see a live preview of each one. When you have finished, click Style 3 to apply that style.

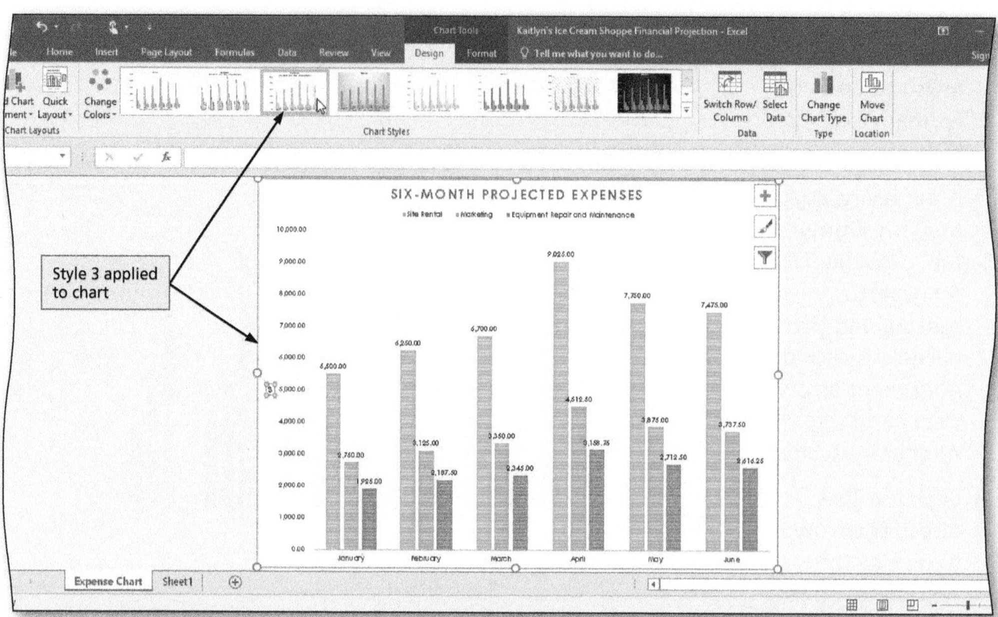

Figure 3–63

To Modify the Chart Axis Number Format

1 ENTER HEADINGS & DATA | 2 ENTER FORMULAS & FUNCTIONS | 3 CREATE SPARKLINE CHARTS
4 FORMAT WORKSHEET | 5 CREATE COLUMN CHART | **6 CHANGE VIEWS** | **7 ASK WHAT-IF QUESTIONS**

Why? The two decimal places in the vertical chart axis numbers are not necessary and make the axis appear cluttered. The following steps format the numbers in the chart axis to contain no decimal places.

- Right-click any value on the vertical axis to display the shortcut menu (Figure 3–64).

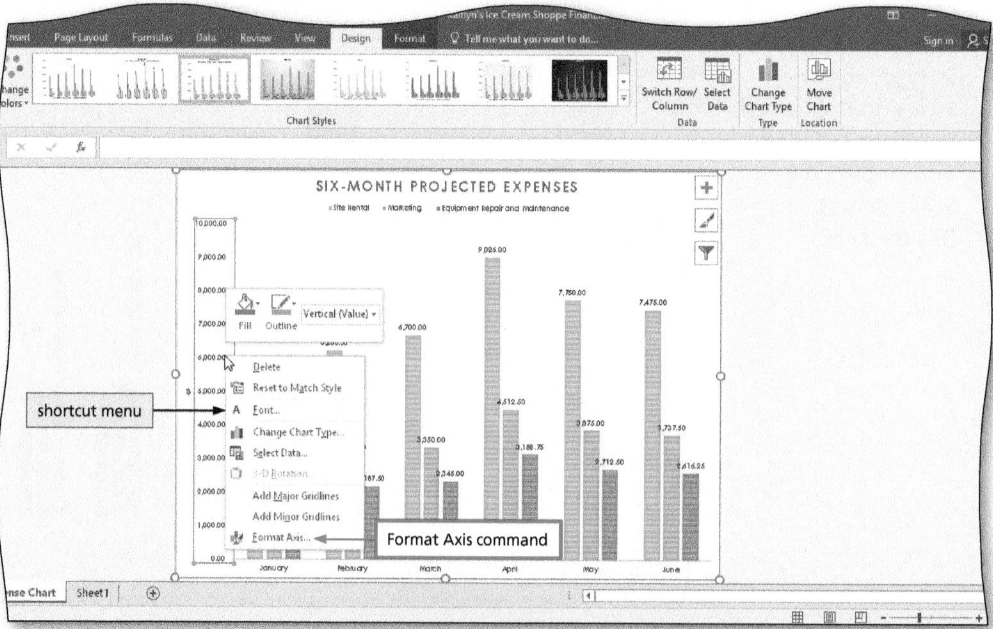

Figure 3–64

2

- Click Format Axis on the shortcut menu to open the Format Axis task pane.
- If necessary, click the Axis Options tab in the Format Axis task pane and then scroll until Number is visible. Click the Number arrow to expand the Number section and then scroll to review options related to formatting numbers.
- Change the number in the Decimal places text box to 0 (Figure 3–65).

3

- Close the Format Axis task pane.

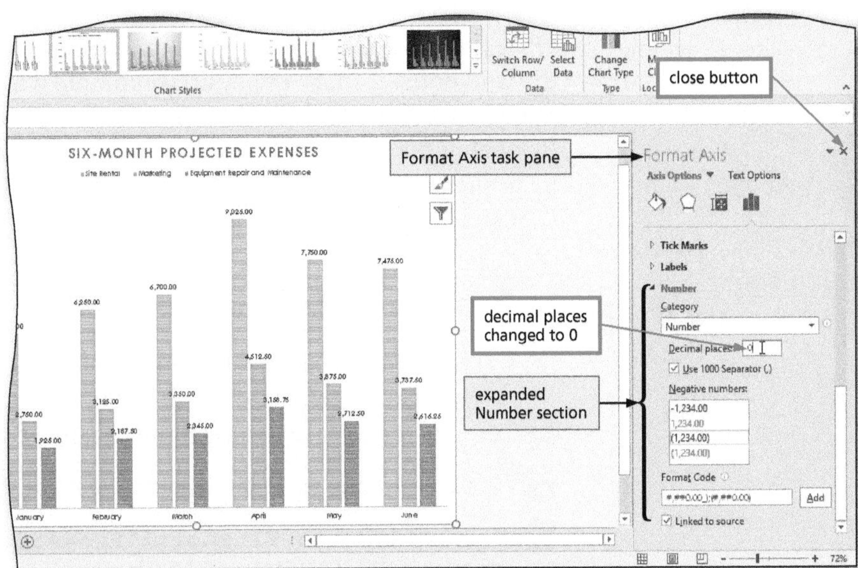

Figure 3–65

To Remove Filters and Data Labels

You decide that the data labels on the bars are distracting and add no value to the chart. You decide to remove the data labels and filters so that all expense data is once again visible. The following steps remove the data labels and the filters.

1. Click the Chart Elements button to display the Chart Elements gallery.
2. Click the Data Labels check box to remove the check mark for the data labels.
3. Click the Chart Elements button again to close the gallery.
4. Click the Chart Filters button to display the Chart Filters fly-out menu.
5. In the Series section, click Bonus and then Commission, click the Apply button to add the compensation data back into the chart, and then click the Chart Filters button again to close the menu (Figure 3–66).

Figure 3–66

BTW

Chart Templates

Once you create and format a chart to your liking, consider saving the chart as a template so that you can use it to format additional charts. Save your chart as a chart template by accessing the chart shortcut menu and then selecting 'Save as Template' from that shortcut menu. The chart template will appear in the Templates folder for Charts. When you want to use the template, click the Templates folder in the All Charts sheet (Insert Chart dialog box) and then select your template.

Organizing the Workbook

Once the content of the workbook is complete, you can address the organization of the workbook. If the workbook has multiple worksheets, place the worksheet on top that you want the reader to see first. Default sheet names in Excel are not descriptive. Renaming the sheets with descriptive names helps the reader find information that he or she is looking for. Modifying the sheet tabs through the use of color further distinguishes multiple sheets from each other.

To Rename and Color Sheet Tabs

The following steps rename the sheets and color the sheet tabs.

1. Change the color of the Expense Chart sheet tab to Green, Accent 4 (column 8, row 1).
2. Double-click the sheet tab labeled Sheet1 at the bottom of the screen.
3. Type **`Six-Month Financial Projection`** as the new sheet tab name and then press the ENTER key.
4. Change the sheet tab color of the Six-Month Financial Projection sheet to Blue, Accent 2 (column 6, row 1) and then select an empty cell (Figure 3–67).

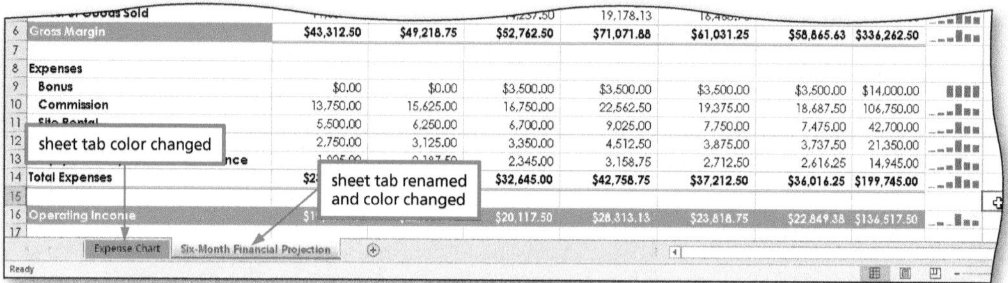

Figure 3–67

To Reorder the Sheet Tabs

Why? You want the most important worksheets to appear first in a workbook, so you need to change the order of sheets. The following step reorders the sheets so that the worksheet precedes the chart sheet in the workbook.

- Drag the Six-Month Financial Projection tab to the left so that it precedes the Expense Chart sheet tab to rearrange the sequence of the sheets (Figure 3–68).

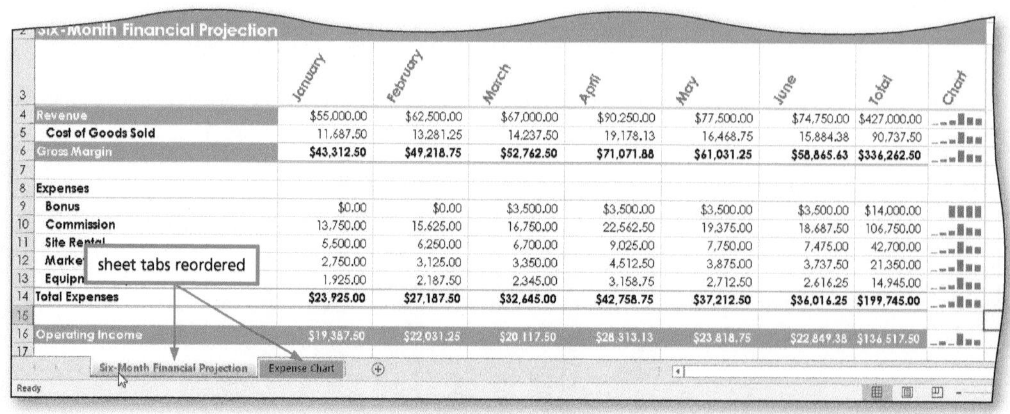

Figure 3–68

Other Ways

1. To move sheet, right-click sheet tab, click Move or Copy on shortcut menu, click OK button

To Check Spelling in Multiple Sheets

By default, the spelling checker reviews spelling only in the selected sheets. It will check all the cells in the selected sheets, unless you select a range of two or more cells. Before checking the spelling, the following steps select both worksheets in the workbook so that both are checked for any spelling errors.

1. With the Six-Month Financial Projection sheet active, press CTRL+HOME to select cell A1. Hold down the CTRL key and then click the Expense Chart tab to select both sheets.
2. Display the Review tab and then click the Spelling button (Review tab | Proofing group) to check spelling in the selected sheets.
3. Correct any errors and then click the OK button (Spelling dialog box or Microsoft Excel dialog box) when the spelling checker is finished.

BTW
Checking Spelling
Unless you first select a range of cells or an object before starting the spelling checker, Excel checks the entire selected worksheet, including all cell values, cell comments, embedded charts, text boxes, buttons, and headers and footers.

To Preview and Print the Worksheet

After checking the spelling, the next step is to preview and print the worksheets. As with spelling, Excel previews and prints only the selected sheets. In addition, because the worksheet is too wide to print in portrait orientation, the orientation must be changed to landscape. The following steps adjust the orientation and scale, preview the worksheets, and then print the worksheets.

1. If both sheets are not selected, hold down the CTRL key and then click the tab of the inactive sheet.
2. Click File on the ribbon to open the Backstage view.
3. Click the Print tab in the Backstage view to display the Print gallery.
4. Click the Portrait Orientation button in the Settings area and then select Landscape Orientation to select the desired orientation.
5. Click the No Scaling button in the Settings area and then select 'Fit Sheet on One Page' to cause the worksheets to print on one page.
6. Verify that the selected printer will print a hard copy of the document. If necessary, click the printer button to display a list of available printer options and then click the desired printer to change the currently selected printer.
7. Click the Print button in the Print gallery to print the worksheet in landscape orientation on the currently selected printer.
8. When the printer stops, retrieve the printed worksheets (shown in Figure 3–69a and Figure 3–69b).
9. Right-click the Six-Month Financial Projection tab, and then click Ungroup Sheets on the shortcut menu to deselect the Expense Chart tab.
10. Save the workbook again on the same storage location with the same file name.

BTW
Distributing a Workbook
Instead of printing and distributing a hard copy of a workbook, you can distribute the workbook electronically. Options include sending the workbook via email; posting it on cloud storage (such as OneDrive) and sharing the file with others; posting it on social media, a blog, or other website; and sharing a link associated with an online location of the workbook. You also can create and share a PDF or XPS image of the workbook, so that users can view the file in Acrobat Reader or XPS Viewer instead of in Excel.

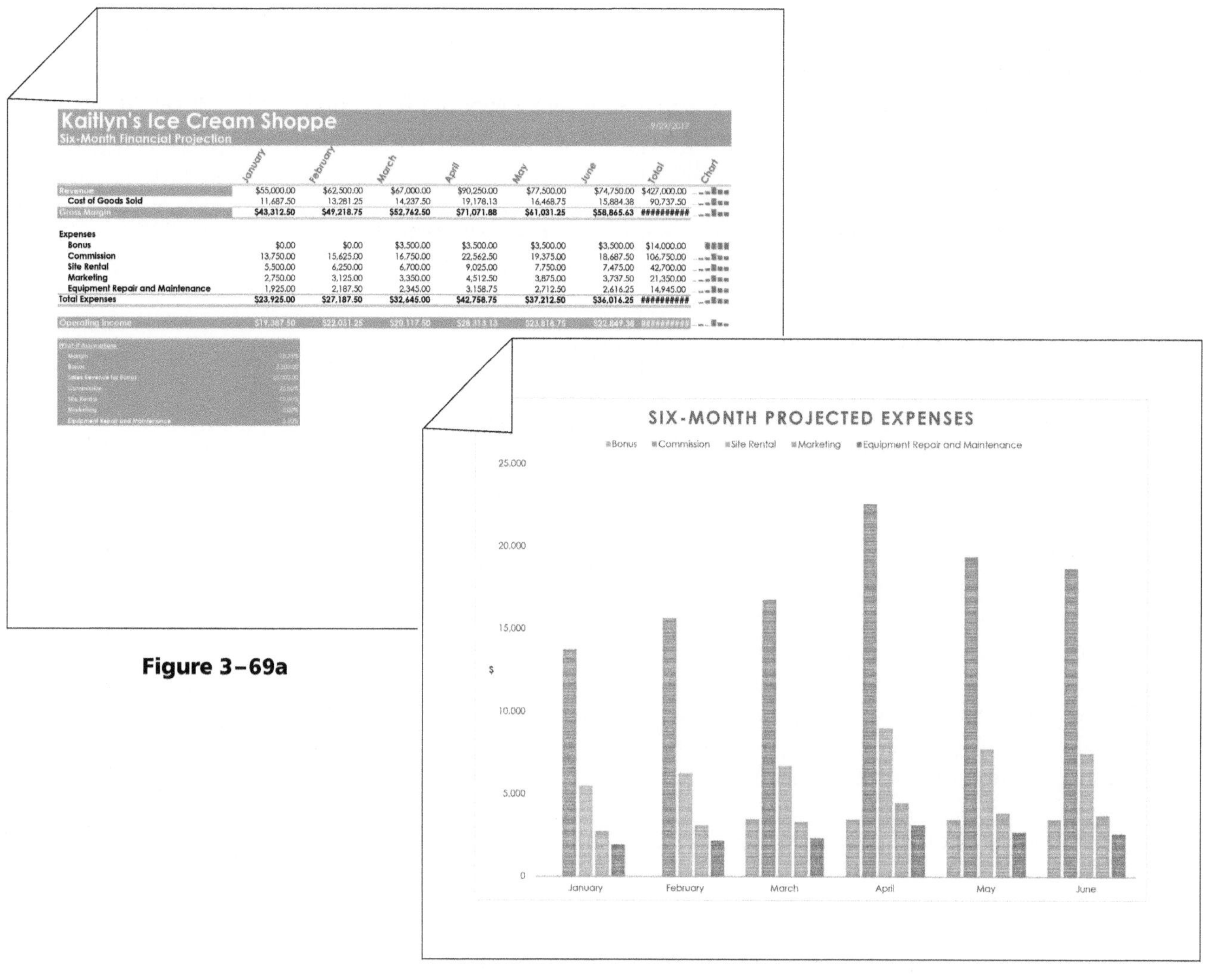

Kaitlyn's Ice Cream Shoppe
Six-Month Financial Projection

	January	February	March	April	May	June	Total
Revenue	$55,000.00	$62,500.00	$67,000.00	$90,250.00	$77,500.00	$74,750.00	$427,000.00
Cost of Goods Sold	11,687.50	13,281.25	14,237.50	19,178.13	16,468.75	15,884.38	90,737.50
Gross Margin	$43,312.50	$49,218.75	$52,762.50	$71,071.88	$61,031.25	$58,865.63	#########
Expenses							
Bonus	$0.00	$0.00	$3,500.00	$3,500.00	$3,500.00	$3,500.00	$14,000.00
Commission	13,750.00	15,625.00	16,750.00	22,562.50	19,375.00	18,687.50	106,750.00
Site Rental	5,500.00	6,250.00	6,700.00	9,025.00	7,750.00	7,475.00	42,700.00
Marketing	2,750.00	3,125.00	3,350.00	4,512.50	3,875.00	3,737.50	21,350.00
Equipment Repair and Maintenance	1,925.00	2,187.50	2,345.00	3,158.75	2,712.50	2,616.25	14,945.00
Total Expenses	$23,925.00	$27,187.50	$32,645.00	$42,758.75	$37,212.50	$36,016.25	#########
Operating Income	$19,387.50	$22,031.25	$20,117.50	$28,313.13	$23,818.75	$22,849.38	#########

Figure 3–69a

Figure 3–69b

Changing the View of the Worksheet

With Excel, you easily can change the view of the worksheet. For example, you can magnify or shrink the worksheet on the screen. You also can view different parts of the worksheet at the same time by using panes.

To Shrink and Magnify the View of a Worksheet or Chart

1 ENTER HEADINGS & DATA | 2 ENTER FORMULAS & FUNCTIONS | 3 CREATE SPARKLINE CHARTS
4 FORMAT WORKSHEET | 5 CREATE COLUMN CHART | **6 CHANGE VIEWS** | **7 ASK WHAT-IF QUESTIONS**

You can magnify (zoom in) or shrink (zoom out) the appearance of a worksheet or chart by using the Zoom button (View tab | Zoom group). ***Why?*** *When you magnify a worksheet, Excel enlarges the view of the characters on the screen, but shows fewer columns and rows. Alternatively, when you shrink a worksheet, Excel is able to display more columns and rows.* Magnifying or shrinking a worksheet affects only the view; it does not change the window size or the size of the printout of the worksheet or chart. The following steps shrink and magnify the view of the worksheet.

1

- If cell A1 is not active, press CTRL+HOME.
- Display the View tab and then click the Zoom button (View tab | Zoom group) to display a list of magnifications in the Zoom dialog box (Figure 3–70).

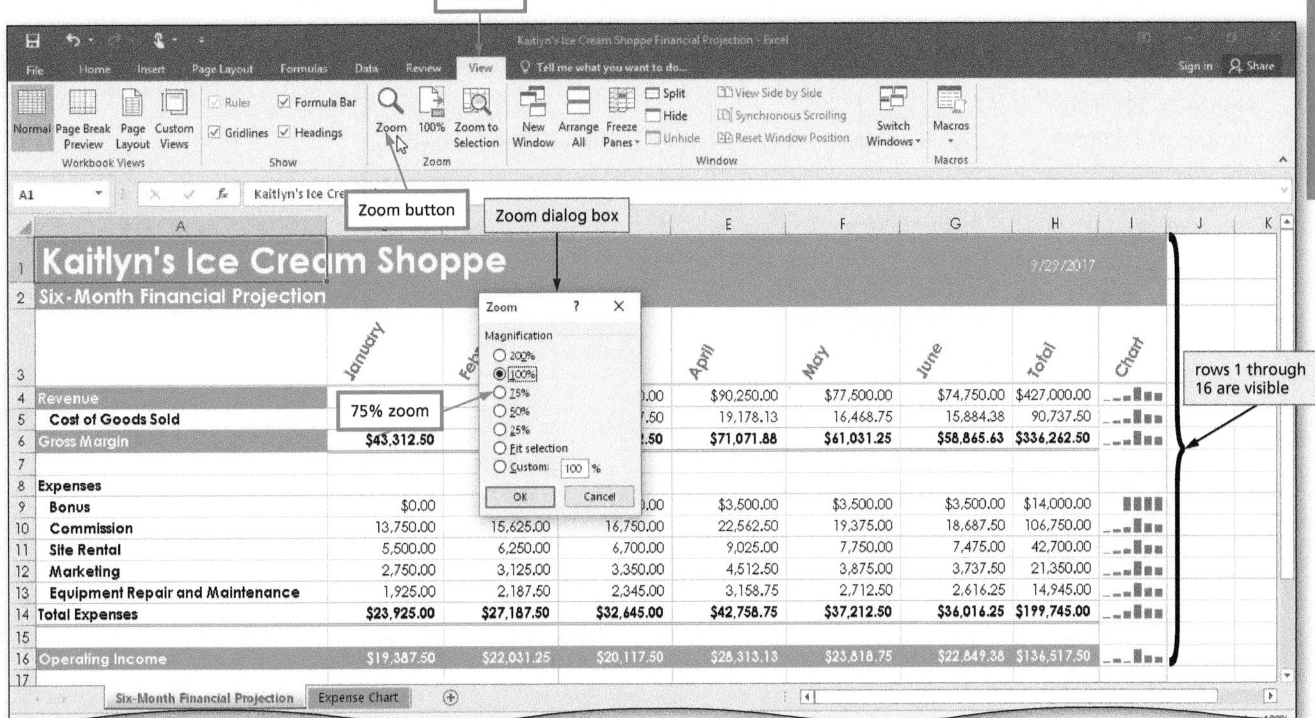

Figure 3–70

2

- Click 75% and then click the OK button (Zoom dialog box) to shrink the display of the worksheet (Figure 3–71). The number of columns and rows appearing on your screen may differ from Figure 3–71.

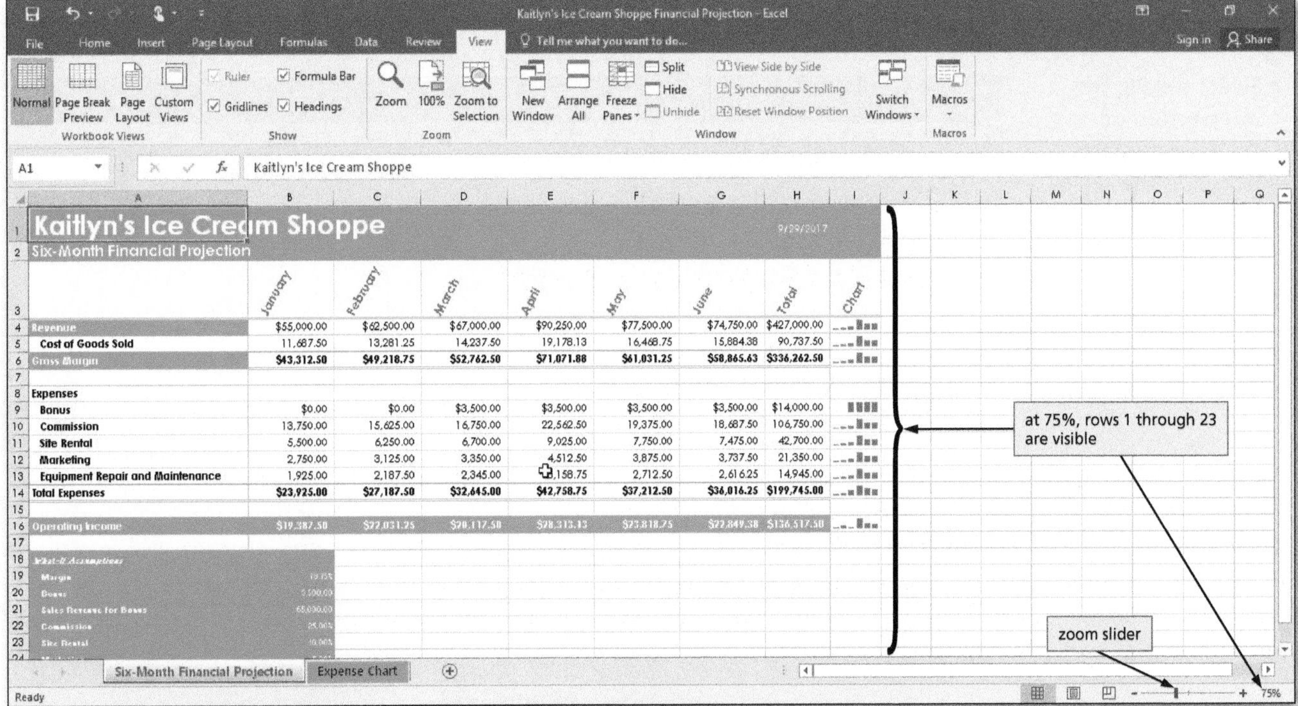

Figure 3–71

- Click the Zoom Out button on the status bar until the worksheet is displayed at 70% and all worksheet content is visible (Figure 3–72). The number of columns and rows appearing on your screen may differ from Figure 3–72.

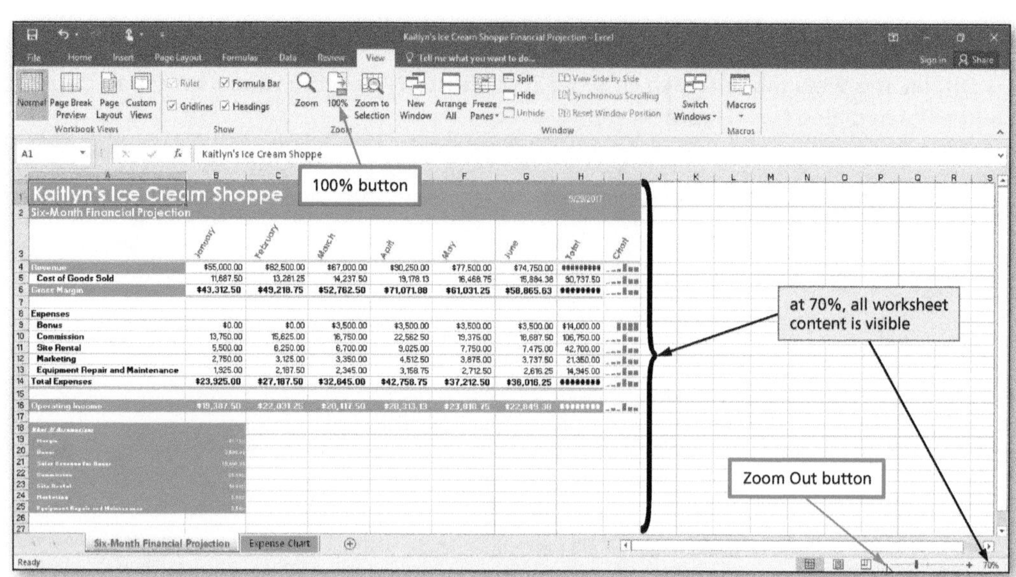

Figure 3–72

- Click the 100% button (View tab | Zoom group) to display the worksheet at 100%.

Other Ways

1. Drag zoom slider to increase or decrease zoom level

To Split a Window into Panes

When working with a large worksheet, you can split the window into two or four panes to view different parts of the worksheet at the same time. ***Why?*** *Splitting the Excel window into four panes at cell E8 allows you to view all four corners of the worksheet simultaneously.* The following steps split the Excel window into four panes.

- Select cell E8, the intersection of the four proposed panes, as the cell at which to split the window.
- If necessary, display the View tab (Figure 3–73).

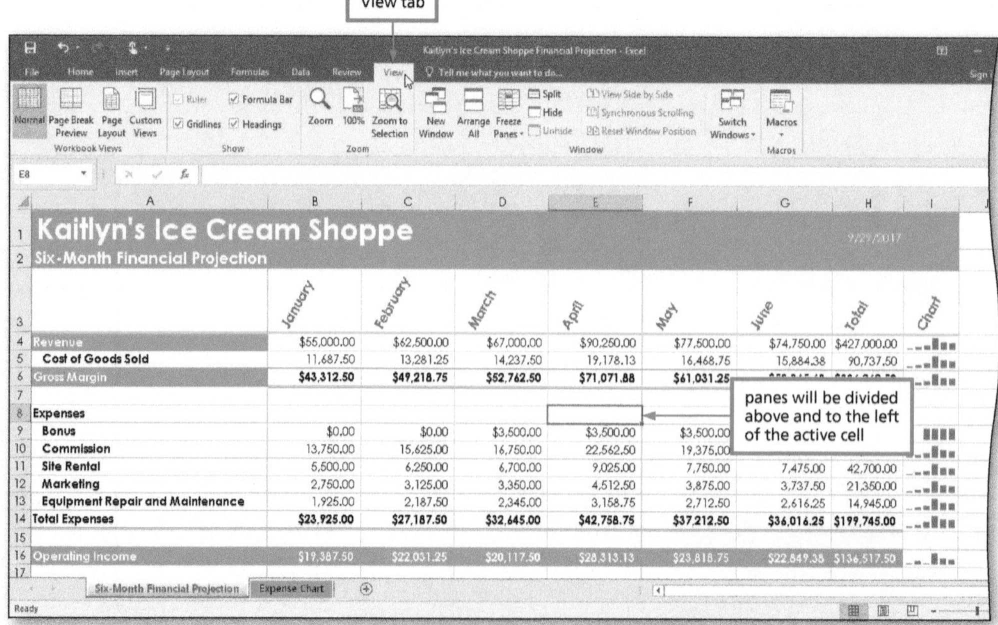

Figure 3–73

2

- Click the Split button (View tab | Window group) to divide the window into four panes.
- Use the scroll arrows to show the four corners of the worksheet at the same time (Figure 3–74).

Q&A

What is shown in the four panes?

The four panes in Figure 3–74 show the following: (1) range A1:D7 in the upper-left pane; (2) range E1:J7 in the upper-right pane; (3) range A17:D25 in the lower-left pane; and (4) range E17:J25 in the lower-right pane. The vertical split bar is the vertical bar running up and down the middle of the window. The horizontal split bar is the horizontal bar running across the middle of the window. If you use the scroll bars below the window, you will see that the panes split by the horizontal split bar scroll together horizontally. The panes split by the vertical split bar scroll together vertically when using the scroll bars to the right of the window. To resize the panes, drag either split bar to the desired location.

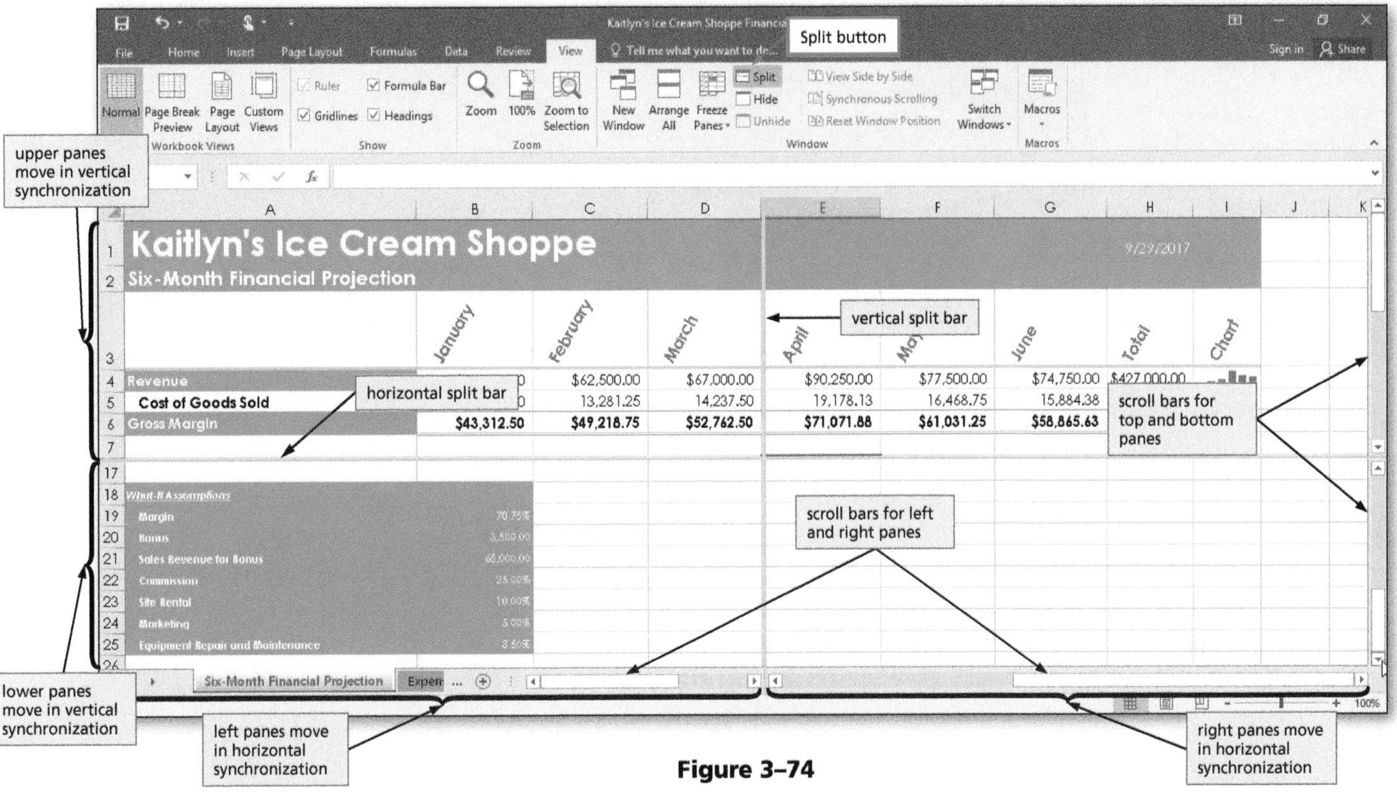

Figure 3–74

To Remove the Panes from the Window

The following step removes the panes from the window.

1. Click the Split button (View tab | Window group) to remove the four panes from the window.

Other Ways

1. Double-click intersection of horizontal and vertical split bars

To Freeze Worksheet Columns and Rows

1 ENTER HEADINGS & DATA | 2 ENTER FORMULAS & FUNCTIONS | 3 CREATE SPARKLINE CHARTS
4 FORMAT WORKSHEET | 5 CREATE COLUMN CHART | 6 CHANGE VIEWS | 7 ASK WHAT-IF QUESTIONS

Why? Freezing worksheet columns and rows is a useful technique for viewing large worksheets that extend beyond the window. Normally, when you scroll down or to the right, the column content in the top rows and the row content in the leftmost columns no longer appear on the screen. When the content of these rows and/or columns helps to identify or define other content still visible on the worksheet, it can make it difficult to remember what the numbers in the visible cells represent. To alleviate this problem, Excel allows you to freeze columns and rows, so that their content, typically column or row titles, remains on the screen, no matter how far down or to the right you scroll. You also may wish to keep numbers visible that you need to see when making changes to content in another part of the worksheet, such as the revenue, cost of goods sold, and gross margin information in rows 4 through 6. The following steps use the Freeze Panes button (View tab | Window group) to freeze the worksheet title and column titles in row 3, and the row titles in column A.

- Scroll the worksheet until Excel displays row 3 as the first row and column A as the first column on the screen.
- Select cell B4 as the cell on which to freeze panes.
- Click the Freeze Panes button (View tab | Window group) to display the Freeze Panes gallery (Figure 3–75).

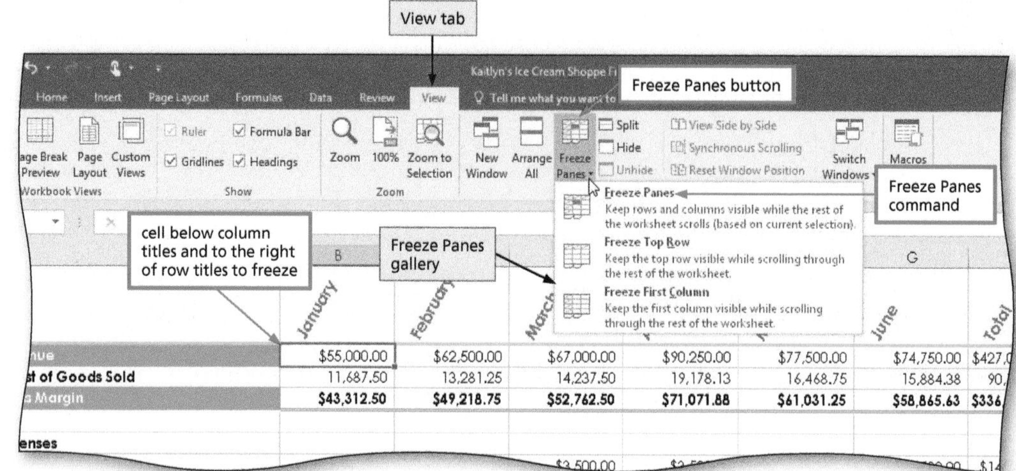

Figure 3–75

Q&A Why should I ensure that row 3 is the first row visible?
Before freezing the titles, it is important to align the first row that you want frozen with the top of the worksheet. For example, if you used the Freeze Panes button in cell B4 while displaying row 1, then Excel would freeze and display the worksheet title and subtitle, leaving only a few rows of data visible in the Six-Month Financial Projection area of the worksheet. To ensure that you can view as much data as possible, always scroll to a row that maximizes the view of your important data before freezing panes.

- Click Freeze Panes in the Freeze Panes gallery to freeze rows and columns to the left and above the selected cell, column A and row 3 in this case.
- Scroll down in the worksheet until row 9 is displayed directly below row 3 (Figure 3–76).

Q&A What happens after I click the Freeze Panes command?
Excel displays a thin, dark gray line on the right side of column A, indicating the split between the frozen row titles in column A and the rest of the worksheet. It also displays a thin, dark gray line below row 3, indicating the split between the frozen column titles in row 3 and the rest of the worksheet. Scrolling down or to the right in the worksheet will not scroll the content of row 3 or column A off the screen (Figure 3–76).

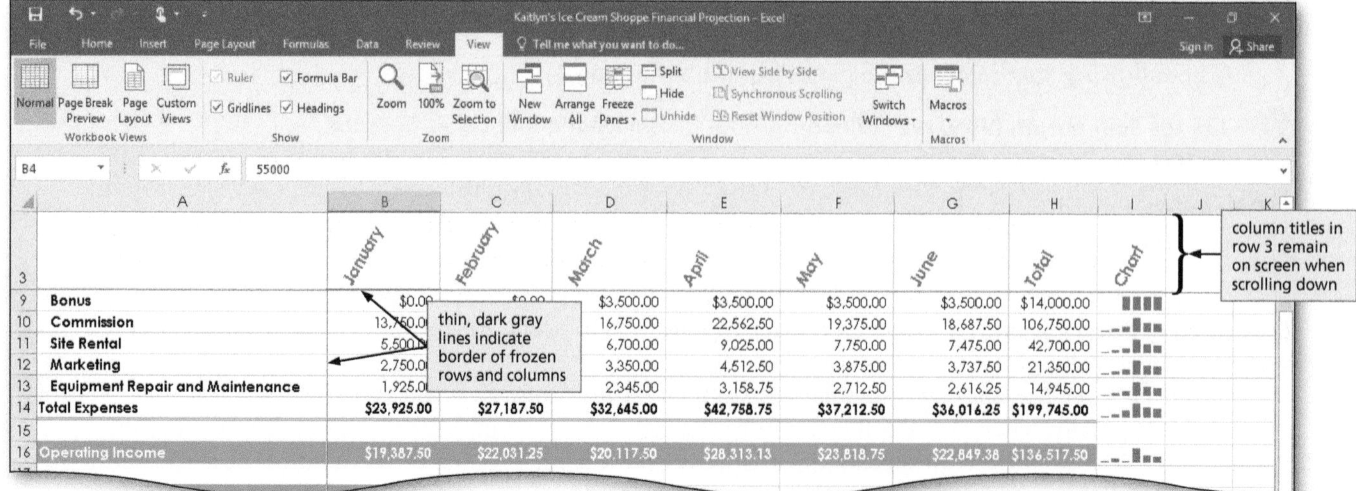

Figure 3–76

To Unfreeze the Worksheet Columns and Rows

Why? Keep columns and rows frozen only as long as you need to view the worksheet in that configuration. The following steps unfreeze the titles in column A and row 3 to allow you to work with the worksheet without frozen rows and columns, or to freeze the worksheet at a different location.

1. Press CTRL+HOME to select cell B4 and view the upper-left corner of the screen.
2. Click the Freeze Panes button (View tab | Window group) to display the Freeze Panes gallery.
3. Click Unfreeze Panes in the Freeze Panes gallery to unfreeze the frozen columns and rows.
4. Display the Home tab.
5. Save the workbook again on the same storage location with the same file name.

Q&A Why does pressing CTRL+HOME select cell B4?
When the titles are frozen and you press CTRL+HOME, Excel selects the upper-leftmost cell of the unfrozen section of the worksheet. For example, in Step 1 of the previous steps, Excel selected cell B4. When the titles are unfrozen, pressing CTRL+HOME selects cell A1.

BTW
Freezing Titles
If you want to freeze only column headings, select the appropriate cell in column A before you click the Freeze Panes button (View tab | Window group). If you want to freeze only row titles, select the appropriate cell in row 1 before you click the Freeze Panes button. To freeze both column headings and row titles, select the cell that is the intersection of the column and row titles before you click the Freeze Panes button.

What-If Analysis

The automatic recalculation feature of Excel is a powerful tool that can be used to analyze worksheet data. Using Excel to scrutinize the impact of changing values in cells that are referenced by formulas in other cells is called **what-if analysis** or sensitivity analysis. When new data is entered, Excel not only recalculates all formulas in a worksheet but also redraws any associated charts.

In the workbook created in this module, many of the formulas are dependent on the assumptions in the range B19:B25. Thus, if you change any of the assumption values, Excel recalculates all formulas. Excel redraws the clustered column chart as well, because it is based on these numbers.

To Analyze Data in a Worksheet by Changing Values

1 ENTER HEADINGS & DATA | 2 ENTER FORMULAS & FUNCTIONS | 3 CREATE SPARKLINE CHARTS
4 FORMAT WORKSHEET | 5 CREATE COLUMN CHART | 6 CHANGE VIEWS | 7 ASK WHAT-IF QUESTIONS

Why? The effect of changing one or more values in the What-If Assumptions table — essentially posing what-if questions — allows you to review the results of different scenarios. In this case, you are going to examine what would happen to the six-month operating income (cell H16) if the following changes were made in the What-If Assumptions table: Bonus $3,500.00 to $5,000.00; Commission 25.00% to 22.50%; Equipment Repair and Maintenance 3.50% to 4.00%. To answer a question like this, you need to change only the second, fourth, and seventh values in the What-If Assumptions table. The following step splits the screen, which allows you to view income and expense figures simultaneously, and then changes values in the worksheet to answer a what-if question. When a new value is entered, Excel recalculates the formulas in the worksheet and redraws the clustered column chart to reflect the new data.

- Scroll the worksheet so that row 4 is the first row visible on the worksheet.
- Click in cell A7 to select the row above which to split the window.
- Click the Split button (View tab | Window group) to split the window after row 6.
- Use the scroll arrows in the lower-right pane to scroll the window content until row 9 is the first row visible in the lower part of the screen, as shown in Figure 3–77.
- Enter **5,000** in cell B20, **22.50%** in cell B22, and **4.00%** in cell B25 (Figure 3–77), which causes the six-month operating income in cell H16 to increase from $136,517.50 to $139,057.50.
- Save the workbook again on the same storage location with the same file name.

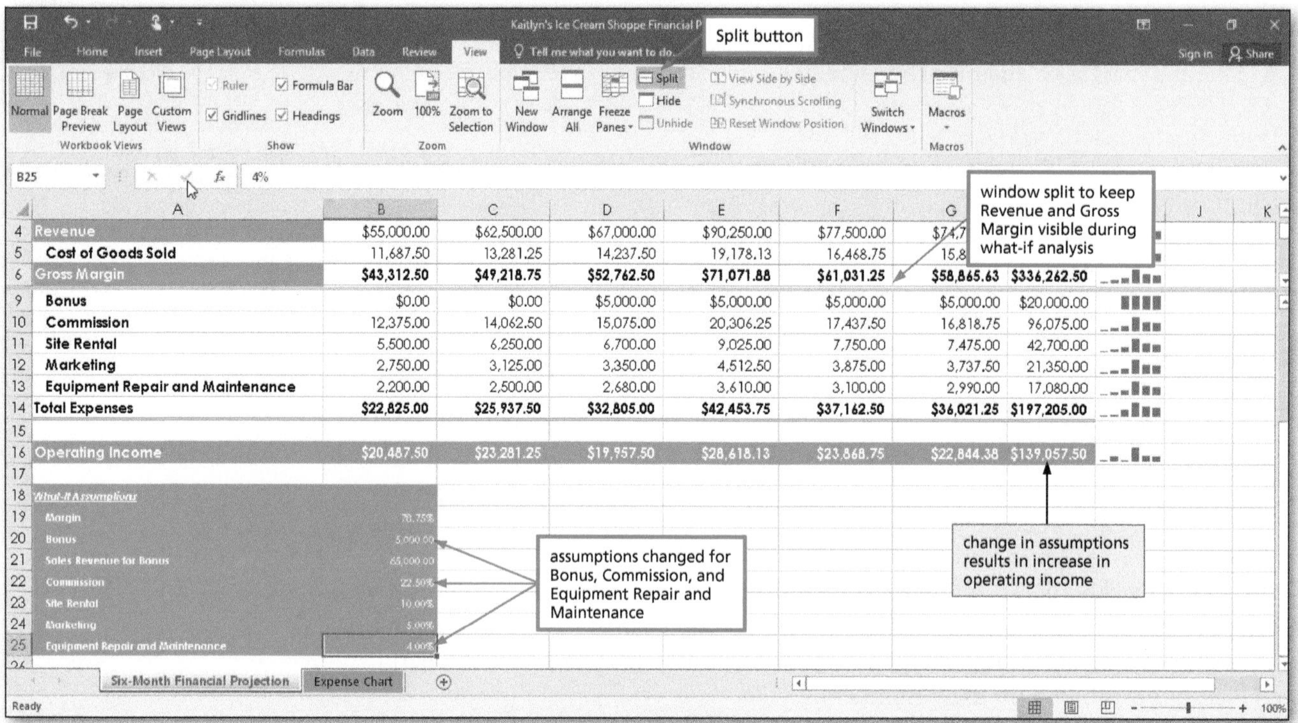

Figure 3–77

To Goal Seek

Why? *If you know the result you want a formula to produce, you can use goal seeking to determine the value of a cell on which the formula depends.* The previous step, which made changes to the What-If Assumptions table, resulted in an operating income that approaches but does not reach $145,000.00. The following steps use the Goal Seek command (Data tab | Forecast group) to determine what Site Rental percentage (cell B23), in conjunction with the earlier changes in assumptions, will yield a six-month operating income of $145,000 in cell H16, rather than the $139,057.50 calculated in the previous set of steps.

1

- If necessary, use the scroll arrows in the lower pane to ensure that you can view all of the What-If Assumptions table and the Operating Income figures.
- Select cell H16, the cell that contains the six-month operating income.
- Display the Data tab and then click the 'What-If Analysis' button (Data tab | Forecast group) to display the What-If Analysis menu (Figure 3–78).

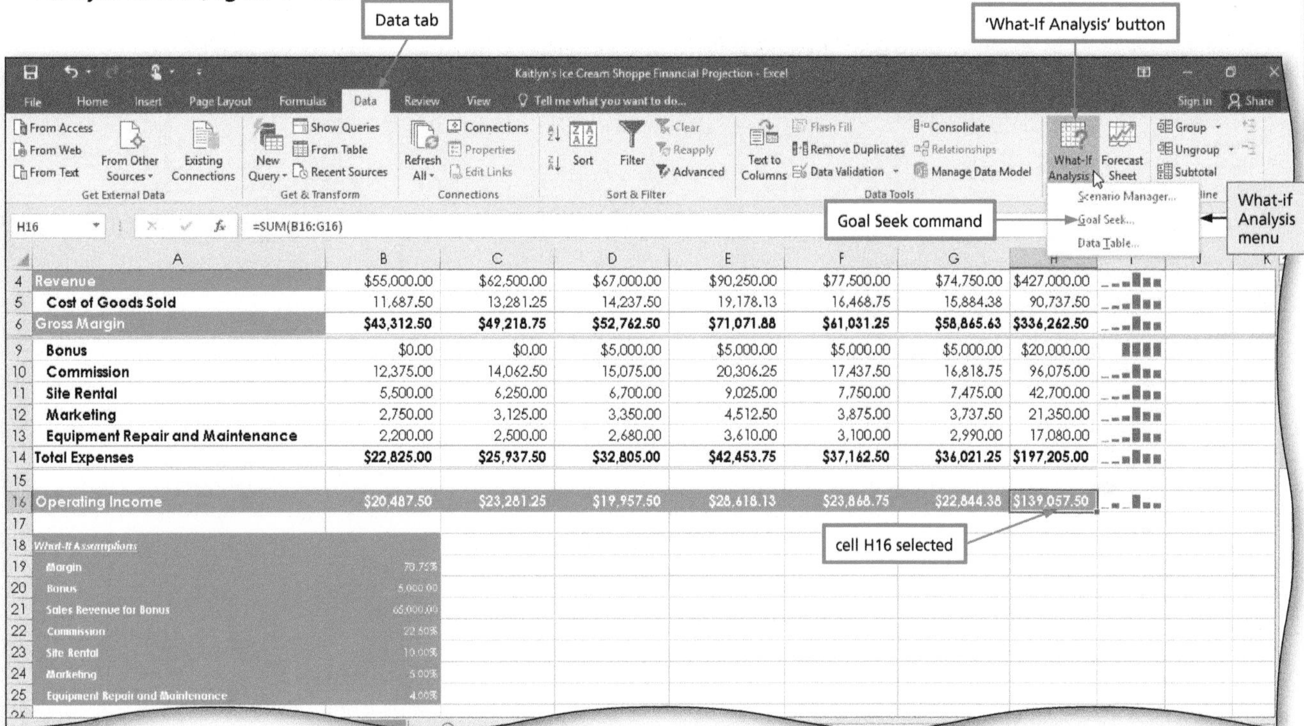

Figure 3–78

2

- Click Goal Seek to display the Goal Seek dialog box with the Set cell box set to the selected cell, H16 in this case.
- Click the To value text box, type **145,000** and then click the 'By changing cell' box to select the 'By changing cell' box.
- Click cell B23 on the worksheet to assign the current cell, B23 in this case, to the 'By changing cell' box (Figure 3–79).

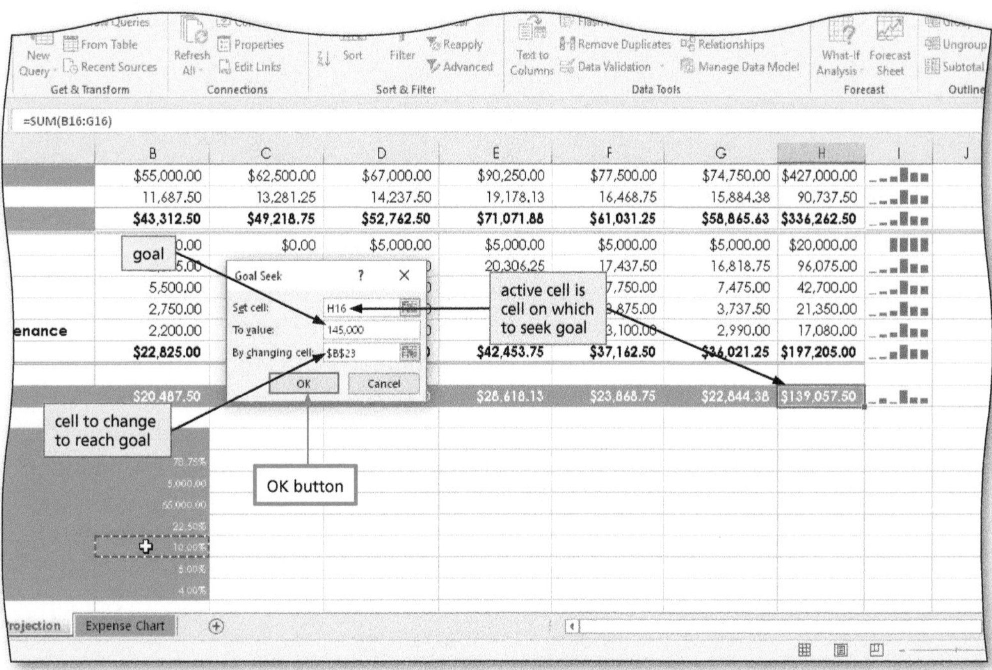

Figure 3–79

- Click the OK button (Goal Seek dialog box) to goal seek for the sought-after value in the To value text box, $145,000.00 in cell H16 in this case (Figure 3–80).

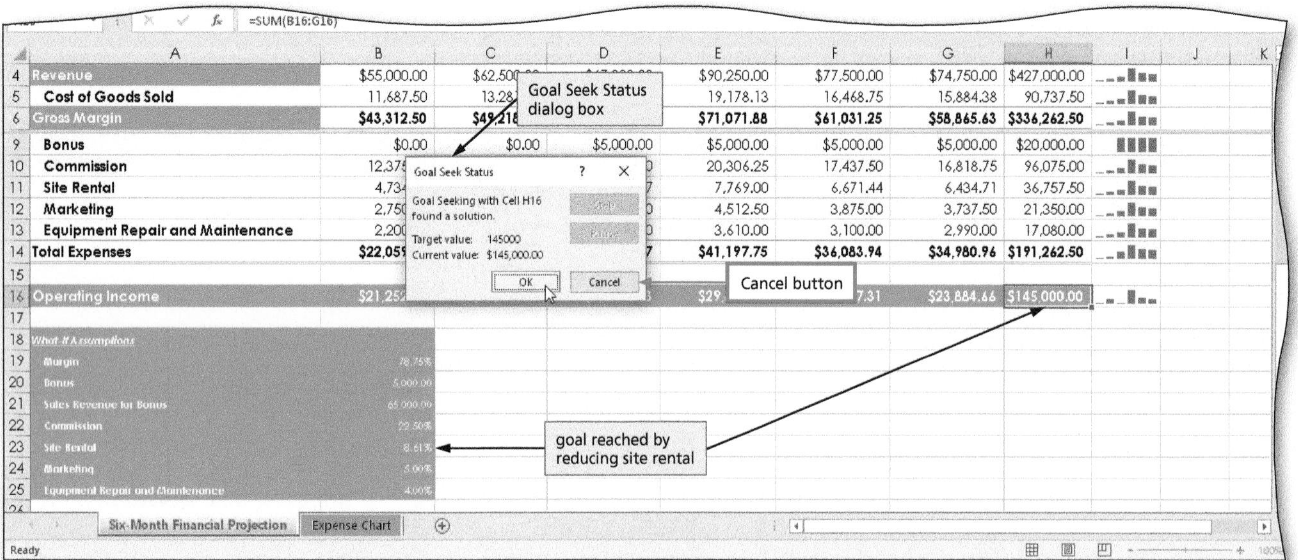

Figure 3–80

Q&A What happens when I click the OK button?
Excel changes cell H16 from $139,057.50 to the desired value of $145,000.00. More importantly, Excel changes the Site Rental assumption in cell B23 from 10.00% to 8.61% (Figure 3–80). Excel also displays the Goal Seek Status dialog box. If you click the OK button, Excel keeps the new values in the worksheet. If you click the Cancel button, Excel redisplays the original values.

- Click the Cancel button in the Goal Seek Status dialog box to redisplay the original values in the worksheet.

- Click the Split button (View tab | Window group) to remove the two panes from the window.

Goal Seeking

Goal seeking assumes you can change the value of only one cell referenced directly or indirectly to reach a specific goal for a value in another cell. In this example, to change the six-month operating income in cell H16 to $145,000.00, the Site Rental percentage in cell B23 must decrease by 1.39% from 10.00% to 8.61%.

You can see from this goal seeking example that the cell to change (cell B23) does not have to be referenced directly in the formula or function. For example, the six-month operating income in cell H16 is calculated by the function =SUM(B16:G16). Cell B23 is not referenced in this function. Instead, cell B23 is referenced in the formulas in row 11, on which the monthly operating incomes in row 16 are based. By tracing the formulas and functions, Excel can obtain the desired six-month operating income by varying the value for the Site Rental assumption.

Insights

The Insights feature in Excel uses the Bing search engine and other Internet resources to help you locate more information about the content in your workbooks. One common use of this feature is to look up the definition of a word. When looking up a definition, Excel uses contextual data so that it can return the most relevant information.

1 ENTER HEADINGS & DATA | 2 ENTER FORMULAS & FUNCTIONS | 3 CREATE SPARKLINE CHARTS
4 FORMAT WORKSHEET | 5 CREATE COLUMN CHART | 6 CHANGE VIEWS | **7 ASK WHAT-IF QUESTIONS**

To Use the Smart Lookup Insight

Smart Lookup uses Bing and other Internet resources to find useful information about text in your spreadsheet and then displays that information in the Insights task pane. ***Why?*** *If you need additional information about some terminology in a workbook you are creating or viewing, Smart Lookup can provide that information.* The following steps use Smart Lookup to look up information about the text in cell A6.

- Select cell A6.
- Display the Review tab and then click Smart Lookup (Review tab | Insights group) to display the Insights task pane containing information about the text in the selected cell (Figure 3–81).

Q&A Why did I see a 'We value your privacy' message?
This message appears the first time you use the Smart Lookup insight. If you agree to the terms, click the Got it button to continue.

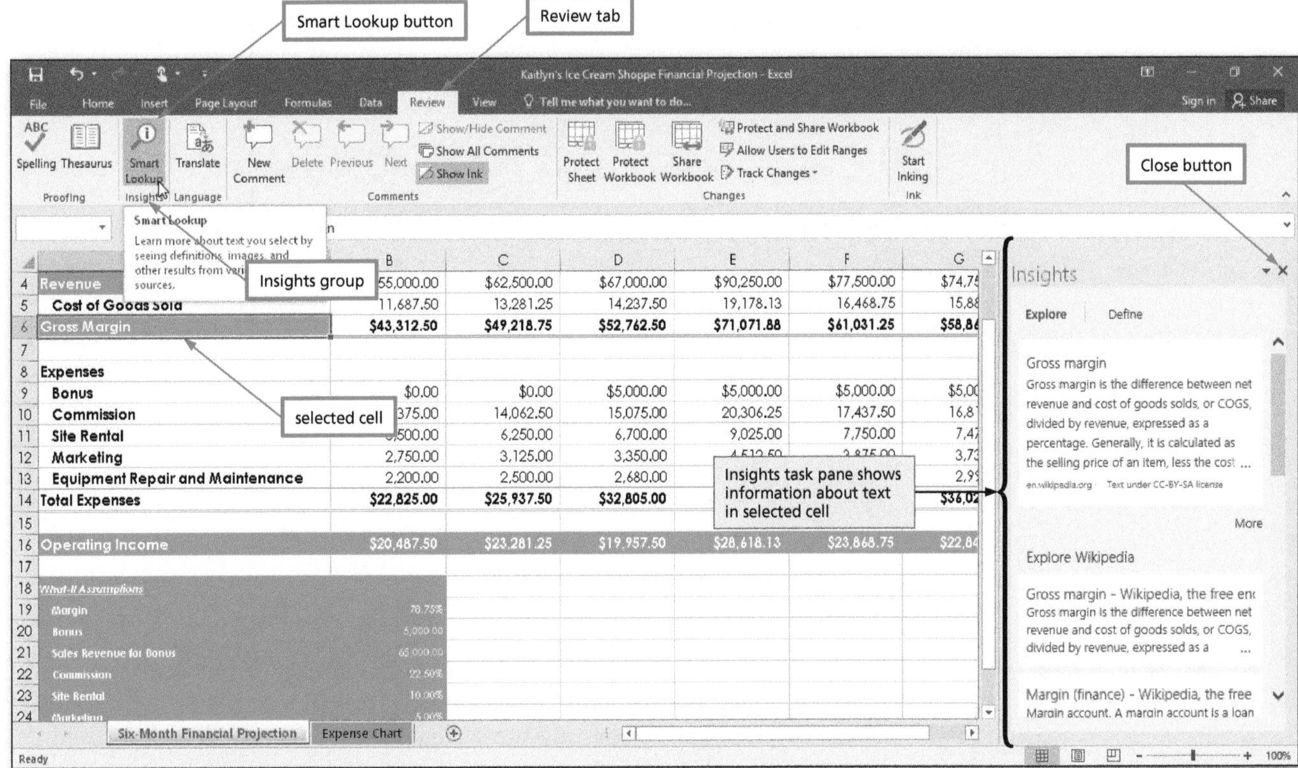

Figure 3–81

- Click the Close button on the Insights task pane to close the task pane.
- If desired, sign out of your Microsoft account.
- Exit Excel.

Accessibility Features

Excel provides a utility that can be used to check a workbook for potential issues related to **accessibility**. Accessibility refers to the practice of removing barriers that may prevent individuals with disabilities from interacting with your data or the app. To use the Check Accessibility command, click File on the ribbon to open the Backstage view, click the Info tab, click the 'Check for Issues' button, and then click Check Accessibility. Excel will check your workbook for content that could prove difficult for people with disabilities to read, either alone or with adaptive tools. The resulting report (Figure 3–82 shows an example) will identify issues and offer suggestions for addressing the reported issues.

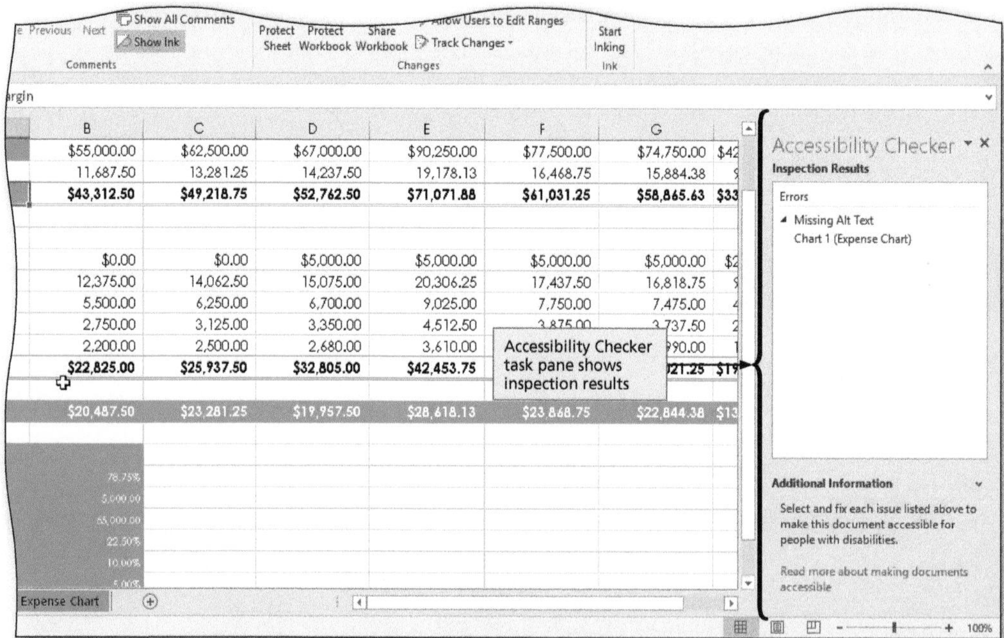

Figure 3–82

Summary

In this module, you learned how to use Excel to create a six-month financial projection workbook. Topics covered included rotating text in a cell, creating a series of month names, entering and formatting the system date, using absolute and mixed cell references, using the IF function, creating and changing sparkline charts, using the format painter, creating a clustered column chart, using chart filters, reordering sheet tabs, changing the worksheet view, freezing and unfreezing rows and columns, answering what-if questions, goal seeking, using Smart Lookup, and understanding accessibility features.

CONSIDER THIS: PLAN AHEAD

What decisions will you need to make when creating your next worksheet to evaluate and analyze data using what-if analysis?

Use these guidelines as you complete the assignments in this module and create your own worksheets for evaluating and analyzing data outside of this class.

1. Determine the workbook structure.
   a) Determine the data you will need for your worksheet.
   b) Determine the layout of your data on the worksheet.
   c) Determine the layout of the assumptions table on the worksheet.
   d) Determine the location and features of any charts.
2. Create the worksheet.
   a) Enter titles, subtitles, and headings.
   b) Enter data, functions, and formulas.
3. Format the worksheet.
   a) Format the titles, subtitles, and headings.
   b) Format the numbers as necessary.
   c) Format the text.
4. Create and use charts.
   a) Select data to chart.
   b) Select a chart type for selected data.
   c) Format the chart elements.
   d) Filter charts if necessary to view subsets of data.
5. Perform what-if analyses.
   a) Adjust values in the assumptions table to review scenarios of interest.
   b) Use Goal Seek to determine how to adjust a variable value to reach a particular goal or outcome.

Apply Your Knowledge

Reinforce the skills and apply the concepts you learned in this module.

Understanding Logical Tests and Absolute Cell Referencing

Note: To complete this assignment, you will be required to use the Data Files. Please contact your instructor for information about accessing the required files.

Instructions Part 1: For each of the following logical tests, indicate whether an IF function in Excel would return a value of True or False; given the following cell values: C2 = 88; H12 = 15; L3 = 24; M14 = 150; and G4 = 5.

1. C2 > H12 Returned value: ______________
2. L3 = G4 Returned value: ______________
3. M14 + 15 * H12 / 10 <= L3 Returned value: ______________
4. M14 – G4 < H12 / C2 Returned value: ______________
5. (C2 + H12) * 2 >= L3 – (C2 / 4) * 2 Returned value: ______________
6. L3 + 300 > H12 * G4 + 10 Returned value: ______________
7. G4 * M14 >= 2 * (H12 + 25) Returned value: ______________
8. H12 = 10 * (C2 / 8) Returned value: ______________

Instructions Part 2: Write cell L23 as a relative reference, absolute reference, mixed reference with the column varying, and mixed reference with the row varying.

______________ ______________ ______________ ______________

Instructions Part 3: Run Excel. Open the workbook Apply 3-1 Absolute Cell References. You will re-create the numerical grid pictured in Figure 3–83.

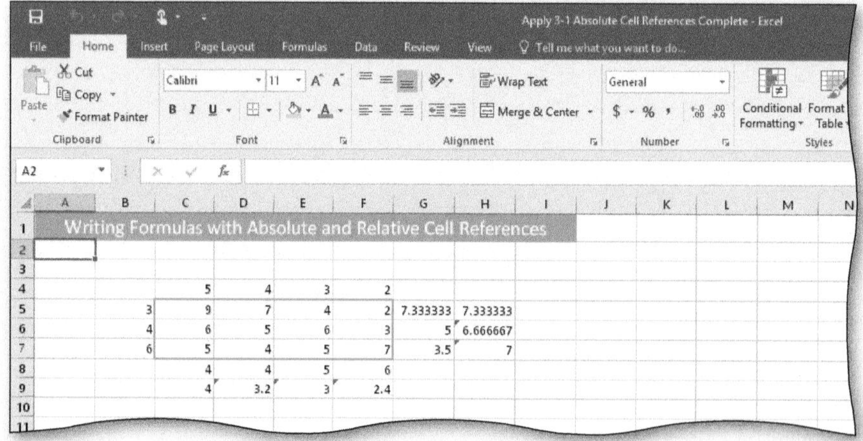

Figure 3–83

Perform the following tasks:

1. Enter a formula in cell C8 that divides the sum of cells C5 through C7 by cell C4. Write the formula so that when you copy it to cells D8:F8, Excel adjusts all the cell references according to the destination cells. Verify your formula by checking it against the values found in cells C8, D8, E8, and F8 in Figure 3–83.

2. Enter a formula in cell G5 that divides the sum of cells C5 through F5 by cell B5. Write the formula so that when you copy the formula to cells G6 and G7, Excel adjusts all the cell references according to the destination cells. Verify your formula by checking it against the values found in cells G5, G6, and G7 in Figure 3–83.
3. Enter a formula in cell C9 that divides the sum of cells C5 through C7 by cell C4. Write the formula using an absolute cell reference so that when you copy the formula to cells D9:F9, cell C4 remains absolute. Verify your formula by checking it against the values found in cells C9, D9, E9, and F9 in Figure 3–83.
4. Enter a formula in cell H5 that divides the sum of cells C5:F5 by cell B5. Write the formula using an absolute cell reference so that when you copy the formula to cells H6 and H7, cell B5 remains absolute. Verify your formula by checking it with the values found in cells H5, H6, and H7 in Figure 3–83.
5. Apply the worksheet name, Cell References, to the sheet tab and apply the Orange, Accent 2 Theme color to the sheet tab.
6. If requested by your instructor, add a dash followed by your name to the worksheet title in cell A1.
7. Save the workbook using the file name, Apply 3-1 Absolute Cell References Complete. Submit the revised workbook as specified by your instructor.
8. How would you rewrite the formula in cell H5 using relative and mixed cell references only, to come up with the same result as showing in Figure 3–83, and to produce the results currently showing in cells G6 and G7 in cells H6 and H7 when the formula in cell H5 is copied to those cells?

Extend Your Knowledge

Extend the skills you learned in this module and experiment with new skills. You may need to use Help to complete the assignment.

The Fill Handle and Nested IF Functions

Note: To complete this assignment, you will be required to use the Data Files. Please contact your instructor for information about accessing the required files.

Perform the following tasks:

Instructions Part 1: Run Excel. Open the workbook Extend 3-1 Fill and IF. If necessary, make Fill the active sheet.

1. Use the fill handle on one column at a time to propagate the 12 series through row 14, as shown in Figure 3–84. (*Hint:* Search in Help to learn more about the fill handle and Auto Fill.) In cells O2:O13, indicate the actions used with the fill handle to propagate the series. For instance, in cell O2, enter `Drag`. For instances where you need to select something other than the cell in row 2 prior to using the fill handle, enter the selection and then the drag action, `A2:A3 Drag` for example.
2. Select cell D20. While holding down the CTRL key, one at a time drag the fill handle three cells to the right, to the left, up, and down to generate four series of numbers beginning with zero and incremented by one.
3. Select cell H20. Point to the cell border so that the pointer changes to a plus sign with four arrows. Drag the pointer down to cell H22 to move the contents of cell H20 to cell H22.
4. If necessary, select cell H22. Point to the cell border so that the pointer changes to a plus sign with four arrows. While holding down the CTRL key, drag the pointer to cell K22 to copy the contents of cell H22 to cell K22.

Continued >

Extend Your Knowledge *continued*

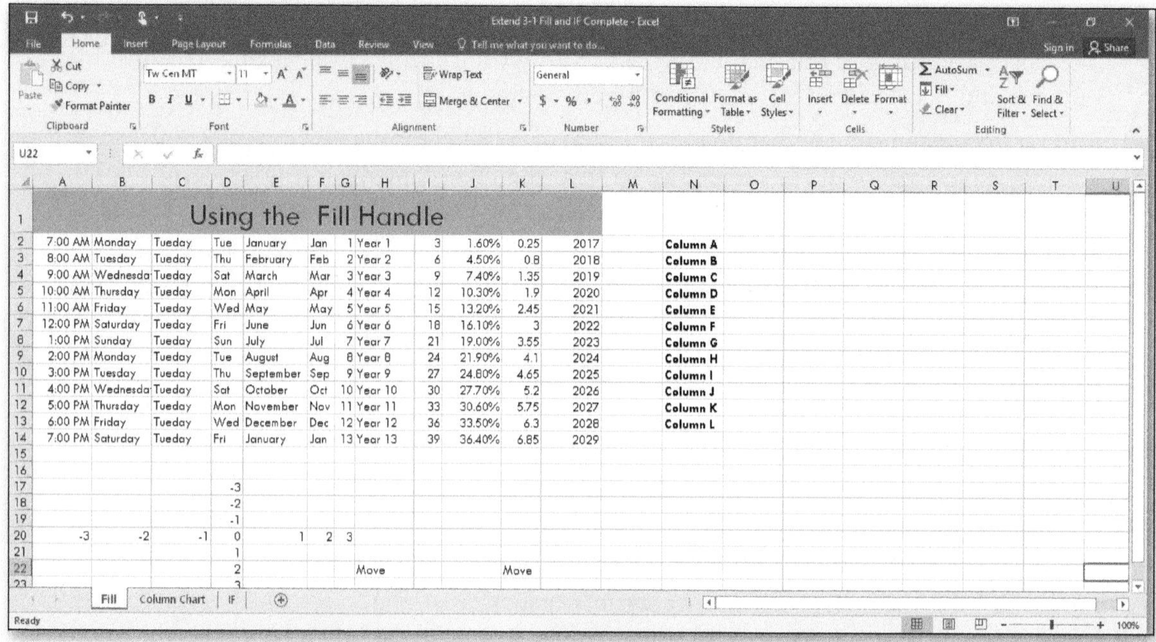

Figure 3–84

5. Select cell K20. Drag the fill handle in to the center of cell K20 until that the cell is shaded and the cell contents are deleted.
6. Select cell range H2:I14, and insert a 3-D column chart on a new sheet.
7. Change the chart title to Annual Breakdown.
8. Add a data table with no legend keys to the chart.
9. Apply the chart sheet name, Column Chart, to the sheet and move the sheet to follow the Fill sheet.
10. Save the workbook using the file name, Extend 3-1 Fill and IF Complete.

Instructions Part 2: Switch to the IF sheet in the Extend 3-1 Fill and IF Complete workbook.

1. Write an IF function in cell C2 that assigns a grade of 'Pass' if the score in cell B2 is 50 or above, and a grade of 'Fail' if the score in cell B2 is below 50. Copy this function to cells C3:C18.
2. Write a nested IF function in cell D2 that assigns a grade of A for scores between 80 and 100, a grade of B for scores between 65 and 79, a grade of C for scores between 50 and 64, and a grade of F for scores below 50. (*Hint*: Search in Help for nested IF when constructing your function.) Copy this function to cells D3:D18.
3. If requested by your instructor, change the student number in cell A3 on the IF sheet to your student number.
4. Save the workbook and submit the revised workbook as specified by your instructor.
5. Students who do not take a test receive a score of NS. How would you include a score of NS as a grade in each of Steps 1 and 2?

STUDENT ASSIGNMENTS

Expand Your World

Create a solution that uses cloud or web technologies by learning and investigating on your own from general guidance.

Analyzing and Graphing Development Indicators

Note: To complete this assignment, you will be required to use the Data Files. Please contact your instructor for information about accessing the required files.

Instructions: You are working as part of a group creating a report on historical education trends in the developing nation of Mali, comparing three related development indicators concerning school enrollment over time. Your task is to format the worksheet containing the historical data, chart the historical education indicators, and make the chart available to your group using OneDrive. Run Excel and then open the workbook, Expand 3-1 Education Indicators.

Perform the following tasks:

1. Save the workbook using the file name, Expand 3-1 Education Indicators Charted.
2. Format the worksheet using techniques you have learned to present the data in a visually appealing form.
3. Create charts that present the data for each of the three indicators. Think about what interested you in these indicators in the first place, and decide which chart types will best present the data. (*Hint:* If you are not sure which types to use, consider selecting the data and using the Recommended Chart button to narrow down and preview suitable choices.) Format the charts to best present the data in a clear, attractive format.
4. Give each worksheet a descriptive name and color the tabs using theme colors. Reorder the sheets so that the data table appears first, followed by the charts.
5. If requested by your instructor, export the file to OneDrive.
6. Submit the revised workbook as specified by your instructor.
7. Justify your choice of chart types in Step 3. Explain why you selected these types over other suitable choices.

In the Labs

Design, create, modify and/or use a workbook following the guidelines, concepts, and skills presented in this module. Labs 1 and 2, which increase in difficulty, require you to create solutions based on what you learned in the module; Lab 3 requires you to apply your creative thinking and problem-solving skills to design and implement a solution.

Lab 1: Eight-Year Financial Projection

Problem: Your supervisor in the finance department at August Online Technology has asked you to create a worksheet for the flagship product that will project the annual gross margin, total expenses, operating income, income taxes, and net income for the next eight years based on the assumptions in Table 3–9. The desired worksheet is shown in Figure 3–85.

Table 3–9 August Online Technology Financial Projection Assumptions	
Units Sold in Prior Year	235,411
Unit Cost	$150.00
Annual Sales Growth	3.25%
Annual Price Increase	3.00%
Margin	29.90%

Continued >

In the Labs *continued*

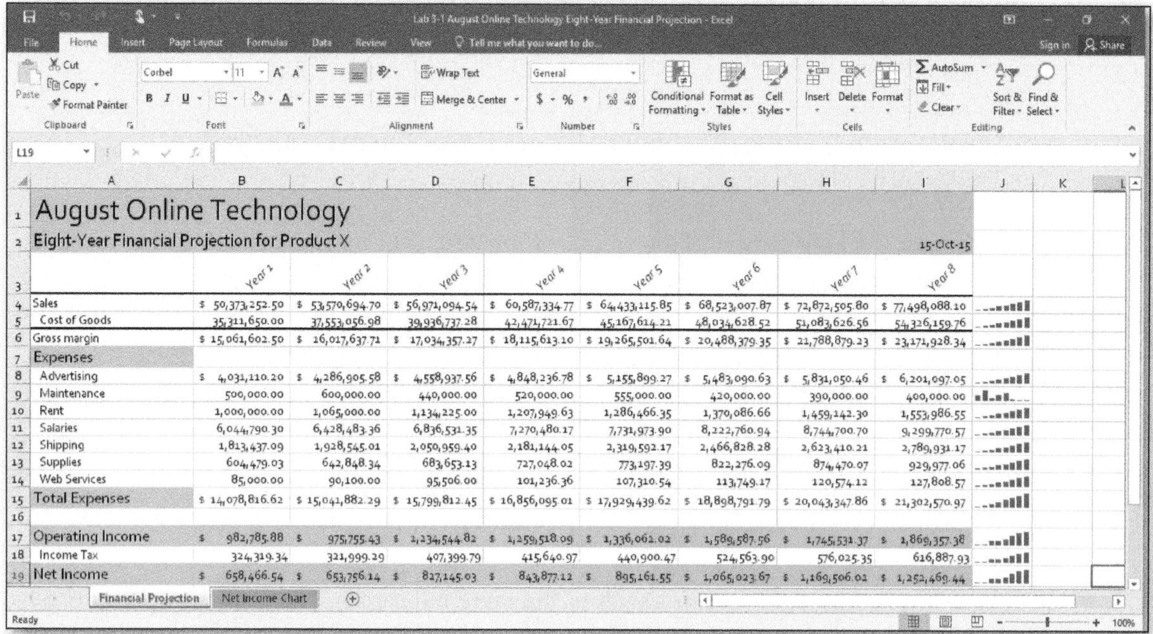

August Online Technology

Eight-Year Financial Projection for Product X 15-Oct-15

	Year 1	Year 2	Year 3	Year 4	Year 5	Year 6	Year 7	Year 8
Sales	$ 50,373,252.50	$ 53,570,694.70	$ 56,971,094.54	$ 60,587,334.77	$ 64,433,115.85	$ 68,523,007.87	$ 72,872,505.80	$ 77,498,088.10
Cost of Goods	35,311,650.00	37,553,056.98	39,936,737.28	42,471,721.67	45,167,614.21	48,034,628.52	51,083,626.56	54,326,159.76
Gross margin	$ 15,061,602.50	$ 16,017,637.71	$ 17,034,357.27	$ 18,115,613.10	$ 19,265,501.64	$ 20,488,379.35	$ 21,788,879.23	$ 23,171,928.34
Expenses								
Advertising	$ 4,031,110.20	$ 4,286,905.58	$ 4,558,937.56	$ 4,848,236.78	$ 5,155,899.27	$ 5,483,090.63	$ 5,831,050.46	$ 6,201,097.05
Maintenance	500,000.00	600,000.00	440,000.00	520,000.00	555,000.00	420,000.00	390,000.00	400,000.00
Rent	1,000,000.00	1,065,000.00	1,134,225.00	1,207,949.63	1,286,466.35	1,370,086.66	1,459,142.30	1,553,986.55
Salaries	6,044,790.30	6,428,483.36	6,836,531.35	7,270,480.17	7,731,973.90	8,222,760.94	8,744,700.70	9,299,770.57
Shipping	1,813,437.09	1,928,545.01	2,050,959.40	2,181,144.05	2,319,592.17	2,466,828.28	2,623,410.21	2,789,931.17
Supplies	604,479.03	642,848.34	683,653.13	727,048.02	773,197.39	822,276.09	874,470.07	929,977.06
Web Services	85,000.00	90,100.00	95,506.00	101,236.36	107,310.54	113,749.17	120,574.12	127,808.57
Total Expenses	$ 14,078,816.62	$ 15,041,882.29	$ 15,799,812.45	$ 16,856,095.01	$ 17,929,439.62	$ 18,898,791.79	$ 20,043,347.86	$ 21,302,570.97
Operating Income	$ 982,785.88	$ 975,755.43	$ 1,234,544.82	$ 1,259,518.09	$ 1,336,062.02	$ 1,589,587.56	$ 1,745,531.37	$ 1,869,357.38
Income Tax	324,319.34	321,999.29	407,399.79	415,640.97	440,900.47	524,563.90	576,025.35	616,887.93
Net Income	$ 658,466.54	$ 653,756.14	$ 827,145.03	$ 843,877.12	$ 895,161.55	$ 1,065,023.67	$ 1,169,506.02	$ 1,252,469.44

Financial Projection | Net Income Chart

Figure 3–85

Perform the following tasks:

Instructions Part 1: Run Excel, open a blank workbook, and then create the worksheet.

1. Apply the Parallax theme to the worksheet.
2. Enter the worksheet title **`August Online Technology`** in cell A1 and the subtitle **`Eight-Year Financial Projection for Product X`** in cell A2. Format the worksheet title in cell A1 to 26-point and the worksheet subtitle in cell A2 to 16-point. Enter the system date in cell I2 using the NOW function. Format the date to the 14-Mar-12 style.
3. Change the following column widths: A = 24.00 characters; B through I = 14.00 characters. Change the heights of rows 7, 15, 17, 19, and 22 to 18.00 points.
4. Enter the eight column titles Year 1 through Year 8 in the range B3:I3 by entering Year 1 in cell B3 and then dragging cell B3's fill handle through the range C3:I3. Format cell B3 as follows:

   a. Increase the font size to 12.

   b. Center and italicize it.

   c. Angle its contents 45 degrees.
5. Use the Format Painter button to copy the format assigned to cell B3 to the range C3:I3.
6. Enter the row titles, as shown in Figure 3-85, in the range A4:A19. Change the font size in cells A7, A15, A17, and A19 to 14-point. Add thick bottom borders to the ranges A3:I3 and A5:I5. Use the Increase Indent button (Home tab | Alignment group) to increase the indent of the row titles in cell A5, the range A8:A14, and cell A18.
7. If requested by your instructor, change the entry in row 14 by inserting your surname prior to the text, Web Services.
8. Enter the table title **`Assumptions`** in cell A22. Enter the assumptions in Table 3–9 in the range A23:B27. Use format symbols when entering the numbers. Change the font size of the table title in cell A22 to 14-point and underline it.

9. Select the range B4:I19 and then click the Number Format Dialog Box Launcher (Home tab | Number group) to display the Format Cells dialog box. Use the Number category (Format Cells dialog box) to assign the appropriate style that displays numbers with two decimal places and negative numbers in black font and enclosed in parentheses to the range B4:I19.
10. Complete the following entries:
    a. Year 1 Sales (cell B4) = Units Sold in Prior Year * (Unit Cost / (1 – Margin))
    b. Year 2 Sales (cell C4) = Year 1 Sales * (1 + Annual Sales Growth) * (1 + Annual Price Increase). Copy cell C4 to the range D4:I4.
    c. Year 1 Cost of Goods (cell B5) = Year 1 Sales * (1 – Margin). Copy cell B5 to the range C5:I5.
    d. Gross Margin (cell B6) = Year 1 Sales – Year 1 Cost of Goods. Copy cell B6 to the range C6:I6.
    e. Year 1 Advertising (cell B8) = 1250 + 8% * Year 1 Sales. Copy cell B8 to the range C8:I8.
    f. Maintenance (row 9): Year 1 = 500,000; Year 2 = 600,000; Year 3 = 440,000; Year 4 = 520,000; Year 5 = 555,000; Year 6 = 420,000; Year 7 = 390,000; Year 8 = 400,000.
    g. Year 1 Rent (cell B10) = 1,000,000
    h. Year 2 Rent (cell C10) = Year 1 Rent + (6.5% * Year 1 Rent). Copy cell C10 to the range D10:I10.
    i. Year 1 Salaries (cell B11) = 12% * Year 1 Sales. Copy cell B11 to the range C11:I11.
    j. Year 1 Shipping (cell B12) = 3.6% * Year 1 Sales. Copy cell B12 to the range C12:I12.
    k. Year 1 Supplies (cell B13) = 1.2% * Year 1 Sales. Copy cell B13 to the range C13:I13.
    l. Year 1 Web Services (cell B14) = 85,000
    m. Year 2 Web Services (cell C14) = Year 1 Web Services + (6% * Year 1 Web Services). Copy cell C14 to the range D14:I14.
    n. Year 1 Total Expenses (cell B15) = SUM(B8:B14). Copy cell B15 to the range C15:I15.
    o. Year 1 Operating Income (cell B17) = Year 1 Gross Margin – Year 1 Total Expenses. Copy cell B17 to the range C17:I17.
    p. Year 1 Income Tax (cell B18): If Year 1 Operating Income is less than 0, then Year 1 Income Tax equals 0; otherwise Year 1 Income Tax equals 33% * Year 1 Operating Income. Copy cell B18 to the range C18:I18.
    q. Year 1 Net Income (cell B19) = Year 1 Operating Income – Year 1 Income Tax. Copy cell B19 to the range C19:I19.
    r. In cell J4, insert a column sparkline chart (Insert tab | Sparklines group) for cell range B4:I4.
    s. Insert column sparkline charts in cells J5, J6, J8:J15, and J17:J19 using ranges B5:I5, B6:I6, B8:I8 – B15:I15, and B17:I17 – B19:I19 respectively.
11. Apply the Accounting number format with a dollar sign and two decimal places to the following ranges: B4:I4, B6:I6, B8:I8, B15:I15, B17:I17, and B19:I19. Apply the comma style format to the following ranges: B5:I5 and B9:I14. Apply the Number format with two decimal places and the 1000 separator to the range B18:I18.
12. Change the background colors, as shown in Figure 3–85. Use Blue, Accent 1, Lighter 40% for the background colors.
13. Save the workbook using the file name, Lab 3-1 August Online Technology Eight-Year Financial Projection.
14. Preview the worksheet. Use the Orientation button (Page Layout tab | Page Setup group) to fit the printout on one page in landscape orientation. Preview the formulas version (CTRL+`) of the worksheet in landscape orientation using the Fit to option. Press CTRL+` to instruct Excel to display the values version of the worksheet. Save the workbook again.

Continued >

In the Labs *continued*

Instructions Part 2: Create a chart to present the data, shown in Figure 3–86. If necessary, run Excel and open the workbook Lab 3-1 August Online Technology Eight-Year Financial Projection.

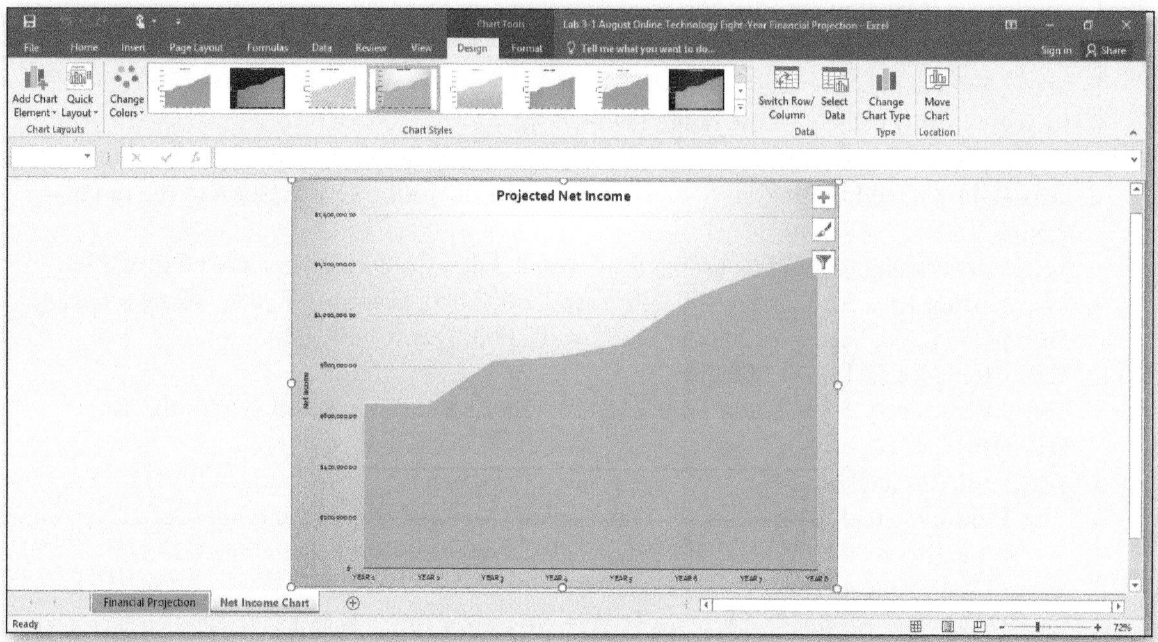

Figure 3–86

1. Use the nonadjacent ranges B3:I3 and B19:I19 to create a Stacked Area chart (*Hint:* use the Recommended Charts button). When the chart appears, click the Move Chart button to move the chart to a new sheet.
2. Change the chart title to **`Projected Net Income`**.
3. Use the Chart Elements button to add a vertical axis title. Edit the axis title text to read **`Net Income`**. Bold the axis title.
4. Change the Chart Style to Style 4 in the Chart Styles Gallery (Chart Tools Design tab | Chart Styles group). Use the 'Chart Quick Colors' button (Chart Tools Design tab | Chart Styles group) to change the color scheme to Monochromatic, Color 5.
5. Rename the sheet tabs Financial Projection and Net Income Chart. Rearrange the sheets so that the worksheet is leftmost and change the tab colors to those of your choosing.
6. Click the Financial Projection tab to return to the worksheet. Save the workbook using the same file name (Lab 3-1 August Online Technology Eight-Year Financial Projection) as defined in Part 1.

Instructions Part 3: Use Goal Seek to analyze three different sales scenarios. If necessary, open the workbook Lab 3-1 August Online Technology Eight-Year Financial Projection.

1. Divide the window into two panes between rows 6 and 7. Use the scroll bars to show both the top and bottom of the worksheet. Using the numbers in columns 2 and 3 of Table 3–10, analyze the effect of changing the annual sales growth (cell B25) and annual price increase (cell B26) on the net incomes in row 19. Record the answers for each case and submit the results in a form as requested by your instructor.

Table 3–10 August Online Technology Alternative Projections

Case	Annual Sales Growth	Annual Price Increase
1	4.25%	2.00%
2	2.25%	3.00%
3	1.25%	4.00%

2. Close the workbook without saving it and then reopen it. Use the 'What-If Analysis' button (Data tab | Forecast group) to goal seek. Determine a margin that would result in a Year 8 net income of $1,500,000. Save the workbook with your needed changes as Lab 3-1 August Online Technology Eight-Year Financial Projection GS. Submit the workbook with the new values or the results of the goal seek as requested by your instructor.
3. How would you use what-if analysis tools to determine what Annual Sales Growth you would need to achieve in order to keep prices steady over the eight-year projection period?

Lab 2: Updating a Weekly Payroll Worksheet

Note: To complete this assignment, you will be required to use the Data Files. Please contact your instructor for information about accessing the required files.

Problem: PHM Reliable Catering is a company that provides catering services to both small and large businesses. You have been asked to update the weekly payroll report to reflect changes in personnel, to update certain mandatory deductions, and to add overtime computations. The final worksheet is shown in Figure 3–87. Run Excel. Open the workbook, Lab 3-2 PHM Reliable Catering Weekly Payroll Report.

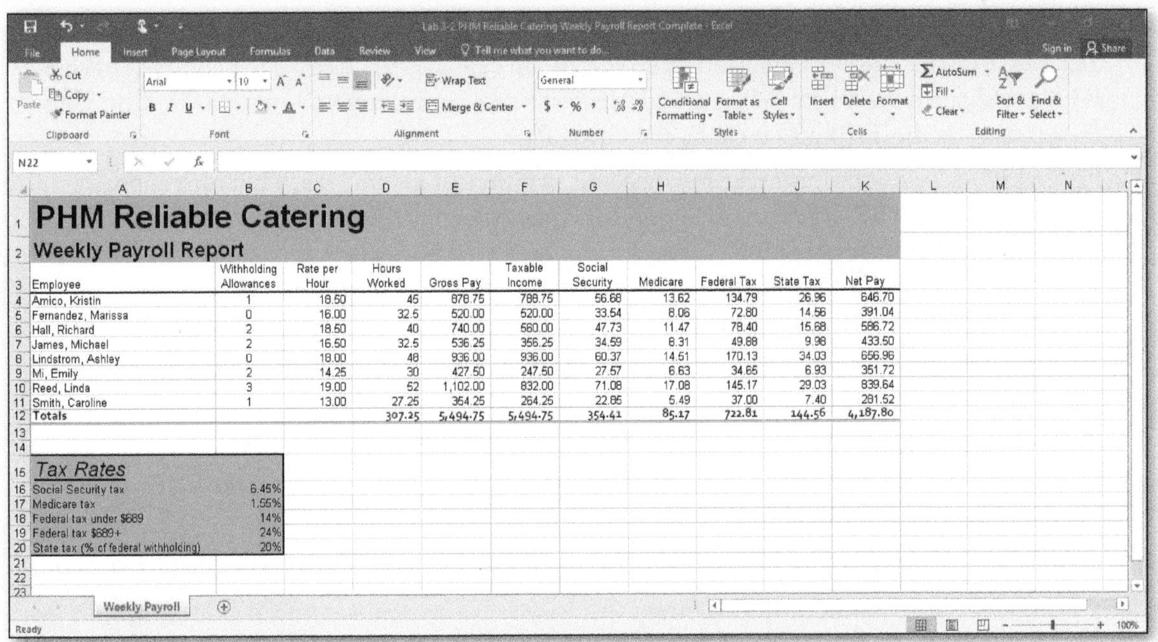

PHM Reliable Catering

Weekly Payroll Report

Employee	Withholding Allowances	Rate per Hour	Hours Worked	Gross Pay	Taxable Income	Social Security	Medicare	Federal Tax	State Tax	Net Pay
Amico, Kristin	1	18.50	45	878.75	788.75	56.68	13.62	134.79	26.96	646.70
Fernandez, Marissa	0	16.00	32.5	520.00	520.00	33.54	8.06	72.80	14.56	391.04
Hall, Richard	2	18.50	40	740.00	560.00	47.73	11.47	78.40	15.68	586.72
James, Michael	2	16.50	32.5	536.25	356.25	34.59	8.31	49.88	9.98	433.50
Lindstrom, Ashley	0	18.00	48	936.00	936.00	60.37	14.51	170.13	34.03	656.96
Mi, Emily	2	14.25	30	427.50	247.50	27.57	6.63	34.65	6.93	351.72
Reed, Linda	3	19.00	52	1,102.00	832.00	71.08	17.08	145.17	29.03	839.64
Smith, Caroline	1	13.00	27.25	354.25	264.25	22.85	5.49	37.00	7.40	281.52
Totals			307.25	5,494.75	5,494.75	354.41	85.17	722.81	144.56	4,187.80

Tax Rates	
Social Security tax	6.45%
Medicare tax	1.55%
Federal tax under $689	14%
Federal tax $689+	24%
State tax (% of federal withholding)	20%

Weekly Payroll

Figure 3–87

Continued >

In the Labs *continued*

Perform the following tasks:

1. Save the workbook using the file name, Lab 3-2 PHM Reliable Catering Weekly Payroll Report Complete.
2. Apply the Depth theme to the worksheet.
3. Delete rows 12 through 14 to remove the statistics below the Totals row.
4. Delete column B. Set column A width to 31.00 and columns B through K to 11.00. Select row 3 and set text to wrap in this row using the Wrap Text button (Home tab | Alignment group), and then set the row height to best fit.
5. Delete the record for the employee Evans, Timothy. Add two blank lines directly above the row for Mi, Emily, and add the information for the two new employees listed in Table 3–11.

Table 3–11 PHM Reliable Catering New Employee Data

Employee	Withholding Allowances	Rate Per Hour	Hours Worked
James, Michael	2	16.50	32.5
Lindstrom, Ashley	0	18.00	48

6. If requested by your instructor, replace one of the employee's names with your name.
7. If necessary, use the fill handle in cell E6 to copy the gross pay formula to the rows of the two new employees.
8. Add the Tax Rates information shown in Figure 3–87 in cells A15:B20 to your worksheet.
9. Change the font size in cell A1 to 28-point. Change the font size in cell A2 to 18-point. Change the font in cell A15 to 18-point italic and underlined. Change the row height for rows 1, 2, and 15 to best fit.
10. Insert three columns to the right of the Gross Pay column. Add the column titles **`Taxable Income`**, **`Social Security`**, and **`Medicare`** in cells F3:H3. Center the contents of cells B3:K3. Calculate the Social Security and Medicare taxes in columns G and H by multiplying the tax rates in the Tax Rates table by the Gross Pay.
11. Federal tax calculations must take into account two tiers of income tax, which are applied to the taxable income. Calculate the taxable income, which is the Gross Pay — (number of withholding allowances × $90).
12. Calculate the federal tax withheld. If an employee has a taxable income of greater than or equal to $689, then the federal tax withheld equals $110.85 plus the federal tax rate found in cell B19 multiplied by the taxable income in excess of $689. If an employees taxable income is $689 or less, the federal tax withheld equals the taxable income multiplied by the federal tax rate found in cell B18. Use the IF function to calculate the federal tax in Column I.
13. State tax is calculated as a percentage of federal tax. Use the tax rate in the Tax Rates table to calculate state tax in column J.
14. Calculate Net Pay in column K, as Gross Pay — Social Security, Medicare, Federal Tax, and State Tax.
15. Use the background color Gold, Accent 5, Darker 25% for the ranges A1:K2 and A15:B20.
16. Center the range B4:B11. Apply the currency style with two decimal places, no dollar signs, and negative numbers in black and parentheses to the range C4:C11 and E4:K12.
17. Apply a Thick Bottom Border to the range A3:K3. Apply the Total cell style to the range A12:K12. Apply a Thick Outside Border to the range A15:B20.

18. Change the sheet tab name to Weekly Payroll and the tab color to match the color used as background color in cell A1.
19. Preview the worksheet. Fit the printout of the worksheet on one page in landscape orientation. Save the workbook again.
20. Submit the workbook as specified by your instructor.

Lab 3: Consider This: Your Turn

Apply your creative thinking and problem-solving skills to design and implement a solution.

Transportation Costs

Instructions Part 1: You are thinking about buying a new vehicle, and you want to make sure that you buy one that offers the highest fuel savings. You decide to research hybrid cars as well as gas-only cars. Your friends are also interested in your results. Together, you decide to research the fuel costs associated with various types of vehicles. Research the gas mileage for six vehicles: three should run only on gas, and the others should be hybrid vehicles, combining gas and battery power. After you find the gas mileage for each vehicle, you will use formulas to calculate the fuel cost for one month, one year, and three years. Assume that in a typical month, you will drive 500 miles. Develop a worksheet following the general layout in Table 3–12 that shows the fuel cost analysis. Use the formulas listed in Table 3–13 and the concepts and techniques presented in this module to create the worksheet. You will need to find the average price of gas for your market. Add a chart showing the cost comparisons as an embedded chart.

Table 3–12 Fuel Cost Analysis

Vehicle	Miles Per Gallon	Fuel Cost 1 Month	Fuel Cost 1 Year	Fuel Cost 3 Years
Gas 1		Formula A	Formula B	Formula C
Gas 2		—	—	—
Gas 3		—	—	—
Hybrid 1		—	—	—
Hybrid 2		—	—	—
Hybrid 3		—	—	—
Assumptions				
Distance per Month	500			
Price of Gas				

Table 3–13 Fuel Cost Analysis Formulas

Formula A = (Distance per Month / Miles per Gallon)*Price of Gas
Formula B = ((Distance per Month / Miles per Gallon)*Price of Gas)*12
Formula C = ((Distance Per Month / Miles per Gallon)*Price of Gas)*36

Instructions Part 2: You made several decisions while creating the workbook for this assignment. Why did you select the chart type used to compare fuel costs? What other costs might you want to consider when making your purchase decision?

Index

X